CONSTRUCTION DETAILING
for Interior Design

CONSTRUCTION DETAILING
for Interior Design

PJ do Val, PhD, LEED AP ID+C

Endicott College

FAIRCHILD BOOKS

NEW YORK · LONDON · OXFORD · NEW DELHI · SYDNEY

FAIRCHILD BOOKS
Bloomsbury Publishing Inc
1385 Broadway, New York, NY 10018, USA
50 Bedford Square, London, WC1B 3DP, UK

BLOOMSBURY, FAIRCHILD BOOKS and the Fairchild Books
logo are trademarks of Bloomsbury Publishing Plc

Copyright © Bloomsbury Publishing Inc, 2019

For legal purposes the Acknowledgments on pp. x–xi
constitute an extension of this copyright page.

Design and illustration by Jasiek Krzysztofiak
Original photograph © Getty Images

All rights reserved. No part of this publication may be reproduced or transmitted in any form or by any means, electronic or mechanical, including photocopying, recording, or any information storage or retrieval system, without prior permission in writing from the publishers.

Bloomsbury Publishing Inc does not have any control over, or responsibility for, any third-party websites referred to or in this book. All internet addresses given in this book were correct at the time of going to press. The author and publisher regret any inconvenience caused if addresses have changed or sites have ceased to exist, but can accept no responsibility for any such changes.

A catalog record for this book is available from the Library of Congress

ISBN: 978-1-5013-5266-9

Typeset by Lachina Creative, Inc.
Printed and bound in the United States of America

To find out more about our authors and books visit
www.fairchildbooks.com and sign up for our newsletter.

Contents

Preface ix

PART I
DETAILING FUNDAMENTALS 1
1 Basics of detailing 1
2 Hand drafting basics 15
3 AutoCAD basics 21
4 Revit basics 35

PART II
DETAIL DRAWINGS 55
5 Walls and openings 55
6 Ceilings 93
7 Millwork detailing 127
8 Cabinetry 147
9 Stairs 173
10 Custom details 229

PART III
THE CONSTRUCTION SET 265
11 Completing the set 265

Appendices 295
Glossary 323
Credits 330
Index 331

Extended Contents

Preface ix

PART I
DETAILING FUNDAMENTALS 1

1 Basics of detailing 1
The importance of detailing 2
Types of detail drawings 2
Detailing characteristics and elements 4
How to place dimensions 10
Starting details 11
Why is this important? 12
Chapter review 14
Chapter terminology 14
Chapter references 14

2 Hand drafting basics 15
Architectural scale 16
Linetype 17
Lineweight 18
Dimensions and annotations 18
Material designations 19
Elevation symbols 19
Section cut markers 19
Detail callouts 20
Why is this important? 20
Chapter review 20
Chapter terminology 20
Chapter references 20

3 AutoCAD basics 21
Chapter disclaimer 22
Scale 22
Linetype 23
Lineweight 24
Dimensioning 24
    Placing dimensions 24
    Editing dimensions 26
Annotations 27
Material designation 27
    Elevation symbols 28
Section cut markers 29
Detail callouts 32
Why is this important? 33
Chapter review 33
Chapter terminology 34
Chapter references 34

4 Revit basics 35
Chapter disclaimer 36
Scale 36
    Model space scale 36
    Sheet scale 36
Linetype 37
Lineweight 38
    Editing lineweights 38
    Altering a single line 38
Dimensioning 39
Annotations 41
Material designations 42
Elevation symbols 44
    Place elevation symbols 44
    Edit elevation symbol style 45
    Edit placement of elevation symbol 46
    Edit direction of elevation symbol 46
    Edit width/depth of elevation 47
Section cut markers 48
    Place section symbol 48
    Edit placement of the section symbol 49
    Edit direction of the section symbol 49
    Edit width/depth of section 50

Detail callouts 50
    Place the detail callout symbol 50
    Edit placement of the callout bubble 52
    Edit placement of the detail callout reference tag 53
Why is this important? 53
Chapter review 53
Chapter terminology 54
Chapter references 54

PART II
DETAIL DRAWINGS 55

5 Walls and openings 55
About walls and openings 56
Drafting stud wall plan and section 62
    Wood stud 62
    Steel stud 64
Drafting stud wall elevations 66
    Technique 1: drafting based on dimensions 66
    Technique 2: drafting from a plan 68
    Technique 3: drafting from an existing elevation 76
Drafting window and opening frames 80
    Wooden frame opening 80
    Aluminum window frame, header, and sill 82
Drafting door frames 84
    Wooden door frame and header 84
    Commercial—aluminum door frame and header 86
Why is this important? 88
Chapter review 89
Example plan updates STUDIO 90
Chapter terminology 91
Wall and opening codes 91
Chapter references 92

6 Ceilings 93
About ceilings 94
Drafting ceiling details 100
    Suspended ACT systems 100
    Suspended GWB systems 102
    Suspended ACT and GWB systems 104
    Suspended GWB cove and recessed ACT system 108
    GWB cove detail 108
    Direct installed GWB 114
    Soffit detail 116

    Box beams 118
    Perpendicular section 118
    Parallel section 120
Why is this important? 122
Chapter review 123
Example plan updates STUDIO 124
Chapter terminology 125
Ceiling codes 125
Chapter references 126

7 Millwork detailing 127
About millwork 128
    Types of wall-mounted millwork 128
    Profiles 132
    Joinery 132
Drafting wall-mounted millwork 135
    Wall-mounted millwork, elevation 136
    Wall-mounted millwork, section 139
Why is this important? 143
Chapter review 144
Example plan updates STUDIO 145
Chapter terminology 145
Millwork codes 146
Chapter references 146

8 Cabinetry 147
About cabinetry 148
    Drafting cabinetry 156
Why is this important? 168
Chapter review 169
Example plan updates STUDIO 170
Chapter terminology 171
Cabinetry codes 171
Chapter references 172

9 Stairs 173
About stairs 174
    Parts of the stair 174
Types of stairs 178
    Residential 178
    Commercial 179
Stair layouts 180
    Direct run 181
    Straight run 181
    L-shaped 181

  U-shaped   182
  Winding   182
  Spiral   182
Calculating stairs   183
  Calculating the number and height of risers   183
  Calculating the number of treads   183
  Calculating tread depth   184
Drafting a wooden direct run—residential   185
  Drafting a direct run—plan   186
  Drafting a direct run—side elevation   190
  Drafting a direct run—front elevation   194
  Drafting a direct run—section   198
  Drafting a run—section   202
  Drafting a direct run—section   206
  Other wooden elements   206
Drafting a steel U-run—commercial   207
  Drafting a U-run—plan   208
  Drafting a U-run—section   212
  Drafting a U-run—elevation   221
  Other steel elements   221
Why is this important?   222
Chapter review   223
Example plan updates STUDIO   224
Chapter terminology   224
Stair codes   225
Chapter references   228

10 Custom details   229

About customizing details   230
Custom tile patterns   233
  Kitchen backsplash   233
  Bathroom floor tile pattern   236
  Bathroom full tile floor plan   238
Custom case piece   240
  Case piece elevation   240
  Drawer stack section   244
  Cubby and bench section   248
Custom reception desk   252
  Reception desk elevation   254
  Reception counter section   256
  Desk hutch section   258
  Full section   260
Why is this important?   260
Chapter review   262
Example plan updates STUDIO   263
Chapter terminology   263
Chapter codes   264
Chapter references   264

PART III
THE CONSTRUCTION SET   265

11 Completing the set   265

About organizing a construction document set   266
  Page numbering systems   266
  Laying out the pages   268
  Adding communicative symbols   271
Completing the construction set   273
  Hand drafting   273
  CAD   275
  Revit   277
Why is this important?   279
Chapter review   279
Chapter terminology   279
Sample CD set STUDIO   279
Chapter references   294

Appendices   295

Appendix A: IBC Codes   296
Appendix B: ADA Standards   299
Appendix C: Symbols, Annotations & Materials   301
Appendix D: Construction Material Guide   304
Appendix E: Wall Types   305
Appendix F: Door Styles   309
Appendix G: Ceiling Types   310
Appendix H: Millwork and Cabinet Styles   314
Appendix I: Stairs, Nosings, and Rails   316
Appendix J: Sample Tile Patterns   318
Appendix K: Project Plan Shell A STUDIO   319
Appendix L: Project Plan Shell B STUDIO   321

Glossary   323
Credits   330
Index   331

Preface

Detail drawings are one of the most fundamental, yet complex, elements of a design project. While it is true that it is the design that sells a project, the details are the communicative elements that allow for that project to be constructed. Before entering the field, students must have a working knowledge of how these detail drawings are created, how to customize them, and how to string them into a cohesive series of illustrations for the construction team. Additionally, students should be aware of the International Building Codes (IBC) put in place by the International Code Council (ICC) and the necessary design standards created through the Americans with Disabilities Act (ADA). If these codes are considered at the start of the detailing process, revisions are kept to a minimum and the detailing process avoids unnecessary setbacks.

With this book, I intend for students to gain confidence in their drafting skills and construction comprehension by practicing easy step-by-step details of typical interior elements. These details can then be edited to meet the needs of their own unique custom designs, providing flexibility to the student. Tables and handy textbox reminders of applicable codes will appear for each topic covered, exposing students to the standards put into place by the ICC/IBC and the ADA Accessibility Guidelines (ADAAG). This combination of practice, flexibility, and regulation are meant to encourage speed, creativity, and practicality when assembling a construction set.

AUDIENCE AND PREREQUISITE KNOWLEDGE

As this book covers a broad range of information for drafting and construction documentation, it is the aim of this text to help design students throughout the course of their studies. Growing with students from the early days of understanding drafting terminology, to developing and customizing details, to creating full CD sets, all while keeping IBC and ADA codes in mind, this book can be used from start to finish in most design programs. The topics and methods discussed within this book have been developed through and integrated into drafting, electronic media, and construction document courses I have taught to undergraduate and graduate students. Additionally, it is my intent that the usefulness of this text extend beyond the classroom for a second life as a functioning guidebook for designers in the field.

Content overview

The main focus of this book is to look in depth at how to illustrate, dimension, annotate, and organize detail drawings for construction sets while adhering to the codes set forth by the ICC. Broken into three parts, this text will allow for you to enhance your skills by first understanding the important characteristics of details and how to use them within the medium of your choice, then how to draw those details, before finally assembling the drawings into a completed set.

Part I: Detailing Fundamentals will focus on how to begin detailing and how to execute detail characteristics by hand, CAD, or Revit. Basic drafting and design terminology will be introduced alongside fundamental drafting techniques. This portion of the text is aimed at those who are new to drafting or in the process of switching to a digital software package.

Part II: Detail Drawings will delve into the specifics of different types of detail drawings. Step-by-step guides for how to detail various construction components will be shown to give you a basis for how to detail different designs on your own. Topics include millwork, stairs, and ceiling construction to name a few.

Finally, Part III: The Construction Set will focus on the assembly of a construction set. The organization of pages and drawings will be discussed in depth with examples showing page layouts, the inclusion of codes and symbols, and how to reference and locate details that relate to other drawings within the set.

Features

While the focus and techniques examined in the three parts will vary, the following features will guide students through the book and support the chapter content:

- Step-by-step illustrated tutorials of construction details feature building code references, definitions of important industry-specific terms, and construction document sets
- Tips and tricks appear throughout each chapter, providing more information about how to simplify the drafting process whether by hand, CAD, or Revit, and offer general rules of thumb (RoT) and relevant building codes and standards (IBC and ADA).
- Chapter reviews pose practical problems to be used as an assessment of your understanding and can be used as a study guide.
- A sample plan is presented at the end of each chapter in Part II for practice, assignments, or examination.
- Fully integrated multimedia STUDIO—when you see the logo, log in to your STUDIO for animations, assignments, and more.
- Appendices offer a wealth of information including ADA standards; IBC codes; guides for symbols, annotations, and materials; reference plans for all of the construction details in the book; and project plan templates

Instructor and student resources

Construction Detailing for Interior Design STUDIO

We are pleased to offer an online multimedia resource to support this text—*Construction Detailing for Interior Design STUDIO*. The online *STUDIO* is specially developed to complement this book with rich media ancillaries that students can adapt to their visual learning styles to better master concepts and improve grades. Within the *STUDIO*, students will be able to:

- Watch video animations to see how certain components are assembled in a three-dimensional space and how each of the two-dimensional drawings are associated with each other to create a series of construction details.
- Review concepts with Visual flashcards of vocabulary terms and detail drawings that reinforce fundamental concepts.
- Download AutoCAD and Revit file templates to complete the example plan updates for each of the tutorials in Chapters 5–11, with each file cumulatively building on the previous chapter to show how the elements come together to create the whole.

STUDIO access cards are offered free with new book purchases and also sold separately through Bloomsbury Fashion Central (*www.BloomsburyFashionCentral.com*).

Instructor resources

- Instructor's guide provides helpful tips for teaching the course, including sample syllabi, additional assignments, and answers to the questions in the book.
- PowerPoint presentations provide a basis for lecture and feature images from the book along with essential vocabulary.
- PDF templates of construction detail fill-in drawings to be used for practice, homework, or testing.
- Suggested building shells for use in residential and commercial studio projects, available in PDF, CAD, and Revit formats.

Instructor's resources may be accessed through Bloomsbury Fashion Central (*www.BloomsburyFashionCentral.com*).

ACKNOWLEDGMENTS

While there are numerous people that I must thank for helping me along the way, I only have enough room in this text to single out a few. First, I want to thank the reviewers who have generously shared their time to provide feedback on my writing and have helped in the vetting of this text: Kristen Arnold, Weber State University; Genell W. Ebbini, University of Minnesota; Wendy Hynes, Purdue University; Donna L. Lusk, University of Akron; Bruce Nacke, University of North Texas; Christopher Manzo, Kansas State University; Cristina McCarthy, Virginia Marti College of Art and Design; Michelle Pearson, Texas Tech University; Saglinda Roberts, Kean University; Stacy Spale, University of Nebraska; Eric Weber, University of Nevada Las Vegas.

To everyone from Fairchild Books that I have had the pleasure to work with for all of your support and patience, especially Corey Kahn, Edie Weinberg, and their teams.

To my mentors in the field and in the classroom, your enthusiasm and knowledge of interior design have shaped who I am as an educator. A special thanks to Kevin Renz, Andrew Brody, and Rosemary Botti-Salitsky for being my teachers and colleagues, for recommending me for this process, and for showing me what type of teacher I want to be.

Thank you to my students, especially those who have had to tolerate my construction document classes before I've finished my first cup of coffee. I appreciate you letting me use you as guinea pigs for projects and assignments, which has shaped how I've approached this book.

For my parents who have encouraged me and made sure that I'm eating and getting enough sleep. I appreciate everything you've done for me, even when I'm stubborn and making you crazy.

To Mike, Lyra, Priya, and Bunsen: Thank you for always being by my side and supporting my dreams. Thank you for being patient, loving, and understanding. Without you, this would not have been possible (or complete). You are the reasons that I've persisted.

The Publisher wishes to gratefully acknowledge and thank the editorial team involved in the publication of this book:

Acquisitions Editor: Wendy Fuller
Senior Development Editor: Corey Kahn
Editorial Assistant: Bridget MacAvoy
Art Development Editor: Edie Weinberg
Designer: Lachina Creative, Inc.
Production Manager: Ken Bruce
Project Manager: Courtney Coffman, Lachina Creative

PART I
Detailing fundamentals

Basics of detailing

CHAPTER 1

CHAPTER OUTCOMES

After completing this chapter you will be able to:

1. Differentiate between the various types of drawings used in architectural drafting and construction document sets.

2. Understand the different elements and characteristics of a detail drawing and the roles they each play in the assembly of a drawing.

3. Recognize the difference between various drawing markers and the types of drawings they relate to.

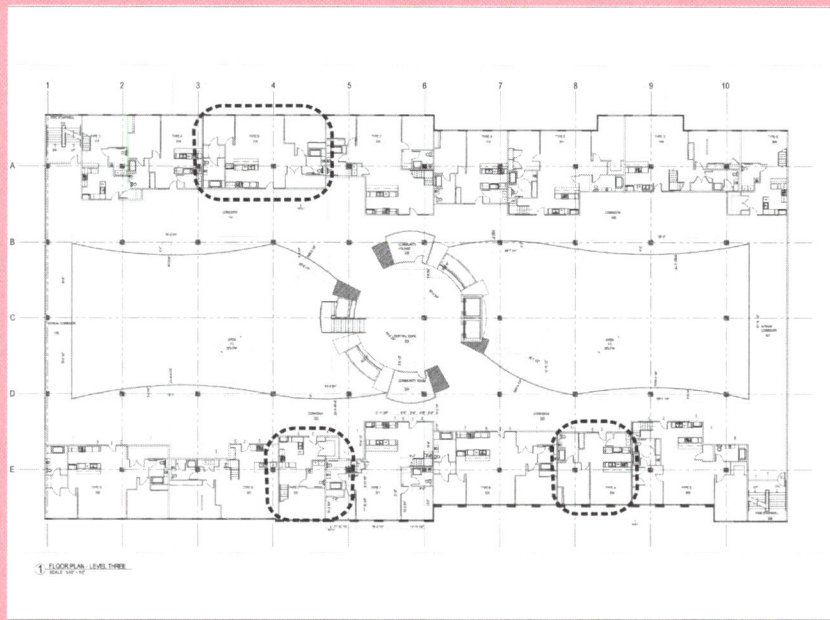

Figure 1.1
Plan view of a mixed use complex.

THE IMPORTANCE OF DETAILING

Defined as a plan, elevation, or section shown at a large scale in order to clarify the dimensions, annotations, and finishes, a **detail drawing** is one of the strongest and most helpful methods of communication in architecture and interior design. These drawings must be clear, direct, and informative as they act as the instructions necessary to create buildings, architectural details, interior construction assemblies, and finishes. The clearer and more precise the drawing, the more streamlined the construction process becomes.

It is important that the drawings are accurate for a few reasons. First, details are the primary source of communication between the client, designer, and contractor. The drawings allow for work to progress without a constant line of communication to be open between the parties. Thus, the drawings must convey all the information needed for the intended final appearance of project.

Second, if there are mistakes in the drawing, the construction team will still build the project according to the document set. This can result in elements that are incorrect and potentially unsafe and will cost time and money to repair. Depending on the contractual clauses in play, this could leave the architecture or design firm at fault and leave you or your bosses financially or legally responsible. It is vital that the details drawn are approved and accepted by all parties involved in the project.

Third, the drawings must adhere to the codes issued by the **International Code Council** (ICC), which develops model codes and standards used in the design, build and compliance process to construct safe, sustainable, affordable and resilient structures. This list of standards, known as the **International Building Codes** (IBC), outlines the minimum safeguards required for each project depending on the construction type and the building's use. These codes must be observed and accounted for within the detail drawings to assure that the individual elements and the project as a whole are compliant with fire and building safety regulations. The smaller scale **International Residential Code** (IRC) focuses on the applicable codes for one- and two-family homes and townhouses and provides clarification for industry regulations.

In addition to the codes put in place by the ICC, the **Americans with Disabilities Act of 1990** (ADA) requires equal or modified accommodations for individuals with disabilities. Enforced by the Department of Justice (DOJ), The **ADA Accessibility Guidelines** (ADAAG) spells out the standards required for construction projects to maintain accessibility and safety for all. By incorporating the IBC and ADAAG codes early in your design process, you can progress from phase to phase efficiently and will reduce the amount of time devoted to redesigning.

TYPES OF DETAIL DRAWINGS

While the total number of detail drawings and the amount of detail needed will vary from one project to the next, certain types of drawings will appear in all construction sets in order for the project to be completed. There are four basic types of detail drawings: plans, elevations, sections, and axonometrics.

Plans are drawings of the space or object as seen from above. These 2D drawings focus on expressing the length and the width of the space as a whole and the placement of individual components within the space. Annotations can be used to call out room names and numbers, materials, height changes, or any additional information that is not readily apparent from the drawing alone. Additional annotations, called elevation markers and section cuts, can be placed on plans to signify that there are other drawings associated with the plan that will give more information than what is

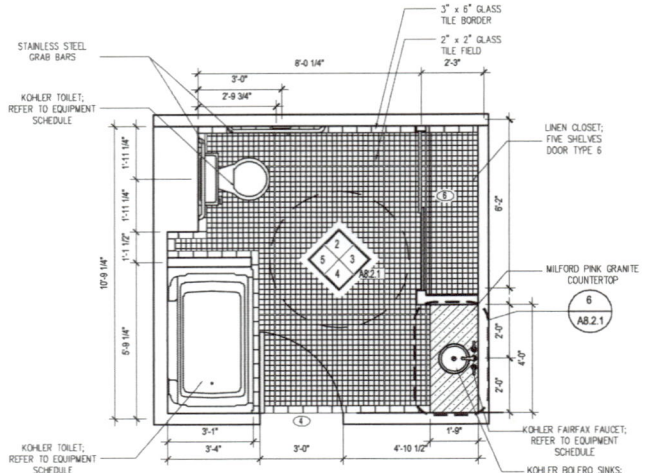

Figure 1.2
Plan view of a residential bathroom.

STUDIO Animation 1.1 Types of Detail Drawings

PART I DETAILING FUNDAMENTALS

visible in this drawing alone. Multiple linetypes and lineweights should be used while constructing plan drawings; refer to Table 1.2 for a breakdown of these elements.

Elevations are another form of 2D drawings, but they differ from the plan in that they show a vertical view of a space or object, allowing for you to indicate overall heights, mounting heights, and other upright details. Elevations appear foreshortened, meaning that objects that appear behind a surface in the foreground will either be hidden or appear closer than it would truly exist. This can be clarified through lineweights and annotation if necessary.

Vertical dimensions are shown in elevation views to call out heights of objects, such as doorframes or window sills, and mounting heights for objects like light switches, thermostats, or other objects attached to the wall. Horizontal dimensions indicating the placement along the wall for the element's location should only be used when they are needed for context or clarification. If an object is being drawn in elevation, it would appear as though you are looking at it straight on or from the side. Elements that appear closer to the viewer should appear as object lines with a standard lineweight while objects in the distance should appear in a lighter lineweight. See Table 1.2 for reference.

The third type of detail drawing is the **section**. A section drawing appears as though the space or object has been physically cut through, showing the individual elements that construct the component, their thicknesses, and the means of connection. While most sections are in a vertical orientation, similar to the elevation, some sections are in a horizontal orientation, similar to a plan view. All dimensions and annotations that are needed to explain how to construct the object should be included but must be well organized so as to prevent the drawing from becoming too cluttered.

It is vital that you incorporate at least four different lineweights into your section drawings to add clarity. The heaviest lineweight is reserved for the section cut elements. Imagine a saw cutting through the object; anything the saw physically touches would appear in the assigned section lineweight. Anything seen in the distance past those section cut lines would appear in elevation. As elevations appear foreshortened and objects appear closer than they would truly exist, two different elevation lineweights are needed. Elements that appear closer to the foreground (but are not being

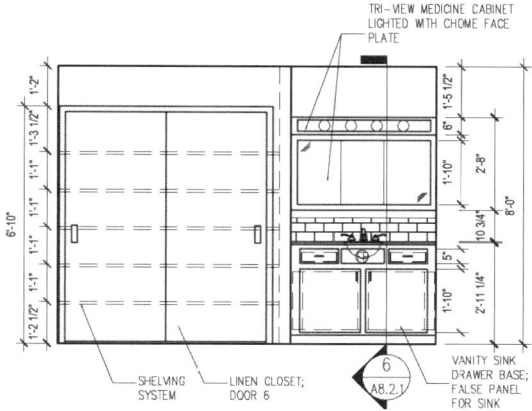

Figure 1.3
Bathroom elevation.

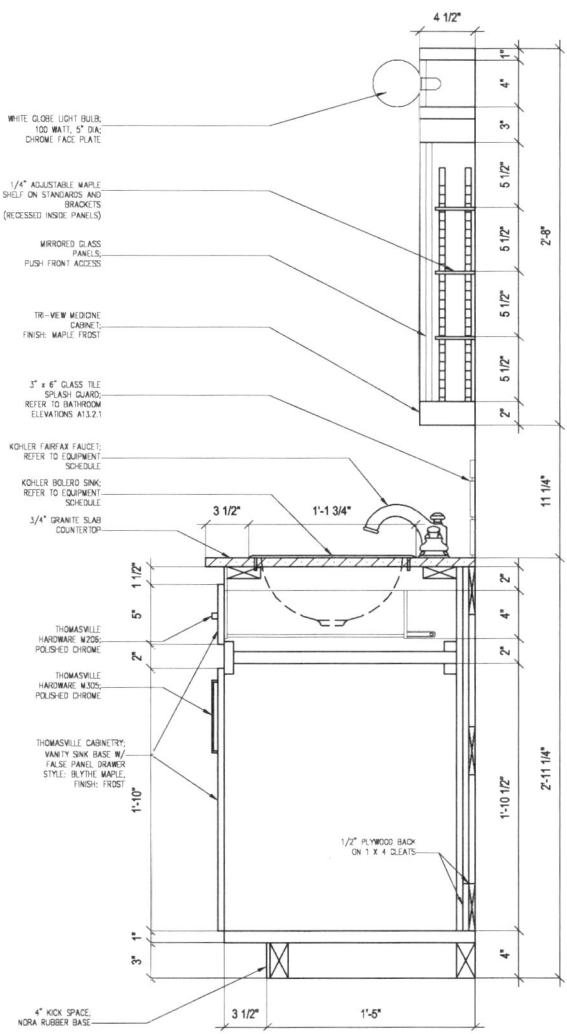

Figure 1.4
Vanity section.

CHAPTER 1 BASICS OF DETAILING | 3

"cut through") will appear as a heavier lineweight than those elevation lines in the distance. Referred to in this text as *elevation near* or *elevation far*, recommended lineweights for these lines can be found in Table 1.2. Finally, finish materials are needed to indicate the makeup of objects in section. The lightest lineweight should be reserved for this purpose so that the communication of the material is present in the view but so that it does not distract from the more important elements in the drawing.

Axonometric drawings, or axons, are the fourth type of detail drawing. These 3D images can be used to show information that cannot be ascertained from the 2D drawings alone, such as a construction joint or a finished assembly. Axons typically will not have dimension stringers but instead can feature annotations for important measurements and finish information.

DETAILING CHARACTERISTICS AND ELEMENTS

A detail can take any form, from plans to sections to axons, but will always include other components that will dictate to the construction team how the designer intends for a part to look and how it is to be built. There are several elements that are necessary for any good detail drawing. Below you will find a description for each of these elements. Refer to Chapters 2–4 for a more detailed explanation of how to incorporate these elements when working by hand or in CAD or Revit.

As a building cannot fit on a piece of paper, it is important to make sure that when it is drawn, the proportions remain consistent to one another. **Scale** refers to the ratio between the size of the physical space being designed and the size the space appears as in the drawing. When reading the scale of a drawing, the first number refers to the unit of length utilized in the drawing while the second number is based on a set, realistic proportion.

For example:

> *Drawing measurement* **1/4"** = **1'-0"** *Real world measurement*

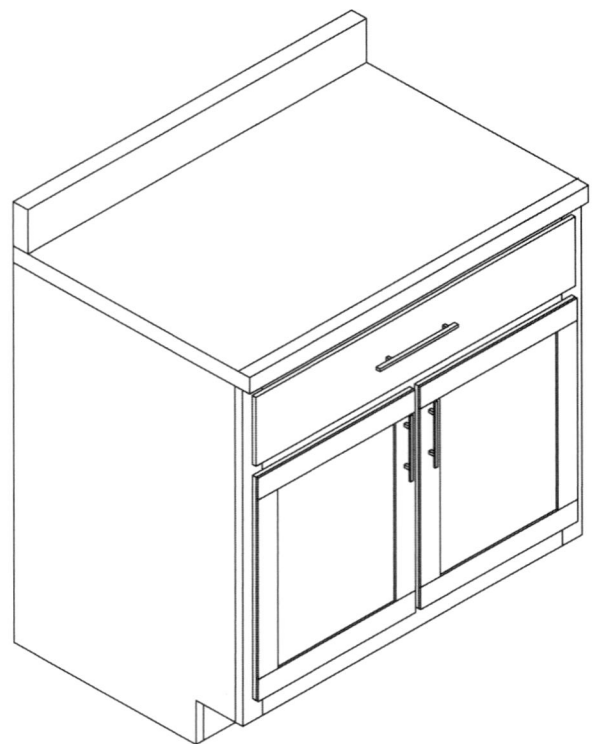

Figure 1.5
Counter and cabinet axon.

This means that every 1/4" measured in your drawing is equal to 1'-0" in reality. For reference, Figure 1.6 shows a side-by-side comparison of the same drawing at 1/8" = 1'-0" scale and at 1/4" = 1'-0" scale.

Various scales can be used for different drawing types but can also be dependent on the amount of detail that needs to show. Larger scale drawings will provide you with more intricate detailing but may become too large for reproduction. Smaller drawings allow for you to create a comprehensive overview, but they may not be large enough to properly detail. Table 1.1 provides a list of recommended scales for each drawing type. Note that these are simply suggested scales, as you must determine the actual scale used based on the drawing type, required detail, and desired size of the detail.

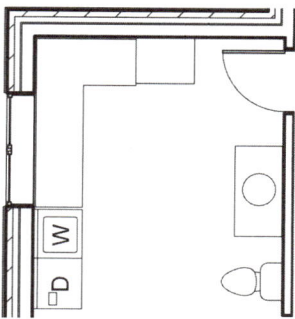
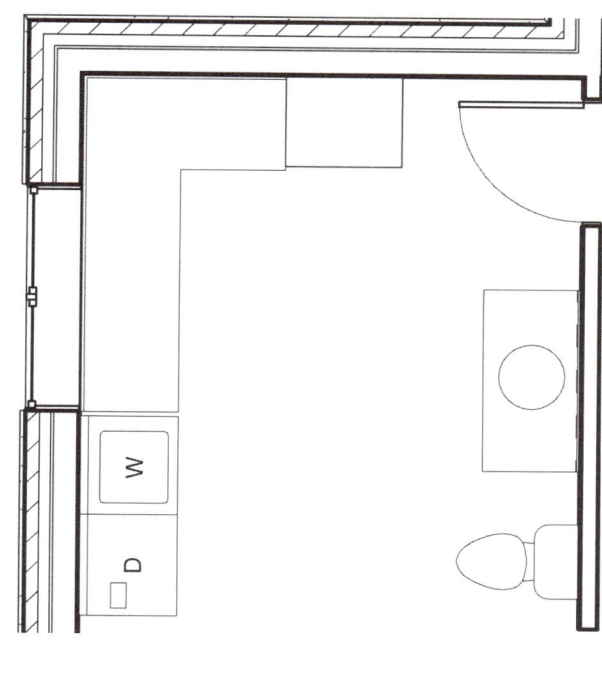

① **1/8" BATHROOM PLAN**
1/8" = 1'-0"

② **1/4" BATHROOM PLAN**
1/4" = 1'-0"

Figure 1.6
A floor plan for a bathroom shown at 1/8" = 1'-0" scale (left) and at 1/4" = 1'-0" scale.

Table 1.1 Typical Drawing Scales		
Drawing Type	**Commercial Scale**	**Residential Scale**
Floor Plan	1/8" = 1'-0"	1/4" = 1'-0"
Enlarged Floor Plan	1/4" = 1'-0" minimum	1/2" = 1'-0" minimum
Reflected Ceiling Plan	1/8" = 1'-0"	1/4" = 1'-0"
Elevations	1/4" or 3/8" = 1'-0"	1/4" = 1'-0"
Building Section	1/4" or 1/2" = 1'-0"	3/4" = 1'-0"
Wall Section	3/4" = 1'-0"	3/4" = 1'-0"
Detail	1/2" to 1" = 1'-0"	3/8" to 1 1/2" = 1'-0"

[a]These scales are suggested and may vary depending on the project, the size of the object/complexity of the detail, and the policy of your supervisor.

Linetype uses a style or pattern to create a visual identifier for what kind of line is being shown. Used in combination with the lineweight, this marking can indicate whether a feature is an object in the foreground, a hidden entity or construction element, or simply a guideline. Below are some of the most common types of lines used in drafting:

Object line

Figure 1.7
Object line.

Objects can refer to anything in your detail drawing, from a wall or opening to a floor tile or furniture piece. The lineweight of this solid line can be manipulated to create a hierarchy, with walls appearing the heaviest, doors and windows appearing slightly lighter, furniture elements next, and flooring being the lightest.

Hidden line

— — — — — — — — —

Figure 1.8
Hidden line.

A hidden line represents objects that are of importance but are for some reason not visible in the view created in the detail drawing. This typically refers to objects that are either below a solid surface, such as shelves below a desk top in a detail, or above a cut plane, such as wall hung cabinets on a floor plan. These lines should be lighter than the object lines.

Guideline

Figure 1.9
Guideline.

Also referred to as a construction line, these lines are used to aid you during the drafting process. Guidelines allow for you to maintain even spacing, proper line placement, and keep lettering aligned, especially when drafting by hand. Guidelines should only be drawn very lightly and should be erased when possible and never inked or transferred to final drawings. It is recommended that you use a lead that is 4H or harder lead for guidelines.

Center line

— — — — — — — —

Figure 1.10
Center line.

These lines mark the center of a symmetrical object, which communicates construction and placement for arcs, circles, or other intricate shapes within a plan. These lines should be drawn lightly enough to not interfere with or deter from the object lines, but they should be heavy enough to be seen when the drawing is reproduced.

Phantom line

——— —— —— — —— — ———

Figure 1.11
Phantom line.

These lines indicate elements that are not actually part of the constructed space but rather aid in the explanation of how to view the space or how elements operate. Section cut markers utilize phantom lines to show where the "cut" through the building or object occurs. These lines should be drawn lightly enough to not interfere with or deter from the object lines, but they should be heavy enough to be seen when the drawing is reproduced.

Lineweight describes the heaviness of a drawn line and creates a hierarchy of importance when combined with different line types. Lineweight influences how crisp the drawing is and affects how easily the instructions for the design can be read by all parties involved. The weight of the line can be manipulated, whether by hand or computer, depending on the type of lead used to draw the line or the designated thickness assigned to the line. Both of these treatments are explored further in the following chapters, but a comparison of different lineweights produced in CAD can be seen in Figure 1.12. Table 1.2 provides a recommended list of lineweights for plans, elevations, and sections and for the different linetypes that appear in each type of drawing.

Figure 1.12
Comparison of different lineweights in CAD.

PART I DETAILING FUNDAMENTALS

| Table 1.2 Recommended Lineweights for Different Drawing Types and Drafting Styles |||||
| Drawing Type | Linetype | Lineweight |||
		Hand	CAD	Revit
Floor Plan & RCP	Object Lines	HB	.20 mm	Thin/Medium
	Hidden Lines	H/HB	.15 mm	Default
	Center Line	2H	.15 mm	Default
	Phantom Line	2H/4H	.09 mm	N/A
	Guide Line	4H	N/A	N/A
	Text	H/HB	Default	Default
Elevations	Object Lines	HB	.20 mm	Thin/Medium
	Hidden Lines	H/HB	.15 mm	Default
	Center Line	2H	.15 mm	Default
	Phantom Line	2H/4H	.09 mm	N/A
	Guide Line	4H	N/A	N/A
	Text	H/HB	Default	Default
Building Section	Section Cut	2B	.30 mm	Wide Lines
	Elevation Lines (Near)	HB	.20 mm	Medium Lines
	Elevation Lines (Far)	H/HB	.15 mm	Medium/Thin
	Materials	2H	.09 mm	Filled Region Default 1

Dimensions are used to indicate the size or thickness of a space or object and mounting heights. When used on a plan, the length and placement of various locations can be called out. Heights for surfaces and mounted elements can be called out in elevations, while length, height, and thickness can each be indicated in a section drawing, as seen in Figures 1.3 and 1.4. The placement of the dimension stringer and how to measure the object will vary depending on the type of drawing you are working on. See the "How to Place Dimensions" section in this chapter or refer to the chapters related to individual topics for more details.

Dimensions are typically shown as part of a comprised set of elements that make a **stringer**, or final dimension notation. The number representing the length is referred to as the *dimension text*, and the line it sits above is called the *dimension line*. When using an architectural scale, the dimension should read in feet and inches with a dash between the two. The *extension line*, also known as a witness line, reaches from the dimension line to the object being measured. It will typically extend 1/8" past the dimension line and the point where these two lines cross will be marked by an *architectural tick*.

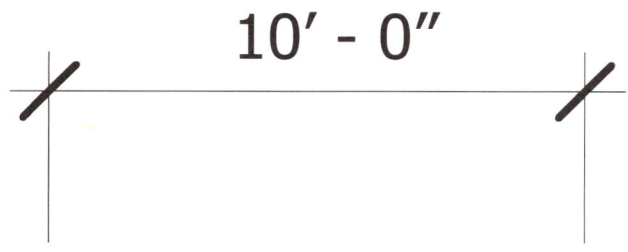

Figure 1.13
Dimension stringer.

CHAPTER 1 BASICS OF DETAILING

Annotations can be used in any type of drawing to add verbal labels or instructions to the illustration. This text should be a short, concise label that indicates a material or finish, size, or construction method. If a lengthier explanation is necessary, you can direct the contractor to refer to a separate note through an annotation.

Leader lines are used to indicate what the annotation is calling out in the detail. Typically shown as one- or two-segment lines, the leader terminates in either an arrowhead or a dot. The lettering used in annotations should be in neatly drafted capital letters, also known as **architectural lettering**.

Material designations are visual depictions of materials that can add clarification between various element layers, create patterns, or indicate finishes. These designations can be shown in two different ways: illustration and annotation. *Illustration* means that a finish symbol will be drawn into the detail. When this method is used, you should remember to remain consistent with your patterns, using each one for a different type of material throughout all of your drawings and creating a new pattern for each additional material. If it becomes necessary for you to reuse patterns, make sure that you annotate the material name within the drawing to ensure that there is no confusion from one image to the next. A sample list of standard material patterns can be found in Appendix C.

The *annotation* method of designating materials means that instead of drawing a finish symbol into the detail, a notation will appear within the drawing to indicate what finish or material will appear in a specific location. The annotation method is typically used to reduce the clutter in a drawing or to increase clarity. Many detail drawings utilize a combination of both the annotation and illustration methods.

Finally, there are multiple markers that are used within the various detail drawings to refer the reader to corresponding drawings that give relevant information to the construction of the space or object. The **elevation symbol** appears on floor plans to indicate the drawing and page number of an elevation, as well as the location and direction of the view. A circle or a square can be drawn on the plan with numbers written inside the shape as references to the exact page and drawing number where the view can be found in the construction set. An arrowhead is added to the shape to specify the direction.

Figure 1.14
Annotation with leader line.

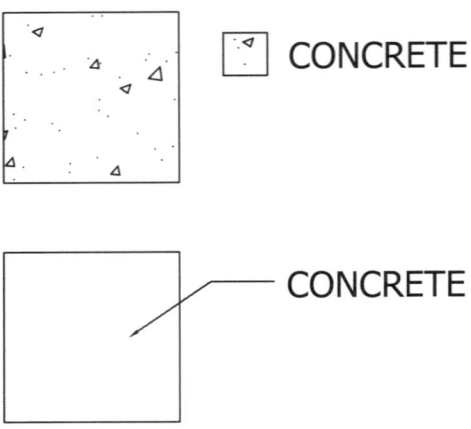

Figure 1.15
Illustration (top) and annotation methods.

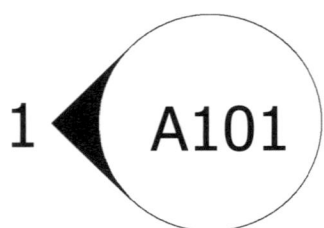

Figure 1.16
Elevation marker.

The view that the elevation gives the reader is as if you were looking at a wall or object straight on, without any perspective. The borders of the drawing are created where the object ends or where walls, ceilings, and floors interfere with the space. This type of view does not allow for the object or space to be cut through; however, a hierarchy of lineweights may be necessary as there can be a layering of elements in the foreground and background based on how much information is visible from the elevation marker. The placement of the marker acts as the exact location from where the view is taken from. A helpful tip for this is to imagine that you are standing on the spot, looking in the direction indicated. Keeping in mind that you cannot see through solid surfaces, the elevation would be drawn as a 2D version of how you see the space.

The **section cut symbol** and the corresponding section drawing are very similar to those for elevations with one huge difference, you cut through the object or space to show how the piece is constructed and the materials that create make it up. The symbol itself is a circle, placed outside of the space, with an arrowhead to indicate the direction of the view. Extending from this circle is a phantom line, showing where the "cut" would be taken. The phantom line terminates with a tail, which is a filled rectangle, extending in the same direction as the view. When thinking of a section, keep the image of a dollhouse in mind. This type of building is one where a wall is literally cut away, allowing one to see all the rooms and how they flow from one space to another. Heavy construction lines are used for anything that has been "cut" through, while the remainder of the drawing is treated in the same manner as an elevation. The view that the section provides can be a small drawing that focuses solely on how specific materials are layered and connected to one another to show how a piece is constructed, as seen in a wall section drawing, or it can be a larger drawing which can be used to show construction, as well as stacked spaces or adjacencies.

A **detail callout** usually appears as a dashed circle, rectangle, or square around a room, construction component, or object to draw the reader's attention to the fact that there is more information to be found on the element in other drawings. As with the elevation marker and the section cut symbol, the page reference circle that is attached to the bubble directs one to the exact page and drawing number where the detail can be found. The detail itself can vary from object to object, being as simple to understand as a floor plan at a larger scale, or being a complicated set of plans, elevations, and sections on how to build a piece of furniture.

Figure 1.17
Section cut symbol.

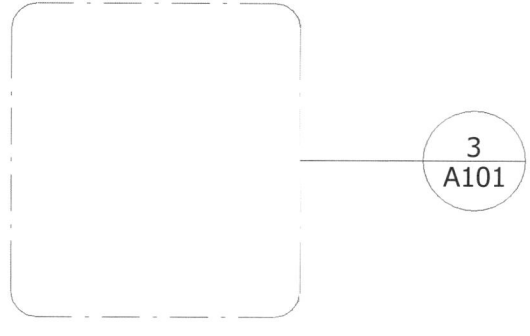

Figure 1.18
Detail callout.

CHAPTER 1 BASICS OF DETAILING | 9

HOW TO PLACE DIMENSIONS

Depending on what you are measuring, the starting and ending points for the dimension stringer will change. It is important to know what objects and drawing types require in terms of dimensioning so that your drawings are annotated properly the first time through. The following is a list of scenarios and how to dimension each of them.

1. An existing shell with new interior partitions (Figure 1.19)
   a. Dimension stringers should measure from the center of one partition to the center of the next, or stud to stud. This measurement accurately determines the placement of the stud, which the partition is constructed around, as will be discussed in Chapter 5.
   b. When dimensioning new partition placements from the shell, begin measuring at the interior face of the exterior wall (where the gypsum board or interior finish begins).

2. Window and door placement (Figure 1.19)
   a. Dimensions should begin or end at the center of the opening (Figure 1.20). Like the placement of the stud, this instructs the contractor where the opening needs to occur and allows them to create the rough opening for the object around this space, as discussed in Chapter 5.

Dimensions should maintain a level of hierarchy with aligned rows of stringers placed neatly around a plan or detail. The dimensions placed closest to the drawing measure the distances between individual objects (windows, doors, walls, etc.). The second tier of dimensions measures individual room sizes (stud to stud or stud to wall face). The final tier provides the overall dimensions of the space for anyone utilizing the plans. Figure 1.19 shows this hierarchy for the construction elements along the 50'-0" wall.

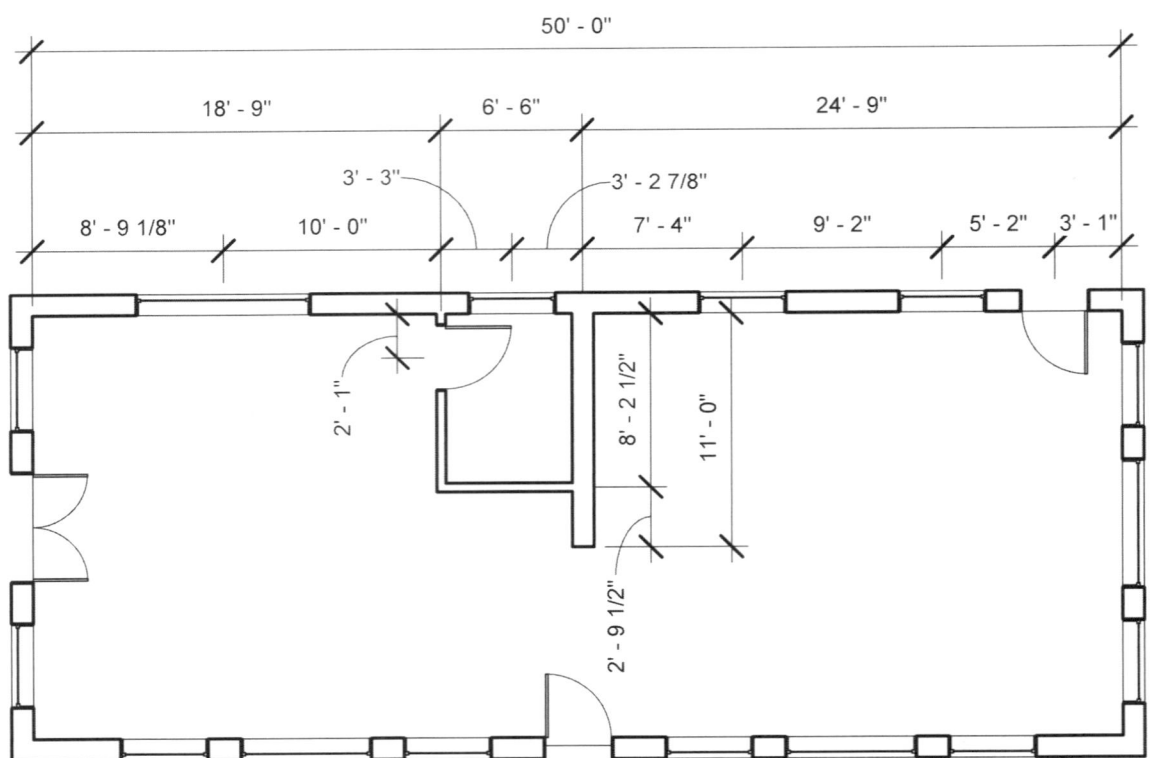

Figure 1.19
Dimension plan showing hierarchy and stringer placement for new partitions and openings.

PART I DETAILING FUNDAMENTALS

3. Objects
    a. Critical distances between objects in a space, such as the countertops and cabinets shown in Figure 1.20, can be measured from edge to edge. This measurement shows the clearances between objects for circulation.
    b. Mounted object (lights, sinks, built-ins, etc.) are typically dimensioned to their center point for accurate installation. This can be seen in the sink measurement in Figure 1.20.
    c. Objects that are placed instead of being installed (furnishings) only need dimensions from edge to edge or edge to wall when certain circulation distances need to be maintained.

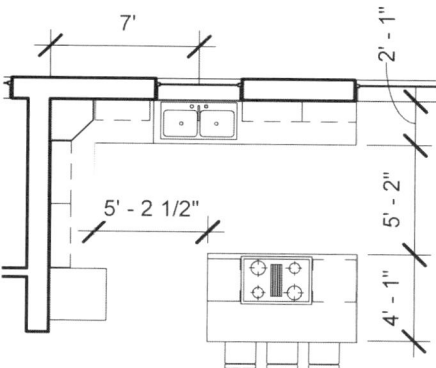

Figure 1.20
Dimension plan showing object installation measurements and clearances.

STARTING DETAILS

When beginning a detail drawing, it is important to either sketch or keep notes on measurements and key annotation information so that you can proceed in an accurate and efficient manner. Once you have compiled your notes, it is recommended that you select the scale you wish to draw and proceed in the following order:

- *Floor plans* will dictate the placement of elements in or on the other drawings. By starting with the floor plan first, you can save yourself time and energy that would otherwise go in to adjusting your other drawings any time an element of the plan changes. Create the shell, then interior walls and openings, dimensions, furniture and fixtures, annotations, and finally finishes. This order will allow for you to make changes to the furniture, fixtures and equipment (FF&E) of the building without having to re-draw or adjust the plan too much.
- *Ceiling plans* can be drawn next, as they are based mainly off of what occurs on the floor plan. Many of the structural elements shown are either identical to the floor plan (such as the shell and interior walls) or will appear between these elements (beams). Fixtures can then be added, followed by dimensions, annotations, and any necessary finishes.
- *Elevations* are derived from the floor plans, and at times from the ceiling plan, too. While the elevation shows what the element looks like from the front, back, and sides, the shape of those pieces are dictated by the plans.
- *Sections*, in a sense, are more detailed elevations. Once you have a completed elevation, you can use the shell of it to create the perimeter of the section drawing. This will allow you to work within a "frame," adding materials and design elements into the drawing, with dimensions and annotations kept mainly on the outskirts of the drawing.
- *Axons* can be created last, once all of the details for sizes and finishes have been completed. This will allow you to create a fully realized 3D drawing without needing to redraw elements that have been edited in other drawings.

If you are working in CAD or Revit, you can begin your drawings anywhere in the model window, as this drawing space will expand to meet your needs. If you are working by hand, it is recommended that you start by selecting trace paper and beginning in the center of your page. Based on the scale and scope of your drawing, determine how big of a sheet of paper you will need. Using trace at this stage allows you to edit mistakes or add additional length or width to your workspace in a relatively inexpensive manner. See Chapter 2 for further details.

WHY IS THIS IMPORTANT?

Understanding the basics of drafting allows you to create good habits in your work. This will enable you to work more efficiently and ensure strong and accurate communication skills with other architects, designers, engineers, and contractors. While the steps will change depending on whether you are drafting by hand or with one of the various computer drafting programs, the drawing types, characteristics and elements will remain consistent. Additionally, the codes established by the ICC and the ADA are updated every three years, so while there are adjustments that you will need to account for, it is vital that you familiarize yourself with the key rules and regulations pertaining to commercial and residential projects.

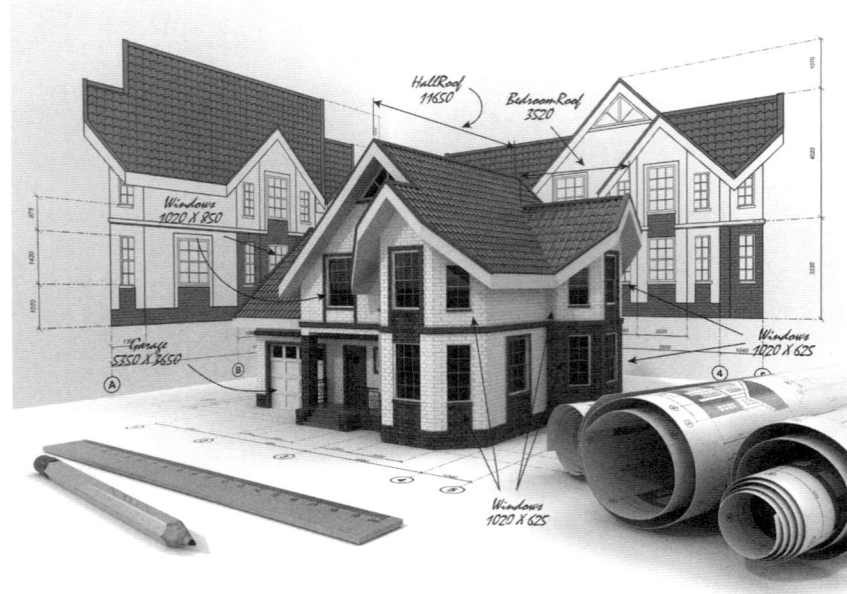

Figure 1.21
3D projection of the drafted exterior elevations of a residence.

Figure 1.22
Close up of construction plans.

Figure 1.23
Hand sketched plan drafts and a finished exterior elevation.

CHAPTER 1 BASICS OF DETAILING | 13

CHAPTER REVIEW

1. What are the differences between elevation and section views?
2. How do the different types of lines impact a drawing and the viewer's understanding of that drawing?
3. Why are the IBC and ADA standards important? Why should you research and implement them early in the design process?

CHAPTER TERMINOLOGY

Americans with Disabilities Act
Americans with Disabilities Act Accessibility Guidelines
annotation
architectural lettering
axonometric
center line
detail callout
detail drawing
dimension
elevation
elevation symbol
guideline
hidden line
International Building Codes
International Code Council
International Residential Code
leader line
linetype
lineweight
material designation
object line
phantom line
plan
scale
section
section cut symbol
stringer (dimensions)

CHAPTER REFERENCES

Ballast, David Kent. *Interior Construction & Detailing for Designers and Architects*. Belmont, CA: Professional Publications, Inc., 2013.

Ching, Francis D. *Building Construction Illustrated*. New York: John Wiley & Sons, 2014.

International Code Council. *International Building Code, 2015*. Chicago: International Code Council Publications, 2014.

International Code Council. *International Residential Code, 2015*. Chicago: International Code Council Publications, 2014.

Kilmer, W. Otie and Rosemary Kilmer. *Construction Drawings and Details for Interiors*. New York: John Wiley & Sons, 2016.

Kruse, Kelsey and Maryrose McGowan. *Interior Graphic Standards*. New York: John Wiley & Sons, 2003.

United States Department of Justice. *2010 ADA Standards for Accessible Design*. Washington, D.C.: Dept. of Justice, 2010.

Hand drafting basics

CHAPTER 2

CHAPTER OUTCOMES

After completing this chapter you will be able to:

1. Determine the proper scales and leads based on the drawing type and lineweight needs.
2. Create annotations and dimensions that are legible and complementary to the drawing.
3. Establish the first step in developing a means of visual communication by connecting one drawing to another through symbols.

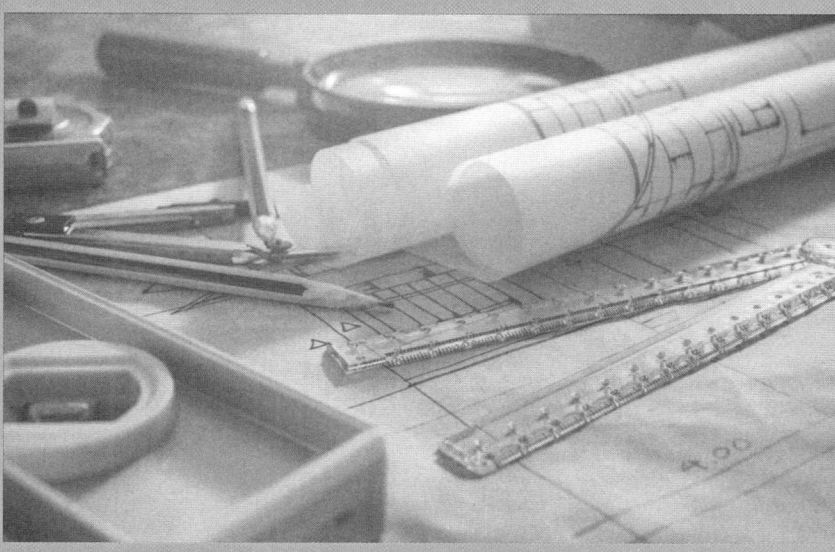

Figure 2.1
Hand drafting on trace.

ARCHITECTURAL SCALE

The **architectural scale** is one of the most important tools for those drafting by hand. This three-sided measuring instrument allows you to quickly switch from one scale to another while providing consistent units of measurement so that your drawings can be accurately produced. Each of the three sides of the scale are broken into four different measurement sizes, each relating to each other on a fractional level. The most used side for interior designers holds the 1"-, 1/2"-, 1/4"-, and 1/8"= 1'-0" scales. Looking at the scale, as seen in Figure 2.2, each end of the scale has two different measurements, meaning that you can rotate the scale around to access each of them. When using each individual strip of the rule, one scale can be read from left to right and overlaps with another scale being read from right to left (Figure 2.3).

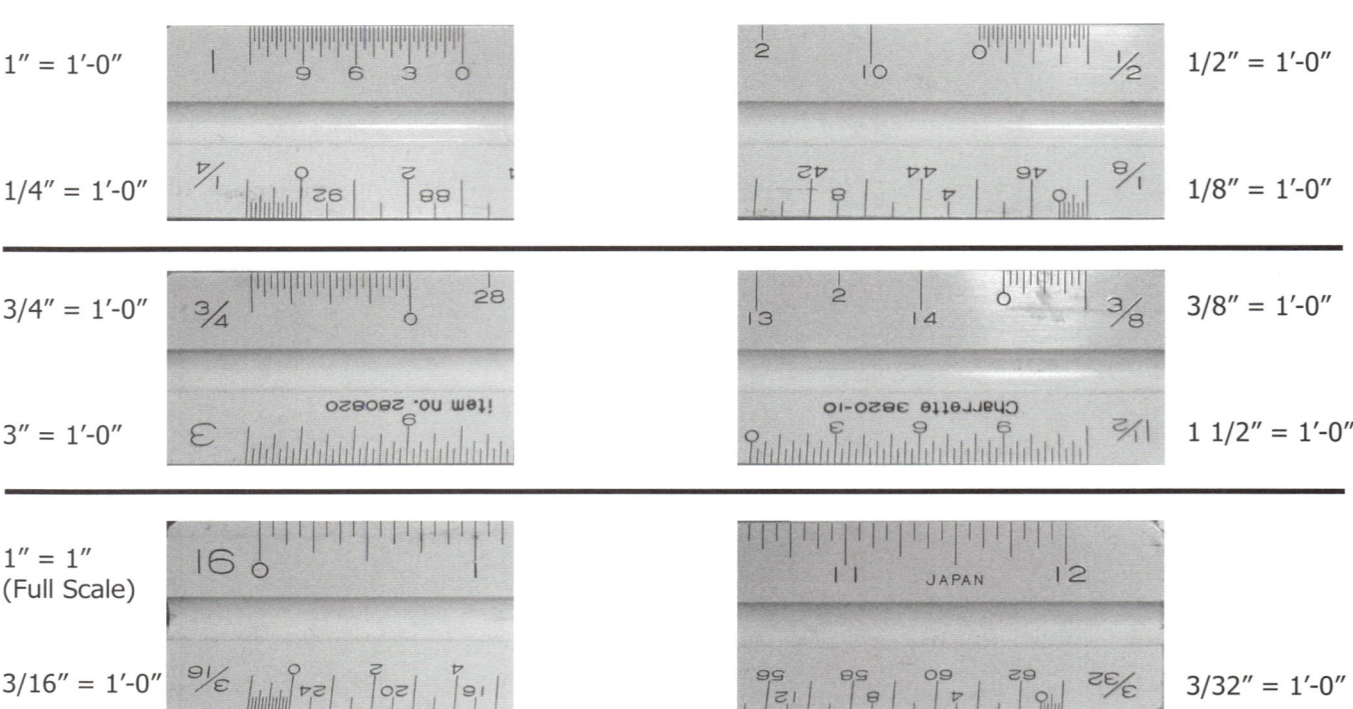

Figure 2.2
Units of measurement on an architectural scale.

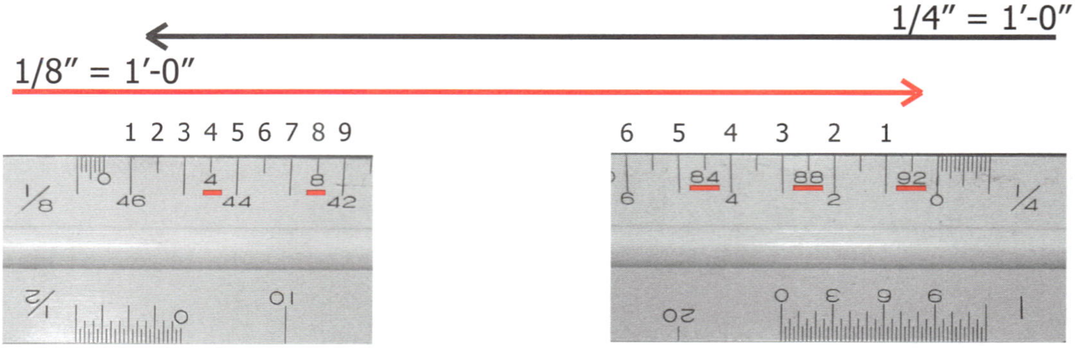

Figure 2.3
A single side of the architectural scale showing both the 1/8" (left) and 1/4" options. The 1/8" scale reads from left to right (shown as the red underlined numbers) while overlapping with the 1/4" scale that reads from right to left.

16 | PART I DETAILING FUNDAMENTALS

Each of the scales is available to aid you in drawing accurately measured, miniature versions of the building or object you are detailing so that a representation of them fits on paper. The scale itself indicates how each foot of the actual project is represented on the page. If you're drawing in 1/4" = 1'-0" scale, every 1/4" measured has the equivalent of 1'-0" in real life.

When using the architectural scale, place the desired unit of measurement along the paper and align the opposite side of the scale with the paraline or a triangle to ensure that the line you measure is straight. If the measurement is a whole foot without any fractional inches, you can measure from the *0* on the number line, as seen in Figure 2.5. If the measurement includes inches, be sure to use the tick marks prior to the *0* to add the fractional inches to the drawing. This segment of the ruler equates to 1'-0" in the specified scale that has been broken down into twelve evenly spaced tick marks, each representing 1".

The exception to the measurement breakdown is the 16 scale, also referred to as a full scale. This side breaks down a real-world 12" measurement into 1" segments that are further broken down into 16 evenly spaced divisions, meaning that each individual tick mark represents 1/16" in both your detail drawing and in the real world. This scale reads from left to right without having to overlap with another measurement.

It is important to remember what scale you are working in and which number line you need when drawing, as it can be easy to accidently switch over to a different scale while working. Make a note for yourself as a reminder of what scale the drawing needs to be in, and always start your measurements from the *0* of the corresponding scale.

LINETYPE

To maintain a consistent linetype from one end of the line to the other, be sure to place your architectural scale alongside your **parallel ruler**, triangle, or T-square. This will ensure that you are able to measure out the dashes that are needed for various linetypes. When drawing a continuous line, simply remove the scale.

For more information on linetypes, refer to Chapter 1.

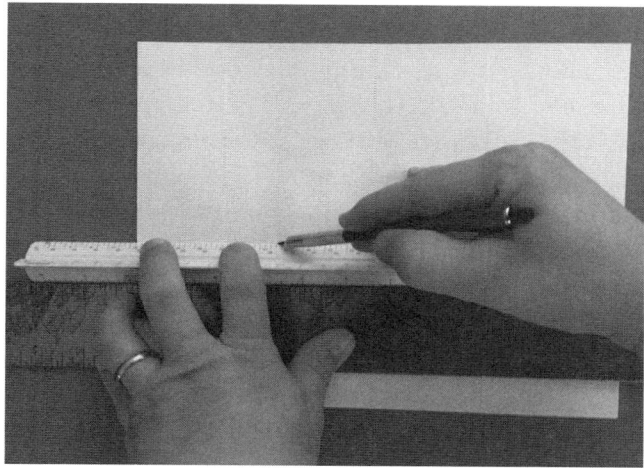

Figure 2.4
Align the architectural scale on the parallel ruler to create your tick marks before drawing lines with the rule.

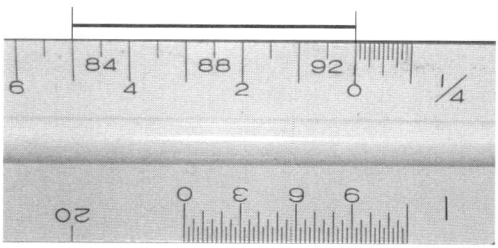

Figure 2.5
A 5'-0" line segment (red) drawn in a 1/4" scale.

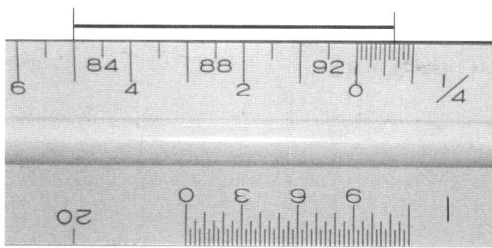

Figure 2.6
A 5'-8" line segment (red) drawn in a 1/4" scale.

Figure 2.7
Different linetypes drawn by hand from top: object line, guideline, hidden line, center line, phantom line.

CHAPTER 2 HAND DRAFTING BASICS | 17

LINEWEIGHT

To maintain a consistent lineweight from one end of a line to another, make sure to sharpen your lead frequently and slowly rotate the pencil as you draw the line. These two methods will maintain a pointed tip on the lead that will keep the line from flaring out. To manipulate your lineweights, you can adjust the pressure from your hand in addition to changing the lead grade you are using.

H leads are hard, meaning that you will have lines that are thin and clean, making these leads ideal for initial drafting work and any technical elements that are to be shown. Be careful not to apply too much pressure or attempt to create your heavier lines with this lead, as you may puncture your paper.

B leads are softer than H leads and should be used when you need thicker, heavier, or darker lines. B leads tends to "bleed" or create dust, so make sure to clean the paper surface with dusting brush after drawing to avoid creating smudges on your work.

HB lead is the neutral lead type between H and B. This lead will read as dark with minimal hand pressure while not bleeding as easily as the Bs, making it ideal for lettering and some technical elements.

For more information on lineweights, refer to Chapter 1.

Figure 2.8
Lineweights can be manipulated by using different leads and pressures. From top: H, B, and HB.

DIMENSIONS AND ANNOTATIONS

When drawing the stringer, make sure to use your parallel ruler to ensure the horizontal lines are straight. For the dimensions, place your triangle on the **parallel ruler** to create a 90 degree angle to draw the vertical lines. Write the dimensions and notations in architectural lettering.

When creating an annotation, make sure to create guidelines for your text so that each individual annotation is straight. This also ensures that each new annotation is aligned with the first. Draw these guidelines very lightly and do not ink them for your final copy.

If the annotation requires a leader line, use your parallel ruler to create the horizontal element and your triangle when drawing the angled portion.

Figure 2.9
Use a triangle to ensure vertical lines are straight.

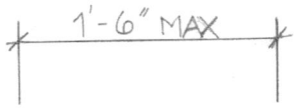

Figure 2.10
Dimension stringers should be drawn with a paraline and triangles.

Figure 2.11
Annotations should be in architectural lettering.

PART I DETAILING FUNDAMENTALS

MATERIAL DESIGNATIONS

Material designations can be created by utilizing a combination of the parallel rule, triangles, templates, and freehand drawing. Once you have selected a pattern, try to make sure that you are as consistent as possible with the design, meaning the more simplistic or representative the easier it is for the drafter and the clearer the communication.

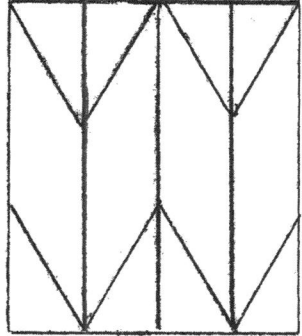 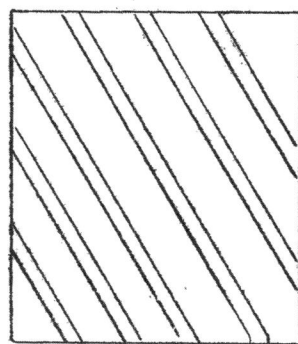 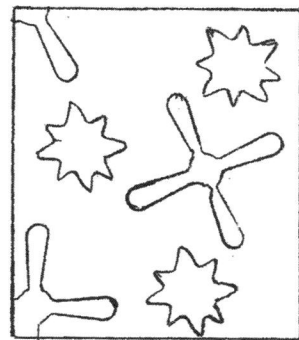 

Figure 2.12
Material designations by hand L–R: plywood (parallel rule), steel (triangles), textile pattern (template), and wood (freehand).

ELEVATION SYMBOLS

The elevation symbol should be placed in the exact location on the plan that you would be standing on if you were to see the views you would draw in elevation. Use your circle template to draw the center of the symbol and the parallel rule and triangle to draw the arrow heads. Draw guidelines to house the numbers in architectural lettering. Remember that these numbers will not be added until you know the order of the drawings in the final construction set, as seen in Part III of this text.

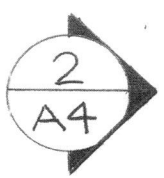

Figure 2.13
An elevation marker indicating that the corresponding drawing will be the second drawing on page A4.

SECTION CUT MARKERS

Begin by drawing a horizontal or vertical line through the plan or elevation to indicate what is being "cut through" for the section drawing. At one end of the line, use your circle template to draw the center of the section cut symbol and the parallel rule and triangle to draw the arrow head pointing in the direction of the view. Draw guidelines to house the numbers in architectural lettering. Remember that these numbers will not be added until you know the order of the drawings in the final construction set, as seen in Part III of this text. At the other end of the cut line, use the parallel rule and triangle again to create a "tail," or rectangle, in the same direction as the arrowhead.

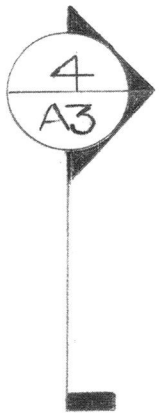

Figure 2.14
A section marker indicating that the corresponding drawing will be the fourth drawing on page A3.

CHAPTER 2 HAND DRAFTING BASICS | 19

DETAIL CALLOUTS

Locate the portion of the plan that you wish to enlarge for the detail callout, and, using a template, draw a dashed circle around it. Use the parallel rule and a triangle to create a leader line extending from this detail callout to a circle, which will be used to record the reference page and drawing numbers for the detail. Draw guidelines in this circle to house the numbers in architectural lettering. Remember that these numbers will not be added until you know the order of the drawings in the final construction set, as seen in Part III of this text.

WHY IS THIS IMPORTANT?

Knowing how to hand draft is an important fundamental for architecture and interior design. It is the first step to reading and comprehending drawings and scales, understanding how to put details together, and it allows you to work through construction documents before learning a computer program to accompany all of this information.

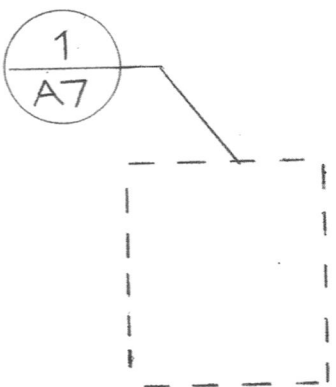

Figure 2.15
A detail callout indicating that an enlarged floor plan will be the first drawing on page A7.

CHAPTER REVIEW

1. Why do line types and lineweights matter? How is this established by hand?
2. What is the importance of dimensions and annotations in a detail?
3. How do the various markers and callouts communicate with one another? Why is this important?

CHAPTER TERMINOLOGY

architectural scale
parallel ruler

CHAPTER REFERENCES

Ballast, David Kent. *Interior Construction & Detailing for Designers and Architects*. Belmont, CA: Professional Publications, Inc., 2013.

Ching, Francis D. *Building Construction Illustrated*. New York: John Wiley & Sons, 2014.

DeChiara, Joseph, Julius Panero, and Martin Zelnik. *Time-Saver Standards for Interior Design and Space Planning*. New York: McGraw-Hill, 2001.

Kilmer, W. Otie and Rosemary Kilmer. *Construction Drawings and Details for Interiors*. New York: John Wiley & Sons, 2016.

Kruse, Kelsey and Maryrose McGowan. *Interior Graphic Standards*. New York: John Wiley & Sons, 2003.

AutoCAD basics

CHAPTER 3

CHAPTER OUTCOMES

After completing this chapter you will be able to:

1. Determine and adjust the properties that are assigned to lineweights and linetypes.

2. Add and edit dimensions, annotations, and materials to a detail.

3. Place and edit markers and views for elevations, sections, and details to ensure accurate communication between drawings.

4. Use shortcut commands other various tips and tricks to streamline the AutoCAD process.

Figure 3.1
CAD drawn floor plans.

CHAPTER DISCLAIMER

While this text provides tips and step-by-step examples of various tools used in CAD, it is not a source for teaching the program. Students should have a working knowledge of AutoCAD and the basic drawing tools noted here. Instead, this chapter should be seen as a reference for shortcuts to and adjustments of the various commands CAD provides in an effort to streamline your workflow when detailing.

SCALE

The **model space** drawing window does not take **scale** into account while you're drawing. As long as you have dictated to the program that you wish to work in architectural scale you can draw with feet and inches.

STEP 1
Type UNITS and press Enter.

STEP 2
In the Length panel, select Architectural in the Type dropdown.

STEP 3
Click OK.

When working in **paper space** to set up your drawings to print, the scale of the **viewport** can be established:

STEP 1
Highlight the viewport. It should appear as a rectangle made up of dashed lines.

STEP 2
In the lower right ribbon, a dropdown menu should appear to allow you to change the scale of the selected viewport. Click on it and choose the scale you wish the drawing to print at.

STEP 3
Note that the drawing will automatically update and it may be necessary for you to resize or reposition what appears on the page to print.

For more about scaling drawings in paper space, see Part III of the text.

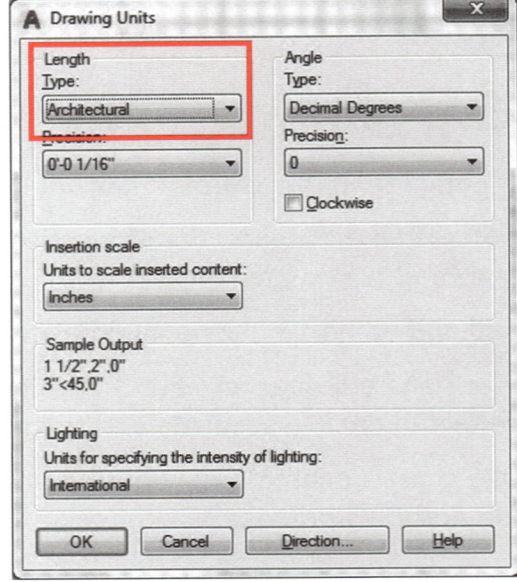

Figure 3.2
Adjust the unit of measurement in the Drawing Units panel.

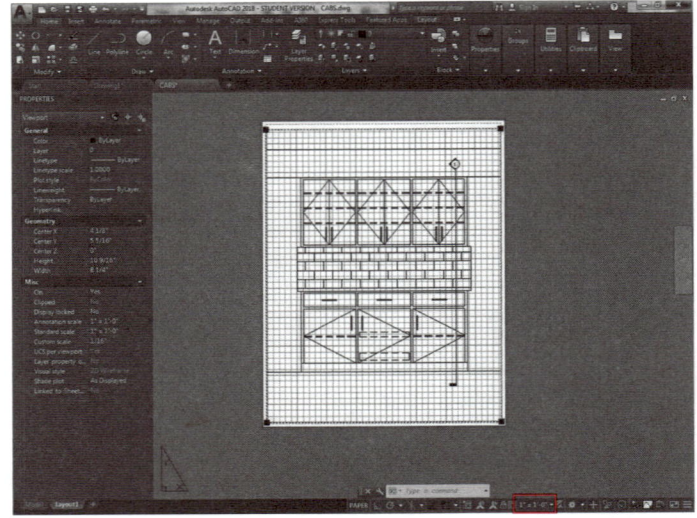

Figure 3.3
Change the scale of the drawing in paper space.

LINETYPE

The linetype can be altered in the same manner as the lineweight, simply by accessing the Layer Properties Manager. Once there, the following differences occur:

STEP 1
Under the Linetype column, click on the Layers option, which should currently read as "Continuous." This will open the Select Linetype window.

STEP 2
If the linetype you need is not yet in the project, click Load . . . , which will open the Load or Reload Linetypes window.

STEP 3
Highlight the linetype you wish to use in the project and click OK.

STEP 4
Once back in the Select Linetype window, highlight the line you need and click OK. Exit out of the Layer Properties Manager.

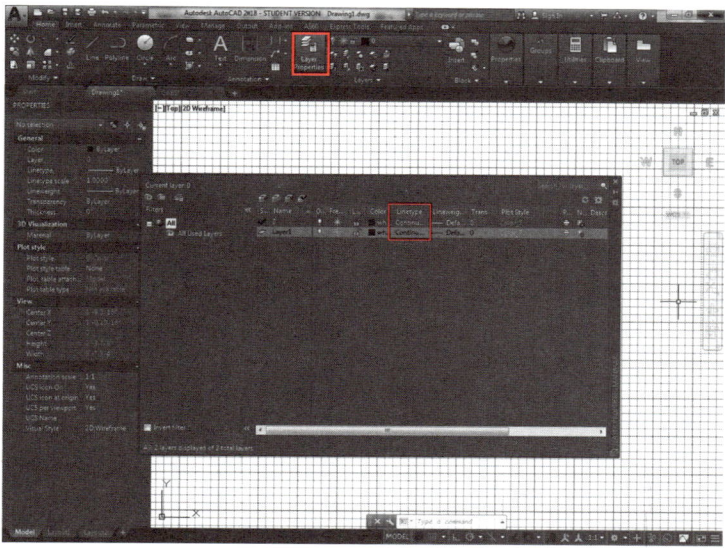

Figure 3.4
Step 1.

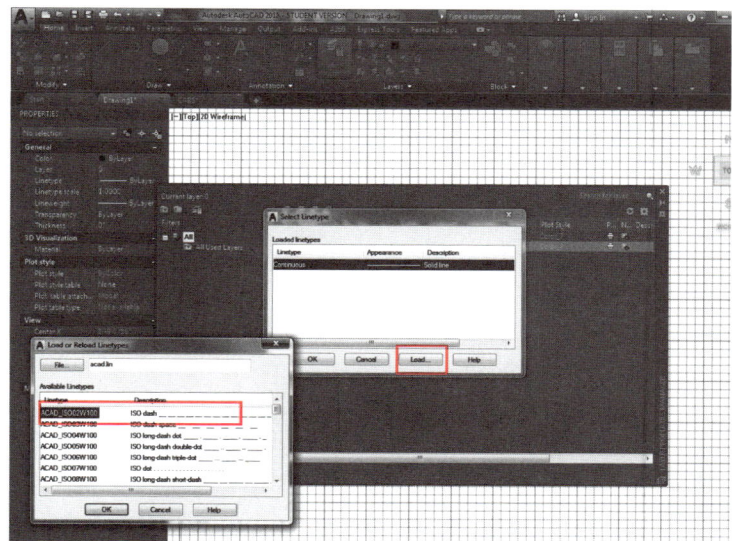

Figure 3.5
Steps 2 and 3.

CHAPTER 3 AUTOCAD BASICS | 23

LINEWEIGHT

The variety of lineweights can be assigned to each "pen," or layer, that you use in the project. These assignments can be altered by accessing Layer Manager in the Layer tab within the Home ribbon, or simply by typing LAYER and pressing Enter. Once the Layer Properties Manager opens, follow these steps to alter the lineweight:

STEP 1
If you have not yet created any layers, click on the icon for New Layer, which can be found at the top of the window. The new layer will be created within the manager, which is where you can alter the color, lineweight, and linetype of the pen.

STEP 2
Under the Lineweight column, click on the Layers option, which should currently read as "Default." This will open a Lineweight Manager.

STEP 3
Select a new weight for the pen and click OK. Exit out of the Layer Properties Manager.

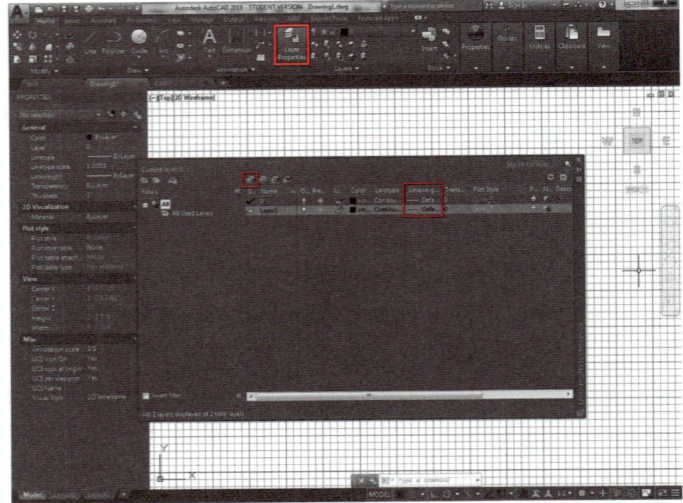

Figure 3.6
Step 1.

Figure 3.7
Step 2.

DIMENSIONING

Placing dimensions

When placing linear dimension stringers in CAD, the system will automatically keep the lines and numbers in order and allow you to place them neatly into your drawing. To do this, follow these steps:

STEP 1
Open the Annotate tab and locate the Aligned or Linear Tools in the Dimension panel.

STEP 2
In the drawing window, hover over the elements you wish to dimension. A green box will appear when your mouse is in a location where you can place a dimension marker, which you can do by clicking.

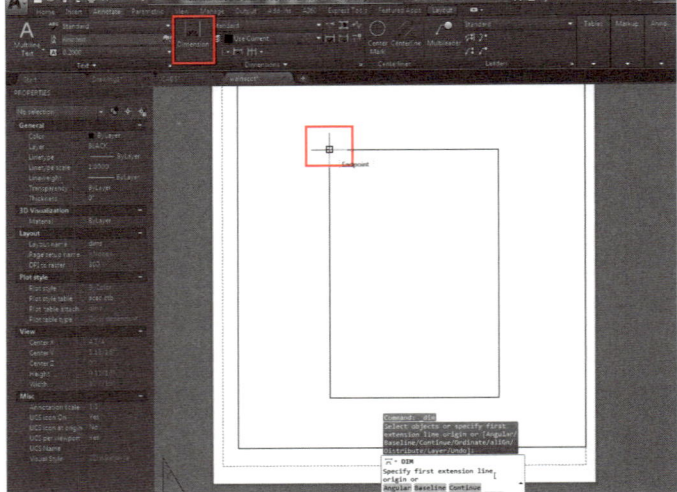

Figure 3.8
Steps 1 and 2.

24 | PART I DETAILING FUNDAMENTALS

STEP 3
A dashed line will appear connecting the dimensioned location to your mouse cursor. Find the end of the measurement you wish to place and click again when hovering over a green box.

STEP 4
Move the mouse a distance away from the measured object and click again to place the stringer. This placement can be adjusted by clicking on the stringer to highlight it and dragging it closer or farther from the elements.

STEP 5
To add additional stringers in line with this first dimension, click on the DIMCONTINUE icon and then carry on placing stringers in your drawing.

At this point, you should also notice that there are a series of blue dots on the stringer lines, which will permit adjustments to the extension lines and placement of the numeric dimension.

STEP 6
To move the placement of the dimension line, click and drag the blue dot in the center of the line. Click to place it in a new location.

STEP 7
To elongate the extension line or change the object that the dimension is connected to, click and drag the blue dots at the end of the extension line. Click to place it in a new location.

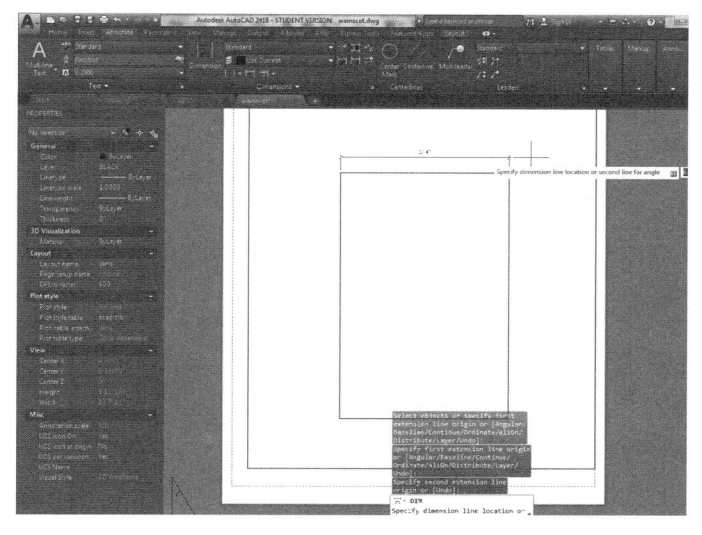

Figure 3.9
Steps 3 and 4.

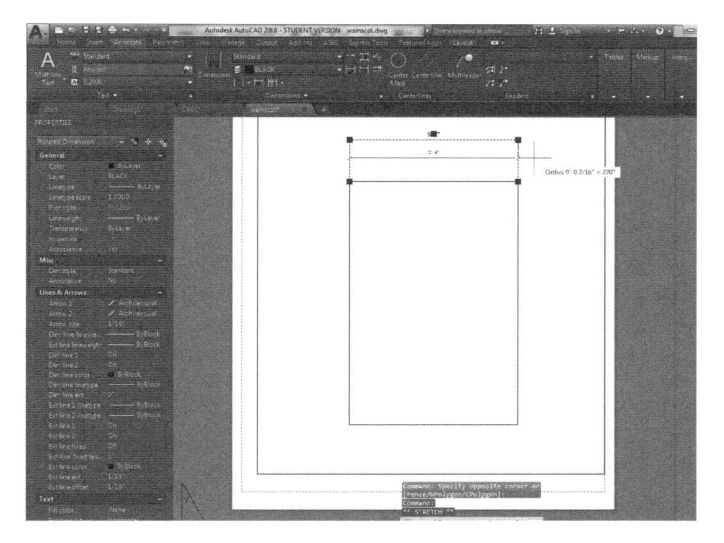

Figure 3.10
Step 6.

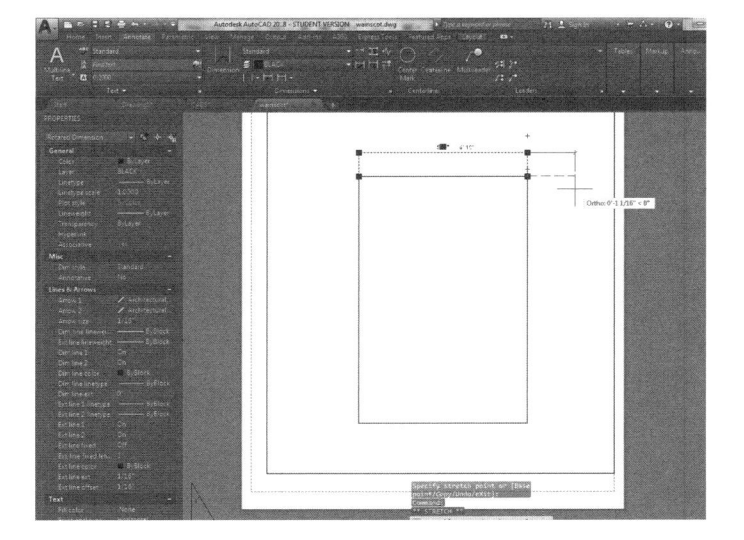

Figure 3.11
Step 7.

CHAPTER 3 AUTOCAD BASICS | 25

Editing dimensions

To edit the style and unit format of the dimensions complete the following steps:

STEP 1
Type DIMSTYLE and press enter. The Dimension Style Manager will open.

STEP 2
Click on Standard on the left hand side of the window and then click Set Current. Finally, click Modify.

STEP 3
In the new window that appears, click on the Symbols and Arrows tab and change Arrowheads from Closed Filled to Architectural Tick. You will see the scale change in the preview window.

STEP 4
On the Text tab, change the following:
a. Text Placement from Vertical: Centered to Vertical: Above.
b. Text Alignment from Horizontal to Aligned with Dimension Line

STEP 5
In the Fit tab, change Text Placement to Over Dimension Line, with leader.

STEP 6
Click on the Primary Units tab and change the Unit Format from Decimal to Architectural.

STEP 7
Click OK and then click Close.

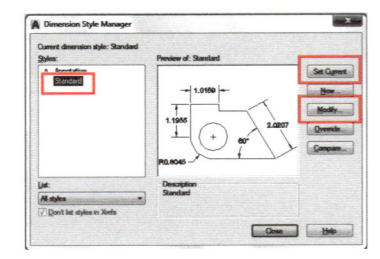

Figure 3.12
Step 2.

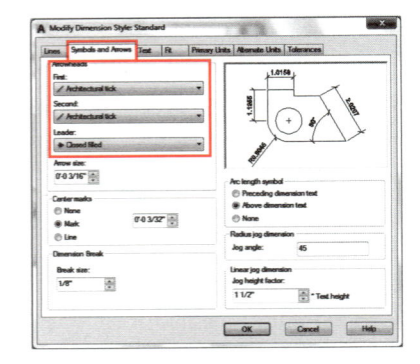

Figure 3.13
Step 3.

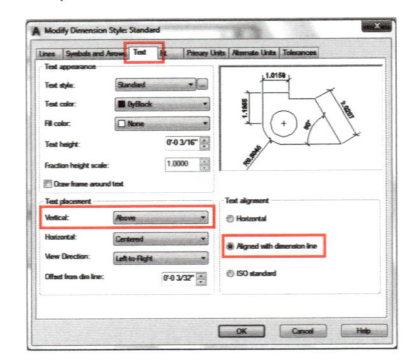

Figure 3.14
Step 4.

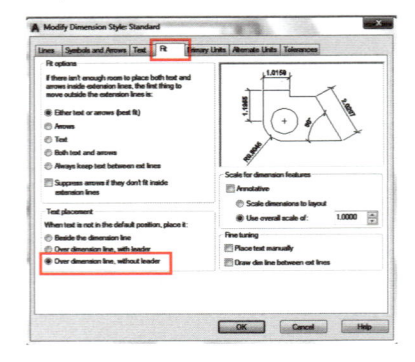

Figure 3.15
Step 5.

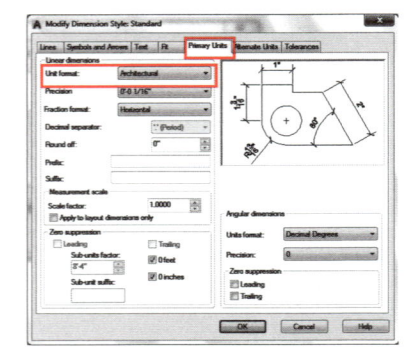

Figure 3.16
Step 6.

PART I DETAILING FUNDAMENTALS

ANNOTATIONS

To add annotations to your drawing, use the Multileader tool, which can be found in the Annotation panel of the Home tab.

STEP 1
After selecting the tool, click once in the drawing window to place the arrow head.

STEP 2
Move your mouse to the location where you wish to place the text. Click once to place it and type the notation in. Click elsewhere in the window to exit from the tool.

STEP 3
If the note needs to point to multiple elements within the drawing, drop down the Multileader selection box and choose Add Leader. Click on the annotation in the model window to add a leader line and click again to place the line.

STEP 4
Press Esc to complete the action.

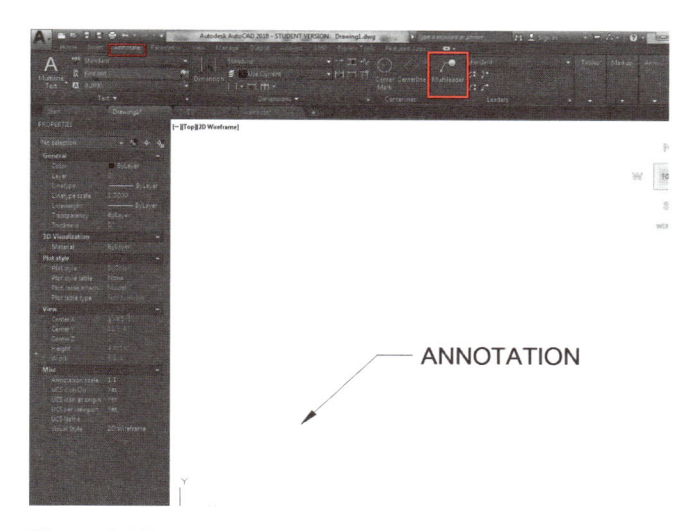

Figure 3.17
Steps 1 and 2.

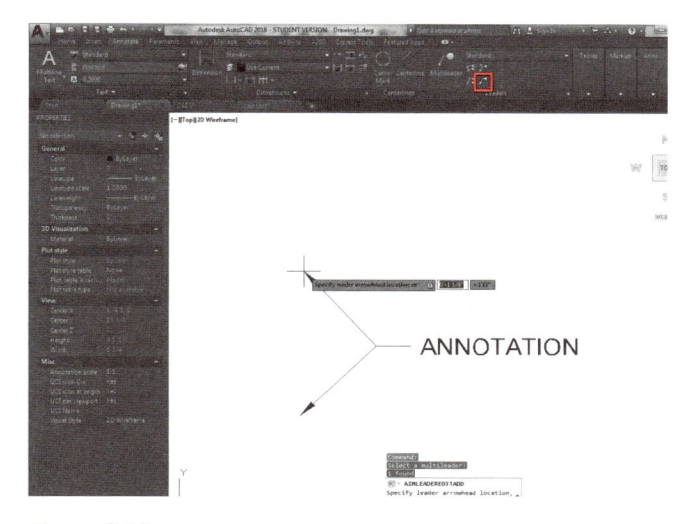

Figure 3.18
Step 3.

MATERIAL DESIGNATION

Material designation patterns can be created two different ways:

a. Use your Line and Circle tools to draw the desired pattern. This can be time consuming, but it will allow you to create custom patterns for your project.
b. Ensure that the shape you are trying to fill is complete and all the lines are connect to each other. Press Escape to terminate all other actions, and then type HATCH and press Enter. This will open the Hatch Creation dialog. Select a **hatch** pattern from the drop-down menu and click inside the shape to fill it. Once the pattern appears, you can press Escape to complete the action.

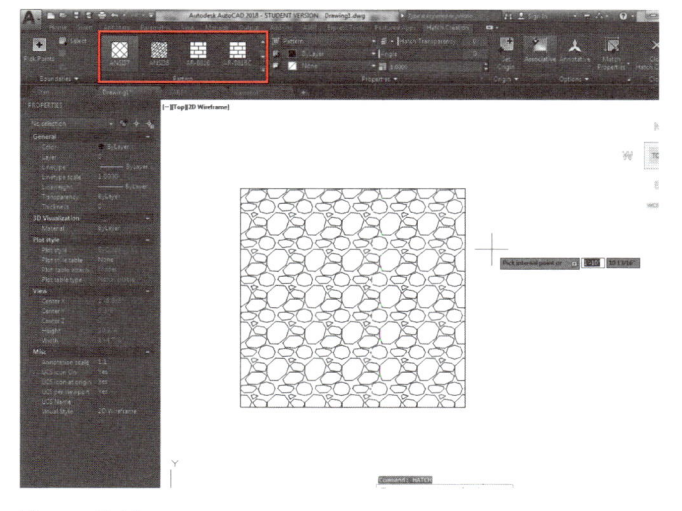

Figure 3.19
Material designation, option B.

CHAPTER 3 AUTOCAD BASICS

Elevation symbols

If you are using AutoCAD, you will need to either download an elevation symbol or draw one yourself using the line, circle, and annotation tools, creating your own block that you can place as needed.

If you are using CAD Architecture, the program will generate the elevation marker for you for quick placement and editing:

STEP 1
Under the Annotate tab, you can find the Callout panel. Locate the Elevation drop-down and select the type of elevation marker you wish to use (this text will use Interior, 1, 2, 3, 4 unless otherwise noted).

STEP 2
In the model space, click on the location where you wish to place the marker. You can see that the marker will remain connected to the cursor.

STEP 3
Move your mouse in the direction of the view for the elevation and click. A Place Callout window will open.

STEP 4
Give your elevation a unique name and click in the box to the left of the Create In option that CAD has assigned or Callout Only.

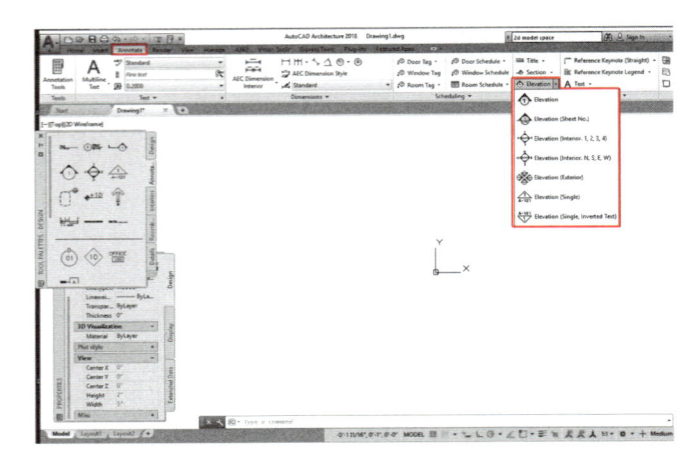

Figure 3.20
Elevation markers can be found in the Callout panel of the Annotate tab.

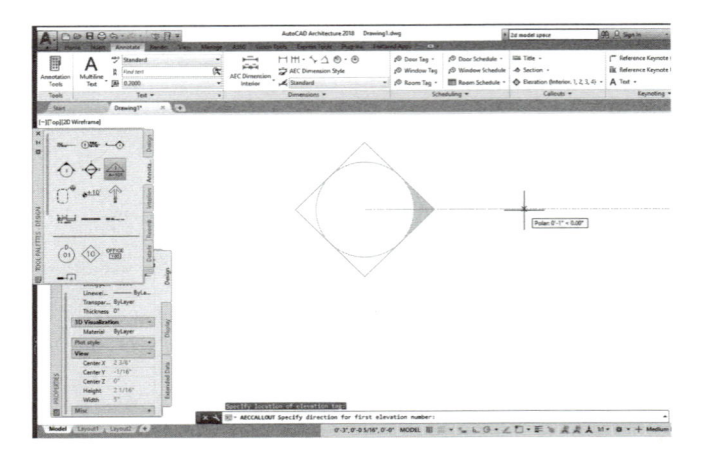

Figure 3.21
Steps 2 and 3.

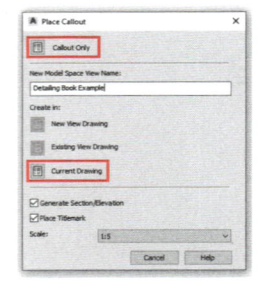

Figure 3.22
Step 4: Place Callout window.

PART I DETAILING FUNDAMENTALS

STEP 5

The tag will appear in your model space with annotative text boxes for the sheet and view numbers. These can be edited by double-clicking on the text.

STEP 6

If a particular view is not needed from the elevation marker, click on the unwanted arrowhead and press Delete.

Additionally, there are two other ways to create elevation markers in CAD. First, you can use the symbol that appears in the Annotation tab of the Tool Palettes—Design Properties box by placing it in a similar manner as above.

Second, if you are using the Build panel from the Home tab or the Tool Palette to create your space, CAD can automatically generate your elevation for you. To place, activate, and use these markers, you will need to utilize the Elevation Line found in the Section & Elevation panel. This technique will allow you to automatically generate an elevation view, similar to what Revit can do, but keep in mind that this drawing will be the bare bones of what your final elevation will look like. The benefit of this action is that you will be able to quickly generate the framework of the elements and will then just need to add the details, dimensions, and annotations.

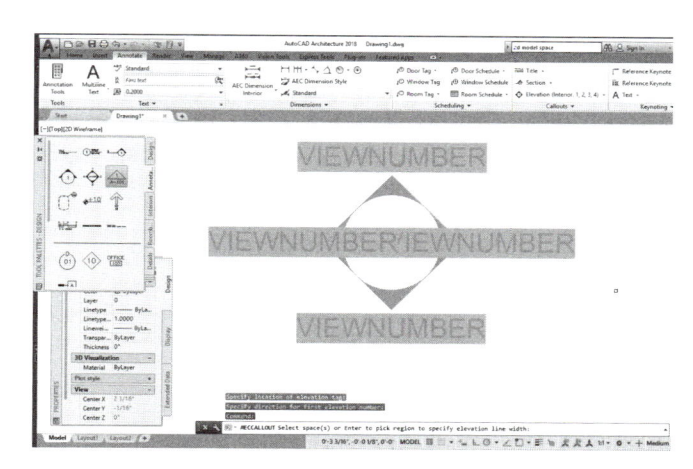

Figure 3.23
Step 5.

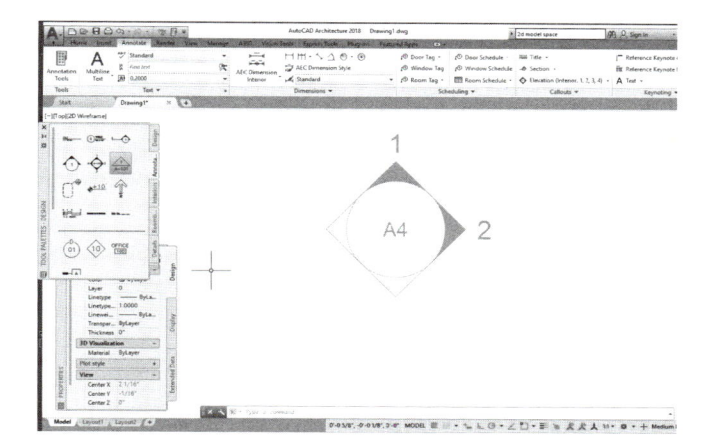

Figure 3.24
Step 6.

SECTION CUT MARKERS

If you are using AutoCAD, you will need to either download a section cut symbol or draw one yourself using the line, circle, and annotation tools, creating your own block that you can place as needed.

If you are using CAD Architecture, the program will generate the section marker for you for quick placement and editing:

STEP 1

Under the Annotate tab, you can find the Callout panel. Locate the section drop-down and select the type of section marker you wish to use (this text will use Sheet Tail unless otherwise noted).

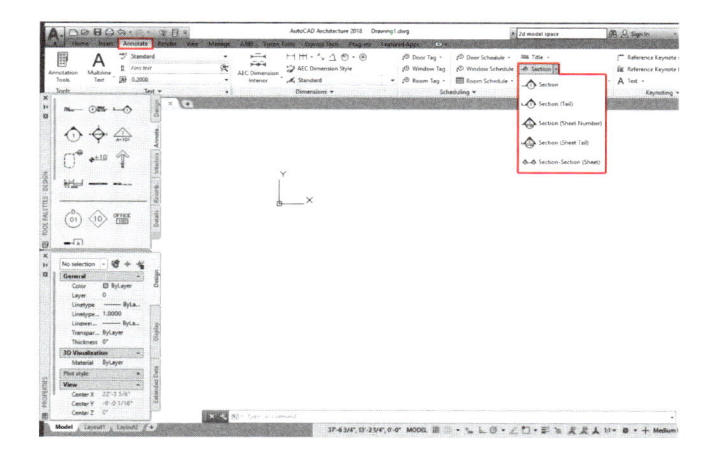

Figure 3.25
Section markers can be found in the Callout panel of the Annotate tab.

CHAPTER 3 AUTOCAD BASICS

STEP 2

In the model space, click on the plan to place the "tail" of the symbol. You will notice that a dashed line will extend from this point to your cursor. This line will illustrate to you what your section marker will cut through before you finalize the placement.

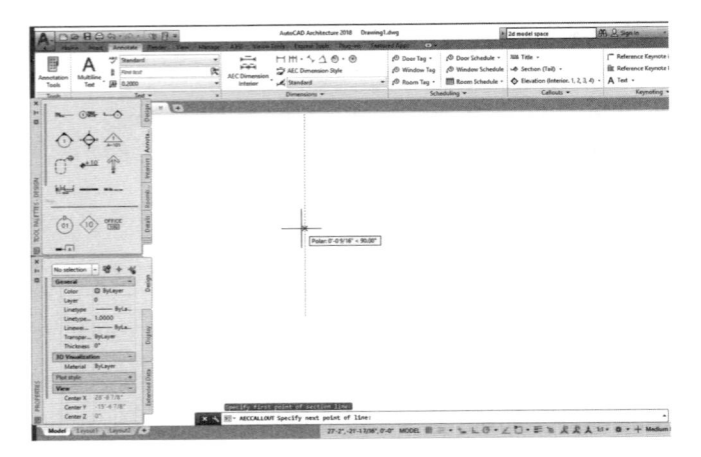

Figure 3.26
Step 2.

STEP 3

Move your mouse past the bounding edge of the element you want to "cut through" and click. You will notice that the cut line has turned purple and the dashed line is still connected to your cursor. You can continue to click and draw cut lines if you choose, but for this example simply press Enter.

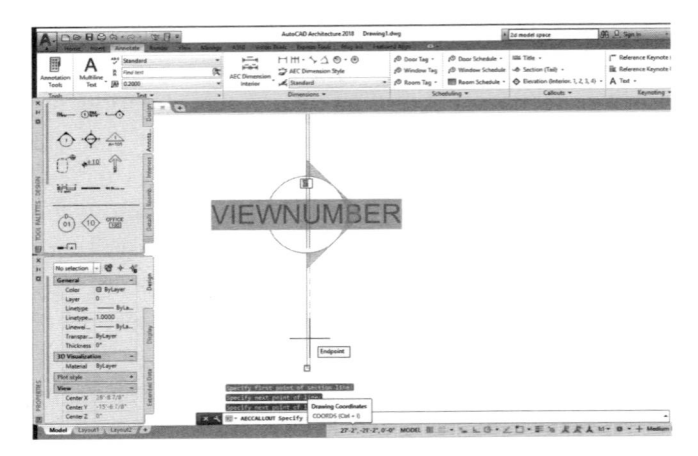

Figure 3.27
Step 3.

STEP 4

The head of the marker will appear, along with a dashed box to indicate the depth of view for the section. Move your mouse in the direction of said view and notice that a solid arrowhead will attach itself to the marker. Move your mouse to extend the depth of view and click, or type in a numeric value for the depth, and press enter. A Place Callout window will open.

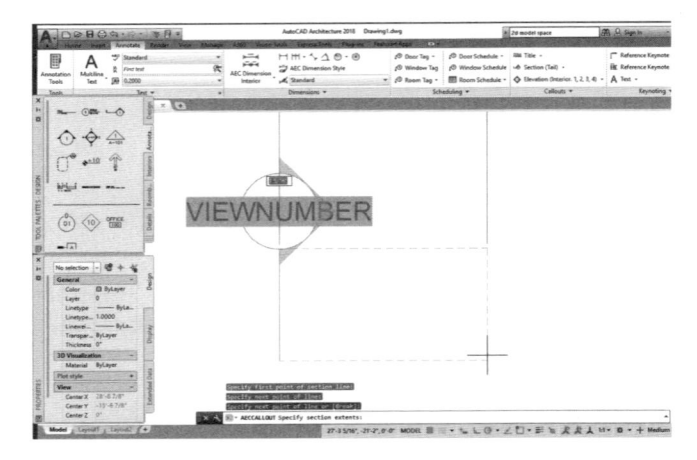

Figure 3.28
Step 4.

PART I DETAILING FUNDAMENTALS

STEP 5

Give your section a unique name and click in the box to the left of the Create In option that CAD has assigned or Callout Only.

STEP 6

The tag will appear in your model space with annotative text boxes for the sheet and view numbers. These can be edited by double-clicking on the text.

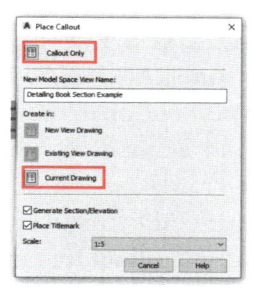

Figure 3.29
Step 5: Place Callout window.

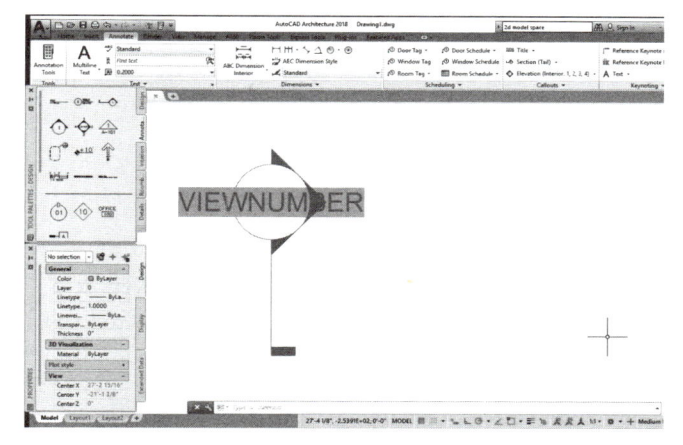

Figure 3.30
Step 6.

Additionally, there are two other ways to create section markers in CAD. First, you can use the symbol that appears in the Annotation tab of the Tool Palettes—Design Properties box by placing it in a similar manner as above.

Second, if you are using the Build panel from the Home tab or the Tool Palette to create your space, CAD can automatically generate your section for you. To place, activate, and use these markers, you will need to utilize the Section Line found in the Section & Elevation panel. This technique will allow you to automatically generate a section view, similar to what Revit can do, but keep in mind that this drawing will be the bare bones of what your final section will look like. The benefit of this action is that you will be able to quickly generate the framework of the elements and will then just require you to add the details, dimensions, and annotations.

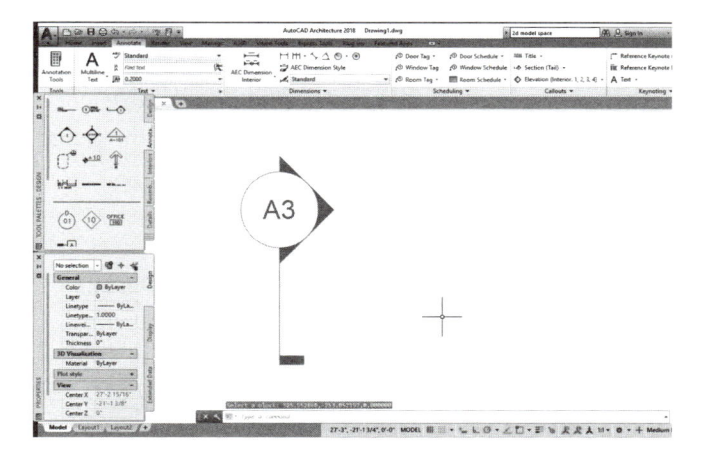

Figure 3.31
Finished section cut marker.

CHAPTER 3 AUTOCAD BASICS   31

DETAIL CALLOUTS

If you are using AutoCAD, you will need to either download a detail callout or draw one yourself using the line, circle, and annotation tools, creating your own block that you can place as needed.

If you are using CAD Architecture, the program will generate the detail callout for you for quick placement and editing:

STEP 1
Under the Annotate tab, you can find the Callout panel. Locate the detail boundary drop-down and select the type of marker you wish to use (this text will use Detail Boundary—Circle unless otherwise noted).

STEP 2
In the model space, click on the center of the location where you wish to place the marker. You can see that the marker will remain connected to the cursor.

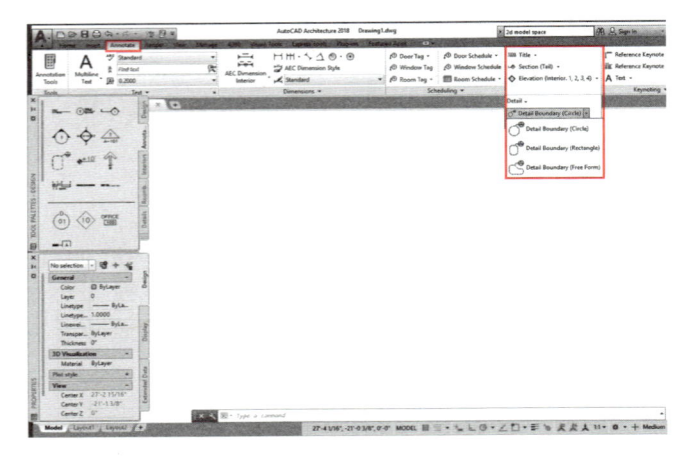

Figure 3.32
Detail markers can be found in the Callout panel of the Annotate tab.

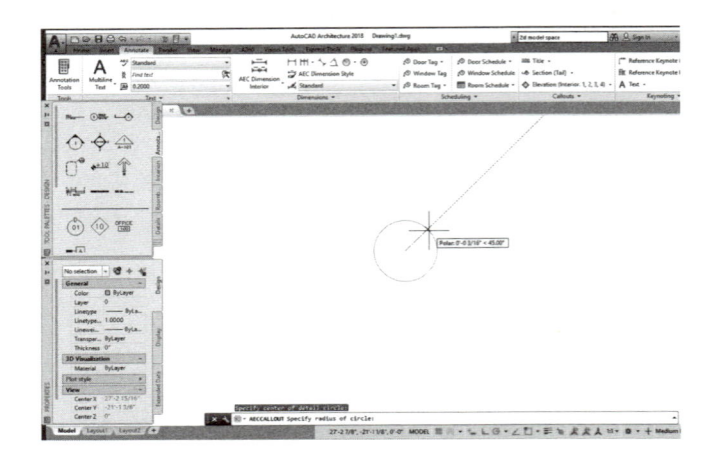

Figure 3.33
Step 2.

STEP 3
Move your mouse outward to enlarge the circle. Once all the elements that will be seen in the detail are within the circle's border, click.

STEP 4
A leader line will attach from the detail callout circle to your cursor; click as many times as necessary to place the leader in the position you wish to have it and then press Enter. A Place Callout window will open.

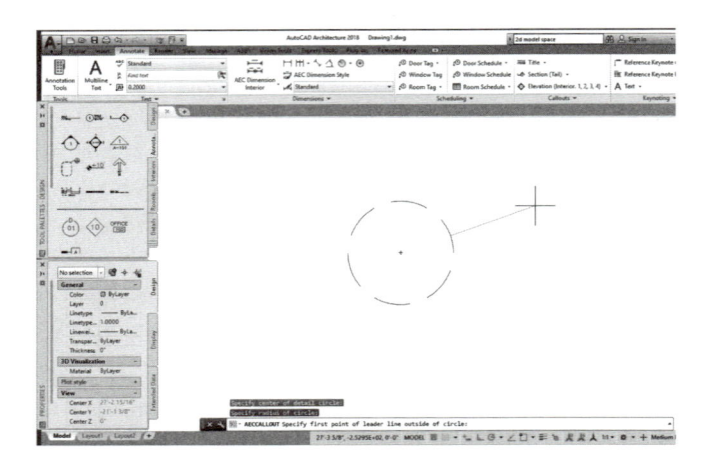

Figure 3.34
Steps 3 and 4.

PART I DETAILING FUNDAMENTALS

STEP 5
Give your detail a unique name and click in the box to the left of the Create In option that either CAD has assigned or Callout Only.

STEP 6
The tag will appear in your model space with annotative text boxes for the sheet and view numbers. These can be edited by double-clicking on the text.

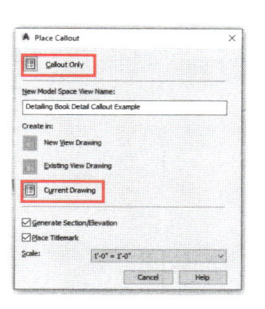

Figure 3.35
Step 5: Place Callout window.

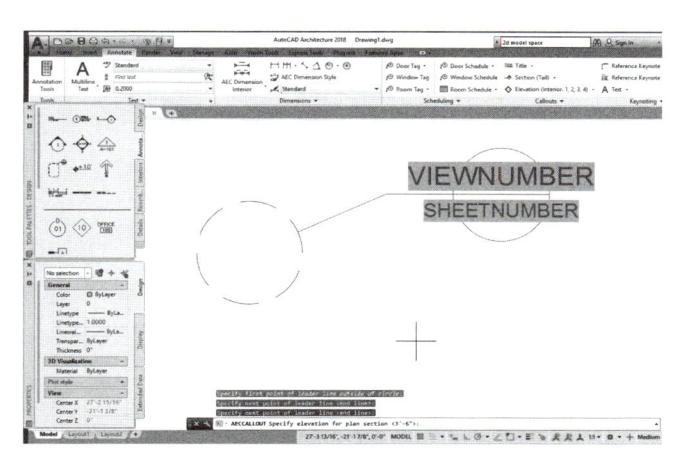

Figure 3.36
Step 6.

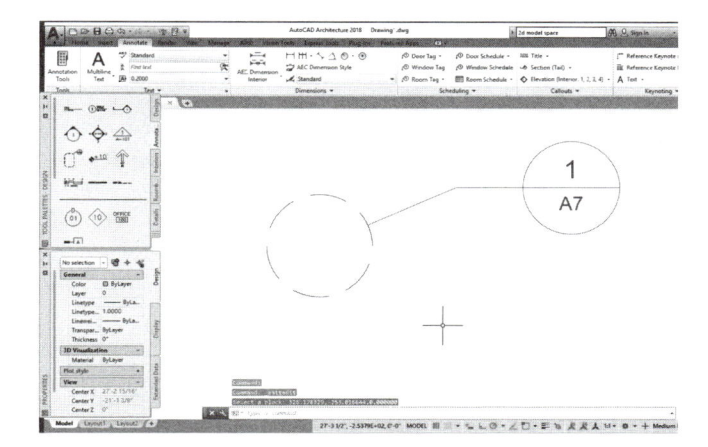

Figure 3.37
Finished detail callout marker.

WHY IS THIS IMPORTANT?

If your school or place of employment uses AutoCAD, it is important that you learn how to manipulate your drawing space and be able to access command shortcuts so that you can work in the most efficient manner possible. When creating detail drawings, it is important to use the tools discussed in this chapter to keep your files organized and consistent from start to finish.

CHAPTER REVIEW

1. Why do line types and lineweights matter? How is this established in CAD?
2. What is the importance of dimensions and annotations in a detail?
3. How do the various markers and callout communicate with one another? Why is this important?

CHAPTER 3 AUTOCAD BASICS   33

CHAPTER TERMINOLOGY

hatch
model space
paper space
viewport

CHAPTER REFERENCES

Ballast, David Kent. *Interior Construction & Detailing for Designers and Architects*. Belmont, CA: Professional Publications, Inc., 2013.

Ching, Francis D. *Building Construction Illustrated*. New York: John Wiley & Sons, 2014.

DeChiara, Joseph, Julius Panero, and Martin Zelnik. *Time-Saver Standards for Interior Design and Space Planning*. New York: McGraw-Hill, 2001.

Kilmer, W. Otie and Rosemary Kilmer. *Construction Drawings and Details for Interiors*. New York: John Wiley & Sons, 2016.

Kruse, Kelsey and Maryrose McGowan. *Interior Graphic Standards*. New York: John Wiley & Sons, 2003.

Revit basics

CHAPTER 4

CHAPTER OUTCOMES

After completing this chapter you will be able to:

1. Determine and adjust the properties that are assigned to lineweights and linetypes.
2. Add and edit dimensions, annotations, and materials to a detail.
3. Place and edit markers and views for elevations, sections, and details to ensure accurate communication among drawings.
4. Use various tips and tricks to streamline the Revit process.

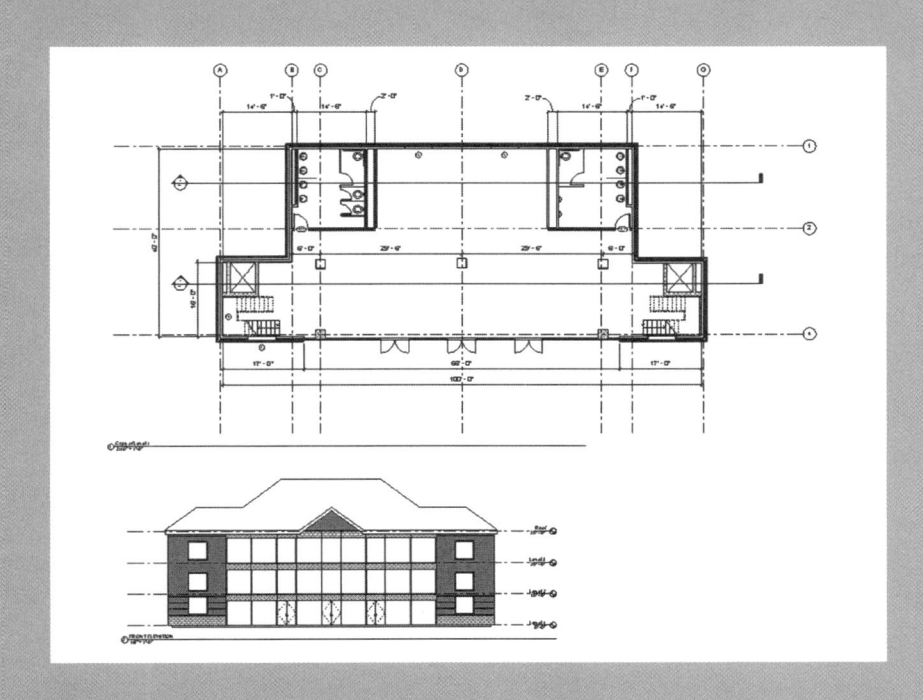

Figure 4.1
Revit-drawn floor plan and elevation.

CHAPTER DISCLAIMER

While this text provides tips and step-by-step examples of various tools used in Revit, it is not a source for teaching the program. Students should have a working knowledge of Revit and the basic drawing tools noted here. Instead, this chapter should be seen as a reference for shortcuts to and adjustments of the various commands Revit provides in an effort to streamline your workflow when detailing.

Furthermore, if you are working in Revit, the program will automatically adjust several elements for you, including the scale of dimensions and annotations in final layouts once you have established project parameters.

SCALE

Model space scale

The model space drawing window does not take scale into account while you are drawing. However, if you know what scale you want your drawing to appear as when printed, you can adjust this in the Properties menu.

STEP 1
Make sure nothing is highlighted in drawing window so that the Properties menu is reading the file and not an object.

STEP 2
Locate the Graphics panel in your Properties menu. The first option will be the View Scale drop-down where you can choose the scale you wish the drawing to be in.

STEP 3
Click Apply. Note that the drawing will not change in size.

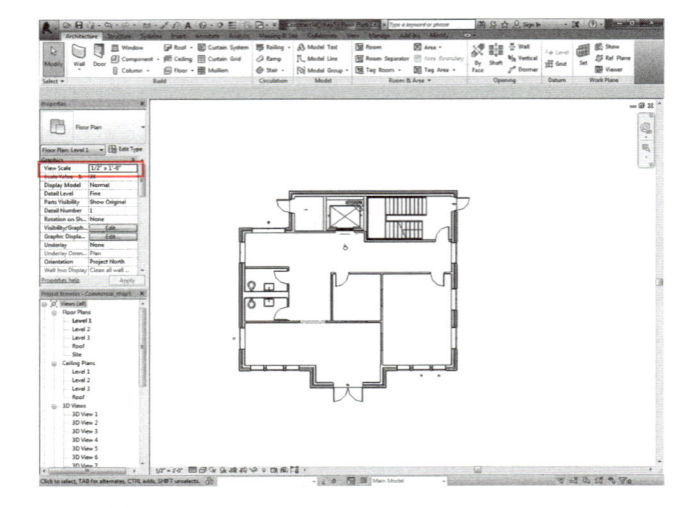

Figure 4.2
Adjust the unit of measurement in the Properties panel by changing the View Scale while in the drawing window.

Sheet scale

When working in a **Sheet** to set up your drawings to print, the scale of the drawing can be established:

STEP 1
Highlight the drawing you wish to change the scale for. The drawing annotation tag will turn blue and the Viewport will become active in the Properties menu, but the drawing itself will appear unaltered.

STEP 2
Locate the Graphics panel in your Properties menu. The first option will be the View Scale drop-down where you can choose the scale you wish the drawing to be in.

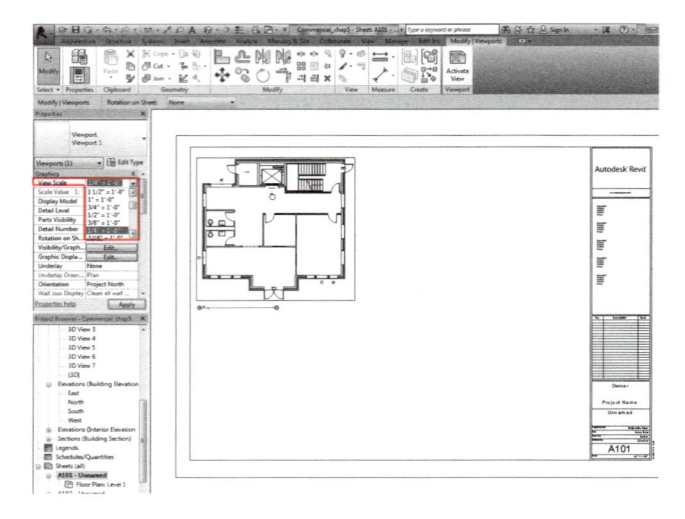

Figure 4.3
Adjust the unit of measurement in the Properties panel by changing the View Scale while in the Sheet view.

STEP 3

Click Apply. Note that the drawing will change size and may need to be repositioned.

For more about scaling drawings on a Sheet, see Part III of the text.

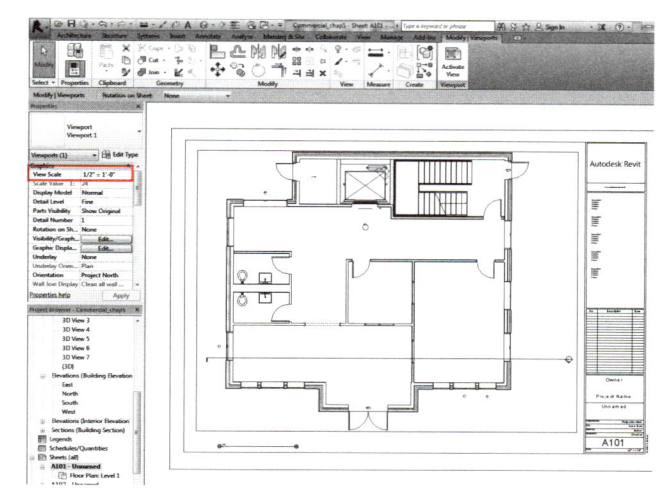

Figure 4.4
The drawing scale will visibly change on the screen.

LINETYPE

Similar to the lineweights, the linetypes are preloaded in the program; however, you can alter the scale, spacing, and pattern of the line:

STEP 1
Click on Manage tab and locate Additional Settings in the Settings panel. Drop-down this menu and click on Line Patterns.

STEP 2
Here, you can edit the spacing or type of line within the pattern by highlighting the name of the line and clicking Edit.

STEP 3
You can create a new linetype by clicking New and using the drop-down menu under Type and manually entering the length of the measurement under Value.

To change the style of an individually drawn line, follow the same steps that are used for editing the lineweight for an individual line. See the following section and Figure 4.9 for more information.

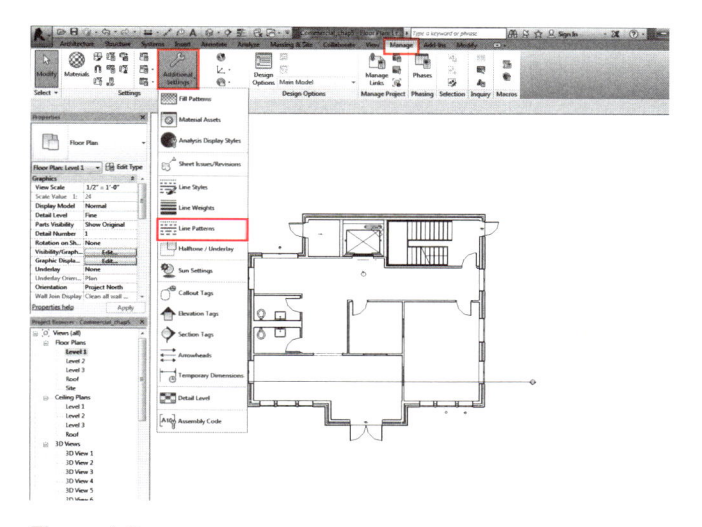

Figure 4.5
Line Patterns from the Additional Settings panel.

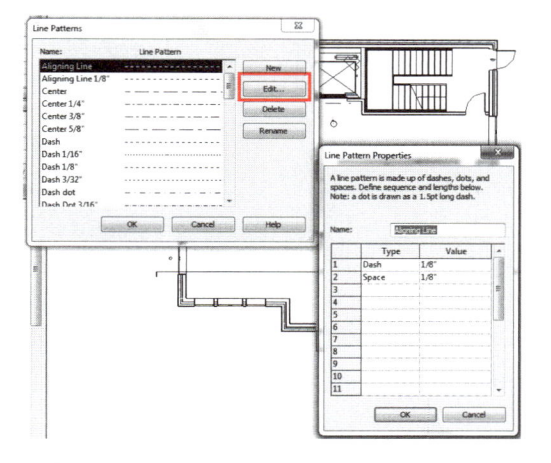

Figure 4.6
Linetype editing panels.

CHAPTER 4 REVIT BASICS 37

LINEWEIGHT

Editing lineweights

Each architectural element and component feature an assigned lineweight that has been preloaded into the program based on the drawing type that is being created. If you choose to change any of these preassigned weights, you can do so through the following steps:

STEP 1
Click on Manage tab and locate Additional Settings in the Settings panel. Drop-down this menu and click on Line Weights.

STEP 2
You will be able to alter the pen weight for lines drawn for modeled components, perspectives, and annotations. Click Apply to see what the changes look like, and click OK to accept the changes. If you applied but choose not to accept the alterations, click Cancel.

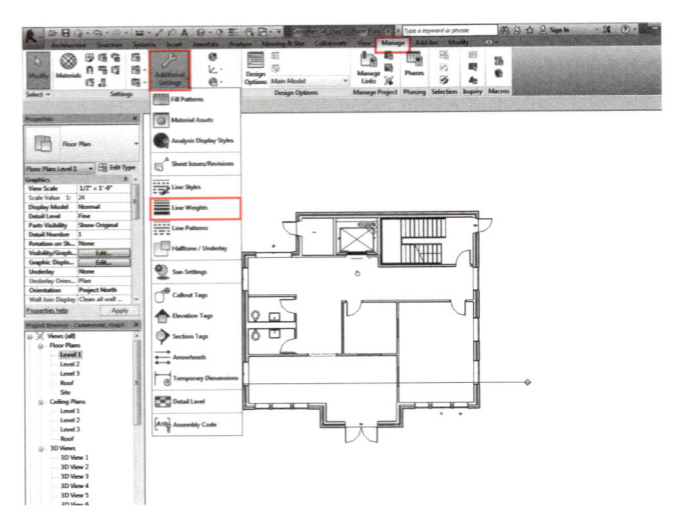

Figure 4.7
Line Weights from the Additional Settings panel.

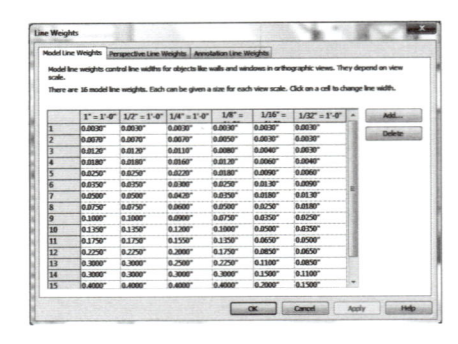

Figure 4.8
Lineweight editing panel.

Altering a single line

To change an individually drawn line within the model or a specific drawing:

STEP 1
Once a line has been drawn, click on it to highlight it.

STEP 2
In the Properties menu on the left side of the screen, locate Line Style under Graphics. Click on the box, which should be in its default setting of Lines, which will show that this is a drop-down option.

STEP 3
Select the weight of line you wish to use.

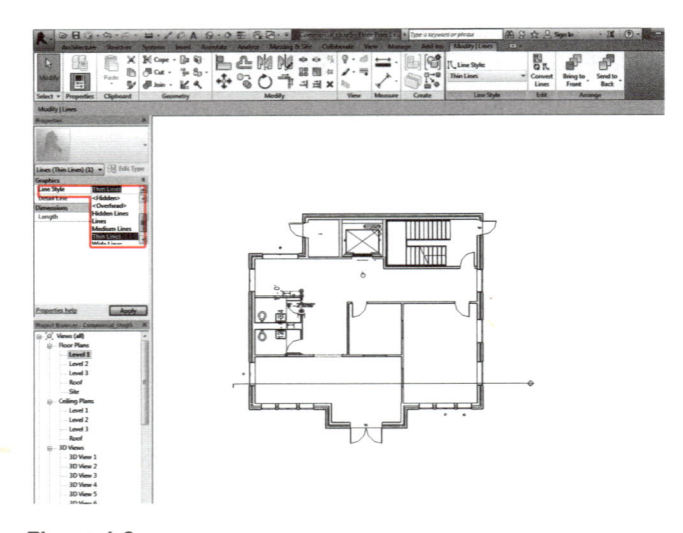

Figure 4.9
Individual lineweights can be altered with Line Styles.

PART I DETAILING FUNDAMENTALS

DIMENSIONING

When placing aligned dimension stringers in Revit, the system will automatically keep the lines and numbers in order and allow you to place them neatly into your drawing. To do this, follow these steps:

STEP 1
Open the Annotate tab and locate the Aligned or Linear tools in the Dimension panel.

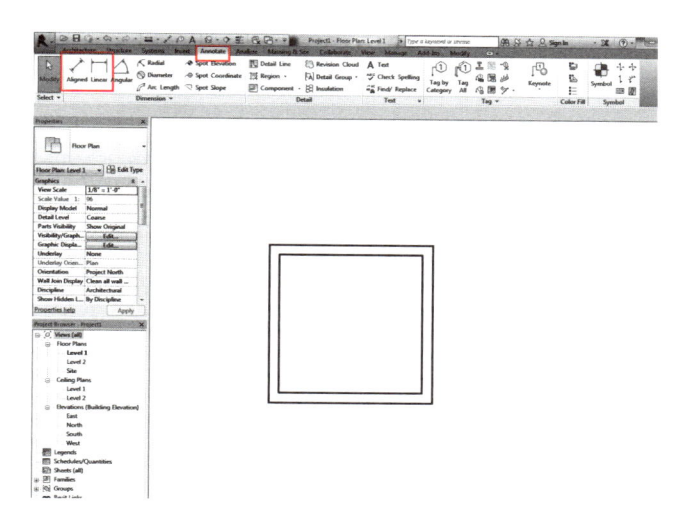

Figure 4.10
Dimensioning tools can be found under the Annotate tab.

STEP 2
In the drawing window, hover over the elements you wish to dimension. A dashed blue line will appear when your mouse is in a location where you can place a dimension marker, which you can do by clicking.

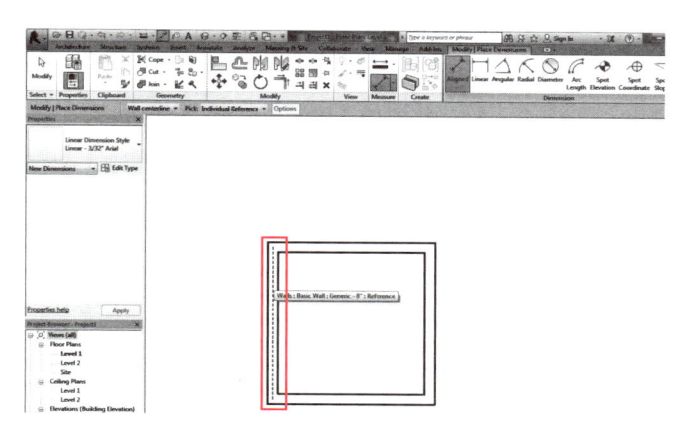

Figure 4.11
Step 2.

STEP 3
The first extension line will appear connecting the dimensioned location to your cursor. Find the end of the measurement you wish to place and click again when hovering over a blue line.

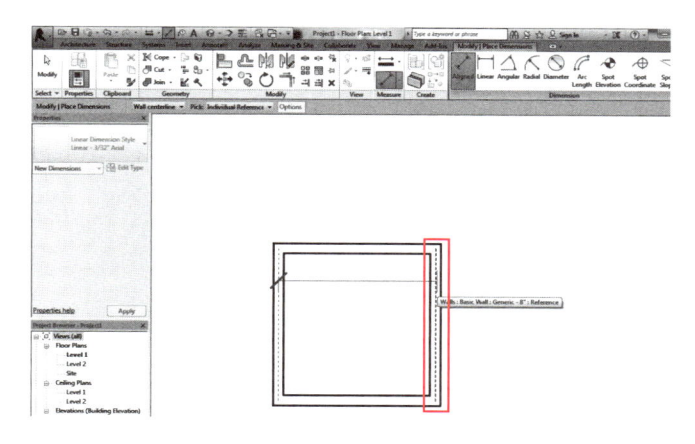

Figure 4.12
Step 3.

STEP 4

Move the mouse a distance away from the measured object and click again to place the stringer. This placement can be adjusted by clicking on the stringer to highlight it and dragging it closer to or farther from the elements.

At this point, you should also notice that there are a series of blue dots on the stringer lines that will permit adjustments to the extension lines and placement of the numeric dimension.

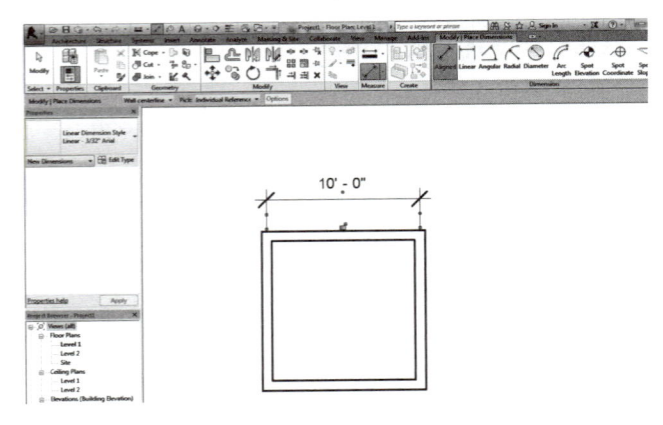

Figure 4.13
Step 4.

STEP 5

To move the numbers, click and drag the blue circle that is directly under the dimension itself. Release the mouse button to place it in a new location.

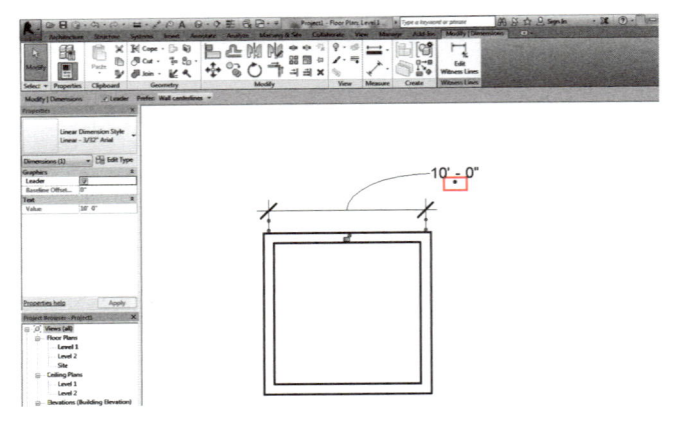

Figure 4.14
Step 5.

STEP 6

To elongate the extension line, click and drag the blue circles at the end of the extension line. Release the mouse button to place it in a new location.

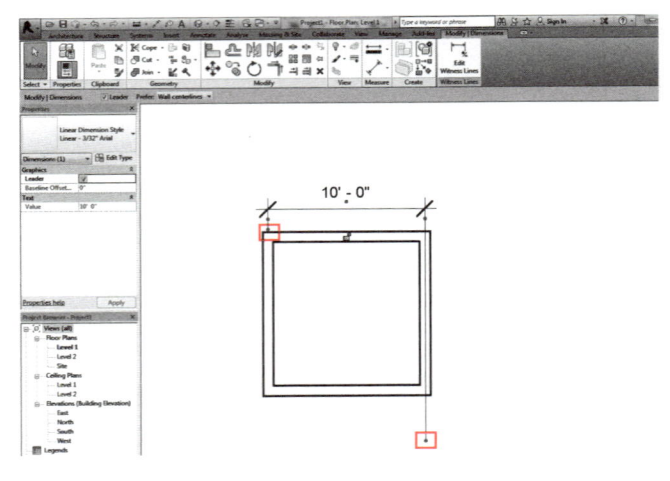

Figure 4.15
Step 6.

PART I DETAILING FUNDAMENTALS

STEP 7
To move the extension line to a new object or other element, click and drag the blue circle that appears in the centers of the extension lines. This can only move in the same direction as the stringer.

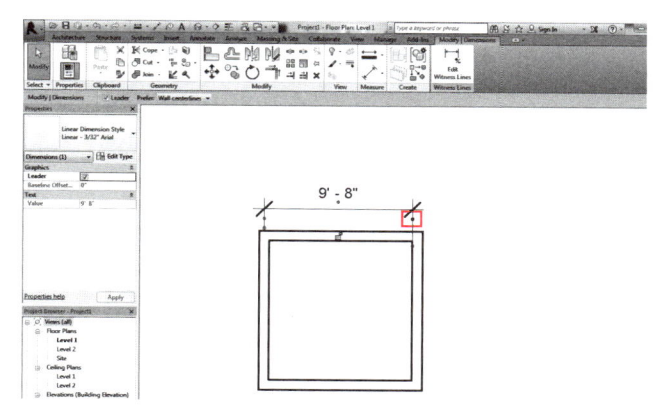

Figure 4.16
Step 7.

ANNOTATIONS
To add annotations to your drawing, use the text tool, which can be found in the Annotation tab.

STEP 1
After locating the text tool, select the One Segment tool from the Format panel.

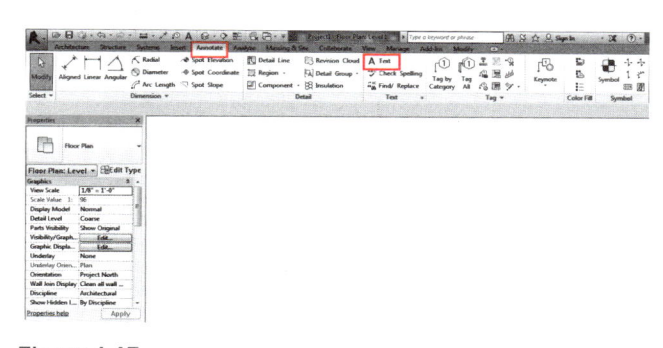

Figure 4.17
Annotation tools can be found under the Annotate tab.

STEP 2
Click once in the drawing window to place the arrow head.

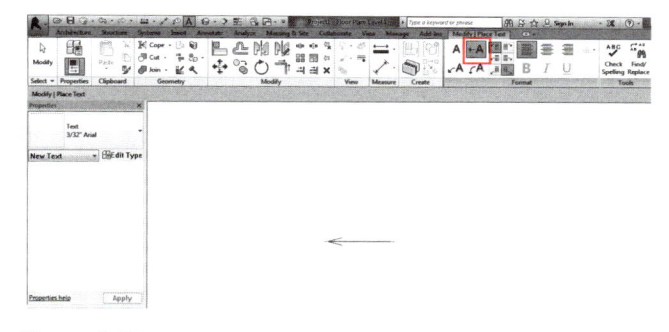

Figure 4.18
Step 2.

STEP 3
Move your mouse to the location where you wish to place the text. Click once to place it and type the notation within. Click elsewhere in the window to exit from the tool.

If you want an arrow that is curved or angled, you can find those within the Format panel for the text tool as well.

Figure 4.19
Step 3.

CHAPTER 4 REVIT BASICS   41

MATERIAL DESIGNATIONS

Revit will let you apply a material in the shape that you wish, but the program has a limited number of preloaded patterns available to use. However, the Materials Palette can be expanded to include customized patterns, colors, and textures. Just because the list of preloaded palettes is short does not mean you are limited.

STEP 1
Go to the Annotate tab and locate the Region drop-down in the Detail panel. Select Filled Region.

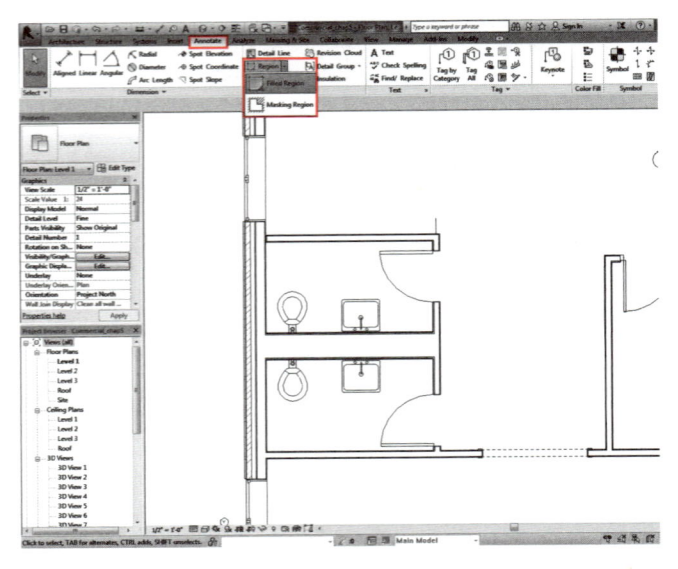

Figure 4.20
Locate the Filled Region tool under the Annotate tab to add material designations to line drawings.

STEP 2
A modification screen will open where you can draw the shape of the object or select the element that you wish to assign a material pattern to. Once you have finished editing, click the green check mark to accept the changes to the drawing.

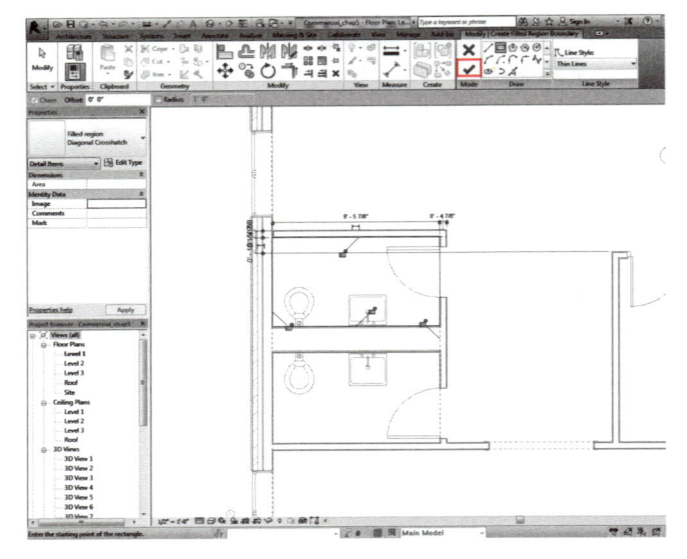

Figure 4.21
Step 2.

PART I DETAILING FUNDAMENTALS

STEP 3

With the new filled region still highlighted, drop-down the Filled Region menu within the Properties panel on the left side of the screen. Here you can change the pattern if necessary.

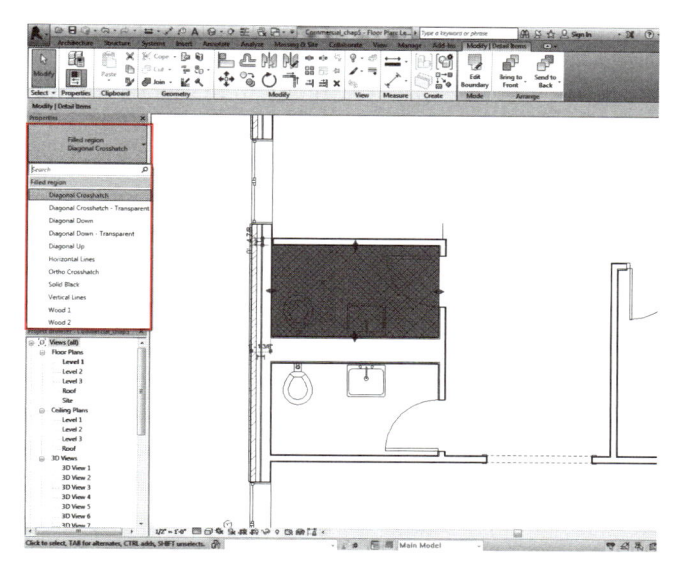

Figure 4.22
Step 3.

STEP 4

To access additional patterns, click on Edit Type in the Properties bar. In the Type Properties window that opens, click in the value cell for Fill Pattern. A . . . icon should appear which will allow you to access a longer list of patterns.

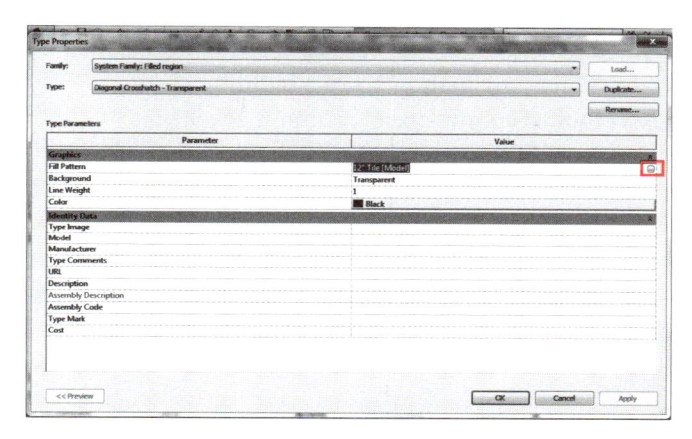

Figure 4.23
Step 4: Edit Type—Fill Pattern window.

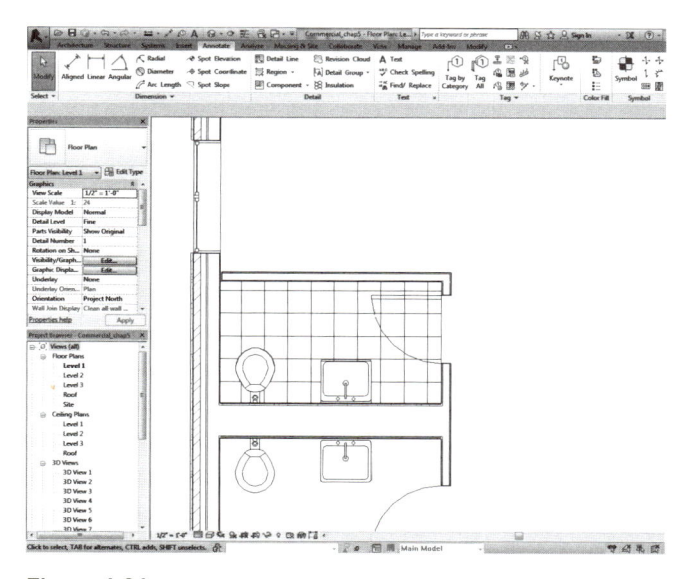

Figure 4.24
Finished filled region.

CHAPTER 4 REVIT BASICS

ELEVATION SYMBOLS

Keep in mind that this elevation will be the bare bones of what your final elevation will look like. The benefit of this action is that you will be able to quickly generate the framework of the elements and will then just be required to add the details, dimensions, and annotations.

Place elevation symbols

STEP 1
Use the Elevation tool, which can be found in the Create panel of the View tab.

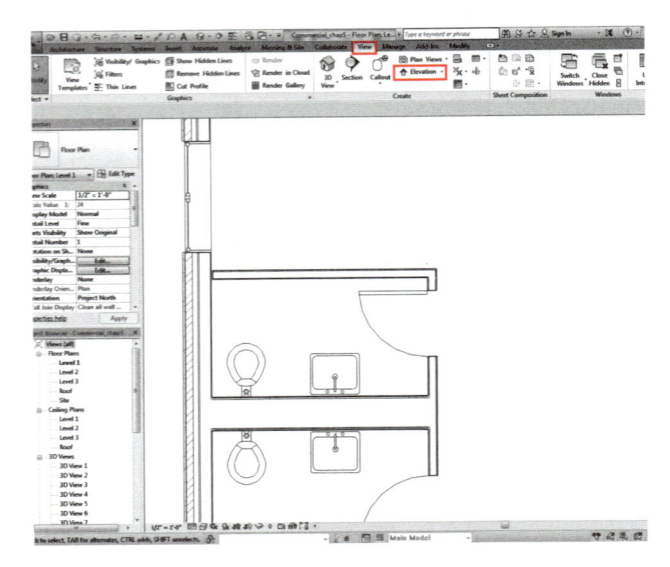

Figure 4.25
Step 1.

STEP 2
In the Properties panel, use the drop down menu to change the marker from a building elevation symbol to an interior elevation marker.

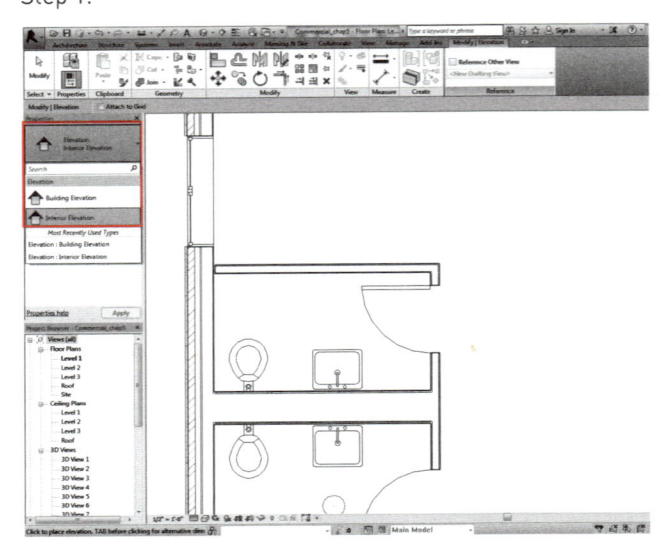

Figure 4.26
Step 2.

STEP 3
You will see the symbol attached to your cursor. Click on the location where you want to make the elevation from. Press Esc to complete the action. Revit will automatically generate an elevation view for you.

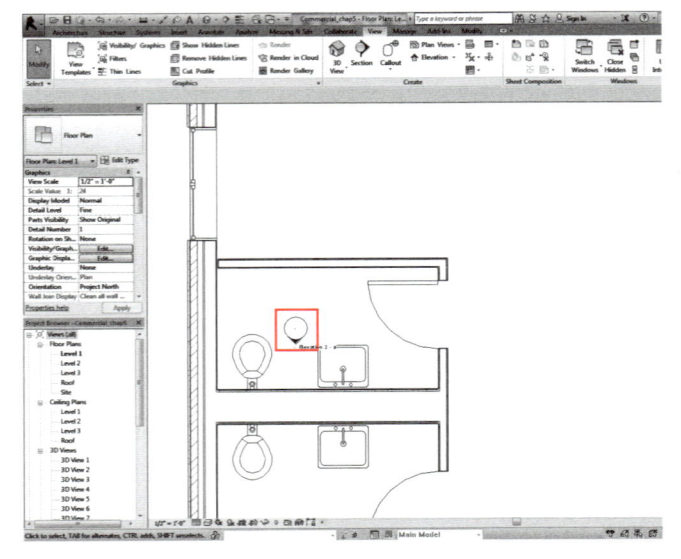

Figure 4.27
Step 3.

Edit elevation symbol style

STEP 1

Hover over the circle indicating the center of the marker. Once it turns blue, click on it. When the Properties menu activates for elevation, click Edit Type.

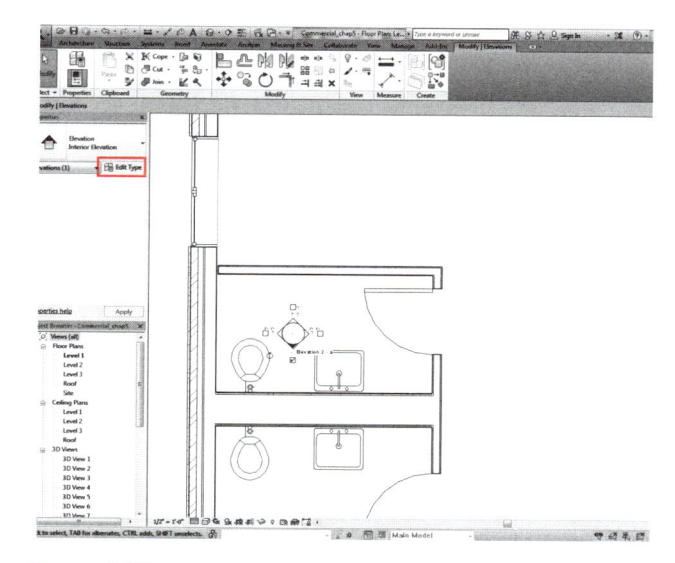

Figure 4.28
Step 1.

STEP 2

In the Type Properties window that opens, locate the Elevation tag under the Graphics heading. Click on the information in the Value column on the right to activate a . . . icon. Click on this icon to open another properties window.

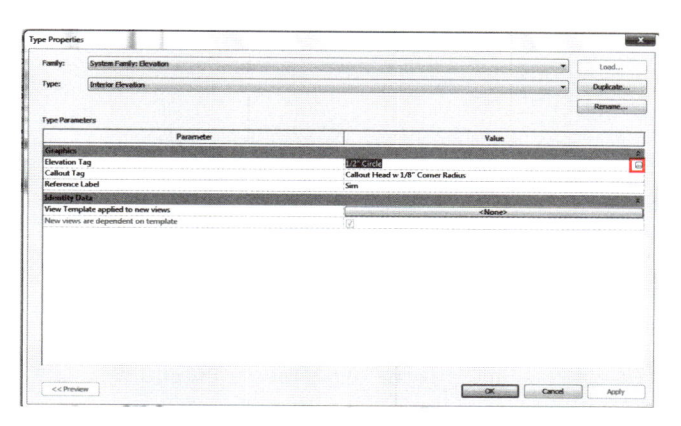

Figure 4.29
Step 2.

STEP 3

Using the drop-down menu under the Value column, select the new style of marker you want to use. The marker used in this text is:

Elevation Mark Body_Circle: Filled Arrow

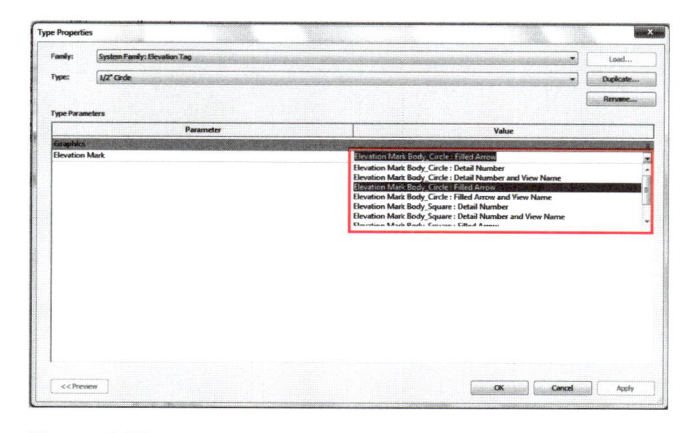

Figure 4.30
Step 3.

CHAPTER 4 REVIT BASICS | 45

STEP 4
Click OK for both windows to close them.

Edit placement of elevation symbol

STEP 1
Hover over the circle indicating the center of the marker. Once it turns blue, click on it.

STEP 2
Using your arrow keys, move the circle in the direction you wish to move the marker.

STEP 3
Press Esc to complete the action.

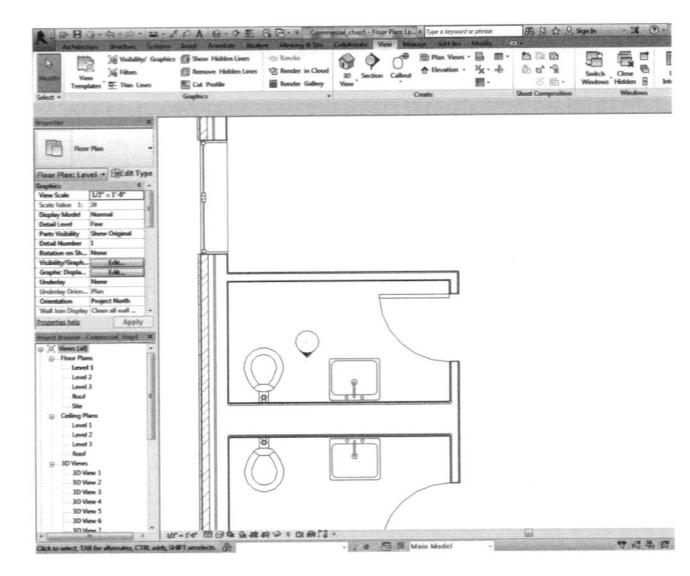

Figure 4.31
Altered elevation marker.

Edit direction of elevation symbol

STEP 1
Hover over the circle indicating the center of the marker. Once it turns blue, click on it and you will see the black arrowhead (existing elevations) and white arrowheads (optional elevations) appear. This can be seen in Figure 4.28.

STEP 2
Blue boxes will be near the points of these arrowheads, which you can click on to activate that arrowhead and create an elevation for that view. Click on the box again to remove the checkmark and you will delete the view.

STEP 3
Press Esc to complete the action.

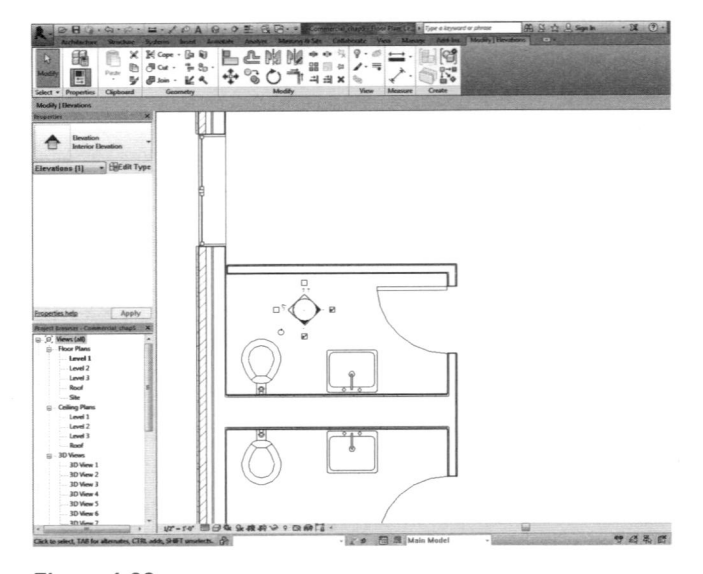

Figure 4.32
Existing (black) and optional (white) elevation locations.

PART I DETAILING FUNDAMENTALS

Edit width/depth of elevation

STEP 1
Click on the active (black) arrowhead pointing in the direction of the elevation view.

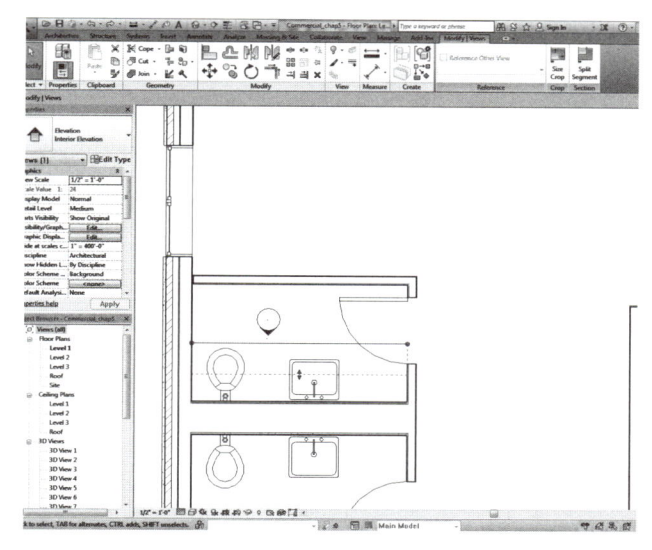

Figure 4.33
Step 1.

STEP 2
A solid blue line will appear at the tip of the arrowhead. This line can be dragged to the center of the elevation marker to indicate where the view begins. The ends of the line can also be dragged to the walls or other bounding objects to create the border of the elevation.

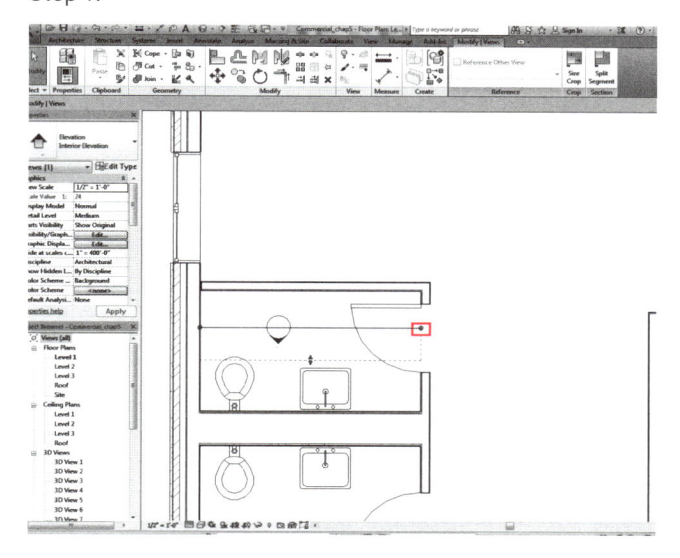

Figure 4.34
Step 2.

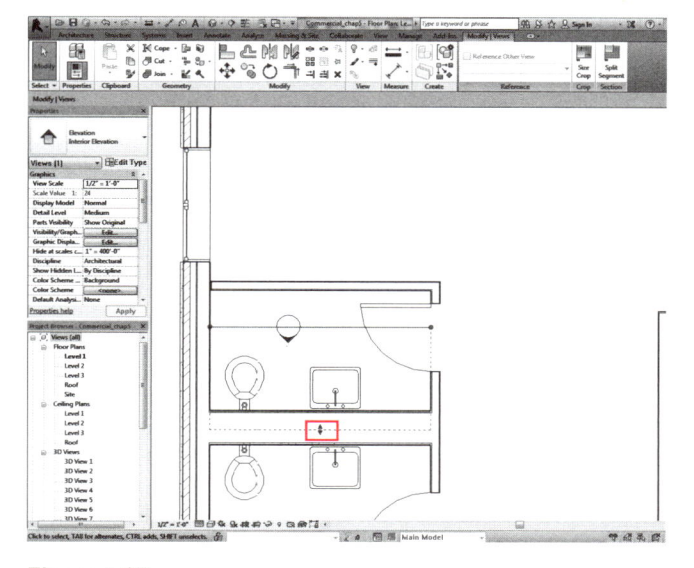

STEP 3
A dashed rectangle will project out from the solid line. This indicates the depth of field and whatever objects fall within this rectangle will appear in your elevation. Click on the blue arrows at the far end of this box and drag the depth of field past the farthest bounding object or wall to pull those elements into view.

STEP 4
Press Esc to complete the action.

Figure 4.35
Step 3.

CHAPTER 4 REVIT BASICS | 47

SECTION CUT MARKERS

Keep in mind that this section will be the bare bones of what your final section will look like. The benefit of this action is that you will be able to quickly generate the framework of the elements and will then just be required to add the details, dimensions, and annotations.

Place section symbol

STEP 1
Use the Section tool, which can be found in the Create panel of the View tab.

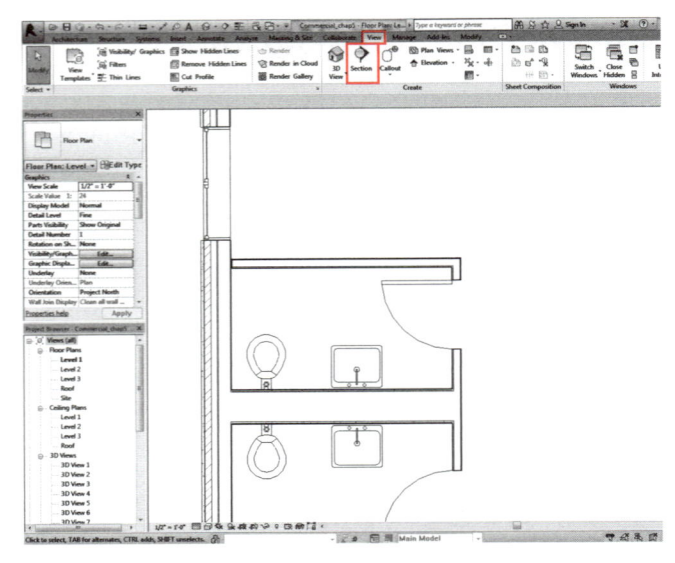

Figure 4.36
Step 1.

STEP 2
Click on the plan to place the head of the symbol. You will notice that the tool will become attached to your cursor.

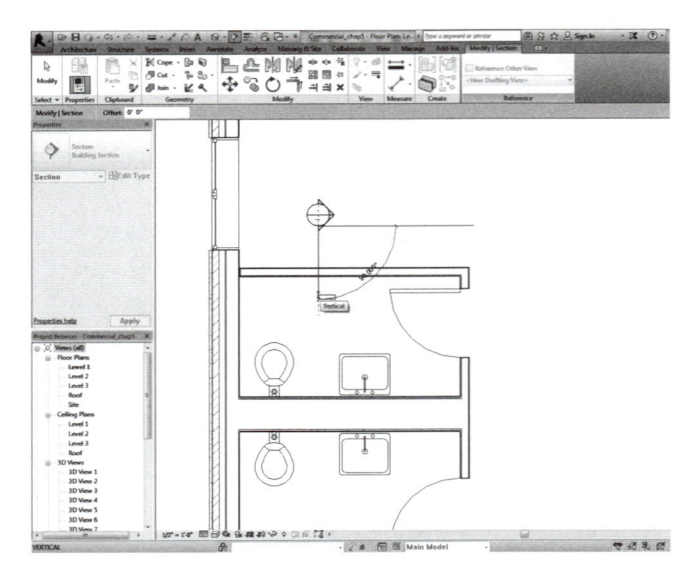

Figure 4.37
Step 2.

48 | PART I DETAILING FUNDAMENTALS

STEP 3
Move your mouse past all the elements that you want to "cut through" in the view, creating a vertical or horizontal line through these objects. Click to place the "tail" of the marker.

STEP 4
Press Esc to complete the action. Revit will automatically generate a section view for you.

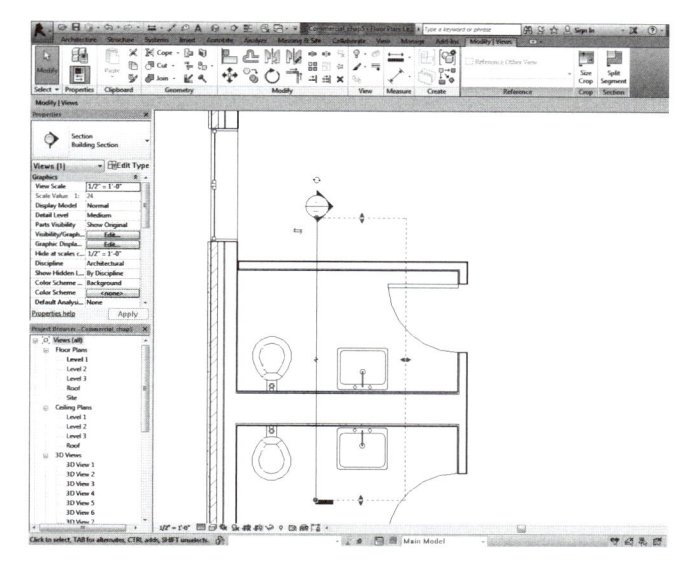

Figure 4.38
Step 3.

Edit placement of the section symbol

STEP 1
Hover over the section marker and once it turns blue, click on it.

STEP 2
Using your arrow keys, move the marker in the direction you wish to move it.

STEP 3
Press Esc to complete the action.

Edit direction of the section symbol

STEP 1
Hover over the section marker and once it turns blue, click on it.

STEP 2
Two parallel arrows pointing in opposite directions will appear just under the head of the marker. Click on them to flip the direction of the view.

STEP 3
Press Esc to complete the action.

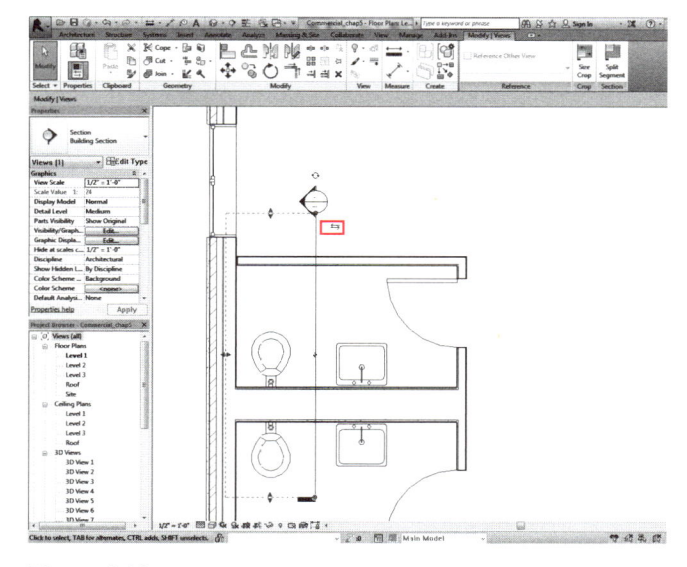

Figure 4.39
Flip the direction of your section view by clicking on the arrows.

CHAPTER 4 REVIT BASICS | 49

Edit width/depth of section

STEP 1
Hover over the section marker and once it turns blue, click on it.

STEP 2
A dashed rectangle will project out from the cut line. This indicates both the width and the depth of field for the section. Click on the blue arrows and drag them past the farthest bounding objects or walls to extend the cut or pull those elements into view.

STEP 3
Press Esc to complete the action.

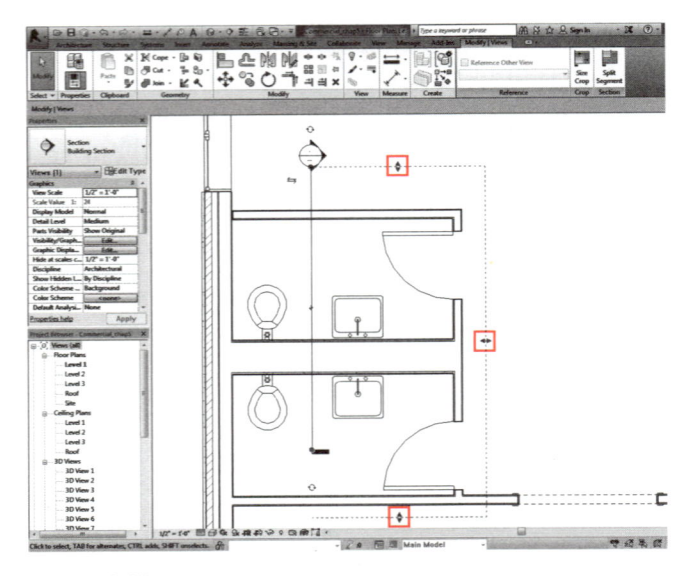

Figure 4.40
Use the drag arrows to adjust the width and depth of the section cut.

DETAIL CALLOUTS

Place the detail callout symbol

STEP 1
To produce an enlarged plan for a detail, use the detail callout tool, which can be found in the Create panel of the View tab.

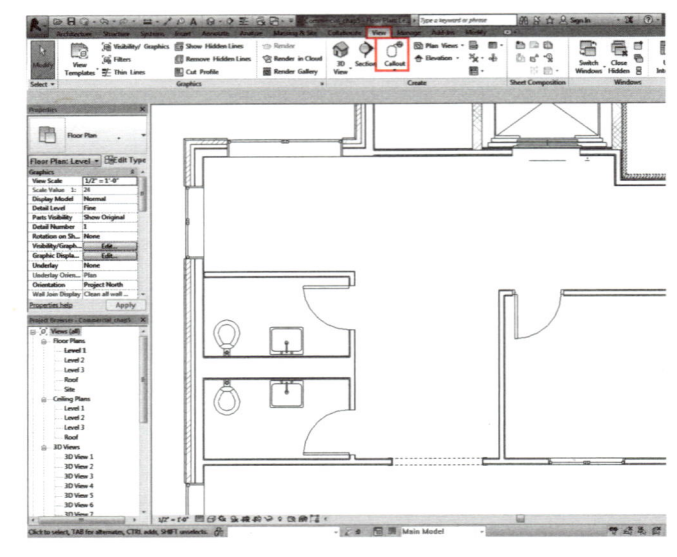

Figure 4.41
Step 1.

50 | PART I DETAILING FUNDAMENTALS

STEP 2
Click on the plan just past the upper left corner of the element you want to detail. You will notice that the tool will become attached to your cursor.

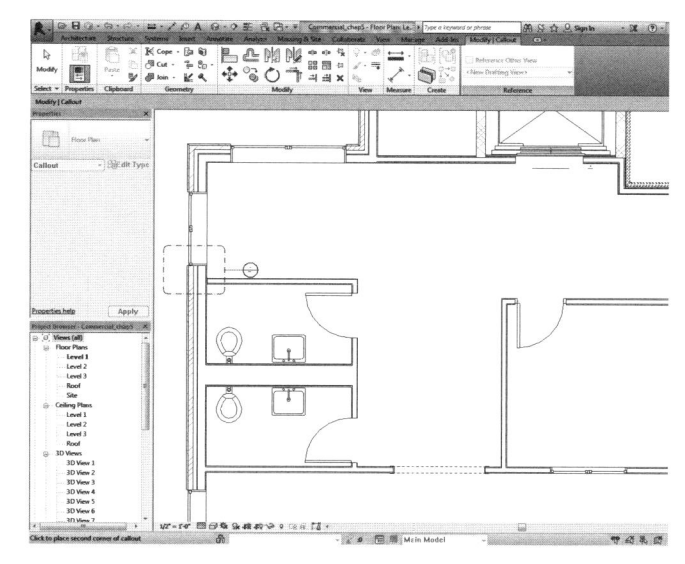

Figure 4.42
Step 2.

STEP 3
Move your mouse past the lower right corner of the element. Click to place the callout bubble.

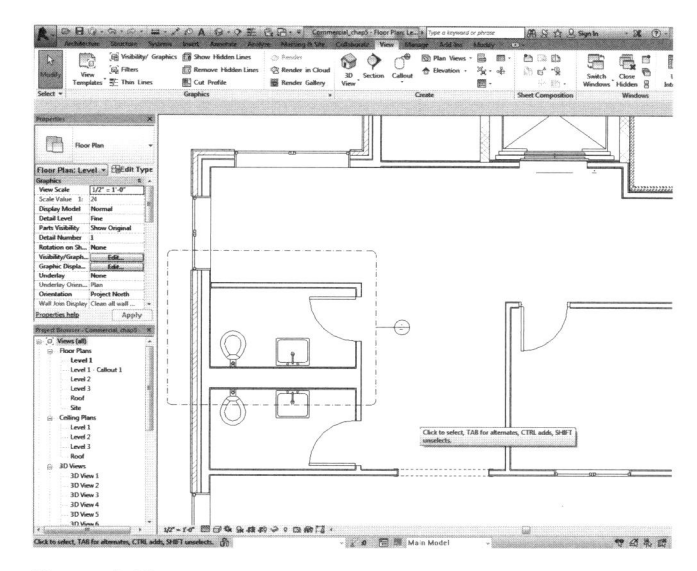

Figure 4.43
Step 3.

CHAPTER 4 REVIT BASICS | 51

Edit placement of the callout bubble

STEP 1
Hover over the callout bubble and once it turns blue, click on it.

STEP 2
Click and drag on the blue dots to change the size of the detail.

STEP 3
Press Esc to complete the action.

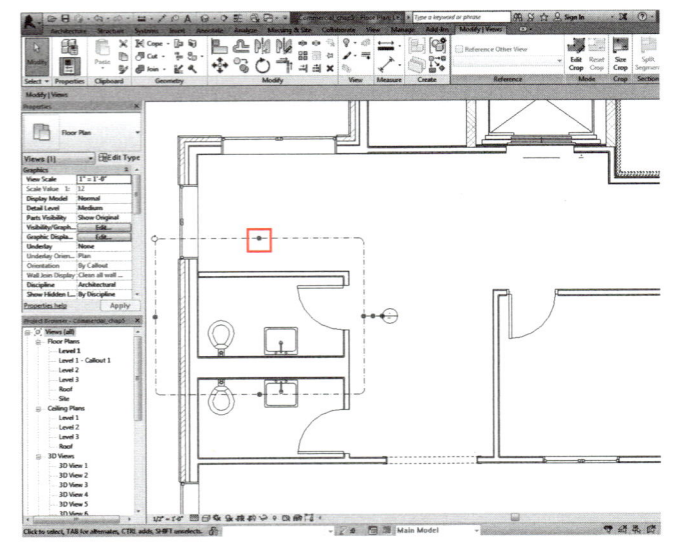

Figure 4.44
Step 2.

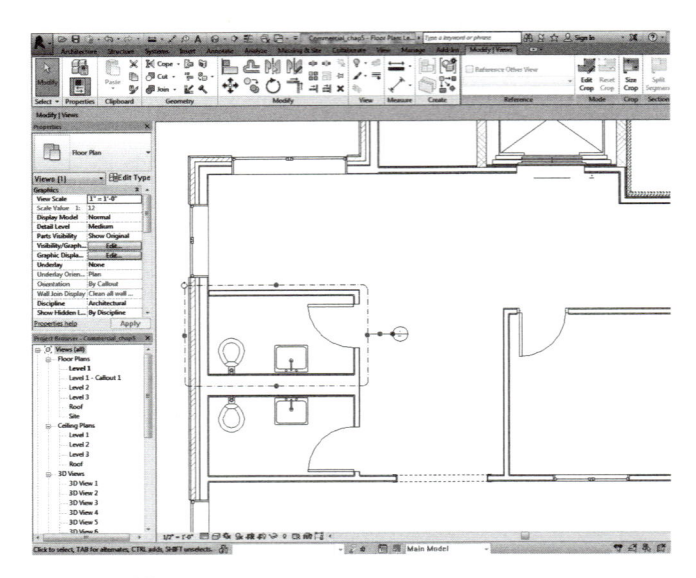

Figure 4.45
Resized detail callout bubble.

Edit placement of the detail callout reference tag

STEP 1
Hover over the callout bubble and once it turns blue, click on it.

STEP 2
Click and drag the blue dot closest to the reference tag to change its placement.

STEP 3
Click and drag on the blue dot in the middle of the leader line to adjust the line's bend.

STEP 4
Press Esc to complete the action.

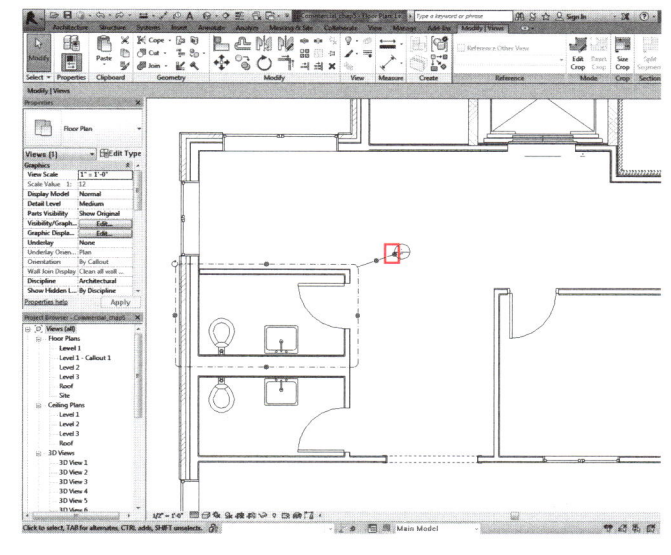

Figure 4.46
Step 2.

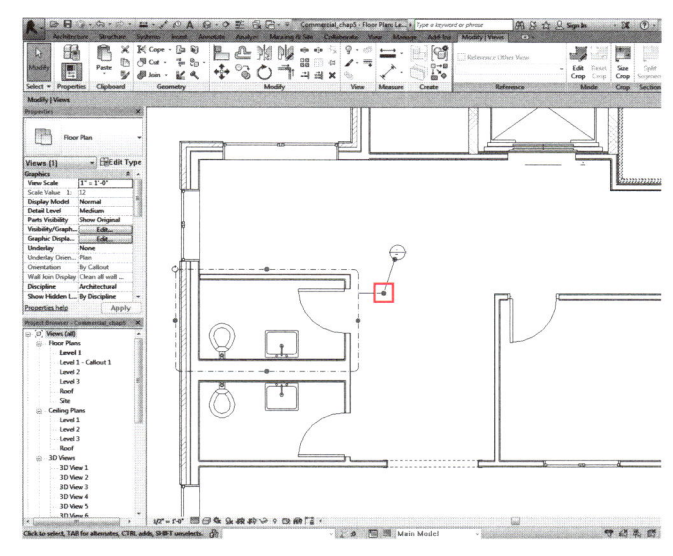

Figure 4.47
Step 3.

WHY IS THIS IMPORTANT?

If your school or place of employment uses Revit, it is important that you learn how to manipulate your drawing space and be able to access command shortcuts so that you can work in the most efficient manner possible. When creating detail drawings, it is important to use the tools discussed in this chapter to keep your files organized and consistent from start to finish.

CHAPTER REVIEW

1. Why do linetypes and lineweights matter? How is this established in Revit?
2. What is the importance of dimensions and annotations in a detail?
3. How do the various markers and callout communicate with one another? Why is this important?

CHAPTER TERMINOLOGY

aligned dimension
Filled Region
marker bubble
model space
Sheet

CHAPTER REFERENCES

Ballast, David Kent. *Interior Construction & Detailing for Designers and Architects*. Belmont, CA: Professional Publications, Inc., 2013.

Ching, Francis D. *Building Construction Illustrated*. New York: John Wiley & Sons, 2014.

DeChiara, Joseph, Julius Panero, and Martin Zelnik. *Time-Saver Standards for Interior Design and Space Planning*. New York: McGraw-Hill, 2001.

Kilmer, W. Otie and Rosemary Kilmer. *Construction Drawings and Details for Interiors*. New York: John Wiley & Sons, 2016.

Kruse, Kelsey and Maryrose McGowan. *Interior Graphic Standards*. New York: John Wiley & Sons, 2003.

PART II
Detail drawings

Walls and openings

CHAPTER 5

CHAPTER OUTCOMES

After completing this chapter you will be able to:

1. Discuss the different components used in walls for steel construction and wood construction.

2. Produce a typical wall for each construction type that can then be edited to create a variety of interior partition types.

3. Detail opening headers, jambs, and sills and how they are supported within the wall structure.

Figure 5.1 Exposed wooden studs with spray insulation for a residential space. Gypsum wallboard will be applied to the framework.

ABOUT WALLS AND OPENINGS

Walls are the framework of a building, acting as both a protective and functional means of supporting the systems and people within it. There are a variety of wall types that are used in specific instances within a project, but each can be edited to meet the needs of the designer and end user. Exterior walls and certain interior walls are **bearing walls**, which support the weight of the roof and upper levels. Removal of these walls requires alternative measures to be taken to support the structure above, and it is recommended that an architect or a structural engineer is consulted. Many municipalities require a permit to remove or alter a load-bearing wall, so it is important to refer to your local laws prior to taking action.

Interior walls that are **nonbearing** act as a space dividers and do not carry the weight of the roof or upper levels. Typically referred to as a **partition**, elements of these nonbearing walls are edited to take on desired characteristics and can then be mixed and matched throughout a space to accommodate specific needs.

Acoustical partitions are constructed with internal layers of sound batt, a soundproofing material that helps to diminish noise transfer from one room to another. The partition itself can be built to ceiling height, but when erected from slab to slab, its ability to lessen sound transfer increases.

Chase walls are constructed to be wide enough to conceal plumbing lines. These walls are typically built where a sink, shower, toilet, washer, or other water fixture is needed. When fixtures will be installed on only one side of the wall, the partition must measure at least 12" wide to account for the plumbing line concealment. If fixtures are to me mounted on both sides of the wall, the wall thickness increases to 16". Chase walls can be finished with a layer of **greenboard** and tiles in areas that are expected to be wet.

Rated partitions are walls constructed with fire-rated materials spanning from slab to slab. These types of walls must utilize steel studs, fire-rated sealants, and **Type X** gypsum board within the assembly. While the combination of these materials will not stop a fire from eventually spreading, they work together to help

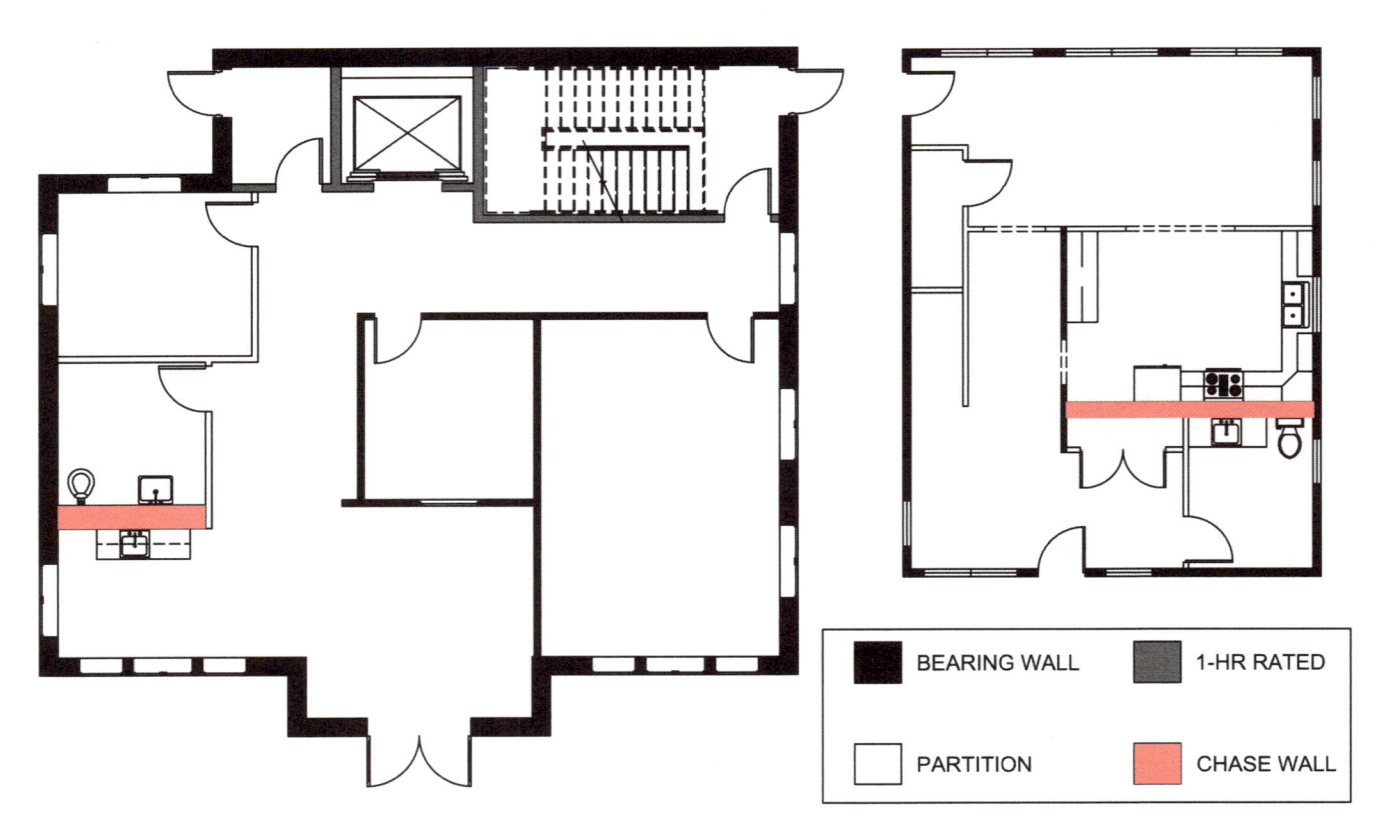

Figure 5.2
Wall types for a commercial project (left) and a residential project. The selected plans are the project examples for this text.

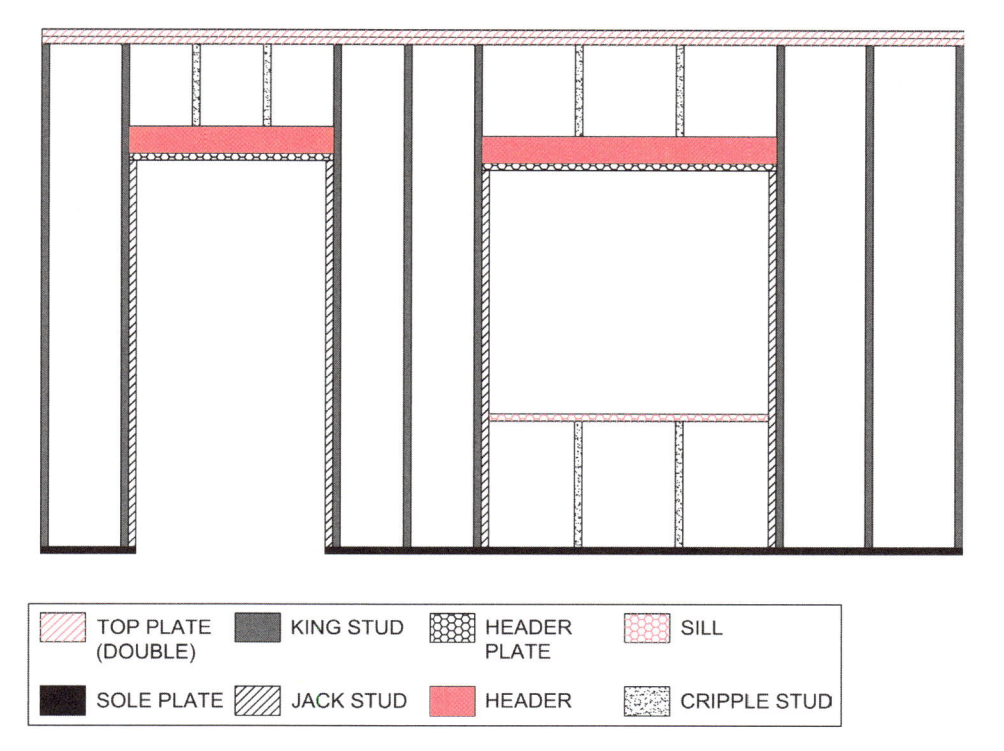

Figure 5.3
Stud wall components.

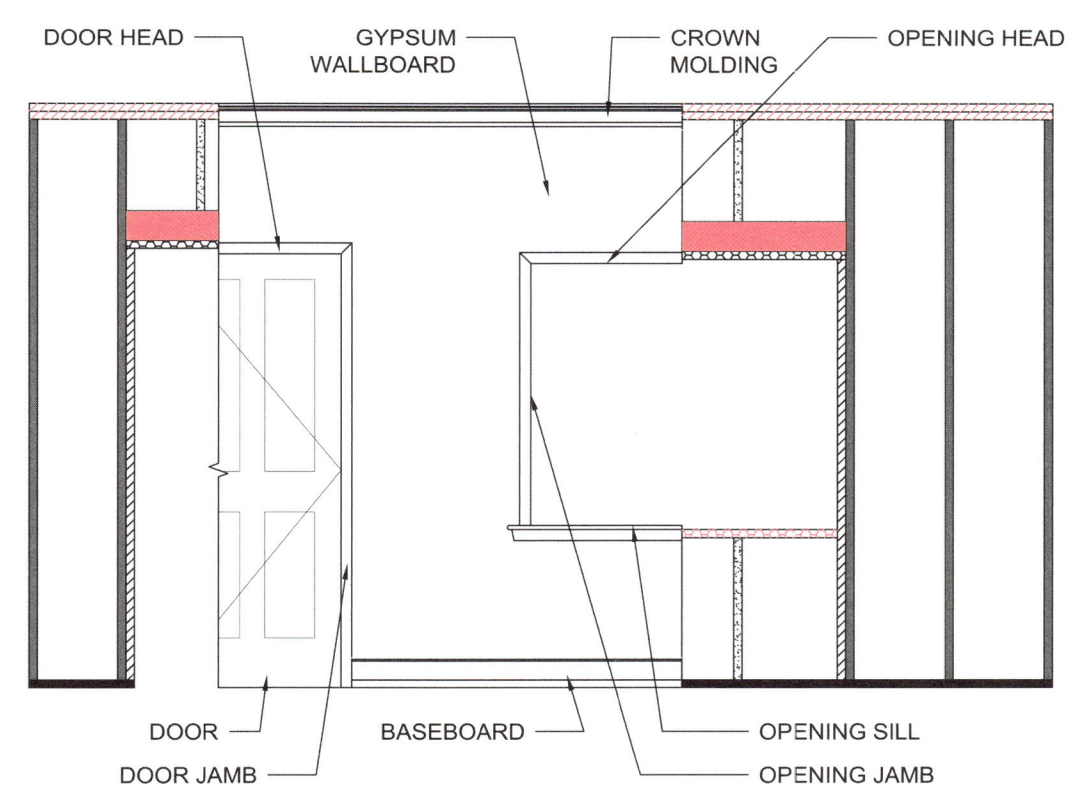

Figure 5.4
Stud wall with finished face and trim overlay.

STUDIO Animation 5.1 Partition components

CHAPTER 5 WALLS AND OPENINGS | 57

Figure 5.5
Residential construction project using a wood stud framing system.

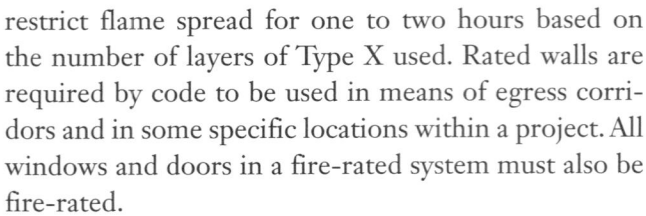

Figure 5.6
Commercial construction project using a steel-stud framing system.

restrict flame spread for one to two hours based on the number of layers of Type X used. Rated walls are required by code to be used in means of egress corridors and in some specific locations within a project. All windows and doors in a fire-rated system must also be fire-rated.

When the surface of a wall is removed, you can see the skeleton constructed below. The most identifiable part of the partition skeleton is the **stud**. This vertical framing member helps to transfer the weight of the load above to the ground and acts as an anchor for the wall face to attach to. Additionally, the type of stud used in construction is dependent on the type of building it is being used for. Commercial buildings must have steel studs, single-family residential buildings are typically wood, and other residential projects can feature either steel or wood studs. While most of the components that make up a stud wall are the same for either a steel or wood project, there are a few exceptions. The information that follows will provide insight into the construction of a wood-stud wall, with any changes for steel construction projects as noted.

The bottommost component of the wall is the **sole plate**, which is a horizontal member that is installed to the floor. When the wall is a wood-stud partition, the sole plate will be a 2 × 4, with the studs abutting the face of the board. Opposite the sole is **top plate**, another horizontal 2 × 4 that forms the top of the partition, anchoring the studs and supporting the ceiling joists. Wood constructions require two 2 × 4s to be used along the top of the wall, forming a **double top plate**. Studs are then spaced between the plates 16" on center to create the vertical plane of the partition. Studs that are full height and are attached to both the top and sole plates are known as **king studs**, which make up a majority of the framework for solid walls. This skeleton framework can then be covered with **gypsum wallboard** (GWB) to create the face of the wall. Made of layers of gypsum and paper, the GWB can also be treated to take on a variety of properties, such as water- or fire-resistance, making different types of GWB applicable for different types of projects.

Steel-stud walls are constructed in a very similar manner to the wood-stud partitions; however, there are different elements used to replace the 2 × 4s. Steel studs are used in place of their wooden counterparts. These studs vary in thickness and can be made taller than the wooden ones. Additionally, they feature holes called **knockouts** for wires to be strung through. Steel studs should be spaced 16" on center, which is typical for all

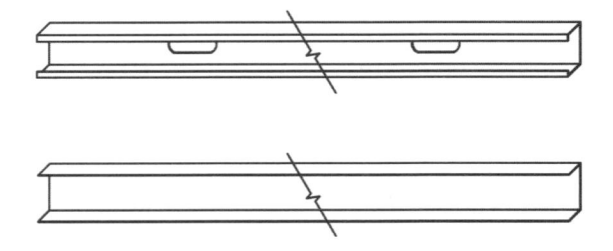

Figure 5.7
Steel stud (top) and steel channel.

PART II DETAIL DRAWINGS

types of commercial buildings. Depending on the codes in your municipality, walls featuring steel studs that are 10'-0" or shorter, may be spaced 24" on center (OC).

In commercial projects, the sole and top plates also substitute steel for wood. Constructed to take on a *C*-shape, the **steel channels** are formed to allow the studs to sit inside the opening portion, creating additional support and protection for the studs. Unlike the wood-stud construction, only one top plate is required for the partition, but an additional horizontal support should be added below the top plate between king studs that frame an opening. This provides the extra strength necessary to support the structure above.

When an opening is needed, a **rough opening** is constructed with an additional 2" height and width allowance to accommodate for doors or windows to be placed. For example, if a 36" × 78" door is to be installed, the rough opening would measure 38" × 80" for the door and the frame to be inserted and installed. In order to achieve this opening, the partition is altered to both frame the gap that is created and help disperse the weight of the load above. First, the sole plate is cut so that the opening can extend to the floor plane. Then, jack studs and a header plate are inserted to frame the opening itself. The **jack stud** is a shortened-height stud that is anchored to the sole plate, but instead of reaching the top plate, it is topped by the header plate. The **header plate** is a horizontal framework member that extends between king studs to support the structure above. It is bolted to the jack studs below, forming three sides of a rectangle. In turn, both the header plate and the jack studs are anchored to king studs to aid in supporting the rough opening as well as allow for weight transfer to occur. As seen in Figure 5.8, interior wood-frame partitions utilize two layers of boards to form the header plate, while only one is need for load-bearing walls as they are strengthened by the addition of a header. The **header** is constructed by rotating two boards on to their sides so that the widest dimension is parallel with the wall plane. One board is then aligned with the front edge of the header plate while the second is aligned with the back edge. The tops of these two header boards are anchored to each other with a wood block, and the remaining space can be filled with insulation. The purpose of the header and the header plate is to accept the weight from the portion of the wall above the opening and carry this load to the king studs they are anchored to. In order to ensure that there are enough studs to carry the weight from above, additional shortened studs, called **cripple studs**, are evenly spaced between the top plate and the header or header plate.

Steel-frame construction differs from its wood-frame counterpart for rough opening headings as the components being used are dissimilar. For an interior partition, a single steel channel is placed across the tops

① WOOD FRAME

② LIGHT GUAGE STEEL

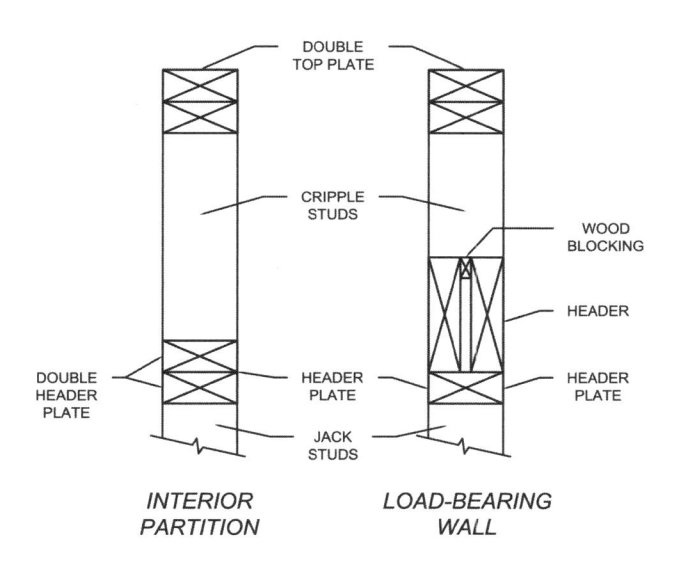

Figure 5.8
Sections of wood-frame headers (left) and steel-frame headers.

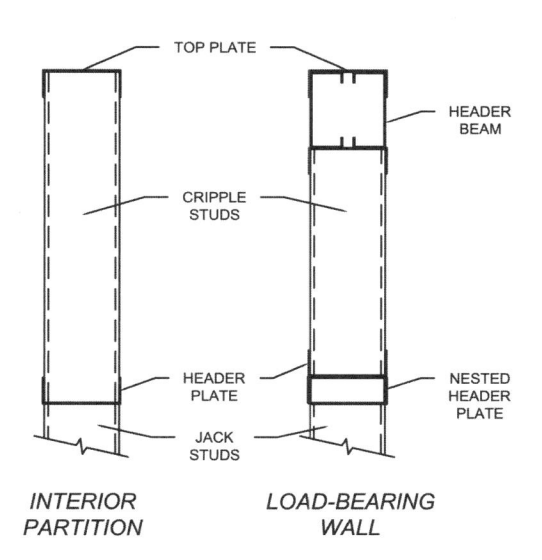

of the jack studs, with its opening facing up, to create the header plate. Then, the cripple studs can be shown fit inside the *C*-shapes created by these channels.

When the steel-frame opening is load-bearing, the top plate requires an additional support similar to the header in wood-frame construction. However, here the support is referred to as a **header beam**, a term used to describe supports that are built to support the strain on the top plate. In light gauge steel, the header beam is built from two C-studs rotated on to their sides so that the widest dimension is parallel with the wall plane. One of these studs is then aligned with the front edge of the top plate while the second is aligned with the back edge. Additionally, a series of steel channels are used to create the **nested header plate** above the rough opening. This component has a steel channel running across two jack studs with its opening facing upward to support the cripple studs above. The flat side of a second steel channel is attached to the bottom of the first with a third channel "nested" into the second. This results in the sides of the second and third channels overlapping and together forming a rectangular shape.

The sides and the top of the rough opening for a window are treated in the same manner as the door, with the use of jack and cripple studs and a header plate, but the main changes occur in the space below the window. Here, the break in the wall is elevated so the sole plate remains intact, with cripple studs extending from the sole to the sill. The **sill** is the horizontal

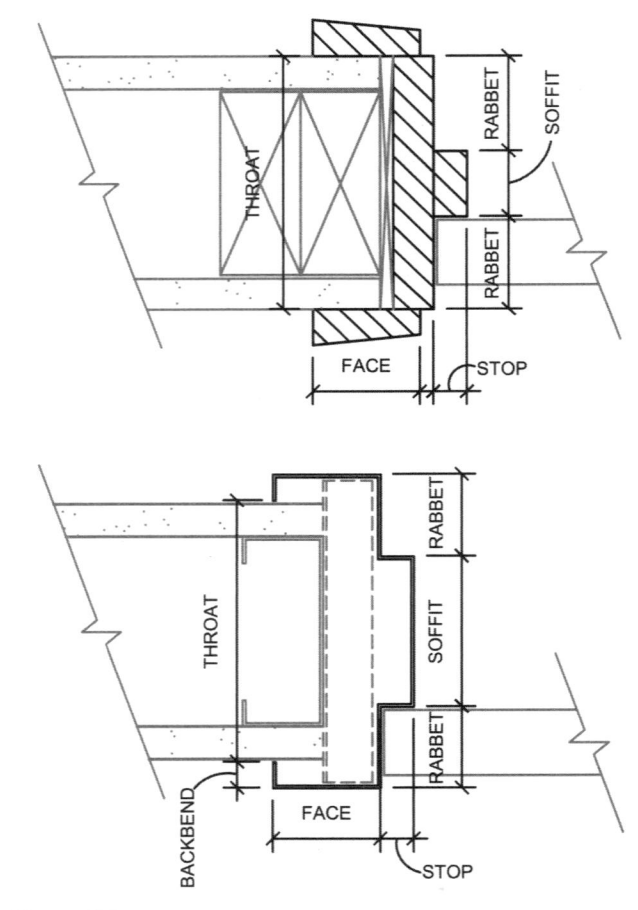

Figure 5.9
Single rabbet jambs in wood (top) and aluminum.

member at the bottom of any elevated opening, which completes the framework around the window.

After the rough opening is constructed, the door or window can be inserted into the void, with the component's frame anchored to the jack studs and header. The **frame** is the assembly around the door itself, made up of the **jamb**, or vertical elements, and the **head**, the horizontal element. The frame is then edged in **casings**, which are the exposed, decorative, and protective trims around the opening. Typically made of wood or aluminum, the casing shields the seams between the framework and GWB from damage, but it also adds a **face** for decorative millwork.

The jamb contains elements that allow for the door to fit within the frame and open and close properly. Instead of being flush with the casing, the jamb is notched to form a groove called a **rabbet**. This space is at least as deep as the door and can be used alone (**single rabbet**) when a door is to be hung only on one side of the frame or in pairs (**double rabbet**) where a door can be place on either side. Next to the rabbet is a **soffit**, or plain edge that is extended from the jamb by the stop. The **stop** provides the closing point, or stopping point, of the door itself. Jambs that are constructed from wood feature individual elements that must be assembled together to form the upright. In contrast, aluminum jambs can be molded from a single sheet with a machine bending the frame to size and combining the jamb and casing into a single unit.

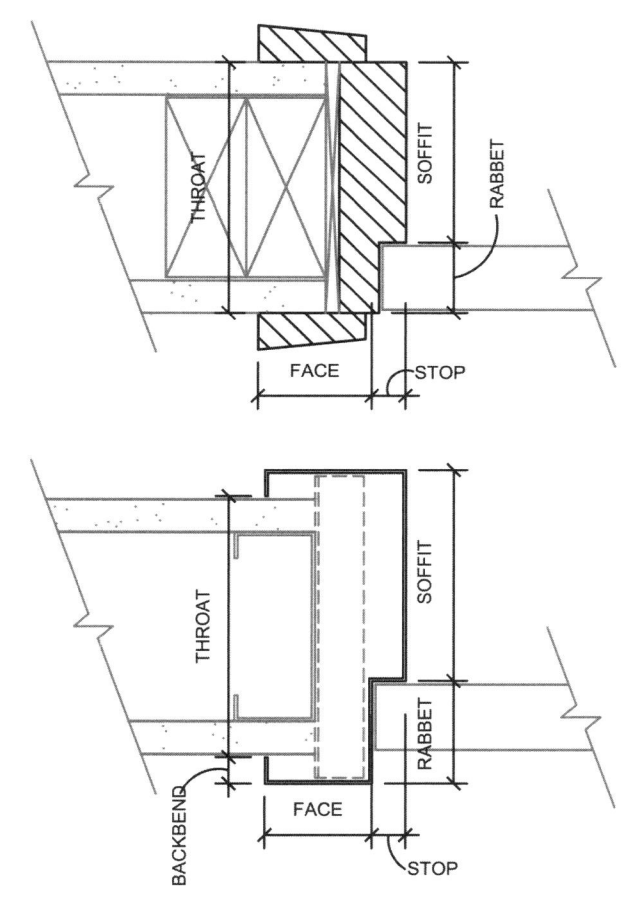

Figure 5.10
Double rabbet jambs in wood (top) and aluminum.

DRAFTING STUD WALL PLAN AND SECTION

Wood stud

This example shows a standard 4 3/4" wood-stud interior partition. All lines should be drawn with a section lineweight unless otherwise noted.

For other types of interior partitions, see Appendix E.

STEP 1
Draw a line to represent the floor plane. Draw two vertical lines 4 3/4" apart, indicating the finished faces of the completed wall width. The remainder of the drawing will be created between these two lines.

STEP 2
To create the width of the GWB, draw another two vertical lines 5/8" away from the ones created in the previous step. Create a 1/4" to 1/2" gap between the bottom of the GWB and the floor plan. This real-life gap accommodates the natural expansion and settling of the materials and building while also protecting the GWB from absorbing moisture from the flooring.

STEP 3
At the top and at bottom of wall, you will need to create the wood plates that hold all the vertical elements together. For this example, the top will require two boards and the bottom needs one. Each plate should measure 3 1/2" wide by 1 1/2" high and will appear as a rectangle with an *X* through it (indicating that it is being cut through in this view). Leave a 1/16" space between the edge of the plate and the gypsum board.

STEP 4
Create two dashed lines running from the edge of the top plate to the edge of the sole plate to indicate the wooden studs in the wall. These dashes should be drawn with an elevation lineweight, as this element is not being cut through.

STEP 5
Draw a section cut of type of ceiling being used in the space. This example uses a gypsum ceiling.

STEP 6
Add four breaklines to the drawing and label the resulting top and bottom segments as SECTION and the middle segment as PLAN. These breaklines should be drawn in an elevation lineweight. The SECTIONs will show how the top plate and sole plate hold the wall together, while the PLAN will show how the studs fit into the space. Change the dashed lines to continuous lines in the PLAN. These will appear in an elevation lineweight.

STEP 7
In the middle of the PLAN segment, create a rectangular stud measuring 3 1/2" wide by 1 1/2" high. Include an *X* through the rectangle to indicate that it is being cut through for this view.

STEP 8
To finalize the drawing, add a hatch pattern within the cut drywall and ceiling using an elevation lineweight. Dimensions and annotations may be added for any key elements. This text also rotates the plan portion of the drawing to emphasize the difference between the section and plan elements.

CAD

Draw the plan portion of the detail in line with the section portions. Once complete, rotate the plan 90 degrees before adjusting lineweights and annotating.

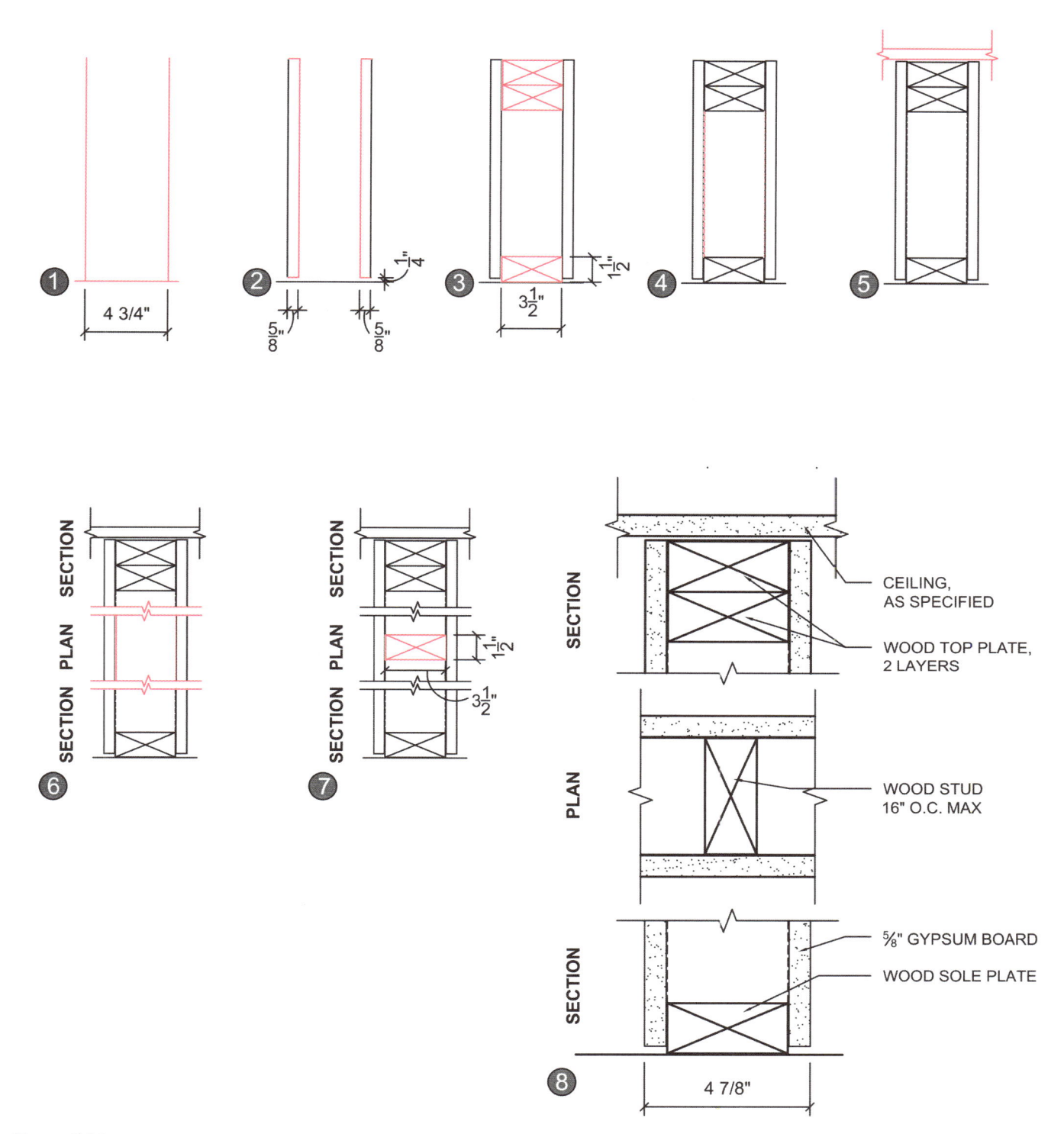

Figure 5.11
Wood stud plan and section, Steps 1–8.

CHAPTER 5 WALLS AND OPENINGS

Steel stud

This example shows a standard 5 1/4" steel-stud interior partition. All lines should be drawn with a section lineweight unless otherwise noted.

For other types of interior partitions, see Appendix E.

STEP 1
Draw a line to represent the floor plane. Draw two vertical lines 5 1/4" apart, indicating the finished faces of the completed wall width. The remainder of the drawing will be created between these two lines.

STEP 2
To create the width of the gypsum board, draw another two vertical lines 5/8" away from the ones created in the previous step. Create a 1/4" to 1/2" gap between the bottom of the GWB and the floor plane.

STEP 3
At the top and at bottom of wall, you will need to create the metal plates that hold all the vertical elements together. For this example, the plates should measure 4" wide and will appear as a *C* on its side.

STEP 4
Measuring 1 5/8" away from the lines drawn in Step 2, create two dashed lines running from the top plate to the sole plate to indicate the steel studs in the wall. These dashes should be drawn with an elevation lineweight, as this element is not being cut through.

STEP 5
Draw a section cut of type of ceiling being used in the space. This example uses acoustical ceiling tile (ACT).

STEP 6
Add four breaklines to the drawing and label the resulting top and bottom segments as SECTION and the middle segment as PLAN. These breaklines should be drawn in an elevation lineweight. The sections will show how the top plate and sole plate hold the wall together, while the plan will show how the studs fit into the space.

Change the dashed lines to continuous lines in the plan. These will appear in an elevation lineweight.

STEP 7
In the middle of the plan segment, create a *C*-shaped stud measuring 3 5/8" × 1 1/4". Remember to include a lip, or slight extension, off of the ends of the stud.

STEP 8
To finalize the drawing, add a hatch pattern within the cut drywall and ceiling using an elevation lineweight. Dimensions and annotations may be added for any key elements. This text also rotates the plan portion of the drawing to emphasize the difference between the section and plan elements.

Revit

Wall sections can be altered through several steps. First, highlight the wall you wish to adjust and click Edit Type. Duplicate the wall and give it a unique name. Under the Construction parameter, locate Structure and click Edit . . .

Then, click the Preview button at the bottom of the Edit Assembly and change the View to Section.

Change the attributes of the wall by adjusting the function, material, or thickness to match the construction you wish to use in your plan.

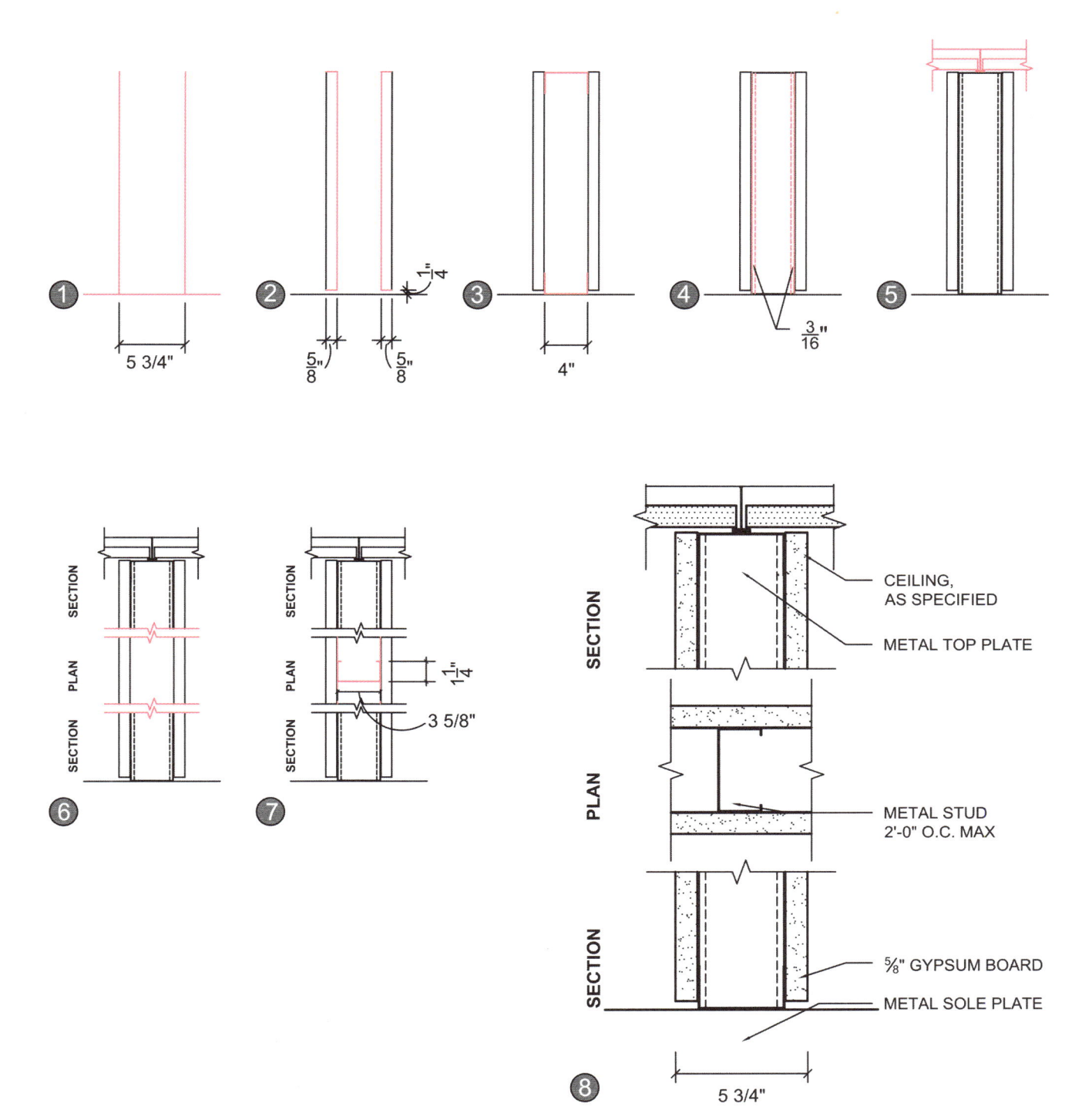

Figure 5.12
Steel stud plan and section, Steps 1–8.

CHAPTER 5 WALLS AND OPENINGS

DRAFTING STUD WALL ELEVATIONS

Technique 1: drafting based on dimensions

For simplicity, this example will use a wood-stud 8'-0" × 8'-0" wall. While this is not taken directly from either the residential or commercial models within the text, the concepts are applicable to both types of projects.

STEP 1
Using the provided dimensions, create vertical guidelines 8'-0" apart for yourself. Connect the top and bottom of those lines to create the floor and ceiling planes, again 8'-0" apart.

Hardline the guidelines at the far left and right to create the walls. Erase any of the guideline that is still visible.

STEP 2
To create the thickness for the top plate and the sole plate, draw lines 1 1/2" away from the ceiling and floor plane lines you drew in Step 1. The 1 1/2" represents the actual thickness of the 2 × 4 or C-stud being used. As seen in this example, a wood-stud wall will require two 2 × 4s for the top plate.

STEP 3
Create the outermost studs by drawing a vertical line 1 1/2" away from the sides of the wall, indicating the stud thicknesses there.

Find the middle of these newly drawn studs, which will be 3/4" from each side, and draw guidelines to indicate those center points for reference.

STEP 4
Locate the middle of the wall (in this case, it is 3'-11 1/4" from each existing stud centerline) and create a guideline from the top to the bottom. This will indicate the center of the stud you are about to draw.

Measure 3/4" on either side of guideline and draw a line from the top plate to the sole plate, creating the sides of your stud. Make sure to keep the guideline at this time.

STEP 5
Working your way from the center of the drawing toward each edge, use the existing guideline to draw a new guideline 16" away. This measurement represents the maximum distance between the centerlines of the studs.

Repeat the 16" measurement, creating guidelines for the remainder of the studs in the wall.

STEP 6
Measure 3/4" on either side of these guidelines, and draw lines from the top plate to the sole plate to draw the remaining studs.

The guidelines can be erased at this time.

IBC

Steel Construction

King studs in nonbearing steel partitions must be spaced 16" on center at most. If the partition is 10'-0" or less in height, the spacing can increase to 24" on center at most. (*IBC 2305.5.3.4*)

Wood Construction

King studs in nonbearing wood partitions must be spaced 16" on center at most. (*IBC 2305.5.1*)

Sole plates must be at least 2" thick. (*IBC 2308.5.3.1*)

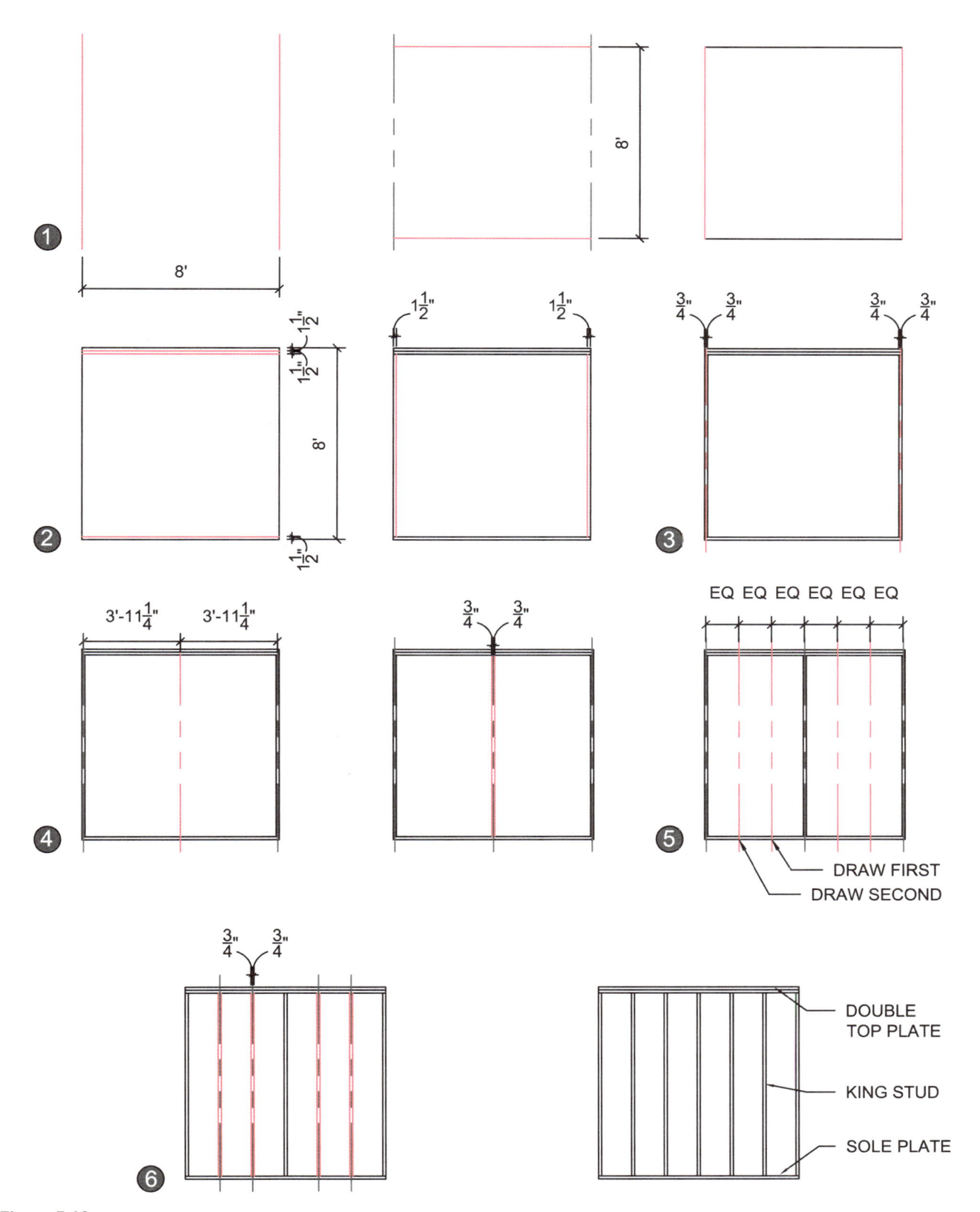

Figure 5.13
Stud wall elevation by dimensions Steps 1–6.

CHAPTER 5 WALLS AND OPENINGS | 67

Technique 2: drafting from a plan

Steel-stud partition with openings

This technique requires that you have a finished plan in order to draw the elevations. The plan should be in the same scale as the elevation you wish to draw. Elevations are typically drawn at a 1/8" = 1'-0" scale, but 1/4" or 1/2" scales can be used if more detail is needed.

STEP 1
Using the plan, create guidelines for yourself extending from the wall face and the sides of the door and window to an area large enough for you to draw on.

STEP 2
Draw a horizontal line to connect the leftmost and rightmost guidelines, creating the floor plane for the elevation. Measure upward 8'-0", as per this example, and draw another horizontal line to create the ceiling plane. This dimension represents the ceiling height and will change depending on the height of the space in your project.

Hardline the guidelines at the far left and far right to create the walls.

STEP 3
To create the thickness for the top plate and the sole plate, draw lines 1 $^3/_8$" away from the ceiling and floor plane lines you drew in Step 2. The 1 $^3/_8$" represents the thickness of the channel stud.

STEP 4
Create the outermost studs by drawing a vertical line 1 $^1/_2$" away from the sides of the wall, indicating the C-stud thicknesses there.

STEP 5
The guidelines that are present in your drawing at this stage represent the widths of the finished door and window. However, for the final drawing you need to show the rough opening that is to be created, meaning that it will measure 2" wider and 2" taller than the component that is to be installed. In this example, the finished door measures 3'-0" × 7'-0", but the rough opening will measure 3'-2" × 7'-2".

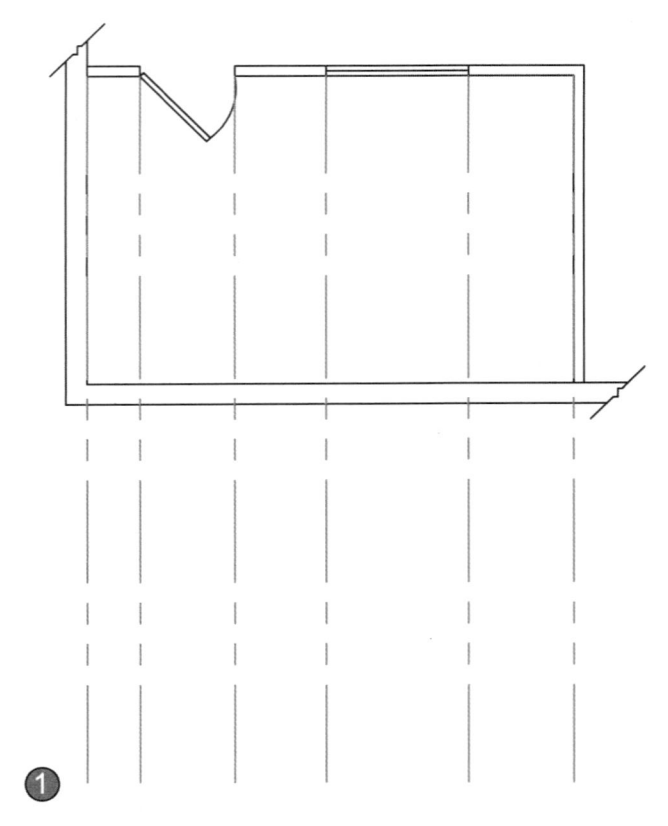

Figure 5.14
Stud wall elevation from plan, Step 1.

First, create the base of the door header by measuring up 7'-2" from the bottom of the sole plate. Draw a horizontal line that extends 1" past each of the door guidelines. This line should measure 3'-2" and will create the width adjustment between the guidelines and the rough opening.

Next, draw vertical lines to connect the bottom of the sole plate to the header line.

The door guidelines and the portion of the sole plate that lies inside of the door opening can now be erased.

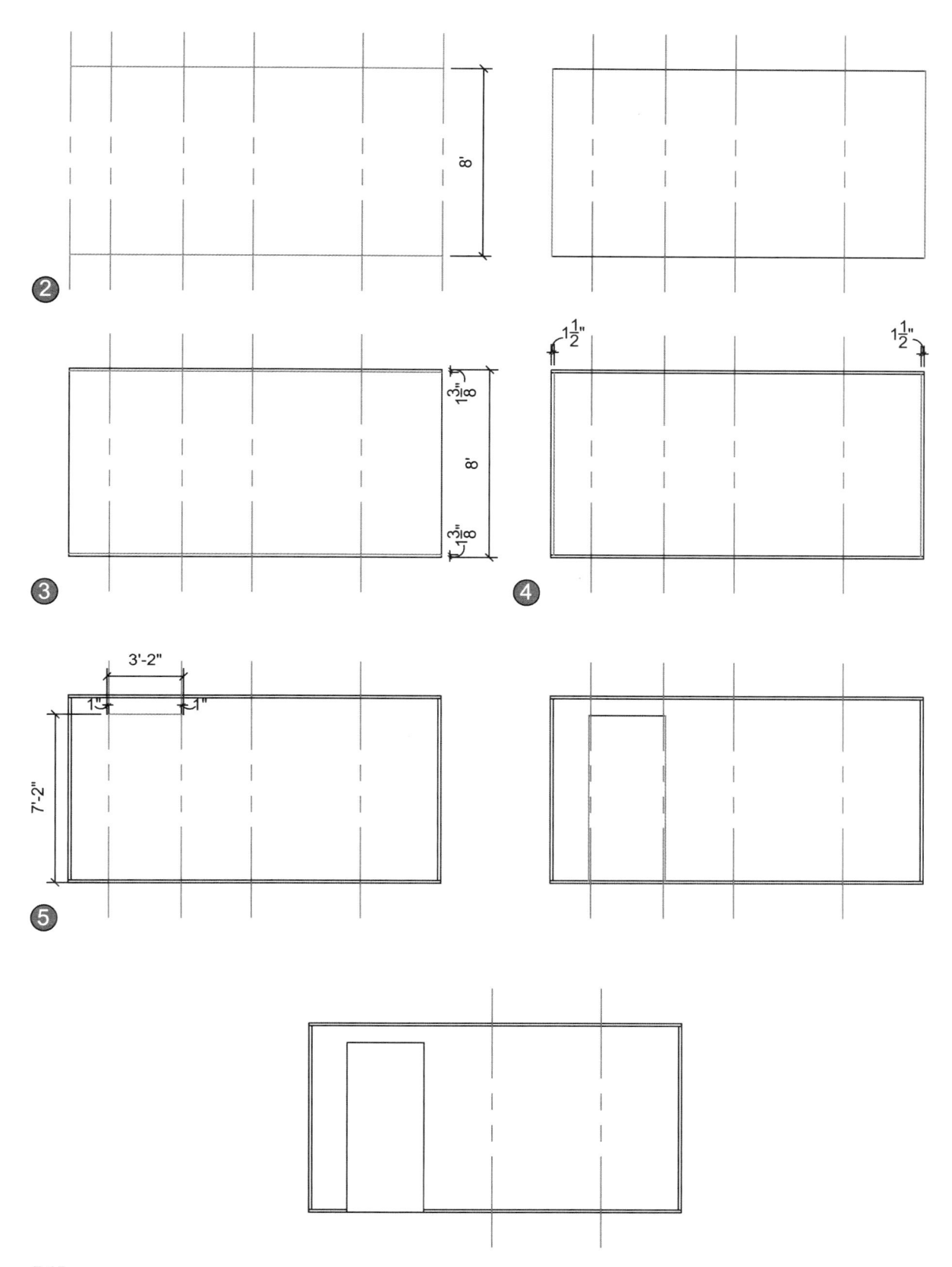

Figure 5.15
Stud wall elevation from plan, Steps 2–5.

CHAPTER 5 WALLS AND OPENINGS

STEP 6

Next to the verticals for the door, you'll need a jack stud attached to a king stud. As mentioned earlier in the chapter, the jack stud will be of a shortened height, measuring even with the top of the rough opening, while the king stud will be full height between the top plate and the sole plate.

To create these studs, measure 1 1/2" from the sides of the rough opening, drawing a line full height between the plates. This will represent the seam between the jack and king studs.

Measure 1 1/2" from these new vertical lines and draw a second set of verticals, which will be the outer edge of the king studs.

STEP 7

Extend the horizontal line from the top of the rough opening to the first set of verticals (the seamline between the two studs). This will be the bottom of the header plate.

Measure upward from the horizontal 1 1/2" and draw a line between the king studs to produce the top of the steel channel that will become the header plate.

STEP 8

Moving to the rough opening for the window, this example uses a fixed 4'-0" × 4'-6" window with a sill height of 2'-6". Keeping in mind that the rough opening requires an additional 2", you will need to make some adjustments based on where the guidelines currently sit, similar to what was done to the door opening in Step 5.

First, draw the horizontal line that will act as the sill support. By accounting for the additional inch needed in the rough opening, this line should be drawn 2'-5" from the bottom of the sole plate and should extend 1" on either side of the guidelines.

Next, measure up 4'-2" from this new line to create the top of the rough opening, again extending the line 1" past each of the guidelines.

Finally, create two vertical lines that connect these horizontals. The lines should measure 4'-8" apart.

The window guidelines can now be erased.

Hand

When drawing dashed lines, place your architectural scale along your straight edge to create even spacing and uniformity for all the lines.

CAD

To create the dashed lines, click on the lines that you wish to change and go to the Home tab and click on Properties and drop down the Linetypes option. Select the dashed line option. If the dashed line option is not available, click on the Other option and find the linetype that you wish to load.

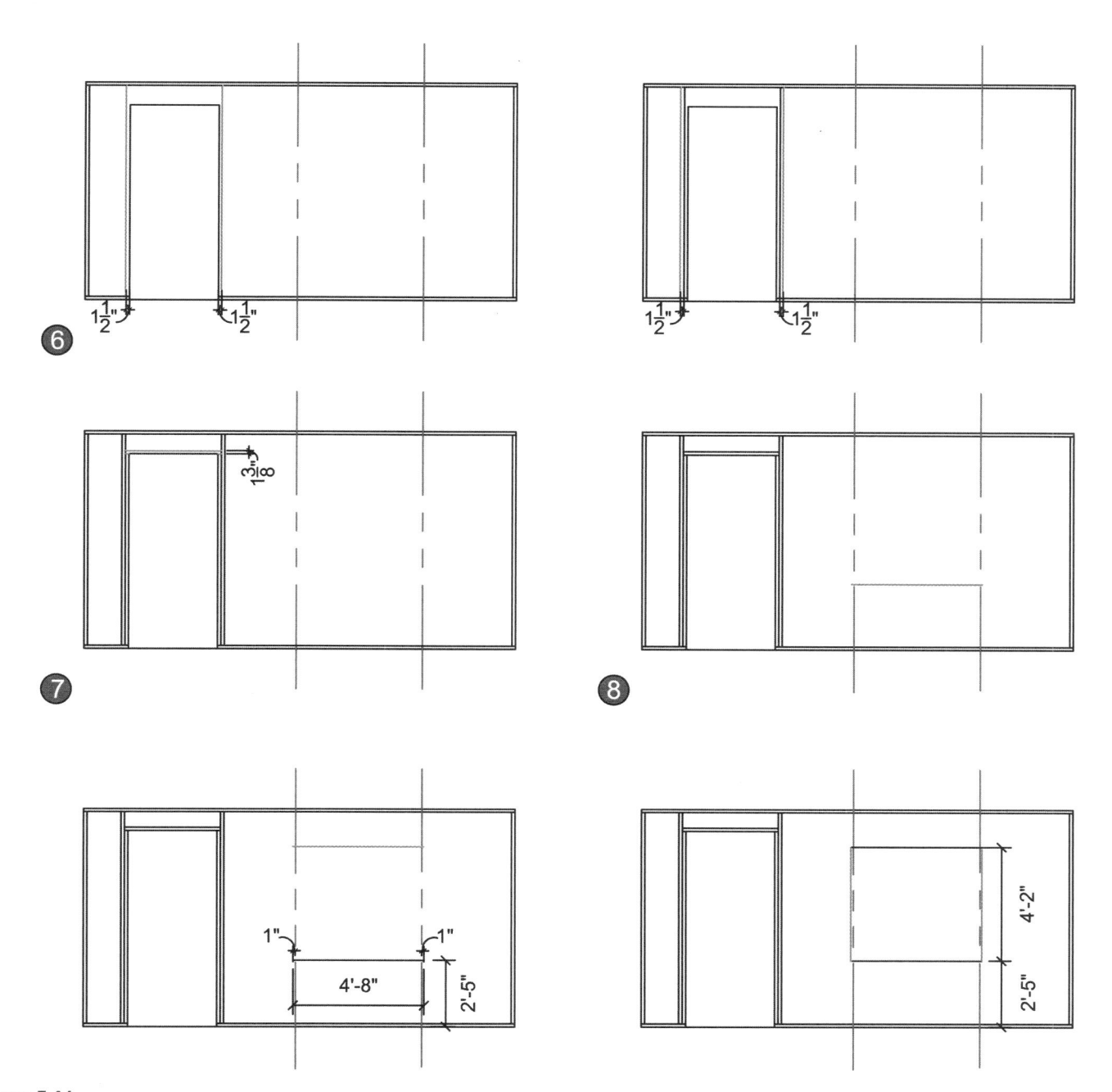

Figure 5.16
Stud wall elevation from plan, Steps 6–8.

CHAPTER 5 WALLS AND OPENINGS

STEP 9
Repeat steps 6 and 7 for the jack and king studs and the header plate for the window.

STEP 10
Make a sill by drawing a line 1 1/2" below the line at the bottom of the window opening. This line should run between the jack studs.

STEP 11
Create guidelines through the center of the existing full-height studs to use as reference points. Measure between these guidelines to determine whether additional studs are necessary, but ignore the space above the door. Keep in mind that in steel-stud construction, the measurement from the center of one stud to the next can be no more than 24" (2'-0"), but if the wall is load-bearing 16" OC is recommended.

In this example, and in most real-life design problems, the distance from the door to window and the window to the wall is not evenly divisible by 24". Because of this, you will need to adjust the spacing pattern and shorten the distance between the final studs. Once you have determined these distances, draw guidelines to help create the new studs.

First, find the location of the stud between the door and the window:

Distance between studs = 2'-4 1/4" = 28.25"

$\qquad$ 28.25"/2 = 14.125"

$\qquad$ 14.125" = 1'-2.125" = **1'-2 1/8"**

Next, find the location of the stud between the window and the wall:

Distance between studs = 2'-11 13/16" = 35.8125"

$\qquad$ 35.8125"/2 = 17.90625"

$\qquad$ 17.90625" = 1'-5.90625" = **1'-5 15/16"**

STEP 12
Using these new guidelines as the centerline for the studs, draw a line 3/4" away on each side of the guide, running from the top plate to the sole plate.

IBC
If the wall opening is wider than 4'-0", you must have a double header to help offset the force of the weight from the floors above. (*IBC 2308.4.4*)

Revit
The easiest way to create a stud wall elevation is to place an elevation marker facing the wall that you wish to detail. Open the Elevation view and hide any elements that may be obscuring the view. Then go to the Annotate tab and select Detail Line from the Detail panel. This will allow you to draw your framework directly onto the Revit walls.

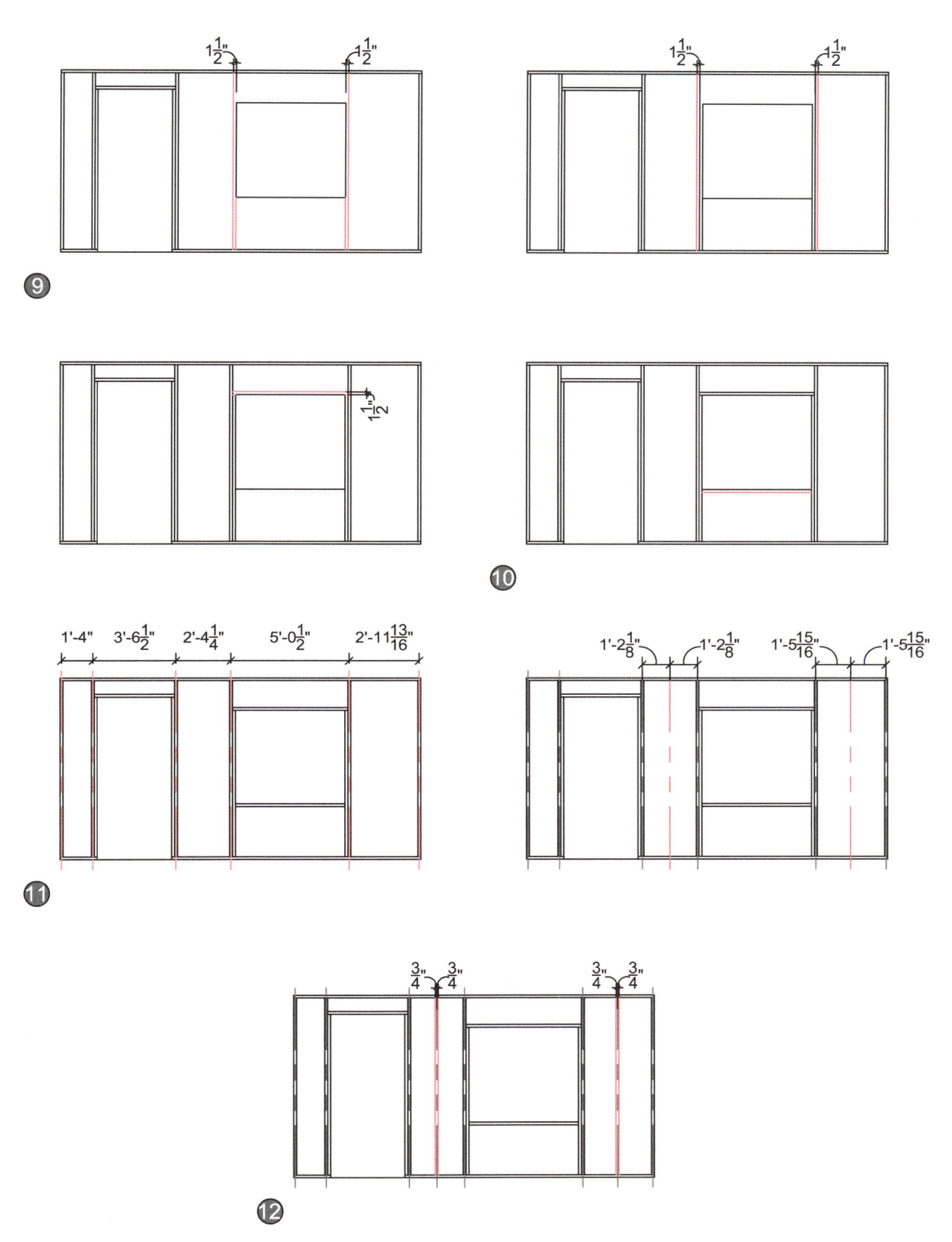

Figure 5.17
Stud wall elevation from plan, Steps 9–12.

STEP 13
Since the distance between the king studs framing the door are more than 24" apart, you will need to create cripple studs above the header plate. In this instance, divide the distance by 3 to determine the spacing for the guidelines:

Distance between studs = 3'-6 $1/2$" = 42.5"

    42.5"/3 = 14.1666

    14.1666 = 1'-2.1666" = **1'-2 $3/16$"**

Using these guidelines, draw a line 3/4" away on each side of the guide, running from the top plate to the header plate.

STEP 14
Repeat Step 13 to draw studs for the window. In this case, you'll need one set of cripple studs between the top plate and the header, and a second set of cripple studs between the sill and the sole plate.

Distance between studs = 5'-0 $1/2$" = 60.5"

    60.5"/3 = 20.1666

    20.1666 = 1'-8.1666" = **1'-8 $3/16$"**

Using these guidelines, draw a line 3/4" on each side of the guide to create the width of the studs.

The drawing is complete once the guidelines are erased.

Hand
Remember to maintain light pressure on all guidelines and tick marks so that you do not have heavy lines marking up your drawing. Lines that will appear in the final drawing can then be darkened.

The easiest way to keep your final drawings clean is to draw the image, step by step, on a piece of trace paper. Then, you can copy your final image on to the vellum, where you can ignore the guidelines and tick marks.

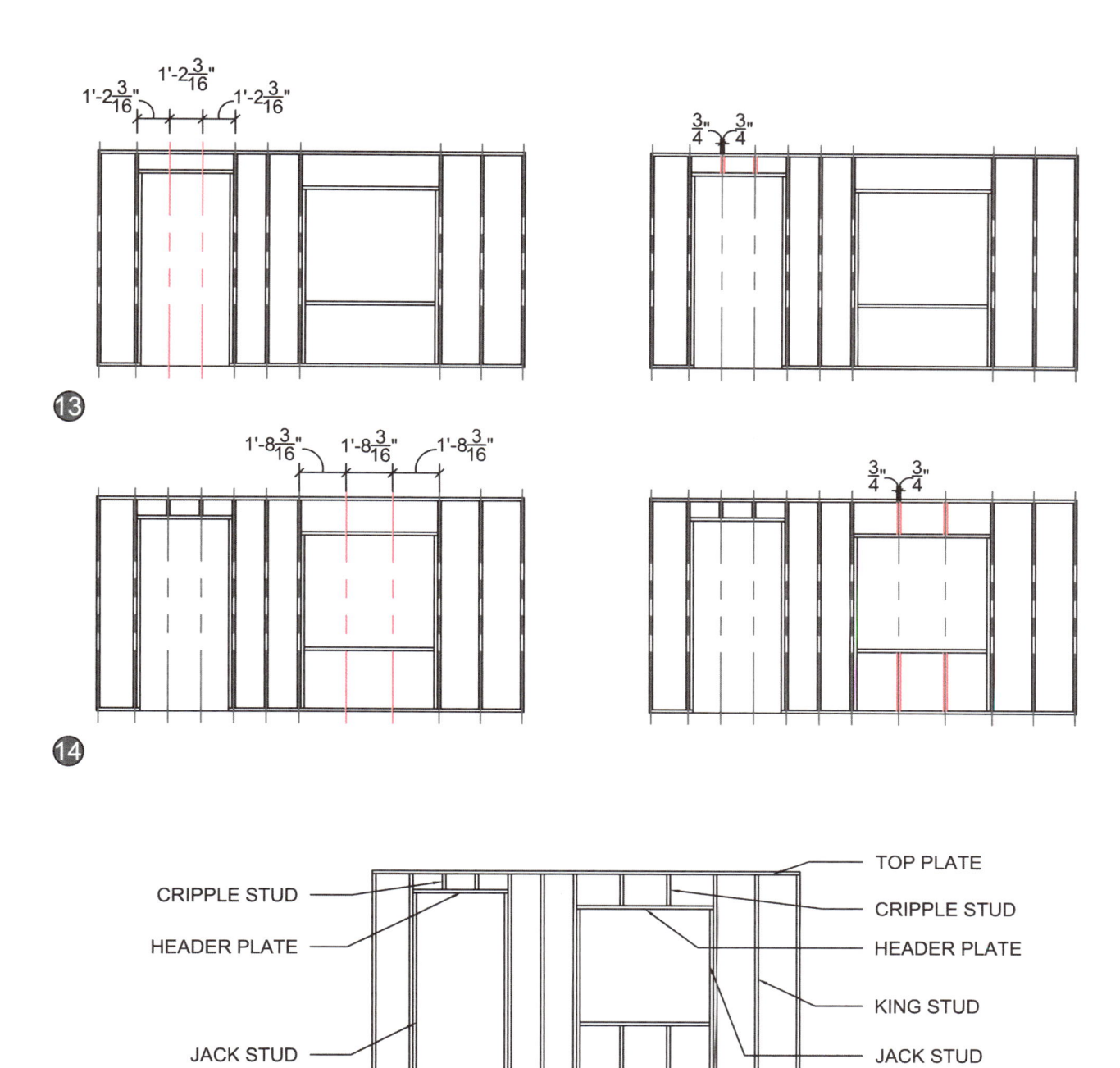

Figure 5.18
Stud wall elevation from plan, Steps 13–14.

CHAPTER 5 WALLS AND OPENINGS | 75

Technique 3: drafting from an existing elevation

Wood-stud partition with openings

Unlike the previous example, this technique utilizes an existing finished elevation for an interior wall to establish the boundaries of what you wish to diagram. The existing elevation should be reproduced at the scale you need for the detail drawing as you will be copying some elements of the original for this diagram.

STEP 1
Using the established elevation, copy the lines indicating the ceiling and floor planes and the edges of the walls. These lines will indicate the outer edge of the detail drawing, with all other line work appearing inside this bounding box.

Lightly copy the lines around any openings that appear, but make sure they are guidelines for now.

STEP 2
To create the thickness for the top plate and the sole plate, draw lines 1 1/2" away from the ceiling and floor plane lines. The 1 1/2" represents the actual thickness of the 2 × 4s being used. As seen in this example, a wood-stud wall will require two 2 × 4s for the top plate.

STEP 3
Create the outermost studs by drawing a vertical line 1 1/2" away from the sides of the wall, indicating the stud thicknesses there.

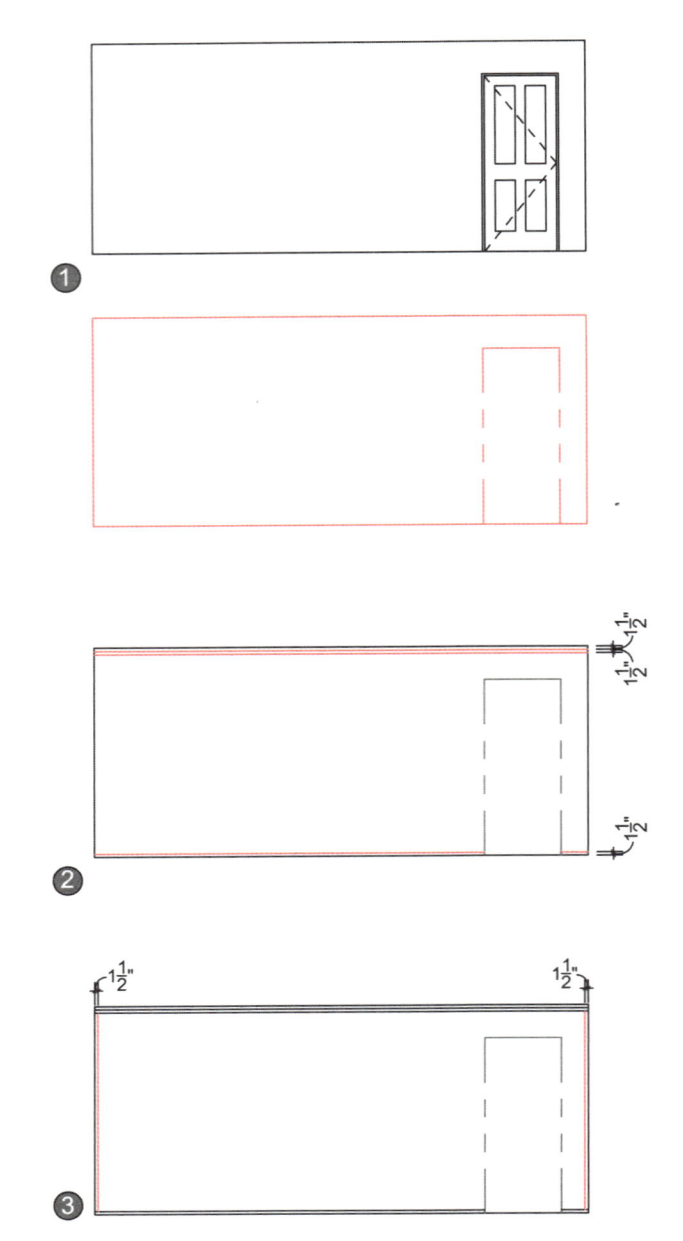

Figure 5.19
Stud wall from an elevation, Steps 1–3.

STEP 4

The guidelines you currently have for the door indicate the finished opening, as opposed to the rough opening needed in this framing drawing. Measure 1" on either side of the door jamb and 2" above the head and hardline these new lines. These will act as the boundaries of the rough opening for the door.

The guidelines can be erased at this time.

STEP 5

Next to the verticals for the door, you'll need a jack stud attached to a king stud. As mentioned earlier in the chapter, the jack stud will be of a shortened height, measuring even with the top of the rough opening, while the king stud will be full height between the top plate and the sole plate.

To create these studs, measure 1 1/2" from the sides of the rough opening, drawing a line full height between the plates. This will represent the seam between the jack and king studs.

Measure 1 1/2" from these new vertical lines and draw a second set of verticals, which will be the outer edge of the king studs.

STEP 6

The header plate of the door will run between the king studs above the top line of the opening. Extend the horizontal line at the top of the door to create the bottom of the header plate. Measure 1 1/2" up from this line and draw a second horizontal line, and then draw a third horizontal 1 1/2" above the second. Together, these three lines will form the two layers of 2 × 4s used to create the header plate.

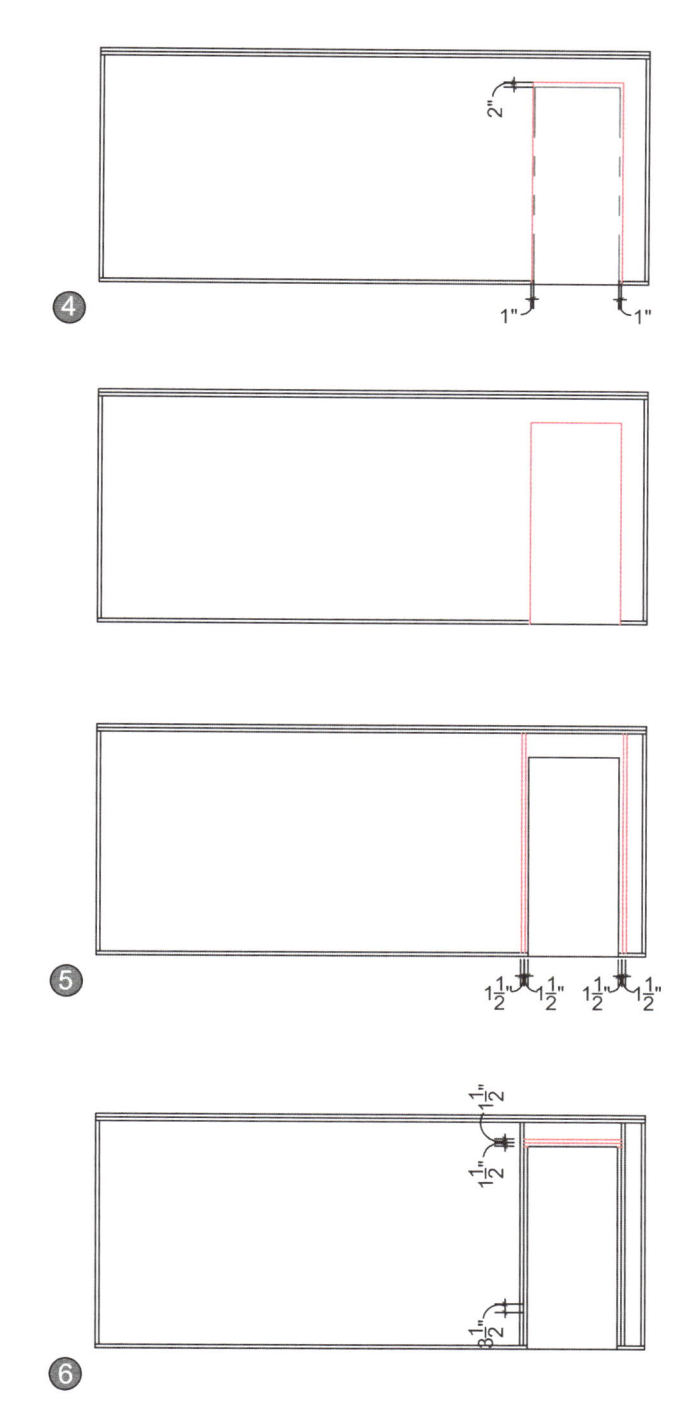

Figure 5.20
Stud wall from an elevation, Steps 4–6.

CHAPTER 5 WALLS AND OPENINGS | 77

STEP 7

Create guidelines through the center of the existing full-height studs to use as reference points. Measure between these guidelines to determine whether additional studs are necessary, but ignore the space above the door. Keep in mind that in wood-stud construction, the measurement from the center of one stud to the next can be no more than 16" (1'-4").

In this example, and in most real-life design problems, the distance between the leftmost wall and the door is not evenly divisible by 16". Because of this, you will need to adjust the spacing pattern and shorten the distance between the final studs.

First, locate the center of this portion of the wall (black guideline):

Distance between studs = 14'-1 $^9/_{16}$" = 169.5625"

$169.5625"/2 = 84.78125"$

$84.78125" = 7'-0.78125" =$ **7'-0 13/16"**

Next, measure 8" to either side of this midpoint (red guidelines). These red lines will indicate the centerlines of two studs that will be drawn in Step 9, which are 16" OC and will also allow for the remaining studs to be laid out in an even pattern.

STEP 8

Draw the remaining guidelines 16" apart from each other. The final guidelines will measure less than 13" from the next stud.

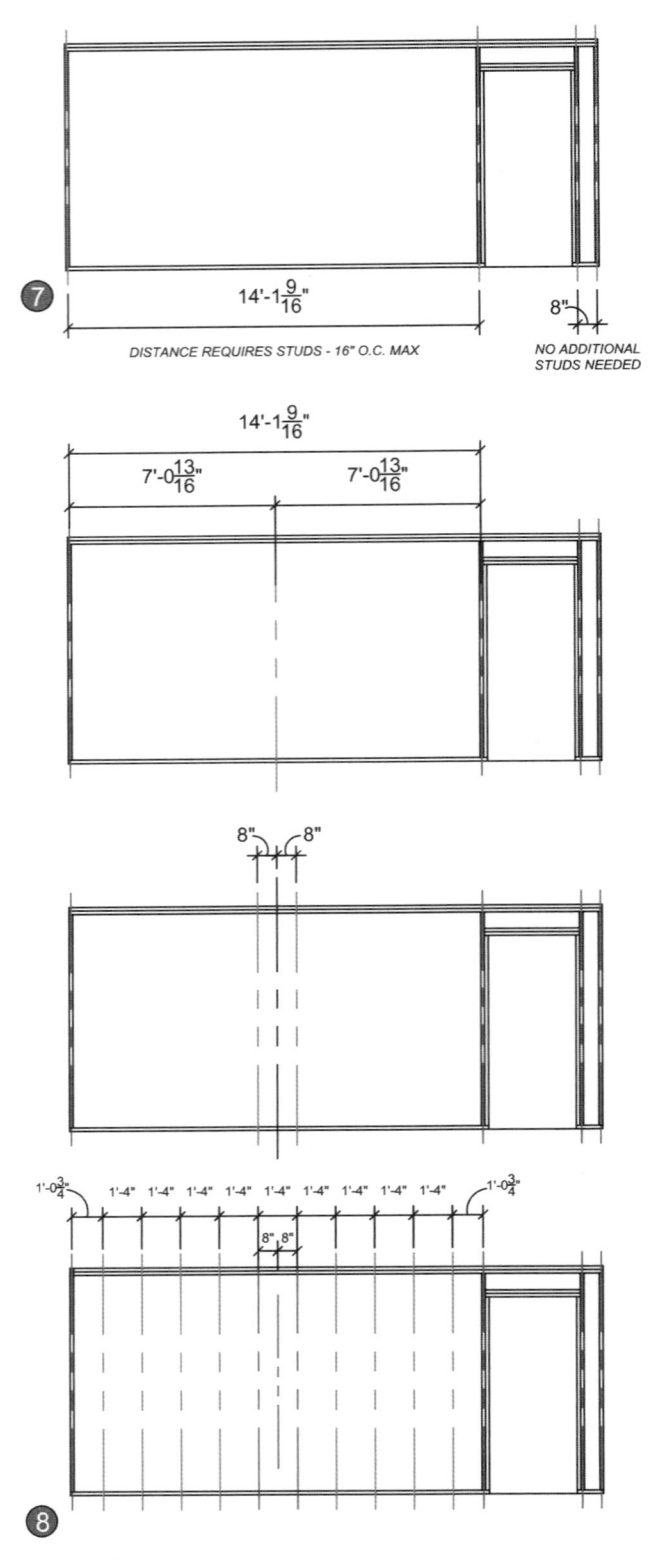

Figure 5.21
Stud wall from an elevation, Steps 7–8.

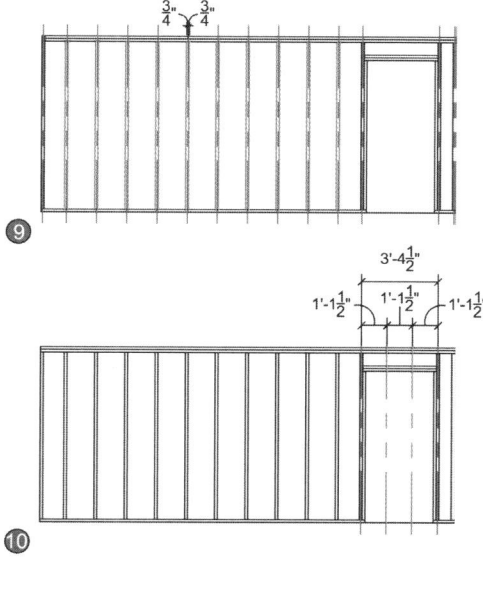

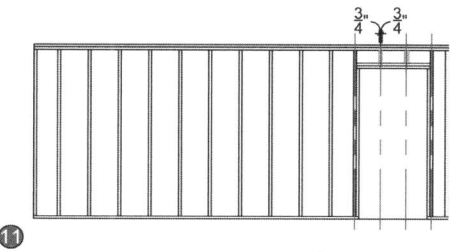

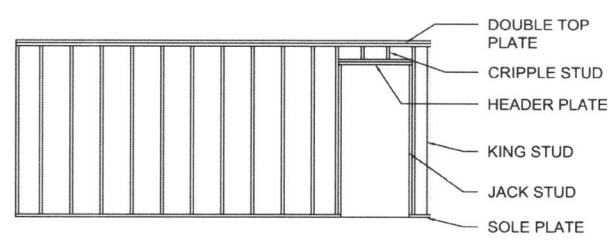

Figure 5.22
Stud wall from an elevation, Steps 9–11.

STEP 9
Using these new guidelines as the centerlines for the studs, draw a line 3/4" away on each side of the guide, running from the top plate to the sole plate.

All of the guidelines can now be erased, except for the ones in the king studs framing the door.

STEP 10
Since the distance between the king studs framing the door are more than 16" apart, you will need to create cripple studs above the header plate. In this instance, divide the distance by 3 to determine the spacing for the guidelines:

Distance between studs = 3'-4 1/2" = 40.5"

$$40.5"/3 = 13.3333$$

$$13.3333 = \mathbf{1'\text{-}1\ 1/2"}$$

STEP 11
Using these guidelines, draw a line 3/4" away on each side of the guide, running from the top plate to the header plate.

All of the guidelines can now be erased.

CHAPTER 5 WALLS AND OPENINGS

DRAFTING WINDOW AND OPENING FRAMES

Wooden frame opening

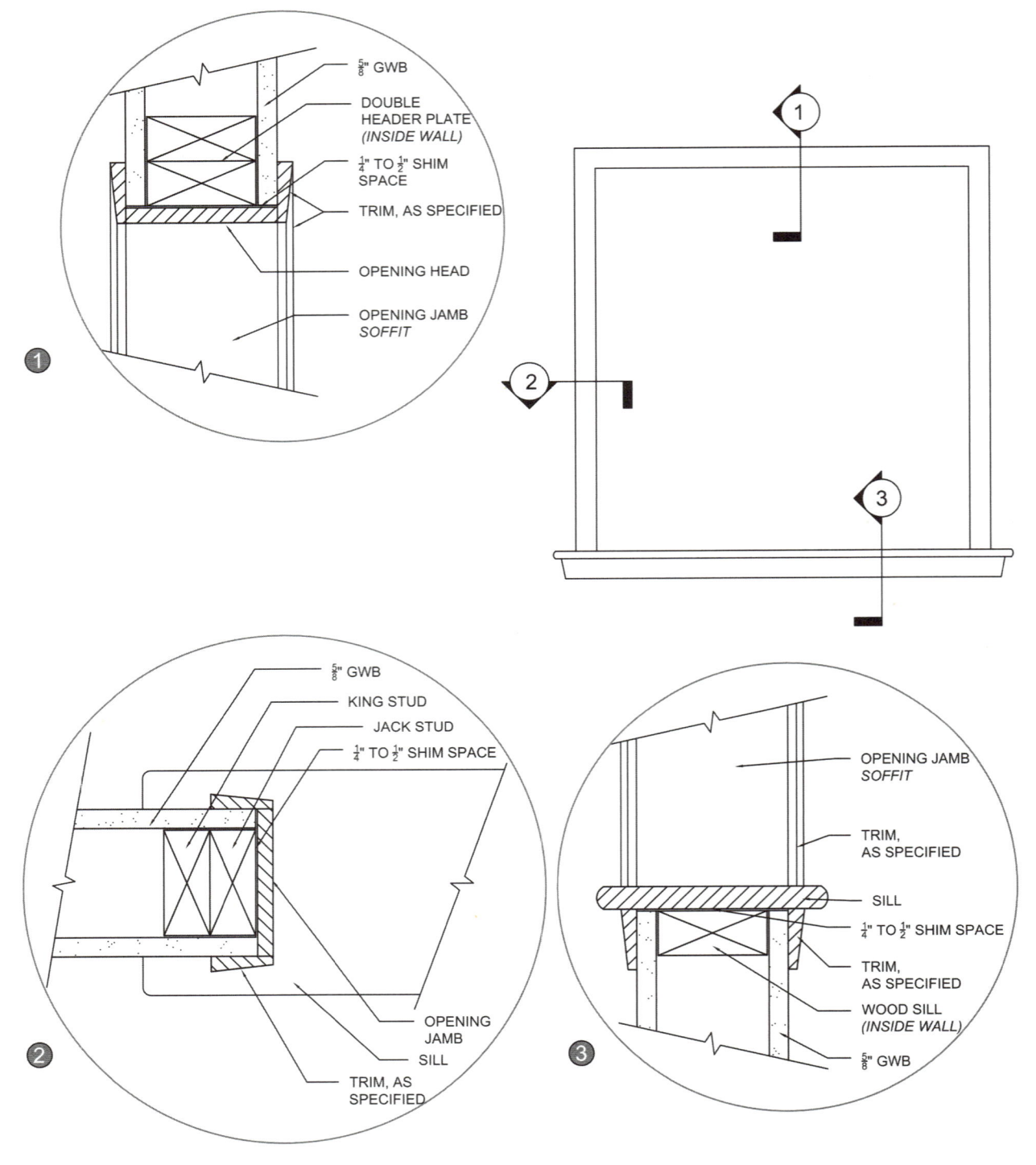

Figure 5.23
Head, jamb, and sill of a wood frame opening.

STUDIO Animation 5.2 Wooden frame opening details

This example documents the head, jamb, and sill details associated for a wall opening with a sill raised 4'-0" above finished floor (AFF). All lines should be drawn with a section lineweight unless otherwise noted.

SECTION 1: head

STEP 1
Draw two 2 × 4s for the header plate of the rough opening. Add 5/8" GWB on either side of the wood block, aligning the bottom of the GWB with the bottom of the header plate. Measure to ensure that this assembly matches the thickness of the wall specified in your plan. Then, create the **shim space** by making a rectangle under the assembly, measuring 1/4" to 1/2" high and running from the face of one GWB to the other. This space allows for leveling strips, or **shims**, to be inserted between the structure and the finish materials to ensure that the final product is level.

STEP 2
Add the opening header below this shim space. This should be a rectangle that runs the same distance and measures as the thickness of the specified wood.

STEP 3
Add your specified trim to either side of the frame, flush with the bottom of the head. This can be of your own creation or from an existing profile. Extend lines for the trim and head down into the drawing. These lines should appear with an elevation lineweight and will occur anywhere there is a seam or a width change.

SECTION 2: jamb

STEP 1
Draw two 2 × 4s with pieces of GWB running along the top and bottom of each board, forming the king and jack studs between the wall faces. Measure to ensure that this assembly matches the wall thickness in your plan.

STEP 2
Create the shim space by making a rectangle next to the jack stud, measuring 1/4"-1/2" high and running from the face of one GWB to the other. Draw the opening jamb next to this shim space. This should be a rectangle the runs the same height and measures as the same thickness as the specified wood.

STEP 3
Add your specified trim to either side of the frame, flush with the outer edge of the jamb. This can be of your own creation or from an existing profile. Add the sill outline in an elevation lineweight below the assembly.

SECTION 3: sill

STEP 1
Draw a 2 × 4 with a 1/4" – 1/2" shim space similar to what you drew for the head's Step 1. Add the GWB to each side of the 2 × 4, but this time align the wallboard with the top of the wood.

STEP 2
Draw the opening sill above this shim space, extending it past the GWB as necessary.

STEP 3
Add the specified trim to either side of the frame, flush with the bottom of the sill. Extend lines for the trim and jamb upward from the sill. These lines will appear with an elevation lineweight.

Aluminum window frame, header, and sill

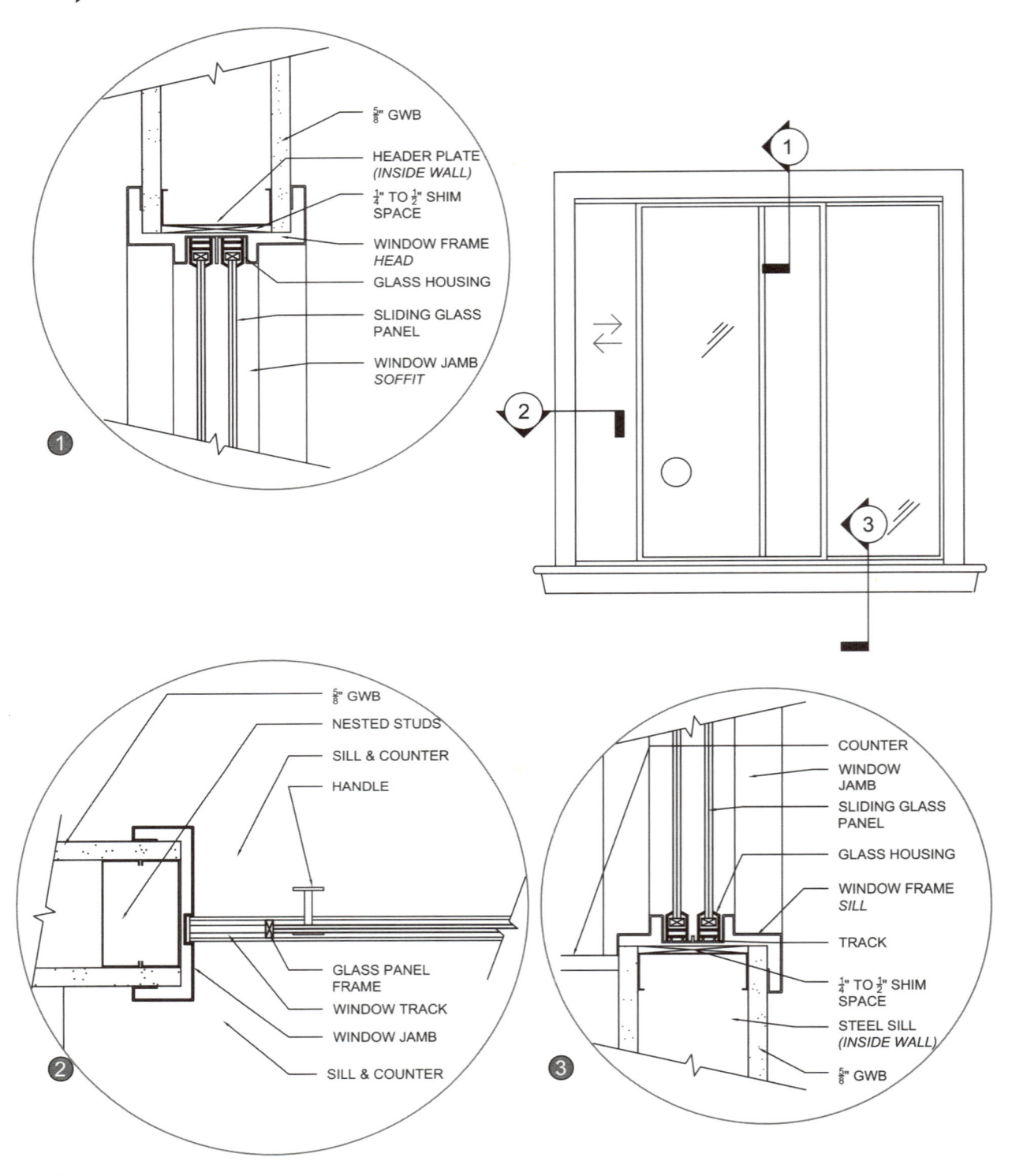

Figure 5.24
Head, jamb, and sill of an aluminum frame window.

STUDIO Animation 5.3 Aluminum window frame details

82 PART II DETAIL DRAWINGS

This example documents the head, jamb, and sill details associated with a sliding window. The elevation is taken from the reception window of the commercial plan. All lines should be drawn with a section lineweight unless otherwise noted.

SECTION 1: head

STEP 1
Draw a C-stud for the header plate of the rough opening. Below the plate, create the shim space by drawing a rectangle measuring 1/4" to 1/2" high and running from one side of one stud to the other. Then, add 5/8" GWB on either side of the plate, aligning the bottom of the GWB with the bottom of the shim space rectangle. Measure to ensure that this assembly matches the thickness of the wall specified in your plan.

STEP 2
Add the aluminum head below the shim space based on a profile supplied by the manufacturer of your specified window. Add in the glass panels based on the manufacturer's information.

STEP 3
Extend lines for the header down into the drawing. These lines should appear with an elevation lineweight and will occur anywhere there is a seam or a depth change.

SECTION 2: jamb

STEP 1
Draw two C-studs with pieces of GWB running along the top and bottom of each. Measure to ensure that this assembly matches the wall thickness in your plan.

STEP 2
Draw the window jamb next to this assembly, overlapping the GWB as necessary. The jamb's profile should match that supplied by the manufacturer of your specified window. Add in the glass panels and any hardware based on the manufacturer's information.

STEP 3
Add the sill outline in an elevation lineweight below the assembly.

SECTION 3: sill

STEP 1
Follow Step 1 for the head section, but place the shim space atop the C-stud and align the GWB with the top of the shim space.

STEP 2
Draw the aluminum sill above this shim space based on a profile supplied by the manufacturer of your specified window. Add in the glass panels based on the manufacturer's information.

STEP 3
Draw any countertops that extend from the opening and the jamb in the distance. These lines will appear with an elevation lineweight.

DRAFTING DOOR FRAMES

Wooden door frame and header

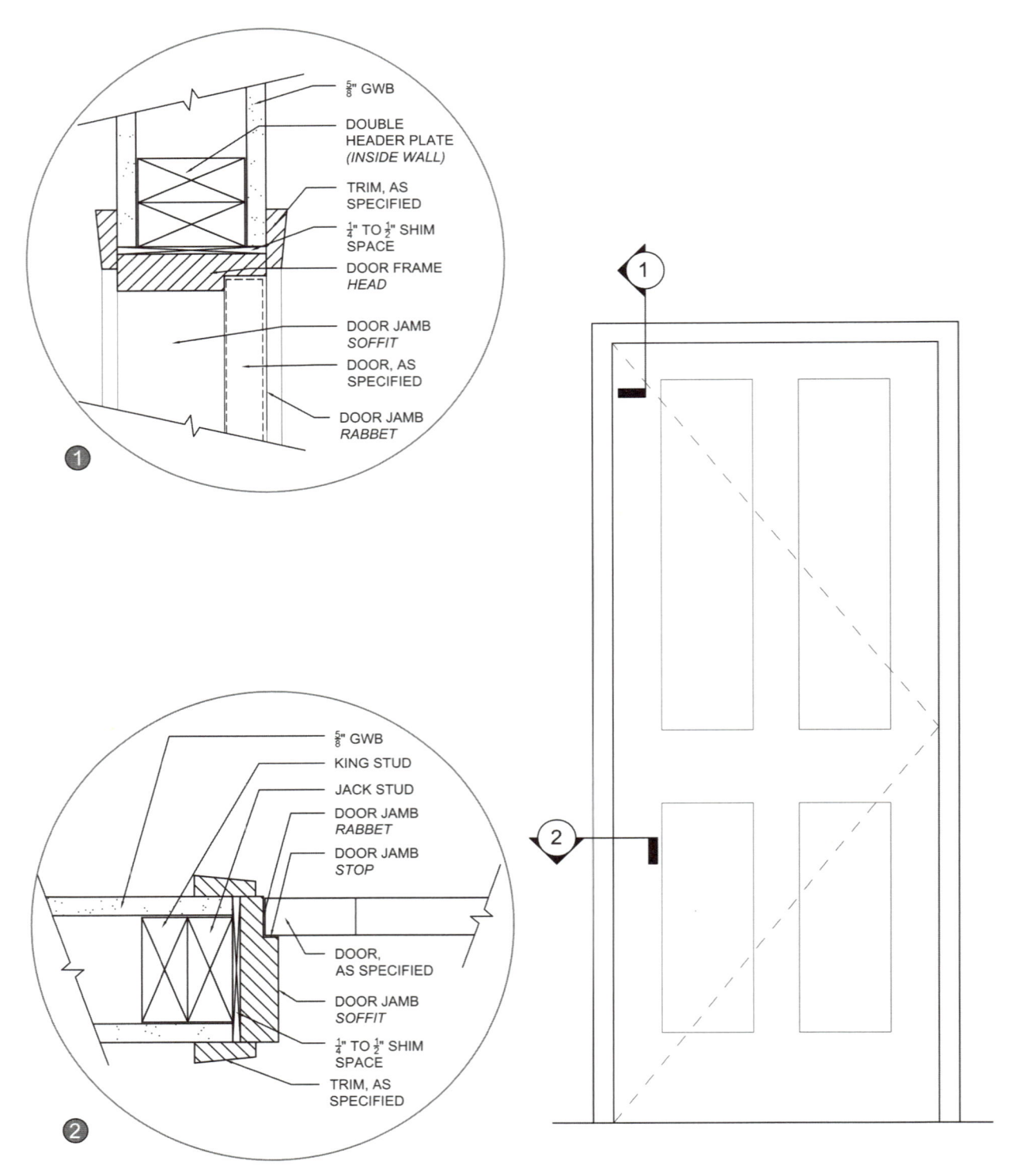

Figure 5.25
Head and jamb of a wood door frame.

STUDIO Animation 5.4 Wood door frame details

This example documents the header and jamb details associated with a wooden interior door frame as used throughout the residential plan. All lines should be drawn with section lineweights unless otherwise noted.

SECTION 1: header

STEP 1
Draw two 2 × 4s for the header plate of the rough opening. Add 5/8" GWB on either side of the wood block, aligning the bottoms of the GWBs with the bottom of the header plate. Measure to ensure that this assembly matches the thickness of the wall specified in your plan. Then, create the shim space by making a rectangle under the assembly, measuring 1/4" to 1/2" high and running from the face of one GWB to the other.

STEP 2
Add the wood header below the shim space based on a profile supplied by the manufacturer of your specified door frame. This portion should align with the edges of the GWB.

STEP 3
Add the trim of your choice. The trim profile can be based on your own design, or can be selected from a typical profile, as seen in Appendix H.

STEP 4
Extend lines from the header down into the drawing to create the appearance of the jamb. These lines should be shown with an elevation lineweight and will occur anywhere there is a seam or a depth change.

SECTION 2: jamb

STEP 1
Draw two 2 × 4s with pieces of GWB running along the top and bottom of each board, forming the king and jack studs between the wall faces. Measure to ensure that this assembly matches the wall thickness in your plan. Then create the shim space by making a rectangle next to the assembly, measuring 1/4" to 1/2" wide and running from the face of one GWB to the other.

STEP 2
Add the wood jamb next to the shim space based on a profile supplied by the manufacturer of your specified door frame. This portion should align with the edges of the GWB.

STEP 3
Add the trim of your choice. The trim profile can be based on your own design or can be selected from a typical profile, as seen in Appendix H.

STEP 4
Add the specified door to the assembly.

IBC

Openings in nonbearing interior partitions can be framed with a single header, but it must be at least 1 1/2" wide. (*IBC 2308.5.5.3*)

Door frames must be at least 78" high. (*IBC 1010.1.1*)

Commercial—aluminum door frame and header

This example documents the header and jamb details associated with an aluminum interior door frame as used throughout the commercial plan.

SECTION 1: header

STEP 1
Draw a C-stud for the header of the rough opening. On either side of the stud, add 5/8" GWB, with the bottom of the GWB extending about 1" past the bottom of the stud. Measure to ensure that this assembly matches the thickness of the wall specified in your plan.

STEP 2
Add the steel header below the GWB based on a profile supplied by the manufacturer of your specified door frame. If using a wraparound frame, as in this example, ensure that there is 1/16" spacing between the header and the GWB for sealant. The wraparound will allow for the edges of the GWB to be encased within the frame, while the butt-frame will unite the edge of the frame to the edge of the wall.

STEP 3
Extend lines from the header down into the drawing to create the appearance of a jamb. These lines should be shown with an elevation lineweight and will occur anywhere there is a seam or a depth change.

SECTION 2: jamb

STEP 1
Draw a C-stud with pieces of GWB running along the top and bottom, aligning the edges of the GWB with the back of the stud. Measure to ensure that this assembly matches the wall thickness in your plan.

STEP 2
Draw the door jamb next to this assembly, overlapping the GWB as necessary, roughly 7/8". The jamb's profile should match that supplied by the manufacturer. Between the wall assembly and the far end of the door jamb there should be a space of at least 3/4" depending on the frame size. Use this space to create a dashed line frame anchor, which runs from face to face on the jamb.

STEP 3
Add the specified door to the assembly.

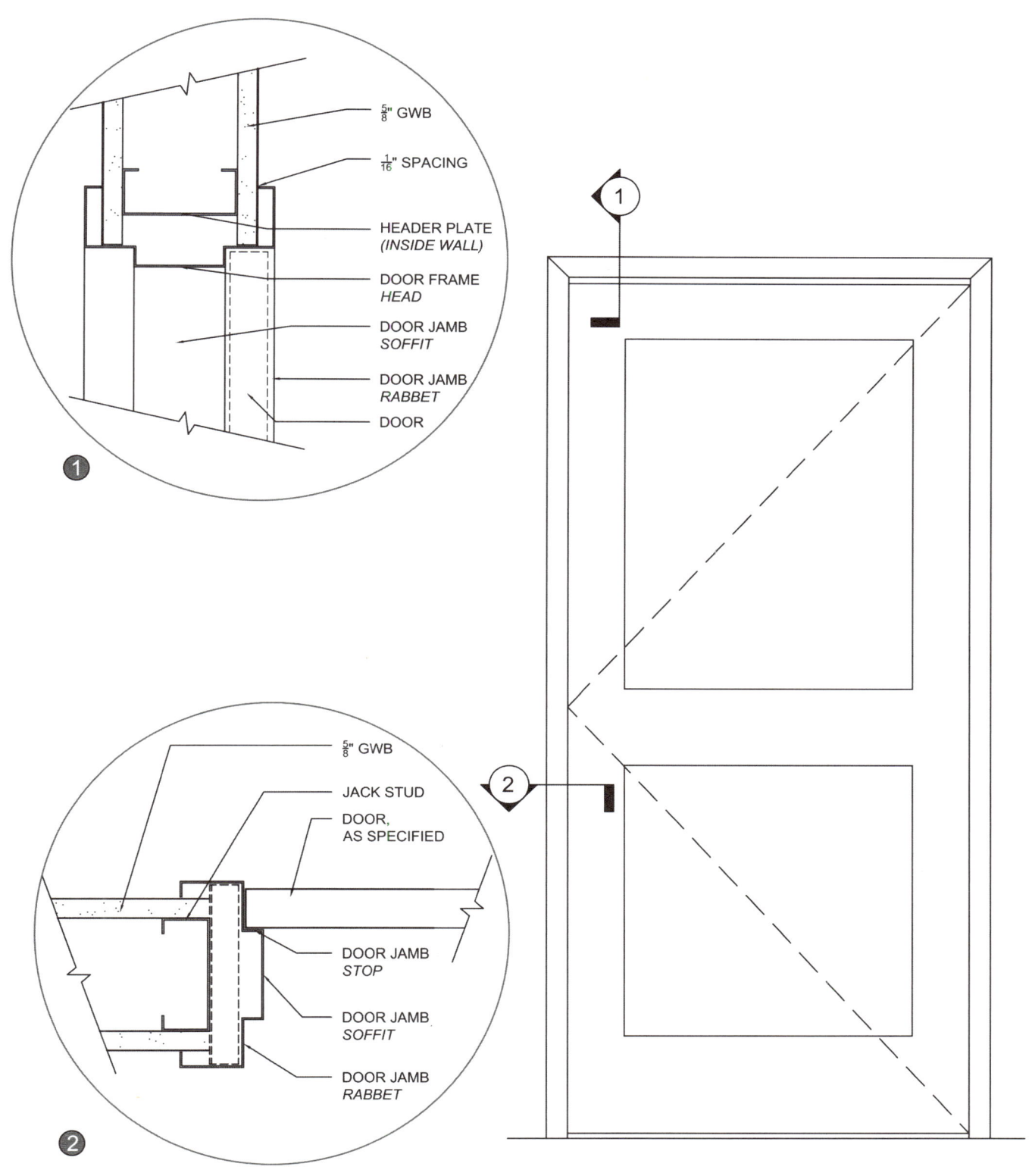

Figure 5.26
Head and jamb of an aluminum door frame.

STUDIO Animation 5.5 Aluminum door frame details

CHAPTER 5 WALLS AND OPENINGS | 87

WHY IS THIS IMPORTANT?

As interior designers, you may never need to draw wall frame diagrams in practice. This is a task typically left to those dealing with the structure of the project. However, when you understand the components that are necessary for partition construction and how they fit together within the wall, you are better equipped to make creative, but feasible, partition alterations. Partitions do not need to be simplistic planes; they can be curved, punctured, tapered, or internally lit. Knowing how to design these creative variables without compromising the integrity of the partition will allow you to be able to manipulate the design to meet your vision.

Figure 5.27
Brick wall featuring an inset wooden wine rack.

Figure 5.28
Angled partition with openings.

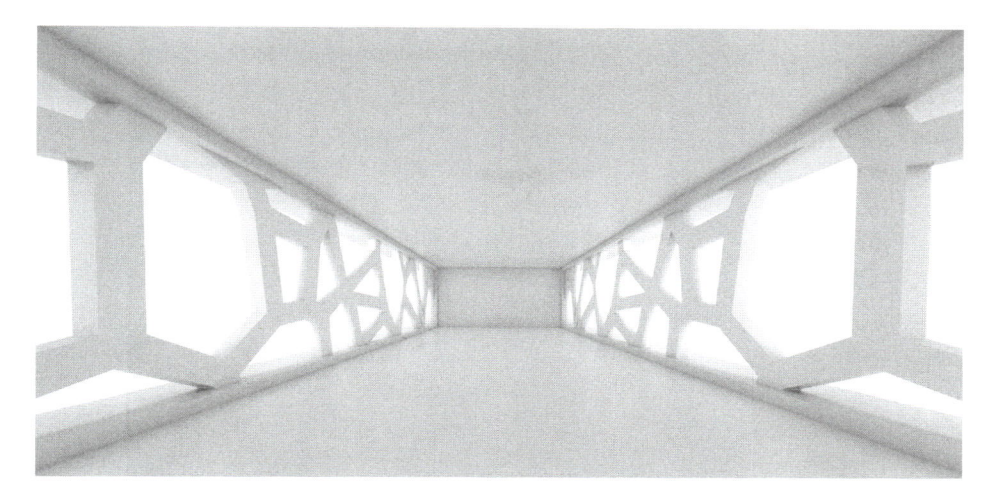

Figure 5.29
Steel frame partitions with irregular openings. Studs and supports are covered with a finish material.

Figure 5.30
Patterned layout of GWB with inset shelves constructed into the extra wide double frame partition.

CHAPTER REVIEW

1. What type of construction features a double header over openings? What is the reasoning behind the double header?
2. How far should the spacing between wood studs be? Between steel studs?
3. Compare and contrast the jamb of a wood-stud assembly to that of a steel-stud construction.
4. What is the importance of the added two inches between door size and the measurement for a rough opening?
5. List the three different types of wall construction, their major elements, and in what instances that type of partition can be used.
6. Create a partition with openings that has the unique feature of your choice (i.e., curved, punctured, etc.). Detail the wall, calling out the construction type and the components needed for the rough openings.

EXAMPLE PLAN UPDATES STUDIO

As this chapter explored the different types of walls used in steel construction (commercial) and wood construction (residential), this first phase of the project focuses on the placement of interior partitions and openings. Here, walls that are poched black are load-bearing, white are partitions, red are chase, and gray are rated. As a reminder, these spaces have been designed with the purpose of providing examples for this text. Students should utilize the author's examples for practice and feel free to be as creative as possible within the shell of their own project.

The commercial plan has been laid out for an office, with the layout containing the following spaces:

- Reception/Waiting
- Restroom
- Office
- Tech room
- Conference room
- Stairs

The walls used in this plan are light gauge steel studs, and there is a 16" chase partition for back-to-back fixtures. All doors have aluminum frames, as does the interior window

The residential plan has been laid out to include:

- Entry/Hall
- Coat closet
- Living room
- Bathroom
- Kitchen
- Under stair storage

The wall types used in this plan are all standard wood-stud partitions with wood frames for doors and openings.

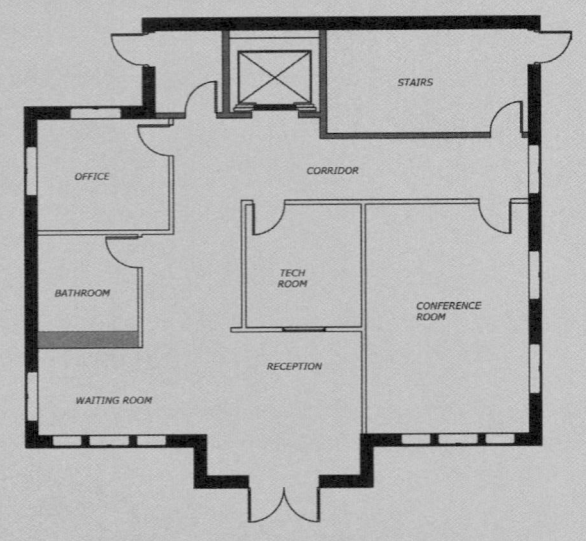

Figure 5.31
Commercial plan with interior walls and openings.

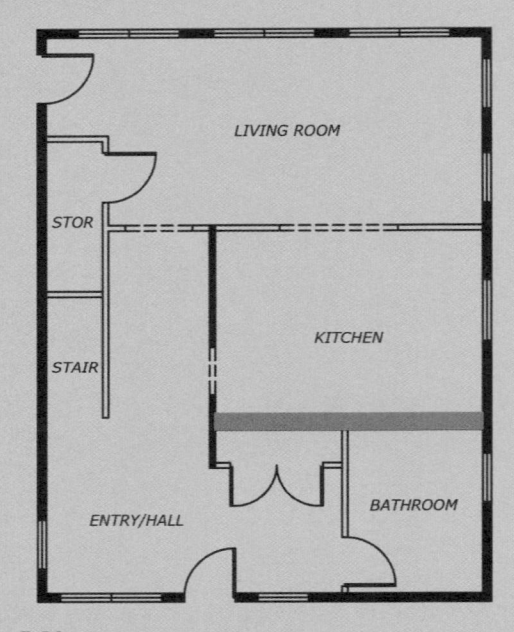

Figure 5.32
Residential plan with interior walls and openings.

CHAPTER TERMINOLOGY

- acoustical partition
- backbend
- bearing wall
- casing
- chase walls
- cripple stud
- double rabbet
- double top plate
- face
- frame
- greenboard
- gypsum wallboard
- head
- header
- header beam
- header plate
- jack stud
- jamb
- king stud
- knockout
- nested double joint
- nested header plate
- nonbearing wall
- partition
- rabbet
- rated partition
- rough opening
- shim
- shim space
- sill
- single rabbet
- soffit (door)
- sole plate
- steel channel
- stop
- stud
- throat
- top plate
- Type X

WALL AND OPENING CODES

This section explored the elements used and how to draw construction details for stud walls and frames for doors, windows, and openings. Below are the ADA standards and the IBC cods that you need to keep in mind when designing and drafting walls and openings.

Table 5.1 ADA Standards for Walls and Openings

ADA Code	Topic	Description
201.1	Scope	All new construction projects and existing projects undergoing alteration must comply with ADA code.
		Exceptions may apply based on the scope of the project and the project type.
403.5.1	Clear width—walking surface	Accessible routes must be at least 36" wide. Corridors should be a minimum of 60" wide.
404.2.3	Clear width—doors	Door openings must be at least 32". When looking at an 80" door, nothing can project into clear width below 34". Between the measurements of 34"–80", only door closers and stops 4" wide or less may project into the clear width.

Table 5.2 IBC Codes for Walls and Openings

IBC Code	Topic	Description
1010.1.1	Door size	Doors that are a part of the egress must be a minimum of 32" wide, but may be required to be wider depending on the occupant load of the building. Door openings must be at least 80" high. Exceptions include doorways in sleeping units (hotels) or dwellings, where doorways must be at least 78" in height.
1010.1.1.1	Projections into clear width	When looking at an 80" door, nothing can project into clear width below 34". Between the measurements of 34"–80", only door closers and stops 4" wide or less may project into the clear width.
1020.1	Corridor construction	Commercial corridors must feature fire-resistance rated materials and must comply with Section 708.
1208.1	Minimum room width	Habitable spaces, or those that the user can live and work in, must be at least 7'-0" wide. This does not include the kitchen.
2308.2.2	Floor-to-floor height	The floor-to-floor height must be 11'-7" or less. Braced interior walls cannot have a floor-to-floor height more than 10'-0".
2308.4.4	Framing around openings	Headers spanning more than 4'-0" are required to be doubled. If it spans more than 6'-0", framing anchors are also needed.
2308.5.1	Wood king studs	King studs in non-bearing wood partitions that are 10'-0" or less in height must run from sole plate to top plate and be spaced 16" OC.
2308.5.3.1	Sole plates	Sole plates must be at least as wide as the stud and must be at least 2" thick.
2308.5.3.2	Top plates	Top plates must be at least as wide as the stud and must be at least 2" thick.
2308.5.3.4	Non-bearing partitions	In partitions that carry no weight, studs must be spaced 24" OC or less.
2308.5.5.3	Nonbearing wood header	Nonbearing interior partitions can be framed with a single header, which must be at least 1 1/2" wide.

CHAPTER REFERENCES

Ballast, David Kent. *Interior Construction & Detailing for Designers and Architects*. Belmont, CA: Professional Publications, Inc., 2013.

Ching, Francis D. *Building Construction Illustrated*. New York: John Wiley & Sons, 2014.

DeChiara, Joseph, Julius Panero, and Martin Zelnik. *Time-Saver Standards for Interior Design and Space Planning*. New York: McGraw-Hill, 2001.

International Code Council. *International Building Code, 2015*. Chicago: International Code Council Publications, 2014.

International Code Council. *International Residential Code, 2015*. Chicago: International Code Council Publications, 2014.

Jefferis, Alan. *Residential Design, Drafting, and Detailing*, 2nd ed. Boston: Cengage Learning, 2013.

Kilmer, W. Otie and Rosemary Kilmer. *Construction Drawings and Details for Interiors*. New York: John Wiley & Sons, 2016.

Kruse, Kelsey and Maryrose McGowan. *Interior Graphic Standards*. New York: John Wiley & Sons, 2003.

United States Department of Justice. *2010 ADA Standards for Accessible Design*. Washington, D.C.: Dept. of Justice, 2010.

Ceilings

CHAPTER 6

CHAPTER OUTCOMES

After completing this chapter you will be able to:

1. Specify and detail suspended and direct installation ceilings as well as create ceilings with varying heights.
2. Design and detail applied ceiling components with wood and steel frameworks.
3. Customize unique ceiling planes and details for projects.

Figure 6.1
A layered suspended ceiling featuring both a recessed acoustical tile grid and a combination box beam cove element.

ABOUT CEILINGS

Ceilings are a compound construction element that includes not only the finish materials that you can see when standing inside of a room but also the support system hidden above it. The principal component is the **girder**, a beam that accepts the weight from above and acts as the main support in the ceiling system. The girder is created by either bolting multiple 2 × 6s (or larger) together or by utilizing a steel **I-beam**. The I-beam is a unit that appears with to have an *I* shape in cross-section, with flanges extending equidistant from the central support. The girders are in turn supported by structural posts below.

Running across or between the girders are the **joists**, or perpendicular beams that support the floor above. These joists can range from 9 $\frac{1}{2}$" to 18" deep but must retain a uniform size across the level. For wood construction, the joists anchor above the girder, with a nominal wood plank acting as a block between runs, as seen on the left-hand side of Figure 6.2. In steel systems, the joists are I-beams that can run across the top of the girder or be anchored into the flanges, as seen on the right side of Figure 6.2.

Depending on the type of ceiling to be installed, materials can be attached directly to the girders and joists, or it may be hung from wires that are tethered to

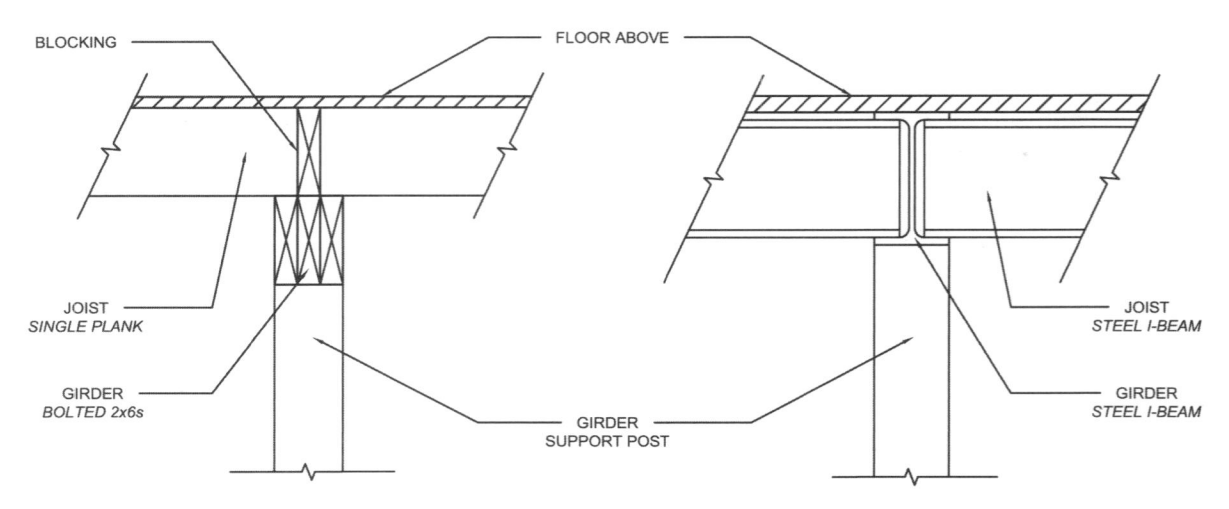

Figure 6.2
Girders and joists creating a ceiling plane and supporting the floor above for wood construction (left) and steel.

Figure 6.3
Wood joists with wires to be hidden once the finished ceiling is installed.

Figure 6.4
Steel girders supporting open web steel joists above.

PART II DETAIL DRAWINGS

those construction components. The following sections will discuss the various types of ceilings, the elements required for the system, and how they are each installed.

Suspension systems are used to hang a finished ceiling from the structure above. These assemblies create a **plenum** space, which is the gap between the finished ceiling and the slab above. This plenum space allows for increased flexibility in the space as it can house and conceal the HVAC and electrical systems. Additionally, the systems allow for the building to naturally expand, contract, and settle, without altering the finished appearance of the ceilings. The two suspension systems to be aware of are the suspended tile system and suspended gypsum system.

The **suspended tile system** utilizes a grid composed of parallel and perpendicular rails that are hung from the joists above to hold a variety of square- or rectangular-shaped panels. Several key pieces are required for this type of suspension system. The **main beam** is a lightweight steel runner that acts as the chief supporting member of the system. It is anchored to the structure above with **wire hangers** that are threaded

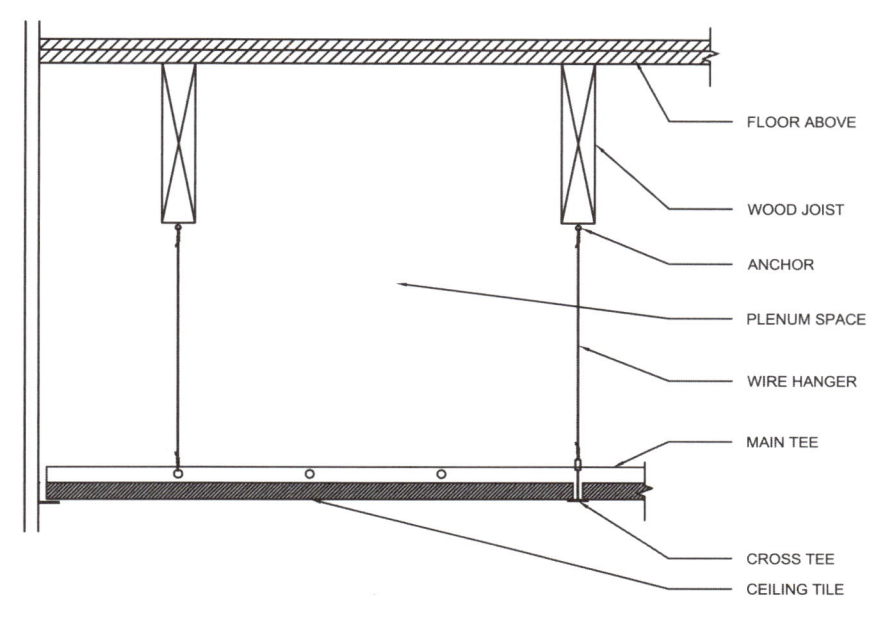

Figure 6.5
The plenum space here is created between the wood joists and the attached suspension system.

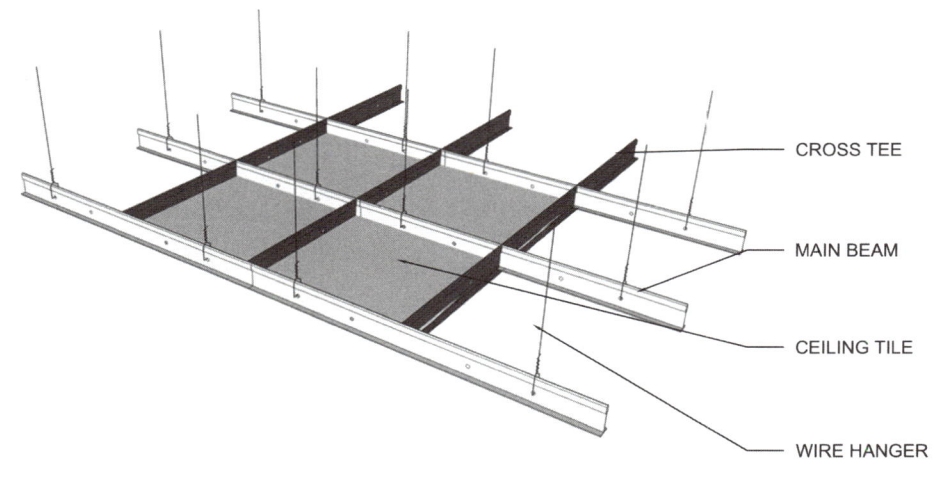

Figure 6.6
The components of a suspended ACT system.

STUDIO Animation 6.1 Suspended ACT system components

CHAPTER 6 CEILINGS | 95

through the main beam and wrapped around the **joist**. Main beams run parallel to each other, spaced 1'-, 2'- or 4'-0" apart depending on the size of the tile. Perpendicular to the main beams are the **cross tees**, the secondary grid members that connect the beams to each other. While the main beams can be up to 12'-0" long, each cross tee is only as long as the tile it supports, holding in place by snapping into the main beam. The bottom portion of the main beam and the cross tee flare out, forming a *T*-shape appropriately referred to as the **T-bar**. This bar creates a lip for the ceiling tiles rest on or hang from.

The finish materials of these ceilings can range from acoustical ceiling tiles to gypsum board to metal panels and more. It is important to remember to consult the manufacturer's instructions when creating details for your ceiling, as each company may have specific elements or sizes for their products.

Acoustical ceiling tiles (ACT) and other panel systems create the greatest amount of flexibility for commercial spaces. These panels can be easily removed for access to the HVAC and electrical wires above, and the grid can hold lighting and other ceiling-mounted elements that can be arranged as needed. Additionally, they aid in the absorption of sound, cutting down on reverberation within the room and diminishing sound transmission from one area to another. Suspended ACT systems are typically the most economical choice for commercial spaces.

The interaction between the grid system and the tiles must be decided upon when a ceiling is specified, as it impacts the look and feel of the ceiling itself. First, it must be determined whether the grid should be seen or be hidden within the space. An **exposed grid** is a suspension system where the users below can see the rails that support the panels, whereas a **concealed grid** is hidden from view by the panels. Second, the type of tile needed for the chosen grid must be specified. The exposed grid can feature either a square edge tile or a tegular tile, while the concealed grid uses a concealed T tile.

Square edge tiles feature a rectangular profile and can be dropped into place above the suspension system, resting on the grid tee. These tiles are the most economical but also have the least dynamic appearance, as there is a flush finish between the tiles and the grid. On the other hand, **tegular tiles** are notched so that when they are installed above the suspension system, the tile extends past the grid tee, creating a layered effect. Because of the increased number of cuts to the tile, tegulars are more expensive than the square edge.

Concealed T tiles are grooved ceiling tiles featuring a dado joint along its sides, allowing it to slide onto the grid tee. Here, the tile grips onto the tee from below with the finished face projecting past the grid

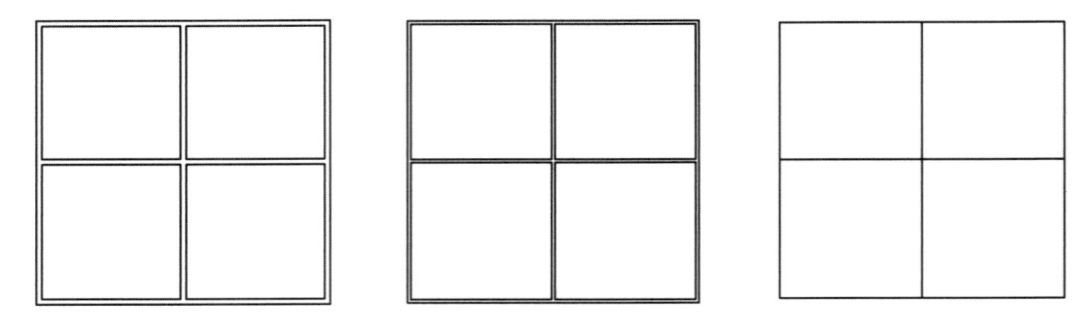

Figure 6.7
Grid system styles, from left: standard 15/16", slimline 9/16", concealed T.

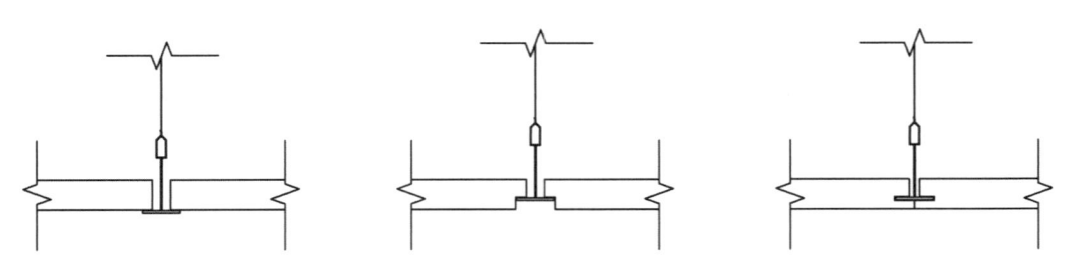

Figure 6.8
Ceiling tile styles, from left: square edge, tegular, concealed T.

PART II DETAIL DRAWINGS

and extending sideways. This creates a flush finish between the tiles while also hiding the grid from view. Concealed T tiles are more expensive than standard tiles, as they feature a more precise cut and are more work to install and remove than their counterparts.

Suspended gypsum systems create a more formal and finished look than are typically associated with exposed grid systems, while still giving the designer control of the ceiling height and placement of mounted elements. These ceilings are typically more expensive to install and maintain as portions cannot be easily removed, repaired, or replaced. Because of this, suspended gypsum wallboard (GWB) systems are usually reserved for dynamic or important spaces in a commercial building, where costs can be justified by the role of the space or the visual and sensory impact.

To create a suspended GWB system, steel channels are suspended on wire hangers from the structure above, in a similar fashion to the main tee in the tile system. Attached to the channels are **furring channels**, hat-shaped metal strips with wide flanges that act as a mounting surface for the GWB. The furrings are tethered to the steel channel by a series of wire hangers while the GWB is screwed to the furring's flanges.

Overall, suspended ceilings provide designers with a healthy amount of flexibility and creativity. The length of the wire hangers can be adjusted across the ceiling, allowing for different heights to be used within the same room. Tiles can be fabricated from a variety of materials, with a wide range of colors and patterns available. As the grids are created from steel, the framework and the tiles can be manufactured in different sizes and shapes. Because of the flexibility of this product, it is ideal for commercial spaces. Suspended ceilings can be used in residential settings, but it is much more likely that direct mount installations will be used in the home.

Direct installation systems are ceiling planes that are anchored directly to the slab above without the use of wire hangers to hold the ceiling in place. These types of ceilings are traditionally used in residential settings with a gypsum board face; however, acoustical and metal panels can also be directly attached to the

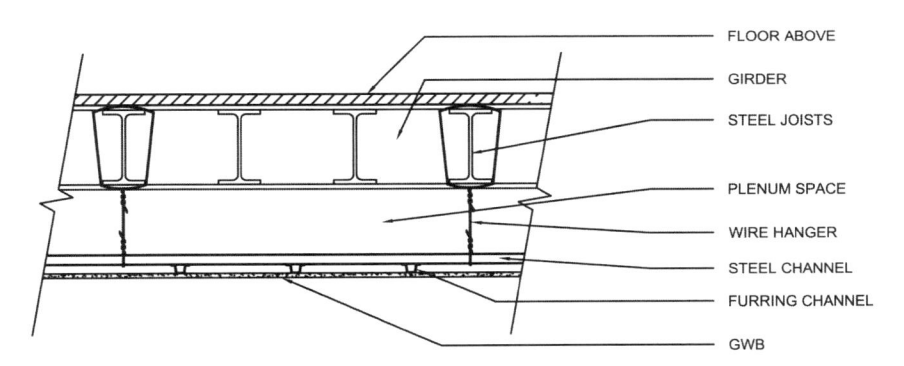

Figure 6.9
The components of a suspended GWB system in a steel frame project.

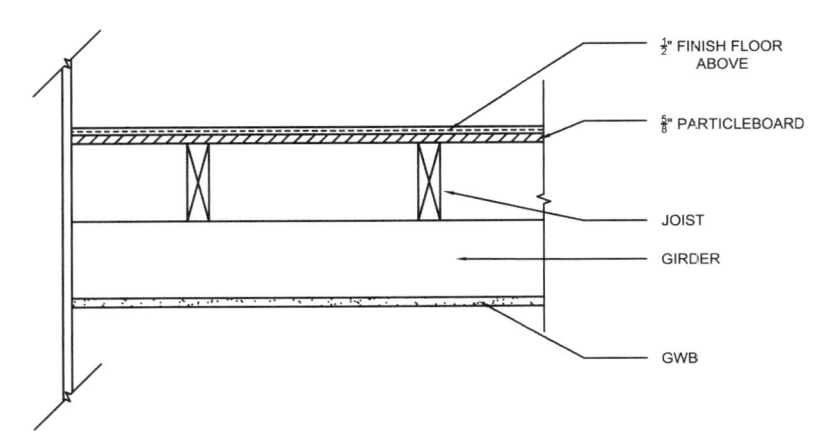

Figure 6.10
The components of a direct install GWB system in a wood frame project.

CHAPTER 6 CEILINGS | 97

structure. Occasionally, direct install may be used in small areas of commercial projects; however, they are not ideal for larger commercial spaces due to the lack of plenum space access.

While direct installation systems are ideal for the home, they can be seen as boring due to their flat, consistent nature. However, by adding constructed elements to the ceiling plane, the surface can become more architecturally interesting. Three of these types of elements are the soffit, the cove, and the box beam.

A **soffit** is a portion of the ceiling built at a lower height than the planes around it, similar to the layered effect created by staggering heights of various suspension systems. Likewise, the soffit acts like a suspension system in that it conceals ductwork and wires from view. The major difference between these systems and a soffit are that the soffit can be anchored directly to the slab above, as opposed to being hung, and it is typically fully enclosed by a finished surface material, usually gypsum board. This creates a lack of access to the elements hidden within, but when used in small or formal areas it can still be a popular choice in commercial settings.

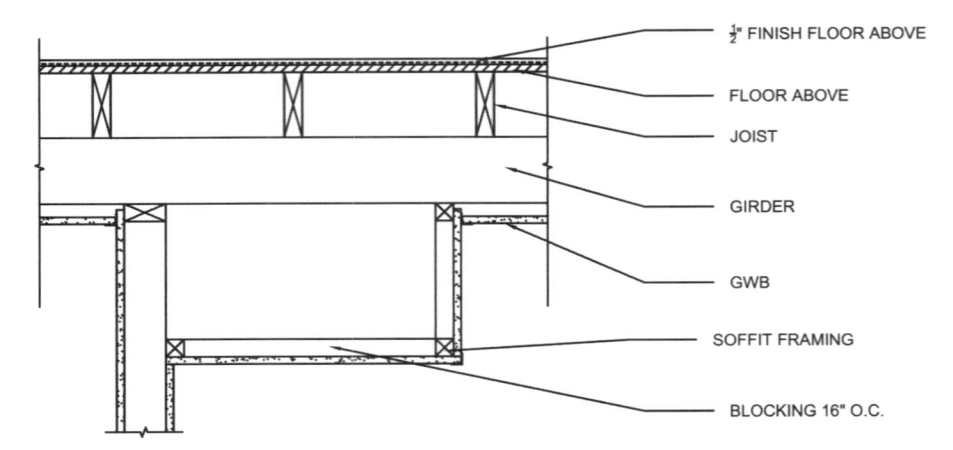

Figure 6.11
Construction detail of a perimeter soffit to a direct install GWB ceiling.

Figure 6.12
A soffit can be seen above the wall cabinets and includes recessed downlights.

98 | PART II DETAIL DRAWINGS

Coves are alcoves created in the ceiling or wall planes that eliminate or disguise the typical 90 degree angle formed between the planes. These nooks may simply be used as a decorative element, but they may also act as housing for hidden lighting within a project. Referred to as **cove lighting**, indirect light is aimed upward and reflected back down to the room below to create ambient lighting. When used in a ceiling, coves can be disguised as soffits or hidden along the edge of a suspended surface.

Box beams are hollow rafters that are applied to finished ceilings for decorative or practical purposes. These beams are nonstructural, meaning that as long as they do not interfere with mechanical or electrical systems, they can be installed at the discretion of the designer or contractor. As a decorative element, box beams can add a formality or visual interest to the space depending on the finishes used and the room they are placed in. As a matter of practicality, these hollow beams are ideal for hiding wires or other ceiling elements and may be used to house light fixtures. Depending on the building type and desired appearance, box beams can be constructed from a mix of 2 × 4s, plywood, and laminate, steel studs, gypsum board, or panels.

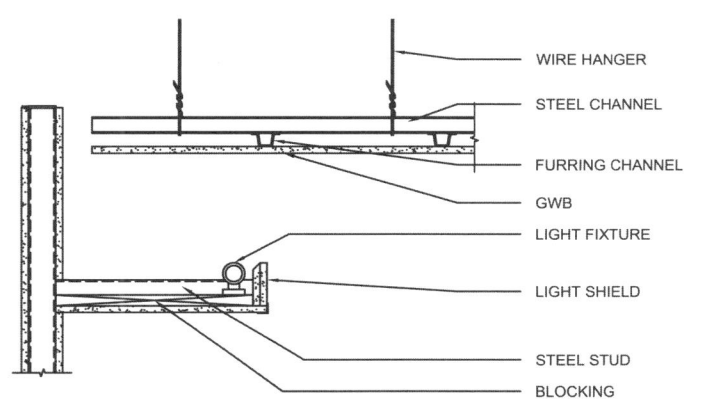

Figure 6.13
Construction detail of suspended ceiling cove with lighting.

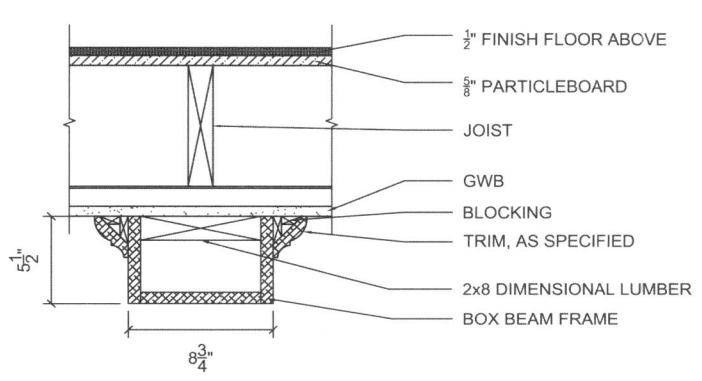

Figure 6.15
Construction detail of a perpendicular cut through a box beam.

Figure 6.14
Suspended GWB concealing a cove which is reflected to the finished ceiling above.

Figure 6.16
A kitchen and dining room with a shared box beam ceiling.

CHAPTER 6 CEILINGS | 99

DRAFTING CEILING DETAILS

Suspended ACT systems

This section detail will focus on the back portion of the commercial space where a suspended 2'-0 x 2'-0" square-edge ACT exposed grid will be hung from a steel frame.

STEP 1

Using a wall for a boundary, measure at least 3/8" away from the face of the wall and create a tick mark. From that tick, draw a rectangle measuring 2'-0" long and 3/4" high. This rectangle will represent the ceiling tile. Refer to Appendix D for additional ACT sizes.

STEP 2

On the far end of the rectangle, create a cross tee for the grid. There is no standard representation for these tees, but they typically appear as an upsidedown *T* shape, topped with an eye opening for the wire hanger. However, there are some basic dimensions to keep in mind when drawing them, as can be seen in the detail callout. If you have a specific manufacturer selected, refer to their drawings for the profile shape and product dimensions.

Create a second ACT on the other side of the cross tee. This tile should retain the 3/4" thickness of the first tile, but a breakline can be added to the drawing to establish the idea of repetitive nature of the grid.

STEP 3

Measure up 3/4" from the top of the tiles, and draw a horizontal line the length of the drawing. This new line represents the top of the main runner for the grid.

To finish the grid, draw an *L*-shaped angle mold between the wall and the first tile. This mold should measure at least 7/8".

STEP 4

Drawing within this main runner portion of the detail, create a series of circular cutouts through which the wire hangers can be inserted. The placement of these cutouts can vary depending on the manufacturer, but the first hanger must be 8" or less from the wall to ensure balance and support

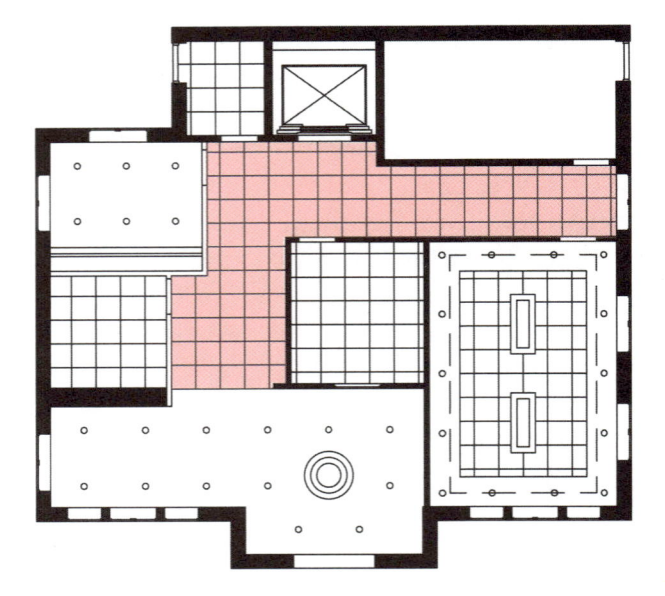

Figure 6.17
Commercial reflected ceiling plan (RCP) with suspended ACT system.

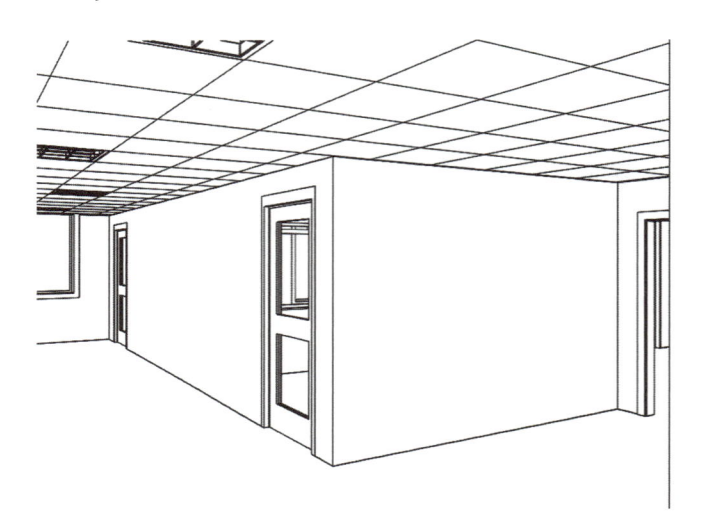

Figure 6.18
Commercial space with suspended ACT system.

for the ceiling. This example shows three such cutouts with the outermost each appearing 8" from the edge and the final one centered.

STEP 5

Finalize the detail by adding any necessary dimensions, annotations, and materials. Lineweights should be adjusted to match the standards established in Part I of this text, with heavier lineweights used on objects that are being cut through and lighter lineweights used for material textures.

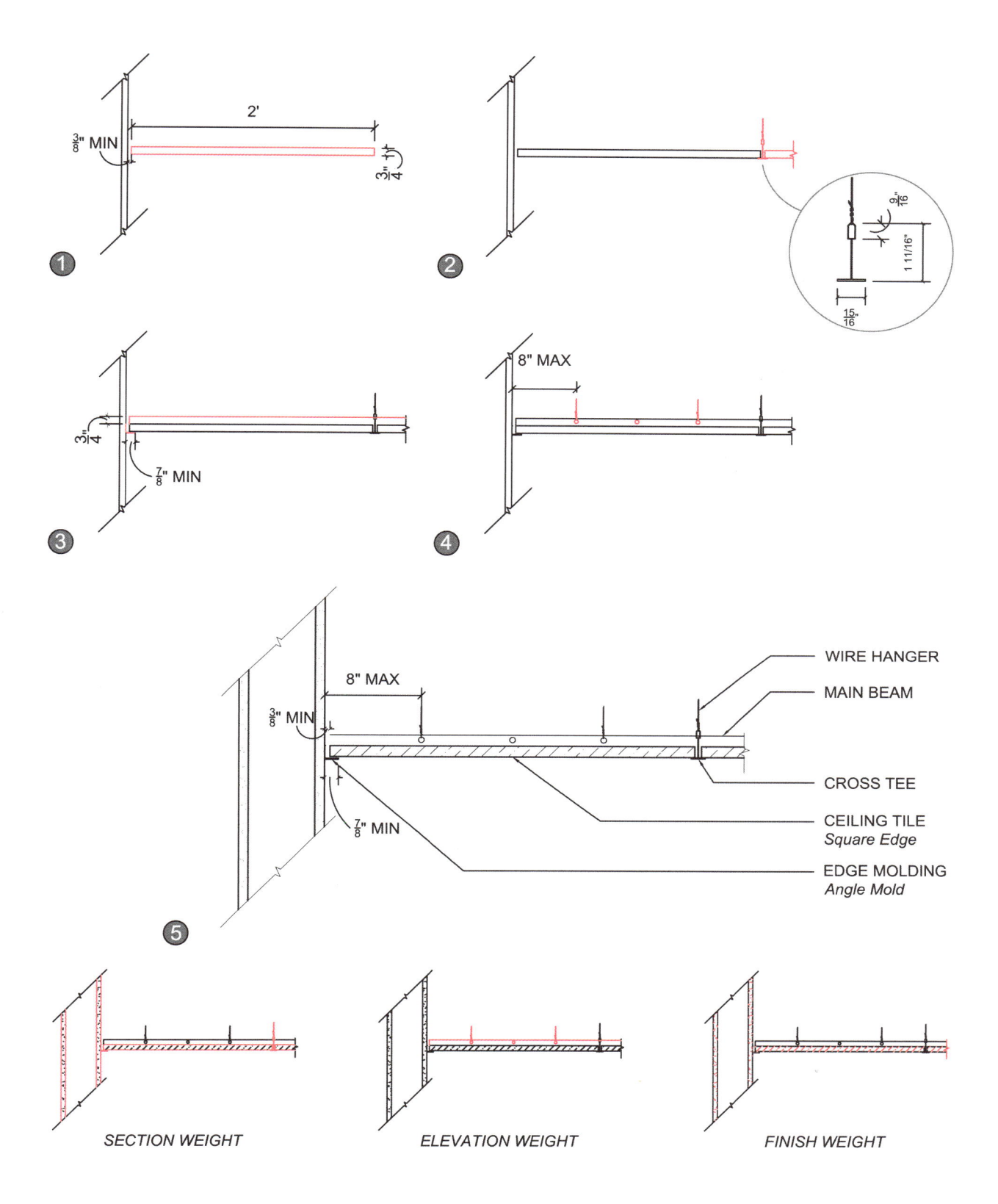

Figure 6.19
Suspended ACT system, Steps 1–5.

Suspended GWB systems

This example will focus on the reception and waiting areas, which will feature a suspended GWB ceiling to be hung from a steel frame.

STEP 1

Using a wall for a boundary, measure at least 3/32" away from the face of the wall and create a tick mark. From that tick, draw a rectangle measuring 5'-0" long and 5/8" high. This rectangle will represent the GWB. A breakline can be drawn at the far end of the GWB to establish the idea of the continuation of the ceiling design.

STEP 2

The furring system, which creates the support for the GWB, will appear above the finished face of the ceiling. Seen perpendicular to the viewer in this example, the furring channels look like a flat-bottomed *U* with flange wings at the top. While there are various sizes available, this example's furrings are 1 1/4" high and 2 1/2" wide from tip to tip of the flanges. These furrings should be spaced evenly across the ceiling but no more than 1'-4" on center (OC). The distance of the furring closest to the wall should not exceed 1'-4" OC from the wall face.

STEP 3

The furrings attach to a steel channel above. While sizes for these channels can be found in Appendix D, this example uses one that is 1 1/2" wide.

STEP 4

Wire hangers are used to attach the steel channel to the structure above. The wire closest to the wall should be no more than 8" away. Any subsequent wires must be 4'-0" or closer.

STEP 5

Finalize the detail by adding any necessary dimensions, annotations, and materials. Lineweights should be adjusted to match the standards established in Part I of this text, with heavier lineweights used on objects that are being cut through and lighter lineweights used for material textures.

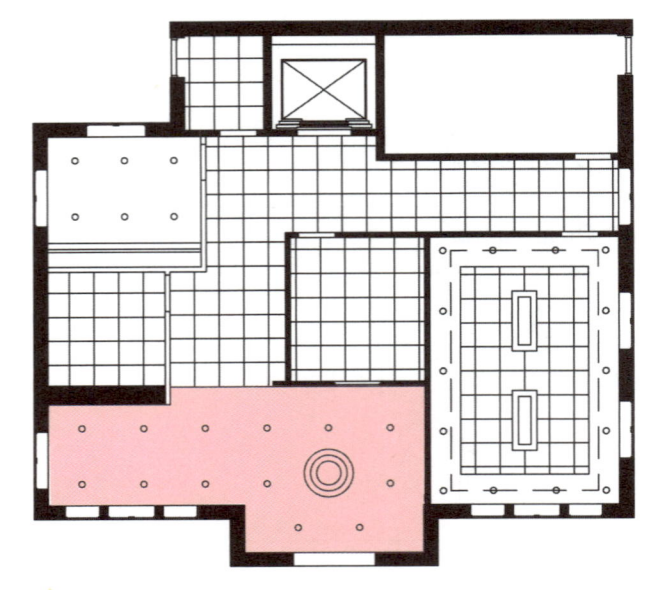

Figure 6.20
Commercial RCP with suspended GWB system.

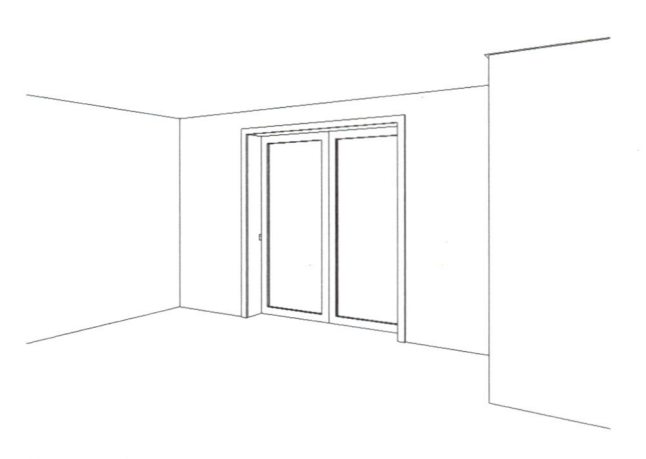

Figure 6.21
Commercial space with suspended GWB system.

IBC

Suspended ceilings that are used in a fire-rated portion of a commercial building must have a Class A rating. (*IBC 803.13.2*)

RoT

In order to maintain the integrity of the products, suspended acoustical ceilings must be used and installed according to the manufacturer's directions. If not, the system could fail, with results ranging from increased expenses to personal injury.

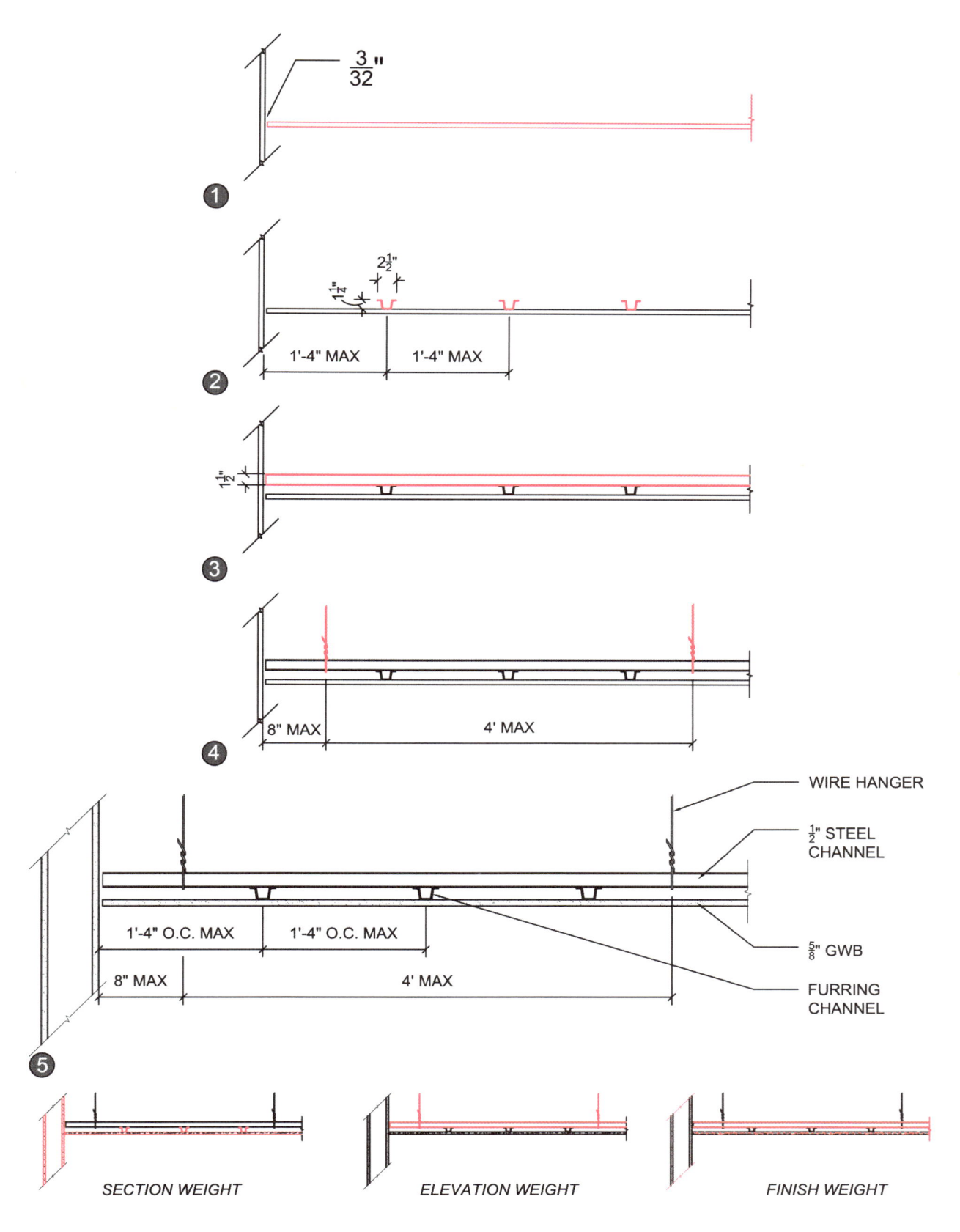

Figure 6.22
Suspended GWB system, Steps 1–5.

Suspended ACT and GWB systems

Suspension systems can be coordinated to be used together to designate separate areas within one room or to create variety and interest within a space. These elements should be treated similarly to the previous sections but with the exception that one or both edges of the plane may not interact with the wall. For designs that feature material planes meeting to create a **flush finish** (abutting at the same height), a different edge treatment should be used to hide the plenum space above.

This example will focus on a flush transition from a suspended GWB ceiling over the reception and waiting areas to the suspended ACT system over the hallway. For other GWB-ACT transition details, see Appendix G.

STEP 1
Beginning with the face of the GWB ceiling, create a rectangle with a height of 5/8". As this drawing shows the meeting point between the GWB and ACT systems, a breakline can be used at the far end of the detail to indicate that the GWB continues on. To give yourself enough drawing space, make sure that the rectangle measures at least 1'-4".

STEP 2
Measuring 6" up from the finished face of the ceiling, create a 5/8" tick mark and then connect it to the existing plane. This will act as a barrier between the finished face of the ceiling and the plenum space above in the real-life event that either the GWB or ACT layers shift.

STEP 3
Measuring 6" away from the vertical GWB, create a rectangle 1 1/4" high. This will act as the furring layer attached to the GWB below. A second horizontal should be drawn 1/8" down in to this rectangle to act as the furring flange thickness.

STEP 4
Next, draw the profile of a steel channel above the furring. This should measure about 4" OC from the leading edge of the furring channel and should be wrapped in a wire hanger. This channel is the support system above the suspended ceiling, anchored to the slab above.

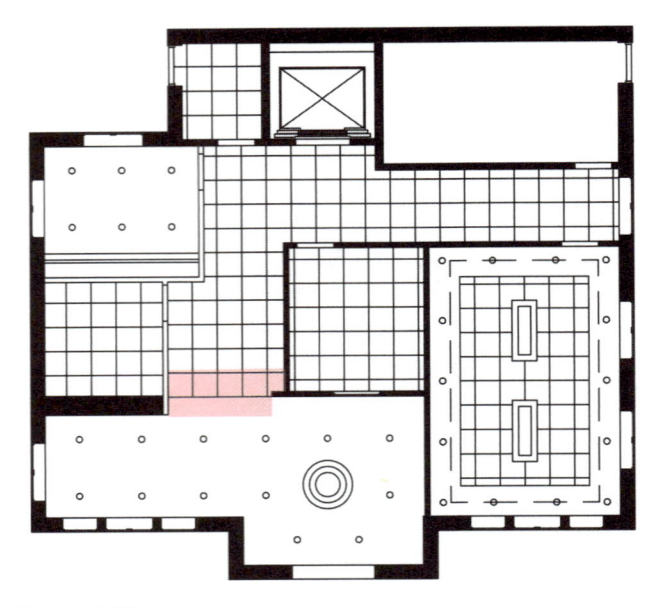

Figure 6.23
Commercial RCP indicating the location where the suspended ACT and GWB systems meet.

STEP 5
Draw another steel channel, this time on its back, at the corner joint created by the two pieces of GWB. While the one in this example measures 3 5/8" wide, you can select a different size; see Appendix D for more options.

STEP 6
Draw two vertical lines on the sides of the newly drawn channel to illustrate support studs running from the ceiling to the structure above.

PART II DETAIL DRAWINGS

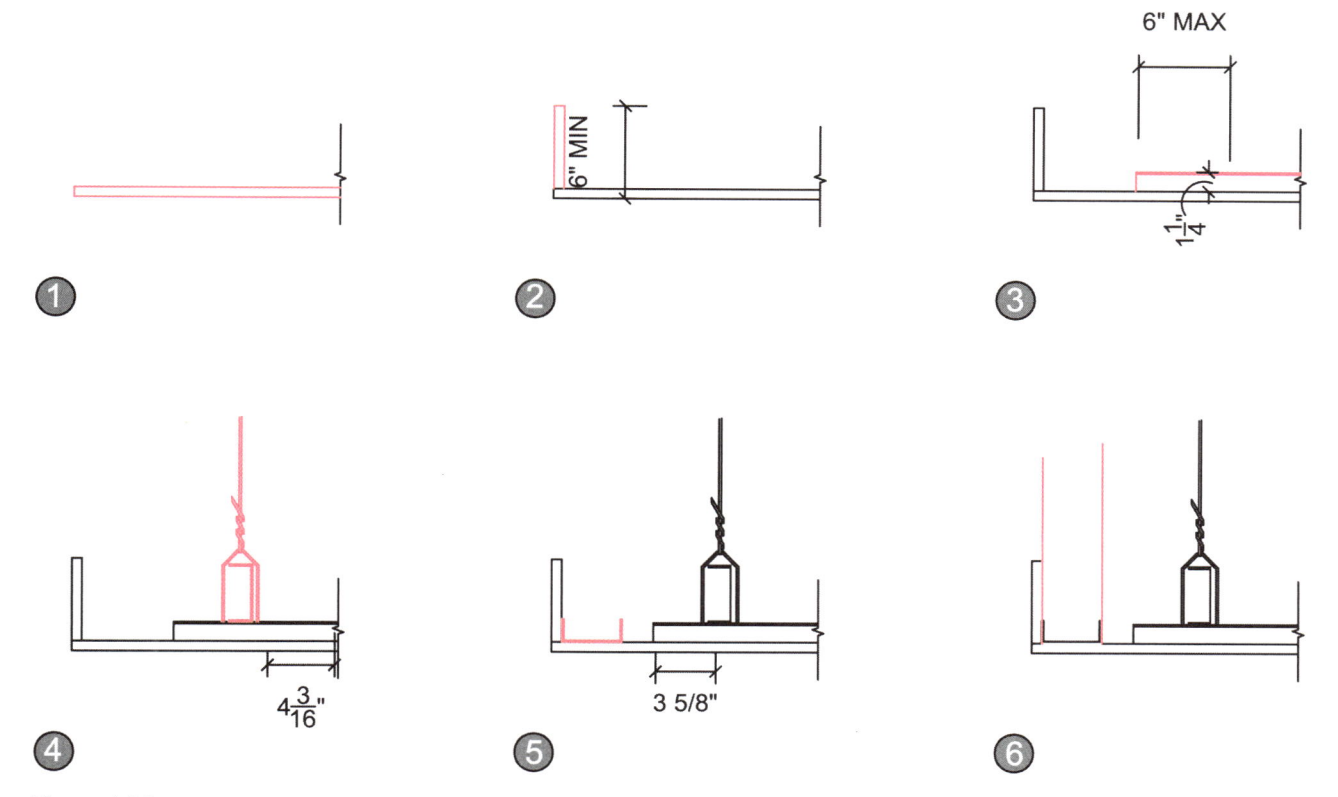

Figure 6.24
Flush ACT and GWB systems, Steps 1–6.

IBC
Ceilings must be at least 7'-6" above finished floor (AFF) for occupiable rooms, corridors, and for the means of egress. (*IBC 1003.2*)

Ceilings may be lowered to 7'-0" in service areas for commercial buildings and in storage spaces. (*IBC 1208.2*)

CAD
Use different colors while you work so that you have a clearer picture of which elements are the face of the ceiling compared to the suspension system. You can still work within a single RCP layer, but you can change the color through a drop-down menu under General in Properties. This will allow you to have a visual distinction between the parts that make up the ceiling, but you will still be able to toggle the RCP level and any of its items on and off.

Hand
Ceiling details are essentially sections of a small portion of the RCP. When drafting these details, use a light lineweight to create the entire image before going back and darkening any portions that need a heavier lineweight. This will make it easier for you to edit the drawing as you go, while also keeping your drawing clean and smudge-free as you work.

Revit
Ceiling details are essentially sections of a small portion of the RCP. Revit recognizes the ceiling plane and its thickness, but unless you have imported a fully designed ceiling, the program will only provide you with an outline of those thicknesses, meaning that most of the detail, and none of the suspension system, will be visible through a simple section cut.

The easiest way to make sure those details appear is to make a section cut and then use detail lines to draw on top of the view that Revit provides for you.

STEP 7
Add the edge trim, the *L*-shaped piece that protects the exposed corner of the GWB, measuring at least 15/16" × 15/16".

STEP 8
Moving on to the ACT portion of this suspended system, measure roughly 1/2" from the finished corner (not the edge mold) of the GWB and create a tick mark. From this mark, draw three horizontal lines, the first even with the GWB, the next 1/16" up, and the third 1/16" above the second. These lines should be at least 1'-0" long, with a breakline at the far end.

The bottom rectangle acts as the ceiling tile, while the top rectangle will serve as the steel runner.

STEP 9
Measuring 3" from the front edge of the runner, draw a circle to act as a cutout for the wire hangers used in the suspension system. Draw a second cutout 6" away from the first.

STEP 10
Similar to the edge trim used for the GWB ceiling, a protective corner element is needed for the ACT. While this example shows a *W*-shaped shadow mold, an *L*-shaped angle mold can be used as well.

The full size of this shadow mold is 1 1/4" × 1 1/4", with longest edge measuring 15/16" to maintain the 3/8" gap between the ACT and the GWB.

STEP 11
Finalize the detail by adding any necessary dimensions, annotations, and materials. Lineweights should be adjusted to match the standards established in Part I of this text, with heavier lineweights used on objects that are being cut through and lighter lineweights used for material textures.

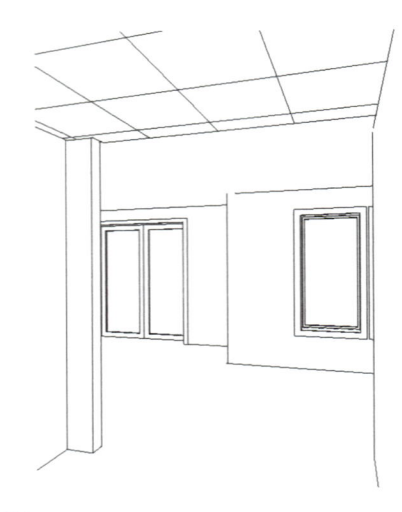

Figure 6.25
Commercial space featuring adjoining suspended ACT and GWB systems.

ADA

In order to meet ADA guidelines, there must be a vertical clearance of at least 80" between the floor and the ceiling plane or between the floor and any ceiling-mounted objects. (*ADA 307.4*)

In the case that the ceiling slopes or a mounted-object reduces the clearance space to less than 80", you must install a guardrail to maintain the physical safety of the end users. (*ADA 307.4*)

Door frames may be as low as 78" high. (*ADA 307.4*)

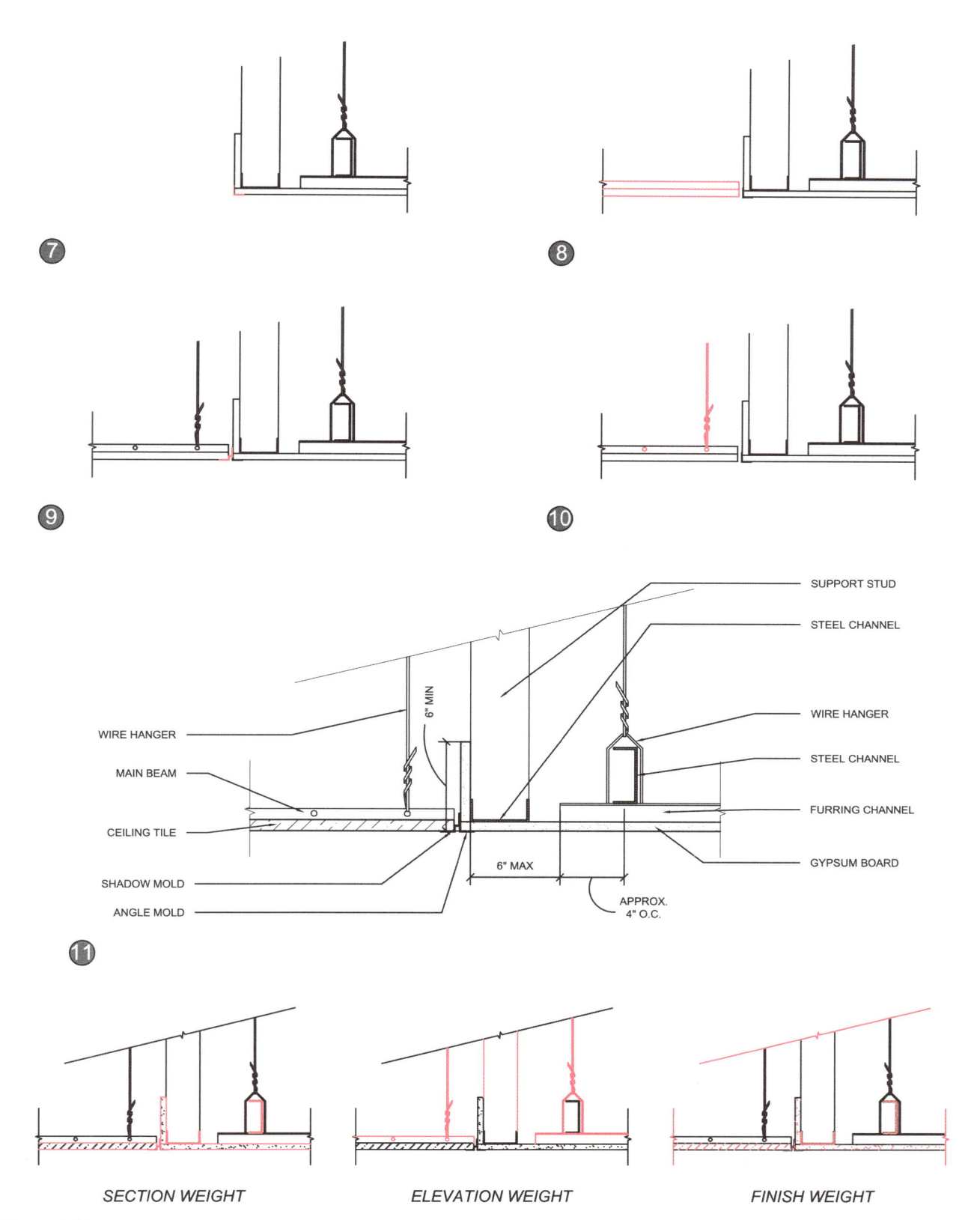

Figure 6.26
Flush ACT and GWB systems, Steps 7–11.

Suspended GWB cove and recessed ACT system

Designers can create visual interest in a ceiling plane by offering a variety of materials, colors, lighting styles, and mounting heights within the project. This can lead to creative opportunities, such as the inclusion of a cove, when varying heights result in surfaces that do not interact directly with one another. Known as **recessed ceiling** or a **dropped ceiling**, this occurs when one plane is installed at a higher or lower height than the standard ceiling height for the room. These instances require not only different edge treatments to finish and protect the ceiling materials, but they also require a coordinated overlap to hide the plenum space above. This example highlights the conference room, featuring a suspended GWB cove ceiling along the perimeter of the room and a recessed ACT system in the center. While Step 1 will indicate how to draw the frame of the room, Steps 2–8 will focus on the cove detail and Steps 9–11 will illustrate how to add the cove and the ACT to the room.

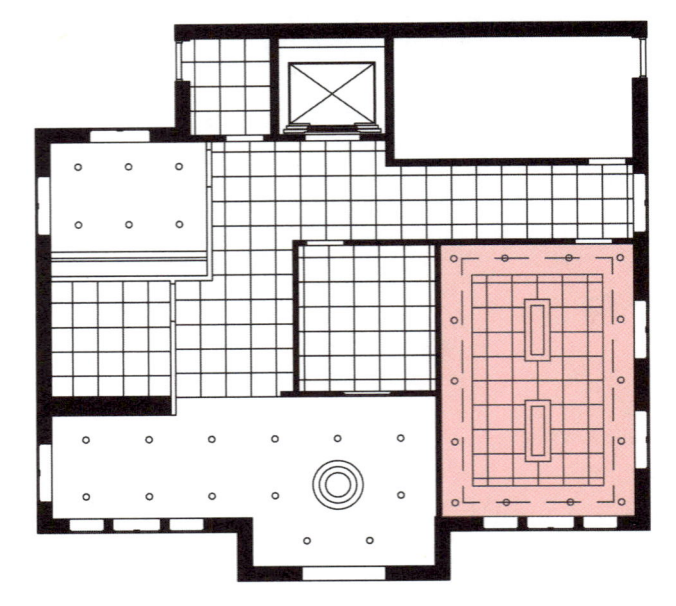

Figure 6.27
Commercial RCP highlighting the conference room where a suspended GWB system coordinates with a recessed ACT system.

GWB cove detail

STEP 1
Create the frame of the room using the plans. This frame, as seen in Figure 6.28, should show a section of the walls, drawn with the specified thickness, and a slab composed of concrete to represent the floor above. From this slab, draw the attached furring channel from which the ceiling will hang.

STEP 2
Moving to the cove detail, draw a horizontal rectangle measuring 2'-0" × 5/8" to create the basis of the GWB ceiling plane. Add angle molds at both ends of this plane.

At one end, add a vertical rectangle measuring 6" × 5/8" to conceal the cove from the room's occupants.

STEP 3
Add a furring channel above the horizontal plane by measuring up 1 1/4" and extending the line the length of the GWB. Add a second horizontal line about 1/8" below the top line to create the thickness of the furring.

STEP 4
Next, draw the profile of a steel channel above the furring. This should measure about 4" OC from the leading edge of the furring channel on the opposite end of the plane from the vertical GWB panel. This channel is the support system above the suspended ceiling and should be wrapped in a wire hanger to anchor it to the slab above.

STEP 5
Draw another steel channel, this time on its back, about 8" OC from the vertical GWB panel. While the one in this example measures 3 5/8" wide, you can select a different size; see Appendix D for more options.

Then draw two vertical lines on the sides of the newly drawn channel to illustrate support studs running from the ceiling panel to the structure above. Once complete, the steel channel will appear in a heavier, section lineweight, while the vertical lines will appear in a lighter, elevation lineweight.

108 | PART II DETAIL DRAWINGS

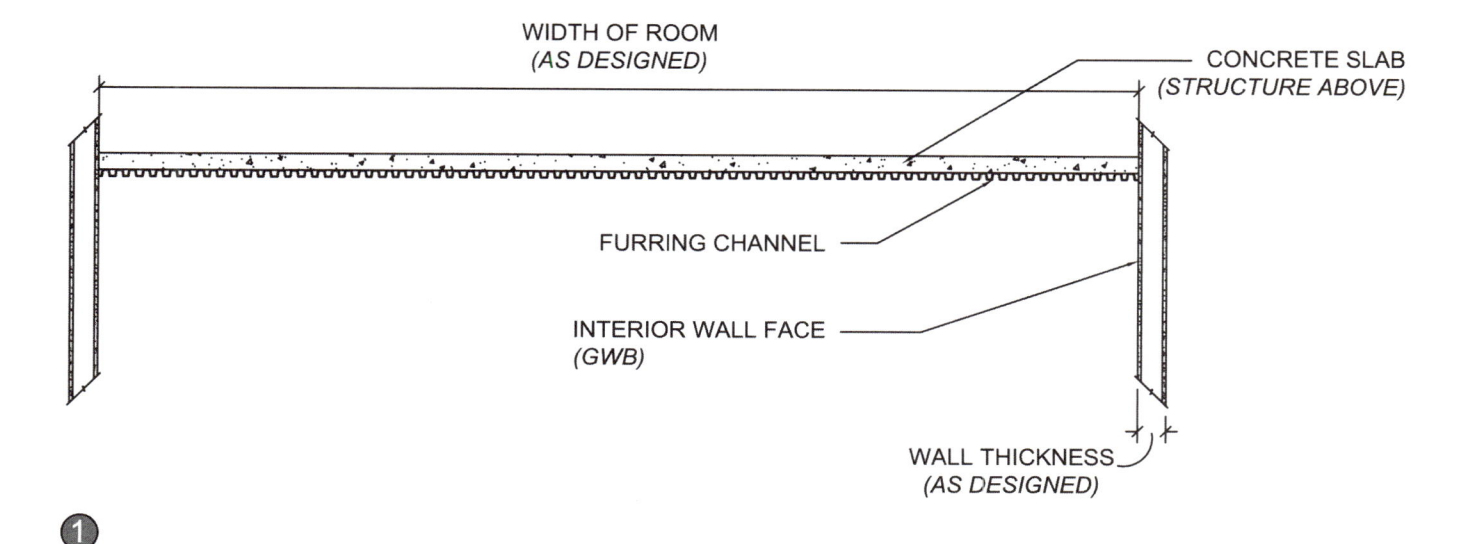

Figure 6.28
Conference room frame based on the commercial building plan. The "frame" is made of section views of the walls and structural slab that will surround the designed ceiling.

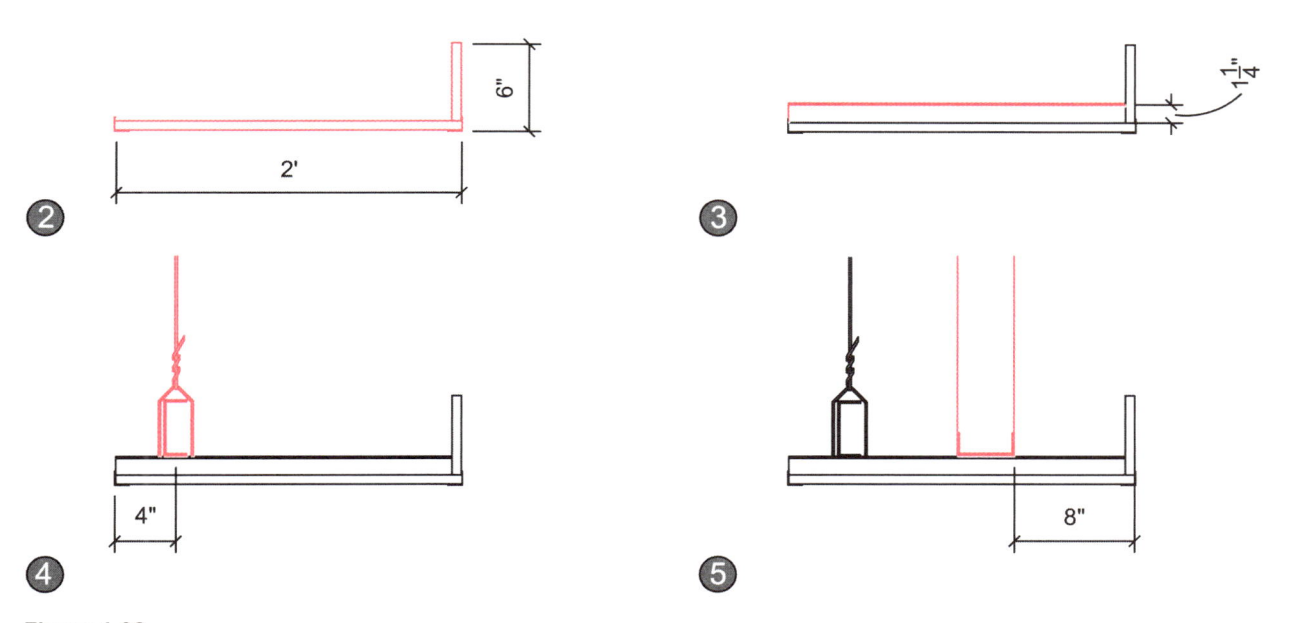

Figure 6.29
GWB cove ceiling, Steps 2–5.

CHAPTER 6 CEILINGS | 109

STEP 6

In order for a cove fixture to work properly, finish materials must be installed to redirect the light from the installed fixture to the room below. At minimum, GWB panels must be installed along the side of the support stud and the top of the furring channel between the support stud and the vertical panel. Aluminum panels may be installed on top of the GWB to increase light reflection if desired.

STEP 7

Add supportive blocking behind the leading GWB panel, both to increase structural support as well as to support the chosen light fixture. Then, add the light source. This should measure a minimum of 3" from the reflection point, but this distance may vary depending on the selected fixture, so it is best to refer to manufacturer's guidelines for this distance.

STEP 8

Finalize the detail by adding any necessary dimensions, annotations, and materials. Lineweights should be adjusted to match the standards established in Part I of this text, with heavier lineweights used on objects that are being cut through and lighter lineweights used for material textures.

STEP 9

Moving back to the frame created in Step 1, measure 2'-6" along the wall from the underside of the slab to the face of the suspended GWB ceiling. Use the instructions for the GWB cove detail from the previous section if necessary.

Create a mirror image of the GWB cove on the opposite side of the drawing.

> **RoT**
>
> In order to maintain the integrity of the products, light fixtures must be used and installed according to the manufacturer's directions. If not, the system could fail, with results ranging from increased expenses to personal injury.
>
> Doublecheck with the manufacturer to ensure that you are using the recommended bulb wattage and size, and that you are specifying the correct spacing from the bulb and the housing to surrounding materials.

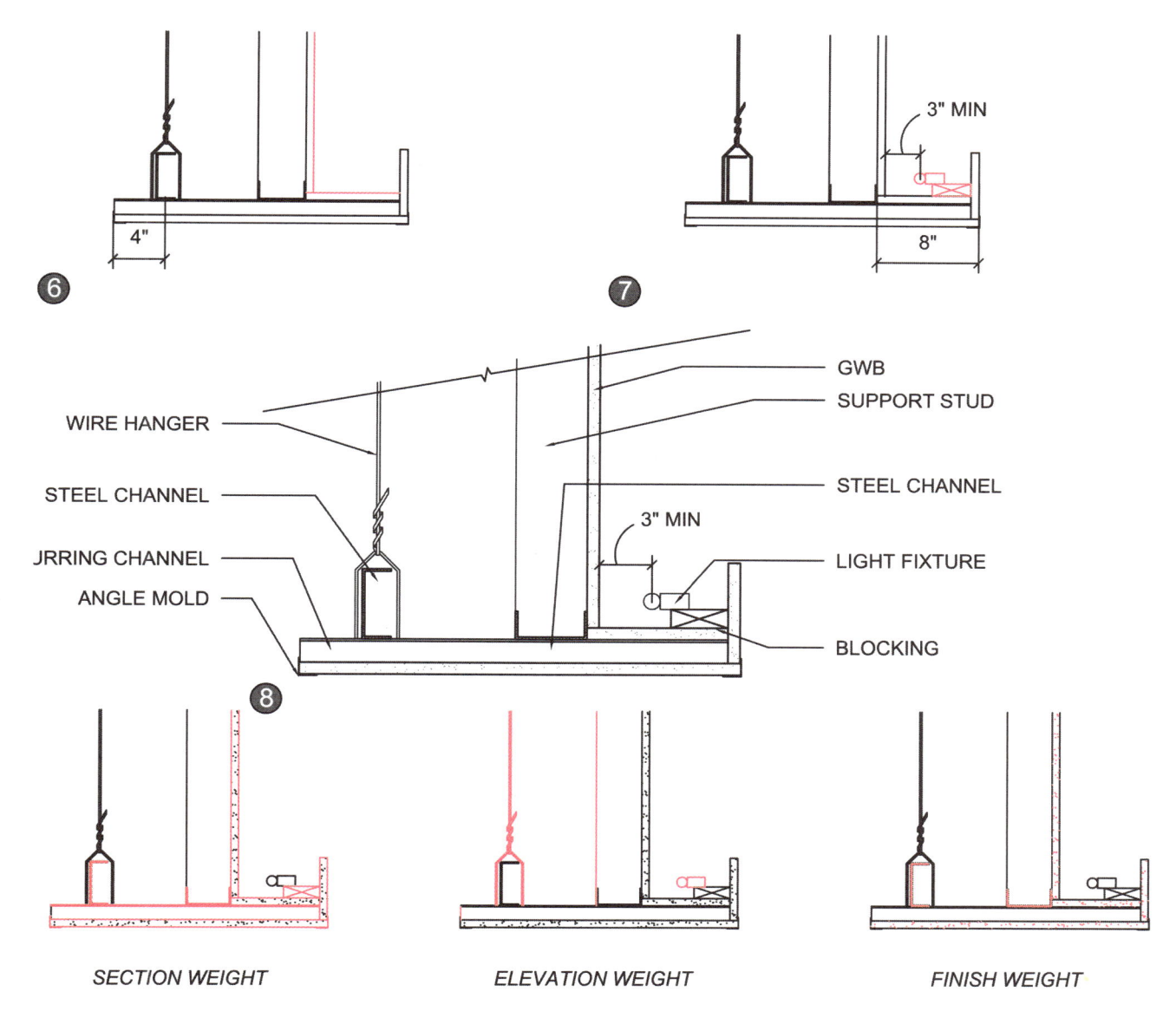

Figure 6.30
GWB cove ceiling, Steps 6–8.

Figure 6.31
Suspended GWB cove and recessed ACT systems, Step 9.

CHAPTER 6 CEILINGS | 111

STEP 10

As designed on the reflected ceiling plan, there should be a 6" overlap of the GWB and ACT components in order to conceal the transition between the two planes. On each side of the room, measure 6" back from the leading edge of the GWB and up 1'-0" and create a tick mark to indicate the starting point of the recessed tiles.

Between these two tick marks, create the ACT suspension system of your choosing, with the finished face of the tiles aligned with the ticks. Use the instructions for the ACT suspension system from earlier in this chapter if necessary.

STEP 11

Finalize the detail by adding any necessary dimensions, annotations, and materials. Lineweights should be adjusted to match the standards established in Part I of this text, with heavier lineweights used on objects that are being cut through and lighter lineweights used for material textures.

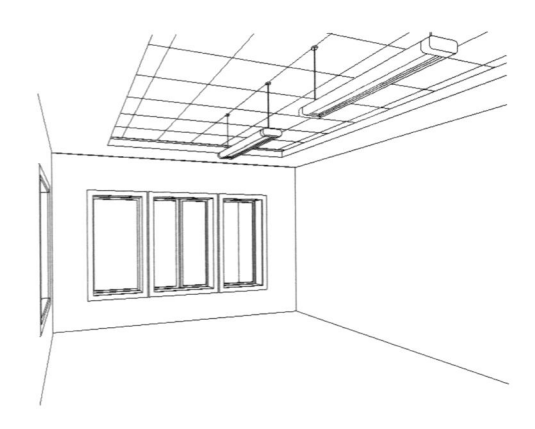

Figure 6.32
A conference room with a suspended GWB system along the perimeter that coordinates with a recessed ACT system.

Figure 6.33 (facing page)
Suspended GWB cove and recessed ACT systems, Steps 10–11.

⑩

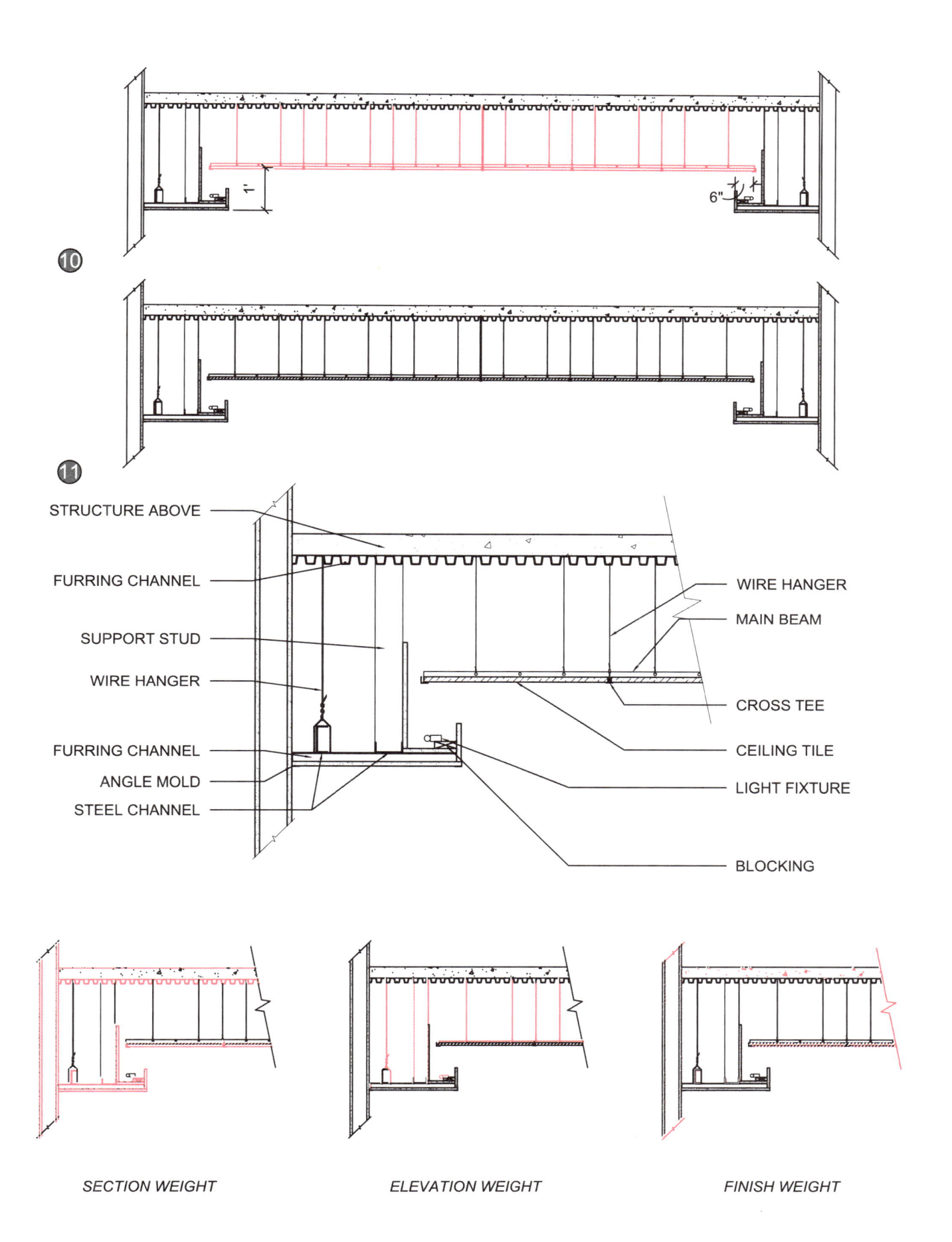

⑪

- STRUCTURE ABOVE
- FURRING CHANNEL
- SUPPORT STUD
- WIRE HANGER
- FURRING CHANNEL
- ANGLE MOLD
- STEEL CHANNEL
- WIRE HANGER
- MAIN BEAM
- CROSS TEE
- CEILING TILE
- LIGHT FIXTURE
- BLOCKING

SECTION WEIGHT   *ELEVATION WEIGHT*   *FINISH WEIGHT*

CHAPTER 6 CEILINGS | 113

Direct installed GWB

This example will focus on the direct installation of a GWB ceiling in the entry and first floor hall of the residential plan.

STEP 1

This example utilizes 2" × 8"s for the ceiling joists, which are typical in residential framing. As these are pieces of dimensional lumber, the rectangles should measure 1 1/2" × 7 1/2".

Draw the two rectangles 1'-4" OC apart, each with an *X* cutting through them to indicate that they are perpendicular to the viewer. If you are planning to include a wall in the drawing, the stud core should be at most 1'-4" OC from the joist.

STEP 2

Draw four horizontal lines below the joists:

One: running along the bottom of the joists, terminating at either a wall or a breakline.

Two: 1/8" down, making a gap to act as the deflection space between elements.

Three: 5/8" below to make the furring channel.

Four: 1/2" down to create the face of the GWB.

STEP 3

Similarly, you will need to draw three lines above the joists:

One: running along the top of the joists, past each of them and terminating at either a wall or a breakline.

Two: 5/8" up, forming the particleboard layer.

Three: 1/2" up, indicating the finished floor above.

STEP 4

Finalize the detail by adding any necessary dimensions, annotations, and materials. Lineweights should be adjusted to match the standards established in Part I of this text, with heavier lineweights used on objects that are being cut through and lighter lineweights for material textures.

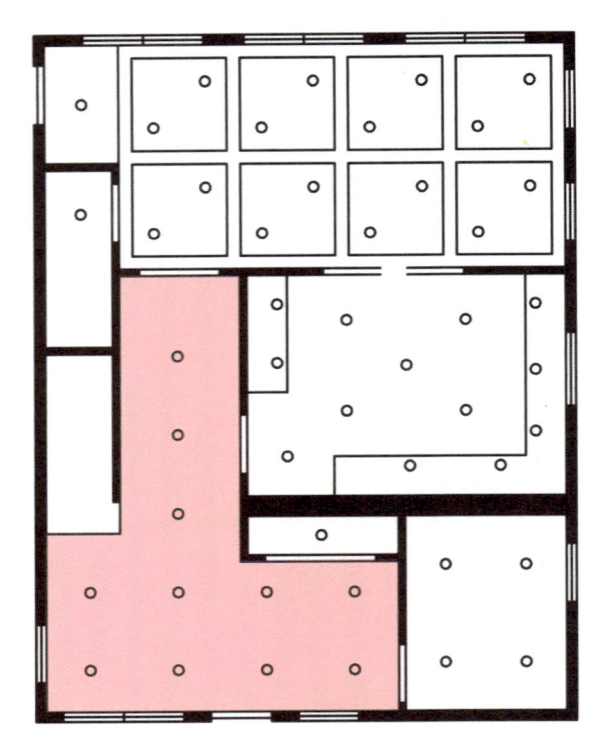

Figure 6.34
Residential RCP highlighting the entry and first floor hall where a direct installation GWB system will be used.

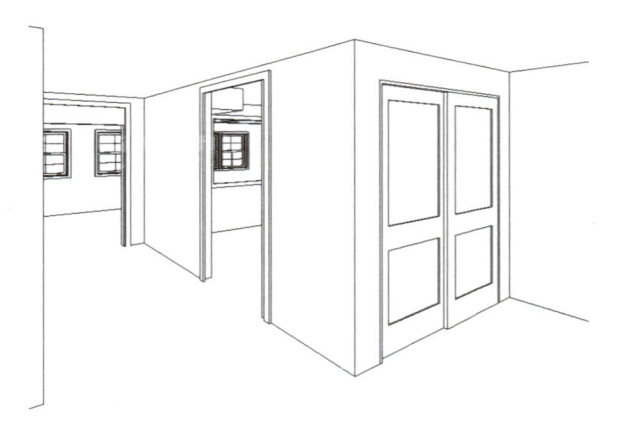

Figure 6.35
View of the residential entry and first floor hall where a direct installation GWB system is used.

Figure 6.36 (facing page)
Direct install GWB ceiling, Steps 1–6.

①

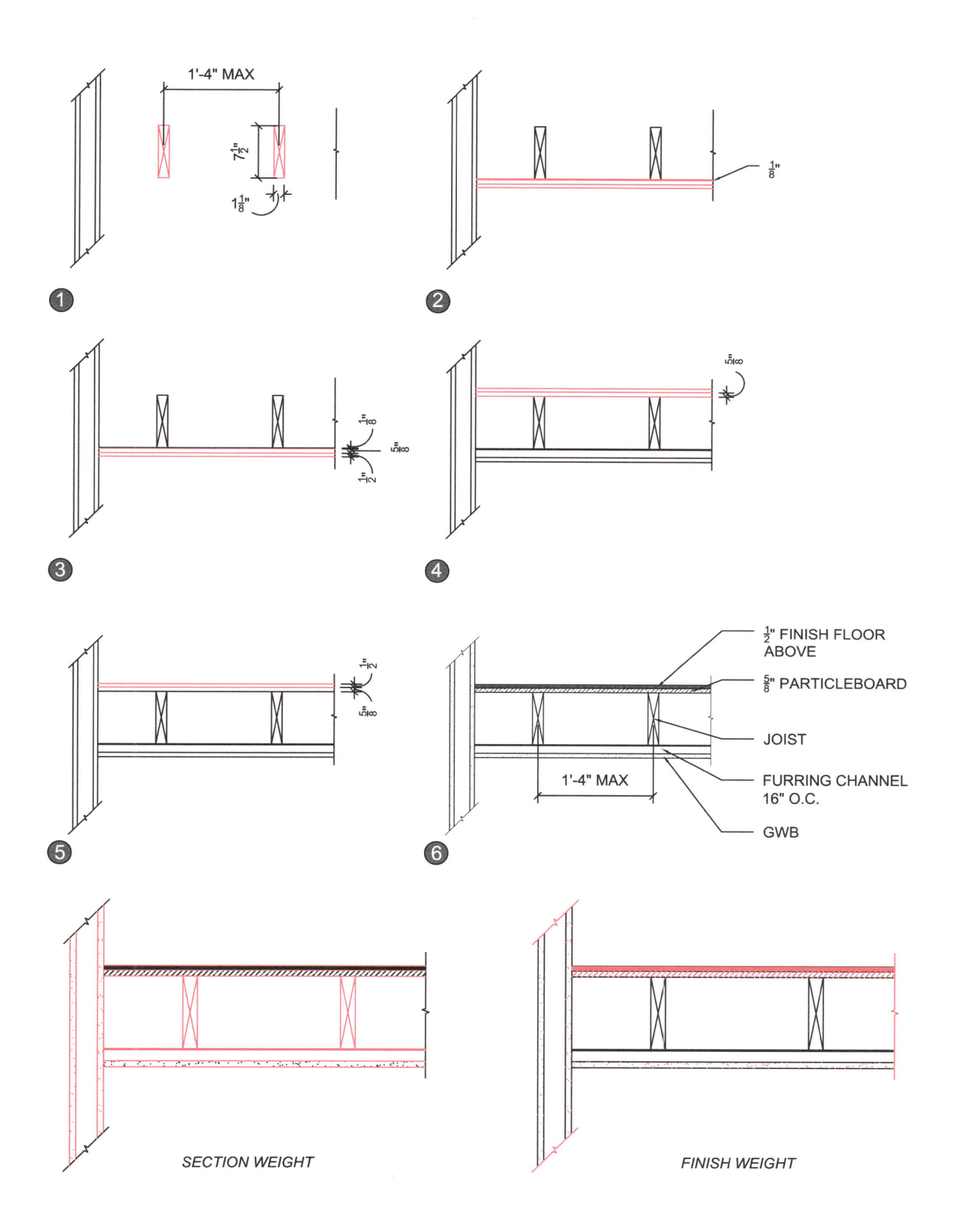

1'-4" MAX
7½"
1⅛"

②

⅛"

③

⅛"
½"
⅝"

④

⅝"

⑤

½"
⅝"

⑥

½" FINISH FLOOR ABOVE
⅝" PARTICLEBOARD
JOIST
FURRING CHANNEL 16" O.C.
GWB

1'-4" MAX

SECTION WEIGHT

FINISH WEIGHT

CHAPTER 6 CEILINGS | 115

Soffit detail

This example will focus on a soffit around the perimeter of the kitchen to be used above the cabinets. This detail will have a wood stud, appropriate for the residential setting. For a finished example of a steel-stud soffit, see Appendix G.

STEP 1

Set up the drawing by creating the boundaries for the soffit. If you have this drawing from a previous detail, use it as the foundation for this drawing. Important elements that are needed are the joists above and the wood stud and top plate from the adjacent wall.

STEP 2

The soffit will be 2'-0" deep and will lower the ceiling in this area by 1'-0". Create the border for the soffit by drawing the finished 5/8" GWB face first.

The lower panel should be placed first, measuring 2'-0" long, 5/8" thick , placed 1'-1 3/4" below the joist.

The vertical panel will be placed on top of the front edge of the horizontal panel and will measure 1'-1 1/4" long and 5/8" thick. This will leave a 1/2" gap between the GWB and the joist above.

STEP 3

Next, the wooden support studs will be drawn to show the framing for the interior of the soffit. Draw 1 1/2" thick rectangle behind the vertical piece of gypsum, running from the horizontal GWB to the joist.

Draw a second rectangle between this new support and the wall stud. This should also measure 1 1/2" high.

STEP 4

Create three squares at the ends of the wood support studs drawn in Step 3, each measuring 1 1/2" × 1 1/2". Draw an *X* through each of these squares to indicate that they are perpendicular to the viewer.

STEP 5

Add the edge trim, the *L*-shaped piece along the outer face of the GWB, measuring at least 15/16" × 15/16". This example also specifies a direct GWB

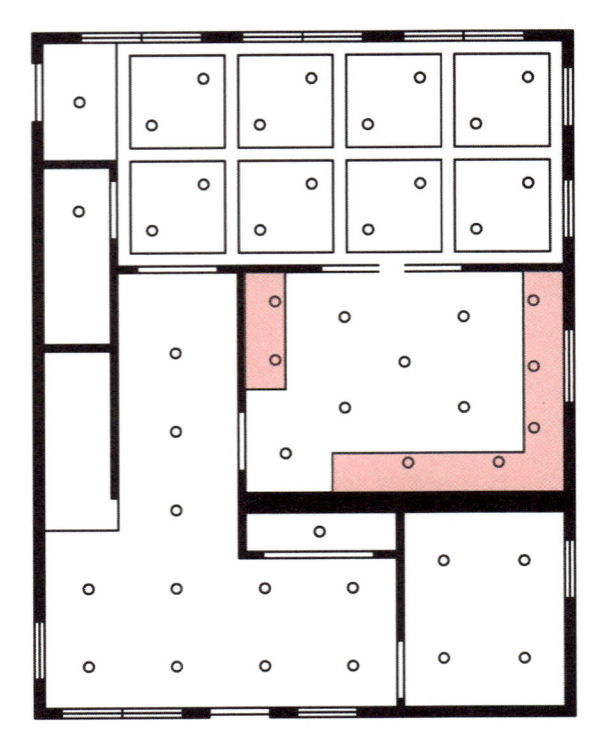

Figure 6.37
Residential RCP highlighting the kitchen where soffits will be installed.

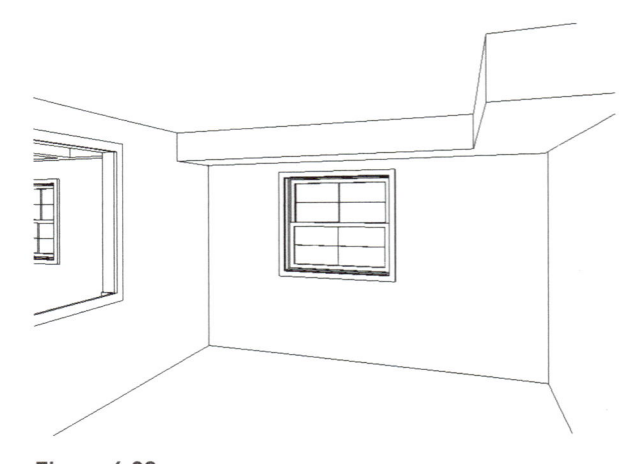

Figure 6.38
View of the residential kitchen showing a soffit. Wall cabinets will be installed below in Chapter 8.

installation for the adjacent ceiling space, which is shown by adding the furring channel and GWB.

STEP 6

Finalize the detail by adding any necessary dimensions, annotations, heavier lineweights, and hatching for any elements that are being cut through.

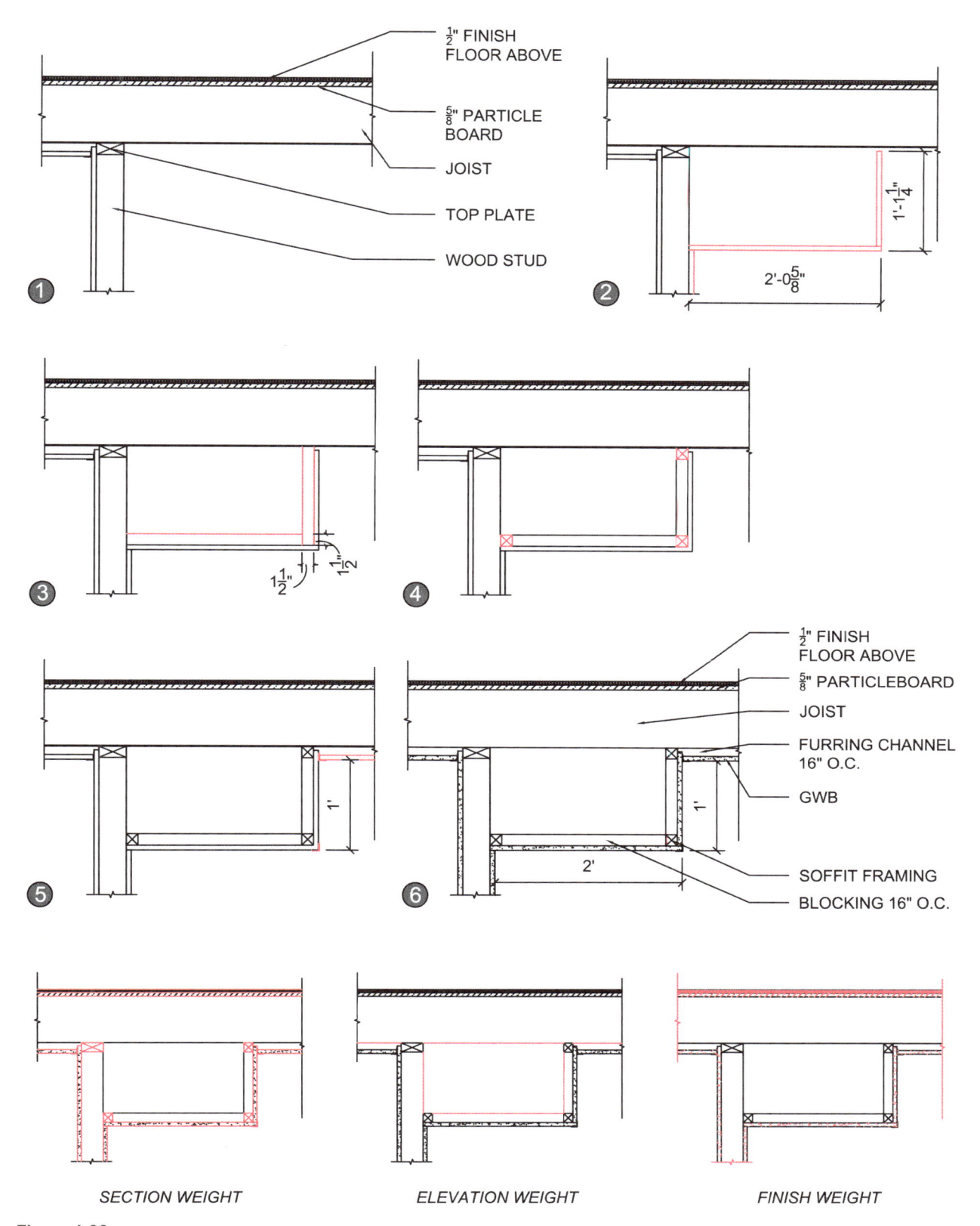

Figure 6.39
Soffit details, Steps 1–6.

CHAPTER 6 CEILINGS | 117

Box beams

This example will be broken into two separate section views. The first will cut perpendicularly through the beam, showing the construction of the width. The second will illustrate the parallel cut, indicating the assembly of the length of the box beam.

Both examples are from the living room ceiling and are constructed from dimensional lumber.

Perpendicular section

STEP 1

The beam will be constructed around a 2 × 8 that will be anchored to the ceiling. Using the finished ceiling plane above, create a rectangle with an *X* through it to show that this piece of lumber is perpendicular to the viewer. As this is a piece of dimensional lumber, it will measure 1 1/2" × 7 1/4". For other sizes, see Appendix D.

STEP 2

The sides of the beam are built from 1 × 6s, each measuring 3/4" × 5 1/2". Draw a rectangle with these dimensions on either side of the anchor beam.

STEP 3

The bottom of the beam will be a 1 × 8 that will anchor in between the side pieces. Draw a rectangle between these sides, flush with the bottom, measuring 3/4" × 7 1/4".

STEP 4

The box beam in this example has crown molding attached to show this possibility as a design option. If you choose not to have molding along the beam, skip to Step 6.

The profile of the selected crown molding is added to either side of the beam, with the back of the molding touching the 1 × 6 and the top touching the ceiling. See Chapter 7 for more information about millwork and Appendix H for additional molding profiles.

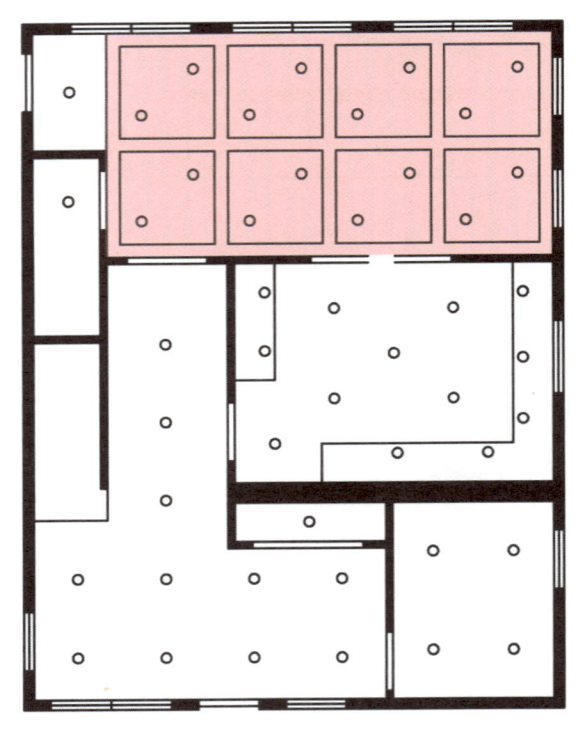

Figure 6.40
Residential RCP highlighting the living room where box beams will be installed.

STEP 5

Add blocking behind the molding, a vertical piece along the box beam, and a horizontal piece along the ceiling.

STEP 6

Finalize the detail by adding any necessary dimensions, annotations, and materials. Lineweights should be adjusted to match the standards established in Part I of this text, with heavier lineweights used on objects that are being cut through and lighter lineweights used for material textures.

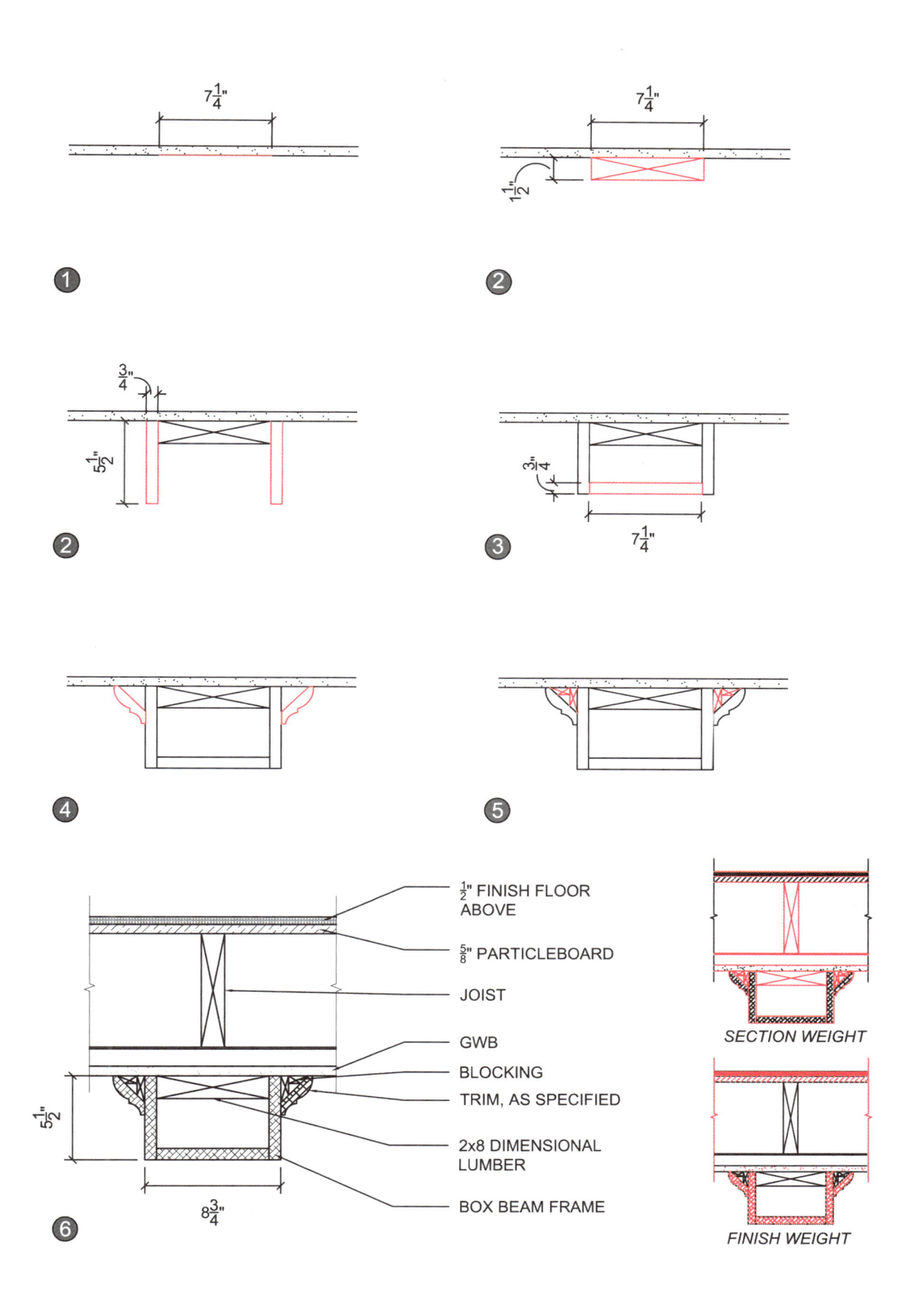

Figure 6.41
Perpendicular section detail of a box beam, Steps 1–6.

CHAPTER 6 CEILINGS

Parallel section

STEP 1
This example uses a vertical line and a horizontal line to indicate the wall and ceiling planes.

Measuring 1 1/2" down from the ceiling plane, draw a horizontal line for the bottom of the 2 × 8 anchor beam.

Draw the next horizontal line 3 1/4" down from the bottom of the anchor beam, indicating the hollow space.

The third horizontal line should be drawn another 3/4" down. This will be the bottom of the box beam.

STEP 2
Starting at the wall, draw a rectangle measuring 1 1/2" wide from the bottom of the anchor beam to the top of the lower plane. Put an *X* through this support block to show that it is being cut through in this view.

Add additional supports throughout the hollow channel, spacing them 1'-0" OC.

STEP 3
Finalize the detail by adding any necessary dimensions, annotations, and materials. Lineweights should be adjusted to match the standards established in Part I of this text, with heavier lineweights used on objects that are being cut through and lighter lineweights used for material textures.

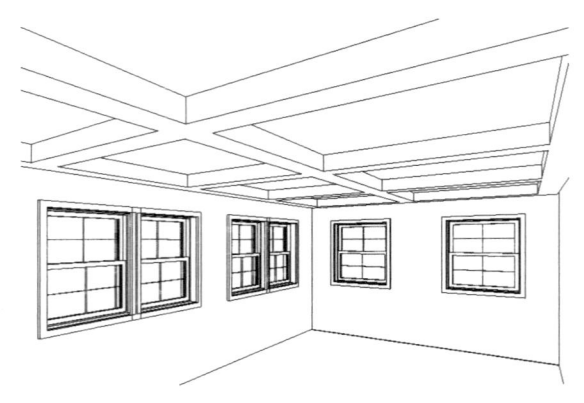

Figure 6.42
View of the residential living room showing the installed box beams.

Figure 6.43 (facing page)
Parallel section detail of a box beam, Steps 1–3.

①

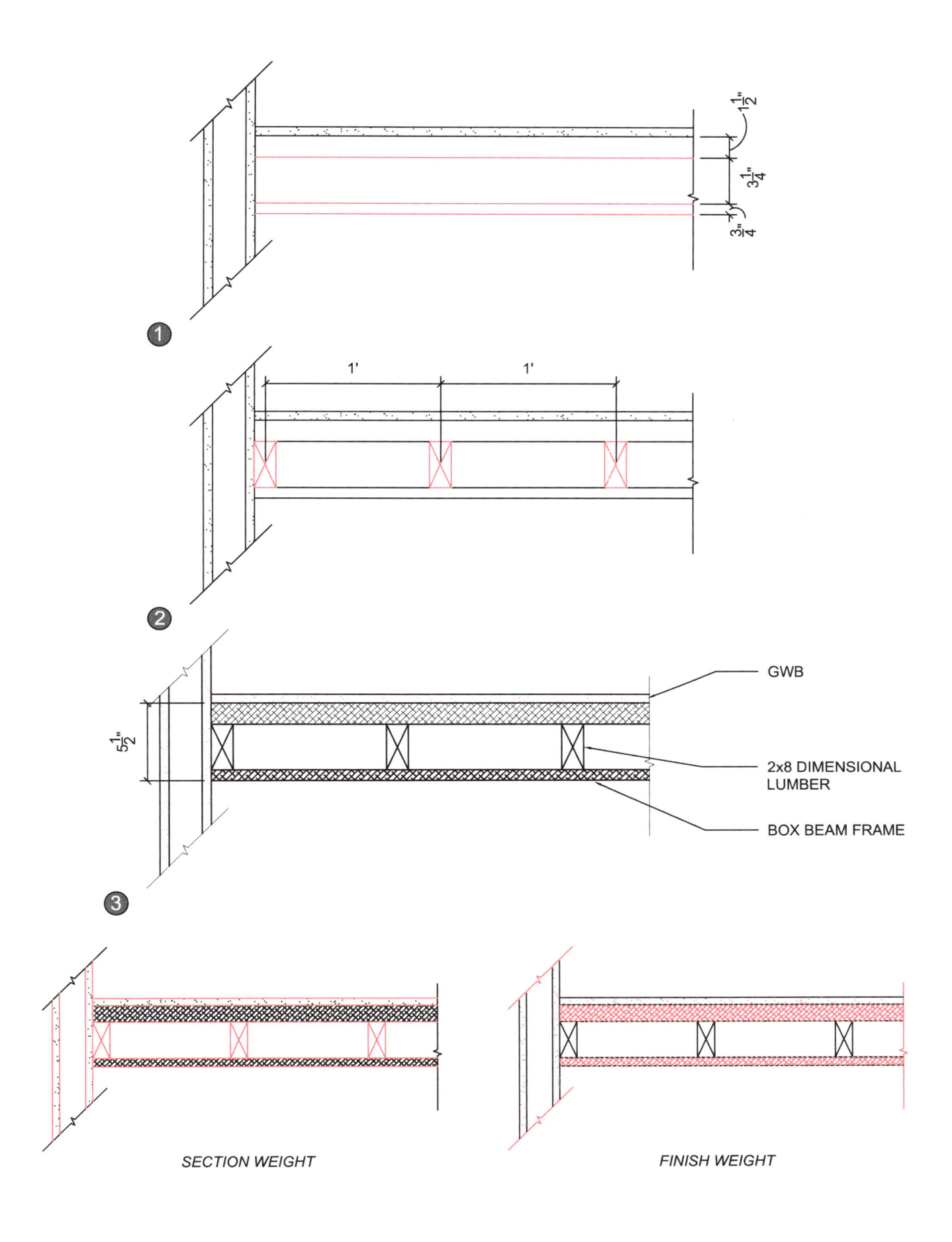

②

③

GWB

2x8 DIMENSIONAL LUMBER

BOX BEAM FRAME

SECTION WEIGHT

FINISH WEIGHT

CHAPTER 6 CEILINGS | 121

WHY IS THIS IMPORTANT?

Interior designers can utilize the ceiling plane as an opportunity to expand upon, strengthen, or support the concept of the room it spans. While there are occasions in which a designer may choose to have one type of ceiling throughout the project, using a single, flat surface can become monotonous or feel unfinished. When a variety of ceiling heights, finishes, and treatments are offered within a project, spaces can be enhanced from efficient and beautiful to dynamic. Understanding how to draw ceiling details allows for a designer to incorporate lighting, HVAC systems, wiring, and plumbing lines within the plenum space, enabling unwanted elements to remain hidden.

Figure 6.44
Suspended wood slat ceilings supporting dispersed light fixtures.

Figure 6.45
Direct installation GWB system with a soffit perimeter surrounding a box beam detail.

Figure 6.46
Office interior highlighted by a wood plank suspension system that supports suspended GWB rings.

Figure 6.47
Suspended GWB panels concealing cove details and recessed GWB channels.

CHAPTER REVIEW

1. Why are suspended tile systems ideal for commercial spaces?
2. What is the edge molding? What shapes are common for these molds?
3. Your client wants accessible ceilings with few visible seams for their office space. What option or options can you offer them?
4. Your client wants the central portion of their conference room to be a recessed ACT system with a GWB perimeter. Sketch and label two designs for your client: GWB as a suspended system and a GWB soffit.

EXAMPLE PLAN UPDATES STUDIO

Building on the progress from the first phase of these projects, this chapter focused on creating different ceiling types and treatments for these plans. Each of the examples called out from these project files has shown various installation techniques and the finish materials appropriate for each building type.
Examples from the commercial plan include:

Suspended acoustical ceiling tiles (ACT)
Corridors

Suspended gypsum board (GWB)
Office

Suspended ACT/GWB flush
Reception/Waiting to Corridor

GWB cove and recessed ACT suspension systems
Conference Room

The residential plan has been laid out to include:

Direct installation (GWB)
Entry/Hallway

GWB soffit
Kitchen

Box beam
Living room

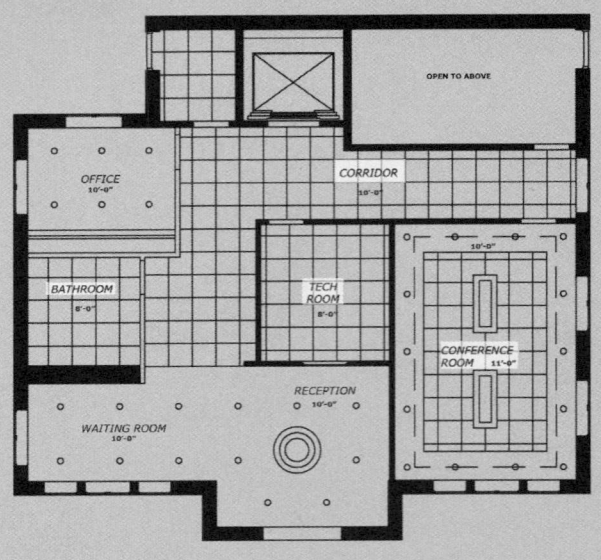

Figure 6.48
Commercial RCP with ceiling heights and light fixtures.

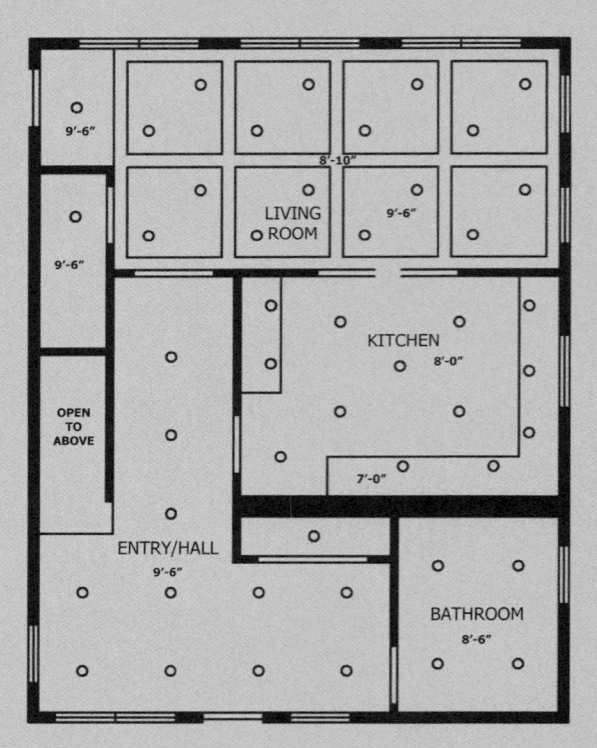

Figure 6.49
Residential RCP with ceiling heights and light fixtures.

124 | PART II DETAIL DRAWINGS

CHAPTER TERMINOLOGY

- acoustical ceiling tile
- angle molding
- box beam
- ceiling
- concealed grid
- concealed T tile
- cove
- cove lighting
- cross tee
- direct installation system
- dropped ceiling
- edge molding
- exposed grid
- flush finish
- furring channel
- girder
- I-beam
- joist
- main beam
- plenum
- recessed ceiling
- shadow molding
- soffit (ceiling)
- square edge tile
- suspended gypsum system
- suspended tile system
- T-bar
- tegular tile
- wire hanger

CEILING CODES

This section explored the elements used and how to draw construction details for a variety of ceiling types. Below are the ADA standards and the IBC codes that you need to keep in mind when designing and drafting ceilings.

Table 6.1 ADA Standards for Ceilings

ADA Code	Topic	Description
307.4	Vertical clearance	Vertical clearance must be at least 80" high. Any spaces that are less than 80" must have a guardrail that is at least 27" AFF.
		Exception made for door frames, which can lower the vertical clearance to 78" AFF

Table 6.2 IBC Codes for Ceilings

IBC Code	Topic	Description
803.13.1	Applying finish materials to rated building elements – Direct attachment	Ceilings that are to be fire-rated must be applied directly to the furring strips above.
803.13.2	Applying finish materials to rated building elements – Suspended ceiling	Suspended ceilings that are to be fire-rated must have a Class A rating.
803.13.4	Material thickness	Materials less than 1/4" can be applied directly to the ceiling without furring strip support, but it cannot be suspended from the ceiling element that supports it. Exceptions include noncombustibles or Class A materials.
808.1	Suspended acoustical ceilings	Suspended ACT must be used and installed according to manufacturer's directions.
1003.2	Ceiling heights for means of egress	The ceiling in a means of egress must be at least 7'-6" high.
1003.3.1	Ceilings and ceiling mounted objects and headroom	Objects are allowed to extend past the minimum ceiling height if the ceiling over any type of passageway is at least 6'-8".
1208.2	Minimum ceiling heights	The ceiling in occupiable rooms and corridors must be at least 7'-6" high. Ceilings for facility and service rooms must be at least 7'-0". These spaces include kitchens, bathrooms, laundry rooms, or storage spaces.

CHAPTER REFERENCES

Armstrong Ceilings. "Suspension Systems." *www.armstrongceilings.com*. Accessed August 2018. https://www.armstrongceilings.com/commercial/en-us/suspension-systems.html.

Ballast, David Kent. *Interior Construction & Detailing for Designers and Architects*. Belmont, CA: Professional Publications, Inc., 2013.

Ching, Francis D. *Building Construction Illustrated*. New York: John Wiley & Sons, 2014.

DeChiara, Joseph, Julius Panero, and Martin Zelnik. *Time-Saver Standards for Interior Design and Space Planning*. New York: McGraw-Hill, 2001.

International Code Council. *International Building Code, 2015*. Chicago: International Code Council Publications, 2014.

International Code Council. *International Residential Code, 2015*. Chicago: International Code Council Publications, 2014.

Jefferis, Alan. *Residential Design, Drafting, and Detailing*, 2nd ed. Boston: Cengage Learning, 2013.

Kilmer, W. Otie and Rosemary Kilmer. *Construction Drawings and Details for Interiors*. New York: John Wiley & Sons, 2016.

Kruse, Kelsey and Maryrose McGowan. *Interior Graphic Standards*. New York: John Wiley & Sons, 2003.

United States Department of Justice. *2010 ADA Standards for Accessible Design*. Washington, D.C.: Dept. of Justice, 2010.

Millwork detailing

CHAPTER 7

CHAPTER OUTCOMES

After completing this chapter you will be able to:

1. Discuss the codes and standards pertaining to millwork and wall-applied details, and design spaces that adhere to these guidelines.

2. Select the appropriate joinery style for your project based on function, structure, and ornamentation.

3. Understand how millwork is designed, fit, and anchored, and be capable of customizing millwork for application in elevation and section details.

Figure 7.1
Interior featuring paneled walls, crown molding, and a detailed mantel.

ABOUT MILLWORK

Interiors feature many different ready-made carpentry components that are installed directly to the walls, ceilings, and floors. These elements, referred to as **millwork**, include trim, cornices, chair rails, and wainscoting that are traditionally carved from wood with a chosen profile. However, modern technology now allows for man-made materials, including various plastics, rubbers, resins, and synthetics to be used. While door and window frames were discussed in Chapter 5, wall-mounted millwork will be discussed in this chapter.

Three important considerations to account for when choosing a project's millwork are the type, the profile, and the joinery techniques.

Types of wall-mounted millwork

Beginning at the top of the wall, the **crown molding** is an element that disguises the seam where the wall and ceiling meet. While it seems as though this molding is mounted along the seam, it is actually one side of a **hollow triangle**, touching both the ceiling and the wall while creating a gap between itself and the corner. Wood backing strips are fastened to the structure, and the molding is then attached to this blocking. The wood backing is simply a 2 × 4 that is trimmed to fit inside of the hollow triangle.

Molding typically features a shaped pattern or detail that runs the length of the surface. These details can vary depending on the architectural style of the project, the height needed for the trim, and the designer's discretion.

In addition to running along the top of a wall, crown molding can also be used at the top of cabinetry or columns. It can also be used in combination with a cornice, frieze, or plate rail to create a more ornate wall topper. The **cornice** is a ledge that is mounted flush to the top wall just below the ceiling, typically sitting above the crown molding or being directly

Figure 7.2
Living room featuring wainscoting, crown molding, chair rail, and baseboard.

incorporated into the profile of the crown. This piece typically features a shaped pattern or detail that runs the length of the surface. The **frieze** is a horizontal band that appears below the crown molding and, while typically left plain, it may be carved. The **plate rail** is a notched shelf that can be installed alone or below the frieze to be used for display. This rail must be installed high enough along the wall to not interfere with the clear space below.

The **chair rail** is molding that is mounted along the mid-section of a wall as a means to protect the wall's finish from damage. The mounting height for the rail is dependent on the height of the walls, as it is installed 32" to 36" above the finished floor (AFF) for standard 8'-0" wall heights and approximately 40" AFF for 10'-0" high rooms. Like the crown molding, the chair rail can feature differently shaped patterns depending on the architectural style of the space and the amount of wall that needs protection.

The chair rail is comprised of at least three parts. The apron is the vertical portion of the rail, typically carved with a decorative design or maintaining a specified profile, that runs along the wall. The apron is adhered to the wood backing, usually a trimmed board, that anchors it to the wall. The whole piece is then topped by the chair rail cap, a board that is flat on three sides and rounded on the fourth, and installed perpendicularly to the apron.

Baseboards are moldings that are used to hide the joint created along the bottom of a wall and the floor, operating similarly to the crown molding; however, the baseboard is applied directly to the wall. Typically measuring 4" to 7" in height, the design of the base is again dictated by the style of the room, the formality of the space, and should be complimentary to the selected crown molding and chair rail, should they be present.

The baseboard is made up of four parts: the baseboard, the base cap, the shoe, and the wood backing. The baseboard panel is the vertical component of the ensemble and, as with the chair rail, is anchored to the wood backing. The base cap is triangular in shape and sits flush with the wall and the baseboard. The angled arm of the triangle can be decoratively carved, giving the baseboard a distinctive profile. The final element is the shoe, a quarter-round that is attached to the bottom of the baseboard panel, disguising the seam between it and the floor.

Figure 7.3
Soffit featuring cornice and crown molding details.

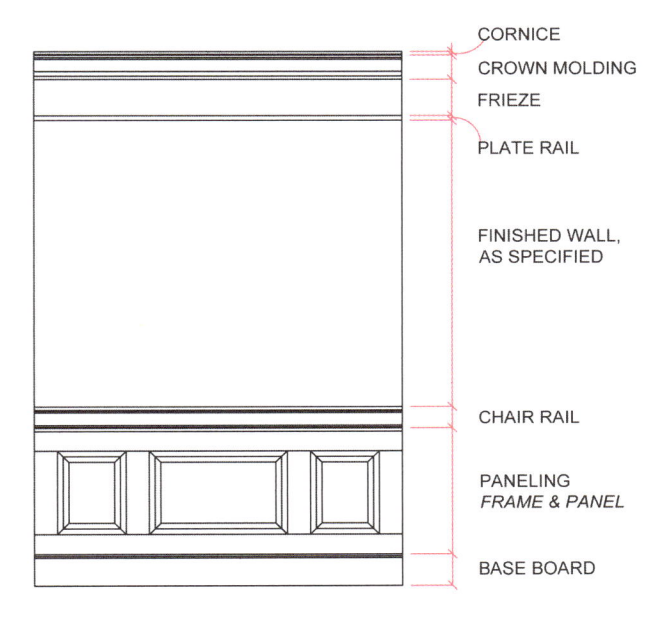

Figure 7.4
Components of wall-installed millwork in elevation.

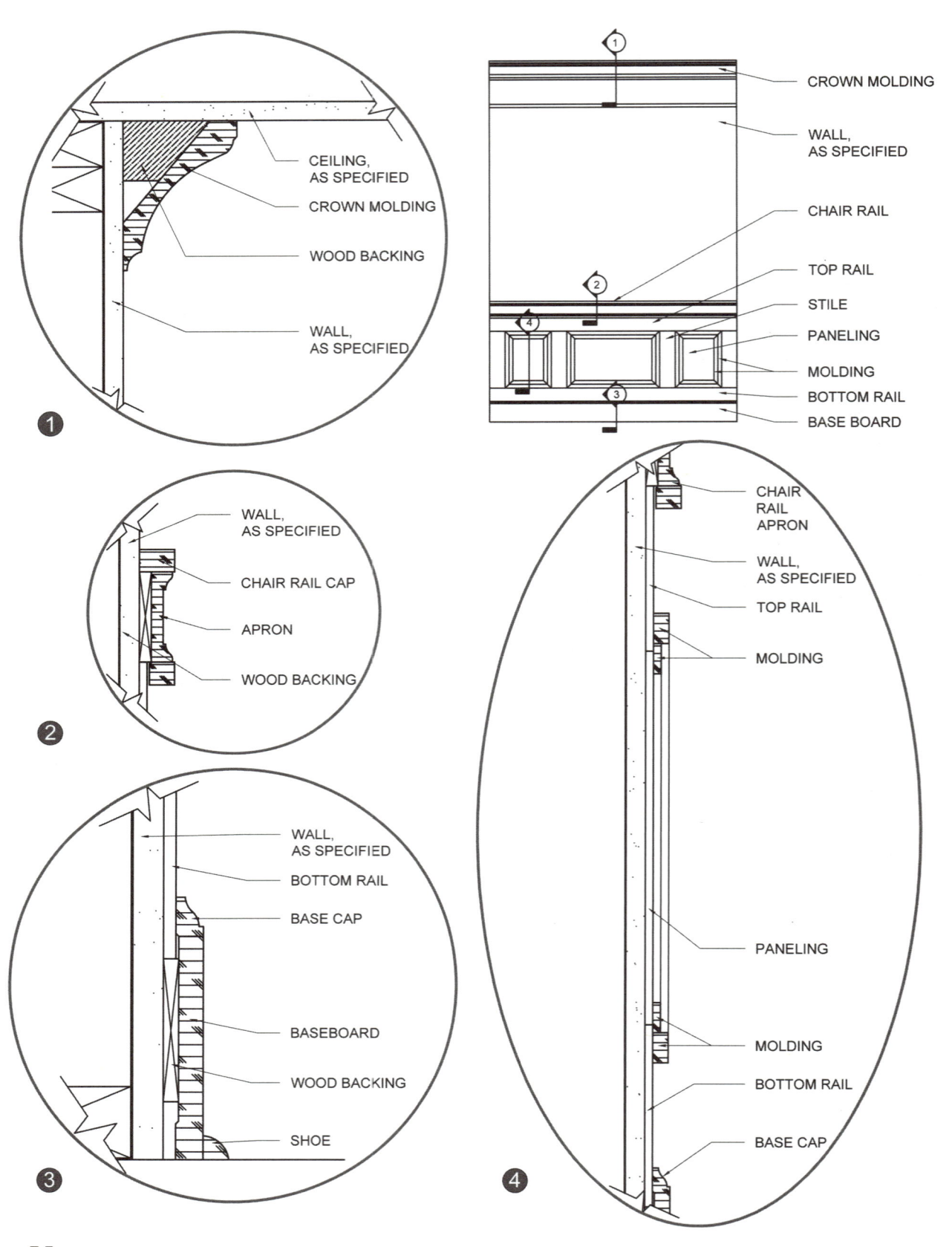

Figure 7.5
Millwork details of 1. crown molding; 2. chair rail; 3. base board; 4. wainscot.

STUDIO Animation 7.1 Wall-mounted millwork details

130 | PART II DETAIL DRAWINGS

Finally, you may wish to include paneling in the space. **Paneling** is a millwork wall cover composed of thin boards that are installed directly to the finished wall. One type of paneling, **wainscot**, appears between the baseboard and the chair rail and can take the form of a decorative panel or a frame and panel design. **Decorative panels** are traditionally made of thin pieces of wood or veneered plywood that are carved or embossed with a repetitive pattern. **Beadboard**, as seen in Figure 7.6, is a type of decorative panel that is carved to give the appearance that it is composed of multiple vertical planks laid side by side.

Frame and panel wainscot are made up of multiple pieces of wood to create a square or rectangle shape with an exposed, or framed, inner element. First, a layer of plywood is applied to the wall over the gypsum wallboard (GWB). Next, trimmed boards are added, with one running near the bottom of the wall and a second running about 3'-0" AFF. These parallel boards are referred to as rails. Between the rails, vertical boards, called stiles, are evenly installed with enough space between them to expose a rectangular panel of the plywood. The seam between the panel and the boards is then covered with a molding trim. The ply and moldings can be painted or stained. A sample of a completed frame and panel wainscot installation can be seen in Figure 7.7 and will be used within this chapter's detail examples.

Figure 7.6
Beadboard paneling installed below a chair rail.

Figure 7.7
Frame and panel wainscot paneling.

IBC

As a general reminder, any trim work that extends into the clear space for a means of egress may not extend more than 1 ½" into the path of travel so not to interfere with anyone trying to exit. (*IBC 1005.7.2*)

ADA

Any trim that extends up to 4" can be mounted between the floor and 27" AFF or above 80" AFF, but must be 1 ½" or less between 27"-80". (*ADA 307.2*)

CHAPTER 7 MILLWORK DETAILING | 131

Profiles

The **profile** is the outline or shape of the trim as seen in section and may be selected for its appearance, historical significance, or simplicity of installation. In elevation, the curves and grooves of the profile traditionally extend in a continuous fashion from one end of the board to the other. The profile can be complex or simplistic and may be selected from a company's existing profile list or can custom made. Figure 7.8 and Appendix H both illustrate a small sampling of profiles, but in reality, there are an endless amount of profiles that can be utilized.

Figure 7.8
A sample of baseboard sizes and profiles.

Joinery

Connection points between pieces of wood, or **joinery**, are important factors in the structure and appearance of millwork. These connection points can abut or interlock with each other, either through tension, fasteners, or bonding agents. The choice of joint style used varies whether the piece is applied decoratively, as in the case of crown molding, or if it is integral to the construction of furniture, such as cabinets or chairs. Designers should consider the type of joint that will be used when they create millwork details in order to determine whether or not the joint will be emphasized within the design. The following section illustrates a handful of joinery options.

The **butt joint** is the most economical joint in that the two boards simply touch each other. The first way is to lay them side by side or end to end and secure them with glue, typically seen in trim work. The second method is to overlap the boards and fasten them to each other with a nail or screw. This technique is primarily used for furniture and cabinetry construction.

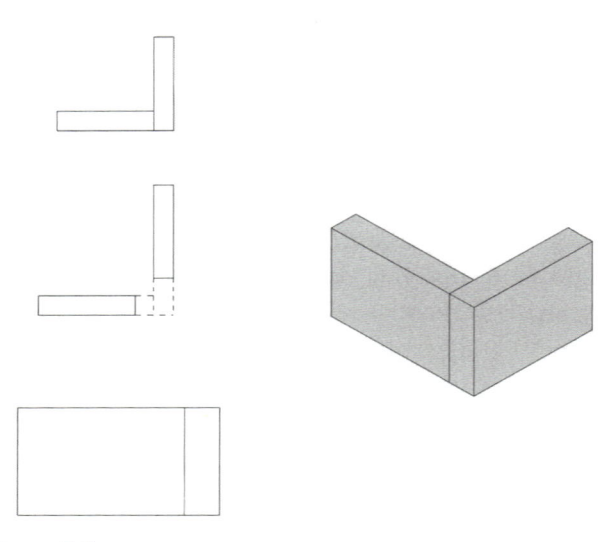

Figure 7.9
Butt joint (continuous); from left: plan, exploded plan, elevation, axon.

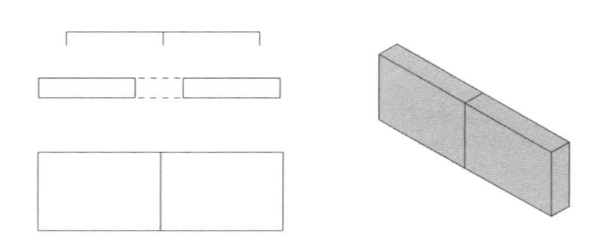

Figure 7.10
Butt joint (90 degrees); from left: plan, exploded plan, elevation, axon.

STUDIO Animation 7.2 Joinery styles

Similar to the butt, the **scarf joint** glues boards end to end to create a continuous line for trim work. The main difference between the previous joint and the scarf is a 45 degree angle cut on these boards that, when overlapped, allows the boards to form a continuous 180 degree line and creates a more discreet seam.

Building off of the scarf joint, the **mitered edge joint** uses 45 degree angle cuts at the ends of the boards. However, instead of allowing these boards to fit in a continuous manner, one can be inverted so that the two cuts form a 90 degree corner. This joint can be used in trim work where walls meet to create frames around panels and to change direction when constructing furniture.

Joinery strength can also be enhanced by creating additional faces for glue or nails to hold on to. Notching the wood so that a part of one board fits into another, or so that a third element can be inserted, creates these faces. While these joints can be used for millwork, most are ideal for furniture construction as the increased strength can withstand additional weights and stresses that occur when intersecting furniture panels and planes meet each other.

One joint that combines the butting technique with notching is the **spline joint**. In this joint, the two pieces of wood are both notched, with a channel carved in each to accept a block of metal or wood. The spline appears similar to the butt joint in elevation, but the inserted piece of wood adds additional faces for glue or nails to help build strength.

Similarly, the **dowel joint** uses channels for a third element to be inserted. However, this technique matches cylindrical lengths of wood, called dowels, with holes that are drilled into each of the boards. Each of the boards slide on to the dowels and abut each other. These joints can be glued together around the dowel or can simply create tension through a tight fit for furniture and cabinetry pieces.

Figure 7.11
Scarf joint; from left: plan, exploded plan, elevation.

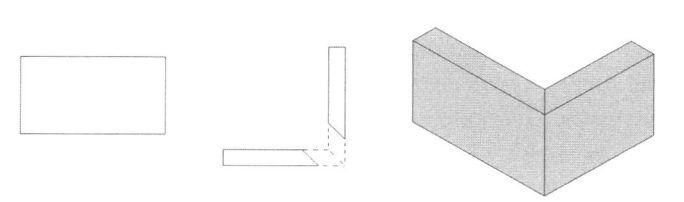

Figure 7.12
Mitered joint; from left: elevation, exploded plan, axon.

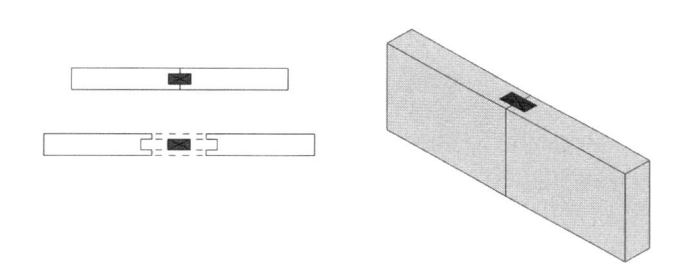

Figure 7.13
Spline joint; from left: plan, exploded plan, axon.

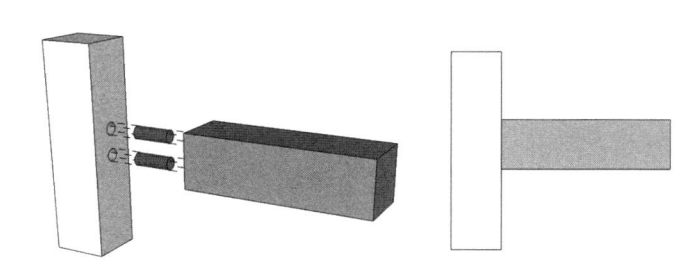

Figure 7.14
Dowel joint; from left: exploded axon, elevation.

The **dado joint** uses a notched cut in one board as a plane to receive a perpendicular board and form a 90 angle. This notch, referred to as the dado, runs perpendicular to the wood's grain, which reduces the risk of the board splintering along the channel. A popular joint, it is typically used within the body of a cabinet or bookcase where a shelf can be slid in to place.

Mortise and tenon joints also form a 90 degree angle between boards, but they can be used in a much more flexible manner as they are one of the strongest joints, can be created with virtually any width of lumber, and can be relatively cost effective. The joint forms between a notched, rectangular, male connector (tenon) being inserted in to a matching female connector (mortise) on the other. The fit should be tight in order to maintain the strength of the joint and can be glued or left without a fastener. The mortise and tenon joint can be seen in furniture and cabinetry.

The joint becomes stronger, but also more costly, when there are more notches cut into the wood. One of these types of joints is the **finger joint**. Here, multiple corresponding 90 degree rectangular wedges are fit together, not unlike puzzle pieces. While it may be used in for continuous lengths, this joint is typically used in furniture and cabinetry, as it can give corners a distinct, decorative look.

An ornate twist on the finger joint is the **dovetail joint**. Using the same concept of fitting multiple coordinating elements together, the dovetail replaces the rectangular wedges with corresponding pins and tails together. These pins feature a broad base and a taper towards the board, creating triangular shapes that intersect with matching tails. The dovetail is typically used in furniture and cabinetry, as it can give corners a desirable look, but as the work is more involved, it is usually reserved for higher-end pieces.

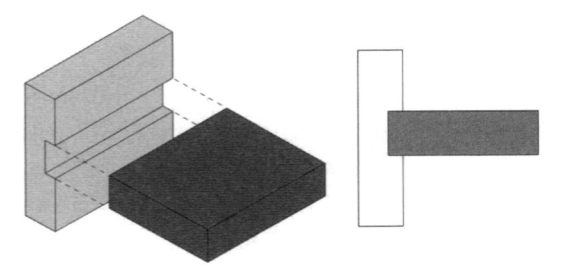

Figure 7.15
Dado joint; from left: exploded axon, elevation.

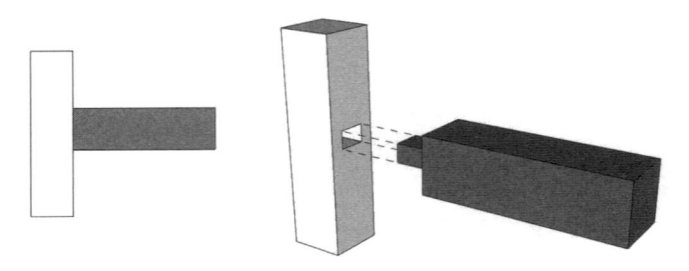

Figure 7.16
Mortise and tenon joint; from left: elevation, exploded axon.

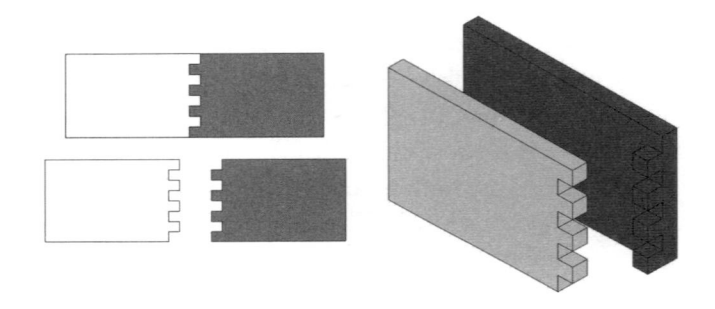

Figure 7.17
Finger joint; from left: elevation, exploded elevation, rectangular pins.

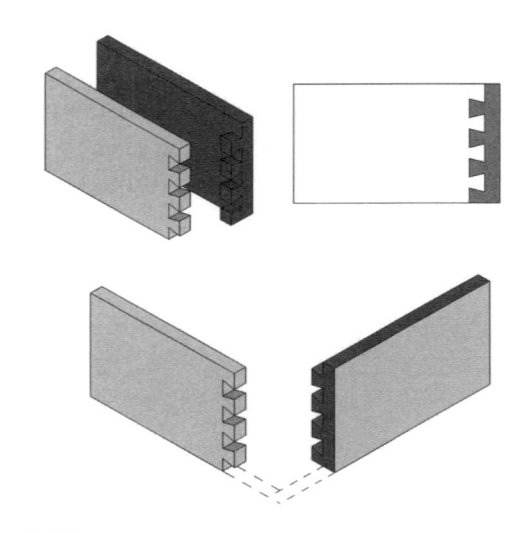

Figure 7.18
Dovetail joint; from left: tails and pins, elevation, exploded axon, plan.

The **French dovetail joint** utilizes the same pin and tail method discussed in the previous example. The major difference here is that the French version utilizes a single dovetail pin that is slid into a corresponding tail. This joint is usually reserved for cabinetry and shelving in high-end furnishings.

The **tongue and groove joint** combines the finger joint with French dovetail. Here, a single rectangular wedge slides into a corresponding channel. This joint can be used in a variety of finishes, from trim work to flooring, and creates a cost-effective solution to the French dovetail for furniture.

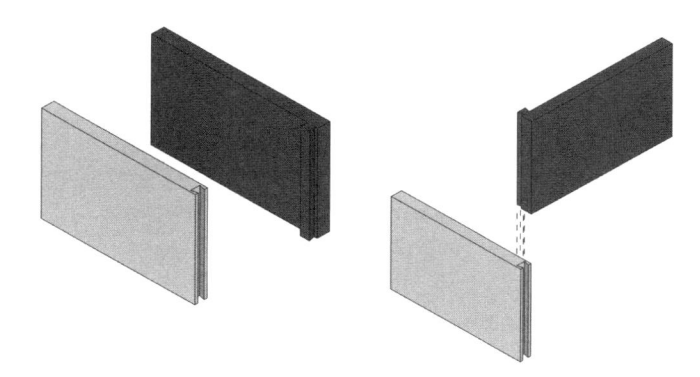

Figure 7.19
French dovetail joint; from left: tail and pin, exploded axon.

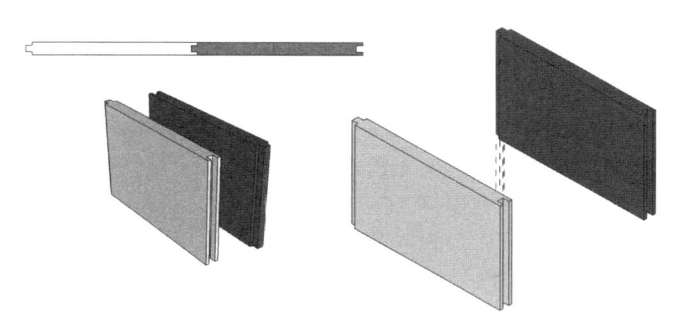

Figure 7.20
Tongue and groove joint; from left: plan, notches, exploded axon.

DRAFTING WALL-MOUNTED MILLWORK

The following sections will examine millwork pieces that can be applied to the wall, first individually and then in combination. While there are only single examples of crown molding, chair rails, baseboards, and wainscot seen here, additional profiles can be found in Appendix H or through your own research and designs.

The examples of each of the four millwork elements will be taken from a hallway wall in the residential plan. Only a portion of this wall will be used for the combination drawings (all four elements in elevation and section) for clarity.

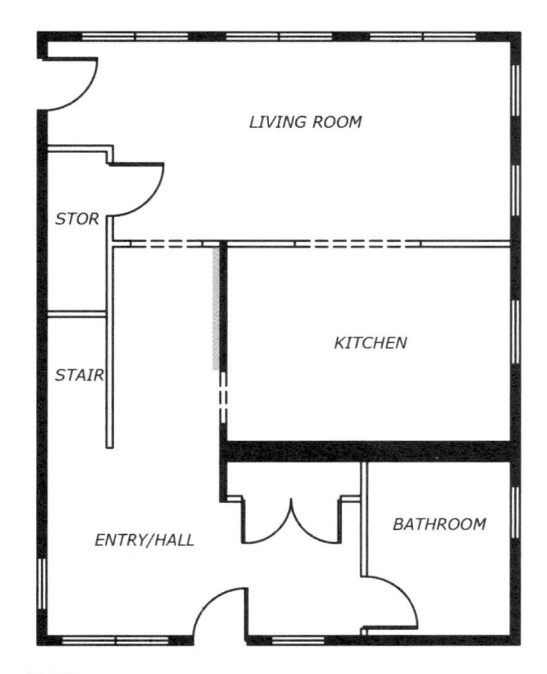

Figure 7.21
Residential plan showing the hallway wall that will be used for the examples in this chapter.

CHAPTER 7 MILLWORK DETAILING | 135

Wall-mounted millwork, elevation

STEP 1
Draw a rectangle to represent the height and length of a wall. As this example is only a portion of the overall wall, we will be using a wall that measures 8'-0" high × 5'-4" wide.

STEP 2
Based on the measurements of the specified crown molding and baseboards for this example, draw a line 5" down from the ceiling and a second line 5 1/2' up from the floor. These lines will designate the bottom of the crown molding and the top of the baseboard.

STEP 3
Create the lines for the chair rail by drawing a line 32" above the floor line and a second line 4 1/8" below the first.

Figure 7.22
Elevation of a portion of the hallway wall, Steps 1–3.

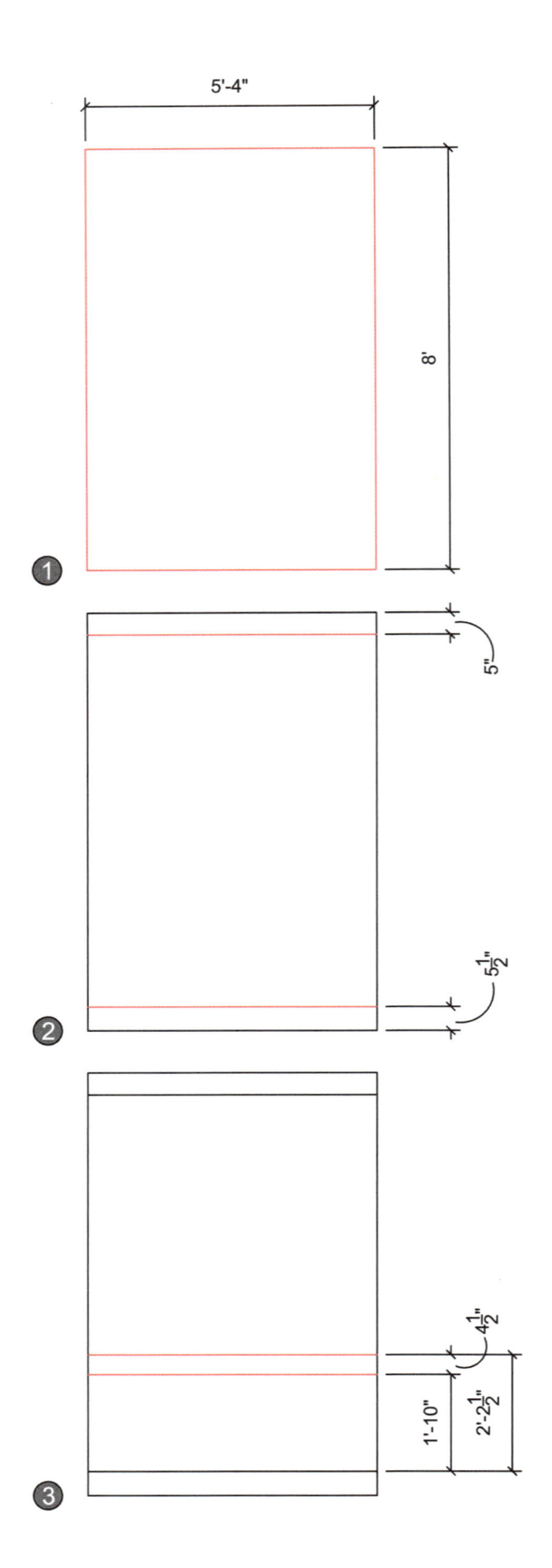

STEP 4

To indicate the wainscoting, first create the horizontal lines that will mark the top and bottom rails. Draw a line 9" down from the top of the chair rail and another 9" up from the floor line. In this example, there should now be a 1'-2" space between these two lines, which is where the stiles and moldings will appear, as seen in the next few steps.

STEP 5

For this example, there will be three wainscot panels which will not be the same size across the wall. The first and the last will be balanced at 1'-0" wide, while the central panel will measure 2'-0" wide. This will leave enough space between each panel for 4" stiles (the vertical elements between panels). Draw these lines in as seen in the example.

STEP 6

Focusing on the molding of the panels, there will be two 1" wide rectangles framing the interior panel. These moldings will be stepped, which will be more important when the section is being drawn. Using the rectangles created by adding the stiles in Step 5 as the outside boundaries, create two smaller rectangles inside each.

Figure 7.23
Elevation of a portion of the hallway wall, Steps 4–6.

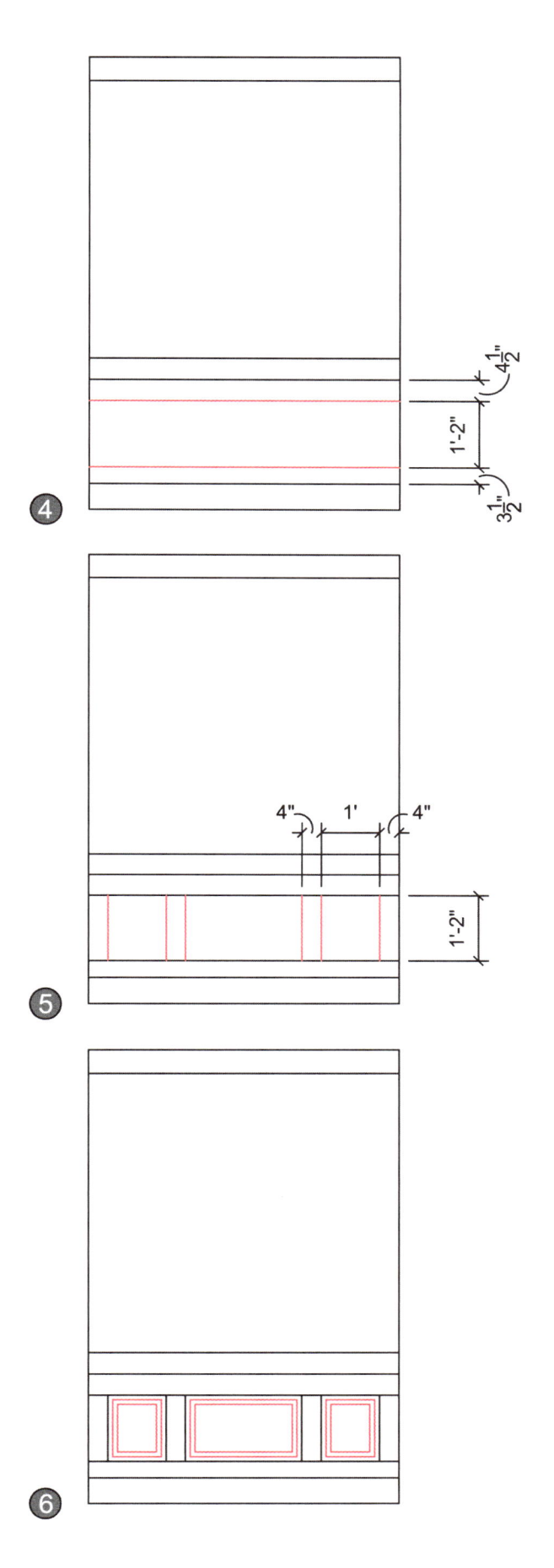

STEP 7

To indicate the mitered edge of each of the panels, draw lines to create the 45 degree angle of the joints.

STEP 8

Based on the pattern of your selected or designed trim, draw horizontal lines within the crown, chair rail, and baseboards to indicate direction changes. The easiest way to do this is to place a profile of each of these elements next to the elevation and draw lines from the element in to the elevation, as seen by in the inset drawing for this step.

STEP 9

Finalize the detail by adding any necessary dimensions and annotations.

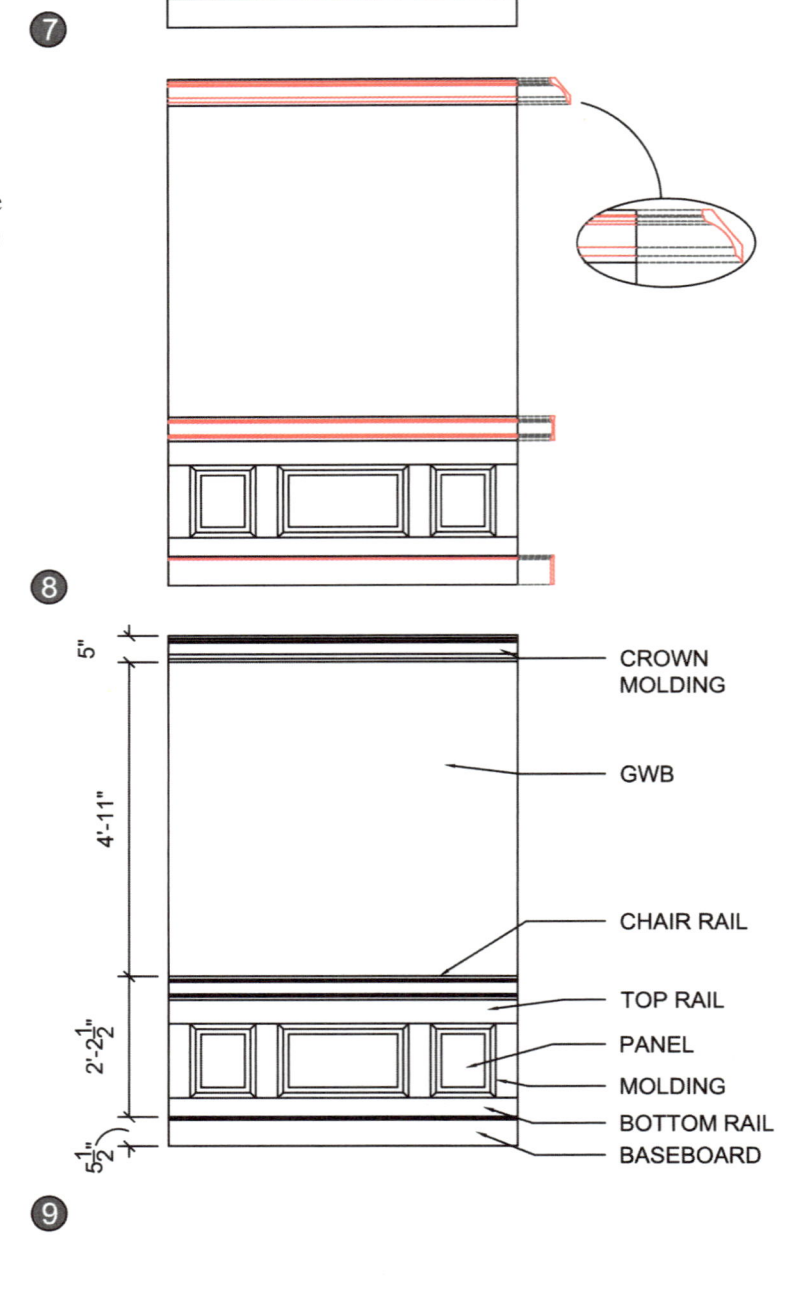

Figure 7.24
Elevation of a portion of the hallway wall, Steps 7–9.

Figure 7.25
Section of a portion of the hallway wall, Steps 1–3.

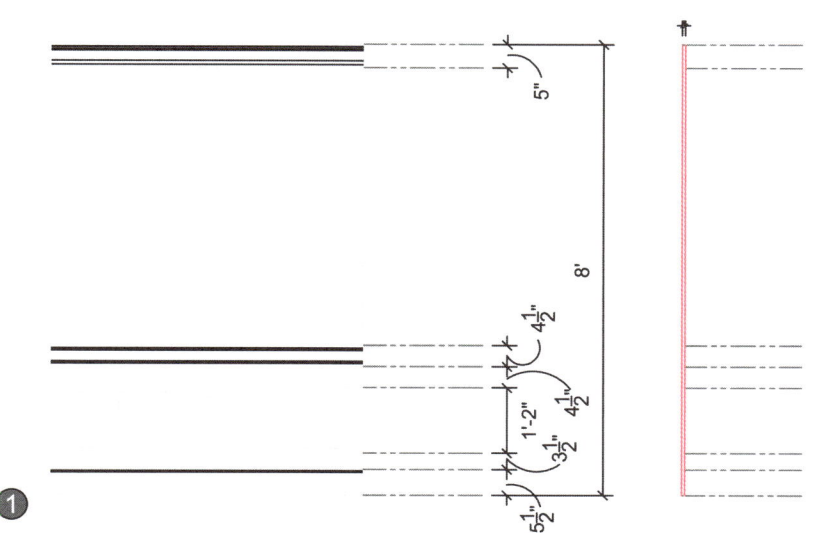

Wall-mounted millwork, section

STEP 1
Using the elevation you just completed, draw guidelines from the top and bottom of each piece of trim work into an open drawing space. This will allow for you to maintain the proper placement of each element.

Once the guidelines are drawn, you can remove the elevation from the drawing space.

Along the side of the guidelines, draw two vertical lines 5/8" apart from the top of the crown molding line to the bottom of the baseboard line. Together, these lines will represent the thickness of the GWB.

STEP 2
Starting at the top portion of the wall, draw the profile of the design you wish to use for the crown molding between the two uppermost guidelines. The hollow triangle should be accommodated for depending on the dimensions of the molding.

STEP 3
Add the wood blocking. Here, it measures 2" high and extends along the ceiling from the GWB to the crown molding profile.

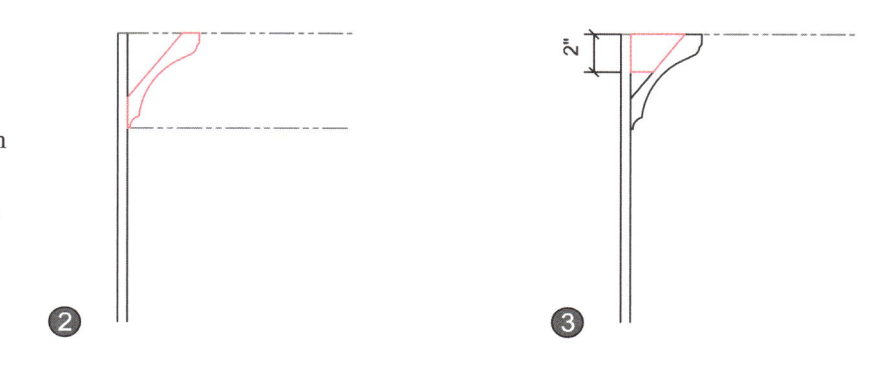

Hand
When drawing the trim profiles, either use an existing template or create your own that can easily be traced for timeliness and consistency.

CAD
A handful of block profiles can be found in the Design Center or imported from Revit. If you choose to use a unique profile, make sure its dimensions meet the IBC and ADA guidelines and create a block that can be dropped into place.

Revit
Profiles can be accessed in the Architecture tab under Component—Load Family—Profiles. They can then be added to the wall as a sweep by highlighting the wall, clicking Edit Type, and editing the Structure. Switch the view to Section and click Sweeps, where you can then load and edit the desired profile.

CHAPTER 7 MILLWORK DETAILING

STEP 4
Moving to the chair rail, draw the profile of the design you wish to use between the top and bottom guidelines you created for this piece.

STEP 5
Add two pieces of wood blocking, each measuring 3" high and 5/8" wide. The first will fit into the hollow space between the GWB, chair rail cap, and apron. The second should measure 1" above the guideline for the floor.

STEP 6
Draw two vertical lines extending from one of the wooden blocks to the other. The first, the plywood layer, will measure 1/4" from the GWB and the second, the finished wood layer, another 1/4" from the ply.

STEP 7
Moving to the baseboard, draw the profile of the base, base cap, and shoe you wish to use at the bottom of the wall. The wood blocking you created in Step 3 should fit along the back of the base, but you may need to adjust it slightly.

STEP 8
To create the molding for the wainscot panels, you must first create the top rail line. This horizontal line should run between the rightmost verticals along the guideline. Draw a second horizontal 1" below this line.

A second horizontal line should extend 1/4" from the top rail and 1/2" down. This will represent the outer molding, which is mounted on top of the finished wall face.

Repeat these steps along the guideline for the bottom rail to create the lower portion of the molding. Then draw a vertical line connecting the outmost corner of the top molding to that of the bottom molding. This will represent the continuation of the molding in elevation.

STEP 9
Convert the topmost guideline to the ceiling plane and the bottommost one to the floor plane. Erase any guidelines that still remain. Since this is a section drawing, remember to give a heavier lineweight to all of the lines of elements that are being cut through. Add any textures, notes, or dimensions necessary to explain how to construct this wainscot panel wall. In this example, break lines have been added to reduce the amount of exposed GWB between the crown molding and the chair rail.

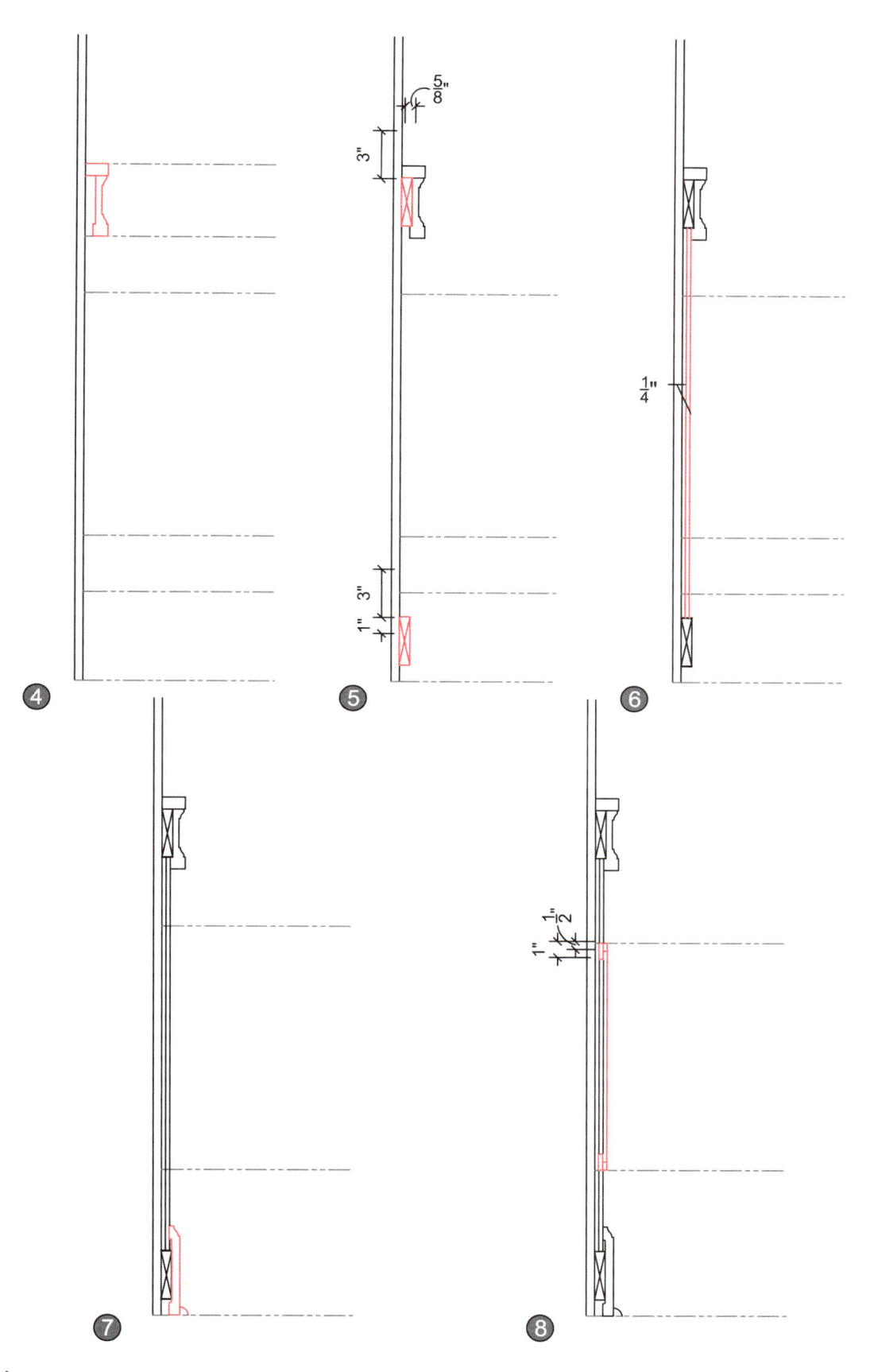

Figure 7.26
Section of a portion of the hallway wall, Steps 4–8.

CHAPTER 7 MILLWORK DETAILING | 141

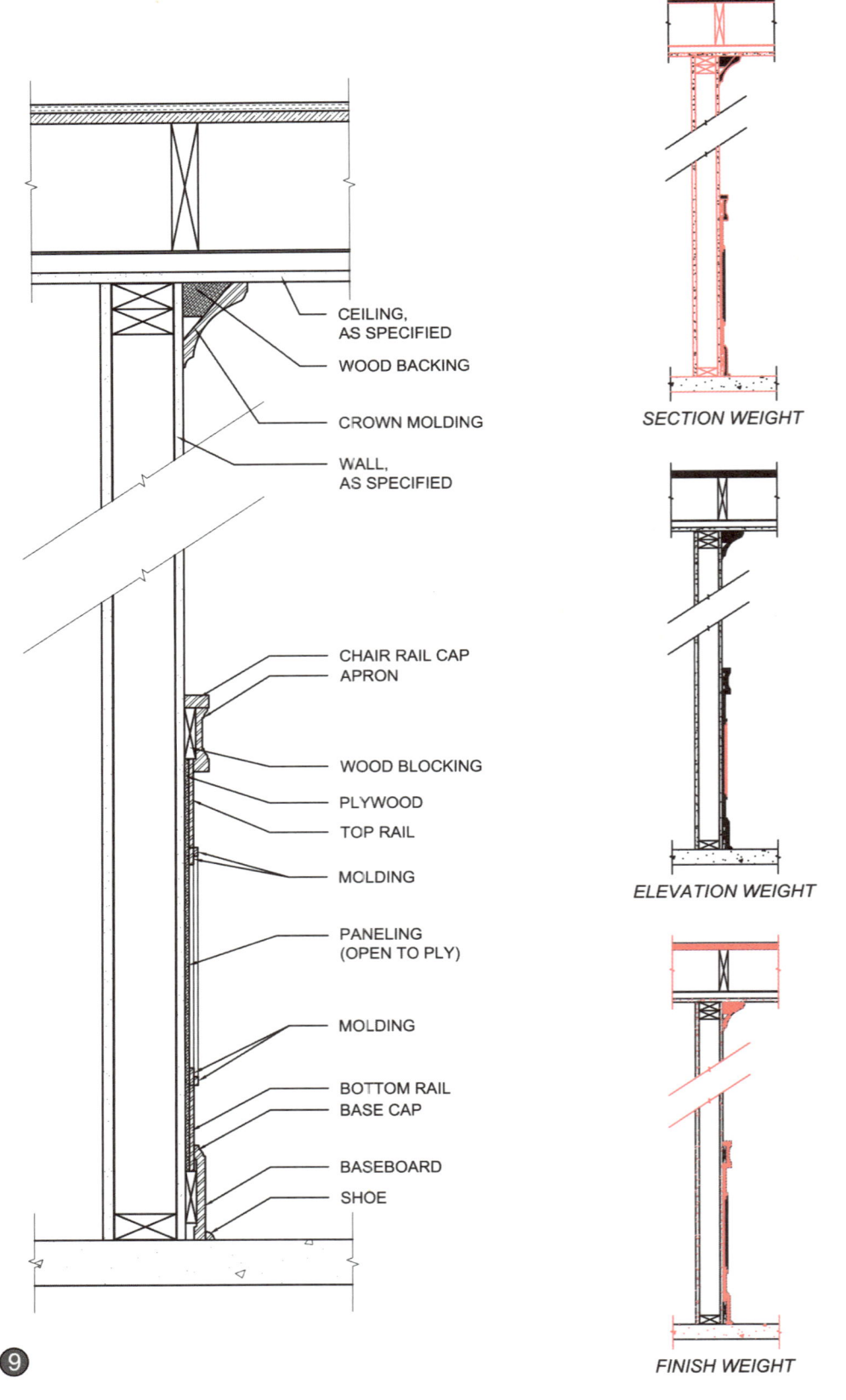

Figure 7.27
Section of a portion of the hallway wall, Step 9.

142 | PART II DETAIL DRAWINGS

WHY IS THIS IMPORTANT?

Historically, millwork details were used to increase insulation, add strength to the walls, and were a sign of care and craftsmanship. Today, millwork is primarily used as a decorative element within an interior and can help create a desired atmosphere depending on how it is implemented. Dark wood colors and full-wall, heavy paneling can be used for more traditional spaces, but lightening the wood color and lower-wall wainscoting gives it a modern feel (see Figure 7.28), as does creating a monochromatic, minimalistic design (see Figure 7.29). Feature walls, such as the abutting planks seen in Figure 7.30 and the full-wall beadboard in Figure 7.31, can be created by installing elements of millwork in unconventional locations, patterns, or sizes. Experiment with different profiles, joints, colors, and placements to find the millwork that is appropriate for your project.

Figure 7.28
Hall and stairwell with frame and panel wainscot.

Figure 7.29
Delicate wall detail made with thin, half-round trim to create wainscot and wall panels.

CHAPTER 7 MILLWORK DETAILING | 143

Figure 7.30
Waiting area featuring a paneled wall with abutting wooden planks.

Figure 7.31
Kitchen paneling created with beadboard to represent tongue and groove planks.

CHAPTER REVIEW

1. What is the hollow triangle? What is its importance?
2. What parts make up the baseboard? How do they fit together and what do they disguise?
3. Your client wants to install a 6" ledge 36" above finished floor around the room. Explain why this is not possible and provide an alternative solution.
4. When can your trim project into a means of egress? What dictates whether or not this is possible?
5. Design complimentary crown molding, chair rail, and baseboard profiles in the style of your choice. See Appendix H for ideas.

EXAMPLE PLAN UPDATES STUDiO

This chapter focused on adding functional and decorative trim to a space. While these examples have focused solely on trims in a residential setting, they can be equally applied to commercial projects. Remember to keep installation heights, widths, and finish materials appropriate for each building type in mind when adding these trims to your projects.

Examples from the commercial plan include:
Chair rail
   Conference room
Baseboards
   Throughout

Examples from the residential plan include:
Crown molding
   Hall/Entry
Chair rail
   Living room
Baseboards
   Throughout
Wainscot
   Hall/Entry
   Living room

For your selected project, it is encouraged that you add a variety of millwork trims throughout the space, not only to practice your skills but to create more dynamic designs. It is important to remember that you must have baseboards in every room to protect the bottom of the wall from damage, but the sizes and profiles of all the millwork are up to you.

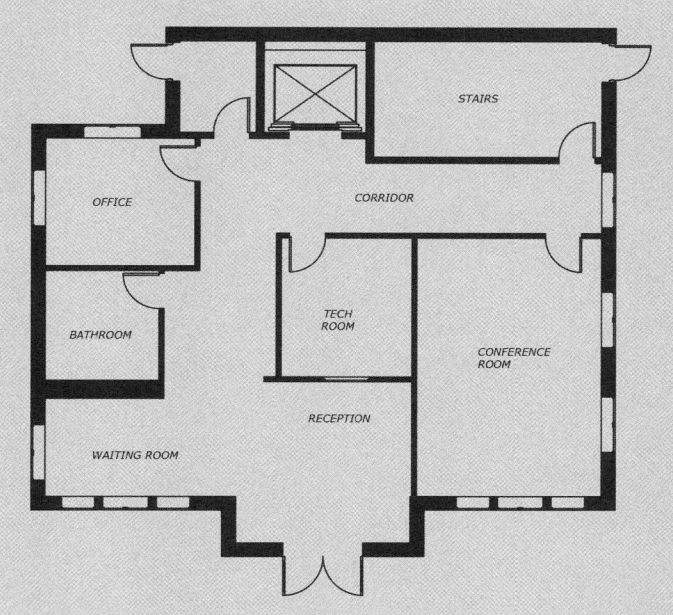

Figure 7.32
Commercial plan after millwork has been added.

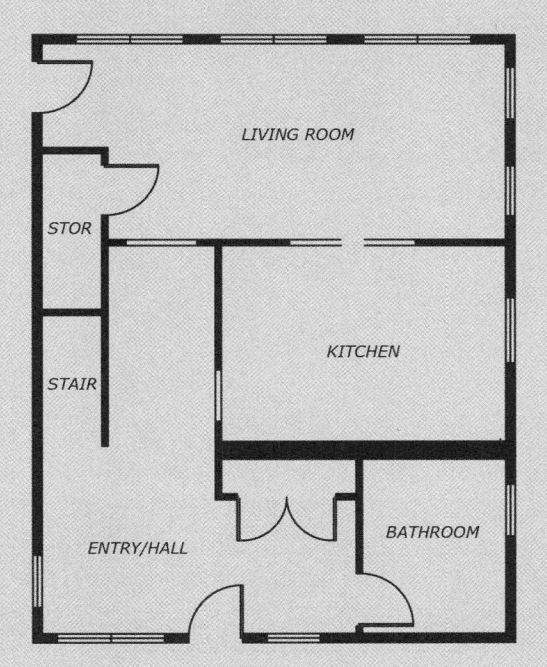

Figure 7.33
Residential plan after millwork has been added.

CHAPTER TERMINOLOGY

baseboard
beadboard
butt joint
chair rail
cornice
crown molding
dado joint
decorative panel
dovetail joint
dowel joint
finger joint
frame and panel wainscot
French dovetail joint
frieze
hollow triangle
joinery
millwork
mitered edge joint
mortise and tenon joint
paneling
plate rail

profile
scarf joint
spline joint

tongue and groove joint
wainscot

MILLWORK CODES

This section will explore the elements used and how to draw construction details for trim and paneling. Below are the ADA standards and the IBC codes that you need to keep in mind when designing and drafting interior millwork.

Table 7.1 ADA Standards for Wall-Mounted Millwork

ADA Code	Topic	Description
307.2	Protrusion limits	Objects mounted 27"-80" AFF can protrude no more than 4" from the wall surface. Handrails may protrude up to 4 1/2".
307.4	Vertical clearance	Vertical clearance must be at least 80" high. Any spaces that are less than 80" must have a guardrail that is at least 27" AFF. Exception made for door frames, which can lower the vertical clearance to 78" AFF.
307.5	Required clear width	Any protruding objects cannot reduce the required clear space.

Table 7.2 IBC Codes for Wall-Mounted Millwork

IBC Code	Topic	Description
803.12	Interior finish stability	Interior finishes, including wall trims, must be fasted to the floor, wall, or ceiling according to manufacturer instructions to ensure that it remains in place during a fire. When furring strips are required, the strips may not exceed 1 3/4".
806.8	Interior floor-wall base	Any floor-wall base that measures less than 6" high must be a Class I or Class II material.
1003.3.4	Trim projections and accessibility	Any trim that extends into an accessible route cannot reduce the minimum clear width requirements.
1005.7.2	Trim projections and means of egress	Trim and wall-mounted decorative elements may project into the means of egress width by 1 1/2" or less.

CHAPTER REFERENCES

Ballast, David Kent. *Interior Construction & Detailing for Designers and Architects*. Belmont, CA: Professional Publications, Inc., 2013.
Ching, Francis D. *Building Construction Illustrated*. New York: John Wiley & Sons, 2014.
DeChiara, Joseph, Julius Panero, and Martin Zelnik. *Time-Saver Standards for Interior Design and Space Planning*. New York: McGraw-Hill, 2001.
International Code Council. *International Building Code, 2015*. Chicago: International Code Council Publications, 2014.
International Code Council. *International Residential Code, 2015*. Chicago: International Code Council Publications, 2014.
Jefferis, Alan. *Residential Design, Drafting, and Detailing*, 2nd ed. Boston: Cengage Learning, 2013.
Kilmer, W. Otie and Rosemary Kilmer. *Construction Drawings and Details for Interiors*. New York: John Wiley & Sons, 2016.
Kruse, Kelsey and Maryrose McGowan. *Interior Graphic Standards*. New York: John Wiley & Sons, 2003.
United States Department of Justice. *2010 ADA Standards for Accessible Design*. Washington, D.C.: Dept. of Justice, 2010.

Cabinetry

CHAPTER 8

CHAPTER OUTCOMES

After completing this chapter you will be able to:

1. Discuss the codes and standards pertaining to base and wall-hung cabinetry, and design spaces, notably kitchens and bathrooms, that adhere to these guidelines.
2. Understand how cabinetry is designed, fit, and anchored for installation.
3. Customize cabinet styles, interior components, and finishes in elevation and section details depending on the needs of the client.

Figure 8.1
A broken *U-shaped* kitchen with base, upper, and wall cabinets along the perimeter and base cabinets within the island.

Figure 8.2
Kitchen with a variety of cabinet styles and varying counter heights.

ABOUT CABINETRY

Cabinets are a type of storage unit constructed from a system of panels, rails, and stiles that can be floor- or wall-mounted. When used in a kitchen, as in the examples for this chapter, the cabinet can be built to accommodate a series of doors, drawers, and shelves, based on the needs of the end user.

Looking first at the **base cabinet**, three solid panels of composite wood are joined together to form a *U*-shape. These are anchored to each other with a series of wood supports, such as cornerblocks and mounting rails. **Cornerblocks** are triangular wedges that, when installed between two pieces of wood, secure those planes at a 90 degree angle. **Mounting rails** are pieces of wood that are installed along the front and back of the assembly and measure the width of the cabinet. While the primary focus of these blocks is to create a surface to attach the countertop to, they also add constructive strength to the cabinet.

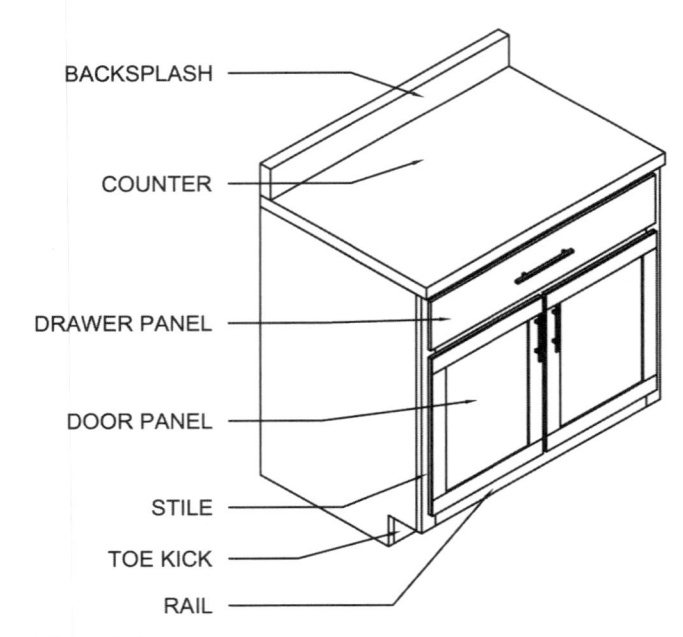

Figure 8.3
Base cabinet axon.

148 | PART II DETAIL DRAWINGS

The face, or front of the cabinet, provides openings for the doors and drawers of the piece. For islands and peninsulas, you may wish to replace the back panel of the cabinet with a second face, allowing access to interior shelves from both sides. The face can be constructed in one of two ways: frameless or face framed. **Frameless cabinet** construction calls for thicker side panels and finished wood supports to be installed across the front, connecting the two sides to each other. Doors can then be installed directly to these supports. This provides a contemporary look with fewer lines and greater access to the interior of the cabinet.

A **face framed cabinet** construction uses a rail and stile system between the structure of the cabinet and the doors. This allows for the interior supports to remain hidden and for the cabinets to have a more finished feel. The horizontal planks, or **rails**, are installed at the top and bottom of the cabinet face, under the counter and above the toe kick respectively. Additional horizontal elements, called **mid rails**, can be used under drawer fronts to help support the drawer. The vertical planks, **stiles**, are installed on either end of the cabinet face and run between the rails. **Mid stiles** can be added as well to help break up the face and allow for a variety of storage options.

The **toe kick** appears at the bottom of the front of the cabinet. This notch, typically 3" to 4" high and deep, creates enough space for the end user to work at the cabinet without damaging the doors or frame by creating a gap for their toes. This feature is used in other types of casework, as seen in Chapter 10.

The **countertop** is the uppermost element of a base cabinet and acts as the work surface of the piece. Counters can be added directly to the top of a base cabinet, attaching to the mounting blocks, or they can be anchored to the wall by bracing it to the studs. Stone slabs and wood composites with a laminate finish are common countertop materials, but plastics and metals are also available.

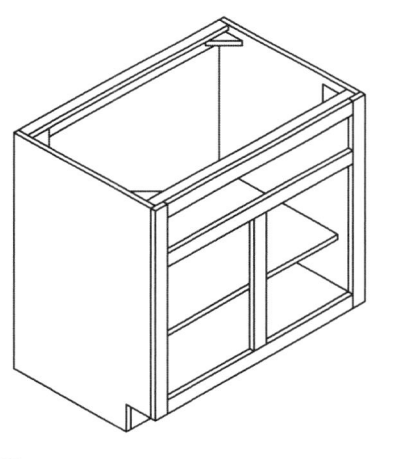

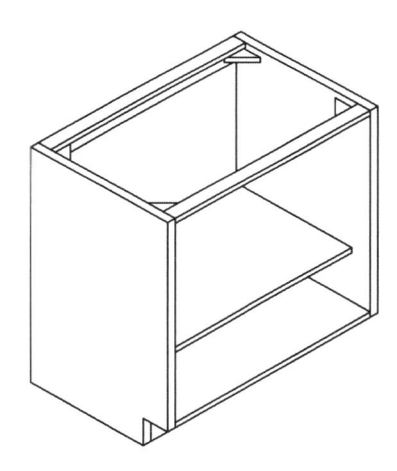

Ⓐ FACE FRAMED　　**Ⓑ FRAMELESS**

Figure 8.4
Cabinet face styles.

TOE KICK

BACKSPLASH 4" MIN

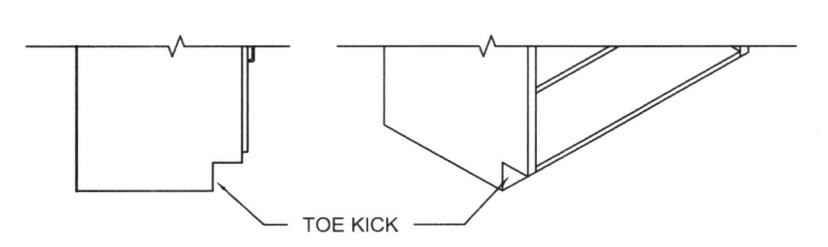

COUNTER

Figure 8.5
Toe kick in elevation and axon.

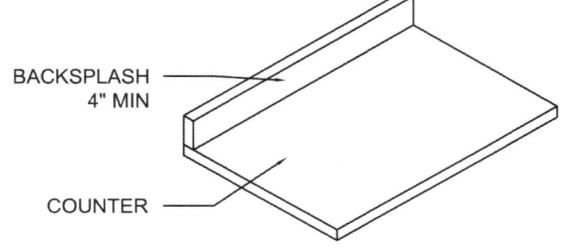

Figure 8.6
Countertop and backsplash.

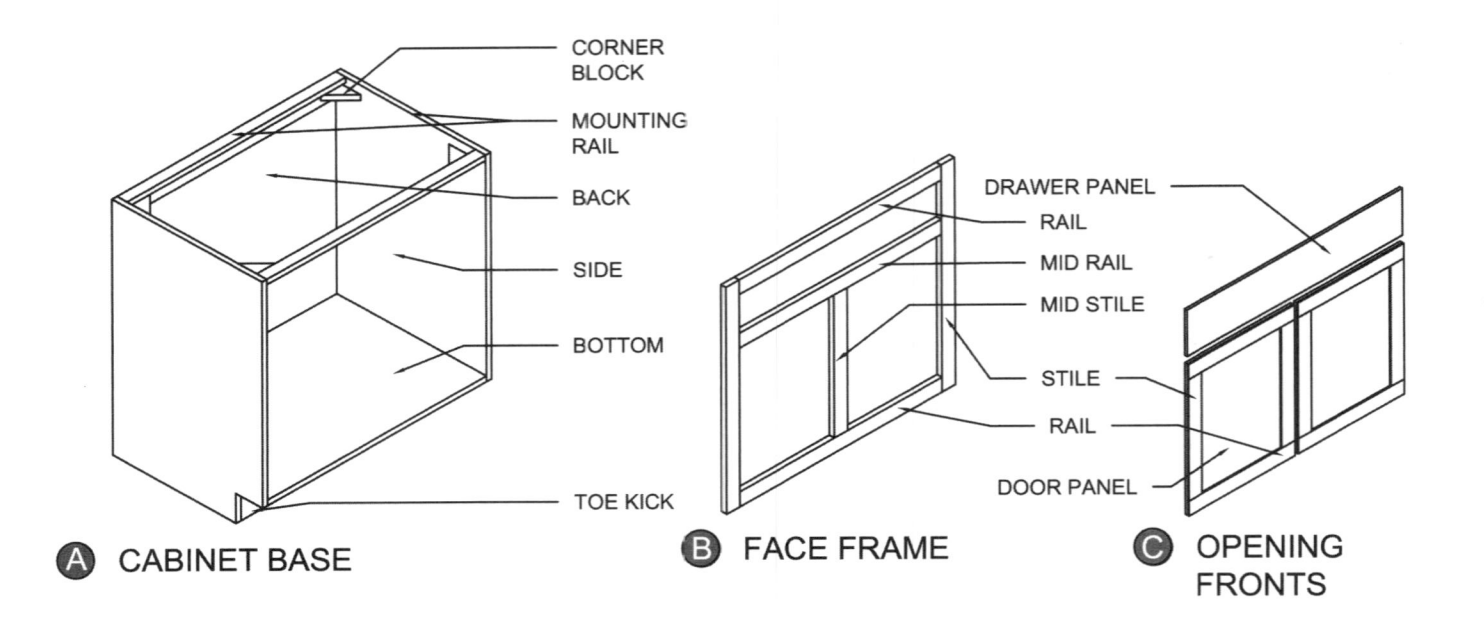

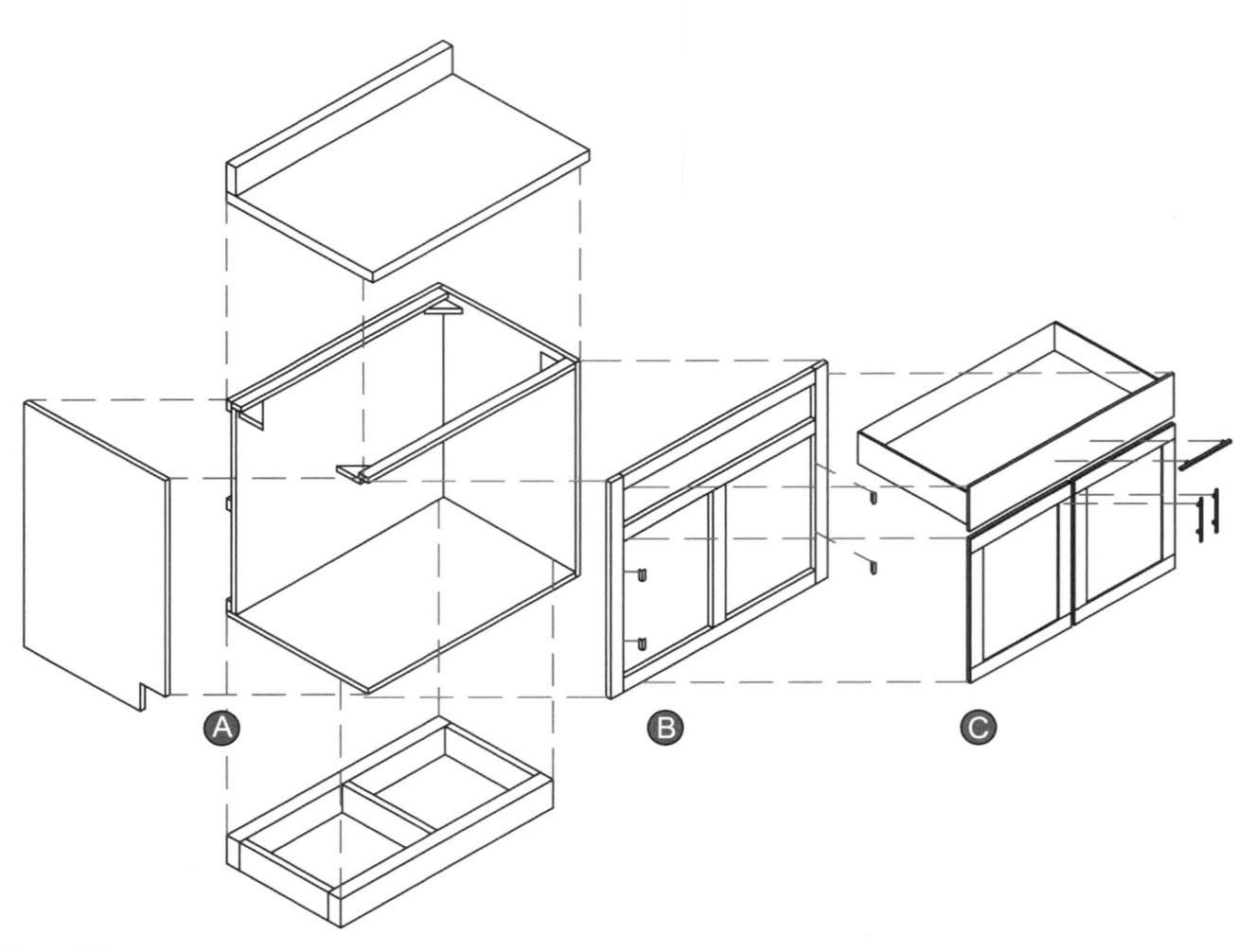

Figure 8.7
Base cabinet exploded axon.

150 | PART II DETAIL DRAWINGS

While the countertop can terminate flush with the cabinet below, as is typical when it abuts a refrigerator, there is usually some sort of extension of the counter past the cabinet. When it extends past the back or to the side, the extension can be seen as a peninsula or an island and is an extension of the work surface. These extensions can be supported by brackets or with individual legs depending on how large the counter is. Any counter extension over the face is known as a **counter edge**, a 1" to 1 ½" overhang that protects the drawer and door fronts from water and food damage. There are numerous profiles for the termination of the countertop, allowing for curves for various patterns and sizes to be used, which protect the end user from being hurt when bumping into the surface.

When installed along a wall, a backsplash should also be used to protect the gypsum board from damage. The **backsplash** is usually a 4" high continuation of the countertop material that can be mounted on to the counter surface, as seen in the examples in this chapter. Custom tile backsplashes can be applied directly to the wall, as seen in Chapter 10.

Wall cabinets are storage units that are elevated off the floor and mounted to the wall. When installed above a base cabinet, they typically hang 4'-8" above finished floor. While constructed in a similar manner to the base cabinets, there are fewer supports needed as wall cabinets are smaller and do not receive the same weight and strain as the working surface of the

Figure 8.8
The installation of a new countertop, which will be supported by the mounting rails.

STUDIO Animation 8.1 Exploded base cabinet

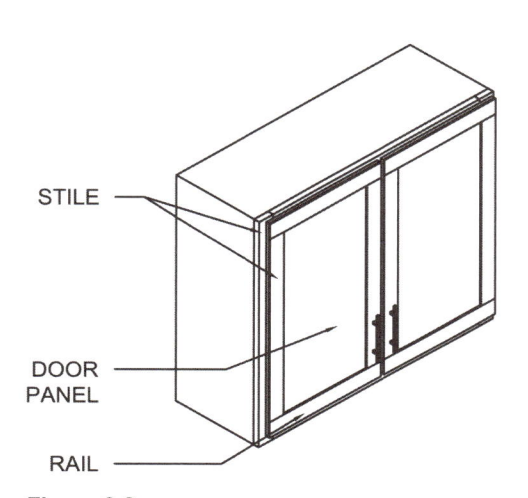

Figure 8.9
Wall cabinet axon.

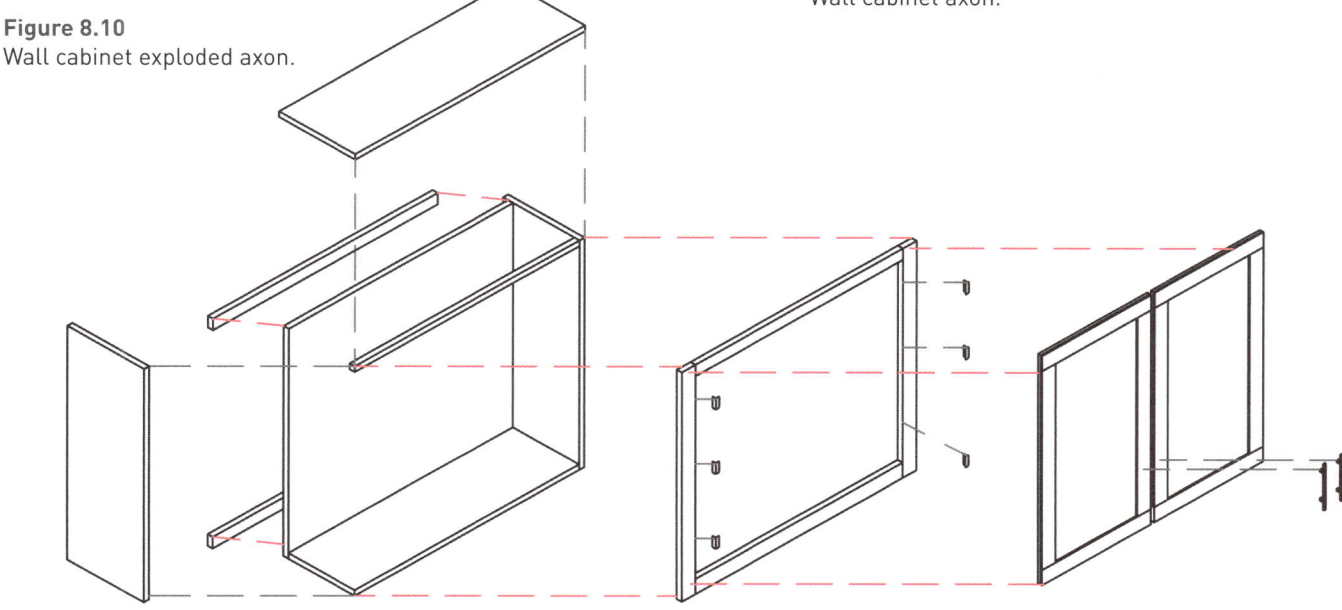

Figure 8.10
Wall cabinet exploded axon.

CHAPTER 8 CABINETRY | 151

base. The box will still have two sides, a back, and a face; however, the mounting rails and the cornerblocks are not present. Instead, interior or exterior **anchoring rails** are installed. These horizontal planks run the width of the cabinet and are located along the top and bottom of the back panel as a connection point for three parts of the cabinet, adding strength to the construction, and creating a plane for wall fasteners. Wall cabinets are also not as deep as base cabinets. As they are typically hung above a work surface, they are usually only 10" to 12" deep to allow for clear work space below.

When possible, cabinetry should be planned for during the early stages of construction in order to ensure that appropriate structural support is provided. In addition to being secured to partition studs, casework is also anchored to **cabinet blocking**. Created out of framing lumber or aluminum measuring at least 2" × 6", the cabinet blocks are installed horizontally between studs within the cavity of the partition, typically at about 33", 54", and 78" high, or aligned with the casework's mounting rails. The cabinet blocking provides a structural plane for the screws to be drilled into. Additionally, **nail plates** should be added along the side of the blocking opposite the cabinet to protect electrical and plumbing lines. Nail plates are plated steel panels that prevent the screw from accidently piercing through the blocking and affecting systems that may be on the other side of the partition cavity.

Cabinet installation requires accurate attention to levelness and support for the project to be successful. The casework should be checked repeatedly for evenness, which can easily be rectified if there is an error. Floors and casework that are uneven can be corrected by inserting **shims** during the installation process. These thin strips of wood fill gaps and elevate portions of the cabinet in small increments so that minor spacing and flatness issues do not interfere with the project. Once the component has been moved into place and shimmed to levelness, it can be scribed to adjust for any unevenness with the wall that it is to be mounted to. **Scribing** is to trim away a portion of the object so that it fits snuggly against the wall while maintaining evenness. In this process, a compass or carpenter's pencil is laid flat against the wall and the side of the shimmed cabinet. While maintaining even pressure, a line is drawn from the top of the cabinet to the floor. Any part of the cabinet that falls between the line and

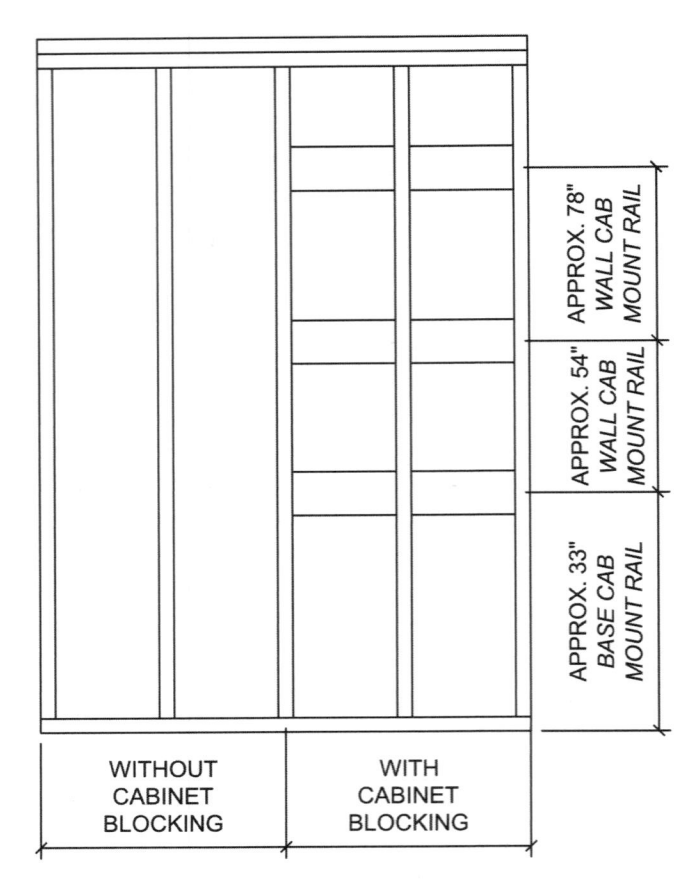

Figure 8.11
Interior partition as typically constructed (left) and with cabinet blocking (right).

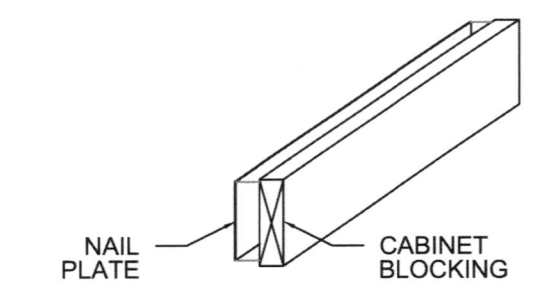

Figure 8.12
Axon featuring a cabinet block backed by a nail plate.

the wall will then be trimmed or sanded off to ensure a perfect fit between the casework and the wall. Comparably, any gaps that appear between the cabinets and the wall that cannot be scribed can be covered with a **filler bar**, which is a piece of wood supplied by the cabinet's manufacturer to match the casework's finish. These bars can be left plain, but they typically will have a design or pattern carved into them to create a decorative, finished appearance.

Cabinetry must be installed in a particular manner to maintain levelness and support. Beginning with the upper cabinets, a **ledger board** should first be installed. This piece of wood should be temporarily mounted about 54" to 56" above the finished floor and will act as a support shelf for the upper cabinets to sit on while they are being installed. Once in place, the cabinet can be shimmed or scribed to ensure levelness and then screws can be drilled through the anchoring rails to the wall studs to mount them. Similarly, floor cabinets must be shimmed or scribed to account for floor or wall unevenness prior to being bolted to the studs. Floor cabinets that are not to be mounted to a wall are required to be placed over **mounting blocks**: 2" × 4" pieces of wood that are anchored to the floor.

When used in combination, base and wall cabinets create an efficient storage and work surface system. Due to variety of sizes, designs, and codes, several elements need to be considered when coordinating cabinetry projects.

First, the style of the cabinet will greatly impact the look and feel of the space. Any carvings or panels present will need to be represented in your drawings, and materials should be annotated. For style ideas, see Appendix H.

Second, the size of the specified cabinet will impact how you choose to layout the pieces in the space. Once you know the dimensions of the kitchen and how many linear feet are available for your project, you may wish to mix and match a variety of cabinet types and widths to determine the layout that is most efficient for your client.

Finally, whether or not the end user needs a standard height or accessible height cabinets should be determined. As seen in Figure 8.15 and Table 8.1, there is a range of heights, depths, and thicknesses that impact the detail drawings.

Figure 8.13
A kitchen cabinet being marked for scribing. The portion to the right of the line will be trimmed away.

Figure 8.14
Contractors installing an upper cabinet. The screws are drilled through the mounting rail in the back of the cabinet to attach it to the wall stud.

CHAPTER 8 CABINETRY | 153

Table 8.1 Combined Cabinet Dimensions for Standard Heights and Accessible Heights

Item	Letter	Standard Range	Accessible Range
Base Cabinet Height	A	36"	34" MAX
Clearance Height	B	18" MIN 24" above sink/stove	No requirement Wall cabinet 48" MAX AFF
Wall Cabinet Height	C	18"-36"	No requirement Bottom 48" MAX AFF
Base Cabinet Depth	D	24"	24"
Countertop Depth	E	25 1/2"	25 1/2"
Wall Cabinet Depth	F	12"	No requirement
Toe Kick Height	G	4"	9" MAX
Toe Kick Depth	H	3"-4"	7"
Knee Space (if applicable)	I	24 1/2"	27"
Countertop Thickness	J	1 1/4"- 1 1/2"	No requirement

Figure 8.15
Cabinet diagram with key dimension locations.

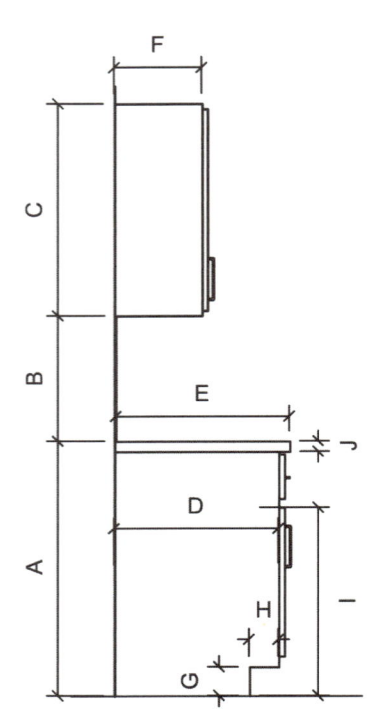

Figure 8.16
Residential kitchen with accessible counter and cabinet heights.

1. The **work triangle** is the design concept that the major appliances (refrigerator, sink, and stove) are close enough for an easy transition from one to the next during the cooking process but spaced out enough that one can still move easily and utilize counter space. The key points to know for the work triangle are:

   - The sum of the three legs of the triangle must fall between 13'-0" and 26'-0".
   - Each leg of the triangle must be at least 4'-0" but no more than 9'-0".
   - Use a clear path when planning the triangle; anything that intersects one of the legs should encroach no more than 1'-0" into the space.

All of this work understanding and determining the type and combination of cabinets and counters to specify is also impacted by the space itself and the selected layout of the kitchen. Figure 8.17 illustrates the various layouts that are typically available for the end user. The following are three things to keep in mind when looking through these layouts:

Figure 8.17 Kitchen layouts.

① Galley Kitchen

② U-Shaped Kitchen
1 entrance

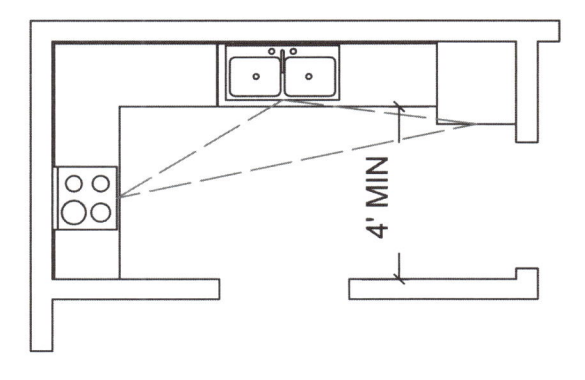

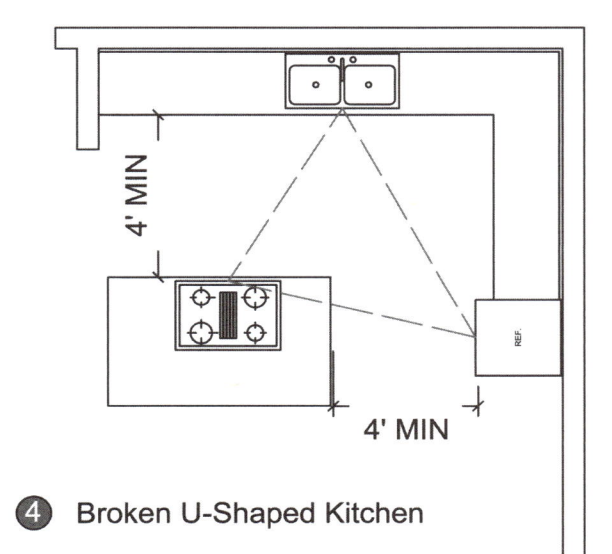

③ L-Shaped Kitchen

④ Broken U-Shaped Kitchen

2. What type of space does your client have? Is it long and narrow or large and open? It is important to ensure that there is enough room for the end user to maneuver efficiently and without obstruction. While counter and storage space is always desired, it may not be practical to add too many elements if the room is tight.
3. If a barrier-free design is preferred, make sure that you plan for the wider paths of travel prior to beginning your drawings.

While it may be a struggle to ensure that all codes are met when working on a layout, remember that the codes and standards are there to benefit the well-being and happiness of the end user and should be thoughtfully integrated into your space.

IBC
When designing a kitchen, remember that there must be at least 3'-0" of clear space between the face of one cabinet and an appliance or face of another cabinet on the other side of the room.

ADA
Barrier-free design calls for at least 3'-0", but preferably 4'-0", of clear space between appliances or cabinet fronts.

Provide two entrances to kitchens when possible. *U*-shaped layouts will require at least a 5'-0" turning radius at its single entrance.

CHAPTER 8 CABINETRY | 155

Drafting cabinetry

The examples from this chapter will focus on the individual base cabinet, wall cabinet, and countertop pieces and how to combine these elements for kitchen details. While all of these components will be taken from the residential project file only, both project types have cabinets in their kitchens and bathrooms. Keep in mind that what is shown here is based on the author's specifications, typical sizes, and installation heights. You should be as creative as possible with the design of the cabinets while maintaining the sizes and heights that are industry standard.

The details shown for the individual units will show one 24" × 24" base cabinet and one 24" × 12" wall cabinet. The details showing a combined installation will have three of each cabinet type.

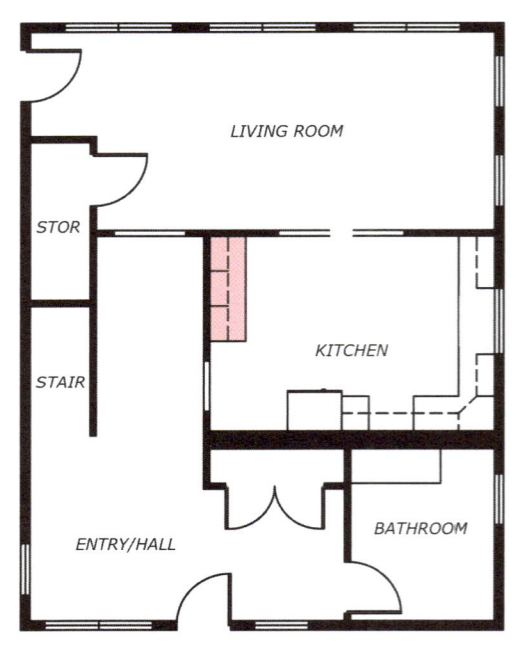

Figure 8.18
Residential plan with focus cabinets located in the kitchen.

Base cabinet, elevation

STEP 1
As this example is for a standard range cabinet, the height from the floor to the top of the counter is 36". However, in order to draw the frame of the base cabinet alone, you will need to subtract the countertop thickness from this height:

Standard height – Counter thickness = Base cabinet height

$$36" - 1\,1/2" = \mathbf{34\,1/2"}$$

Draw a vertical line 34 1/2" up from the floor to indicate the left side of the cabinet. Next, measure 24" to the left of this line and draw another vertical line 34 1/2" up from the floor for the right side of the cabinet.

Add the toe kick by drawing a horizontal line 4" up from the floor, running between the verticals.

STEP 2
Add the countertop by drawing a horizontal line across the top of the two verticals, extending the line 1" on each end to account for the nosing. The line will measure 2'-2".

Measure up 1 1/2" from this new horizontal line and draw a second. This will indicate the thickness of the counter. Draw a third horizontal 4" above the counter for the top of the backsplash. Connect the ends of the lines to one another.

STEP 3
In this view, you will not be able to see where the door and drawer panels overlap the rail and stiles of the frame. Because of this, you need only draw in the panels to indicate that there are openings. Measure inward 1" from the edges of the cabinet and draw vertical lines to show where the panels overlap the stiles. Then measure 3/8" down from the bottom of the counter top and connect the new verticals to form the top of the drawer panel. Draw another horizontal 6" down to create the bottom of the drawer, and another 1" down from there to make the top of the door. The door height measures 1'-10", meaning that there will be a 1 1/8" reveal of the bottom rail.

STEP 4
Add the handles of your choice.

STEP 5
Create a shelf inside of the cabinet. For this example, there is one central shelf. Make sure to use dashed lines to indicate that the shelf is present behind the door.

STEP 6
To show the way the cabinet opens, a phantom line can be drawn from the top corner of the handle

side of the door to the midpoint of the hinge side of the door. Repeat this phantom line from the bottom corner of the handle side to the midpoint of the hinge side.

STEP 7
Finalize the detail by adding any necessary dimensions and annotations.

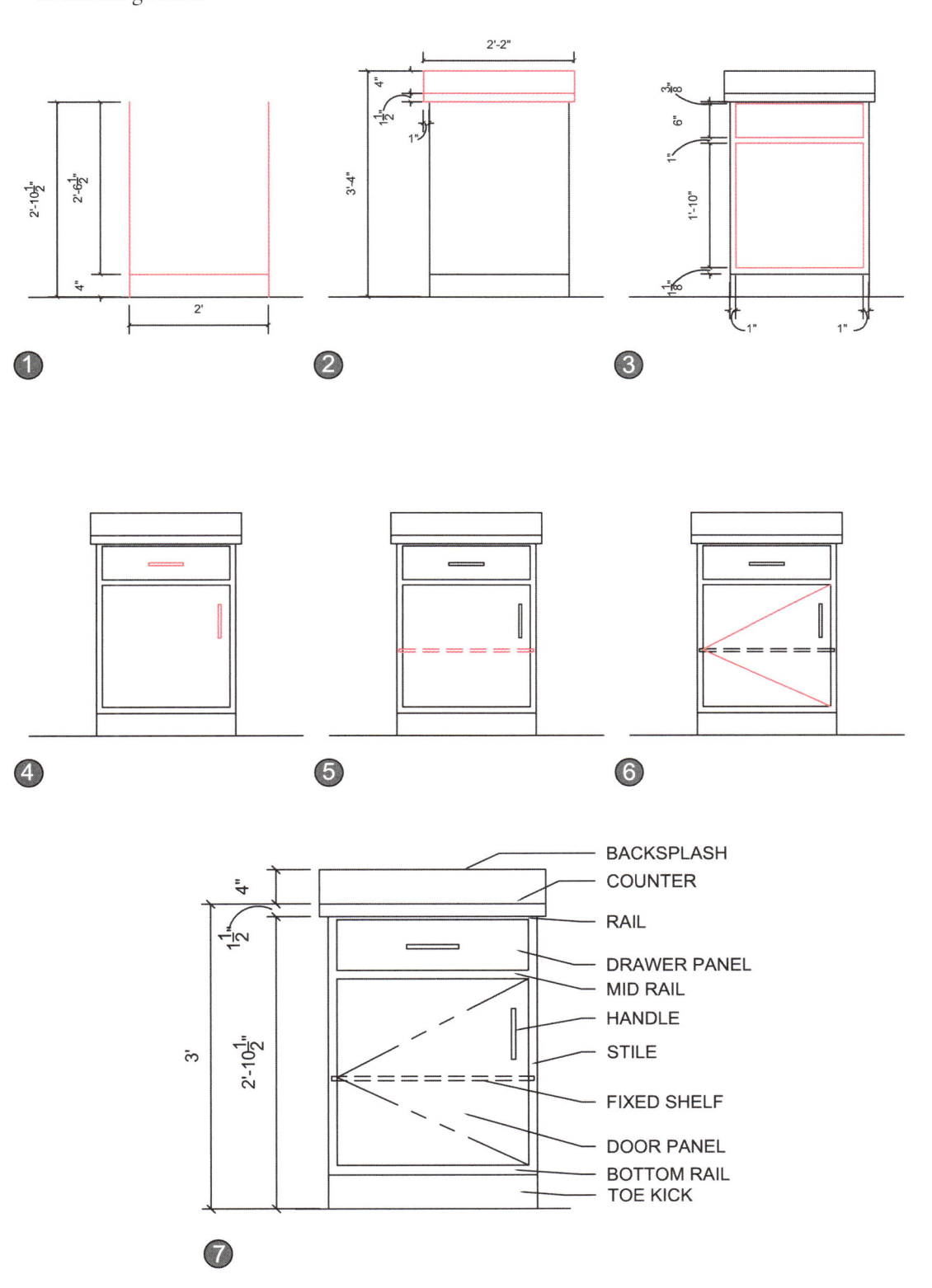

Figure 8.19
Base cabinet elevation, Steps 1–7.

Base cabinet, section

STEP 1
Set up your drawing so that you have a floor plane and wall plane to "anchor" the cabinet to. Measure 3'-0" up the wall and create a tick mark. Draw a second tick mark 1 1/2" below the first. These ticks represent the thickness of the countertop. Extend lines out from these tick marks measuring 2'-1" and connect the ends of these lines. This portion will represent the work surface of the countertop.

Add the backsplash by drawing a rectangle measuring 4" high by 1 1/2" wide along the wall.

STEP 2
Create two vertical guidelines where the front face of the cabinet will appear. As the base cabinet is 24" deep, measure 1" in from the nose of the countertop for the first line. Draw the second guideline another 3/4" in from the nose. The space between these guidelines will become the cabinet face and can be used as a baseline for the development of the remainder of the detail.

STEP 3
Draw the toe kick at the base of the cabinet by creating two lines: the first a horizontal extending 4" from the outer guideline into the cabinet and the second from the edge of this line down 4" to the floor.

STEP 4
Form the bottom of the cabinet with a horizontal line running from the inner guideline to the wall 4" above the floor. Measure up 3/4" and draw a second horizontal line to indicate this board's thickness.

STEP 5
2" × 4" support blocks are needed under the bottom of the cabinet, the first located along the wall and the second 3/8" in from the toe kick.

STEP 6
Draw interior mounting rails as rectangles measuring 3 1/2" × 3/4" in size just under the countertop, one at the wall and one at the first guideline. Using the same size rectangles for the anchoring rails along the wall, draw one directly below the mounting rail and the other touching the bottom of the cabinet.

STEP 7
To create the back panel, draw a vertical line alongside the anchoring rails from the underside of the counter to the bottom of the cabinet. This should measure 3/4" from the wall. Indicate the panel's thickness by drawing a second vertical 3/8" in from the first.

STEP 8
Moving to the front of the cabinet, create the drawer panel by adding a tick mark on the outermost guideline 3/8" below the counter. Draw a vertical line extending down 6" from this mark. Duplicate this line 3/4" away from the guideline and connect the verticals to finish the panel.

STEP 9
Show the drawer extending into the cabinet. The size of this drawer can depend on your design choices or the manufacturer's specifications. To illustrate this, draw a horizontal line approximately 1 1/2" below the top of the drawer panel, and the other two 1/8" apart, about 3/4" up from the bottom of the panel.

Then, connect the topmost and bottommost of these lines to illustrate the back of the drawer. Duplicate this line inward 1/8" to create the thickness of this board. Keep in mind that when you finalize this drawing, the bottom and back of the drawer are in section and should be shown with a heavier lineweight than the topmost line, which remains in elevation.

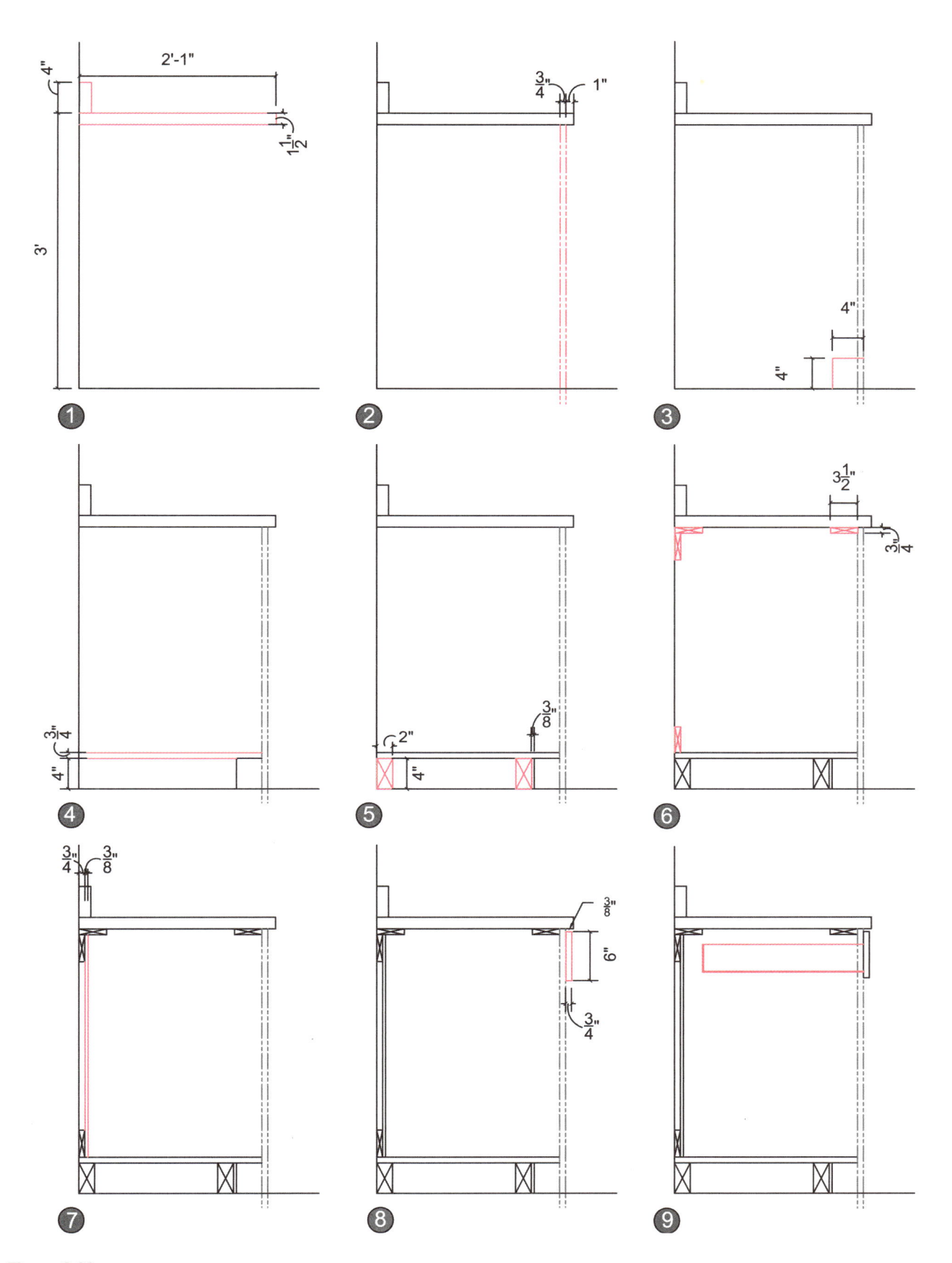

Figure 8.20
Base cabinet section, Steps 1–9.

CHAPTER 8 CABINETRY

STEP 10

Draw the door panel in the same manner as you did the drawer panel. This rectangle will measure 1'-10" high and be spaced 1" down from the bottom of the drawer front.

STEP 11

Add two additional supports within the body of the cabinet, both measuring 3 $1/2$" × 3/4". The first should align with the bottom of the drawer and the first guideline and will act as a support for both the drawer and the mid rail. The second aligns with the bottom of the cabinet and the first guideline to support the bottom rail.

STEP 12

Next, add the rails and stile that can be seen in this view by hardlining portions of the guidelines. As seen in the illustration for this step in Figure 8.21, there will be a top rail measuring 1 $1/2$" under the counter, a mid rail under the drawer, and a bottom rail aligned with the base of the cabinet, each measuring 2". When the drawing is finalized, these rails will appear with a heavier lineweight, as they are in section.

The stile in this view will appear with a lighter lineweight, as it is in elevation. Aside from the portion of the guideline that runs through the drawer, the guidelines can be changed to continuous lines. Any portion of these guides outside of the cabinet can now be erased.

STEP 13

Much like the drawer, interior shelving can be added at your discretion or at the direction of the manufacturer. Here, a fixed shelf has been added to the cabinet by showing two rectangles. The top rectangle represents the shelf itself and will appear with a heavy lineweight in the finalized drawing. The bottom rectangle represents a support for the shelf and will be seen in elevation.

Add a 3 $1/2$" × 3/4" anchoring rail for the shelf to attach to.

STEP 14

Finalize the detail by adding any necessary dimensions, annotations, materials, and a partition assembly along the back of the cabinet. Lineweights should be adjusted to match the standards established in Part I of this text, with heavier lineweights used on objects that are being cut through and lighter lineweights used for material textures.

ADA

When designing an accessible residential kitchen, countertops should measure 34" high with clearance for the end user's knees. (*ADA 804.4.3*).

Dining counters must measure between 28" and 34" high. (*ADA 902.3*).

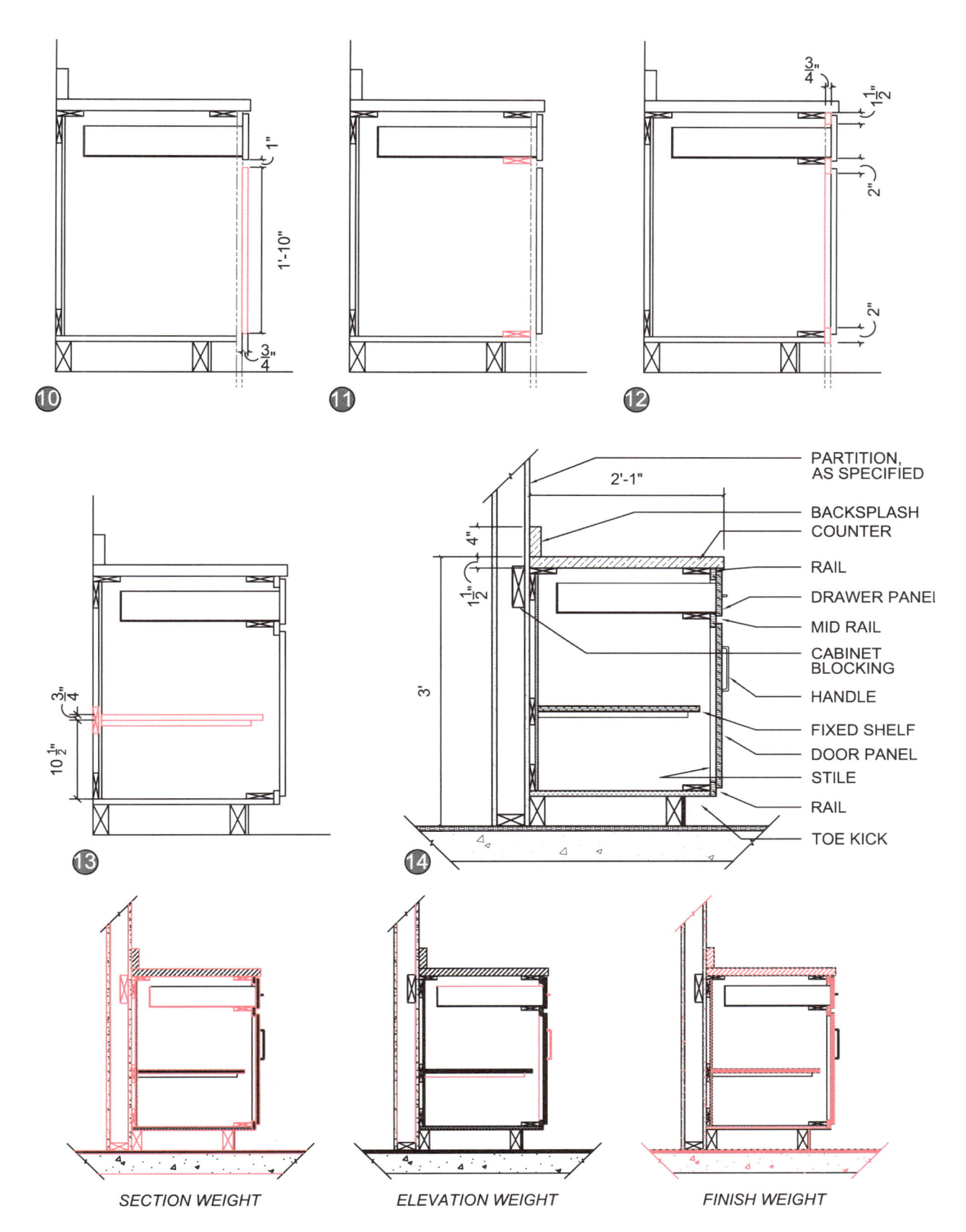

Figure 8.21
Base cabinet section, Steps 10–14.

CHAPTER 8 CABINETRY | 161

Wall cabinet, elevation

STEP 1
Draw a rectangle measuring 2'-6" high by 2'-0" wide to form the outline of the wall cabinet.

STEP 2
Add the door by creating a second rectangle 1" in from each side of the first. This new rectangle should measure 2'-4" × 1'-10".

STEP 3
Add the handles of your choice.

STEP 4
Create shelves inside of the cabinet. For this example, there are two equally spaced shelves. Make sure to used dashed lines to indicate that they are present behind the door.

STEP 5
To show the way the cabinet opens, a phantom line can be drawn from the top corner of the handle side of the door to the midpoint of the hinge side of the door. Repeat this phantom line from the bottom corner of the handle side to the midpoint of the hinge side.

STEP 6
Finalize the detail by adding any necessary dimensions and annotations.

Hand
Use your trace paper! It will ensure that you are happy with all of the elements in the detail and allow you to transfer the final drawing to vellum with fewer mistakes. Once you are on the vellum, you can fix the lineweights and notations without needing to worry about having to erase or lighten, as you've already made those decisions.

CAD
Draw elements that appear in section on a different layer than those that appear in elevation. This will allow you to assign a different lineweight to each layer so that you will not need to select individual lines to adjust later. You can also give each of these layers a different color to make them more distinguishable from one another.

Revit
Use the components that Revit provides you with for your cabinets. Once you have selected a cabinet, you can edit the size, profile, and finishes to customize the look to your liking.

The program will automatically generate an elevation for you, but when you create a section through a cabinet, it will only draw the frame without any of the shelves or drawers, supports, or panel thicknesses. Open the section view for the cabinet and select Model Lines from the Annotate tab. Use these lines to detail the interior elements of your cabinets. When one of these lines is highlighted, you can change the lineweight under Line Style in the Modify tab that appears. Medium represents elements in section and thin can show those that appear in elevation. Wide line is very thick and should be used sparingly.

The program also supplies you with components to create the interior elements of the cabinets. Under the Annotate tab, locate the Detail panel and drop-down the options for Component. Here, you will find Detail Components, which will open a Modify/Place ribbon and allow you to click on Load Family to select items from the Detail Items folder.

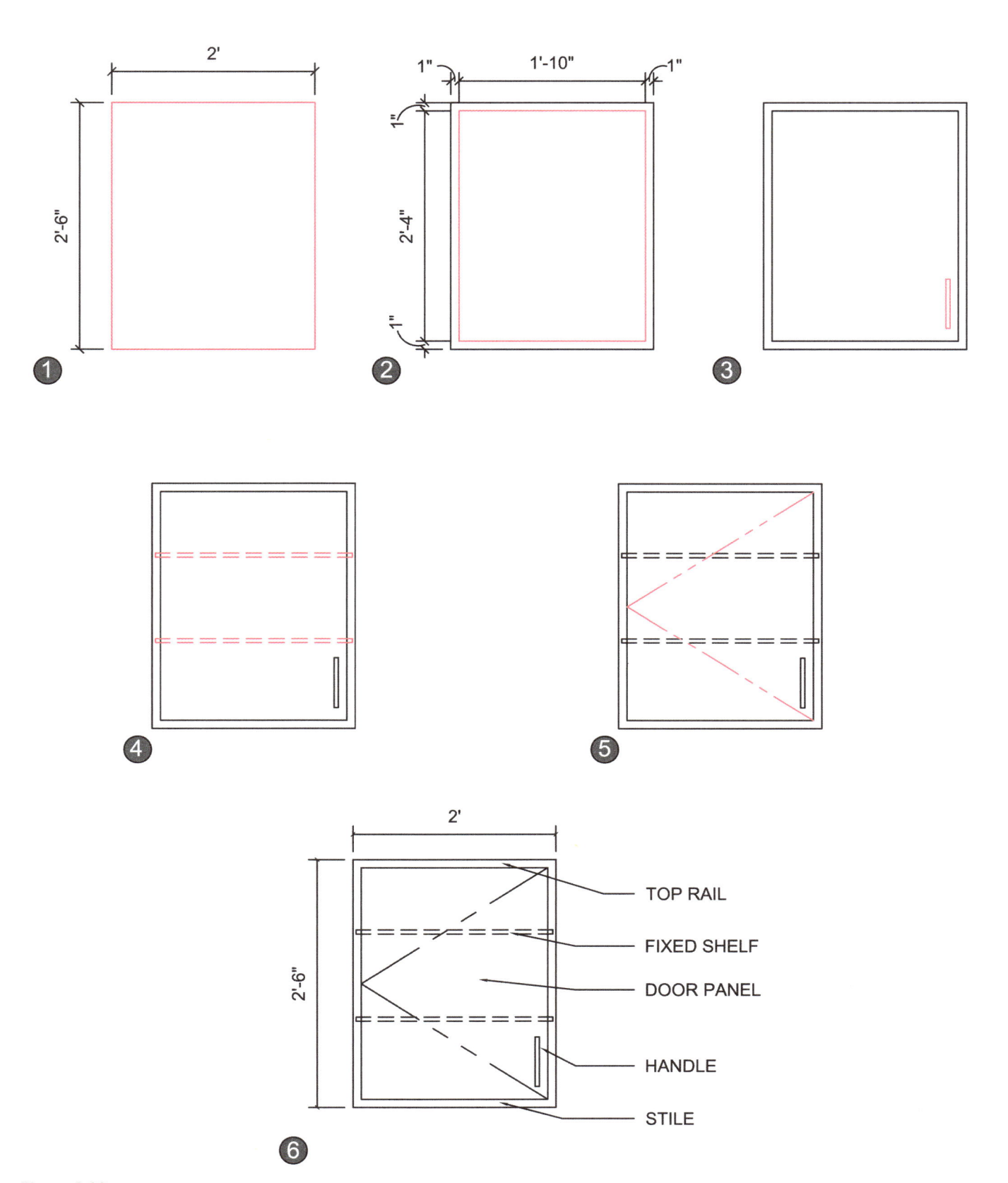

Figure 8.22
Wall cabinet elevation, Steps 1–6.

Wall cabinet, section

STEP 1
Set up your drawing so that you have a wall plane to "anchor" the cabinet to. Draw a vertical line measuring 2'-6", then draw a 11 1/4" horizontal line at each end of the vertical. These lines form the top, bottom, and back of the cabinet.

Add one vertical guideline running past the end of the horizontal lines and a second guideline 3/4" away from the first.

STEP 2
Indicate the thickness of the top and bottom of the cabinet by drawing lines spanning from the back of the cabinet to the first guideline. These lines should be 3/4" away from the cabinet's outer frame.

STEP 3
Draw anchoring rails as rectangles measuring 3 1/2" × 3/4" along the leftmost line, one directly below the cabinet top and the other touching the bottom of the cabinet. Add a vertical line running along the inner edge of each of these rails and then a second vertical 3/8" away from it. These two new lines illustrate the thickness of the back panel.

STEP 4
Moving to the front of the cabinet, add the rails by hardlining portions of the guidelines. As seen in the illustration for this step in Figure 8.23, there will be two rails measuring 1 1/2" high at top and bottom of the cabinet. Draw these rails in between the guidelines. When the drawing is finalized, these rails will appear with a heavier lineweight as they are in section.

STEP 5
The stile in this view will appear with a lighter lineweight as it is in elevation. Hardline the portion of the guidelines that run between the rails to form the stile. Any portion of these guides outside of the cabinet can now be erased.

STEP 6
Draw the door panel as a rectangle that measures 3/4" thick and 2'-4" high, meaning that the rail reveals will measure 1".

STEP 7
Interior shelving can be added at your discretion or at the direction of the manufacturer. Here, two fixed shelves have been added to the cabinet by showing each formed by two rectangles. The top rectangle represents the shelf itself and will appear with a heavy lineweight in the finalized drawing. The bottom rectangle represents a support for the shelf and will be seen in elevation. These shelves have been evenly spaced.

Add 3 1/2" × 3/4" anchoring rails for the shelves to attach to.

STEP 8
Finalize the detail by adding any necessary dimensions, annotations, materials, and a partition assembly along the back of the cabinet. Lineweights should be adjusted to match the standards established in Part I of this text, with heavier lineweights used on objects that are being cut through and lighter lineweights used for material textures.

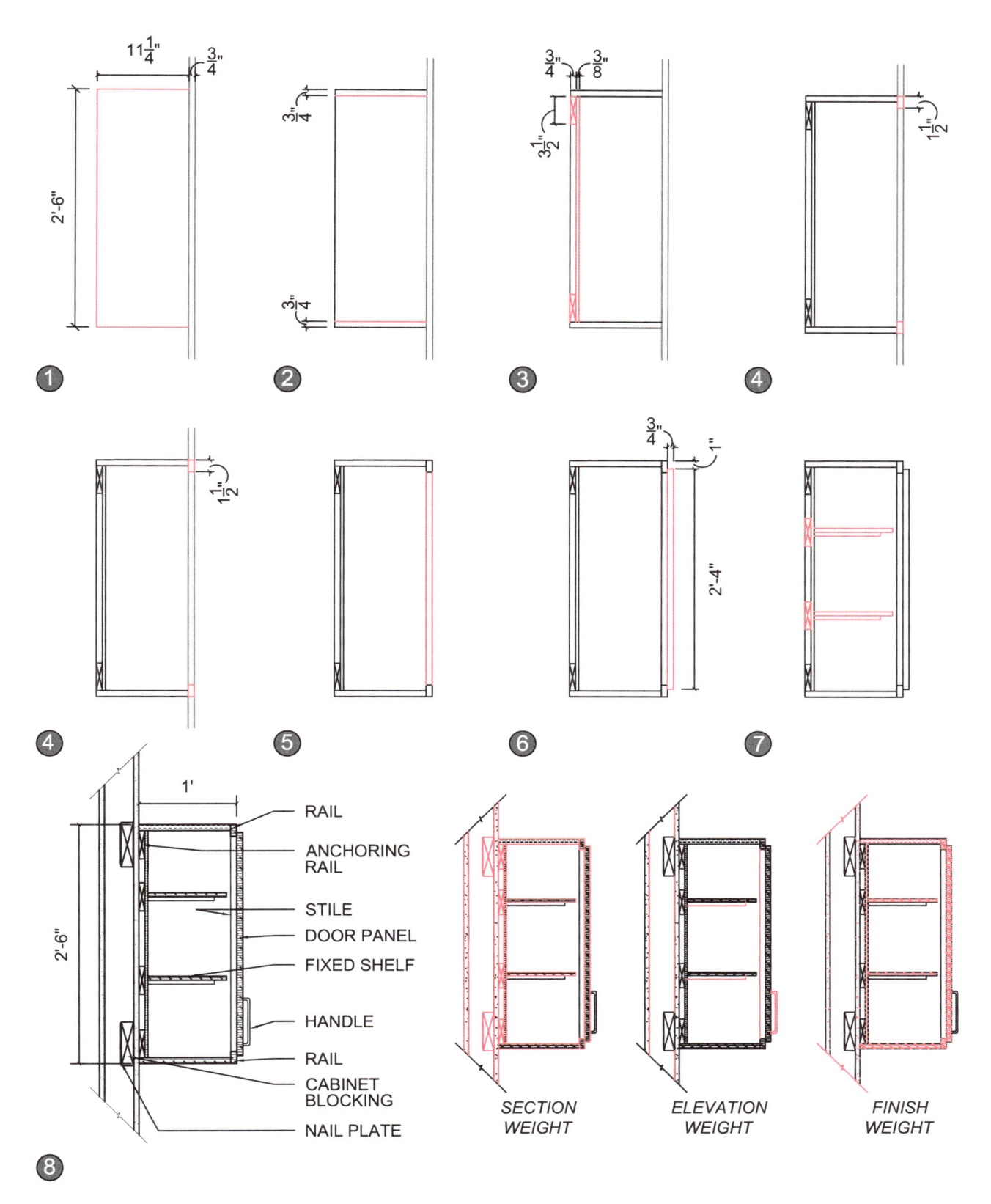

Figure 8.23
Wall cabinet section, Steps 1–8.

CHAPTER 8 CABINETRY | 165

Base/wall combination, elevation

STEP 1
Draw a horizontal line for the floor plane and a horizontal line for the ceiling. An additional ceiling line should appear below the first to represent the soffit height that was added in the residential project kitchen file.

STEP 2
Add the base cabinets you have drawn in elevation. As seen in this example, additional cabinet units have been added to the single unit drawn earlier in this chapter.

STEP 3
Block out 1'-6" of clearance space to appear between the base cabinet and the wall cabinet above.

STEP 4
Add the wall cabinets you have drawn in elevation. As seen in this example, additional cabinet units have been added to the single unit drawn earlier in this chapter.

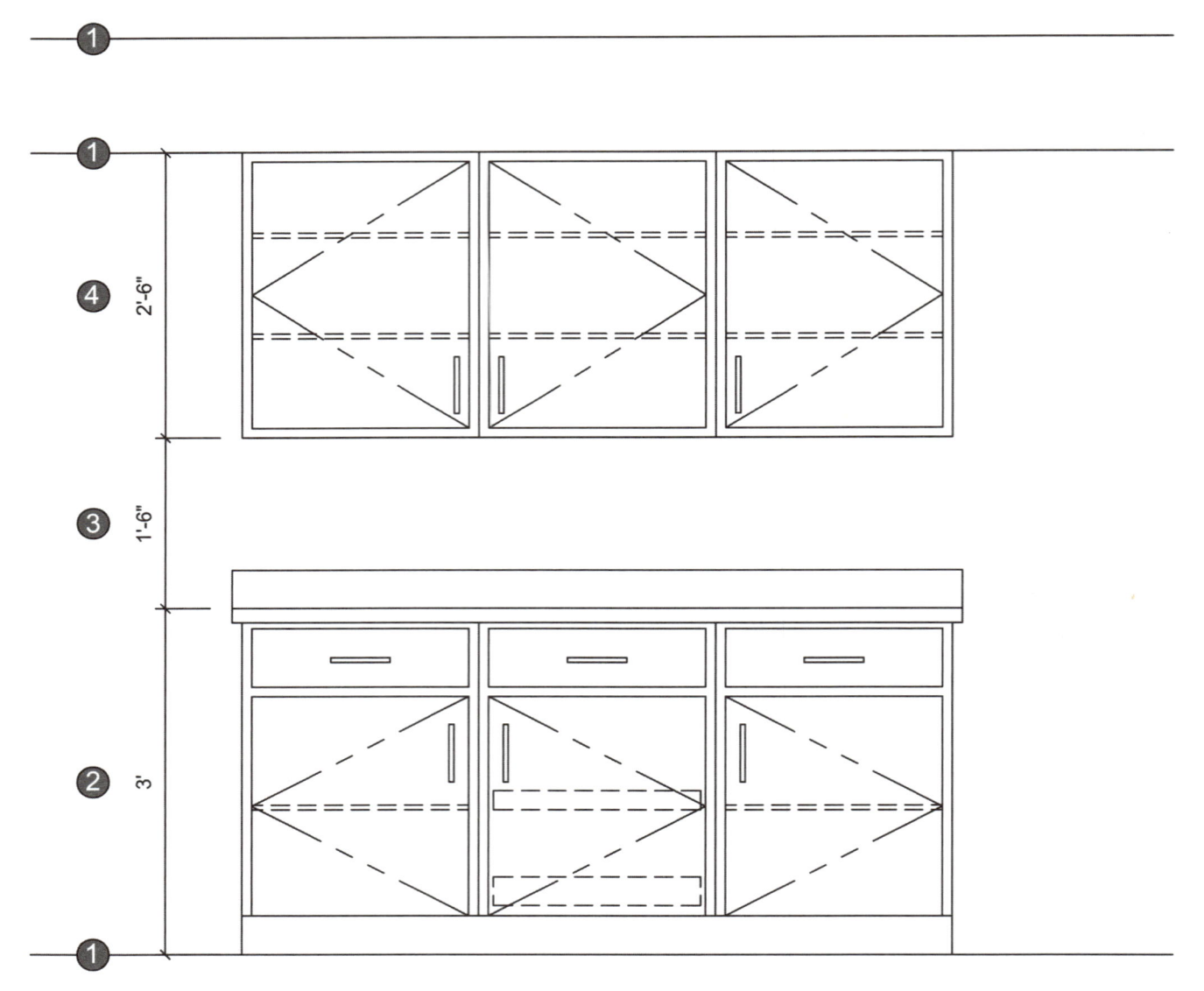

Figure 8.24
Wall and base cabinets, elevation.

STUD!O Animation 8.2 Base and wall cabinet details

Base/wall combination, section

STEP 1
Create the framework (floor, partition, and ceiling) for the cabinets to be placed in to. Based on the example from the residential kitchen used for this section view, there needs to be a soffit 1'-0" below the ceiling. Remember to include the cabinet blocking and nail plates to the interior cavity of the partition. For examples, see Chapter 5 for wall sections and Chapter 6 for ceiling details.

STEP 2
Add the base cabinet you drew in section. Lineweights should distinguish section elements from elevation.

STEP 3
Block out 1'-6" of clearance space to appear between the base cabinet and the wall cabinet above.

STEP 4
Add the wall cabinet you drew in section.

STEP 5
Finalize the detail by adding any necessary dimensions, annotations, and materials. Lineweights should be adjusted to match the standards established in Part I of this text, with heavier lineweights used on objects that are being cut through and lighter lineweights used for material textures.

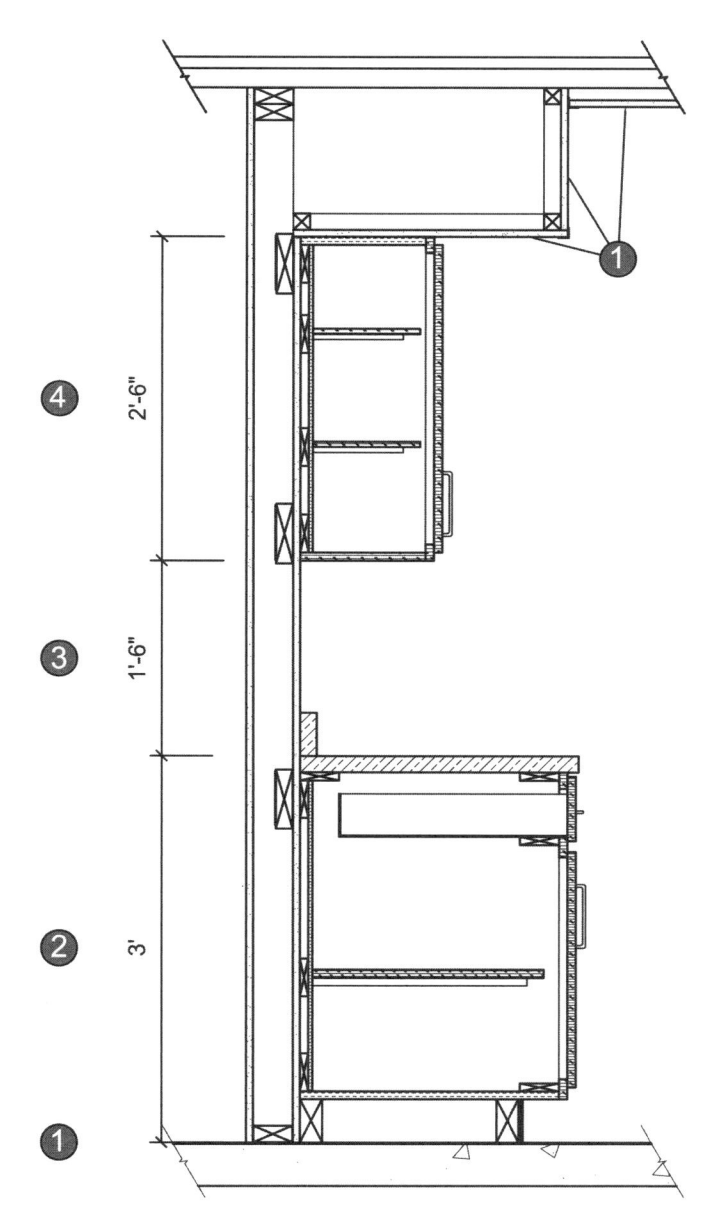

Figure 8.25
Wall and base cabinets, section.

WHY IS THIS IMPORTANT?

Cabinetry can greatly impact many interiors as they undergo an immense amount of use and can carry a heavy price tag. Depending on the project type and the needs of the end user, your design may range from simplistic and orthodox to intricate and unique.

Cabinets used in commercial projects can vary greatly; workplace kitchenettes are typically prefabricated, standard size units that are chosen for being efficient and economical, while commercial kitchens need to be constructed from durable materials and provide ample workspace and flexible storage. These types of designs do not offer as much creativity, apart from layout, as do residential cabinets, but they are no less important.

In residential real estate, kitchen design and cabinetry are major factors in home values. Because the kitchen enjoys daily use and plays a prominent role in homemaking and entertaining, homeowners look for the room to be laid out efficiently and are concerned with the durability of the cabinetry and finish materials. Because of this, it is often recommended to update kitchens prior to placing homes on the market in an effort to drive up the asking and selling price and increase the likelihood that the home sells quickly. While prefabricated cabinets can still be used and look great in residences, they may not always result in the desired appearance that the homeowners are striving for. Professionally designed kitchens allow for customizable layouts for not only the look and layout of the cabinets, it can also result in unique details, such as top hinge cabinets that open upward (Figure 8.26) or open upper wall shelves (Figure 8.27).

While cabinetry describes more than kitchen and bathroom casework, customizable types of storage and built-ins will be discussed more in-depth in Chapter 10.

Figure 8.26
These upper cabinets feature a top hinge, where the door swings upward instead of to the side.

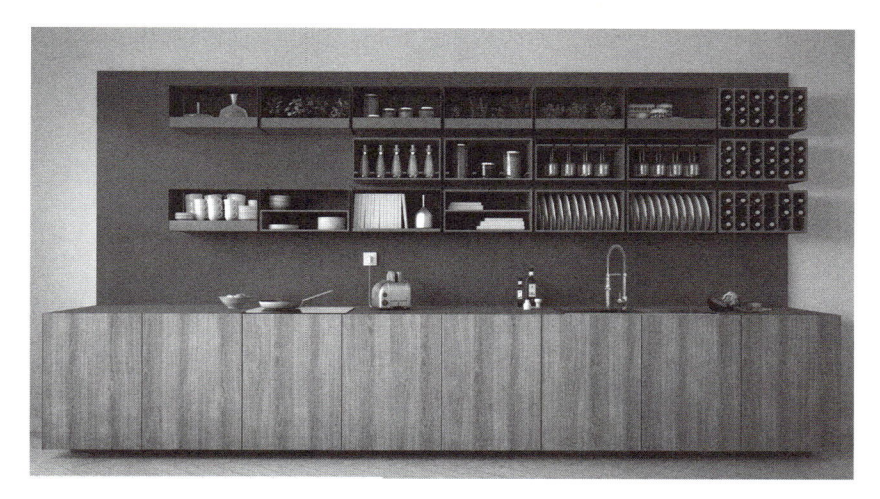

Figure 8.27
Minimalistic kitchen design featuring base cabinets with hidden hardware and open shelves in place of wall cabinets.

Figure 8.28
Full height storage options with stacked cabinets and drawers.

Figure 8.29
Modern kitchen designed with classical details.

CHAPTER REVIEW

1. What is the difference between a face framed cabinet and a frameless cabinet? What are the advantages of each?
2. What impact does a cabinet have on the layout of the kitchen?
3. What are the minimum and maximum standard cabinet heights based on IBC? ADA?
4. Design a set of door and drawer panels in the style of your choice. See Appendix H for ideas.

EXAMPLE PLAN UPDATES STUDIO

While this chapter investigated only base and wall cabinets, the construction and detailing techniques explored here can be applied to full-height cabinets as well. For a deeper look at detailing built-ins, reference Chapter 10.

Examples of cabinetry added to the commercial plan include:

Base cabinets
> Kitchenette
> Bathroom

Wall cabinets
> Kitchenette

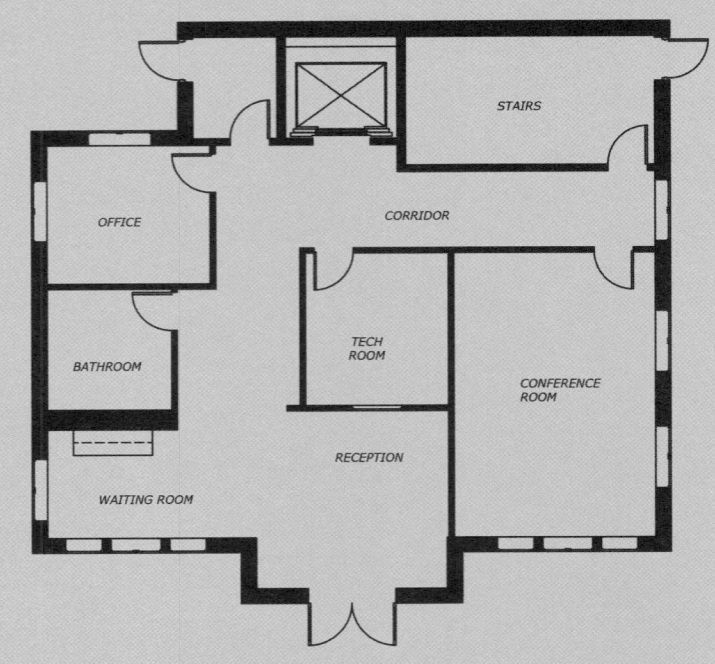

Figure 8.30
Commercial plan with cabinets located in the bathroom and kitchenette.

Examples from the residential plan include:

Base cabinets
> Kitchen
> Bathroom

Wall cabinets
> Kitchen

For your selected project, it is encouraged that you add different cabinet types and layouts, which will allow you to practice your skills, and create a variety of storage and work solutions. It is important to remember that you must maintain at least 4'-0" of clearance in front of cabinets in a kitchen layout, but the sizes and design of these cabinets are up to you.

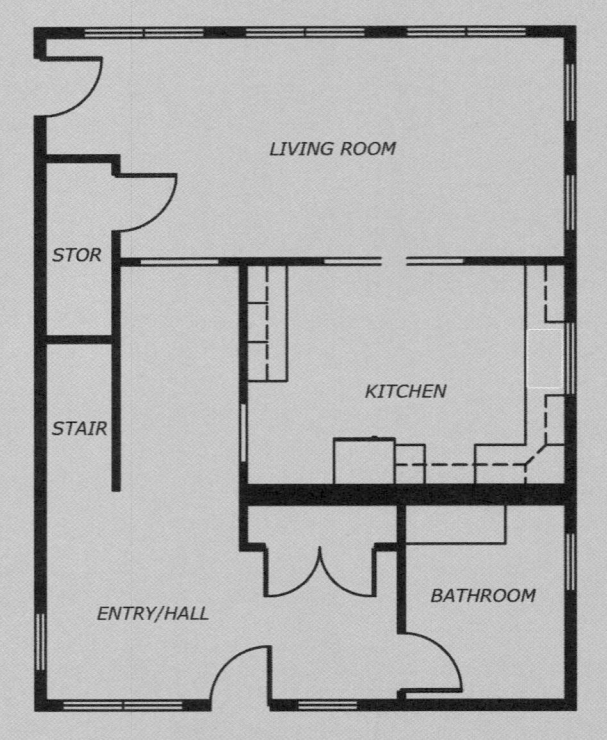

Figure 8.31
Residential plan with cabinets located in the bathroom and kitchen.

CHAPTER TERMINOLOGY

- anchoring rails
- backsplash
- base cabinet
- cabinet
- cabinet blocking
- cornerblock
- counter edge
- countertop
- face frame cabinet
- filler bar
- frameless cabinet
- ledger board
- mid rail
- mid stile
- mounting blocks
- mounting rails
- nail plate
- rail
- scribing
- shim
- stile
- toe kick
- wall cabinet
- work triangle

CABINETRY CODES

This section will explore the elements used and how to draw construction details for cabinetry. Below are the ADA standards and the IBC codes that you need to keep in mind when designing and drafting cabinets.

Table 8.2 ADA Standards for Cabinetry

ADA Code	Topic	Description
804.2.1	Pass through kitchen	Kitchens must have at least 3'-4" of open space between counter fronts and appliances on opposite sides, and feature two entrances.
804.2.2	U-shaped kitchen	When kitchens are enclosed on three sides by walls, cabinets, counters, or appliances, the entrance must be at least 5'-0" of clear space.
804.4.3	Residential kitchen counters	If a residential unit is accessible, there must be clear space for a forward approach to at least 2'-6" of counter that is 34" AFF with knee clearance.
902.3	Dining/work surface height	Surfaces for dining or work must be 28-34" or less AFF.

Table 8.3 IBC Codes for Cabinetry

IBC Code	Topic	Description
1107.3	Accessible spaces	Spaces that are open to the public or units for people with mobility impairments must have kitchens and bathrooms that are for accessible use.
1107.7.2	Multistory units	Residential units that are constructed to be accessible must have a kitchen and bathroom on the same level as the entrance.
1109.4	Kitchens	Buildings that are accessible must have accessible kitchens.
1109.9	Storage	At least 5% of fixed storage (stationary cabinets and drawers) in accessible buildings must be accessible.
1109.11	Seating at counters	At least 5% of fixed counters in public spaces must be accessible.
1208.1	Minimum room widths	Kitchens must have at least 3'-0" of open space between counter fronts, appliances, and walls.

CHAPTER REFERENCES

Ballast, David Kent. *Interior Construction & Detailing for Designers and Architects*. Belmont, CA: Professional Publications, Inc., 2013.

Ching, Francis D. *Building Construction Illustrated*. New York: John Wiley & Sons, 2014.

DeChiara, Joseph, Julius Panero, and Martin Zelnik. *Time-Saver Standards for Interior Design and Space Planning*. New York: McGraw-Hill, 2001.

International Code Council. *International Building Code, 2015*. Chicago: International Code Council Publications, 2014.

International Code Council. *International Residential Code, 2015*. Chicago: International Code Council Publications, 2014.

Jefferis, Alan. *Residential Design, Drafting, and Detailing*, 2nd ed. Boston: Cengage Learning, 2013.

Kilmer, W. Otie and Rosemary Kilmer. *Construction Drawings and Details for Interiors*. New York: John Wiley & Sons, 2016.

Kruse, Kelsey and Maryrose McGowan. *Interior Graphic Standards*. New York: John Wiley & Sons, 2003.

United States Department of Justice. *2010 ADA Standards for Accessible Design*. Washington, D.C.: Dept. of Justice, 2010.

Stairs

CHAPTER 9

CHAPTER OUTCOMES

After completing this chapter you will be able to:

1. Discuss the various elements that comprise the stairs and understand the codes that impact those components.
2. Determine the materiality and construction of a staircase depending on the building type.
3. Calculate the footprint and proportions for different stair layouts to ensure the best fit.
4. Illustrate the overall stairway in plan, elevation, and section views, as well as detail drawings for the construction of an individual stair.

Figure 9.1 A residential direct run stairway constructed from wood with a single-side handrail.

ABOUT STAIRS

Parts of the stair

Stairs are a means of vertical circulation that allow the end user to travel from one level to another through a calculated set of steps. When discussing stairs, it is important to understand the various terms that describe the portions and dimensions of the staircase, especially before talking about the parts specific to wooden or steel stairs. First, a flight of stairs, from the first to the last, is referred to as a **run**. The **total rise** is the vertical distance from the finished floor below the first step to the finished floor of the slab above. This height affects the **total run**, or the length of the flight of stairs, which is measured from the front of the first step (nose of the tread) to the front of the last (nose of the landing). The total run is a careful calculation that is derived from dividing the total rise by IBC code heights for each individual step. This set of calculations will be explored later in this chapter.

The **landing**, which is a level area equal to or greater than the width of the staircase, appears at the top and bottom of a run and when necessary can break up a continuous run of stairs. IBC states that if the total rise for a staircase is greater than 12'-0", you must install a landing, or multiple landings, so that the travel distance between resting points, or **vertical rise**, is less than 12'-0". The landing placement and the how the runs interact with it can give the stair a distinct look, as you can see from the various stair layouts later in this chapter.

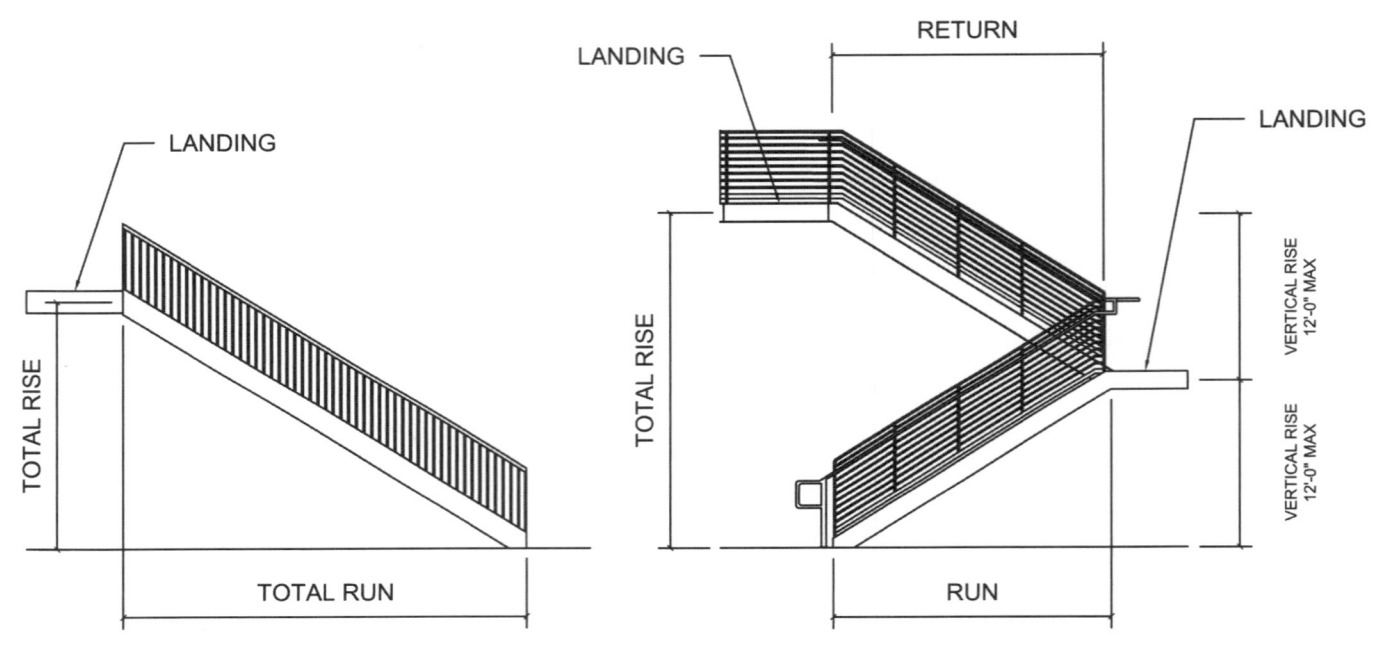

Figure 9.2
Stair terminology for direct run (left) and U-run.

Figure 9.3
View from the central landing of a commercial U-run stairwell.

174 | PART II DETAIL DRAWINGS

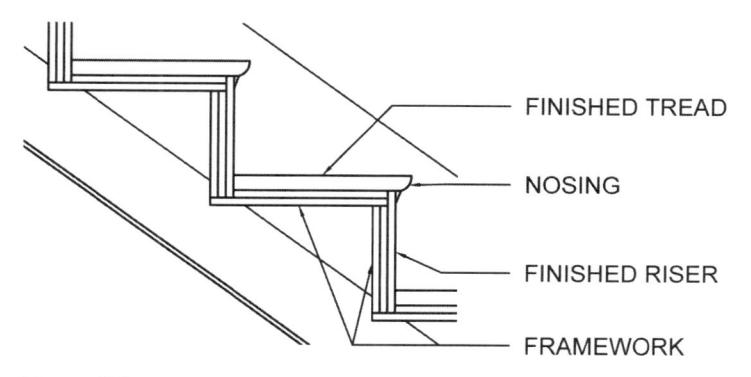

Figure 9.4
Treads and risers.

Figure 9.5
Constructed treads and risers.

The most recognizable parts of the staircase are the tread and the riser. The **tread** is the horizontal portion of the stair that you place your foot on. Constructed from a single plank or slab, the tread is anchored to a framework and supports below, and occasionally to the side. Code dictates how deep the tread must be depending on the building type, measuring at least 9" for a residence and 11" for commercial project. The depth of the tread is measured from nose to nose to maintain consistency. The tread can be finished or treated according to the material used: wood treads can be stained or painted, stone can be polished or smoothed, and rubber applications can be raised in a variety of anti-slippage patterns. The back of the tread should be a snug fit with the construction it abuts to, typically achieved with a straight edge cut to form a 90 degree angle. The front of the tread is referred to as the **nosing**, a curved edge that extends 1 1/2" at most over the riser below. The nose must feature a curve or angle in profile in order to reduce tripping and injury. Acceptable nosing profiles can be found in Appendix I.

The **riser** is the vertical counterpart to the tread, acting as a support at the front of the step, under the nosing. Much like the tread, the riser is typically fabricated from a single plank or slab, but the framework may also be exposed depending on the construction materials. It is important to remember to conform to IBC codes for the height of the riser, which states that in commercial projects the height cannot exceed 7", while in a residence it may be as high as 7 3/4". The tread and the riser intersect with each other through a combination of butt and dado joints. When installing the riser, it can either sit on top of the tread below or can extend past the tread and fit into a groove created in the framework structure below the tread. Likewise, the top of the riser can either abut the tread above, or it can fit into a dado joint notched behind the tread's nose.

The materiality and the construction style are dependent on the project building type. While residential projects may have either wood or steel stairways, commercial projects are required to be built from steel according to code.

The basis of the wooden stair framework is the **carriage**, which supports both the risers and the treads. Typically constructed from a 1 × 12 or 2 × 12, the wood is held at an angle and notched so that two to three layers of ply and then the treads and risers can be affixed directly to the carriage. This allows for it to carry and distribute the combined weight of the flight and users. The number and size of the carriages depends on the width of the flight.

In some cases, the carriage may be visible from a side view of the staircase, but in most instances, it is covered with a **stringer**. This finished element runs along the outer edge of the carriage, acting as a termination point for the treads and risers. If the element follows the pattern of the treads and risers without blocking

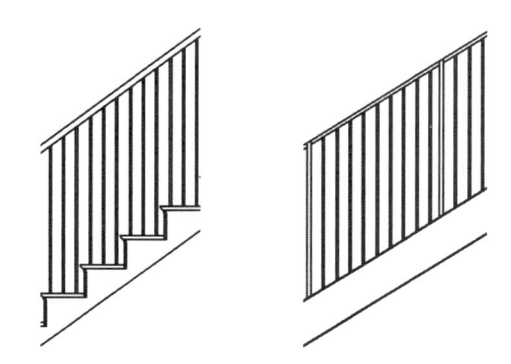

Figure 9.6
Open (left) and closed stringers.

CHAPTER 9 STAIRS | 175

① FULL STRINGER

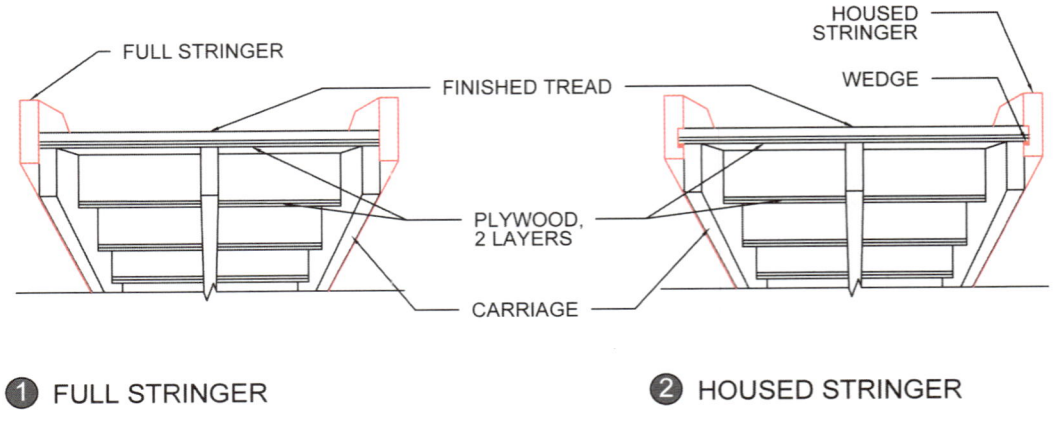

② HOUSED STRINGER

Figure 9.7
Comparison of a full stringer (left) and a housed stringer.

them from view, this is called an **open stringer**. Likewise, a **closed stringer** will obscure the stairs from view, which can be done two different ways. The first type of closed stringer is a full stringer. The simpler of the two types, the **full stringer** is an angled board that is cut to form a 90 degree angle with the floor at its base and the slab above, and other than the possible carved design, remains uncut, and simply butts against the carriage, treads, and risers. The other type of stringer is the housed stringer. Made similarly to the full stringer, the **housed stringer** features shallow notches to receive the tread and risers into it, creating a dado joint. This protects the edges of the stairs and disguises the edge seams of the steps. Within the notches for the treads, wedges are inserted to act as shims, ensuring that there is a tight fit among the various elements.

Steel staircases, which are required in commercial projects and occasionally used in residential ones, are constructed differently than their wooden counterparts. Replacing the stringers and carriages are **steel channels**, *C*-shaped beams measuring at least 10" deep. While they are not directly connected to the tread and riser, they are bolted or welded to the **angle supports**, *L*-shaped supports that provide space for the support and anchoring of the treads and risers, which in turn abut the steel channels. The channels are hung from the floor above or sit on bearing plates in order to support the weight of the stairs. Regardless of how the weight of the channel is carried, it is anchored with a **clip angle**, an *L*-shaped metal element that bolts the channel to the floor. Runs that require landings also feature a **channel support** between the landing and the highest riser. This steel tube is another welded point of contact and creates additional strength for the staircase.

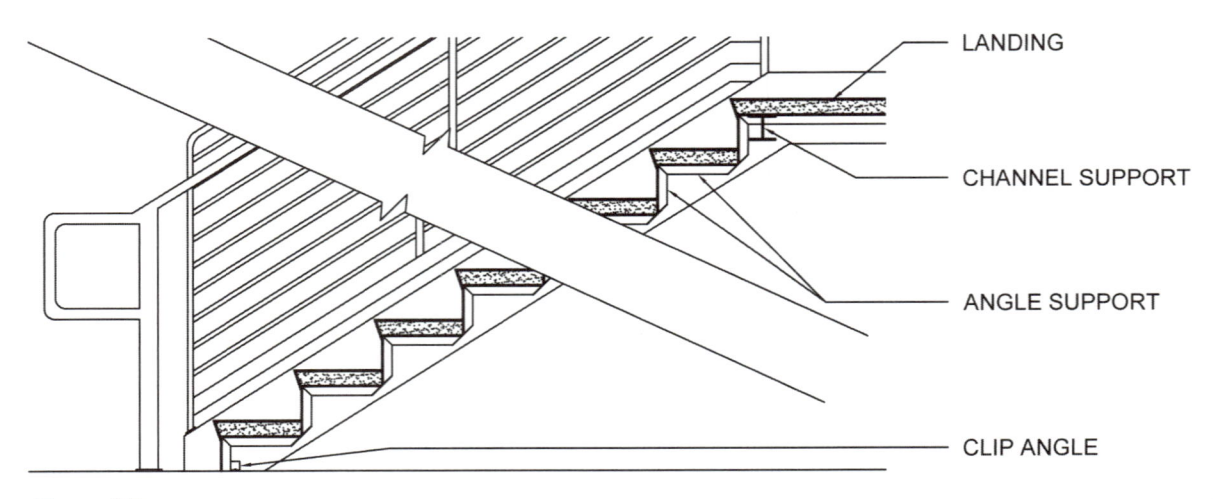

Figure 9.8
Steel stair elements.

Both wood and metal stairs utilize **handrails**, supportive bars that are installed 34" to 38" above the nosing on one or both sides of the staircase, but codes stipulate differences between the rails used in commercial and residential projects. IBC code 1011.11 dictates that commercial buildings must have handrails on both sides of the stairway, while residential projects are only required to have it along one side. Furthermore, the IBC and the ADA both require that commercial stairs have added **handrail extensions** that are not present for residences. The extensions are the portions of the rail that continue past the top and bottom risers in an effort to provide prolonged support for the end user. While the extension at the top of the stairs must extend 12", the rail bottom of the flight must extend 12" plus the depth of one riser for the specified staircase. Finally, one planning element that must be kept in mind while designing a staircase is to account for distance that the rail infringes on the **clear space** of the stair, as the width of the walking path may not be interrupted by the rail.

In commercial settings and some residential projects, a **guardrail** is needed in place of or in addition to, the handrail. It is a barrier or rail that is used on landings or along stairs to protect an individual from a fall. The guardrail is mounted 42" above the nose or finished floor.

Balusters are installed between the rail and the stair or landing. These vertical members support the rail above and aid in both safety and decoration. As a matter of safety, the balusters enhance the guardrail by ensuring that the user cannot fit or fall through the guardrail. IBC dictates that the balusters must be spaced so that a 4" sphere cannot pass between them. Decoratively, the balusters can be made of various profiles and materials, allowing for the designer to customize the final product. The **newel post** is the largest, and typically the most decorative baluster, found at the top and bottom of a rail, acting as both an anchoring point and a termination point for the rail.

IBC

Commercial projects require handrails on both sides of a staircase. *(IBC 1011.11)*

Commercial handrails must extend at least 12" past the top riser and 12" plus the depth of one tread past the bottom riser. *(IBC 1014.6)*

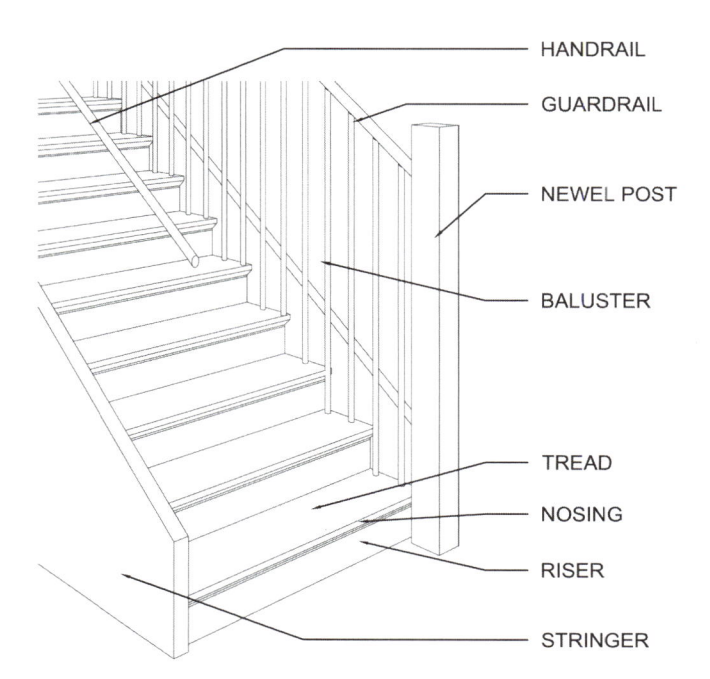

Figure 9.9
Stair and rail parts.

Figure 9.10
Residential stair with a single handrail without an extension.

Figure 9.11
Commercial stair with extensions at the top and bottom of the flight.

CHAPTER 9 STAIRS

TYPES OF STAIRS

This chapter will cover three different types of stairs: residential, commercial, and egress. Each stair type has its own set of codes that dictates everything from tread depth to construction type to finish materiality. This section will cover the major differences among each type of stair so that you can select the one that is the best fit for your project type.

Residential

Residential stairs refers to any staircase in a one- or two-family home. Typically, these stairs are framed of wood, as their construction material should match that of the building frame, but they may also be of steel construction. As these types of stairs are located within a personal residence, they are not subject to the same capacity load or strict code guidelines as those in a commercial building. While it is recommended that you refer to both the International Building Code and the International Residential Code, the important policies that will impact your stair design are provided in Table 9.1 for your convenience.

As per IBC, residential stairs must have at least 36" of clear space for the path of travel; however, the handrails can infringe into this space by up to 4 1/2", reducing this width to 31 1/2". This can be seen as dimension *A* of Figure 9.12. The clear space can be further reduced to 27" if the staircase is designed to have only one continuous handrail, as is allowed in homes.

When calculating the quantity and dimension of treads and risers, as seen later in this chapter, it is important to note the size requirements issued by IBC. Residences must have a tread depth (*B*) of at least 10", while the riser height (*C*) cannot exceed 7 3/4". When designing the appearance of the residential stair, you can use opened or closed risers.

The calculations also impact the layout of the stair, as any landings that are present must have the same width as the stairway but are required to be at least 36" in depth. Landings are to be used for any *L*- or *U*-shaped layouts but are also required by code for straight runs when the vertical rise of the stair exceeds 12'-3". Layouts will be discussed in the following section.

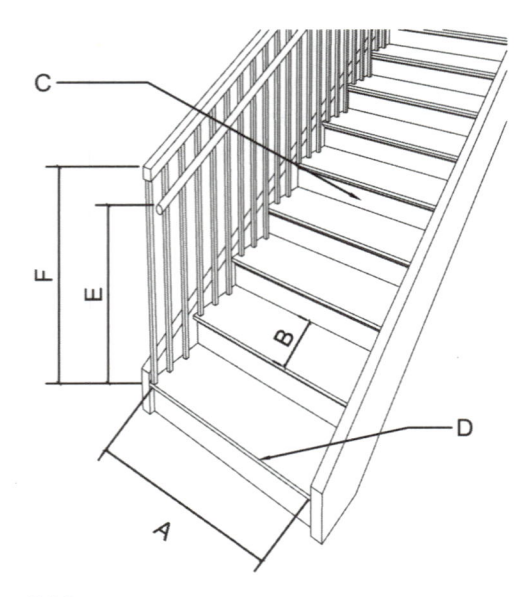

Figure 9.12
Dimension guidelines for residential stairs.

Table 9.1 Dimension Guidelines for Residential Stairs

Letter	Subject	Residential
A	Tread width	36" min
B	Tread depth	9" min
C	Riser height	7 3/4"
D	Nosing depth	1 1/2" max
E	Handrail height	34"–38" One side required
F	Guardrail height	34"–38" min

Figure 9.13
Residential stair with a single handrail and two landings.

PART II DETAIL DRAWINGS

Commercial

Commercial stairs are any of the main staircases in a multi-family home, such as an apartment building or public building. These stairs must be of steel construction, matching the material that makes up the framework of the building. Wood is not permitted to make up the components of the staircase, but the material is allowed to be used on the handrail. While commercial stairs are customizable and interesting, they are subject to stricter codes due to fire codes and the increased volume of people using the space. While it is recommended that you refer to both the International Building Code and the International Residential Code, the important policies that will impact your stair design are provided in Table 9.2 for your convenience.

As per IBC, commercial stairs must have at least 44" of clear space for the path of travel. This can be seen as dimension *A* of Figure 9.14. However, if the commercial project is small, and the number of people utilizing the building is less than fifty, the stair width can be reduced to 36". Handrails are required to be installed on both sides of the stairs, but in addition to the continuous rail running from the first tread to the last, extensions are required in commercial spaces. The extension that appears at the top of the stair must measure at least 12" past the last riser, while the extension at the bottom of the stair must measure 12" *plus* the depth of one tread. Furthermore, guardrails must also be installed in cases that the stair is 30" or more off the ground and does not border a wall.

When calculating the quantity and dimension of treads and risers, as seen later in this chapter, it is important to note the size requirements issued by IBC. Commercial staircases must have a tread depth (*B*) of at least 11", while the riser height (*C*) cannot exceed 7". Risers are permitted to be open, only if the stairs are not a designated egress stair *and* a 4" sphere cannot pass through the opening.

The calculations also impact the layout of the stair, as any landings that are present must have the same width as the stairway *and* must be at least as deep as the stairs are wide. Landings are to be used for any *L*- or *U*-shaped layouts, but they are also required by code for straight runs when the vertical rise of the stair exceeds 12'-0". Layouts will be discussed in the following section.

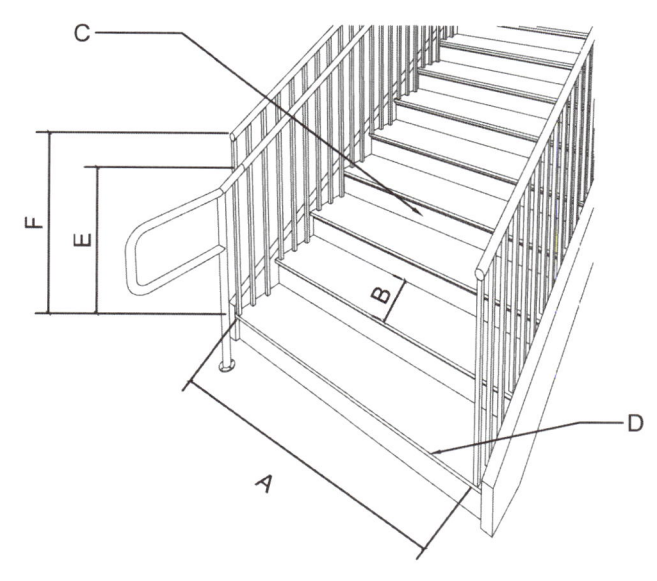

Figure 9.14
Dimension guidelines for commercial and egress stairs.

Table 9.2 Dimension Guidelines for Commercial and Egress Stairs

Letter	Subject	Commercial	Commercial Egress
A	Tread width	44" min	48" min
B	Tread depth	11" min	11" min
C	Riser height	7" max	7" max
D	Nosing depth	1 ½" max	1 ½" max
E	Handrail height	34"–38" Both sides required	34"–38" Both sides required
F	Guardrail height	42" min	42" min

Figure 9.15
A commercial staircase constructed from steel with handrails and guardrails along both sides.

Egress stairs are a type of commercial stair that are constructed in an enclosed, fire-protected area of a building to be used as an emergency stair. For the most part, egress stairs are very similar to commercial stairs; however, there are a few differences due to the vital importance of these stairs. The similarities and differences between the required dimensions for the two stair types can be found in Table 9.2, but the key information can be found below.

The major difference is that the egress stairs must be protected within a fire-rated enclosure. This means that the assemblies that make up the walls, ceilings, and any openings must meet fire code and be constructed out of materials that have been certified for their fire-resistant properties. Additionally, egress stairs must be of steel construction, as wood is not permitted to make up the components of the staircase. Instead, treads should be constructed from steel or concrete and be finished with a non-slip surface. Risers must be closed.

The last key difference between the egress and commercial stairs is that the egress stairway must be wider than commercial stairs. They must measure at least 48" of clear space for the path of travel, as seen as dimension *A* of Figure 9.14.

STAIR LAYOUTS

The layout of a staircase is influenced by many factors, including the travel distance from one floor to the next, the number of landings required, the headroom, and the desired appearance. The following generic diagrams show basic stair layouts, which can then be customized to fit your project needs by adjusting the length and width of each step and the addition of handrails, rail extensions, and guardrails.

Figure 9.16
An egress stair in a commercial building.

IBC

A minimum headroom clearance of 80 inches is needed. This must be measured from the edge of the nosing vertically to the ceiling or landing above and must be maintained for the whole width of the flight. *(IBC 1011.3)*

RoT

If 80" cannot be maintained, you may need to determine if a different stair layout can rectify the problem or if the staircase must be moved to a different location.

Direct run

This type of stair allows for the user to travel from one floor to the next without any landings or returns. **Direct runs** can only be used when the total rise is less than 12'-0".

Figure 9.17
Direct run plan and axon.

Straight run

Laid out in a similar manner to the direct run, the **straight run** features landings between runs, allowing this staircase to be used when the total rise is more than 12'-0".

Figure 9.18
Straight run plan and axon.

L-shaped

The *L*-shaped stair features two runs separated by a landing. The first run is a straight run to the landing, while the second run attaches to the landing perpendicular to the first.

Figure 9.19
L-shaped plan and axon.

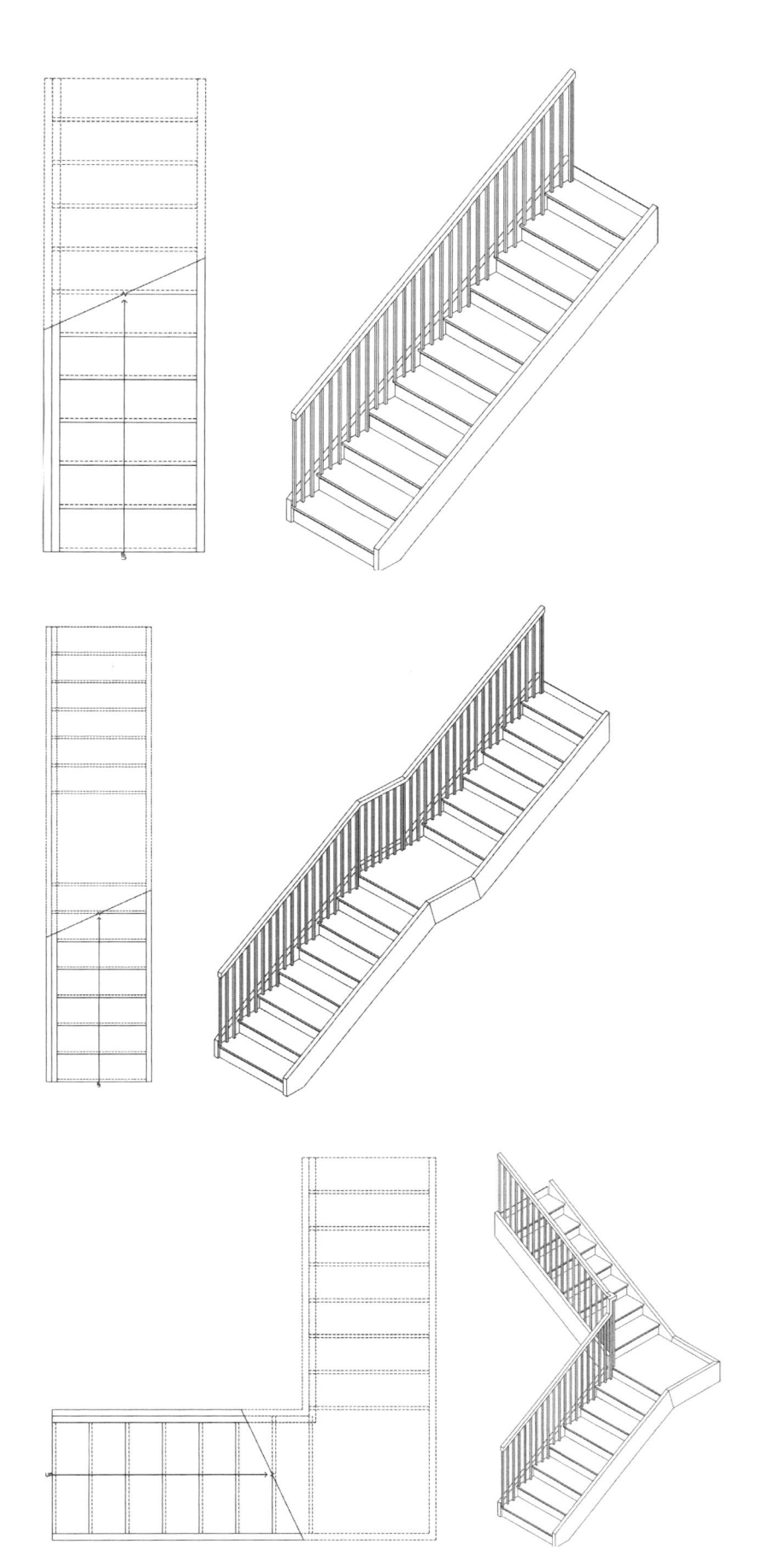

CHAPTER 9 STAIRS | 181

U-shaped

The *U-shaped* stair features two runs separated by a landing. The first run is a straight run to the landing, while the second run becomes a return, running parallel to the first. The **return** is the second portion of a staircase, which extends from the first landing to the second landing, allowing the user to reverse direction and end up directly above where they started.

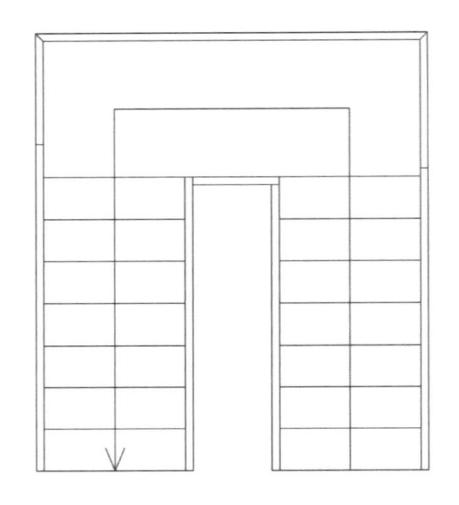

Figure 9.20
U-shaped plan and axon.

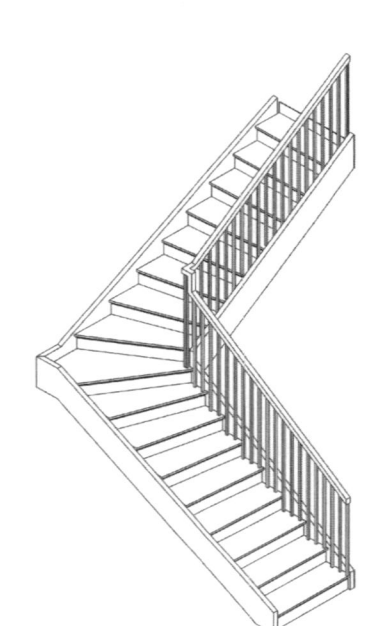

Winding

Winding stairs take the shape of an L- or U-stair, but wedged shaped treads replace the central landing. By code, winders cannot be used as a means of egress for commercial buildings, but they may be used in residential projects. These runs are best used in homes where space is at a premium.

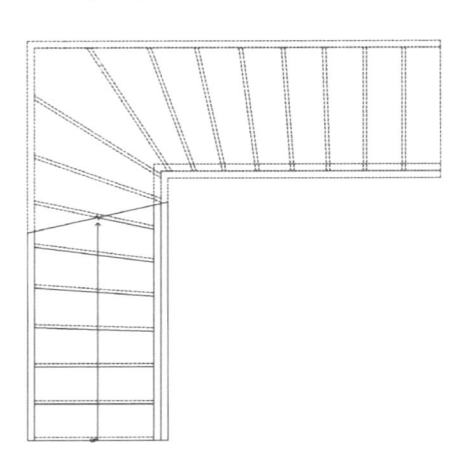

Figure 9.21
L-shaped winder plan and axon.

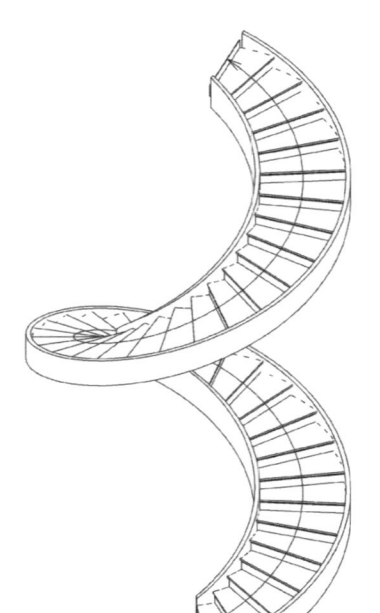

Spiral

A **spiral stair** is a circular or oval staircase featuring regular, wedge-shaped treads that are installed in a rotating manner around the central axis. These runs are best used in homes where space is at a premium.

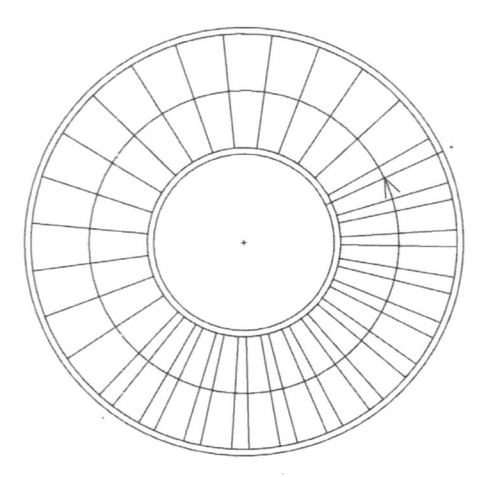

Figure 9.22
Spiral plan and axon.

PART II DETAIL DRAWINGS

CALCULATING STAIRS

IBC requires treads and risers to be a uniform shape and size for a set of stairs, meaning that they each must be the same dimensions from the bottom to the top of the flight. In order to ensure that they are the same size, a series of calculations must be performed. The example calculations performed in this section are not based on the project files but does use the commercial tread minimum (11") and riser maximum (7") dimensions.

Calculating the number and height of risers

1. Determine the total rise, the measurement from floor to floor, where the staircase is needed. For this example, a total rise of 10'-5" will be used, as seen in Figure 9.24. Convert this number into inches.

    10'-5" = 125"

2. Divide the total rise by the maximum riser height allowed for your project. This will allow you to determine the quantity and height of the risers. In this case, use the commercial riser height of 7".

    125/7 = 17.857

    If the calculated number is a whole number, that will be the number of risers, each measuring 7"

3. As you cannot have .857th of a riser, you must determine the correct whole number of risers.

    To do this, round up the number of risers calculated and divide the total rise by that number.

    17.857 ≈ 18

    125/18 = 6.94"

    Based on this calculation, there will be 18 risers, each measuring 6.94".

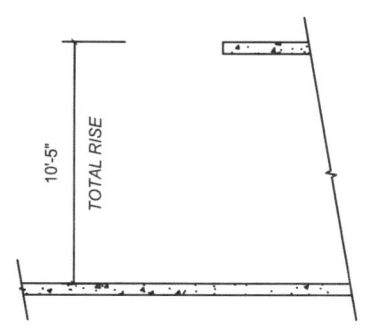

Figure 9.23
Total rise for this section's example. The total rise should measure from slab to slab.

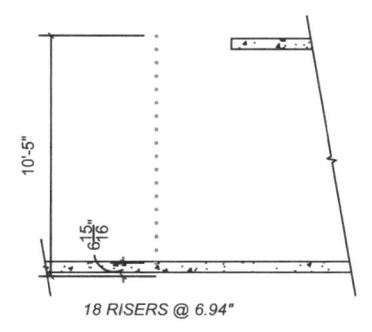

Figure 9.24
Each dot represents the 18 risers spaced out for the calculated distance between them.

Calculating the number of treads

If the total rise is less than 12'-0"

Take the number of risers necessary for the run and subtract 1 (the second-story landing will not be counted here).

18 – 1 = **17 treads**

If the total rise is more than 12'-0"

Take the number of risers necessary for the run and subtract 1 for each landing in the run.

Mid-flight landing and second-story landing

18 – 2 = **16 treads**

Two mid-flight landings and second-story landing

18 – 3 = **15 treads**

Calculating tread depth

Keep in mind that as long as the depth of the tread is at least 11 inches, your design will be to code. By using this equation, you can find the "best fit," a ratio of riser height to tread depth that is the most comfortable for a majority of the population. While you do not need to use the "best fit" number, it is recommended that you design the treads to be as close to this number as possible.

In this equation, T = depth of tread and R = riser height.

$$T = 25 - 2R$$
$$T = 25 - 2(6.94)$$
$$T = 25 - 13.88$$
$$\mathbf{T = 11.12"}$$

For this example, a direct run with a total rise of 10'-5" results in the following:

$$18 \text{ risers @ } 6.94"$$
$$17 \text{ treads @ } 11.12"$$

CAD

Save yourself from a headache by setting up your drawing space before you begin the detail. In the Home tab, click Layers and then Layer Properties to create new layers for your file.

By creating these five layers of different colors you will keep your drawing organized: *treads, nosings, handrails, annotations,* and *guidelines*.

Revit

While Revit will automatically calculate the best fit risers and treads for your staircase, it is important to know how to hand-calculate. Custom, nontraditional layouts can be calculated and sketched out by hand before being drafted. Exams such as the NCIDQ and the ARE include questions about staircases, best fit scenarios, and how to calculate the rise and run.

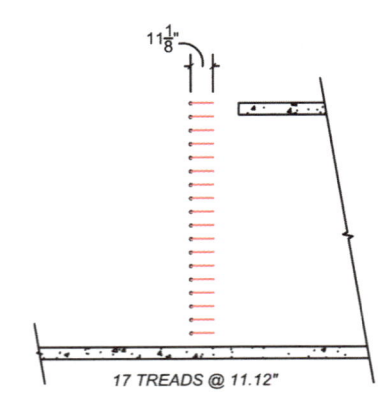

Figure 9.25
Each line extending from the dots represents the depth of each calculated tread.

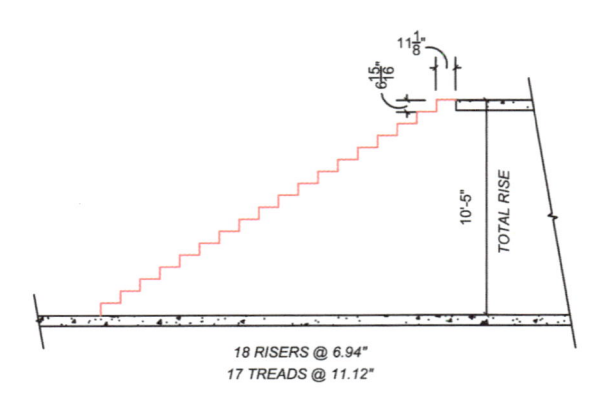

Figure 9.26
Outline of the proposed staircase based on the provided calculations.

DRAFTING A WOODEN DIRECT RUN—RESIDENTIAL

The example for a direct run staircase has been taken from the residential project. As designed, the desired staircase will run between two walls, one of which starts after the sixth tread, resulting in an open stringer. Because of this, the width of the treads will change, with the bottom of the stairs measuring 3'-8" wide, while the top measures 3'-4". The total rise for this project is 10'-0", with a desired tread depth of 10". Using the stair calculations seen earlier in the chapter, the size and quantity of risers and treads can be determined.

Riser height and quantity

Total rise = 10'-0" = 120"
120 / 7.75 = 15.48 risers, rounds up to 16
120 / 16 = 7.5"
16 risers @ 7.5"

Tread quantity

Number of risers = 1
16 -1 = 15 Treads

Total run

Number of Treads × Depth of Tread = Total Run
15 × 10" = 150"
150" = 12'-6"

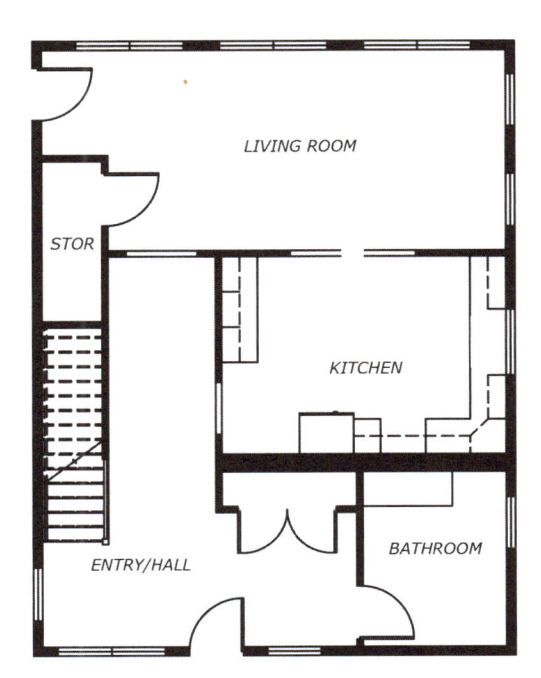

Figure 9.27 Direct run stairs, residential plan.

IBC
Residential stairways

Landings (*R311.7.6*)
The total rise cannot exceed 12'-0" without either connecting to the upper level or a central landing being created.

Handrails (*R311.7.8*)
Stairs must have at least one handrail running from the nosing of the first step to the last.

Nosing (*R311.7.8*)
1 ½" with 60 degree slope under nose MAX.

Materials (*IBC 1011.7*)
Wood or steel construction for frame or rails accepted.

Width (*R311.7.1*)
36" minimum clear space.

Treads (*R311.7.5*)
10" minimum nose to nose.

Risers (*R311.7.5*)
7.75" max.

Revit

Use Detail Lines to create the bounding box for the staircase to allocate the amount of space needed for it. Detail Lines can be found in the Detail panel of the Annotate tab or can be accessed by typing DL. Using the Stair button found in the Architecture tab, you can quickly create a flight of stairs with handrails. After activating the tool, click once in the drawing window and move your mouse in the direction of travel and click again to create the stairs. Items can be edited in Properties, but for best results and increased ease, parameters should be set prior to beginning the sketch.

For staircases that have different widths at the top and bottom, you will need to utilize the Stair by Sketch tool and create a custom boundary for the stair.

RoT

Landings must be as deep as the width of the staircase they serve, meaning that if the staircase is 60" wide, the landing must be 60" deep.

Drafting a direct run—plan

STEP 1

Typically, as with this example, there will be walls for the stairs to either run along or fit between. Isolate this area from your project floor plan. Next, block out the space needed for the run of stairs and landing based on the desired stair widths and the calculation you completed for the total run.

First, determine where the landing will be located and its dimensions. As the stairs at the top of the run are to be 3'-4" wide, the landing needs to at least match this measurement for its depth and width. Using either continuous lines or guidelines, create a rectangle as a placeholder for the landing.

Next, use a continuous line to extend a second rectangle from the landing. This rectangle should measure 12'-6" long, as dictated by the total run calculation that was completed for this run of stairs. The width of this rectangle should also match the desired tread widths of 3'-4" near the top and 3'-8" at the bottom.

Once the footprint of the stair run is in place, you can erase any guidelines used.

STEP 2

Drawing inside of these guidelines, measure 10" from the bottom of the rectangle and draw a line to create the first tread.

Repeat this step for the remaining treads in the run, making sure they are 10" apart from one another. The last line should overlap the front of the landing.

> **IBC**
>
> IBC states that a flight of stairs cannot have a vertical rise more than 12'-0" between landings or floor levels. This means that if the total rise of your staircase is 12'-6", you must have a landing breaking up the runs. (*IBC 1011.8*)

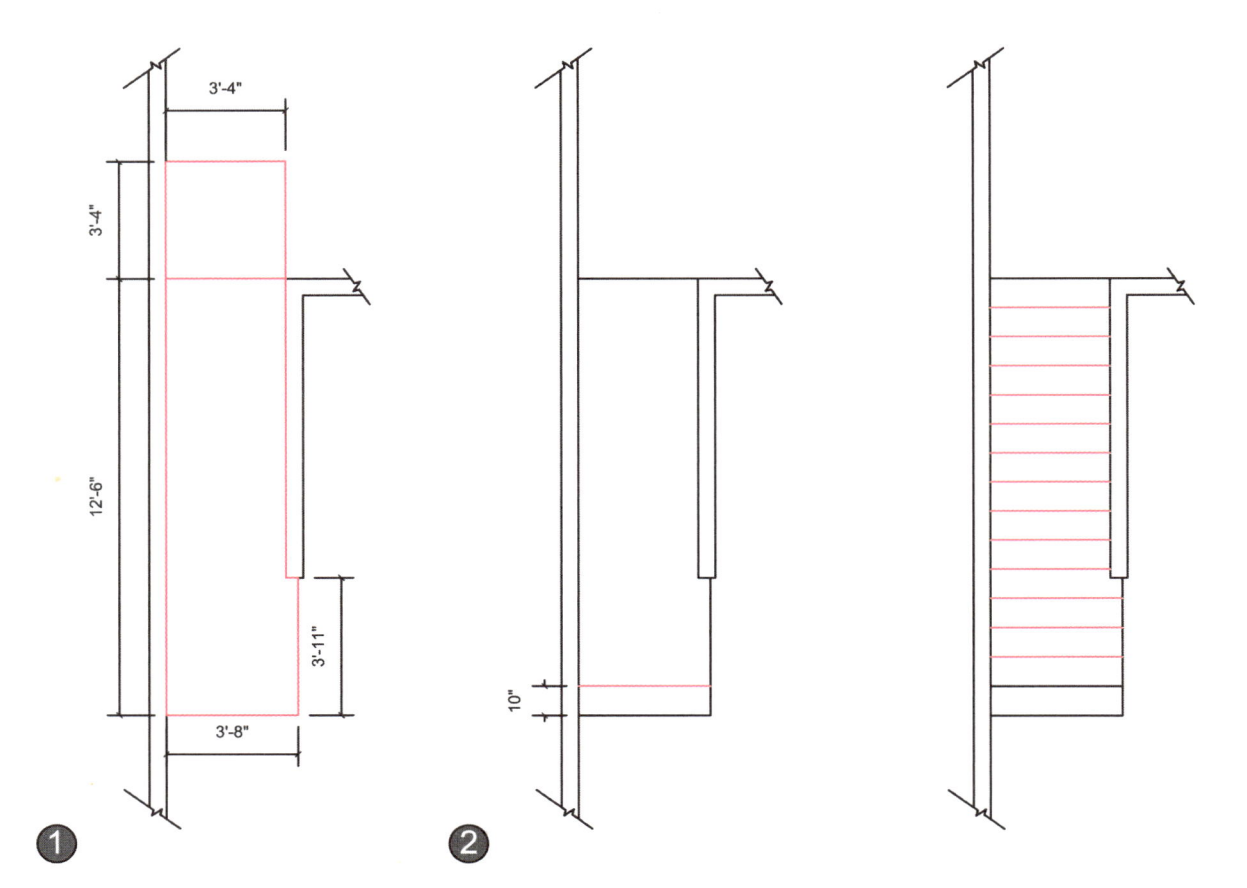

Figure 9.28
Direct run stairs, plan, Steps 1–2.

CHAPTER 9 STAIRS | 187

STEP 3

To indicate the nosing and the riser underneath, measure 1" from the front of the first tread and draw a dashed line. This creates the illusion that the tread hangs over the riser that supports it. Repeat this process for the remaining risers, making sure they are 1" in from the front line of each tread. The last one should appear 1" into the landing.

STEP 4

To create the handrail against the full wall, measure 1 1/2" from the side of the staircase and draw a line from the bottom of the flight to the top. Draw a second line 1 1/2" in from the rail line you just drew. Together, these two lines will indicate the handrail. Connect these lines at the top and bottom of the stairs and erase the treads and risers that appear between the lines. As this is a residential stair, only one handrail is required and it does not need to extend past the top or bottom riser.

STEP 5

At the bottom of the staircase, you can see that there are six treads that are open on one side. This area needs a guardrail to ensure safety, with the newel post built into the bottom step. Draw a 4" × 4" box to represent the newel post for the guardrail.

STEP 6

Connect the newel post to the wall by drawing two lines between them. This example uses a 2" handrail, spaced 1" in from either side of the newel post. Erase the treads and risers that appear under this handrail.

STEP 7

Annotate the staircase by adding UP and a directional arrow to indicate the path of travel, dimensions, and any necessary drawing symbols.

IBC

Handrails must be continuous, meaning there cannot be a break or a post unless it is on the lowest tread or landing. *(IBC 1014.4)*

If the stairwell has one handrail, the run must have at least 31.5" of clear travel space. If the stairwell has two handrails, the clear space must be at least 27". Handrails must be at least 1 1/2" away from the wall. *(IBC 1015.3)*

CAD

In CAD you can draw a line along the edge of the staircase and then move it 1 1/2" away from that edge. After it has been moved, copy the line over another 1 1/2" to create the width of the railing.

Revit

Even though the handrails are drawn with the stairs, some elements of the rail can be edited separately. In the drawing window, hover over the stairs and select the railing once it becomes highlighted. Editing options include the shape of the rail and whether it is flipped into the path of travel or is against the wall.

You can also eliminate the autogenerated rail and create your own component if you want to further customize it.

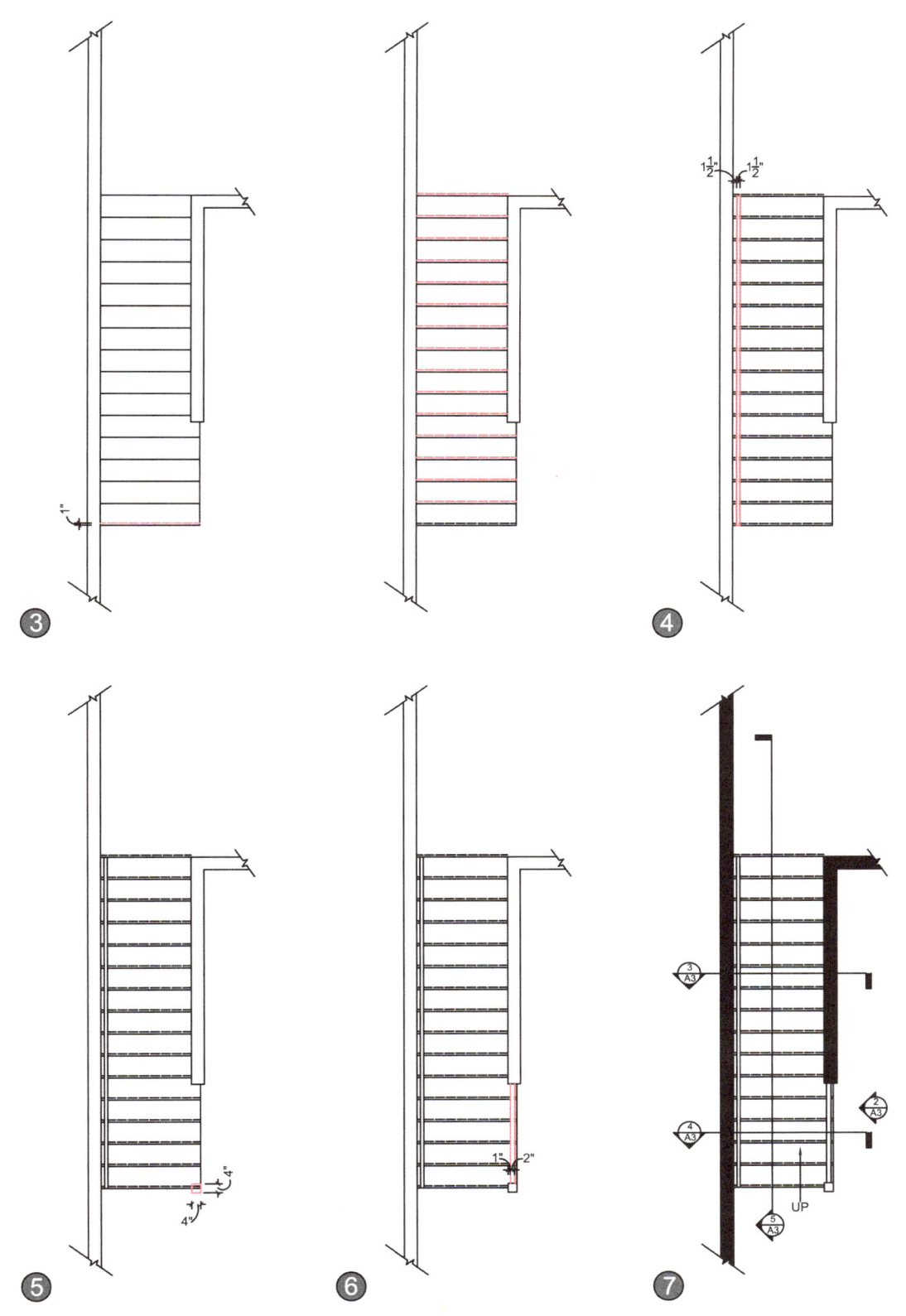

Figure 9.29
Direct run stairs, plan, Steps 3–7.

CHAPTER 9 STAIRS | 189

Drafting a direct run— side elevation

The callout marked 1/A3 refers to an elevation drawing that shows a view of the stairs from the side or how the user would see it from the first floor hallway.

STEP 1

Rotate your stair plan so that the wall to be shown in elevation is facing downward. Extend guides from wall corners or terminations into drawing space below.

Draw two horizontal lines to represent the floor and ceiling planes. These lines measure 9'-6" apart (the ceiling height for the residential project) and should extend between the outermost guidelines.

Once the floor and ceiling are in place, hardline the walls and erase any of the guides that are still visible.

STEP 2

Create a new set of guidelines from the nosing and riser lines in the plan to the floor plane.

As the staircase will feature an open stringer, this example will now focus on the stairs themselves, which will occupy the space shown in the dashed gray circle, which is not to be drawn.

STEP 3

Starting at the leftmost guideline, which represents the nosing of the first step, measure up 7 1/2" and place a tick mark. Then, draw a horizontal line from this tick to the riser guide for the next step, which in this example is 11" away to indicate the top of each tread. As a reminder, the tread depth of 10" is measured from nose to nose, whereas the constructed tread must include the space under the nose above, which in this case will make the tread measurement 11".

Continue this process of drawing 11" horizontal lines between nosing guides, ensuring that they are each 7 1/2" apart, until you reach the wall.

STEP 4

To create the thickness of each tread, measure 1" below the horizontal lines you just drew and add a tick mark. Add the nosing profile of your choice in this space, keeping in mind the IBC requirements for the nose. Then extend a horizontal line from the end of the nose past the guide for the next riser. As seen in this example, when measured from the left guide past the right guide, the line will measure 11 1/2". This will allow for bottom of the next riser to align with the bottom of the tread.

Repeat this for the other stairs.

STEP 5

Next, add the riser thickness by drawing a vertical line along the second guideline 1" in from the front of the nosing. Draw a second vertical 1/2" in from this line.

Repeat this for the other stairs. The back of the risers should align with the end of the bottom of the treads. Once all the stairs are in place, erase the remaining guidelines.

STEP 6

Returning to the plan, extend two new guidelines from the newel post into the elevation. The dashed circle indicates the focal area for Steps 7–10.

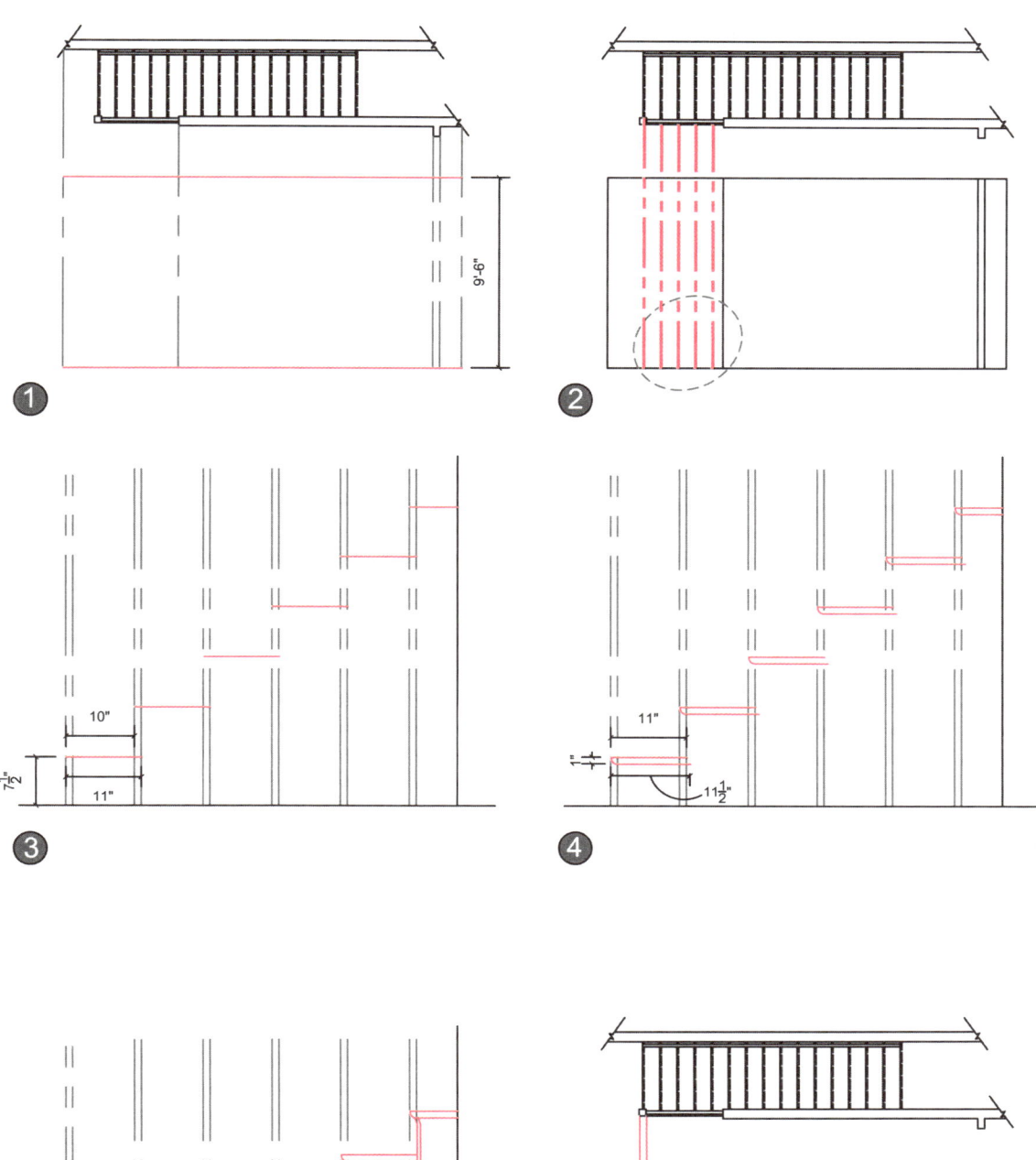

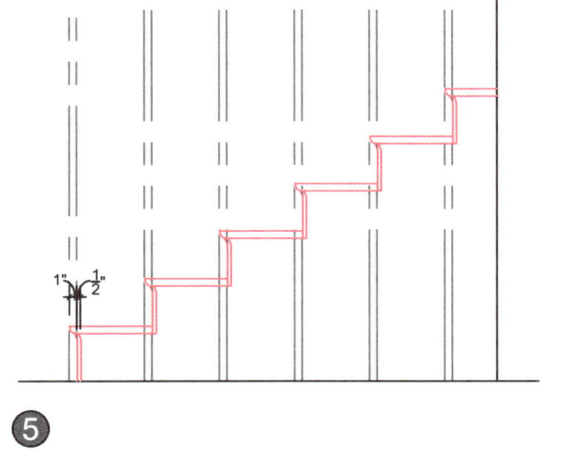

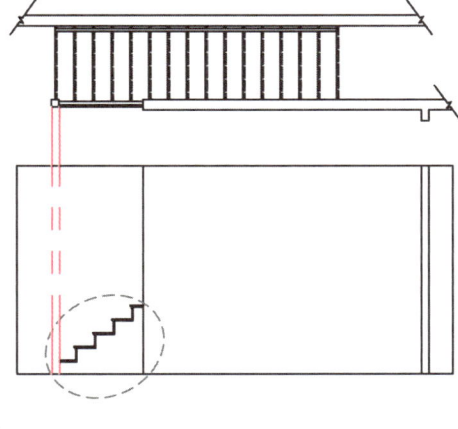

Figure 9.30
Direct run stairs, side elevation, Steps 1–6.

CHAPTER 9 STAIRS | 191

STEP 7
Then, following the guides, draw two vertical lines measuring 50" high to build the sides of the newel. Connect the tops of these lines to finish the post.

STEP 8
Measuring up 3'-2" from each tread's nose, draw a line for the top of the guardrail from the newel post to the wall. Draw a second line 2" below the first to finish the guardrail.

STEP 9
Add the balusters of your choice. Remember to ensure that they are spaced so that a 4" sphere cannot pass between them.

STEP 10
A handrail runs along the far side of the stairs, meaning that while it will be in view, it will be edited to appear behind the balusters. Measuring up 2'-10" from each tread's nose, draw a line for the top of the handrail from the newel post to the wall. Erase any of the rail that appears behind the balusters.

STEP 11
To finish the drawing, add any trim or millwork details present in your design.

IBC

Residential guardrails are required when there is an opening located 30" above the floor. When a residential guardrail doubles as the handrail, the rail must be between 34" to 38" above the nose of the tread and is typically the same height as any specified rail along the other side of the staircase. (IBC 1015.3)

Revit

Existing handrails can be changed to a guardrail through the Properties menu. Simply highlight the existing handrail and change the drop-down option from Railing to Guardrail.

The height and style can then be altered by clicking on Edit Type and changing the given parameters.

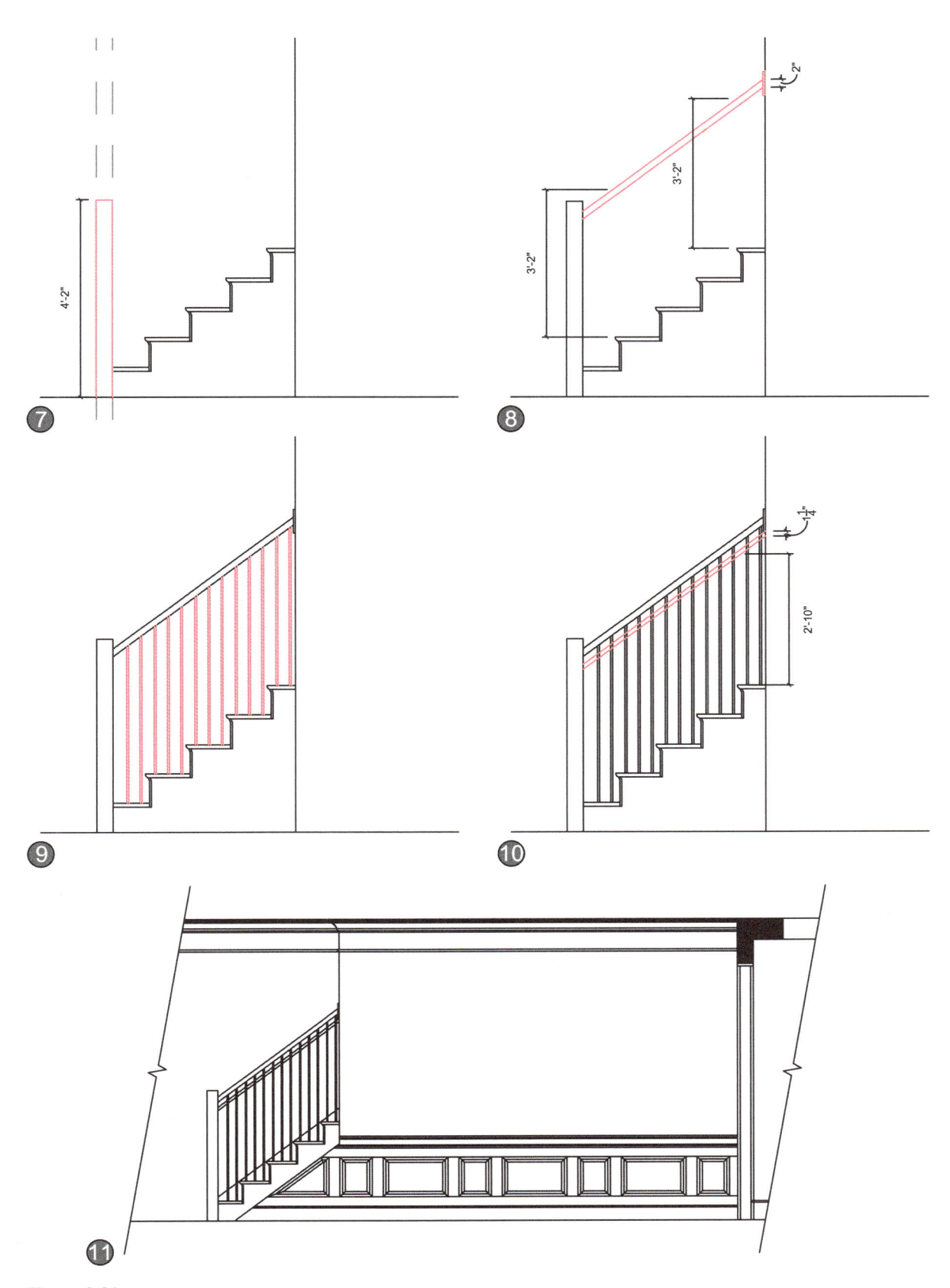

Figure 9.31
Direct run stairs, side elevation, Steps 7–11.

CHAPTER 9 STAIRS | 193

Drafting a direct run—front elevation

The callout marked 2/A3 refers to an elevation drawing that shows a view of the stairs from the front, or how the user would see it from the main entrance.

STEP 1

Rotate your stair plan so that the first step is closest to the drawing space. For this example, there is no rotation needed from the plan layout. Extend guides from wall corners or terminations into drawing space below. While a room elevation would include the hall and closet for this space, those elements will not be added until the final step, once the elevation of the stairs has been completed.

Draw two horizontal lines to represent the floor and ceiling planes. These lines measure 9'-6" apart (the ceiling height for the residential project) and should extend between the outermost guidelines.

Once the floor and ceiling are in place, hardline the walls and erase any of the guides that are still visible.

STEP 2

Extend two new guidelines from the plan for either side of the newel post. Once the guides are in place, measure 50" up from the floor line and draw a horizontal line connecting the guides. This will form the top of the newel post, and by hardlining the portions of the guides between the floor and the horizontal will form the sides. Erase any of the guides that are still visible.

> **Hand**
>
> When drawing dashed lines, place your architectural scale along your straight edge to create even spacing and uniformity for all the lines. An example of this technique can be seen in Chapter 2, Figure 2.4.

PART II DETAIL DRAWINGS

①

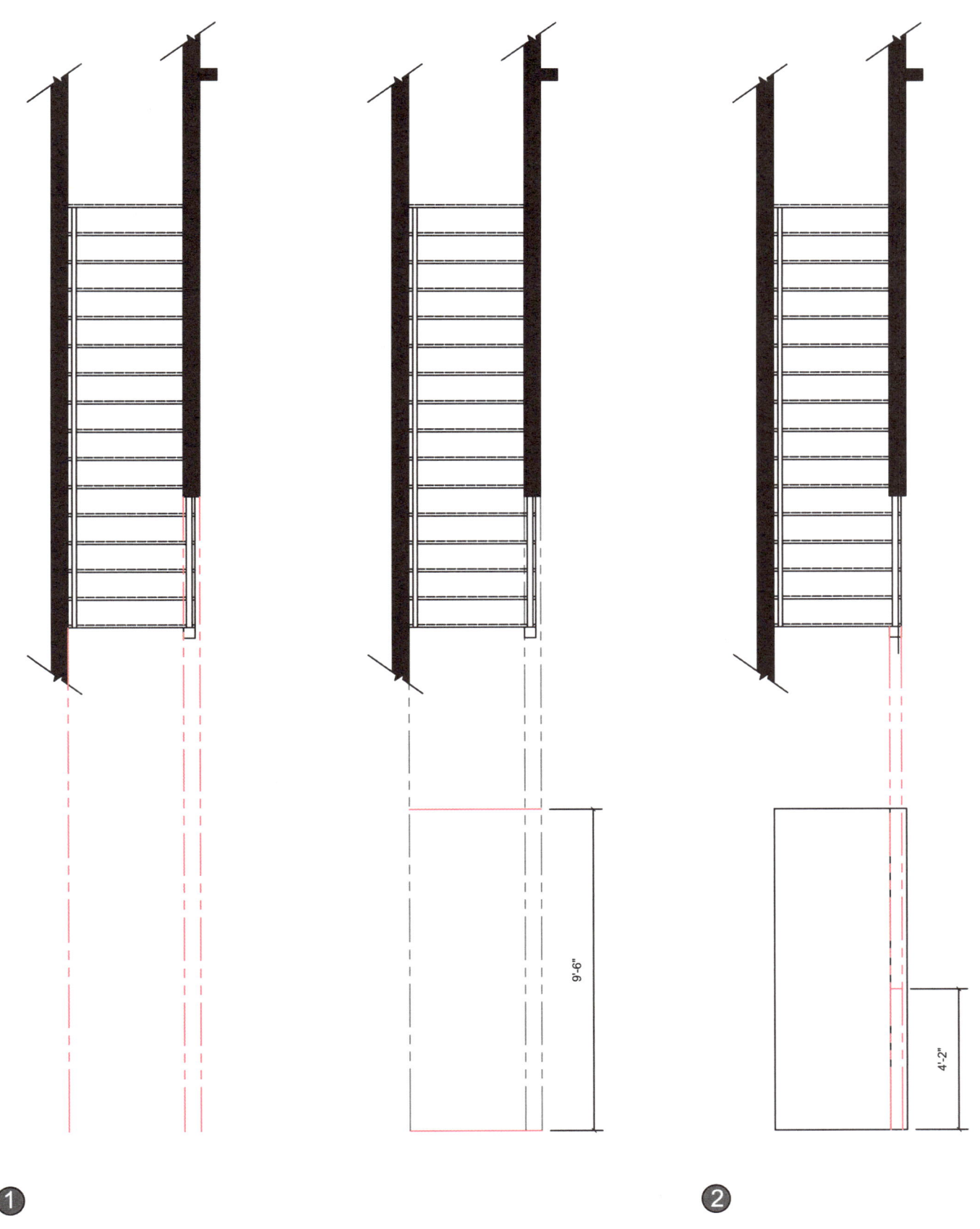

Figure 9.32
Direct run stairs, front elevation, Steps 1–2.

②

CHAPTER 9 STAIRS | 195

STEP 3

In the space allotted for the flight of stairs, draw two horizontal lines to form the bottommost tread. The first line will measure 6 1/2" above the floor line, with the second 1" above the first. Doublecheck that the top of these two lines measures 7 1/2" above the floor line, consistent with the height of the risers based on this example's calculations.

Continue to add the rest of the treads in this fashion. As the flight is taller than your ceiling height, you will not see all of the steps or the landing at the top of the staircase.

STEP 4

Add the guardrail that extends from the newel post to the wall by measuring up 6'-7 1/2" from the floor line and creating a tick mark on the face of the wall behind the newel. This measurement is based on mounting height of the guardrail being 42" above the nosing of the fifth tread.

Extend vertical lines from this tick to the newel, ensuring that they are 2" apart, with 1" spacing between the edges of the newel and the guardrail.

STEP 5

On the opposite side of the stairway, add the handrail profile 2'-10" above the nosing of the first tread. Per code, it needs to be at least 1 1/2" from the wall and should be about 1 1/2" thick. Then extend lines from each side of the rail up to the ceiling line. As with the stairs, the handrail will appear to end at the ceiling plane because in reality it terminates past the sight line for this view.

Erase any treads that appear under the rail.

STEP 6

Add any trim or details necessary to the stairs. The front elevation of the stairs is now complete and can be added to any building drawings that contain this angle of the stairs, as seen in the room elevation in Figure 9.33.

IBC

Handrails should have a circular cross-section or a rounded topmost element and a diameter between 1 1/4" and 2". *(IBC 1014.3)*

Handrails must be mounted 34" to 38" above the nosing of the tread. *(IBC 1014.2)*

Handrails must have a clearance of at least of 1 1/2" from the wall. *(IBC 1014.7)*

CAD

To change the lineweight of individual lines, click on the line to highlight it and under the Properties tab, change the lineweight to the desired weight.

Revit

To dictate the lineweights, go to the Manage tab → Settings panel → Additional Settings → Line Weights.

Once this dialog is open, you can adjust or add lineweights as necessary.

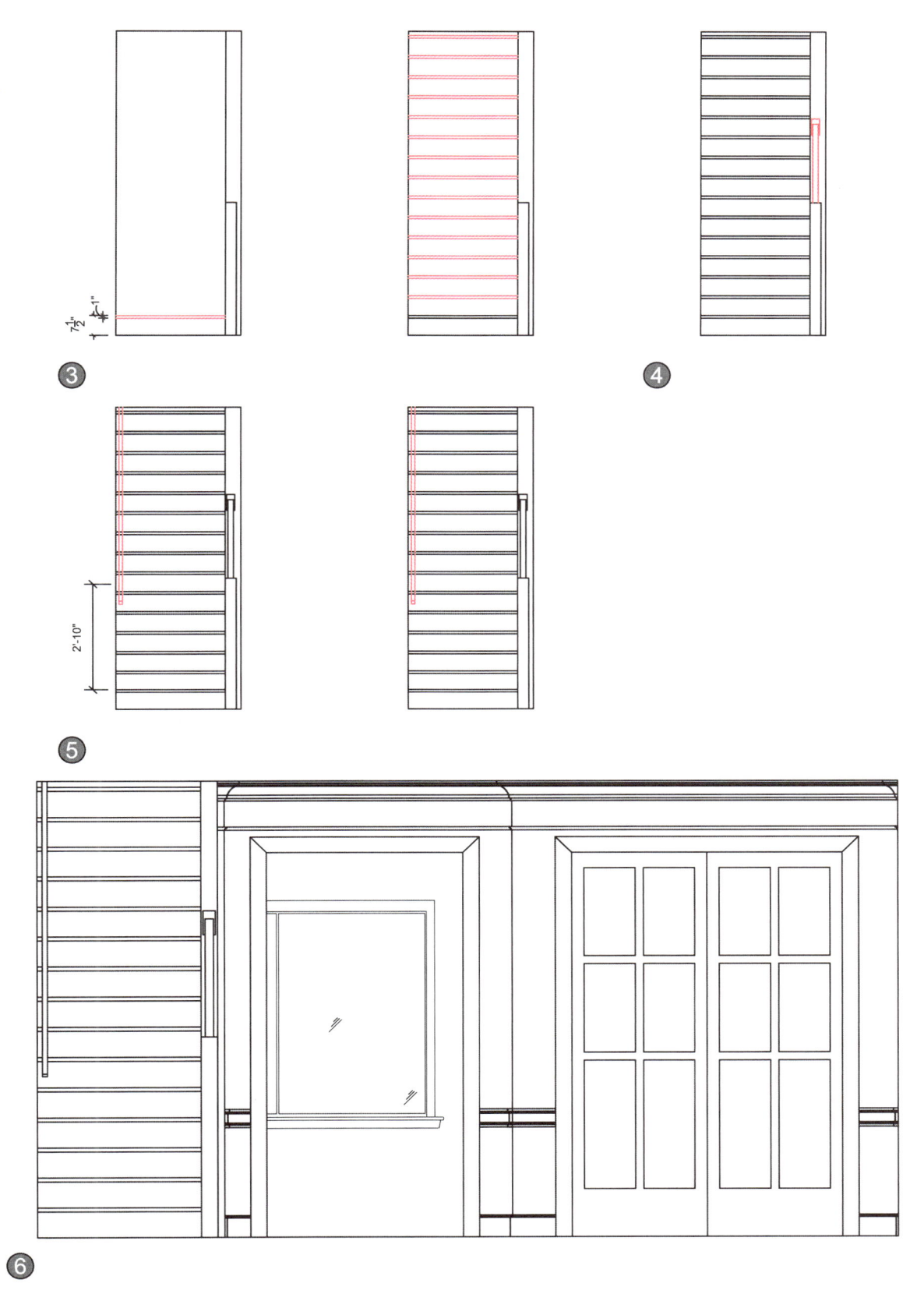

Figure 9.33
Direct run stairs, front elevation, Steps 3–6.

CHAPTER 9 STAIRS | 197

Drafting a direct run—section

Full stringer and housed stringer

The callout marked 3/A3 refers to a section drawing that cuts through the stairs in a location that would show how the stairs connect to the walls on either side of the path of travel. The step-by-step drawings for this callout will be a split view so that you can draw the stringer type of your choice. *The elements on the left will be a housed stringer, while those on the right will be a full stringer.*

STEP 1
Copy and rotate the stairs to show them in the direction the section cut is looking toward. In this case, the stairs have been rotated 180 degrees.

Erase anything from the original plan that falls below the section cut line. This will leave you with only the necessary elements to create the drawing.

STEP 2
Draw vertical lines extending from the walls into your drawing space. This will give you enough room to work while also creating the boundaries of your staircase. Draw another line 5/8" in from the boundary lines to create the gypsum wallboard (GWB) thickness.

STEP 3
Measure 1" in from the interior face of the walls you just created, and draw a guideline down into your work plane.

Leaving yourself space to work below, Create two horizontal marks from the wall to the new guideline, spacing them 12" from each other.

Erase the main guidelines you just drew, leaving the 1" horizontal lines and the 12" vertical lines between them. These lines will create the stringers for either side of staircase, measuring 1" × 12" each.

STEP 4
Measure 4" and 5" down from the top of each stringer and draw horizontal lines to connect the stringers, indicating the thickness of the tread. *This is where the two sides of the drawing will begin to differ.*

Housed: Create a notch in the stringer where it meets the tread by drawing a rectangle that is 1/4" wide by 1 1/2" high. Extend the tread into this notch and place a wedge in the remaining space, which aids in holding the tread in place.

Full: This step is complete.

STEP 5
Both sides of the staircase need blocks placed for additional support. Blocks can vary in size within a project and any sizes used here are for the sake of the example used.

Housed: Two small blocks are needed, one directly below the tread, the other aligned with the bottom of the stringer.

Full: Place a block under the stringer, in this case, it measures 1" × 5".

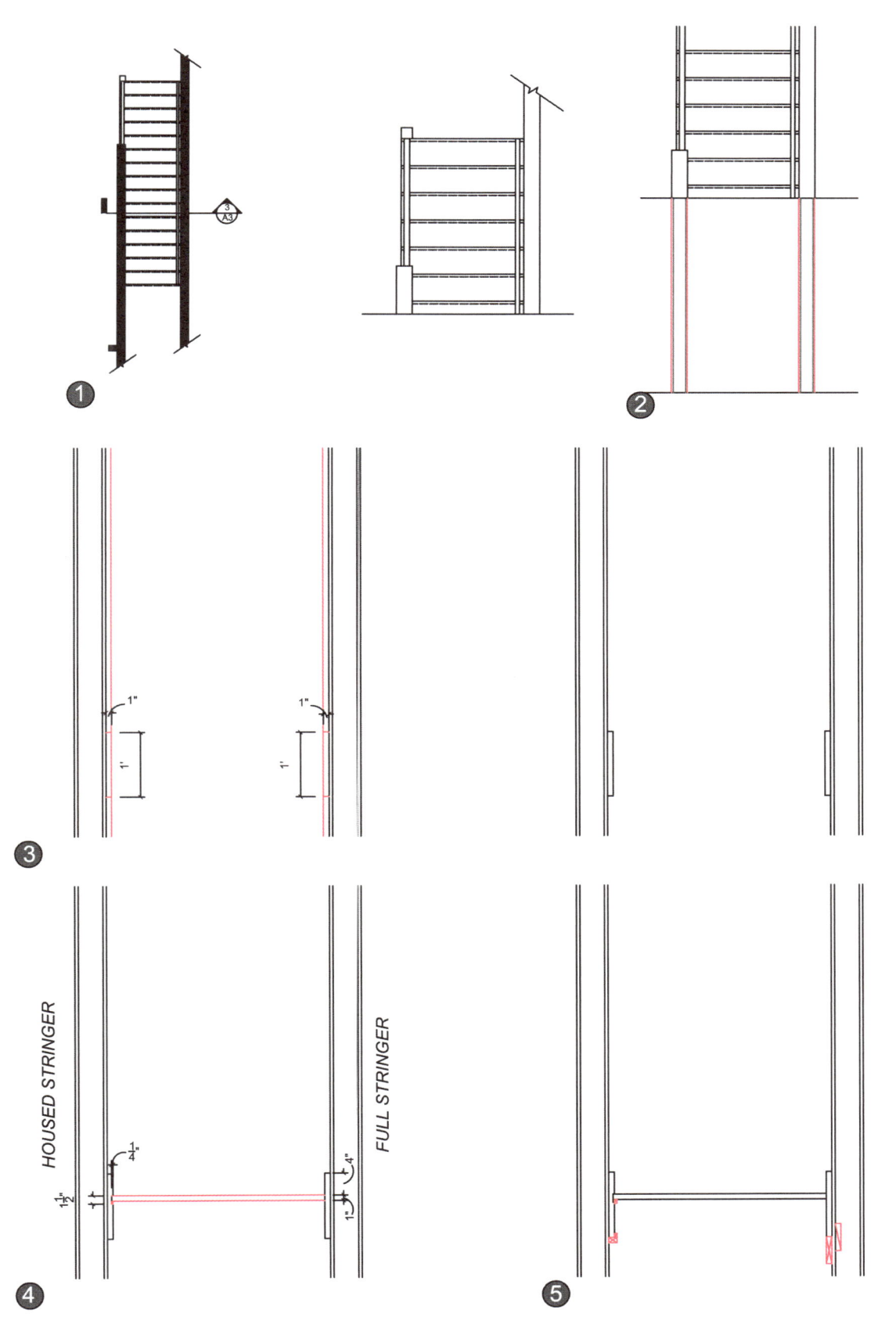

Figure 9.34
Direct run stairs, housed stringer and full stringer, Steps 1–5.

CHAPTER 9 STAIRS | 199

STEP 6

Next, the carriages will be added on both sides of the staircase as close to the existing stringers and blocks as possible.

The carriage is typically made from a 2" × 12" board, and will be drawn as a rectangle. As the board is being "cut through" in this drawing, indicate this action by drawing an X in the board.

Extend the sides of the carriage past its bottom line. This will allow for it to appear as if it recedes from view and continues along with the stairs once Step 9 is complete.

STEP 7

Between the carriages, multiple horizontal lines will be drawn to indicate the plywood substructure. Immediately below the tread, draw two horizontal lines, spaced 1/2" apart from each other. These lines will appear as section cut lines.

Based on the calculations for the staircase, measure 9 1/2" down from the top of the tread and draw another horizontal line. This line indicates the very bottom of the plywood support for the step's riser. Draw a second horizontal line 1/2" above this new line to create the thickness of the board. These lines are not being cut through, meaning they will appear in elevation.

STEP 8

The handrail for this staircase appears only on one side in this area. Measure 34" up from the top of the tread and draw a circle. The circle must appear 1 1/2" from the wall and have a diameter of 1 1/2". The top of the circle must touch the top of the guideline.

Add a supportive bracket to the circle to complete the handrail.

A block should be placed in the wall, adjacent to the handrail, to indicate where the handrail is anchored.

STEP 9

Finalize the detail by adding any necessary dimensions, annotations, materials, and a partition assembly along the back of the staircase.

Lineweights should be adjusted to match the standards established in Part I of this text, with heavier lineweights used on objects that are being cut through and lighter lineweights used for material textures.

As the main elements of this drawing are not on the floor or ceiling, you can also add breaklines to finish the image.

RoT

Each stringer can project into the clear space of a stairway a maximum of 1 1/2".

If the stair width is already at the minimum size, the stringers cannot project into the clear space.

The carriage can be created from various sized boards, but it is recommended that you use 2" × 12" or 2" × 14".

Hand

The cleanest way to work with section drawings is to create a draft of the section on trace paper. You can then copy the lines you wish to keep and use the proper lineweights on to vellum.

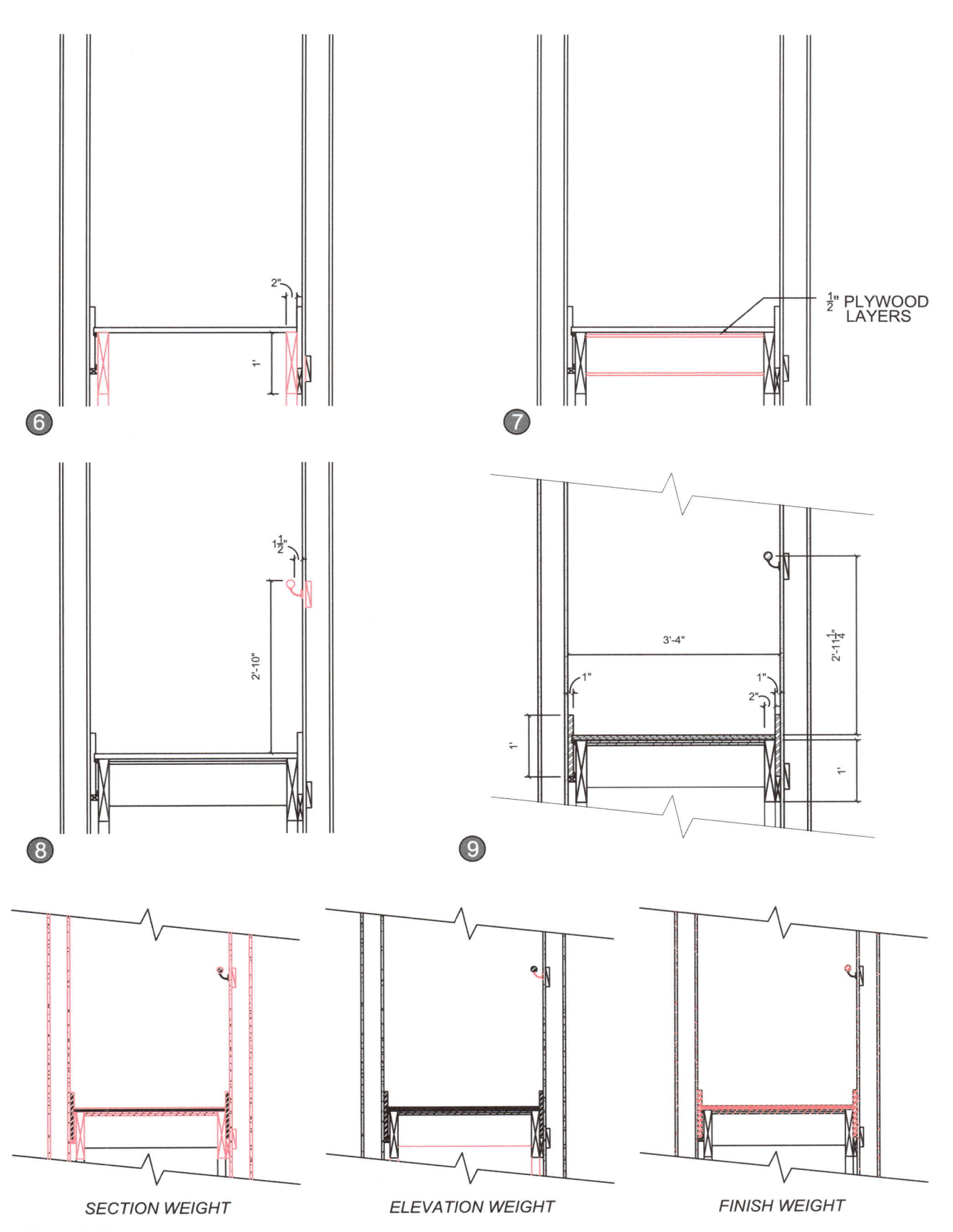

Figure 9.35
Direct run stairs, housed stringer and full stringer, Steps 6–9.

CHAPTER 9 STAIRS | 201

Drafting a run—section

Open stringer with rail

The callout marked 4/A3 refers to a section drawing that cuts through the stairs in a location that would show the open stringers and guardrail at the bottom of the flight.

While the right side of the drawing featuring the full wall will be developed, the following instructions will focus solely on the open stringer on the left side. For instructions on full or housed risers, see the previous section.

STEP 1
Copy and rotate the stairs to show them in the direction the section cut is looking in to. In this case, the stairs have been rotated 180 degrees.

Then erase anything from the original plan that falls below the section cut line.

STEP 2
Draw vertical guidelines extending from the wall and open riser tread edge into your drawing space.

STEP 3
This example indicates that the section is cutting through the third tread, which would measure 1'-10 1/2" from the ground. Draw a horizontal line to indicate the top of the tread and a second line 1" below this line to indicate the tread's thickness.

As this is an open stringer, the edge of the tread will extend past the stringer. Draw two vertical lines from the bottom of the tread to the floor, spaced 1" apart from each other and 1" from the edge of the tread. An edge detail can be added to the side of the exposed tread, typically a continuation of the nosing detail.

STEP 4
The carriage is typically made from a 2" × 12" board, and will be drawn as a rectangle.

Place the carriage 1/2" away from the stringer. As the board is being "cut through" in this drawing, indicate this action by drawing an X in the rectangle.

Extend the sides of the carriage to the floor. These two lines represent the carriages continuing on with the staircase past the section cut and will appear in elevation. Draw a horizontal line 2" up from the floor plane connecting these two carriages. This line creates the thickness of the block used to anchor the carriages to the floor.

STEP 5
Between the carriage and the stringer, add two small blocks, one directly under the tread and the other closer to the bottom of the carriage.

Place a larger block directly below the carriage. Trim the line that you extended to the floor in the previous step.

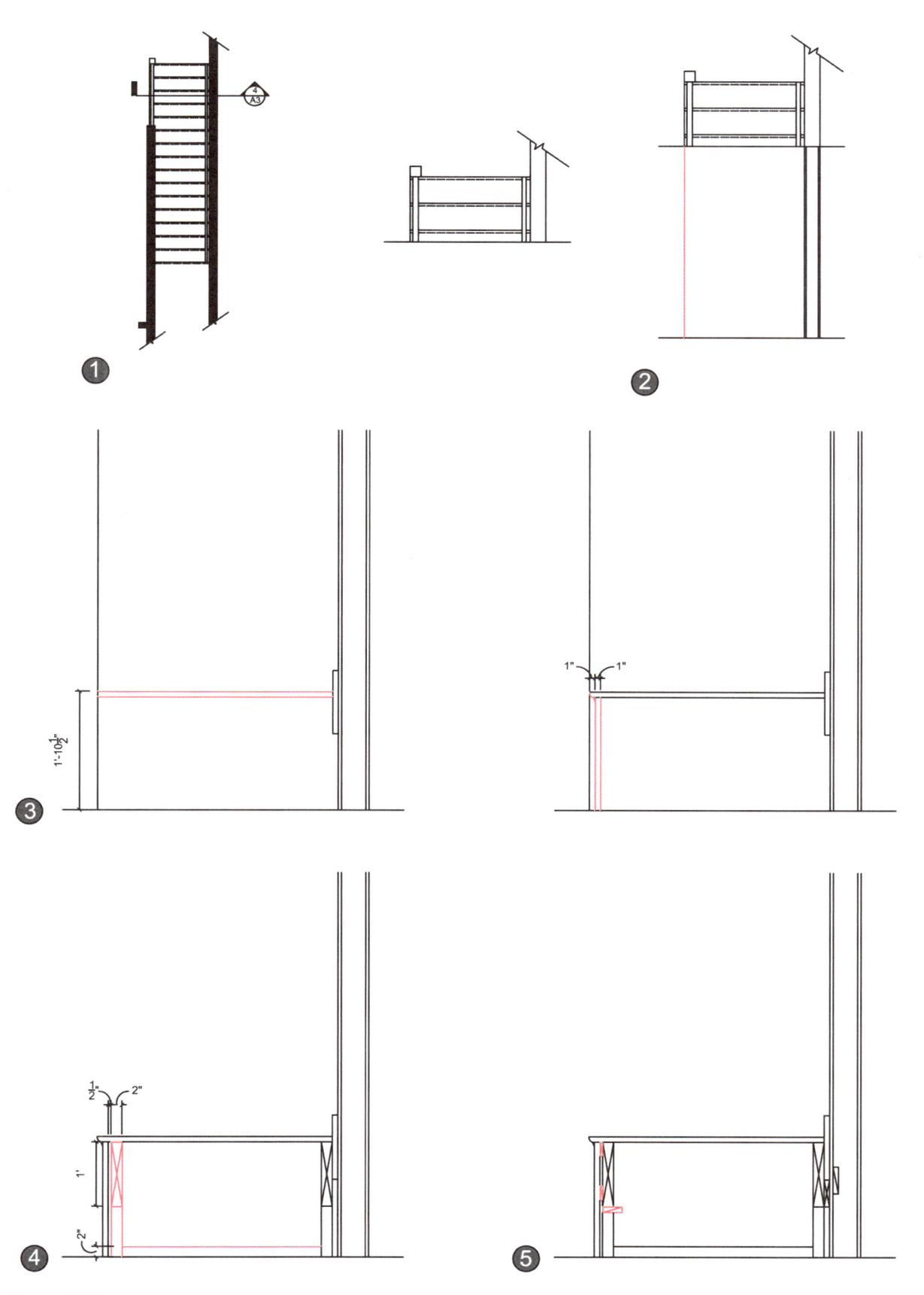

Figure 9.36
Direct run stairs, open stringer, Steps 1–5.

CHAPTER 9 STAIRS

STEP 6

Between the carriages, multiple horizontal lines will be drawn to indicate the plywood substructure. Immediately below the tread, draw two horizontal lines, spaced 1/2" apart from each other. These lines will appear as section cut lines.

Based on the calculations for the staircase, measure 9 1/2" down from the top of the tread and draw another horizontal line. This line indicates the very bottom of the plywood support for the step's riser. Draw a second horizontal line 1/2" above this new line to create the thickness of the board. These lines are not being cut through, meaning they will appear in elevation. Repeat this process for the lower steps.

At this time, add the edges of the treads over the side of the stringer, extending them no more than 1".

STEP 7

The guardrail for this staircase appears only on one side in this area. Measure 38" up from the top of the tread and draw the desired shape of the rail, the top of which must touch the top of the guideline. The rail will appear with a heavier lineweight, as it will be cut through in section.

Place the newel post into the drawing, measuring 4" wide and up 42" from the finished floor plane. The newel will appear in elevation, as it is not being cut through in this detail.

STEP 8

Connect the guardrail to the newel post with a series of lines in a standard lineweight. A baluster can also be added, shown in elevation, between the tread and the bottom of the guardrail.

STEP 9

Finalize the detail by adding any necessary dimensions, annotations, materials, and a partition assembly along the back of the staircase. Lineweights should be adjusted to match the standards established in Part I of this text, with heavier lineweights used on objects that are being cut through and lighter lineweights used for material textures. As the main elements of this drawing are not on the ceiling, you can also add a breakline to finish the image.

CAD

Depending on how you work, there are two ways to ensure clarity for yourself when drawing details such as stairs:

1. Create individual layers for each element so that you have one for the stringers, one for treads, etc.

2. Create a stair layer so that the stairway can be turned on and off or frozen all at the same time, but change the color of individual lines within that layer. This can be done by clicking on a line to highlight it and then changing the color from By Layer to the one of your choice under the General section of the Properties menu.

RoT

The closed-riser stair features a tread that overlaps the stringer. This edge can be flat or can feature the same detailing as the nosing that appears on the front of the tread.

For examples of acceptable nosing designs and measurements, refer to Appendix I.

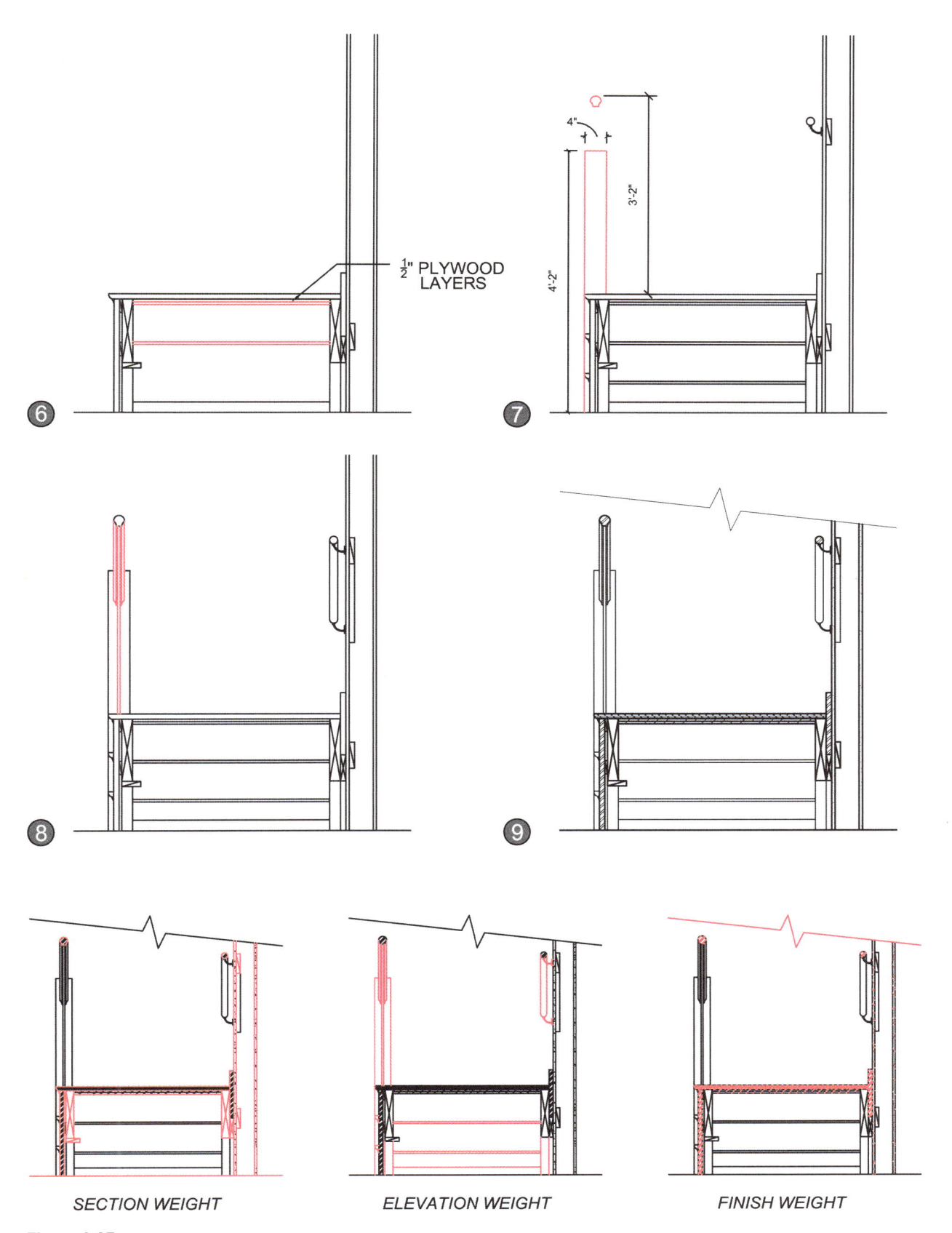

Figure 9.37
Direct run stairs, open stringer, Steps 6—9.

SECTION WEIGHT

ELEVATION WEIGHT

FINISH WEIGHT

½" PLYWOOD LAYERS

CHAPTER 9 STAIRS | 205

Drafting a direct run—section

Full flight

The callout marked 5/A3 refers to a section drawing that cuts through the full flight of stairs. The completed section that is called out in the direct run floor plan can be seen below. For information on sections, see Part I of this text. For instructions on drawing a *U*-shaped stair section, which can be adapted for your needs, see the section on steel stairs for commercial use.

Other wooden elements

For acceptable nosings and rails, see Appendix I.

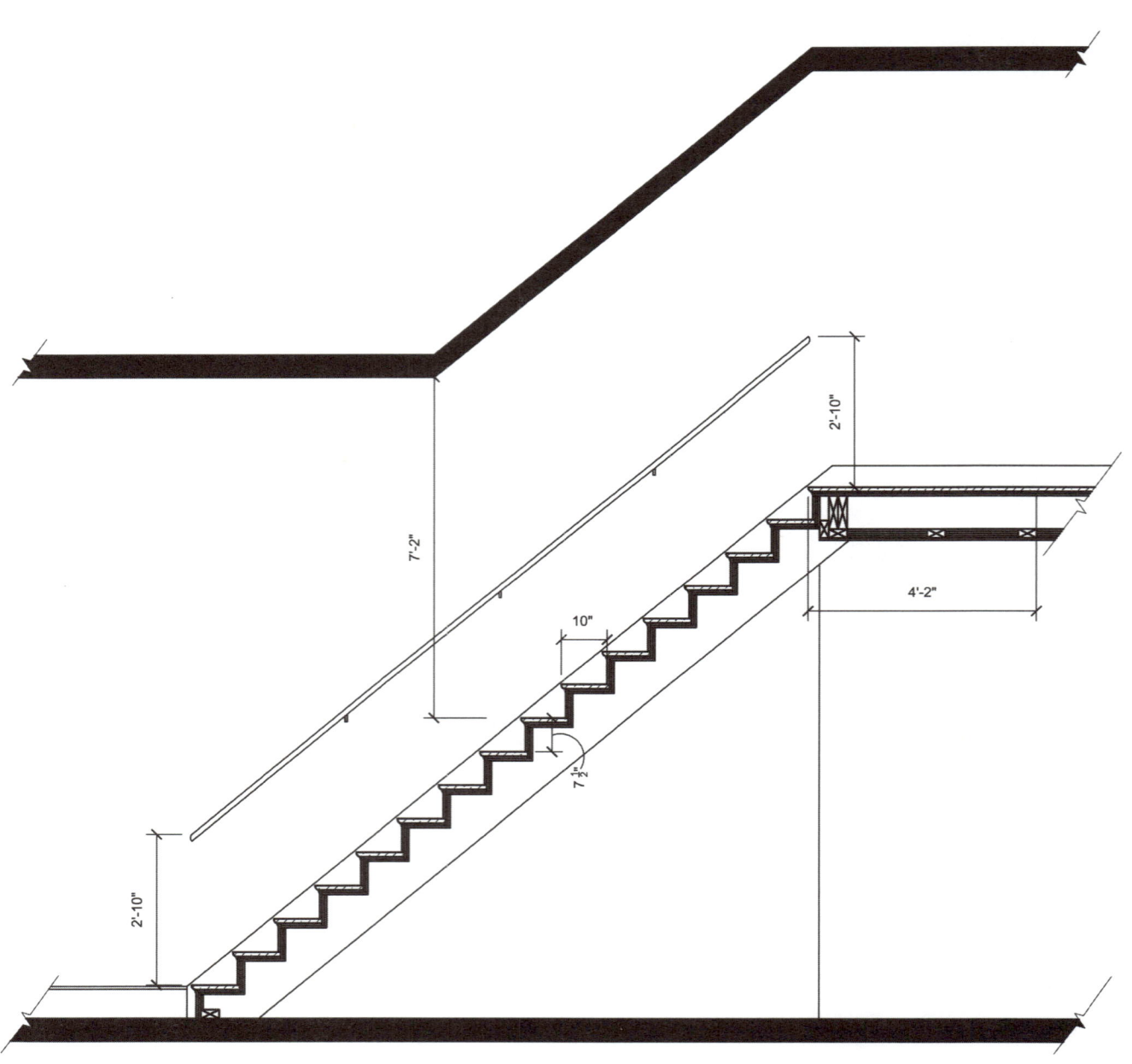

Figure 9.38
Direct run stairs, full flight section.

STUDIO Animation 9.1 Direct run full flight details (wood)

DRAFTING A STEEL U-RUN—COMMERCIAL

Steel stairs, while appearing similar to wooden stairs, have several changes in their construction, as discussed earlier in this chapter. This section will explore the elements used in steel stairs and how to draw a steel U-run flight, the handrails, and the necessary callouts and construction details. The stair used for this example has been taken from the egress stair in the commercial project file.

A U-Run is flight of stairs that utilizes two runs that travel in opposite directions and are connected by a centralized landing. These types of runs are ideal when the total rise is more than 12'-0", as a central landing provides both a resting point and creates a shorter total run than if a direct flight were to be used.

For this example, an exit stair will be drawn with a total rise of 12'-3" and the landing depth will be 48", as it must measure at least the width of the clear space of the run. While the stair calculations discussed earlier in the chapter can be used to determine the dimensions and number of risers and treads, there are some important changes to note.

First, as there will be a landing for this set of stairs, when calculating the number of treads, subtract two from the number of risers: one for the landing at the top of the stairs and one for the landing in the middle of the flight.

Second, as there will be two halves to the full flight of stairs, the total run calculation will not need to include all of the treads to determine the length of the staircase. Instead, the number of treads will be divided by two. If this results in a fraction, round up to the next whole number. Then, to find the length of the space that the staircase will occupy, the depth of the landing will be added on.

Finally, it is important to remember that there are key differences in the codes that are implemented for egress stairs than those that are used for ornamental stairs.

Riser height and quantity

Total rise = 12'-3" = 147"
147/7 = 21
21 risers @ 7"

Tread quantity

Number of risers = 2
21 − 2 = **19 Treads**

Tread depth

T = 25 − 2R
T = 25 − 2(7)
T = 25 − 14
T = 11"

Run

Depth of treads × Number of treads
11 × 10 = 110" = **9'-2"**

*Add the landing depth to the run to find the distance from the first nose to the landing:

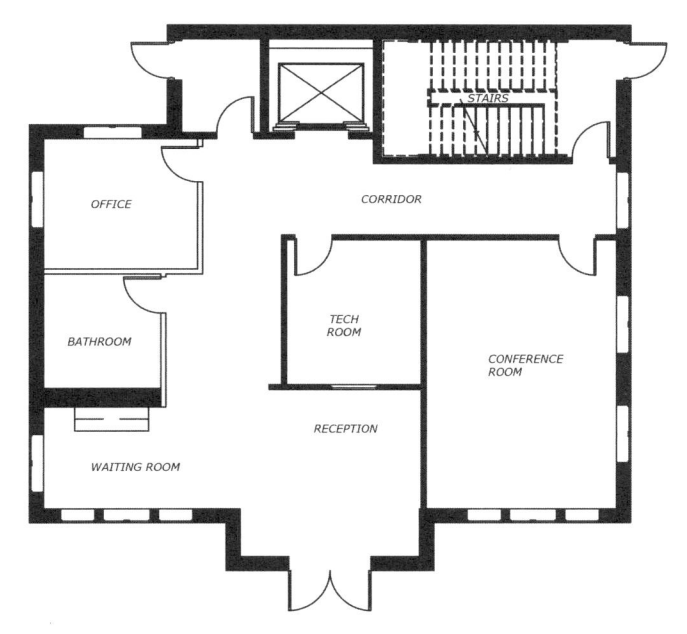

Run + Landing depth
9'-2" + 4'-5" = **13'-7"**

Figure 9.39
U-run stairs, commercial plan.

Drafting a U-run—plan

STEP 1

Draw a rectangle on the floor plan to designate the footprint, or area, that the stairs will occupy. For this example, the rectangle should measure 13'-7" long by 10'-0" wide, as determined in the previous section. The dashed line indicates the landing on the second story.

STEP 2

Draw a line 4'-5" from the rear wall to indicate where the landing will be. This dimension is based on the spacing required for the depth of the clear space for the landing plus the steel channel and railing:

$$2" \quad + \quad 48" \quad + \quad 1\,{}^1/_2" \quad + \quad 1\,{}^1/_2" \quad = \quad 53"$$

Channel   *Landing*   *Handrail*   *Spacing*

STEP 3

Because this staircase will be used as a means of egress, each run must measure 48" of clear space and have handrails on both sides. If you add the spacing from the wall and the handrail width, each run should measure at least 54" wide, as seen in this equation:

$$1\,{}^1/_2" \quad + \quad 1\,{}^1/_2" \quad + \quad 48" \quad + \quad 1\,{}^1/_2" \quad + \quad 1\,{}^1/_2" \quad = \quad 54"$$

Spacing   *Handrail*   *Stairs*   *Handrail*   *Spacing*   *Run width*

Using this dimension, measure 54" from the outer lines of the original rectangle and draw a line. This will create the outline for each run of the flight. The 1'-0" notation indicates the spacing between runs, which can be eaten into by the runs if you want a wider tread.

STEP 4

This example has an odd number of required treads (19), so the first run will be shorter than the second, which will also allow for improved spacing with the exit door. For the first run, move the line indicating the start of the stairs 11" toward the central landing, shortening the run by one tread.

STEP 5

Draw lines 2" from the edge of both runs and the landing. These lines will represent the steel channels.

STEP 6

Measure 11" from the bottom of the first run rectangle and draw a line to create the first tread. Repeat this for the remaining treads in the first run and secnd run, making sure they are 11" apart from each other, until you reach the landings.

IBC

Commercial stairways

Landings (*IBC 1011.6*)

The total rise cannot exceed 12'-0" without either connecting to the upper level or a central landing being created.

Landings must be as deep as the width of the staircase they serve, meaning that if the staircase is 60" wide, the landing must be 60" deep.

Nosing (*IBC 1011.5.5*)

1 ½" with 60 degree slope under nose max

Maximum 1/2" radius at edge

Materials (*IBC 1011.7*)

Steel construction only

Wood or steel rails

Width (*IBC 1011.2*)

44" minimum clear space

Exit stairway 48" clear

Treads (*IBC 1011.5.2*)

11" minimum nose to nose

Risers (*IBC 1011.5.2*)

7" max

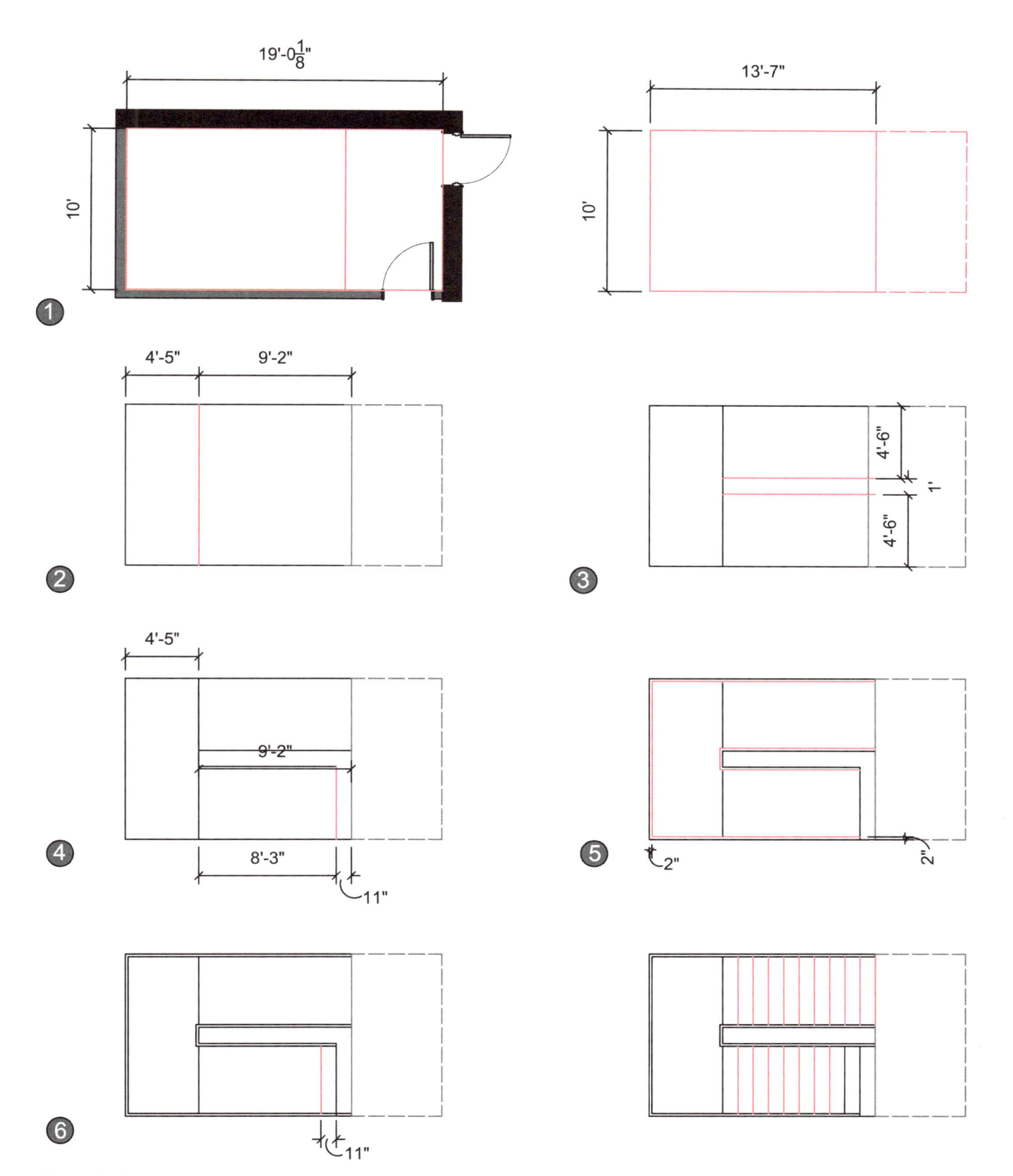

Figure 9.40
U-run stairs, plan, Steps 1–6.

STEP 7

To indicate the nosing and the riser underneath, measure 1" from the front of the first tread and draw a dashed line. This creates the illusion that the tread hangs over the riser that supports it.

Create the remaining noses by drawing dashed lines 1" in from the front of the tread for the remaining stairs, both in the first run and in the second.

STEP 8

To create the handrail, draw a line 1 1/2" from the side of the staircase along the wall. Then draw a second line 1 1/2" in from the line you just drew.

Repeat this along the opposite side of the first run and on both sides of the second run.

STEP 9

At the bottom of the staircase, the handrail along the wall needs to be extended *12"+T*. In this example, the *T* = 11", so the handrail is to be extended a total of 1'-11".

At the top of the first run, the handrail along the wall needs to be extended 1'-0".

Repeat this for the side along the wall of the second run of stair.

STEP 10

Along the central landing between the two runs, the rails must be connected to each other.

STEP 11

To create the guardrail, draw two lines, spaced at least 1" apart, along the steel channels between the two runs and along the open edges of the landings.

STEP 12

Annotate the staircase by indicating the path of travel and dimensions to complete the drawing.

A breakline can be added to indicate what appears as a solid line in plan and what appears as a dashed line (typically anything 4'-0" above finished floor [AFF]).

Erase the tread and riser lines that pass through the handrail if you have not already done so.

If detail drawings of certain aspects of the plan are needed, add section cuts, elevation markers, or create a callout bubble around those objects. The numbers that go into the tag indicate the drawing number and page number for locating the drawings in a set, as will be discussed in Part III of this text.

CAD

Using the line tool and creating groups within the drawing will make it easier to edit your stair drawings.

The ability to see and edit individual layers can be toggled on and off through the Layer drop-down. Using the drop-down, click on the light bulb to turn it on or off, making the layer hidden or visible. Click on the sun to change it to a snowflake, freezing the ability to edit the layer and locking its elements in place.

Revit

Using the Stair button found in the Architecture tab, you can quickly create a flight of stairs with handrails. After activating the tool, click once in the drawing window and move your mouse in the direction of travel to create the first run. Once you have created the desired number of treads, click once to generate them and move your mouse parallel to the last tread created. Click again to start the second run and click for a fourth time to complete the staircase. The landing should be automatically generated between the runs.

Figure 9.41
U-run stairs, plan, Steps 7–12.

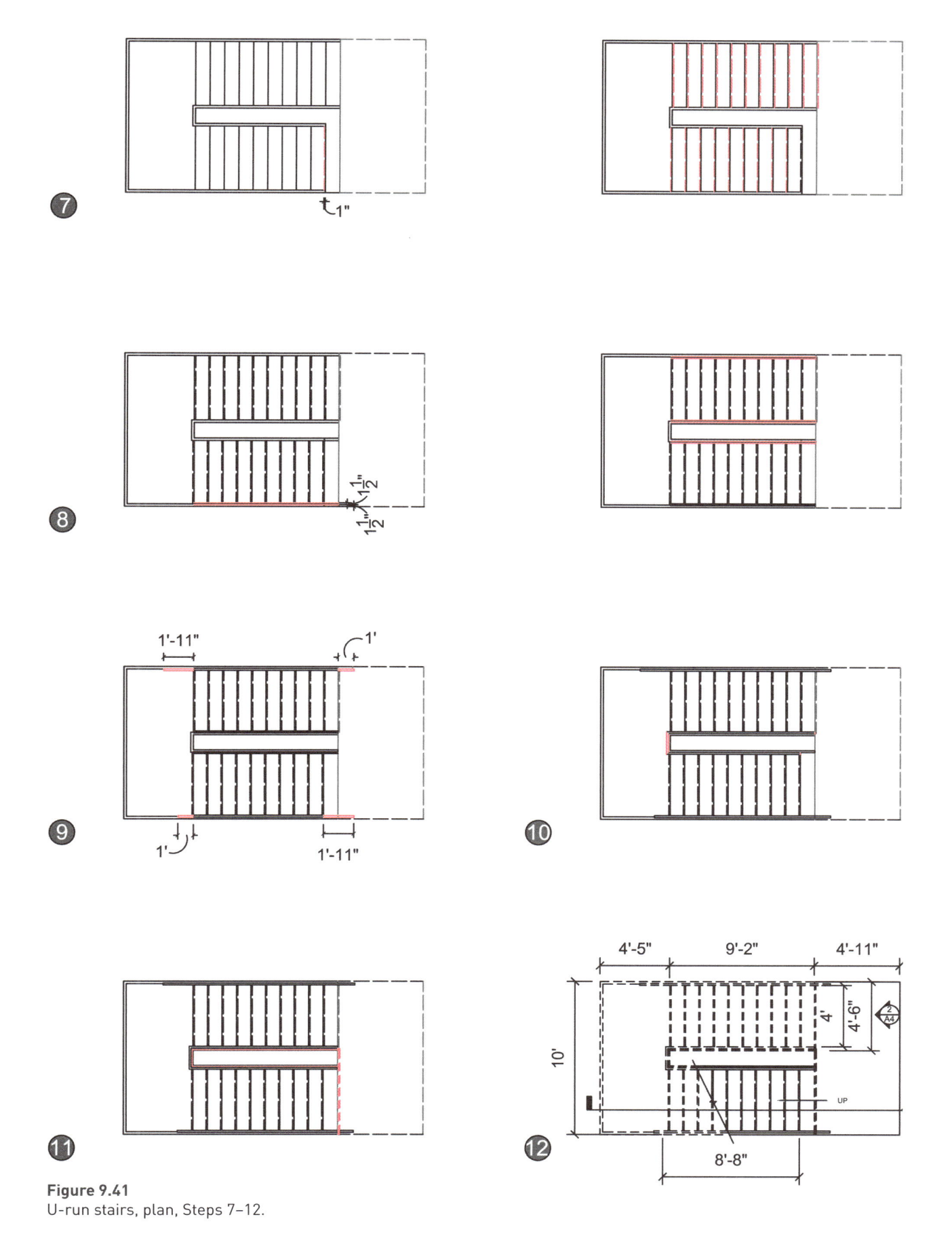

CHAPTER 9 STAIRS

Drafting a U-run—section

The callout marked 3/A4 refers to a section drawing that cuts through the first run of stairs and central landing. From this view, you will be able to see the interior construction of the staircase as well as the second run in elevation behind it.

STEP 1
Copy and rotate the stairs to show them in the direction the section cut is looking in to. In this case, the stairs do not need to be rotated to be in the desired orientation.

Then erase anything from the original plan that falls below the section cut line.

STEP 2
Draw vertical guidelines extending from the walls and noses of both the central landing and the top landing into your drawing space. Also add guidelines from the nosings and risers for the first two steps.

STEP 3
Draw horizontal lines from the first guideline to the last to create the floor and ceiling planes, measuring 21'-3" apart. The vertical guidelines that represent the walls can be hardlined at this time.

Between these two lines, indicate the central landing and the top landing by adding horizontal lines from the exterior walls to their noses. Based on the dimensions for this example, the central landing line will be 5'-10"AFF, while the top landing will be 12'-3" AFF.

This example will now focus on the stairs themselves, using the four guidelines drawn in Step 2, which will occupy the space shown in the dashed red circle.

STEP 4
This step will focus on creating the first step. When complete, parts A–C will appear in section, while part D will appear as an elevation.

A. Draw a horizontal line 7" up from the floor line spanning from the first guideline to the last. Next, draw a vertical line along the third guide up 4 3/4" from the floor. Connect the top of this line to the end of the first line, creating a diagonal to form the nosing. This line should be approximately 2 1/2" and should create an angle of 30 degrees or less.

   Copy these same lines 3/16" away from the originals to create the tread's rubber finish thickness.

B. Add the tread slab below the finish by drawing a horizontal line 2" from the bottom of the rubber finish. This line should extend 1/8" past the first guideline to accommodate for framework in future steps.

C. To form the steel framework below the treads, draw another horizontal line 1/8" below the tread slab, extending it 1/4" past the first guideline. Add another vertical line 1/8" behind the riser. Ensure that these two lines connect.

D. Add the final vertical and horizontal lines 1 1/8" in from the framework, extending them until they intersect. The vertical should hit the ground plane while the horizontal will measure 8 1/2", making it 1/4" shy of the second guideline. Create a diagonal connecting these lines to form the support angle.

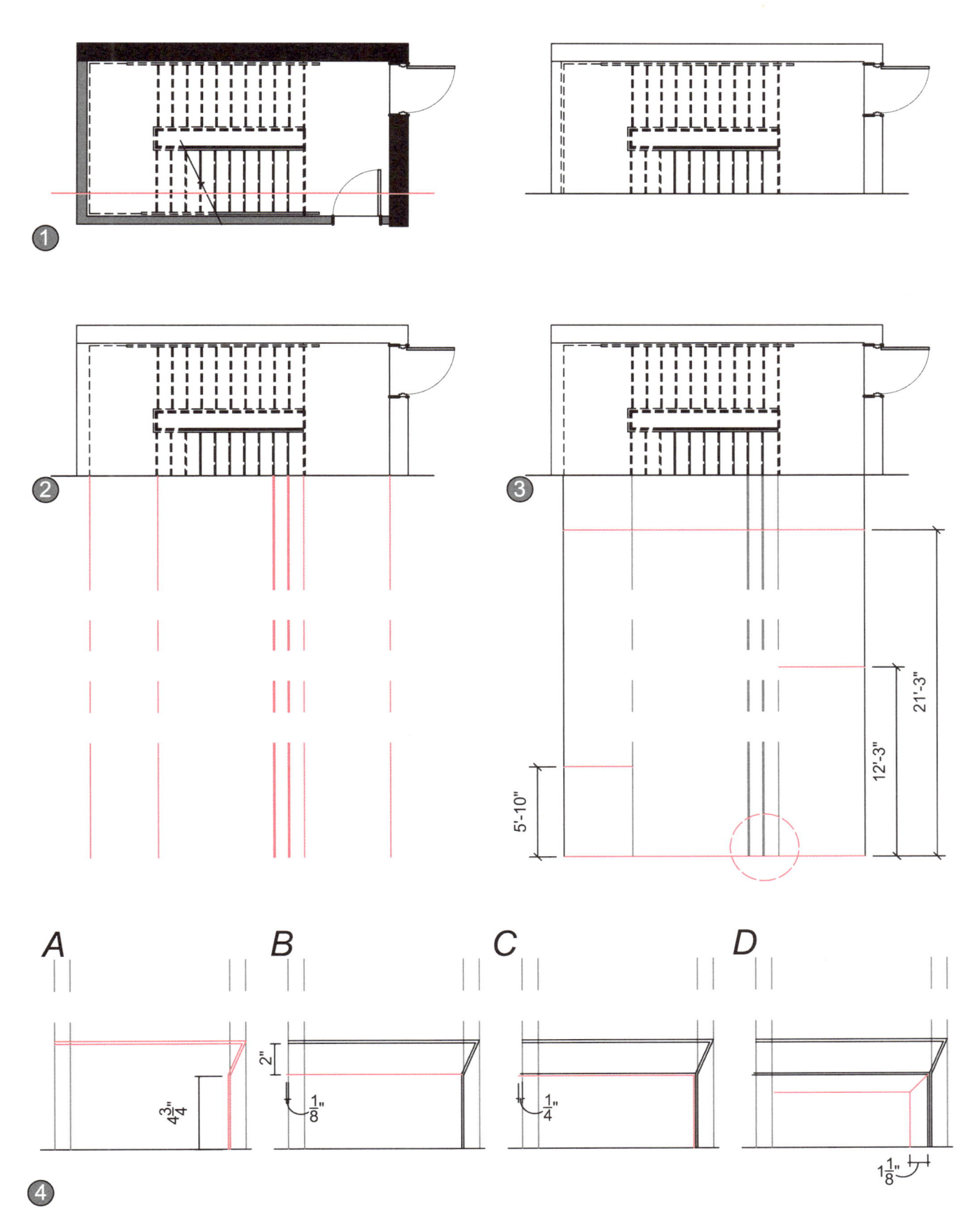

Figure 9.42
U-run stairs, section, Steps 1–4.

CHAPTER 9 STAIRS

STEP 5

This step will focus on adding the second step of the first run.

A. Copy the first step and place it so that the top of the tread is 1'-2" above the floor, with the front of the riser aligned with the first guideline (touching the top back corner of the tread) and the nose is aligned with the second guideline. The guidelines can now be erased.
B. Connect the framework for the second step to that of the first step.
C. Elongate the vertical line for the angle support so that it measures 4 1/2". At the end of this line, draw a horizontal line to connect the vertical to the bottom of the framework for the step below. Trim any piece that cuts through the step's framework.
D. The final view of these two steps alone shows the heavier lineweight and hatch patterns that pertain to the portions seen in section view, with the lighter elevation lines shown in the distance.

STEP 6

Complete the first run of stairs up to the landing by copying the second step up the remainder of the flight. Add an extra one to account for the central landing, minus the steel angle, extending its lines to the wall.

STEP 7

This step will focus on adding supports around and under the central landing.

A. Create a 10" high by 2" wide rectangle at the wall, with 3" appearing above the landing. Erase any of the landing that passes through this rectangle.

 Offset lines 1/4" into the rectangle, forming what looks like a *C*. This will make the steel channel that runs around the staircase.
B. Draw a 3 1/2" × 3 1/2" square under the front and back of the landing. Within these squares, draw a second square measuring 3" × 3", creating the appearance of a hollow tube to represent the channel support.

Hand

When an object is in the background of a section, it should appear with your standard lineweight to imply that the object is being seen in elevation and is not being cut through.

CAD

Use the default lineweights when you are creating the section drawings. When you complete the drawing, simply click on the lines you wish to give a heavier weight, and in the Properties panel of the Home tab, you can alter the lineweight from By Layer to the weight of your choice.

Revit

While Revit has saved you quite a bit of time when drawing the stair plans, the program only creates an outline of the drawing in section, not filling in the carriages, blocking, or any other interior elements.

The easiest way to add these details is by opening the section views that you have created and adding the individual elements with Detail Components. These premade construction elements can be found by accessing the Annotation toolbar and using the Component drop-down. You can also utilize Detail Lines, which can also be found in the Detail panel of the Annotate toolbar, and will allow you to draw directly onto the existing section. These components and lines will not appear in any other drawing.

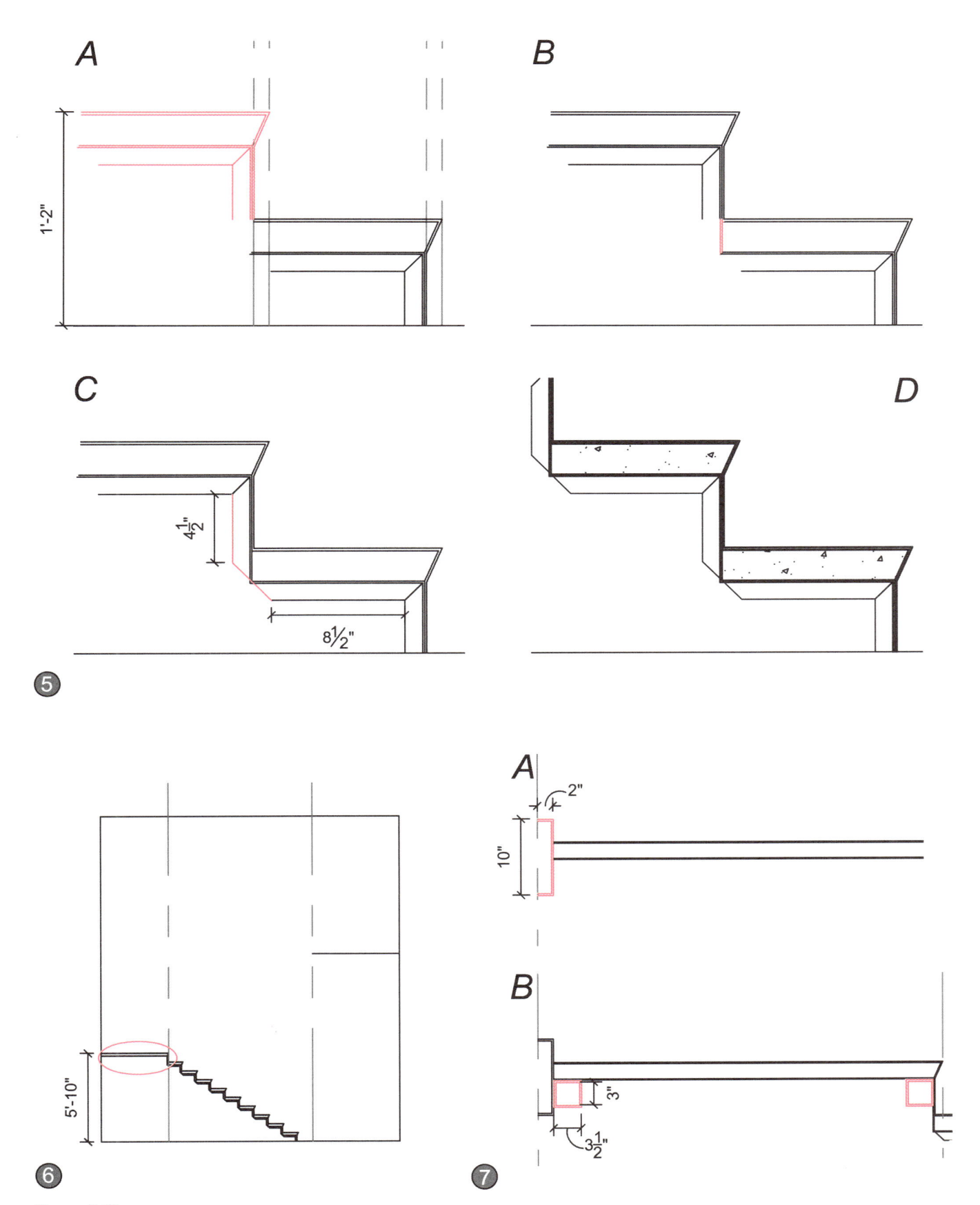

Figure 9.43
U-run stairs, section, Steps 5–7.

CHAPTER 9 STAIRS | 215

STEP 8
Create the steel channel along the side of the staircase:

A. Extend the steel channel from Step 7 by drawing horizontal guidelines from the *C*-shape to the guideline for the landing's nose. This guideline can now be erased.

B. Draw a diagonal guideline connecting all of the noses for the stairs. At the base of the stair, run the diagonal 5" past the first nose and then create a vertical to connect the diagonal to the floor plane. At the landing, intersect the diagonal with the horizontal drawn in Step 8.A. Trim the portion of the horizontal that runs past the diagonal.

    Measure this angle as it will be needed in a moment. The angle used in this example is 32 degrees from horizontal.

C. For the portion of the steel channel that is visible under the staircase, utilize the same 32 degree angle, ensuring that it is 10" away from the first diagonal. This can be done by creating guidelines running in the opposite direction (add 180 degrees to the original degree angle you used) from the diagonal, through the nosing, to the space below the stair. In this example, as the original angle was 32 degrees, the opposite angle for the guides will be 212 degrees.

    Connect the ends of the guidelines to create the underside of the steel channel.

    Trim the diagonal where it crosses the floor plane and adjust the intersection of the diagonal and the steel channel under the landing.

D. Hardline the steel channel, remembering that it will appear in elevation in this view. Add the clip angle to the bottom of the stairs, in front of the steel channel.

STEP 9
Add the second run of stairs from the first landing up to the second. As this run is not being cut through, the stairs are blocked from view by the steel channel, which will be seen in elevation. For reference, the stairs have been dashed in, but due to the complicated nature of this drawing, they make the image muddy and will not appear in the rest of this example. However, it is important to note where several of the nosings are located for reference in the next few steps.

The placement of the section cut in this example does result in the second landing being cut through and will be treated in the same manner as the central landing.

RoT
The steel channel must be at least 10", but larger sizes are available depending on design and construction.

The channels will be bolted together and create the frame around the entire staircase.

Hand
You may choose to tape the elevation of the staircase next to the work space. This will allow you to carry horizontal lines over to the section or to simply act as a reference.

When an object is in the background of a section, it should appear with your lineweight to imply that the object is being seen in elevation and is not being cut through.

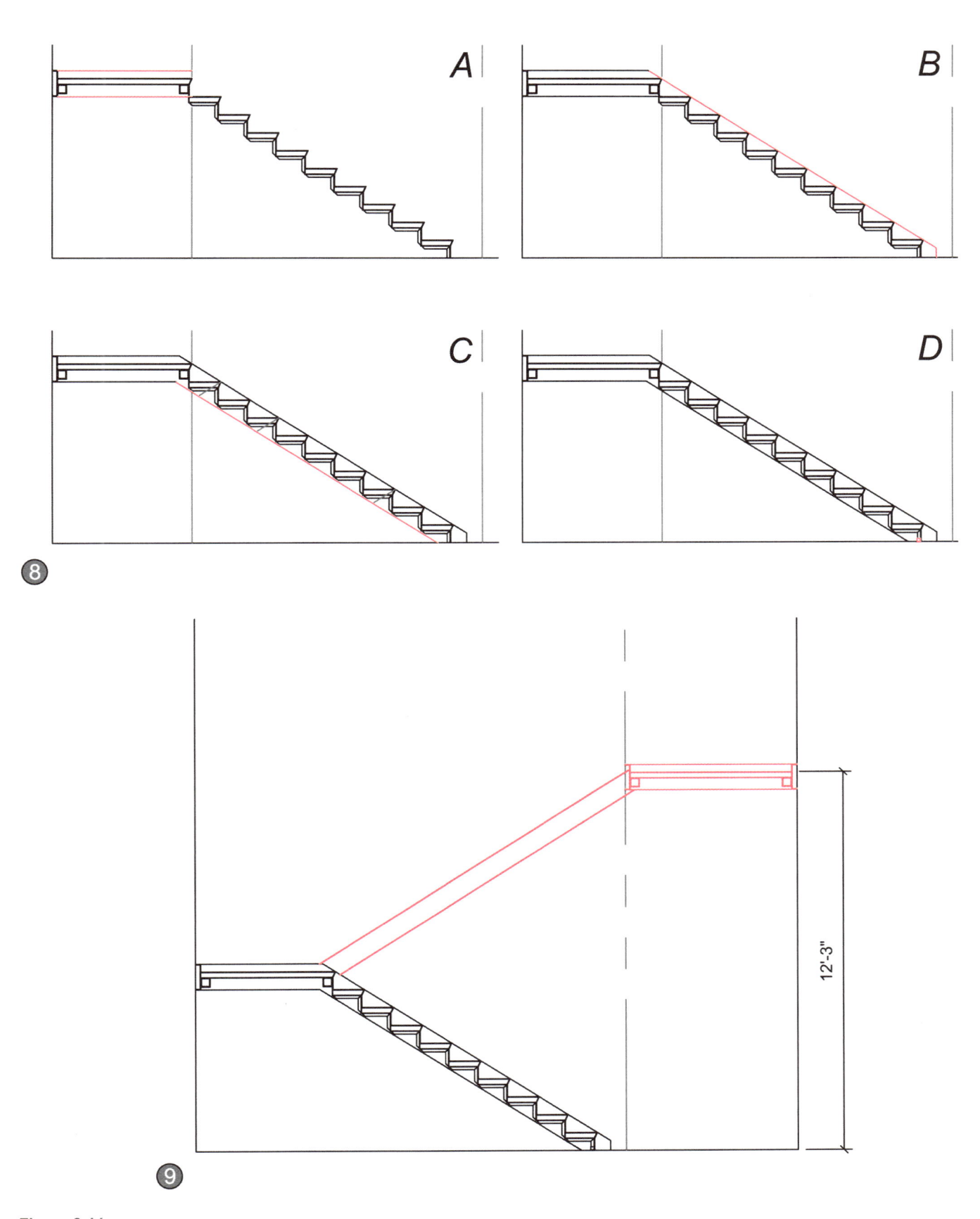

Figure 9.44
U-run stairs, section, Steps 8–9.

CHAPTER 9 STAIRS | 217

STEP 10
Draw the handrail of your choice up both runs. Make sure that the top of the rail measures 34" to 38" above the tread nosings, with this example using a 36" high rail. The easiest way to ensure this is to draw a guideline from several of the noses up to the height of your chosen rail, connecting these guides with a diagonal to indicate the slope and the top of the rail. Acceptable handrail profiles can be found in Appendix I.

Additionally, handrail extensions are required by code when used in a commercial building. At the bottom of each run, the rail must extend 12" plus the depth of one tread. As the treads in this example are 11" deep, the handrail must extend 1'-11".

Rails at the top of the flight must extend 12".

The rail at the central landing will extend 12", but because it needs to be continuous between the two runs, it will appear to loop up to the second run.

STEP 11
Draw the guardrail of your choice up both runs. Make sure that the top of the rail measures at least 42" above the tread nosings. This can be done in a similar fashion to the placement of the handrail in Step 10. You will also need to include balusters or panels within the guardrail to ensure that the user cannot sustain a fall from the stairs.

The guards should run the length of each run, but they may also be used around the landings if necessary, as seen near the nosing of the second landing.

Acceptable guardrail profiles can be found in Appendix I.

STEP 12
To complete the drawing, darken the lineweights for all the objects that are being cut through. This will indicate which elements are being cut (section) and which are in the background for contextual aids (elevation). Add any necessary annotations or dimensions.

IBC

Handrails must be continuous, meaning there cannot be a break or a post unless it is on the lowest tread or landing. *(IBC 1014.4)*

Handrails must be at least 1 ½" away from the wall. *(IBC 1014.7)*

CAD

Save time by copying lines instead of redrawing them. You can draw lines several balusters and then copy them up to the next few steps. Make sure to continuously measure to ensure that the elements are spaced properly.

You can then copy and mirror the lines up to the second run of stairs to save even more time.

Revit

Even though the handrails are drawn with the stairs, some elements of the rail can be edited separately. In the drawing window, hover over the stairs and select the railing once it becomes highlighted. Editing options include the shape of the rail and whether it is flipped into the path of travel or appears against the wall.

Revit does not create the extensions, leaving you with two options in plan view:

1. Using Detail Lines, draw the extensions on to the image.
2. Create or import a component of an extension and attach it to the existing rail.

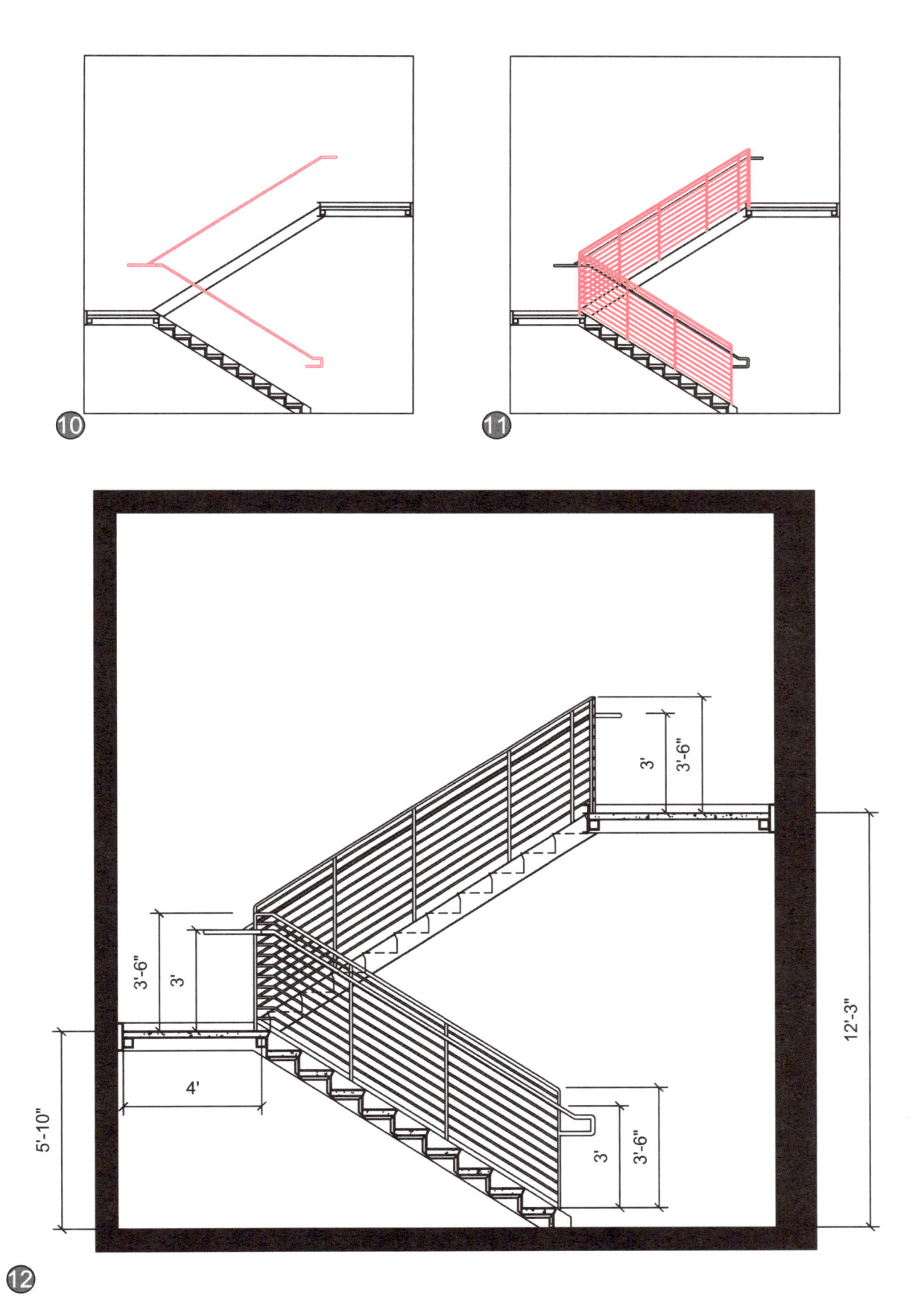

Figure 9.45
U-run stairs, section, Steps 10–12.

CHAPTER 9 STAIRS | 219

SECTION WEIGHT

ELEVATION WEIGHT NEAR

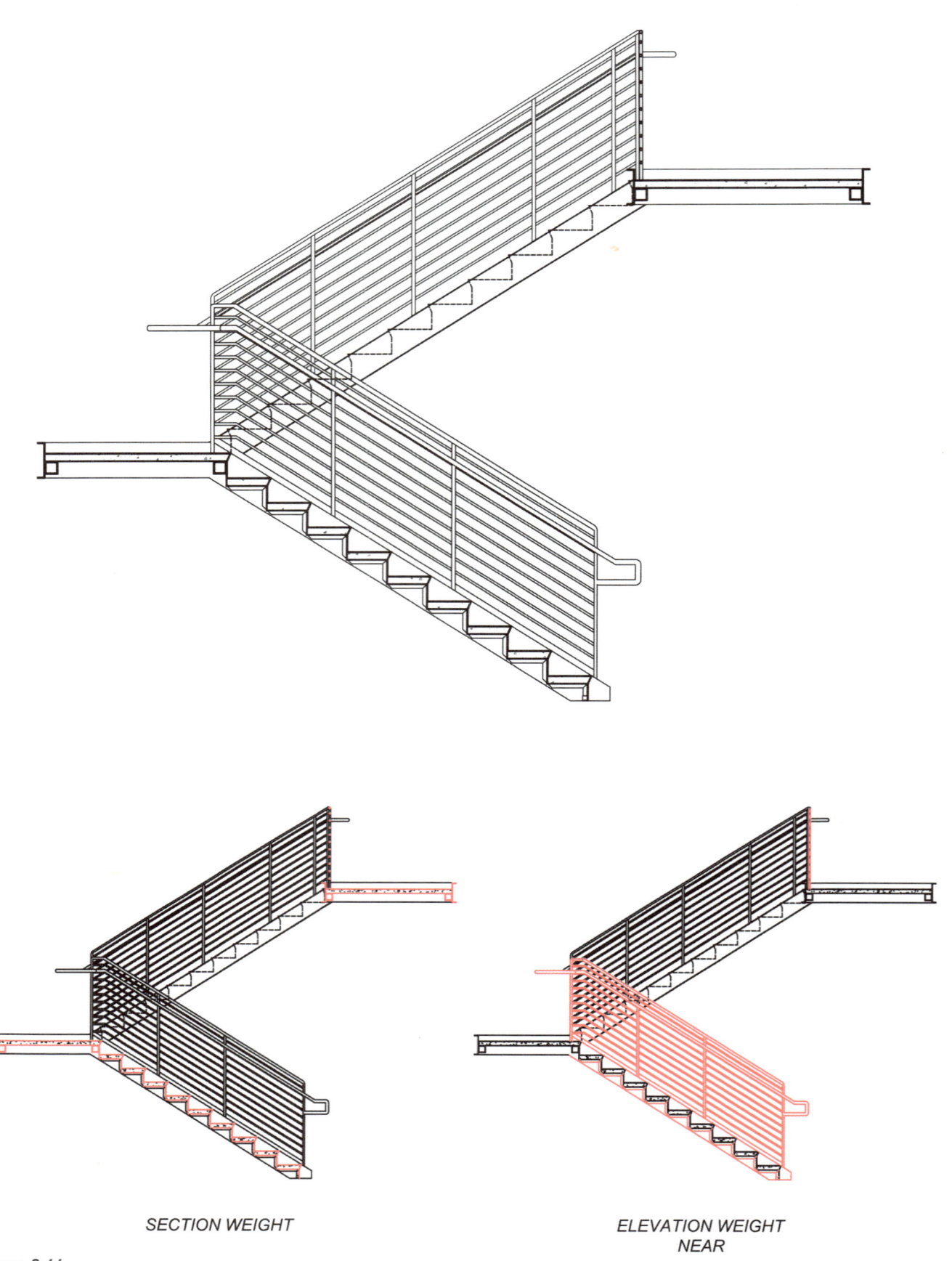

Figure 9.46
U-run stairs, section line weight assignments.

PART II DETAIL DRAWINGS

ELEVATION WEIGHT
FAR

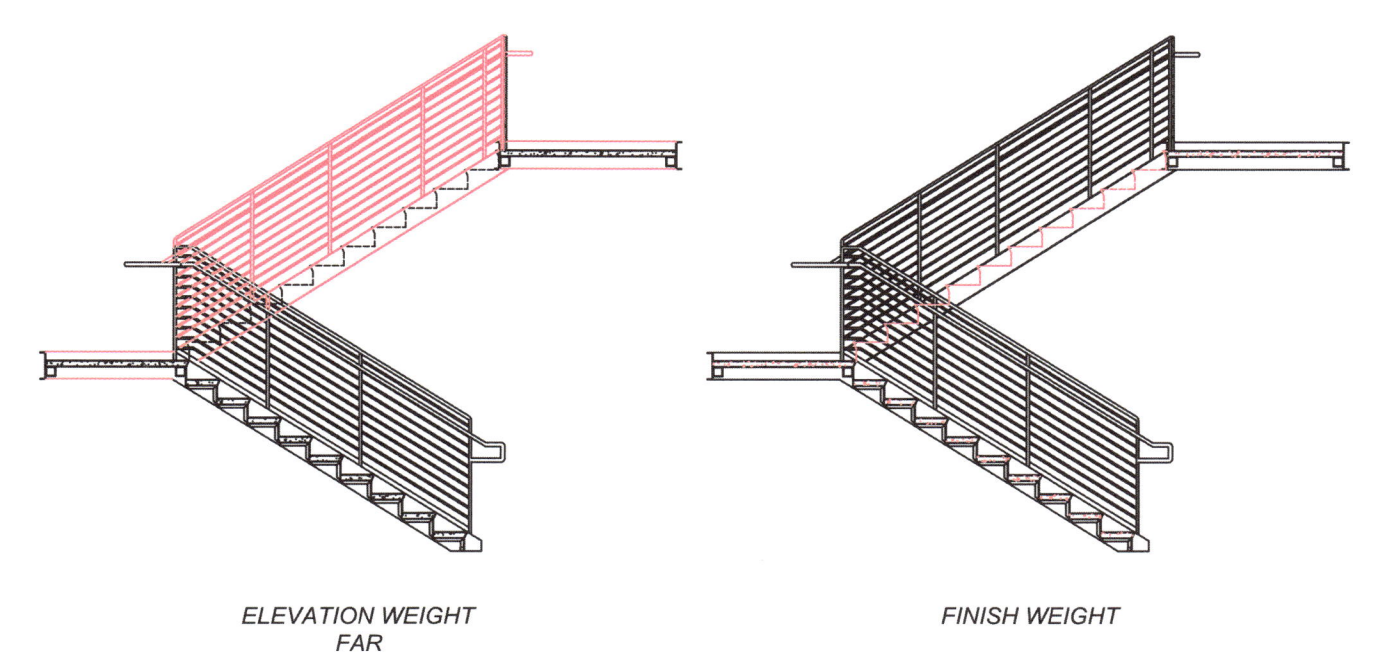

FINISH WEIGHT

Figure 9.47
U-run stairs, section line weight assignments.

Drafting a U-run—elevation

The completed elevation that is called out as drawing 2/A4 in the U-run floor plan can be seen here for your reference. This view illustrates how the user would see the staircase from the exterior doorway. For information on elevations, see Part I of this text. For instructions on drawing a direct run stair section, which can be adapted for your needs, see the section on wood stairs for residential use.

Other steel elements

For acceptable nosings and rails, see Appendix I.

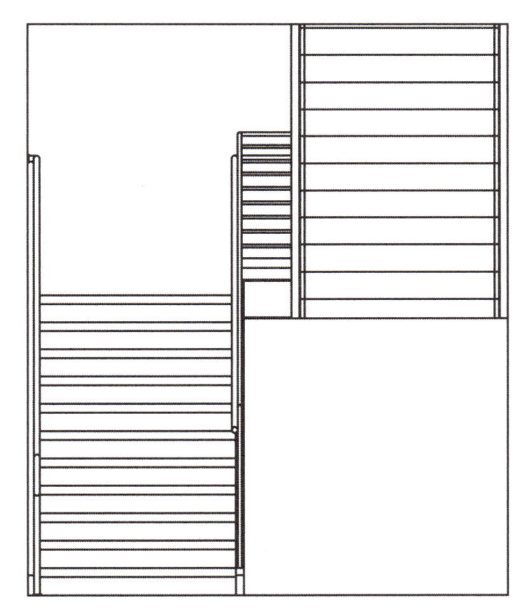

Figure 9.48
U-run stairs, elevation.

STUDIO Animation 9.2 U-run full flight details (steel)

CHAPTER 9 STAIRS | 221

WHY IS THIS IMPORTANT?

Stairs are a critical element of architectural design. Not only do they serve as a means to get from one floor to another, they can be lifesaving tools or opportunities for statement design. It is important to understand and incorporate codes in the design process to ensure that the finished product is useable. They must also be drawn accurately so that both the designs and code adherences are communicated clearly from the designer to the construction team. However, due to the large square footage footprint they can take up, designers can take advantage of the customizable nature of the layouts, materiality, and rails for residential and commercial stairs to use the space creatively. For the best, most accurate results, it is recommended that you calculate and sketch the stairs you wish to design prior to drafting them.

Figure 9.49
Curved commercial L-stair with two handrails and a guardrail.

Figure 9.50
Multi-story commercial U-stair.

Figure 9.51
Residential L-stair with a single handrail and guardrail and open risers.

Figure 9.52
Residential L-stair with a single handrail, double guardrail, and closed risers.

Figure 9.53
Double staircase in a commercial lobby.

CHAPTER REVIEW

1. What stair layout options do you have for a commercial building with a total rise of 7'-4"? Which one(s) can you still use if the footprint of the staircase is 10'-0 × 16'-10"?
2. What type of project requires only one handrail?
3. What is the name of the element that acts as a stringer in a steel staircase? How wide must it be?
4. What layout options can you have for a residential project with a total rise of 8'-9"? Calculate the size and quantity of the treads, the number and depth of treads, and the total run for each.

EXAMPLE PLAN UPDATES STUDIO

Calculate and construct the staircases for your selected project type based on the construction type, layout need, total rise, and whether or not it is a means of egress. Depending on the size of your project and placement of stairs, you may need a second flight in order to satisfy fire codes.

While this chapter investigated only a direct run and a U-run, the construction and detailing techniques explored here can be applied to all nonspiral staircases.

Example of stairs added to the commercial plan:

U-run
- *Central landing*
- *Handrail*
- *Guardrail*
- *Means of egress*

Example from the residential plan:

Direct run
- *Full stringer*
- *Housed stringer*
- *Open stringer*
- *Handrail*

Remember to double-check codes for tread and riser dimensions, handrail and/or guardrail heights, and headroom when designing your stairs.

CHAPTER TERMINOLOGY

angle supports
balusters
carriage
channel support
clear space
closed stringer
clip angle
commercial stair
direct run
egress stair
full stringer
guardrail
handrail

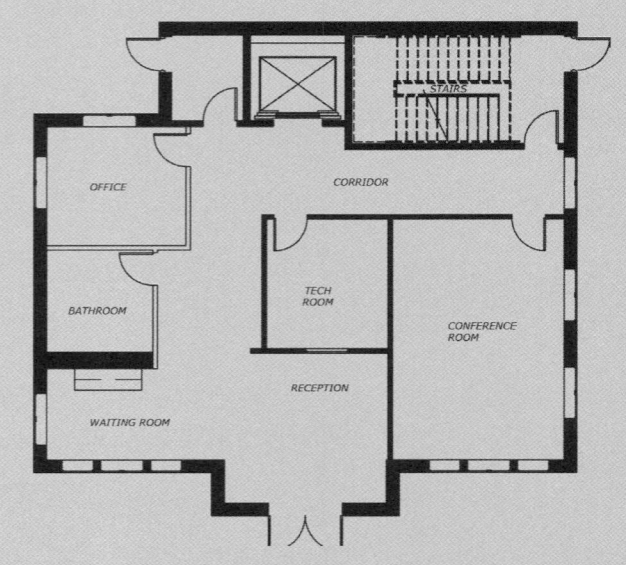

Figure 9.54
Commercial plan with U-run egress stairs.

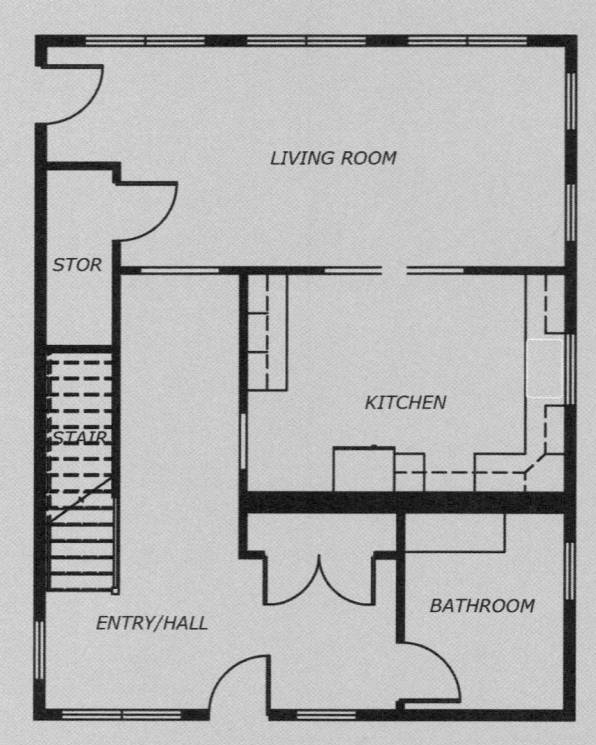

Figure 9.55
Residential plan with direct run stairs.

handrail extension
housed stringer
L-shaped stair
landing
newel post
nonegress stair
nosing
open stringer
residential stair
return
rise
riser
run

spiral stair
stair
steel channel
straight run
stringer (stairs)
total rise
total run
tread
U-shaped stair
vertical rise
wedge
winding stair

STAIR CODES

This section will explore the elements used and how to draw construction details for stairs. Below are the ADA standards and the IBC codes that you need to keep in mind when designing and drafting stairs. While the IBC codes that are listed include information on both commercial and residential stairways, portions of the International Residential Code have been included for your convenience. These codes are designated with an *R* before the code number at the end of Table 9.3.

Table 9.3 ADA Standards for Stairs and Rails

ADA Code	Topic	Description
504.2	Treads and risers	Treads must be at least 11" deep. Risers must measure between 4"–7" high. Both treads and risers must be uniform in their chosen measurement for the length of the stair run.
504.3	Open risers	Open risers are not allowed in commercial spaces.
504.4	Tread surface	It is recommended that a visual or textural contrast is provided along the nosing of the stair to aid individuals with visual disabilities.
504.5	Nosings	Nosings may project up to 1 1/2" over the tread below. Nosing curvature may have a maximum 1/2" radius. Projecting nosings must be curved or beveled. Risers may slope up to 30 degrees from vertical.
505.4	Handrail height	Rails must measure between 34"–38" above the nosings of each stair.
505.5	Handrail clearance	A clear space of at least 1 1/2" must be present between the rail and the wall.
505.7.1	Handrail cross section – Type I	Circular cross section handrails must have a diameter between 1 1/4"–2"
505.7.2	Handrail cross section – Type II	Non-circular rails must have a perimeter between 4"–6 1/4" and a cross-section up to 2 1/4".
505.10.2	Handrail extension – top of stairs	Handrails must extend at least 12" past the top riser and return to the wall, guard, or a newel post.
505.10.3	Handrail extension – bottom of stairs	Handrails must extend at least 12" plus the depth of one tread past the bottom riser and must connect to the wall, guard, or newel post.

Table 9.4 IBC Codes for Stairs and Rails

IBC Code	Topic	Description
1005.3.1	Capacity based on occupant load—stairs	Calculate the stair capacity by multiplying the occupant load by 0.3" per person, using the occupant load for each floor that would be serviced.
1009.3	Accessible means of egress—stairs	A flight must have a minimum clear width of 48" between handrails and an area of refuge in order to be considered an accessible means of egress.
1011.2	Stairway width and capacity	Stairways must be at least 44" wide, unless fewer than 50 people will use the stairs as an accessible means of egress, in which case the minimum width becomes 36".
1011.3	Stairway headroom	A minimum headroom clearance of 80 inches is needed. This must be measured from the edge of the nosing vertically to the ceiling or landing above and must be maintained for the whole width of the flight.
1011.5.2	Riser height and tread depth	Commercial riser heights must be between 4"–7" and the minimum depth a tread can be is 11".
1011.5.5	Nosing and riser profile	Nosings must curve or bevel between 1/16"–9/16" and connect to a solid riser with an angle of 30 degrees or less.
1011.5.5.1	Nosing projection	Nosings can project up to 1 1/4" past the riser below.
1011.5.5.3	Solid risers	Commercial risers must be solid. Stairways that are not a means of egress may have openings between treads, but they must be small enough that a 4" sphere cannot pass through.
1011.6	Landings	Landings must be as deep as the stairway is wide. Commercial straight run stairs may have landings up to 48". Doors that open into landings can project up to 7" into that landing.
1011.7	Stairway construction	Stairs must be built with the same materials permitted for the shell construction of the building. Wood handrails are permitted in all project types.
1011.8	Vertical rise	The vertical rise of a run of stairs cannot exceed 12'-0" without a landing being used.
1011.11	Handrails	Commercial projects require handrails on both sides of a staircase.
1014.2	Handrail height	Handrails must be between 34"–38" above the nosing of each tread.
1014.3.1	Handrail graspability – Type I	Circular cross section handrails must have a diameter between 1 1/4"–2". Non-circular rails must have a perimeter between 4"–6 1/4" and a cross-section between 1"–2 1/4".
1014.3.2	Handrail graspability – Type II	Non-circular rails with a perimeter greater than 6 1/4" must have finger recesses on both sides of the rail. The recess must measure 3/4" from the tallest portion of the rail's profile. This rail must measure between 1 1/4"–2 3/4" wide.
1014.4	Handrail continuity	Commercial handrails must provide continuous support from the bottom to the top of the run without being interrupted by newel posts. Residential handrails may be interrupted by a newel post at a landing.

Table 9.4 IBC Codes for Stairs and Rails

IBC Code	Topic	Description
1014.6	Handrail extensions	Commercial handrails must extend at least 12" past the top riser and 12" plus the depth of one tread past the bottom riser. These rails must then connect to the wall, guard, or newel post.
		Residential handrails may run from the top riser to the bottom riser with no needed extension.
1014.7	Handrail clearance	A clear space of at least 1 1/2" must be present between the rail and the wall.
1014.8	Handrail projections	Accessible routes require a clear width between handrails of at least 36". Rails may project up to 4 1/2" on each side of the stair.
1015.2	Guardrail placement	Guardrails are required along mezzanines, stairs, ramps and landings that are more than 30" above the floor below.
1015.3	Guardrail height	Guardrails must be at least 42" high when measured from the floor of a landing or a nosing of a tread.
		Single residential units require guards of at least 34". If the guardrail also acts a handrail, the height must be between 34"–38".
1015.4	Guardrail openings	Commercial guards must be designed so that a 4" sphere cannot pass through any openings.
		Residential guards cannot allow a 4 3/8" sphere to pass through.
R311.7.1	Residential stairway width	Stairs must have at least 36" of clear width above the hand rail. Rails may project up to 4 1/2" into the clear width.
		When handrails are installed on both sides, the clear width can measure at least 31 1/2".
		When a handrail is installed on one side, the clear width can measure 27".
R311.7.3	Residential vertical rise	The vertical rise of a run of stairs cannot exceed 12'-3" without a landing being used.
R311.7.5	Residential treads and risers	For residential projects, the maximum riser height can measure 7 3/4", the minimum tread depth can be 10", and a nosing must be between 3/4" and 1 1/4".
R311.7.5.3	Residential nosings	Nosings may curve up to 9/16" and may project between 3/4"–1 1/4" past the riser.
		Residential treads that are deeper than 11" do not require a nosing projection.
R311.7.6	Residential stair landings	Residential straight run stairs must have landings of at least 36".
R311.7.8	Residential handrails	Residential projects require a handrail on only one side of a staircase, but handrails are permitted to be on both sides.

CHAPTER REFERENCES

Ballast, David Kent. *Interior Construction & Detailing for Designers and Architects*. Belmont, CA: Professional Publications, Inc., 2013.

Ching, Francis D. *Building Construction Illustrated*. New York: John Wiley & Sons, 2014.

DeChiara, Joseph, Julius Panero, and Martin Zelnik. *Time-Saver Standards for Interior Design and Space Planning*. New York: McGraw-Hill, 2001.

International Code Council. *International Building Code, 2015*. Chicago: International Code Council Publications, 2014.

International Code Council. *International Residential Code, 2015*. Chicago: International Code Council Publications, 2014.

Jefferis, Alan. *Residential Design, Drafting, and Detailing*, 2nd Ed. Boston: Cengage Learning, 2013.

Kilmer, W. Otie and Rosemary Kilmer. *Construction Drawings and Details for Interiors*. New York: John Wiley & Sons, 2016.

Kruse, Kelsey and Maryrose McGowan. *Interior Graphic Standards*. New York: John Wiley & Sons, 2003.

United States Department of Justice. *2010 ADA Standards for Accessible Design*. Washington, D.C.: Dept. of Justice, 2010.

Custom details

CHAPTER 10

CHAPTER OUTCOMES

After completing this chapter you will be able to:

1. Design and annotate custom tile patterns for use on floors and walls.
2. Create sets of furniture construction drawings, complete with dimensions, material specifications, and joinery details.
3. Utilize existing drawings and shortcuts to speed up your drafting time and reduce the repetitive nature of detail drawing.

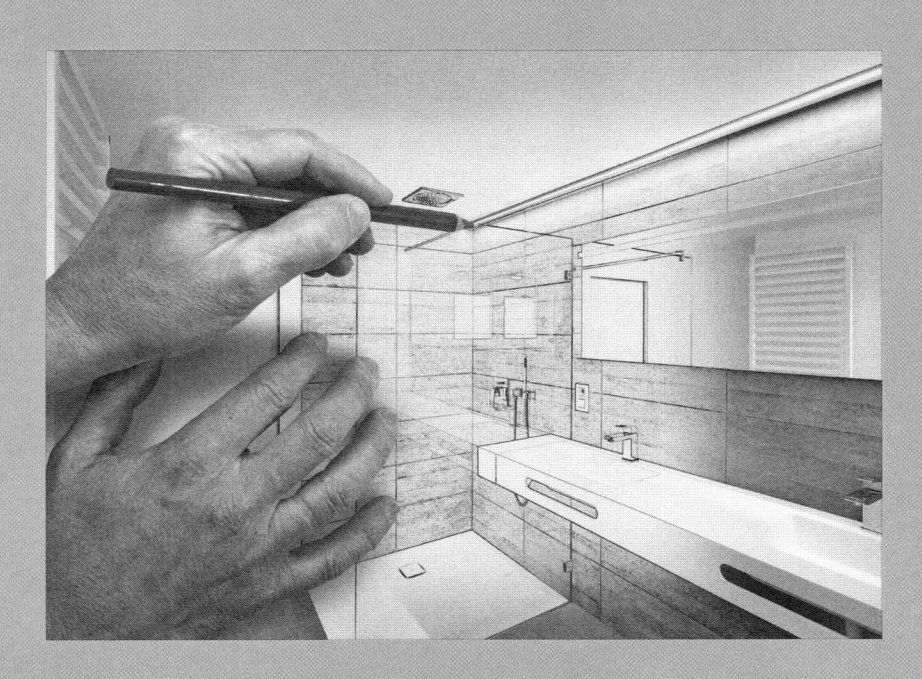

Figure 10.1 Custom bathroom design from conception to reality.

ABOUT CUSTOMIZING DETAILS

Custom designs can be some of the most fun to create and are major selling points to a client. However, the detailing process for these unique pieces can be daunting when you are either unsure of how the piece can be constructed or overwhelmed by the detailing process. This chapter will illustrate how customized details can be completed quickly, efficiently, and accurately.

The first type of customization that will be explored is the tile pattern. Custom tile patterns can be used for floor, wall, or ceiling fields to add visual interest in a variety of colors and materials. This chapter will look at two different customized patterns: a backsplash featuring a subway tile pattern and an intricate floor pattern for a bathroom. Custom tile applications can easily be adjusted or altered depending on the size of the tiles and the needs of the client, allowing for a quick impact with high flexibility. While there are no drawings from earlier chapters to base these details on, tile pattern drawings are simple in nature, even when the final product appears complex. It is important to note that some tiles are only to be used on a specific plane or location. You should refer to a tile professional or the manufacturer's instructions when there are any questions about the use of a tile in certain circumstances, as disregard for these specifications could result in injury or product failure.

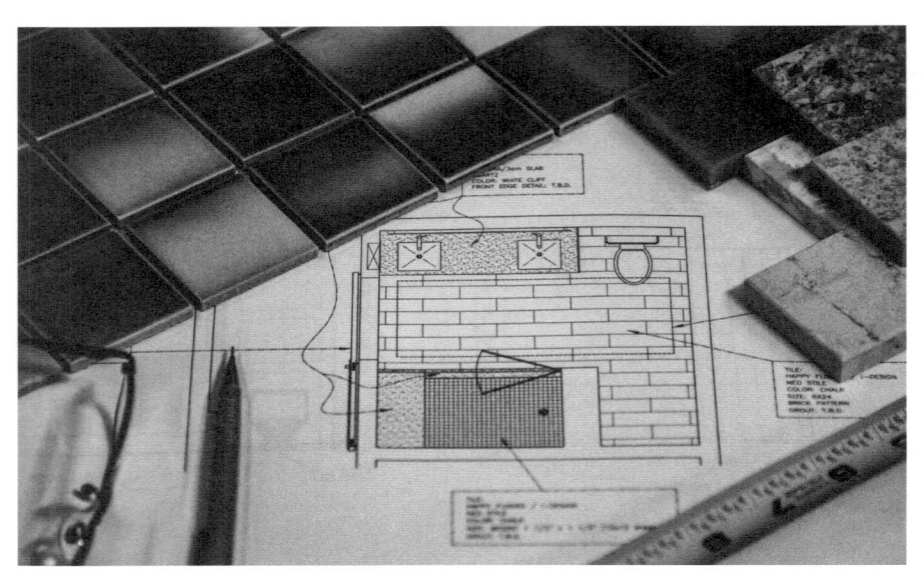

Figure 10.2
Bathroom layout for custom tile with finish options.

Figure 10.3
Backsplash layout running from counters to upper cabinets.

230 | PART II DETAIL DRAWINGS

Case pieces and built-in storage can be customized by editing the cabinets seen in Chapter 8. By adjusting these units, end users are given diverse storage options to meet their needs, and designers can find unique ways to occupy what would otherwise be dead space. This chapter will investigate how to customize existing cabinetry drawings, resulting in storage cubbies and a built-in desk. This process will allow for you to utilize an existing drawing that will help save you valuable drafting time.

Finally, a custom reception desk will be created. Many commercial projects require reception desks that are both user friendly and dynamic. Reception desks provide quite a bit of creative flexibility as sizes, shapes, and materials can all be customized by the designer. Customizable elements of a reception desk include the work surface layout, storage options, and materials. Keep in mind that there are certain ADA guidelines that need to be accounted for in the final detail drawings. Particularly, the desk needs to be approachable via wheelchair and provide all users with a comfortable work surface. Table 10.1 shows the various dimensions that are necessary when creating your desks.

Figure 10.4
Custom built-in laundry center.

Figure 10.5
Reception desk constructed specifically for a client's space.

CHAPTER 10 CUSTOM DETAILS | 231

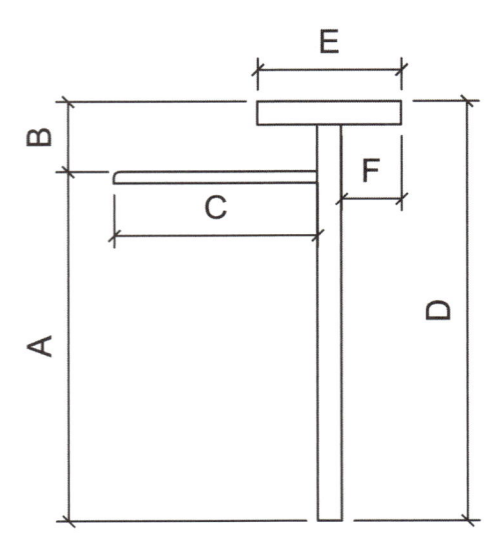

Figure 10.6
Height differences between the work surface and the reception hutch.

Figure 10.7
Reception desk dimensions.

Table 10.1 Combined Reception Desk Dimensions: Desk Height, Counter Height, and Accessible Range.				
Item	**Letter**	**Desk**	**Counter**	**Accessible**
Work surface height	A	29"–30"	36"–39"	28"–34"
Work surface to reception hutch	B	10"–12"	10"–12"	10"–12"
Work surface depth	C	26"–30"	22"–30"	20"–25"
Floor to reception hutch	D	39"–42"	44"–48"	28"–36"
Reception hutch depth	E	12"–15"	12"–15"	12"–15"
Kick/knee depth	F	6"–9"	2"–4"	4"–12"

It is recommended that custom pieces are illustrated in perspective prior to beginning the detailing process. It is much easier to create the detail drawings once you have an image of what you want the final product to look like as opposed to trying to draw the details and making up the product as you go along. This will also ensure that you have considered heights, depths, and unique features before boiling it down to construction jargon.

Once the piece has been illustrated, you have additional decisions to make before drafting the details. First, you must determine the materials that are to be used for each part of the project. When choosing materials, make sure that the finishes selected are appropriate for their roles in the project, as per the manufacturer's recommendation. Elements that are to be covered in **veneers** or other lightweight finishes can be constructed from **plywood** or **particleboard** which create the smooth plane necessary for the finish to be adhered. Using multiple layers of these boards can also create strength and rigidity for the project.

Second, you must determine how the planes will be connected. If you want the planes to overlap, you will need to decide what types of fasteners or supports you wish to have and whether you want them to be exposed or concealed. If you choose to have the planes intersect, you will need to plan out what type of joint you want to use. Refer to Chapter 7 for a list of joints.

Once you know your design, the materials, and how the major planes will interact with one another, you can begin your details. It is recommended that in this case, you design from the outside in: draw an outline of the custom piece before you draw its interior makeup. This will ensure that you retain the proper size of the design from start to finish.

CUSTOM TILE PATTERNS

Kitchen backsplash

The backsplash for this example is taken from the kitchen in the residential project and uses 3" × 6" tiles to create a subway tile pattern. By using the kitchen cabinet elevations you have already created, you can save yourself drafting time because you have already dictated the area that the tiles must fit into. While this drawing is straightforward and simplistic, the tile itself can have a visual impact in the room. To see other tile layout ideas, refer to Appendix J.

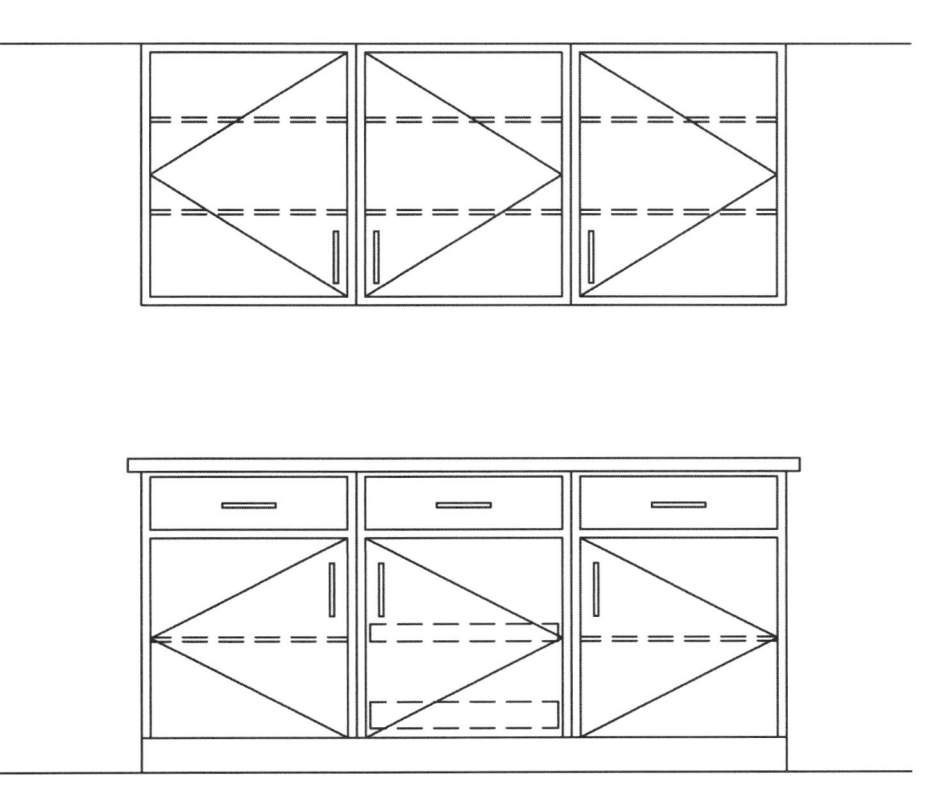

Figure 10.8
Existing kitchen cabinet elevation.

CHAPTER 10 CUSTOM DETAILS | 233

STEP 1
Using the elevation you created for the base and wall cabinets, block out the area that the tiles will appear in. In this example, this area is a rectangle measuring 6'-3" long by 1'-6" high, and will be 3'-0" above finished floor (AFF). For simplicity sake, the cabinets will be hidden for the remainder of this example and the tile boundary will be drawn in guidelines.

STEP 2
Draw a vertical guideline down the center of the boundary; in this case, measuring 3'-1 1/2" from each end.

STEP 3
Center a single tile along the bottom of the boundary box and the vertical guideline you just drew.

STEP 4
Finish the bottom row of tiles by adding 3" × 6"s on either side of the first tile until you reach the edges of the boundary box. For this example, the tiles will be shown to overhang the boundary box so that they retain their dimensions.

STEP 5
Add a row of tiles above the first, offsetting them by 3". The easiest way to do this is to use the central guideline you created in Step 2 and draw a full tile on each side of it. Continue with full tiles until you hit the boundary box.

STEP 6
Copy these two rows upward until you hit the top of the boundary box.

STEP 7
If you have not yet trimmed the tiles that overhang the boundary box, you can do it at this time. Hardline the boundary box.

STEP 8
Add the tile pattern and any necessary dimensions and annotations to the elevation drawing.

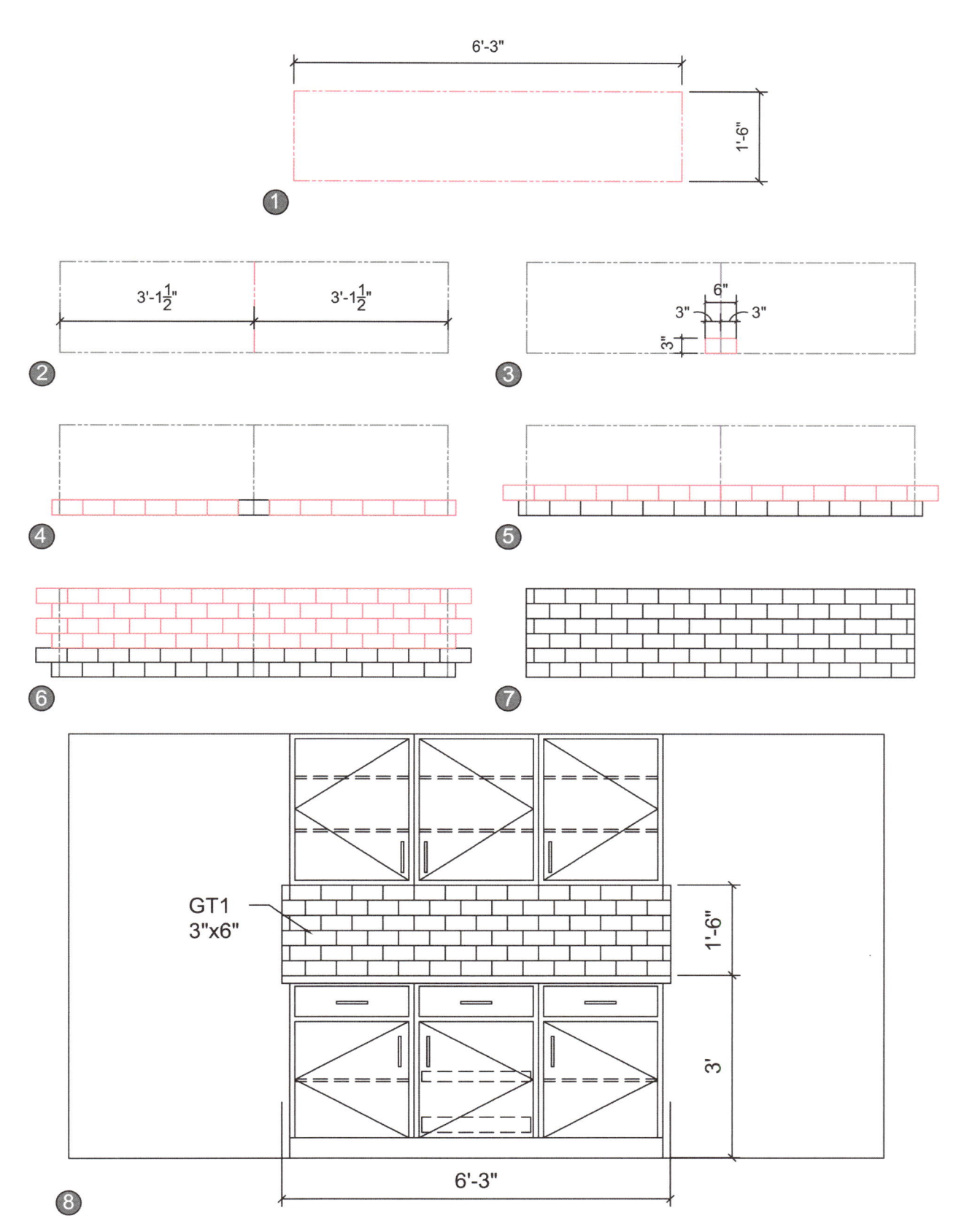

Figure 10.9
Kitchen backsplash elevation, Steps 1–8.

CHAPTER 10 CUSTOM DETAILS | 235

Bathroom floor tile pattern

This example is the first of two phases to create a custom floor pattern for the residential bathroom. Here, the pattern itself will be established before it is installed into the room in the next section. While this example uses three types of tiles arranged in a 2'-0" × 2'-6" layout, the pattern can be altered to incorporate a variety of tile sizes, shapes, materials, and colors to meet your client's needs. To see other layouts, refer to Appendix J.

STEP 1
Draw a guideline rectangle measuring 2'-0" × 2'-6" to illustrate the boundaries of the pattern.

STEP 2
Draw the first tile in the corner of the of the boundary box. For this pattern, the tile will be a 12" × 12".

STEP 3
Add a 6" × 12" along the bottom of the boundary box, finishing the first row.

STEP 4
Place a 6" × 6" tile in the corner created by the two tiles already present.

STEP 5
In the 6" space left in the second row, draw a rotated 6" × 12" so that it runs alongside the boundary box and extends upward into the third row.

STEP 6
Add a 6" × 12", which will be the center tile in this pattern.

STEP 7
In the 6" space left in the third row, draw a rotated 6" × 12" so that it runs alongside the boundary box and extends upward into the fourth row.

STEP 8
Draw the last 6" × 12" by placing it in the top corner, running along the boundary box and the previously installed tile.

STEP 9
Complete the pattern by extending the leading edge of the tile from Step 8 downward. This will simultaneously create a 6" × 6" tile and a 12" × 12" tile.

STEP 10
Complete the detail by adding any necessary textures and annotations. This example uses an illustrated material designation by incorporating hatch patterns into the final drawing to show where each type of tile should be used. The patterns can then be placed into a key to easily call out the size and assigned specification code for the tile types, streamlining communication between the designer and the installer.

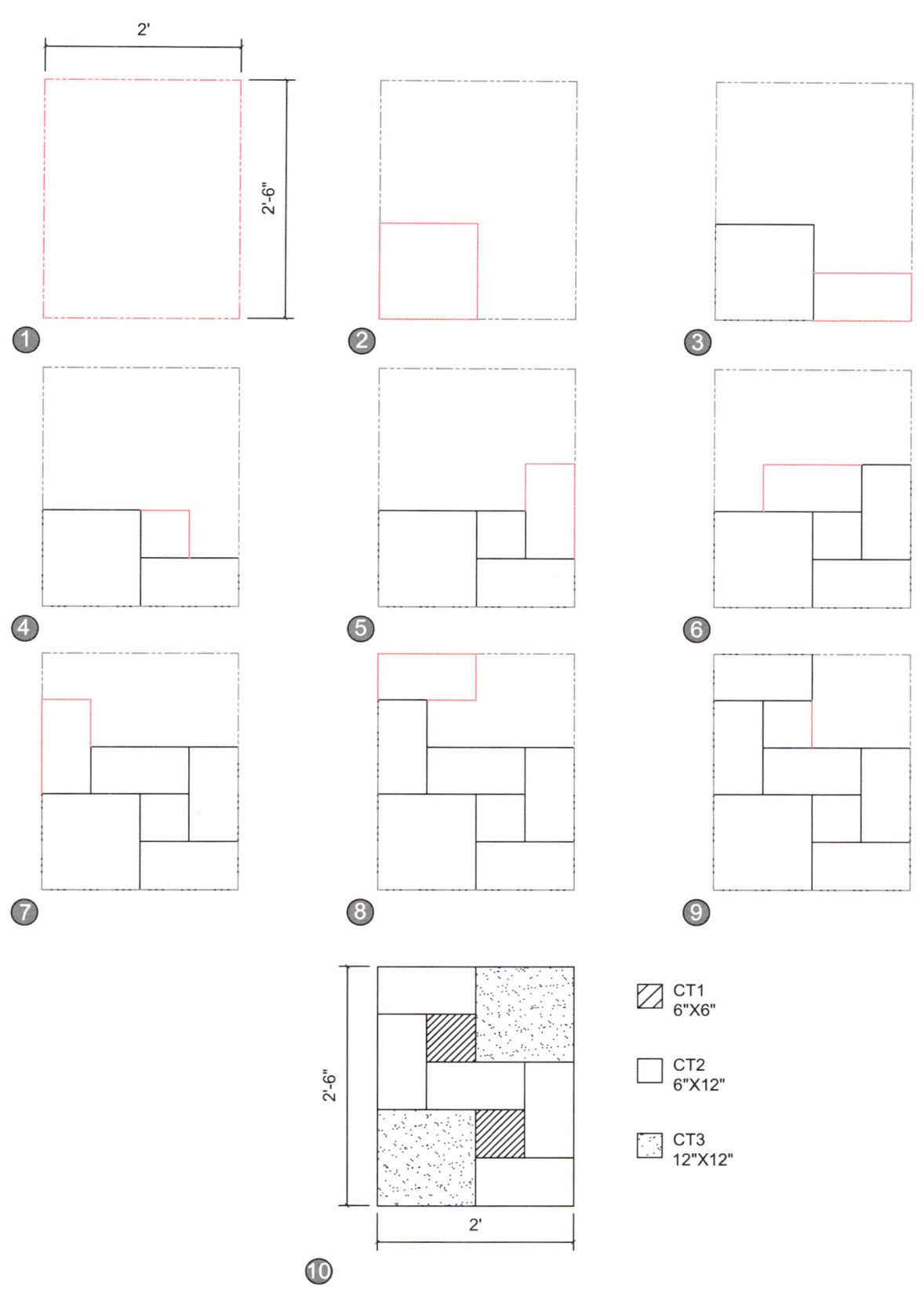

Figure 10.10
Floor tile pattern, Steps 1–10.

Bathroom full tile floor plan

This example is the second of two phases to create a custom floor **pattern** for the residential bathroom. Here, the pattern that was designed in the previous section will be installed into the room as a **repeat**. The pattern, which measures 2'-0" × 2'-6", will be centered in the 8'-0" × 10'-0" bathroom.

STEP 1
Using the floor plan for the residential bathroom, draw a vertical guideline and a horizontal guideline to locate the center of the room. For simplicity sake, the door and window will be hidden for the remainder of this example.

STEP 2
Take the pattern you created in the previous section and align the center of the pattern with the center of the room. This was completed here by using guidelines to connect the corners of the pattern to find the midpoint of the tiles and then placing that on top of the central point of the floor plan.

STEP 3
Use the tile layout you placed onto the floor plan as a fixed point and repeat the pattern on all sides of this fixed point until you run into the wall. For this example, the full pattern is shown to overhang the boundary box so that they retain their dimensions.

STEP 4
Trim the tiles so that they are retained within the room. Complete the detail by adding any necessary textures and annotations, which may or may not include the guidelines indicating the center of the room, as seen here. This example uses an illustrated material designation by incorporating hatch patterns into the final drawing to show where each type of tile should be used. The patterns can then be placed into a key to easily call out the size and assigned specification code for the tile types, streamlining communication between the designer and the installer.

RoT

This example is shown simply to have students practice patterns, placements, and detail organization. In reality, when detailing a floor pattern, you do not need to show the entire pattern. Typically, you would show a portion of the pattern (as created in the previous section) on the floor plan with measurements from walls to the placed pattern to inform the installer of the positioning. You would also supply the contractor with the tile specifications and quantities so that they have all the supplies they need to fully tile the area based on your communication.

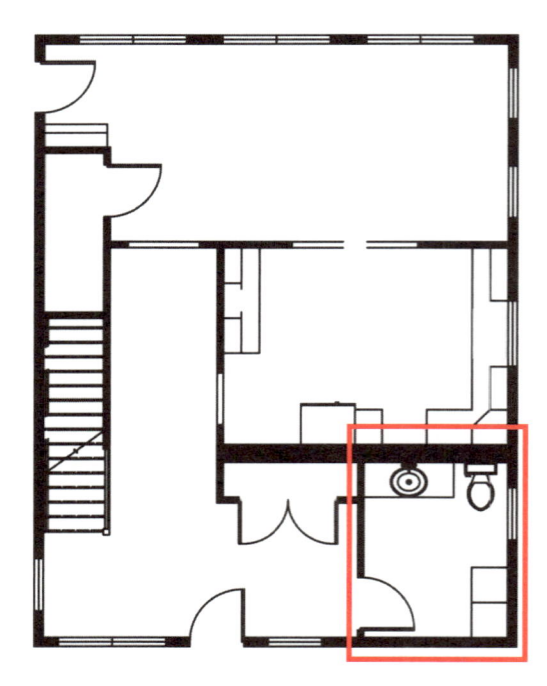

Figure 10.11
Residential bathroom.

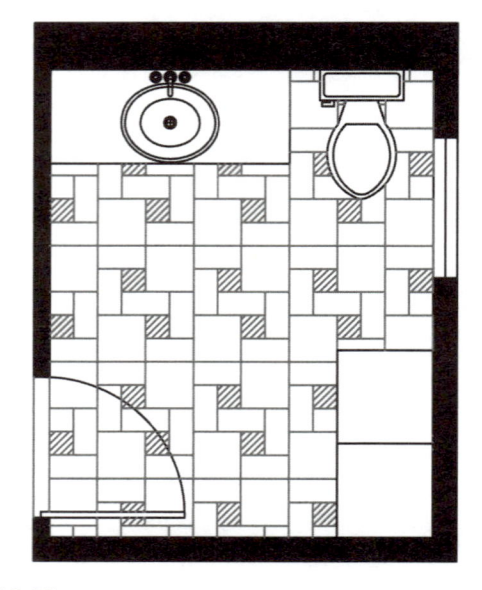

Figure 10.12
Tile pattern applied to bathroom floor plan.

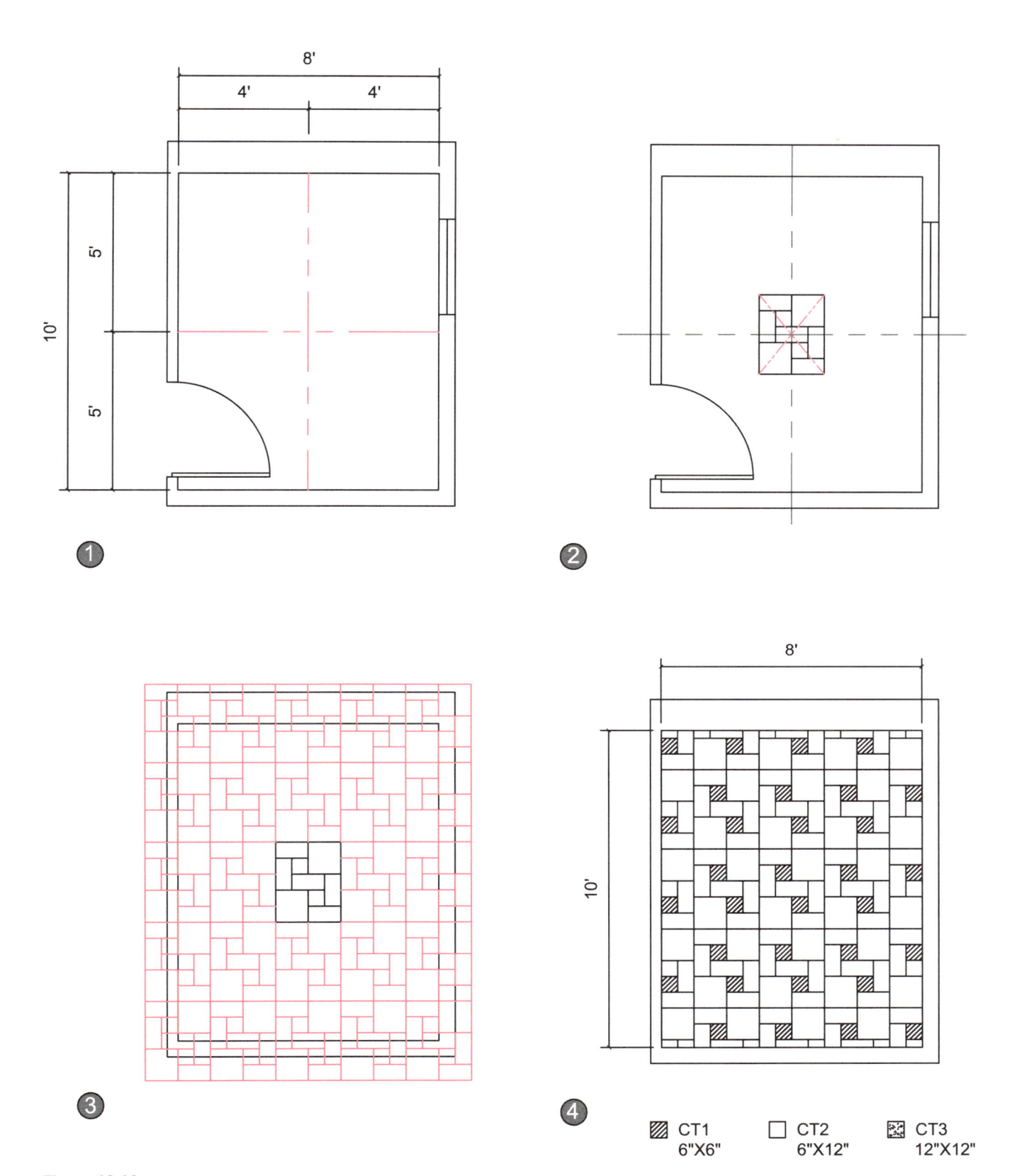

Figure 10.13
Creating a repeat with the tile pattern in the bathroom.

CT1 6"X6"   CT2 6"X12"   CT3 12"X12"

CHAPTER 10 CUSTOM DETAILS | 239

CUSTOM CASE PIECE

The residential project features a small mudroom space at the back of the house, requiring a combination case piece to provide the most flexibility for the end user. Figure 10.9 shows a perspective of the proposed piece, a unit that houses multiple levels of cubbies, a **drawer stack**, an upper cabinet, and a bench, finished with beadboard paneling. While this may seem like a massive undertaking, the detail drawings for this unit can be created by editing the cabinets drawn in Chapter 8. The following details will show how to alter the drawings you already have in order to speed up your drafting time. Lines for the existing drawings will be shown in gray, edits will be in red, and new hardlines will appear in black.

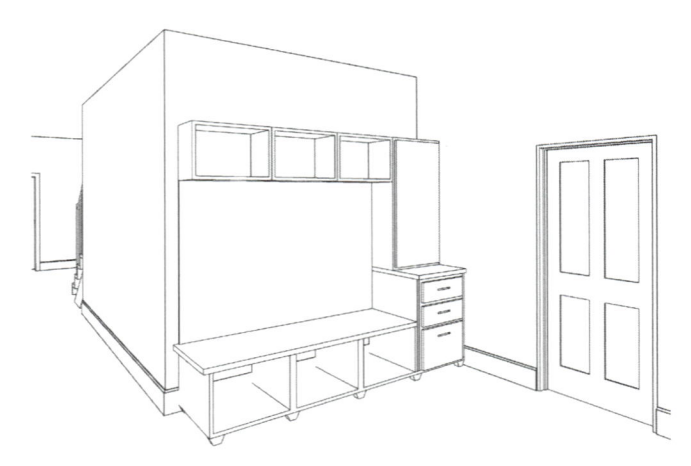

Figure 10.14
Custom bench with cubbies and storage.

STUDiO Animation 10.1 Custom case piece details

Case piece elevation

STEP 1
Obtain a copy of the elevation you created of upper and lower cabinets for the kitchen. If you have not previously created these cabinets, refer to Chapter 8.

STEP 2
The example from Chapter 8 called for three 24" cabinets, which together would measure 6'-0" in length. As the case piece being constructed here measures 8'-0", copy one of the original cabinets over so that you now have four 24" cabinets.

STEP 3
Erase any extraneous information that the existing elevation is providing you, including hidden lines and pulls.

STEP 4
Beginning with the base, a series of spade feet have been added to the bottom of the cabinets, occupying where the kick space had previously been. These feet measure 2" high and are 4" at their widest point, tapering to 2" at the floor.

STEP 5
The original three base cabinets are going to be repurposed as cubbies under the bench. To do this, lower the countertop so that it is 1'-8" AFF and trim anything that crosses over it.

The fourth cabinet will remain at 3'-0" AFF, but may need additional lines added to it to fill in any spaces or gaps that should not be present.

STEP 6
Add a horizontal 3" AFF along the bottom of the drawer stack and cubbies to form the thickness of the pieces.

To complete the base, add the drawer panels and handles.

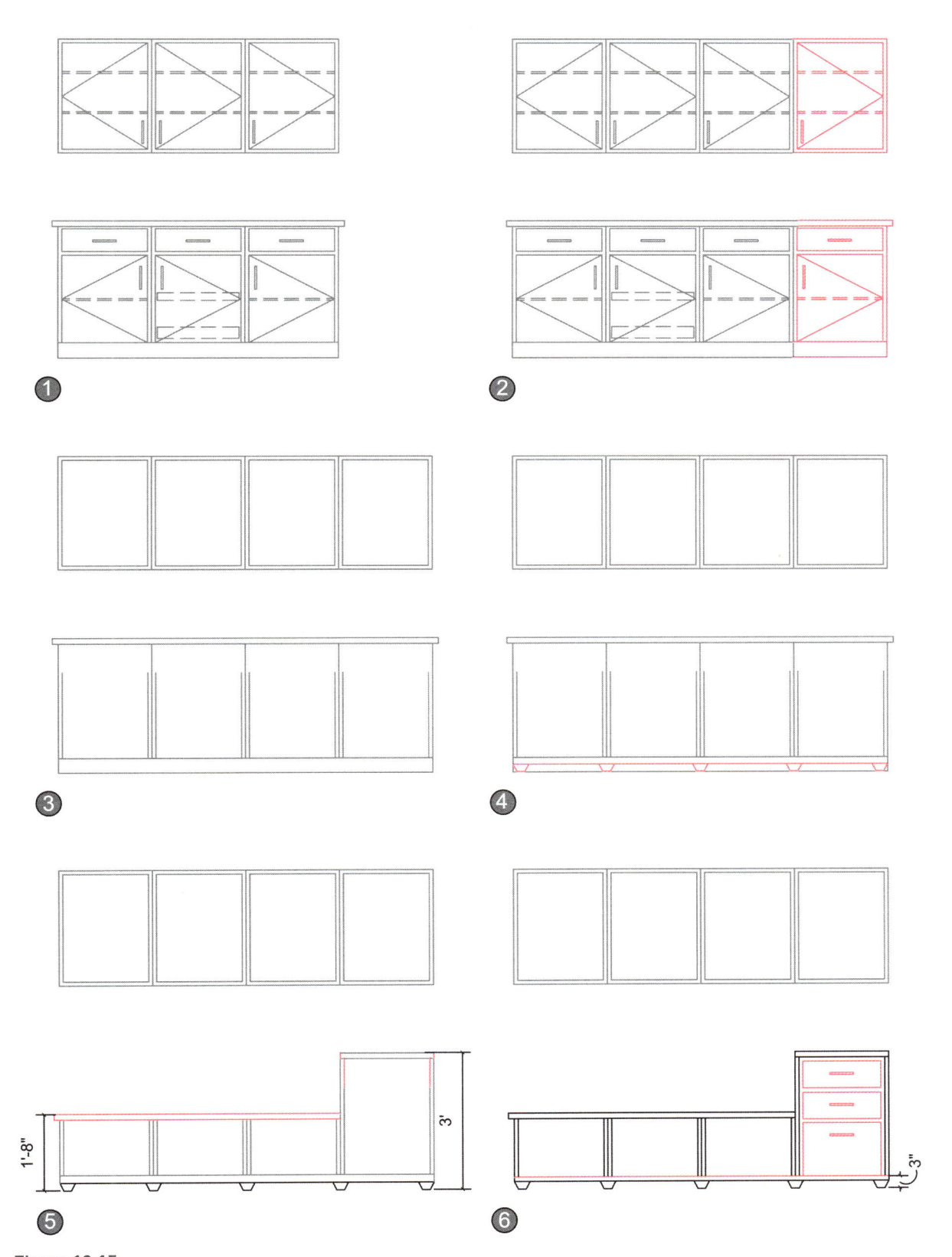

Figure 10.15
Case piece, elevation, Steps 1–6.

STEP 7

Moving to the upper cabinets, shorten the first three so that they measure 1'-4" high, forming the cubbies that will appear above the bench. Add a vertical line from the bottom of the first shortened cubby to the bench below as the edge of the beadboard panel.

Extend the bottom of the fourth cabinet to the stack of drawers below. Here, the upper cabinet will now measure 4'-0".

STEP 8

Add handles for anything you wish to illustrate as a door. Using hidden lines, draw a series of hooks into the cabinet to turn it into a mini coat closet.

STEP 9

Finalize the detail by adding any necessary dimensions and annotations.

ADA

Seating should have a surface that measures 17"-19" AFF.

If bench seating is to be used in public, it must measure at least 42" long and be 20" to 24" deep.

While not a part of the ADA guidelines, it is recommended that chairs and benches have a back and/or arms in order to provide additional support and comfort to the user, while also acting as a hold for aid when standing.

Hand

Use your paraline, triangles, and templates to create the leader lines and symbols for your drawing.

Do not fill in the drawing number or page number until you have created your final layout sheets to ensure that they are numbered properly.

CAD

To create the notations for a drawing in CAD, use a Multileader, which can be found in the Annotate tab.

The callout and section cut symbols can either be imported from CAD block sites or drawn by hand.

Do not fill in the drawing number or page number until you have created your final layout sheets to ensure that they are numbered properly.

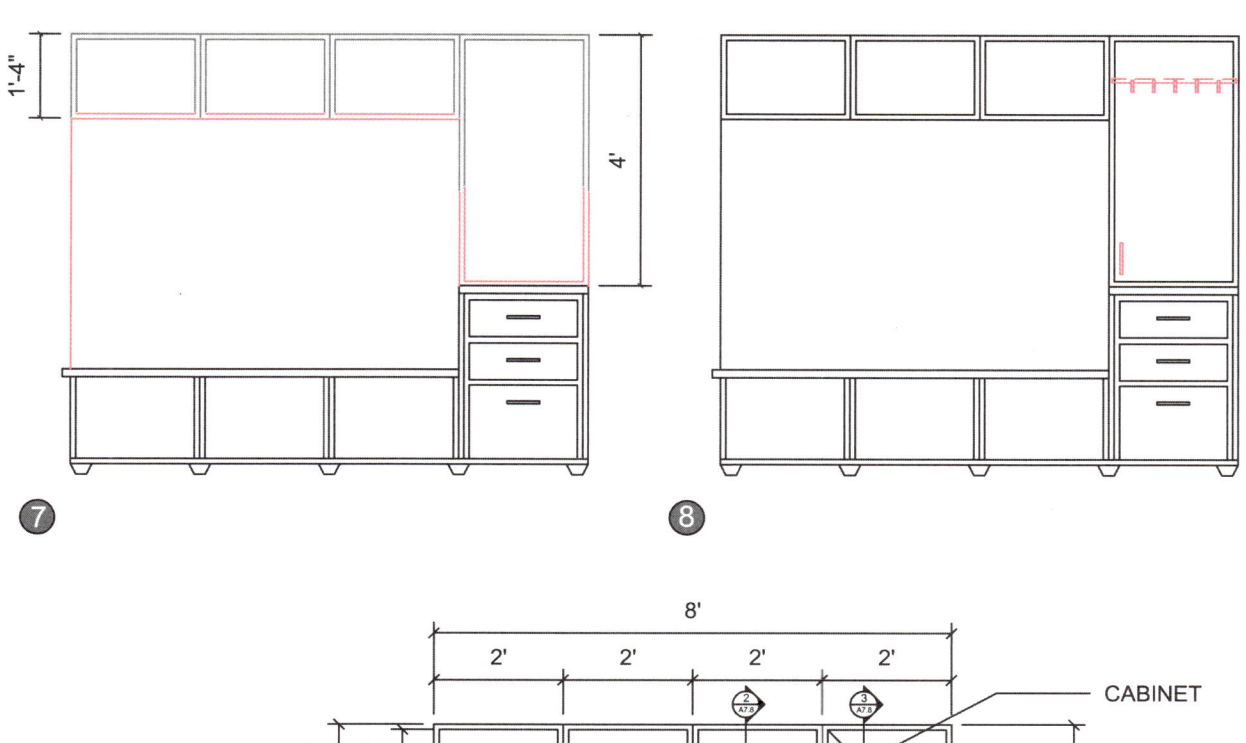

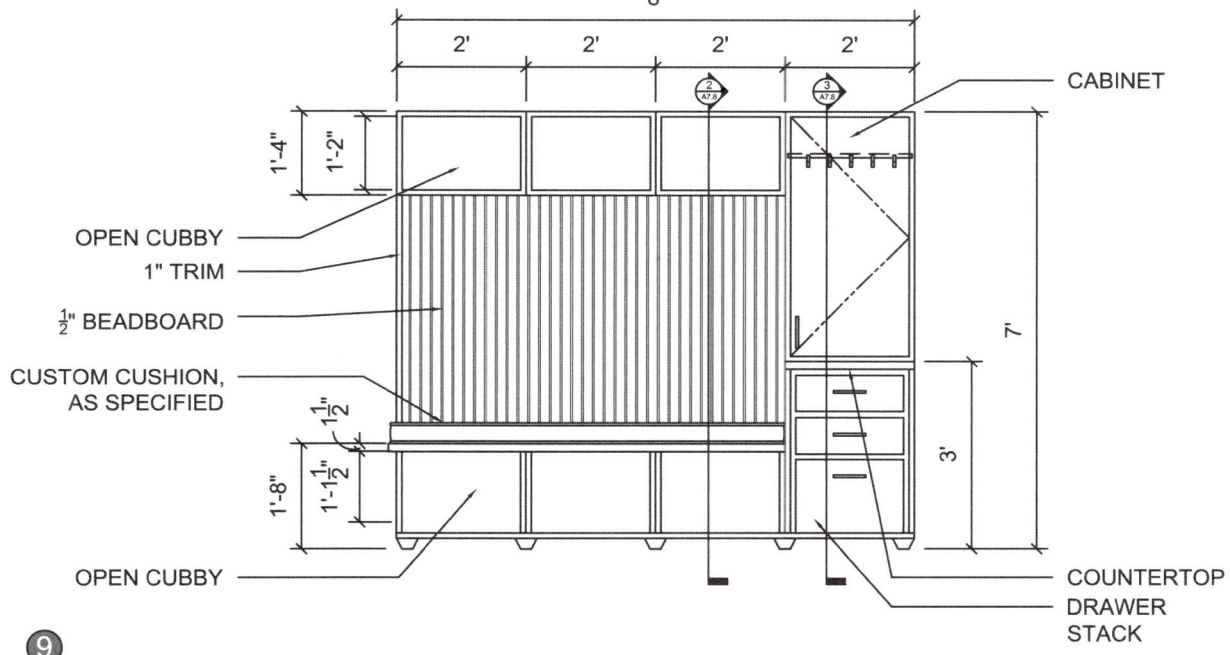

Figure 10.16
Case piece, elevation, Steps 7–9.

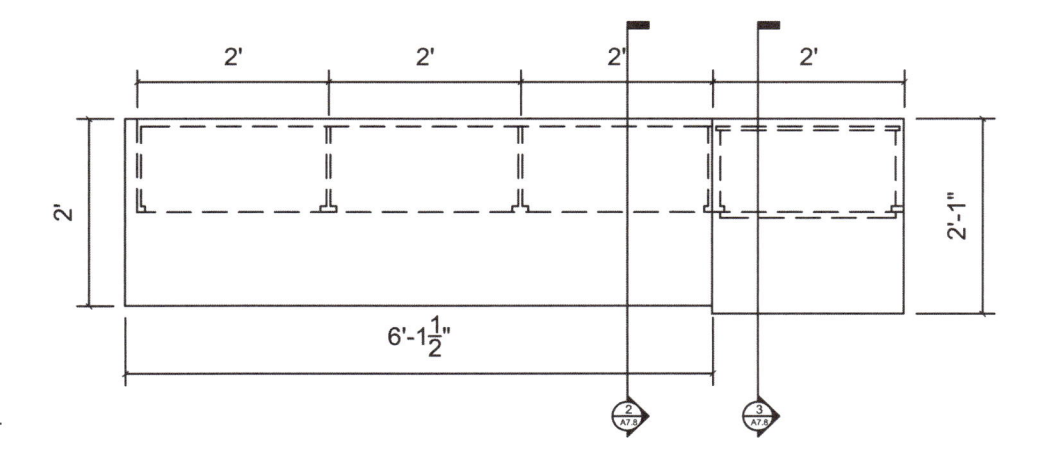

Figure 10.17
Case piece, plan.

CHAPTER 10 CUSTOM DETAILS | 243

Drawer stack section

STEP 1
Obtain a copy of the section you created of upper and lower cabinets for the kitchen. If you have not previously created these cabinets, refer to Chapter 8.

STEP 2
Erase any extraneous information that the existing section is providing you, including any interior shelves and anchoring rails. If you have drawers in the base cabinet, keep them for this example.

STEP 3
Reduce the height of what was the toe kick space to 2" high, adding a spade foot at the front of the cabinet. This foot should measure 4" at its widest point, tapering to 2" at the floor, and should be set about 2" back from the front of the cabinet.

The foot supporting the back of the case piece will be a simple block foot placed 1" from the edge and measuring 2" × 2".

STEP 4
Use the existing drawer as a template to add other drawers in the stack. While this example uses two 7" drawer panels and one 14" drawer, these can easily be rearranged into different size configurations.

STEP 5
Add a 3/4" piece of particle board to the drawer stack, running from the countertop to the base. Include blocking at the top and bottom of the stack where the sides will connect.

STEP 6
Moving to the upper cabinet, extend the lines for the door panel to the countertop below. Reposition the door handle as necessary.

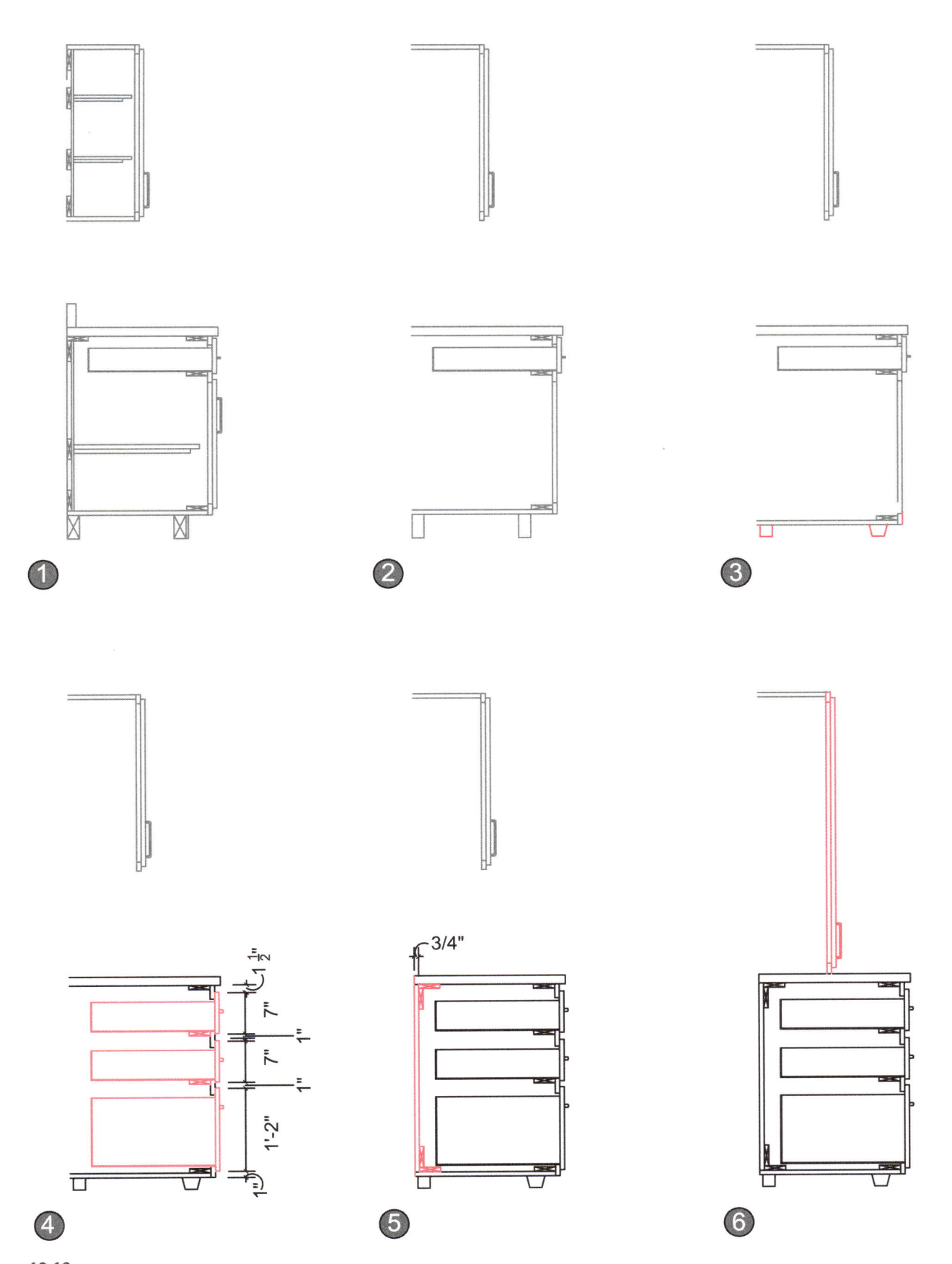

Figure 10.18
Case piece, section through drawers, Steps 1–6.

CHAPTER 10 CUSTOM DETAILS | 245

STEP 7
Repeat Step 5 by adding particle board to the back of the cabinet. Then add 1/8" veneer and blocking.

STEP 8
Add any hooks or racks in the cabinet.

STEP 9
Since this is a section drawing, remember to give a heavier lineweight to any elements that are being cut through. Add textures, notes, or dimensions as necessary to explain how to construct this cabinet.

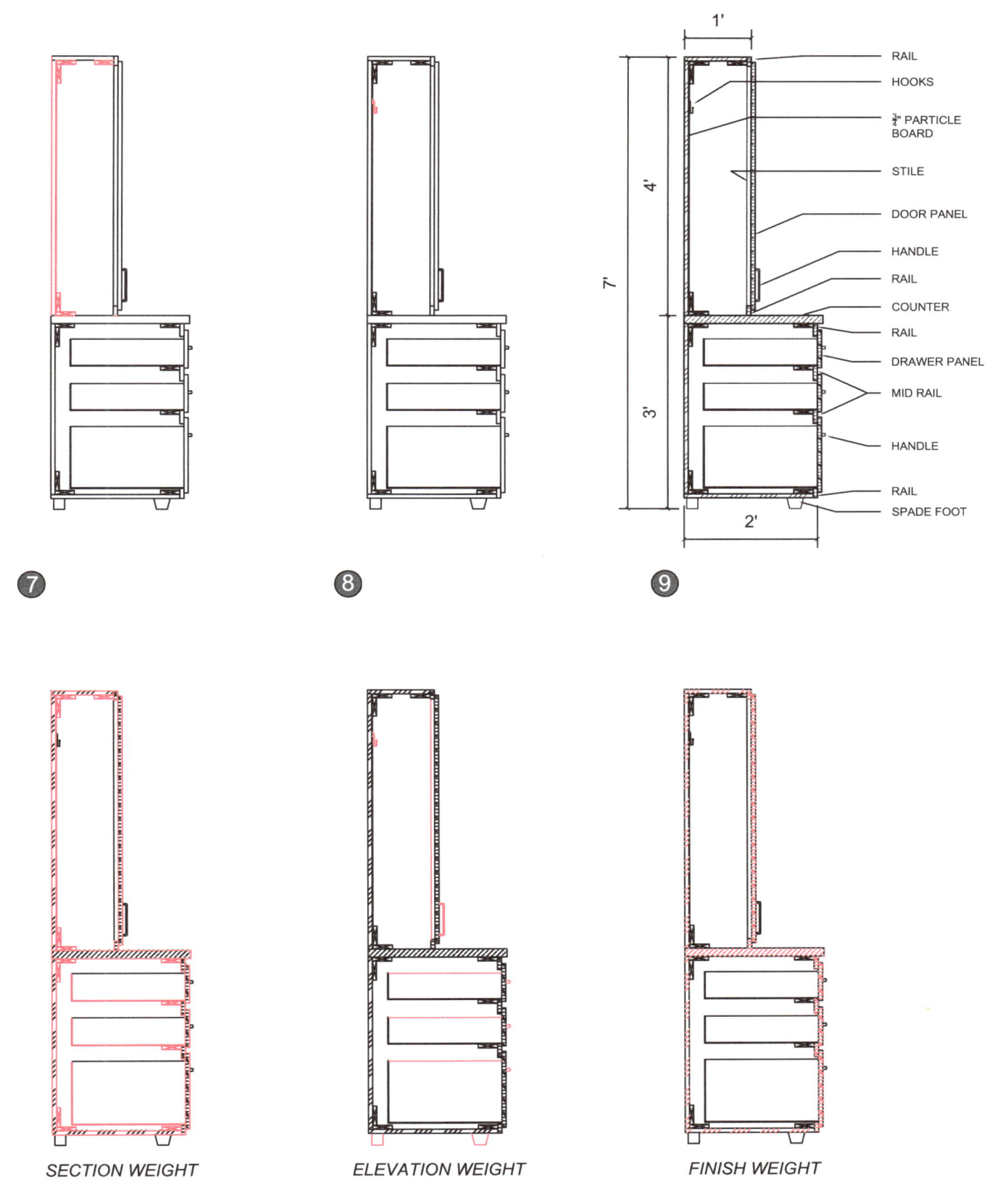

SECTION WEIGHT *ELEVATION WEIGHT* *FINISH WEIGHT*

Figure 10.19
Case piece, section through drawers, Steps 7–9.

CHAPTER 10 CUSTOM DETAILS

Cubby and bench section

STEP 1
This section will be built in front of the drawer stack section you completed in the last example. Erase everything except the framework and the feet, door, and drawer panels, which will be seen in elevation.

STEP 2
Form the lower cubby by creating a *C*-shape out of horizontal and vertical planes. Keep the bottom line of the original base of the framework and draw two horizontal lines above it, each 1/2" apart. These lines will indicate the particle board structure and the veneer finish.

Keep the existing cabinet framework at the back of the cubby, which should have measured 3/4" thick. Draw a second vertical line another 3/4" away from the framework.

Next, create the top of the cubby, which is also the bench seat. This can be done by drawing two horizontal lines that run from the front of the cabinet to the back. These lines will be 1 1/2" apart and will rest on top of the back of the *C*-shape. The top of the bench should be 17" to 20" AFF.

All the lines in this step will appear in section when the drawing is complete.

STEP 3
Add 1/8" veneer to the interior of the cubby and around the bench seat. Add a horizontal line through the center of the bench slab to indicate that there are two pieces of particleboard.

STEP 4
Add the cubby frame by drawing two vertical lines from the top of the *C*-shape to the bottom along the front of the cubby opening, measuring 3/4" thick. Place a corner block at both the front and back of the cubby. All elements added in this step will appear in elevation when the drawing is complete.

STEP 5
Build the back panel for the bench by drawing two vertical lines measuring 5'-3 3/4" long. They should be 3/4" apart from each other, with the first line at least 1/4" from the edge of the bench. The lines should start 1/4" into the bench seat, indicating that there is a dado joint present.

The top of the case piece can also be added at this time. These two horizontal lines will measure 1'-0" long and be 3/4" apart from each other. These horizontals should align with the cubbies below, meaning that they will start 1/4" before the back panel and 1/4" below the top of those verticals, housing a dado joint.

STEP 6
Measure 1'-4" from the top of the cubby and draw a horizontal line to form the bottom of the cubby. This line should start 1/4" into the back panel and extend for another 11". Add another horizontal line 3/4" above the first.

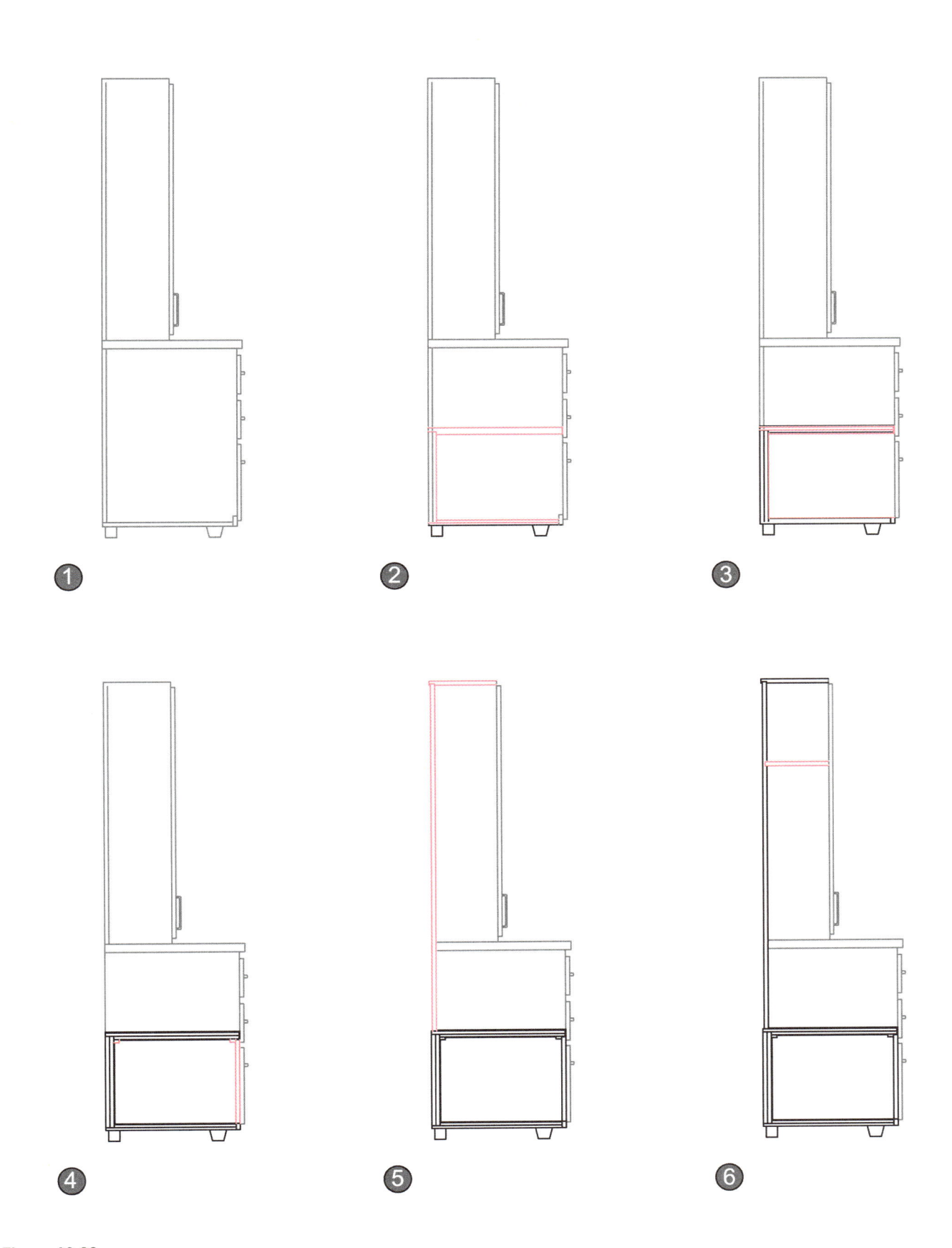

Figure 10.20
Case piece, section through cubbies and bench, Steps 1–6.

CHAPTER 10 CUSTOM DETAILS | 249

STEP 7

Trim the top and bottom of the cubby with veneer by adding lines 1/4" around the shelves.

STEP 8

The first image for this example shows the cubbies and bench in black with the existing cabinetry shown in gray. All of the black lines will receive a heavier lineweight to indicate the section cut, with the exception of the feet and the elements drawn in Step 4. The second image illustrates the finished section with the proper lineweights and textures, as well as annotations and dimensions.

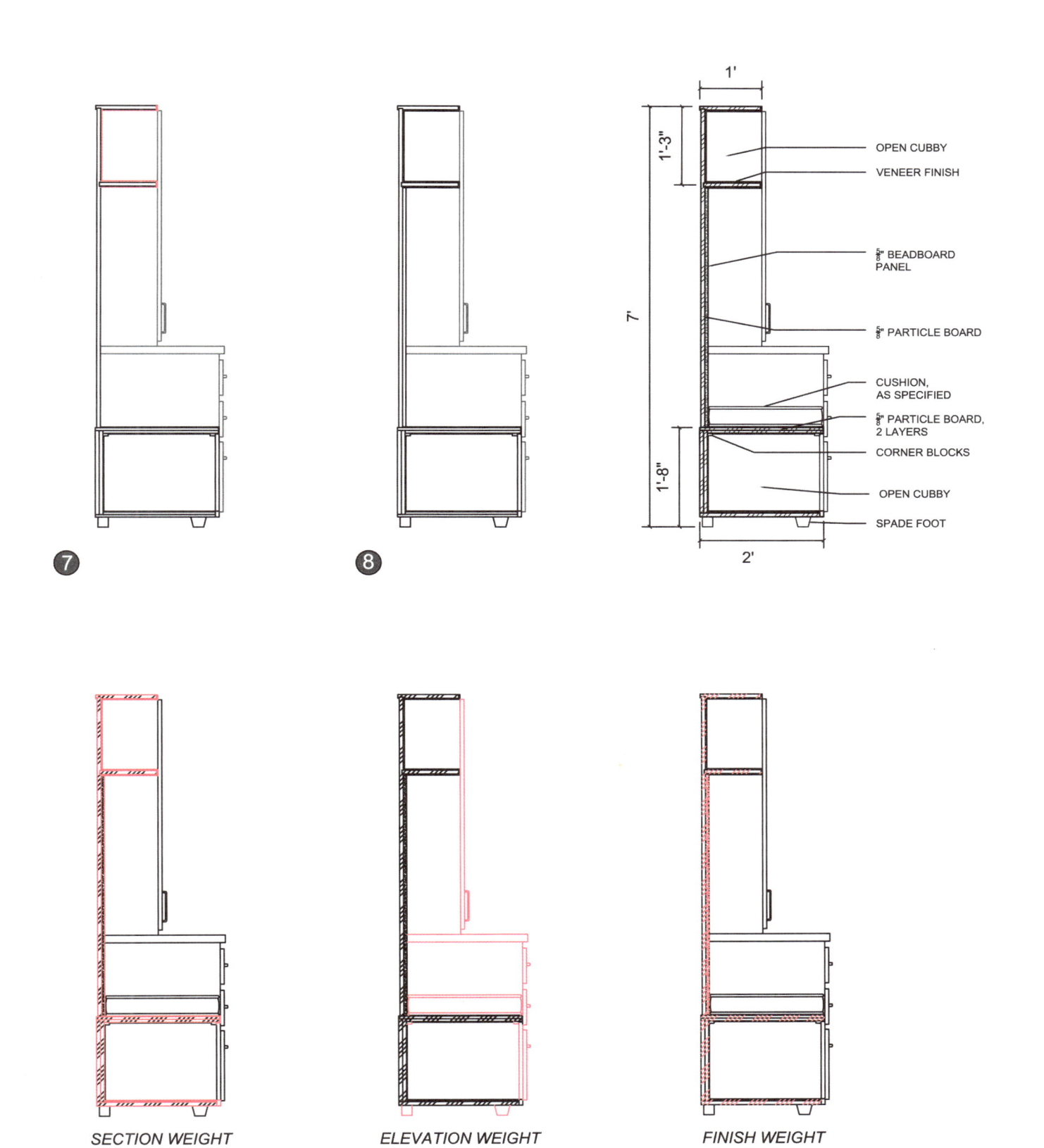

SECTION WEIGHT *ELEVATION WEIGHT* *FINISH WEIGHT*

Figure 10.21
Case piece, section through cubbies and bench, Steps 7–8.

CHAPTER 10 CUSTOM DETAILS | 251

CUSTOM RECEPTION DESK

The last example for this chapter is a reception desk for the main entrance of the commercial project. As seen in Figure 10.22, the desk features three elements that are important to understand. First, the **reception counters** are staggered in height so to meet the requirements of ADA for wheelchair approach, accommodate typical ergonomics, and extra advertising space. Here, these counters curve, creating another layer of interest and difficulty for this detail.

Second, the desk includes a **return** that runs along the wall, connecting the back desk with the reception counters. Many desks in both commercial and residential settings feature a return, and while it may seem unimportant in the section and elevation drawings that it appears in, the return serves multiple functions, from added workspace to support and balance.

Third, the desk features a **hutch** on the back, which is also typical in work stations. While the one provided in this example is a series of open shelves, hutches can also be enclosed, with doors and drawers treated in a similar manner to the details discussed in Chapter 8. Many times, hutches or various storage elements provide the designer with creative freedom for storage solutions and impact. Most hutches are 12" deep and should have a clearance space of at least 16" between the work surface and any shelves.

The initial perspective and plan drawings for the desk can be seen in Figures 10.22 and 10.23, providing the information needed for the look and size of the piece. When combined with the height and width details ascertained from the elevation drawn in the next section (Figure 10.25), the full scope of the design can be seen. Additional construction details can be determined through the section drawings in Figures 10.24 and 10.28, allowing for the commissioned contractor to understand the interaction of materials for the desk and the designer's intent.

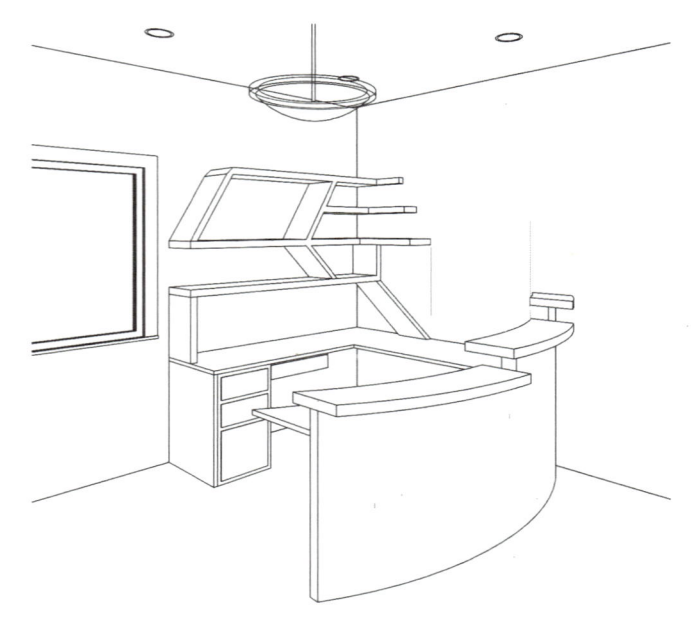

Figure 10.22
Custom reception desk with return & storage hutch.

STUDiO Animation 10.2 Custom reception desk details

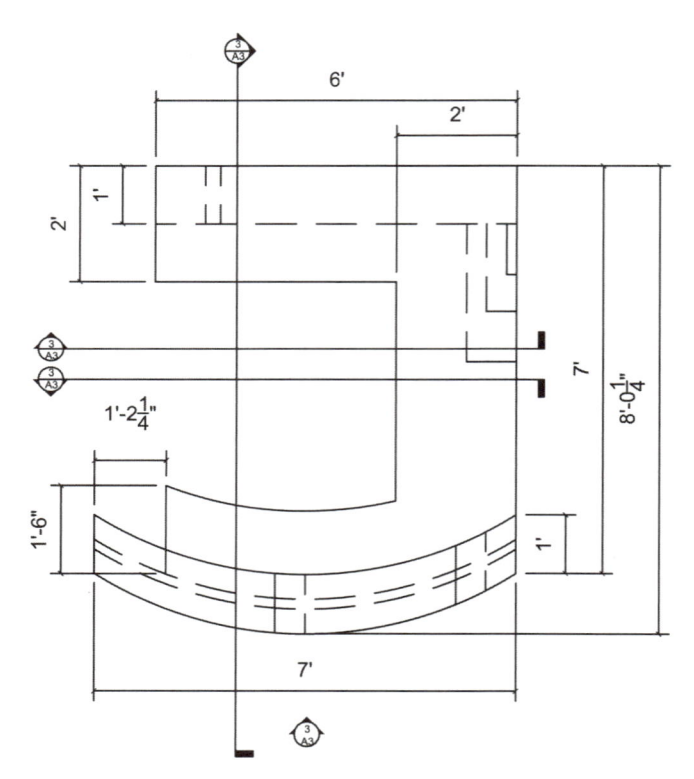

Figure 10.23
Reception desk plan.

PART II DETAIL DRAWINGS

Figure 10.24
Reception desk sections.

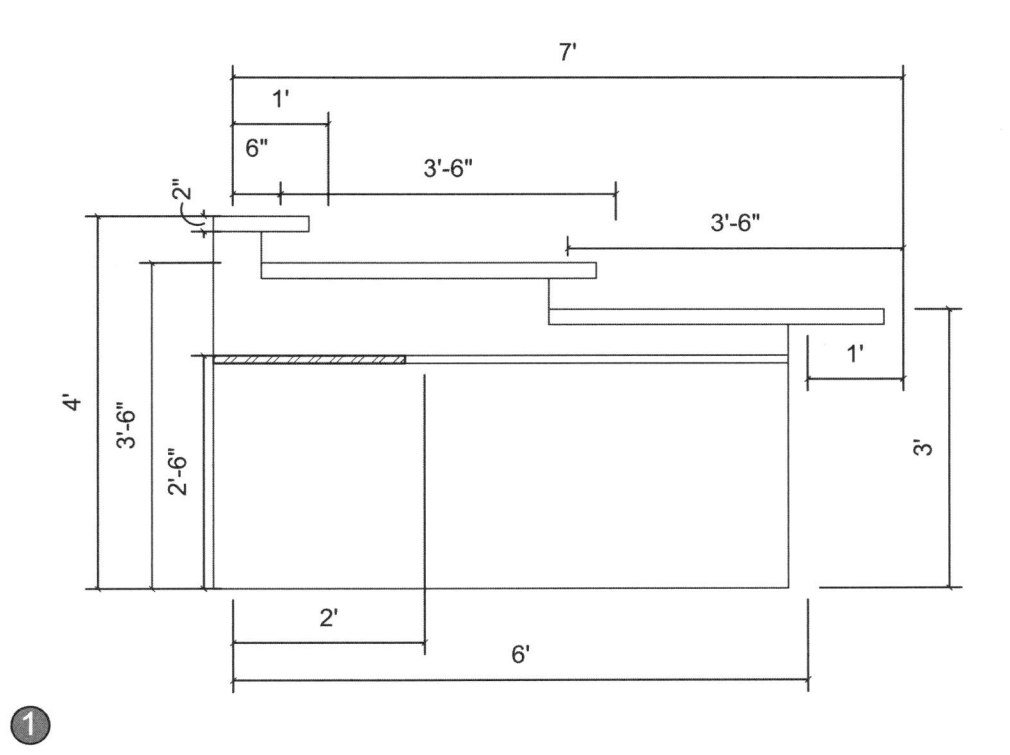

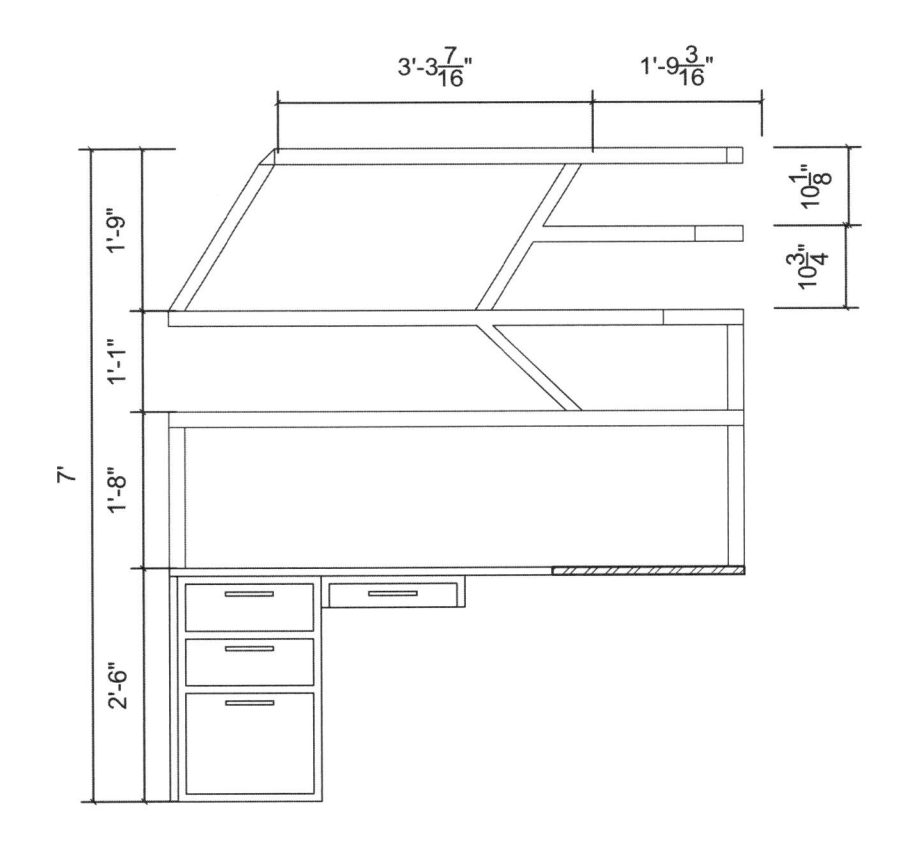

CHAPTER 10 CUSTOM DETAILS | 253

Reception desk elevation

STEP 1
If necessary, rotate the desk plan so that the reception hutch (front of desk) is facing downward. Then draw guidelines from the edge of each tier of the reception hutch and the edge of the work surface to a ground plane below.

STEP 2
Draw horizontal lines between the first and last guidelines to indicate the top and bottom of each tier of the reception hutch. In this example, there are three tiers, each measuring 2" thick. The top of each tier will appear at 3'-0", 3'-6", and 4'-0" AFF, meeting requirements for ADA wheelchair approach, serving typical ergonomics, and adding advertising space.

STEP 3
Use the remaining guidelines to create overhangs from each tier, the most important of which occurs between the first and second guides. This overhang serves as an extended countertop for wheelchair access, allowing the user to pull up as close to the work surface as possible without having to make a side approach. While not required, this **barrier-free** detail makes it easier for all guests to utilize the space. The other overhangs are decorative and may be altered at the discretion of the designer.

The front of the desk is now complete for the purposes of this example and will not be altered in the remaining steps.

STEP 4
Returning to the plan, extend guidelines from the storage hutch and rear work surface to the elevation.

STEP 5
Using the guidelines, customize the hutch to meet the needs of the end user. The clearance between the first set of hutch shelves or doors and the work surface should be at least 15", but the remaining dimensions here are arbitrary and should be determined by the designer based on the desired appearance and the building height restrictions.

STEP 6
Remove any remaining guidelines and add any necessary dimensions and annotations.

ADA
If a service counter is to be approached from the side, the counter must be at least 36" long and measure 36" AFF.

If the service counter is to be approached from the front, the counter must be at least 30" long and 36" AFF.

Revit
You can create custom furniture pieces in Revit by creating a new Family file from the program's Start menu. Here, you can draw in 2D and extrude to 3D while assigning dimension parameters to the piece prior to importing it to your floor plan. This will allow you to build the furniture without it becoming "stuck" to the floor and walls, which could become a headache if you do not notice it early enough!

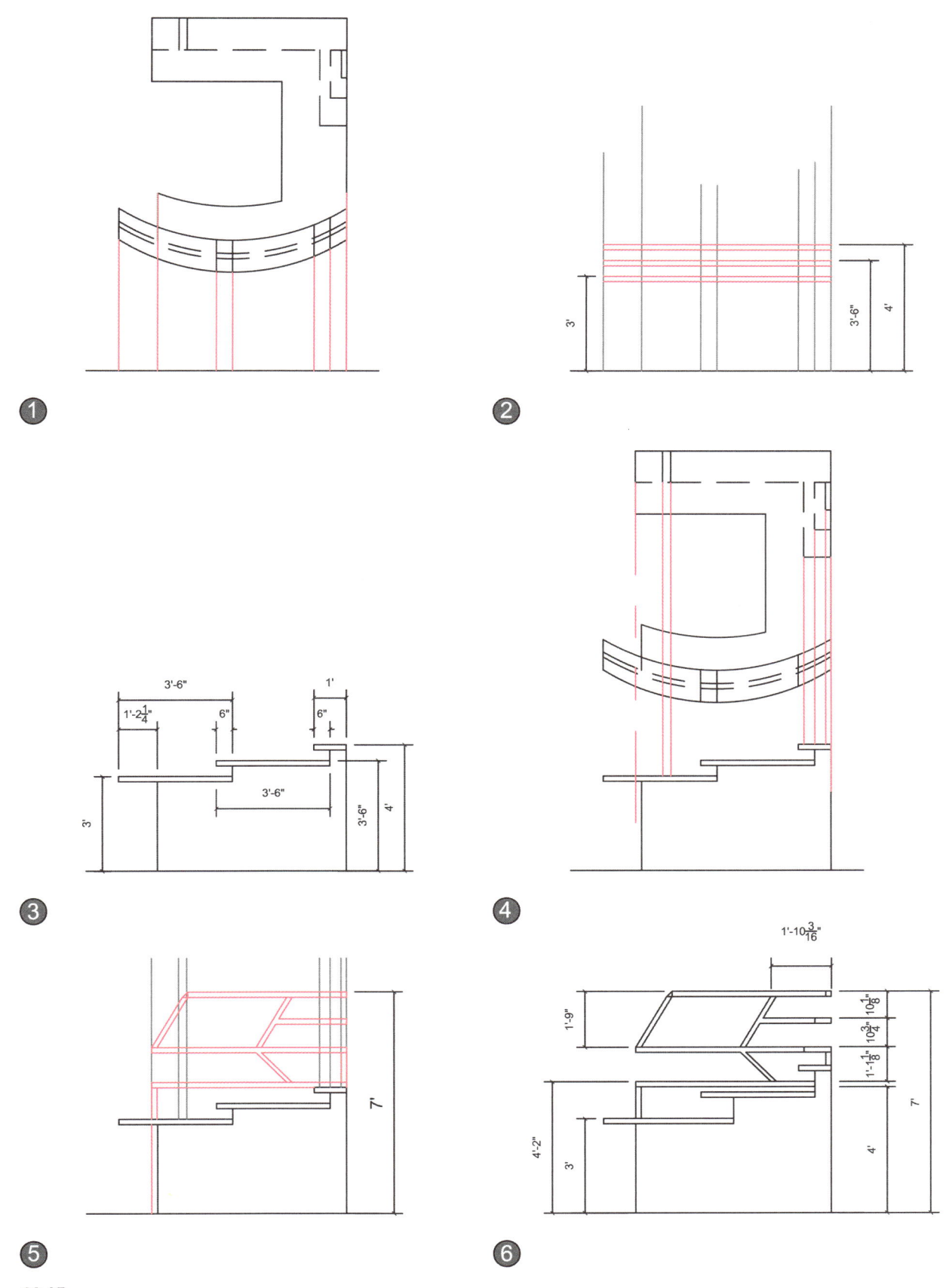

Figure 10.25
Reception desk elevation.

CHAPTER 10 CUSTOM DETAILS

Reception counter section

Marker 4/7.2 seen in Figure 10.23 indicates a section that cuts perpendicularly through the reception hutch and storage hutch on the desk. The following examples will break the section into two separate details, focusing first on the front portion of the desk and then on the back. See Figure 10.28 for the final combined section.

It is recommended that you rotate the plan so that you are facing the direction of the section cut marker and extend guidelines from the desk to the drawing space below.

STEP 1
Based on the dimensions of the reception hutch that were provided earlier in this chapter, we know that the surface is 2" thick and 1'-0" wide. Draw a rectangle with these dimensions 3'-0" AFF, as the section is cutting through the tier at ADA height.

STEP 2
Add a centralized, 2" thick vertical plane from the floor to the reception hutch. Create a dado joint between the vertical plane and the surface above by extending the vertical lines 1" into the reception hutch above. The dado will create a concealed connection between the two pieces and allow any fasteners to be hidden below the hutch surface. Refer to Chapter 7 for other types of joints.

STEP 3
Draw the work surface on the receptionist's side of the desk, measuring up 2'-6" AFF. Here, the plane starts 1" into the vertical plane and extends 1'-6", terminating with a curved counter edge.

Add an L-bracket below the work surface at the intersection of these two planes. Available in various sizes, this metal *L*-shaped support anchors the two pieces together while also efficiently transferring weight loads.

STEP 4
Due to the curvature of the desk, a small amount of the first tier is visible in elevation behind the elements drawn in Steps 1–3. Extend guidelines into the detail to achieve the desired placement.

STEP 5
Add tier two into the drawing. This level will appear in elevation.

STEP 6
Add tier three into the drawing. This level will appear in elevation.

Extend a vertical line from the underside of the third tier to the floor to indicate the far edge of the reception hutch. Trim any of this line that passes through the second tier or work surface.

STEP 7
Clean up any remaining guidelines and any lines that need to be trimmed. Give a heavier lineweight to the portions of the desk that are in section, which in this case are the first tier, the work surface, and the vertical plane drawn in Steps 1–3.

STEP 8
Finish the drawing by adding any necessary dimensions, annotations, and textures.

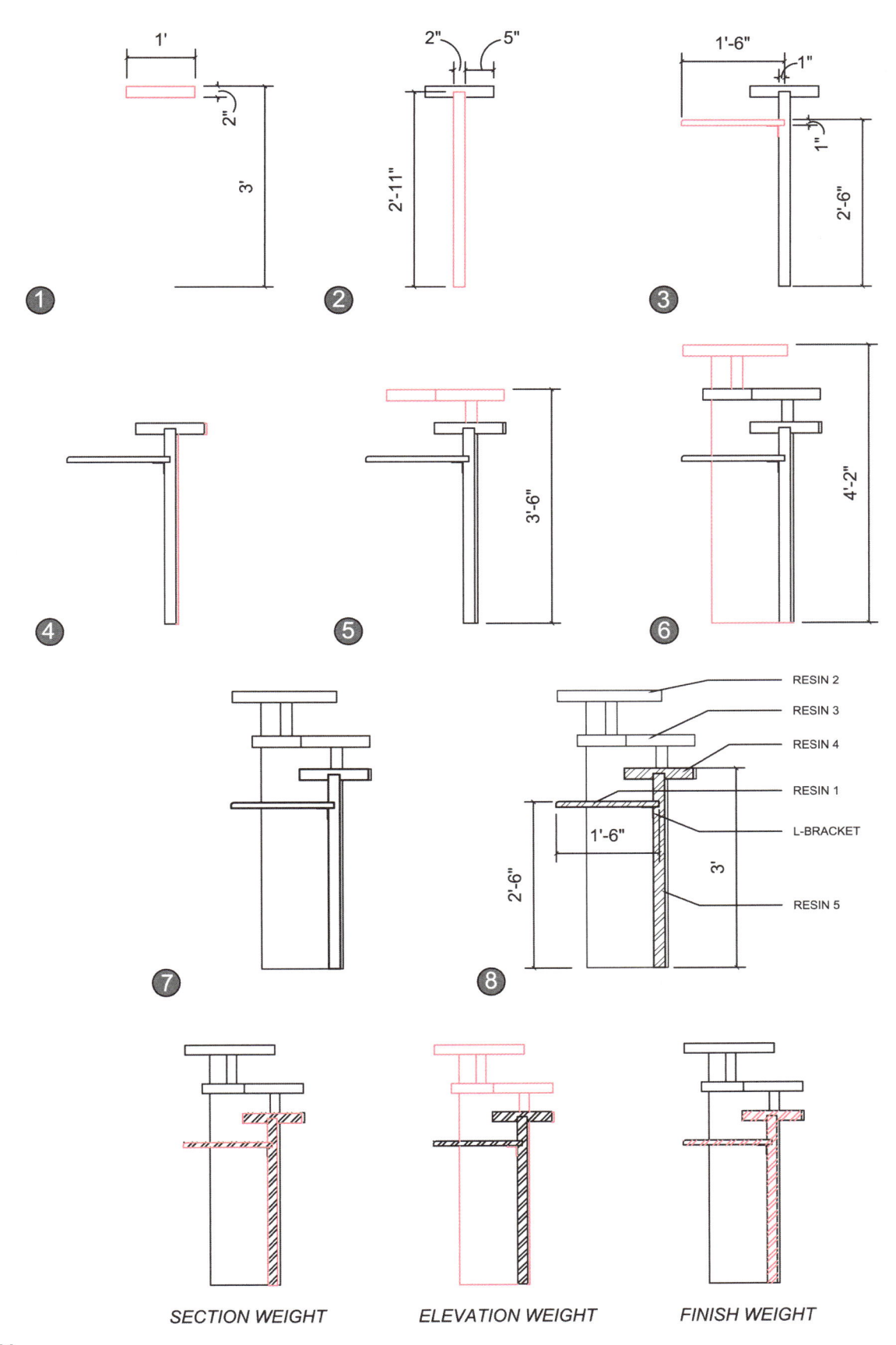

Figure 10.26
Reception hutch and counter section.

CHAPTER 10 CUSTOM DETAILS

Desk hutch section

STEP 1
Draw a work surface measuring 2'-0" deep and 1" thick. The counter edge should match the one that you selected for the first half of the desk section example. Elevate the surface so that it is 2'-6" AFF.

STEP 2
Create a vertical support that measures 1 1/8" thick. The support should run from the floor to the underside of the work surface. Illustrate an L-bracket to join the two planes.

STEP 3
Add any drawers or cabinets that are cut through depending on the storage options that you have added for the desk. A pencil drawer can be seen in this example. Refer to Chapter 8 for examples on drawers and shelves.

STEP 4
Moving up to the storage hutch, there are three open shelves that are being cut through in this section. Each shelf measures 1'-0" deep and 2" thick. As seen from the diagram, the shelves vary in height from the work surface, which can be determined by the designer.

STEP 5
Add any parts of the storage hutch that can be seen in elevation past the section cut.

STEP 6
Finish the drawing by adding any necessary dimensions, annotations, and textures. The lineweights for anything being cut through should also be darkened at this time.

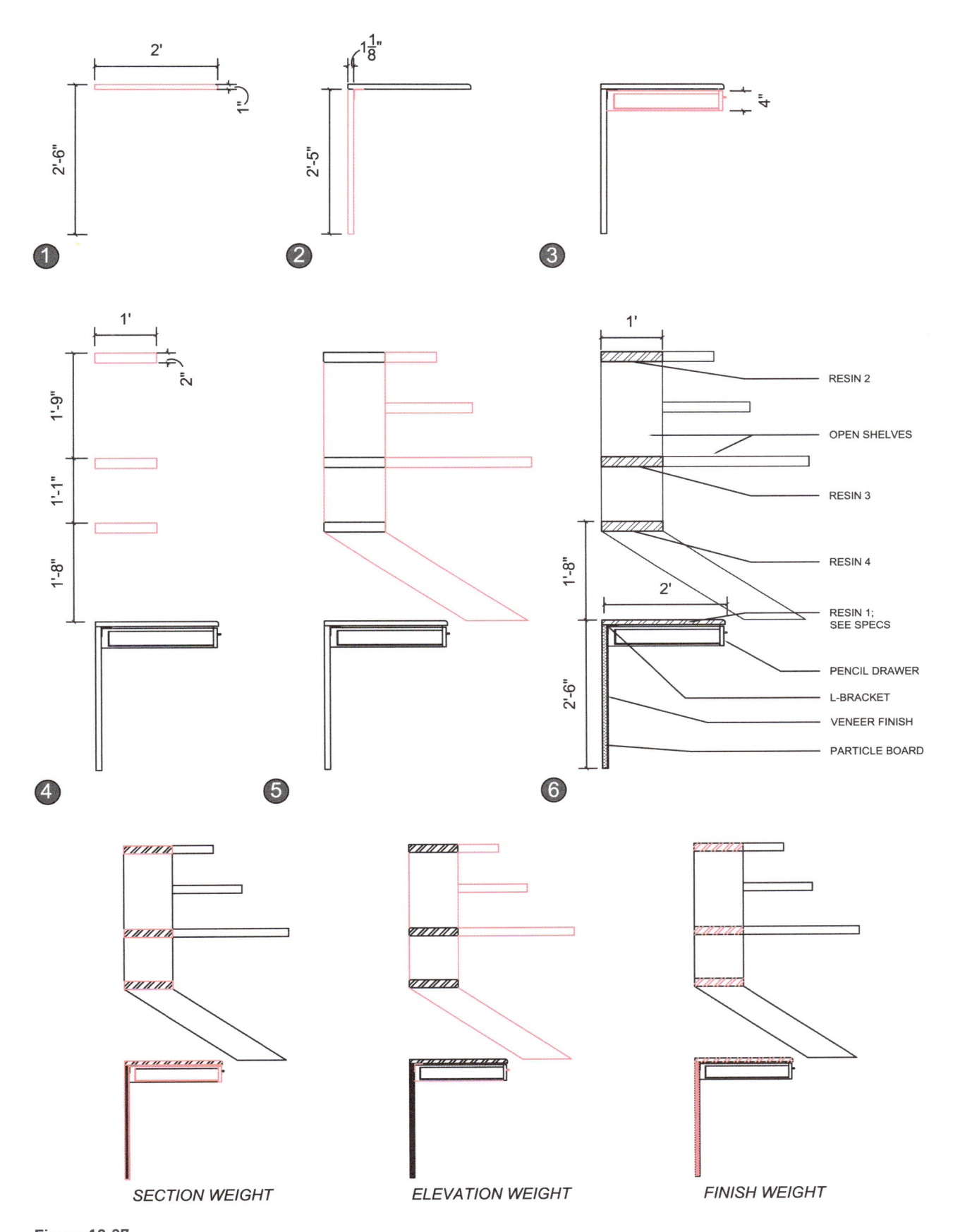

Figure 10.27
Storage hutch and work surface section.

CHAPTER 10 CUSTOM DETAILS

Full section

Combine the two sections you just created to form the overall desk section. Place the desk plan above the drawing space to aid in the alignment of the two drawings. Finish the detail by adding the return and any storage or design elements as elevation in the background.

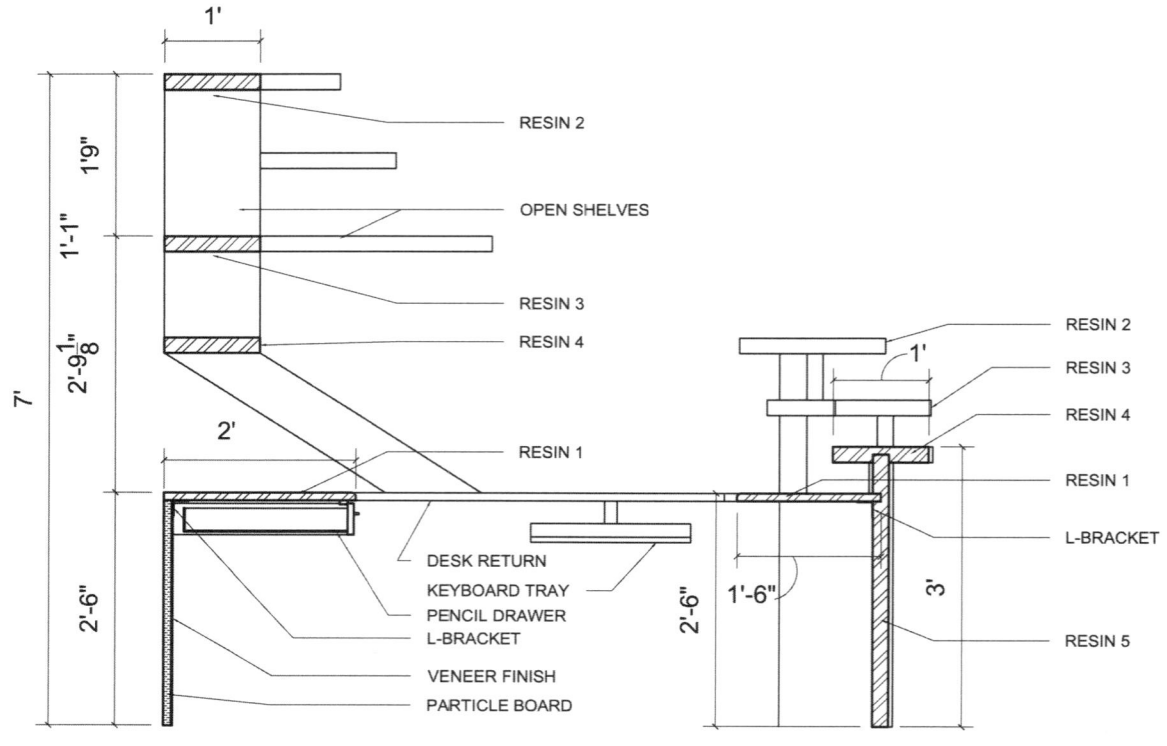

Figure 10.28
Combined section showing the full desk.

WHY IS THIS IMPORTANT?

Clients seek out the expertise of a designer to ensure that a project efficiently meets their needs while also providing them with unique touches. The key selling points on a custom design are how well the piece fits the project and the attractiveness of the end results. There is no limit to the number of different customizable elements that could be included in an interior project, so it is recommended that you consider what components are needed to create the biggest impact and whether or not there are readily available substitutions.

260 | PART II DETAIL DRAWINGS

Figure 10.29
Custom desk seating with built-in planters.

Figure 10.30
Abstract wall shelving at a café.

CHAPTER 10 CUSTOM DETAILS | 261

Figure 10.31
Storage options utilizing the space under a flight of stairs.

Figure 10.32
Conceptual bar design.

CHAPTER REVIEW

1. What ADA guidelines apply to reception desk design? Why is it important for typical and custom designs to be accessible?
2. Why is it important to understand the manufacturer's suggested use for a material prior to specifying it for a project? What negative results can occur if you misuse a product?
3. What custom elements can you integrate into your own project? Examine your plans and indicate areas where potential customization is possible.

EXAMPLE PLAN UPDATES STUDIO

This chapter investigated only four of the many customizable elements that can appear in a project. Treat this chapter as a jumping off point for your own exploration into the different patterns, materials, and combinations that you can use to create a unique design.

Based on the topics included in this chapter, the commercial plan added:

Reception desk
> *ADA reception hutch*
> *Storage hutch*
> *Return*

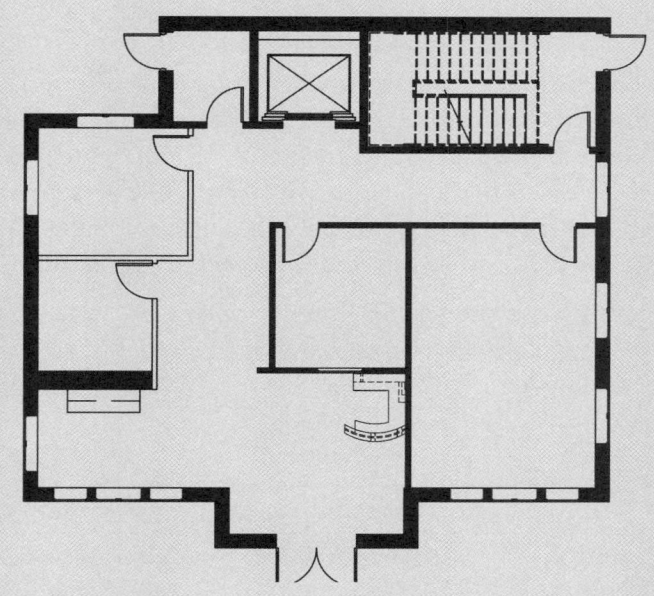

Figure 10.33
Commercial plan with custom desk.

Examples from the residential plan:

Tiles
> *Kitchen backsplash*
> *Bathroom floor*

Case piece
> *Bench with cubbies, drawer stack, and cabinet*

Remember to double-check if there are applicable IBC or ADA codes before you start detailing. This step will save you time up front and keep you from becoming frustrated in the long run!

CHAPTER TERMINOLOGY

barrier-free
drawer stack
hutch
particleboard
pattern
plywood
reception counter
repeat
return
veneer

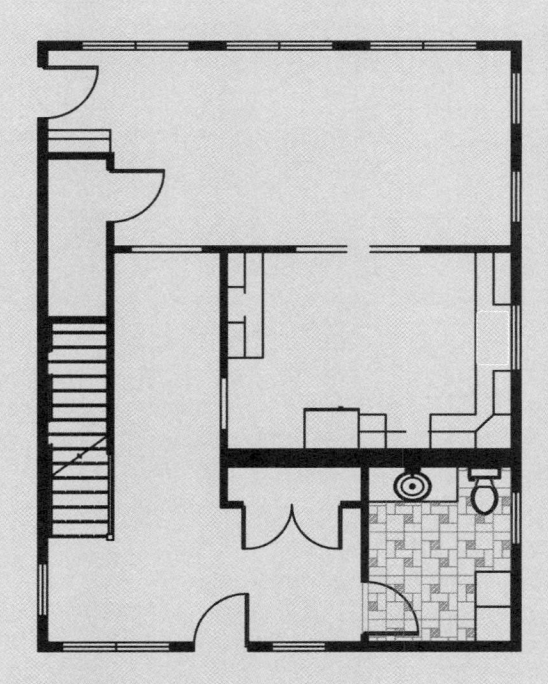

Figure 10.34
Residential plan with custom tile pattern and storage unit.

CHAPTER 10 CUSTOM DETAILS | 263

CHAPTER CODES

This section explored the elements used and how to draw construction details for a handful of custom elements. Below are the IBC codes and the ADA standards that pertain to the items *in this chapter*. The personalized nature of these types of drawings makes it impossible for codes for every scenario to be listed here, which is why there are no specific IBC codes for this chapter. It is important to note that it is your responsibility to determine whether or not any additional codes impact the heights, construction, or materials of any custom elements you create.

Table 10.2 ADA Standards for Custom Elements in this Chapter

ADA Code	Topic	Description
306.2	Toe clearance	A space measuring at least 9" deep and 30" wide must remain clear between the floor and a constructed element above.
902.3	Work surface height	The top of a work surface must be between 28"–34" AFF.
903.3	Bench size	Benches in public facilities must be at least 42" long and between 20"–24" deep.
903.5	Bench height	Benches in public facilities must have a seating surface between 17"–19" AFF.
904.4	Service counter depth	Accessible service counters must measure the same depth as non-accessible service counters.
904.4.1	Service counter, parallel approach	Accessible service counters are required to be at least 36" long and measure 36" AFF MAX with clear ground space for a side approach to the work surface.
904.4.2	Service counter, forward approach	Accessible service counters are required to be at least 30" long and measure 36" AFF MAX with under counter space meeting code 305 and clear ground space for a forward approach to the work surface.

CHAPTER REFERENCES

Ballast, David Kent. *Interior Construction & Detailing for Designers and Architects*. Belmont, CA: Professional Publications, Inc., 2013.

Ching, Francis D. *Building Construction Illustrated*. New York: John Wiley & Sons, 2014.

DeChiara, Joseph, Julius Panero, and Martin Zelnik. *Time-Saver Standards for Interior Design and Space Planning*. New York: McGraw-Hill, 2001.

International Code Council. *International Building Code, 2015*. Chicago: International Code Council Publications, 2014.

International Code Council. *International Residential Code, 2015*. Chicago: International Code Council Publications, 2014.

Jefferis, Alan. *Residential Design, Drafting, and Detailing*, 2nd ed. Boston: Cengage Learning, 2013.

Kilmer, W. Otie and Rosemary Kilmer. *Construction Drawings and Details for Interiors*. New York: John Wiley & Sons, 2016.

Kruse, Kelsey and Maryrose McGowan. *Interior Graphic Standards*. New York: John Wiley & Sons, 2003.

United States Department of Justice. *2010 ADA Standards for Accessible Design*. Washington, D.C.: Dept. of Justice, 2010.

PART III
The construction set

Completing the set

CHAPTER OUTCOMES

After completing this chapter you will be able to:

1. Organize drawings by grouping details and efficiently laying out the images within a title block.
2. Direct others to detail drawings within the set by accurately adding communicative symbols.
3. Complete and assemble a full construction document set.

CHAPTER 11

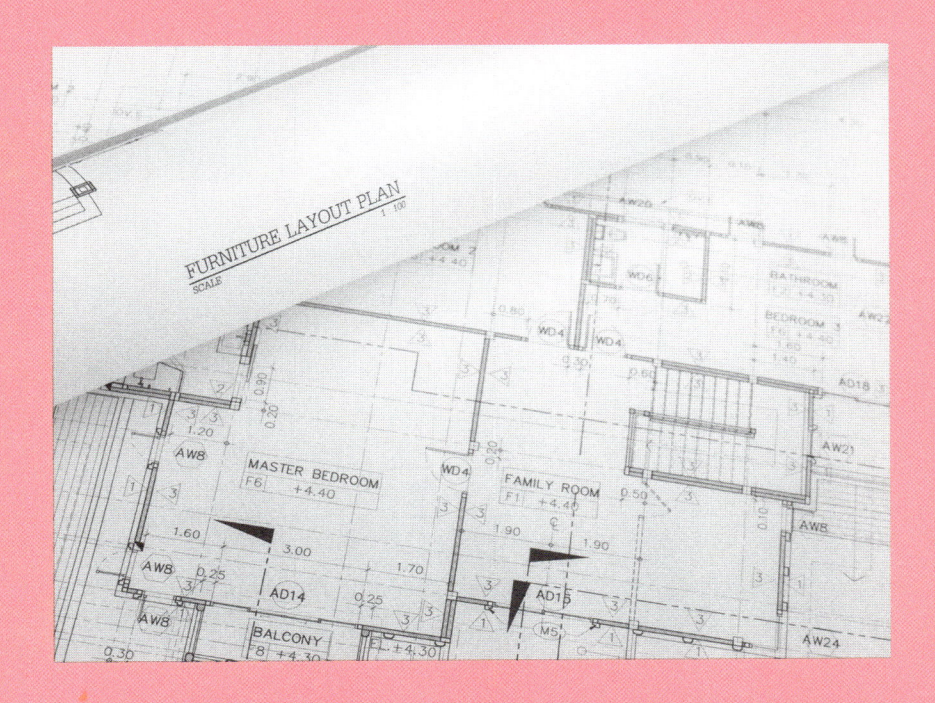

Figure 11.1 A detail drawing page from a construction set.

ABOUT ORGANIZING A CONSTRUCTION DOCUMENT SET

Based on the details drawn through this text, you have completed individual drawings telling the general contractor (GC) where walls are to be placed, how the millwork should appear, the dimensions of staircase, and so on. However, these drawings are currently stand-alone details and would be an ineffective construction tool at this moment. In order for the details to tell the construction story, you must compile them into a **construction document (CD) set**. The CD set is a collection of interrelated drawings that will act as the instructions for the GC and their team to build the project as specified. This is done by organizing individual drawings into groups and laying out pages in an orderly manner.

Page numbering systems

Page numbers are derived by grouping details into content groups based on multiple factors. The first factor results in an alphabetical abbreviation for the discipline the content relates to, usually associated with the type of contractor responsible for the drawings or work.

Figure 11.2
Reviewing a construction set.

Table 11.1 Alphabetical Abbreviations for Discipline Designations

Alphabetical Designator	Discipline	Drawing Types
A	Architecture	Plans, sections, elevations, details
C	Civil Engineering	Site, water, sewage
E	Electrical	Lighting, wiring, security, telecommunications
F	Fire protection	Sprinklers
I	Interiors	Furniture, Finish & Equipment plans (FF&E)
L	Landscape	Site, plantings, water drainage
M	Mechanical	HVAC
P	Plumbing	Pipes, fixtures, and equipment
S	Structural	Load-bearing, framing

For simplicity sake, all pages contained within this text will utilize the A designation.

Drawing designations are groups of details that are organized into sections as indicated by a numerical code. This allows drawings of similar content to be located with each other within the CD set. These sections can be broken into in one of the following two manners:

Table 11.2 Numerical Group Codes for Uniform Drawing System (grey) and Interiors (red) Designations.

Group Number	Contents	Group Number	Contents
0	General	1	Cover
1	Plans	2	Demo/Existing
2	Elevations	3	Dimension plan
3	Sections	4	Building sections & partition types
4	Enlarged views	5	Building elevations
5	Details	6	Door & window types
6	Schedules	7	Detail drawings
7	User-defined	8	Furniture plan & schedule
8	User-defined	9	Finish plan & schedule
9	3D images	10	Ceiling plan, schedule & details

The first set of group designations are based on the Construction Specifications Institute's Uniform Drawing System (CSI's UDS), as seen in the grey/white portion of Table 11.2. This set combines drawings based strictly on the type of drawing being explored, meaning that dimension plans, finish plans, and electrical plans will all be in group 1. There are fewer sections with more information in each group.

The second set of group designations, which are derived by what you may see in place for a small interiors firm, breaks the drawings into groups based on both the type and the discipline. As seen in the red/white portion of Table 11.2, plans are grouped apart from not only the other drawing types but also from each other. The dimension plan is separate from the furniture plan, making it easier to provide individual groups of drawings to the contractor associated with it. There are more sections with less information in each group.

This text will utilize the second type of grouping.

At times, all of the drawings within a group can fit on to one page, which makes labeling the pages much more simplistic. If there are too many drawings within a group to fit onto one page, a second numerical tag is required to indicate that there are multiple pages of that drawing type. This can be done by adding *01, 02, 03...* to the end of the existing tag, or, as seen in this text, by adding *.1., .2., .3....*

Based on the information provided, the page designation *A5.2* would direct you to a second page of elevations.

Next, the drawings must be organized within the group so that they are easy to locate and in a logical sequence. It is recommended that smaller drawings, such as sections and elevations, are organized by room number within the set in order to maintain clarity. Each page of a construction set can hold multiple drawings, so those drawings should be placed in a sequential manner, in columns and rows, from top left to bottom right. Based on the information provided, any notations you have that specifically refer to the fourth drawing on the second page of elevations should be written as *4/A5.2*.

The above instructions may differ from one class or firm to the next, so it is important to verify the layout standards applicable to your situation.

Laying out the pages

Construction sets are typically produced on 24" × 36" sheets of paper but can also be produced on 11" × 17". By using larger sheets, you allow for large construction projects to be illustrated in a legible manner, for detail drawings to be shown at a large scale, or small projects to be seen in just a few sheets. Once you have selected the page size for your CD set, a border must be drawn around the page with a 1/4" margin along the top, bottom, and right sides. Use a 1/2" border along the left as extra space is needed to accommodate the binding.

Next, the **title block** is added along either the right side or bottom of the sheet. The title block holds project information, such as the client's name and the building's location. Additional information, such as the page number, the contents of the page, and the scale of the drawings on the sheet are also present.

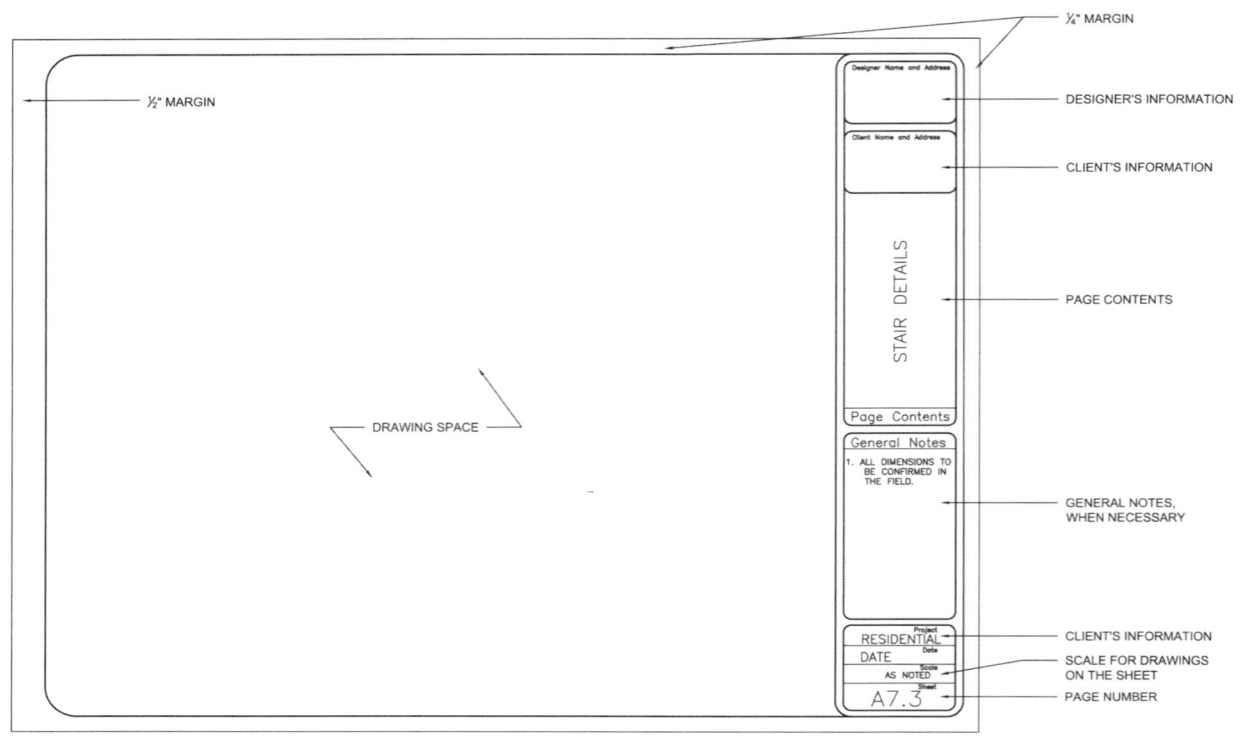

Figure 11.3
Drawing sheet with title block and drawing space.

When organizing and laying out your pages, you want to keep your drawings in as orderly a fashion as possible. This means that drawings should be kept in columns and rows based on the center of the page. To find the center of a page, use Figure 11.4.

If you are placing a single drawing on the page, locate the center of the drawing you wish to place (as shown with the X) and copy the drawing onto the sheet by overlapping the center of the X on the sheet with the X on the detail.

If you are placing multiple drawings on the page, determine how much space they each require on the sheet and align them so that they are in left-justified columns and rows. Then, find the center of the collection of details and overlap X on the sheet with the center of the details.

268 | PART III THE CONSTRUCTION SET

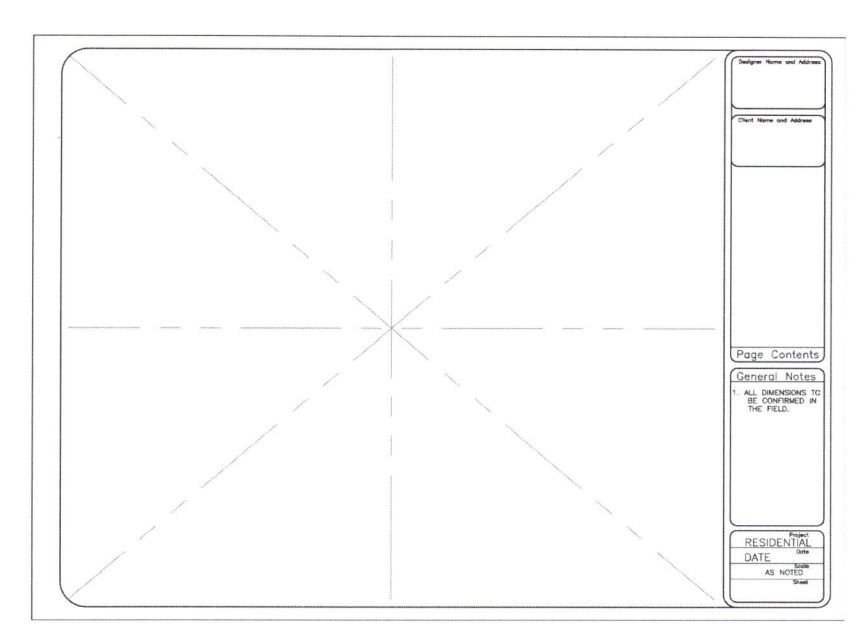

Figure 11.4
Locating center on a drawing sheet.

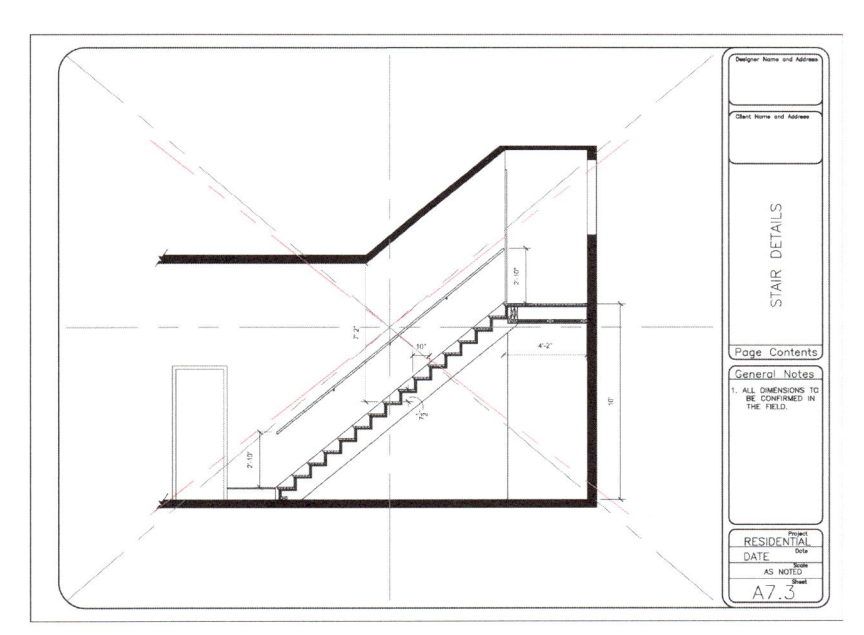

Figure 11.5
Layout with a single drawing.

CHAPTER 11 COMPLETING THE SET | 269

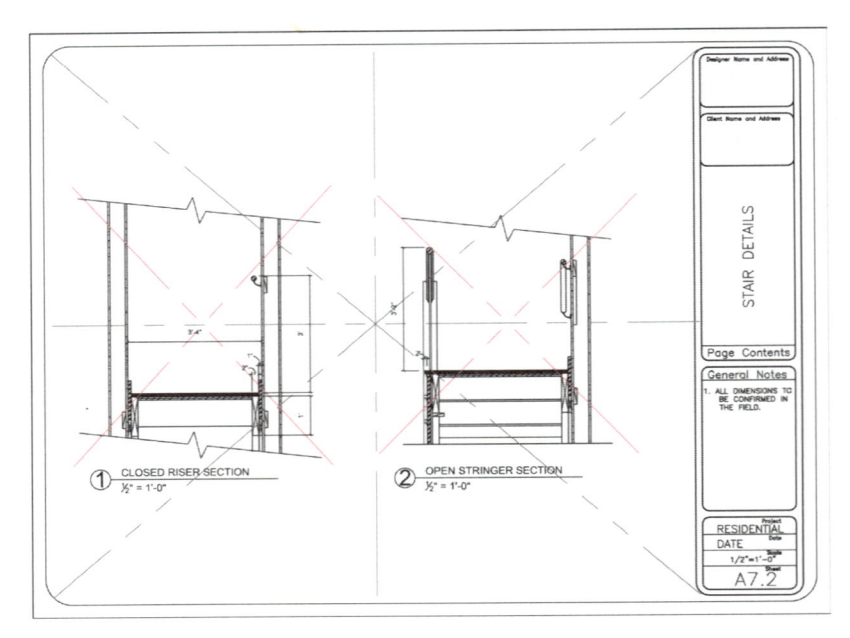

Figure 11.6
Layout with multiple drawings.

Each drawing requires a label that will give the GC information to ensure that they are viewing the correct detail and measuring properly. Labels begin with a bubble that contains the number assigned to an individual drawing. The first drawing on each page will be numbered *1*, with the drawings being labeled consecutively from left to right, row by row. A line will extend from the center of the label bubble to provide a guideline for the remaining information.

The drawing title will appear along the top of the drawing label line. This title should be more descriptive than simply *Elevation* but should be as concise and descriptive as possible, at times containing room numbers and the direction of the view. For example, if Room 3 is the dining room and the elevation is showing the west wall in the space, the detail label could be *Room 3 Elevation—West* or *Room 3, Dining Room, West*.

Below the label line, the drawing scale should be indicated so that the GC can utilize an architectural scale if necessary. If the drawing is only for reference and there is no set scale to the drawing label it as *Not to Scale*, or *NTS*.

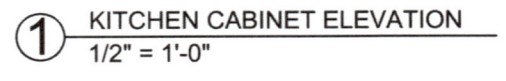

Figure 11.7
Drawing label.

PART III THE CONSTRUCTION SET

Adding communicative symbols

Now that the drawings are grouped into sections based on the information that they pertain to and numbered based on their order on the page, it is time to add **reference symbols** to the individual details. The purposes of each of the reference symbols, which include elevation markers, section cut markers, and detail callouts, were previously discussed in Chapter 1, but the placement of any of these symbols within a drawing indicates to the GC that they can ascertain more information about the element they are to construct from other drawings within the set. However, simply placing the symbols into drawings does not mean that they actually "talk" to one another until content has been added to their bubbles. As seen in the elevation marker shown on the floor plan of Figure 11.8, the content is divided into two sets of numbers: the bottom number references the page that the elevation drawing can be found on, while the top number specifies which drawing on the page is the elevation for that view. By combining these two numbers within a symbol that indicates the type of drawing being called out, the designer is directing the GC to all of the information needed to construct the element in question.

Placement of each type of marker is crucial for effective communication. The center of the elevation marker should be located on the exact spot that the viewer's feet would be if one were to stand on the plan and look in the direction of the detail. Elevation markers are only used on floor plans. The line connecting the bubble and the tail of the section marker cuts through the plan so that whatever the line touches is in section view and anything else still visible appears in elevation in the distance. Section markers and detail callouts can be used on plan, elevation, or section drawings. There is no limit to the number of reference symbols that can be placed on a drawing, but there are instances where symbols can overlap with each other or important information.

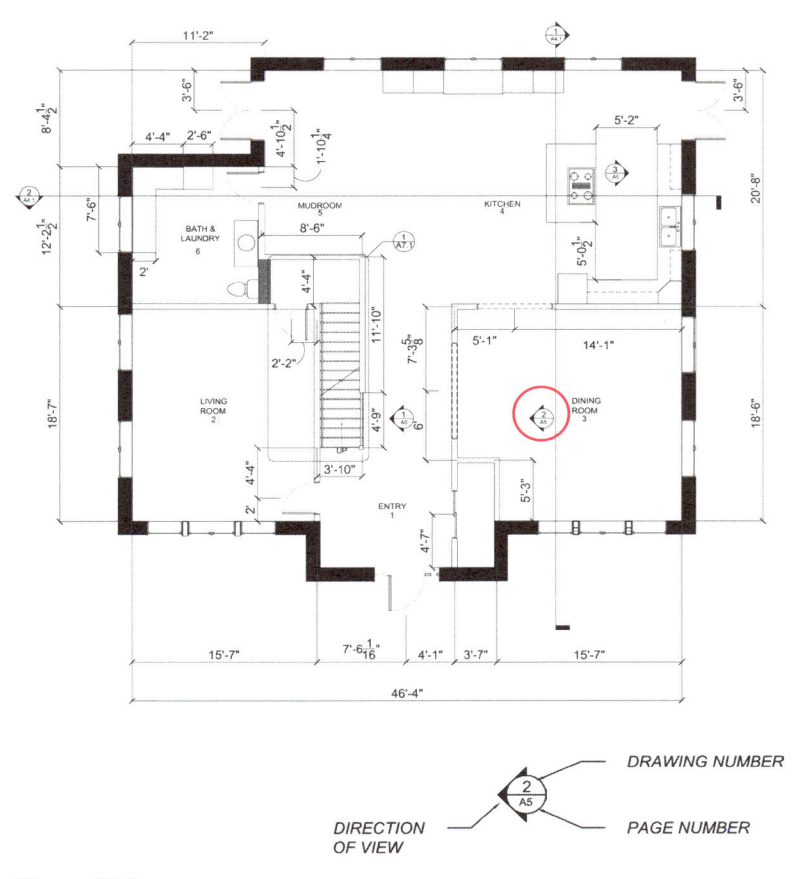

Figure 11.8
Elements of an elevation marker.

CHAPTER 11 COMPLETING THE SET | 271

When multiple markers of the same kind overlap, additional bubbles or arrowheads may be needed. Typically, rooms that have elevations views of different walls from the same fixed space will have a single bubble with an arrowhead for each direction that drawings are needed for. The placement of the marker content can vary, but should remain as a consistent style throughout your drawing set. Figure 11.9 illustrates how to add content for elevation markers for multiple views.

Section cuts that result in drawing muddiness from the added lines can be simplified to a broken line. This line will enter the drawing as an extension from the marker bubble and stop shortly into the drawing, ending without a tail. The line will restart near the other end of the section view, passing through the object's boundary and terminating with a second marker bubble, as seen in Figure 11.10.

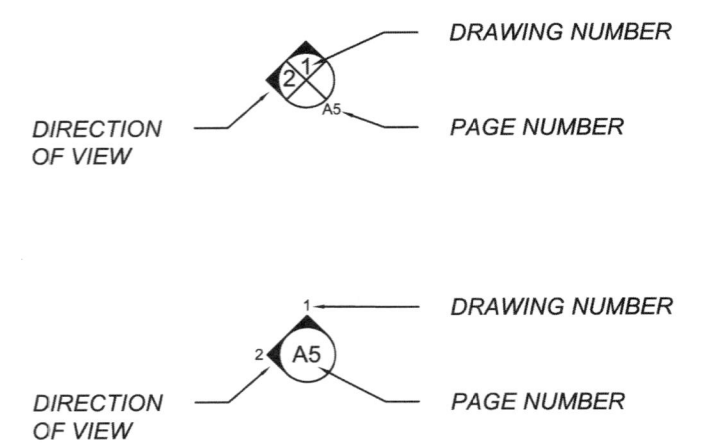

Figure 11.9
Single elevation markers for multiple details.

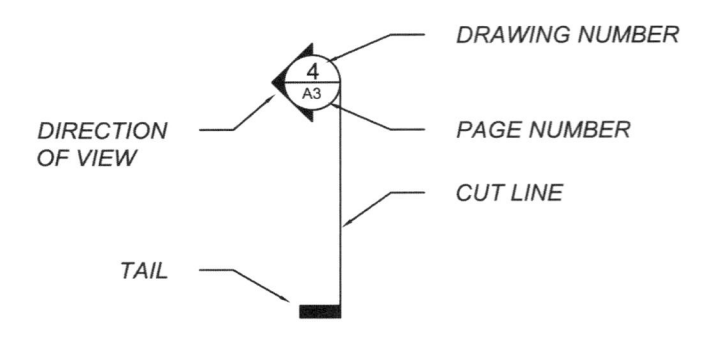

Figure 11.10
Typical section marker and broken section marker.

Detail callouts have the most flexibility in placement as they need only be drawn around an object to indicate an enlarged detail is available. These enlargements are typically associated with plan views that are blown up for clarity or so that additional, usually complex, information can be added. Callouts can also refer to enlarged elevation and section details when additional information on a particular element is needed.

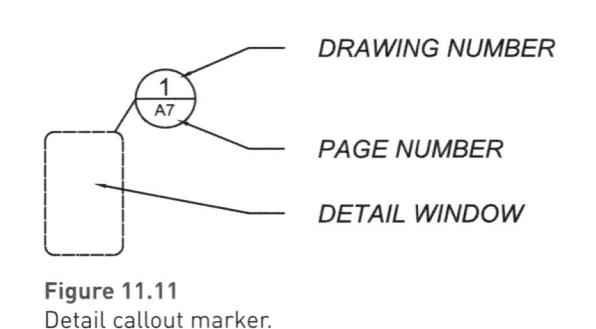

Figure 11.11
Detail callout marker.

272 | PART III THE CONSTRUCTION SET

COMPLETING THE CONSTRUCTION SET

Hand drafting

1. When drafting by hand, it is important to remember that your final set will require quite a bit of math and trace paper. Use the trace paper to record measurements for each drawing that will appear on the sheet and create a sketch to use as a guide. Remember to include spacing for the title block, borders, and any labels. This will ensure that your spacing is accurate.

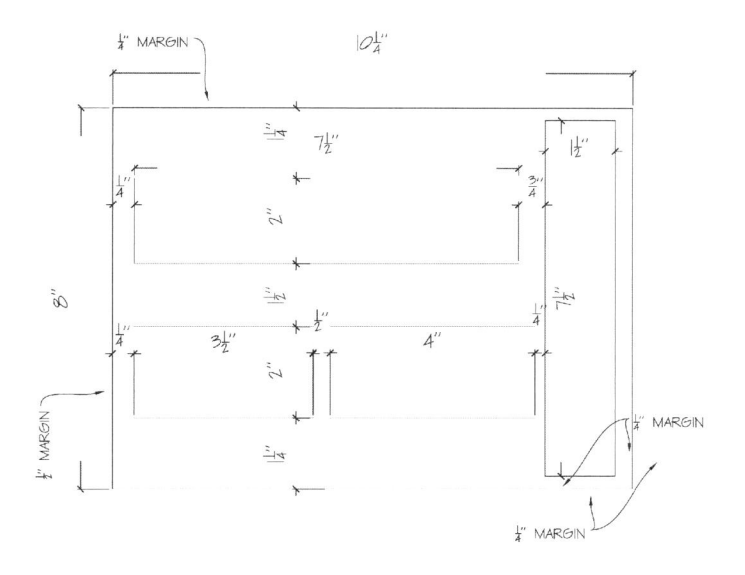

Figure 11.12
Layout notes.

2. To save yourself time and a headache, draft your title block and sheet borders onto trace paper that has been cut to the same size as your vellum. If your trace roll is not the same size, you can utilize a small seam between trace sheets for the same effect. By creating a template of your title block and borders, you can ensure that they will have a consistent appearance from one final sheet to the next. When your template is complete, secure it to your drafting table.

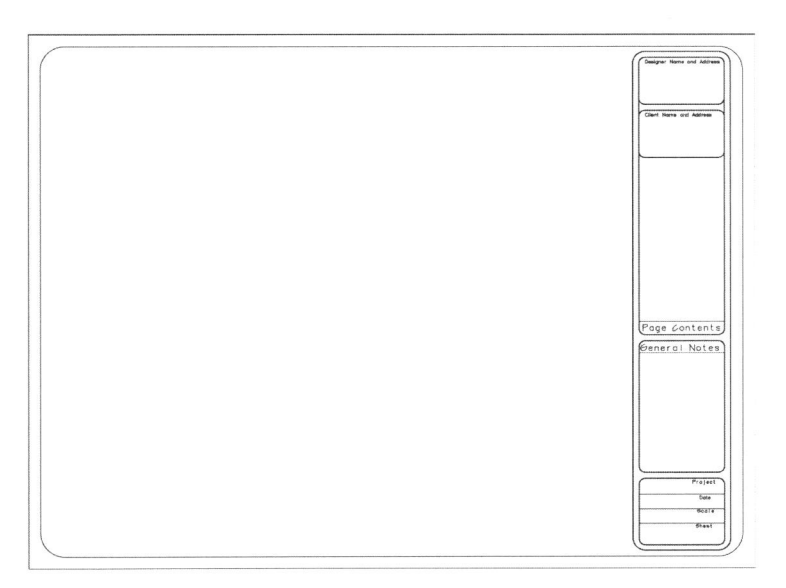

Figure 11.13
Title block template for spacing purposes.

CHAPTER 11 COMPLETING THE SET | 273

3. Next, tape your preliminary detail drawings to the drafting table. Measure as you place each detail so that the spacing is accurate and consistent from one image to the next. Use your paraline and triangles to guarantee that your lines appear at 90 degree angles.

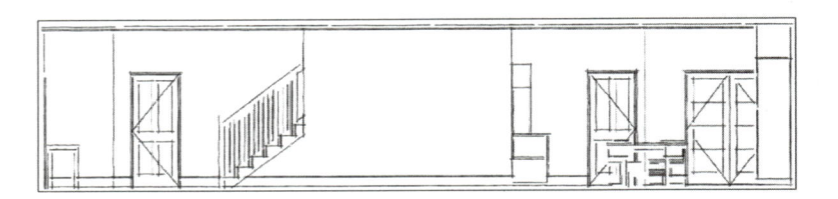

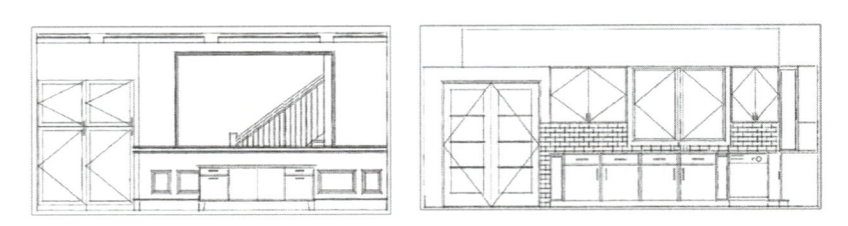

Figure 11.14
Hand-drafted elevations.

4. Once the guides for your borders, title block, and details are in place, lay your vellum sheet on top of the images below. Secure the vellum to the drafting table once you double checked that the page is aligned with the paraline and triangles. You can begin tracing the images at this time. Make sure to keep your lineweights and linetypes accurate to their role and importance within the drawing, with the heaviest lineweights being added last in an effort to reduce smudging. If necessary, ink the drawings in place of using lead.

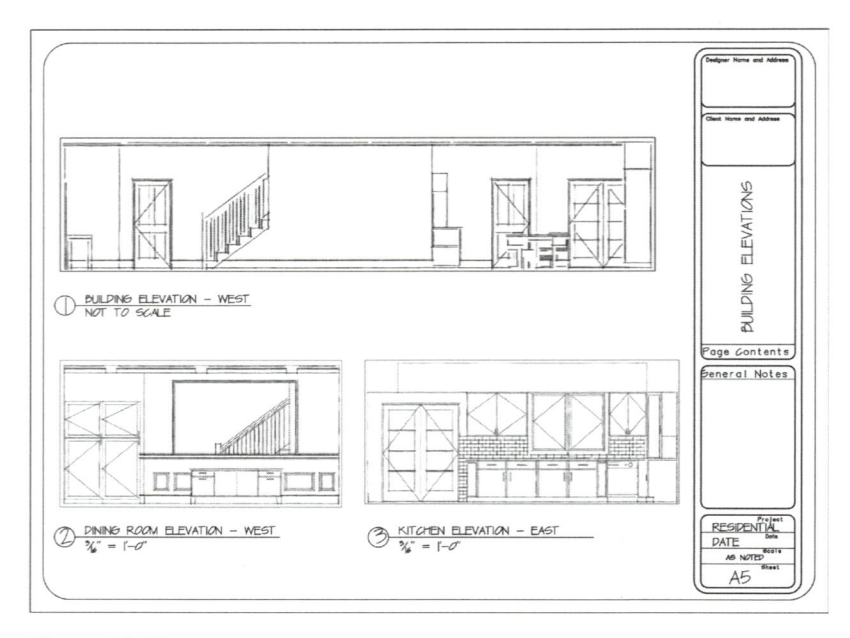

Figure 11.15
Hand-drafted elevation sheet with title block.

Hand

Keep a piece of trace under your hand while you work. This will keep the lead dust or wet ink from bleeding on to your hand, which will cut down on smudging.

CAD

Organizing the drawing set in CAD can be streamlined by setting up a single sheet and then simply copying it to create new pages.

STEP 1
This can be done through the tabs at the bottom of your screen, currently labeled Layout1 and Layout 2. Click on the Layout 1 tab to open your paper space window, which is essentially your "sheet."

STEP 2
The rectangle in the middle of the page is **viewport**, which is the window from the sheet to your model space. Reduce the size of the viewport so that a majority of the paper space is visible. Here you can draw or import the title block of your choice.

STEP 3
Once drawn, highlight the frame and border of the title and block them together. Then, while keeping the frame highlighted, click on all the text and create a group out of these elements. This will allow you to move the entire title block without worrying about any issues in spacing. To change how the text reads from one sheet to the next, simply type X to explode the group.

STEP 4
Click on the viewport to highlight it. Change the layer from the default Layer 0 to the new viewport layer. You can then double-click inside the viewport, which will create frame to change from light (inactive) to bold (active), indicating that you are in model space. Scroll or pan around within the viewport to locate the drawing you wish to focus on. Return to the paper space by either double-clicking outside of the viewport or clicking on the MODEL icon on the bottom of the screen, turning it to PAPER.

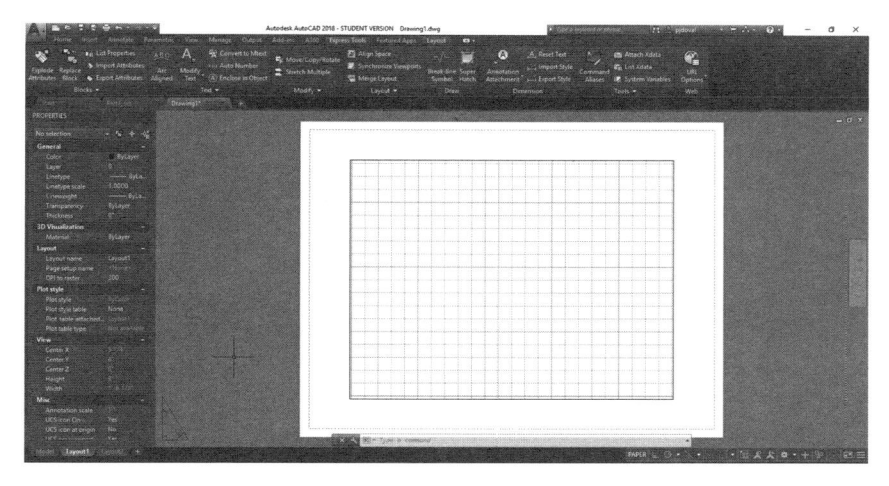

Figure 11.16
Step 1.

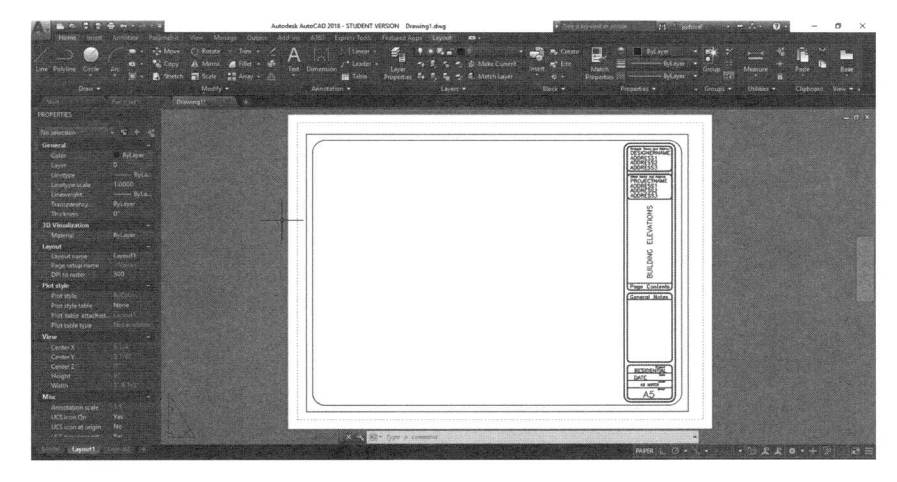

Figure 11.17
Steps 2 and 3.

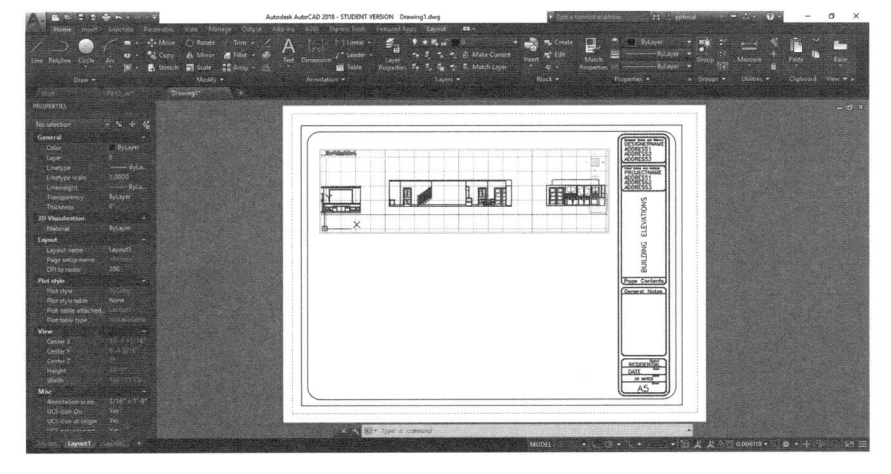

Figure 11.18
Step 4.

CHAPTER 11 COMPLETING THE SET | 275

STEP 5

Click on the viewport frame to highlight it. Using the adjustment tool in the lower ribbon that was discussed in Chapter 3, change the scale of the drawing as necessary. The viewport can then be adjusted around the detail as well.

STEP 6

Add any labels or annotations necessary for this drawing.

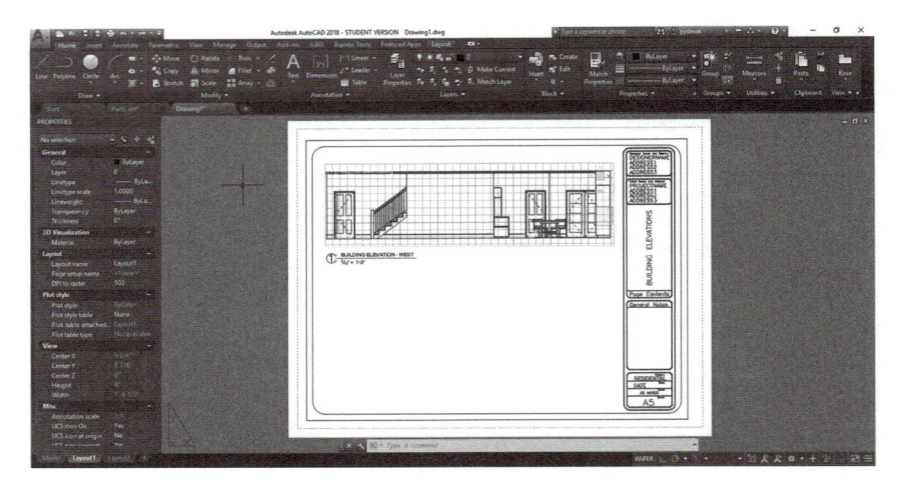

Figure 11.19
Steps 5 and 6.

STEP 7

Viewports can be copied and pasted across the sheet. After each new drawing is scaled, measure the distance between it and its neighbors to ensure proper placement.

STEP 8

New sheets can be created by right-clicking on the Layout tab and copying it. Give each page its own name and then change the content of the viewports from sheet to sheet.

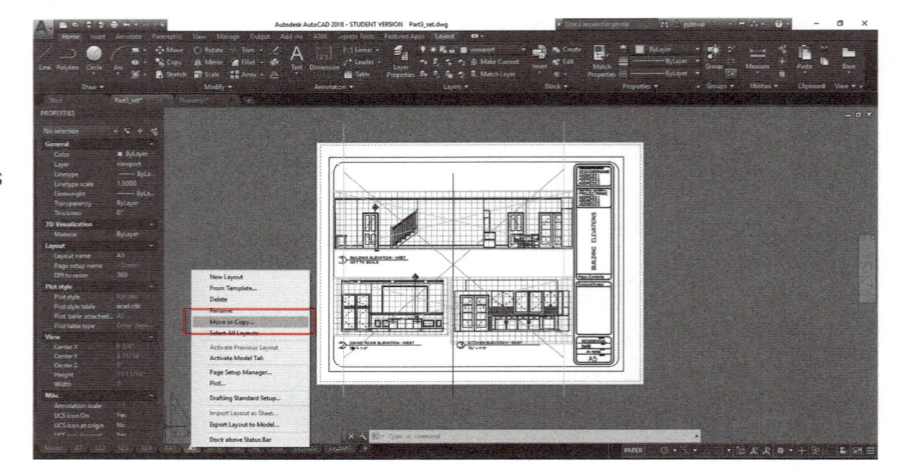

Figure 11.20
Steps 7 and 8.

CAD

Go to Layer Properties and create a viewport layer. Make sure that you give the layer a unique color so that you can easily see it while spacing the individual details on the sheet. If you do not want the viewport to print, find the Plot column in the Layer Properties window and click on the printer icon for the layer to toggle its visibility on and off.

Revit

Organizing the drawing set in Revit is by far the quickest of the three methods as the program generates so many elements for you.

STEP 1
Scroll to the end of the Project Browser and right-click on Sheets, choosing New Sheet. Then select or load a new title block and click OK. A complete page will be generated for you.

STEP 2
Scroll back up in the Project Browser and locate a file you wish to add to the sheet. Drag the drawing name from the Project Browser to the sheet in the drawing window and click to place it. The drawing will automatically be given a label.

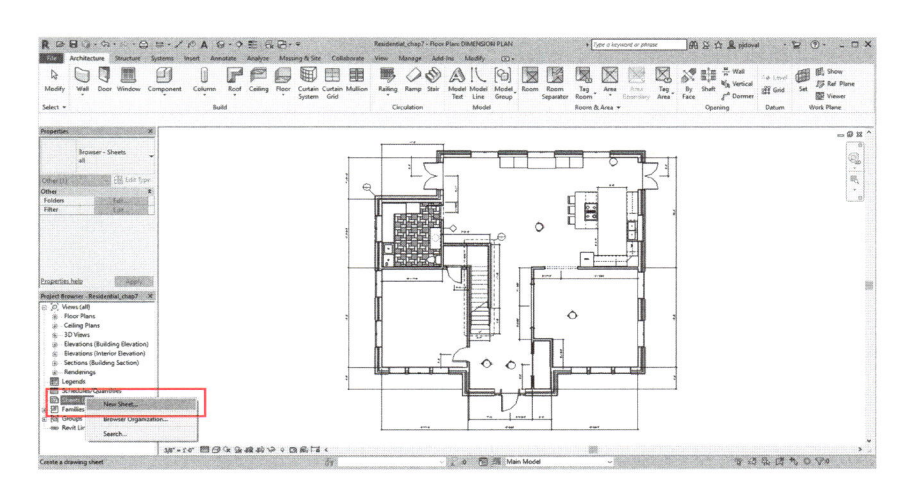

Figure 11.21
Step 1, Project Browser sheets.

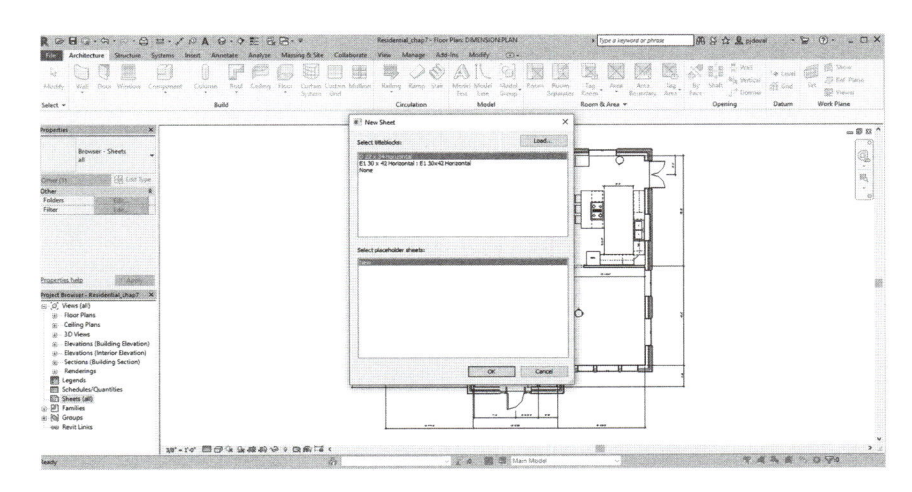

Figure 11.22
Step 1, sheet size and title block files.

> **Revit**
>
> Revit makes the drafting process even less stressful by automatically updating the elevation, section, and detail callout markers in all of your drawings to reflect the label and page numbers assigned to any image that appears on a sheet. All you need to do is double-check that the symbols have updated within the other drawings and that there are no left-over symbols, indicating that a view was forgotten somewhere along the way.

STEP 3

With the detail highlighted on the sheet, the Properties menu will provide you with information on the viewport and its contents. Here you can change the scale of the drawing with the View Scale drop down. You can also adjust the detail level and visibility if necessary.

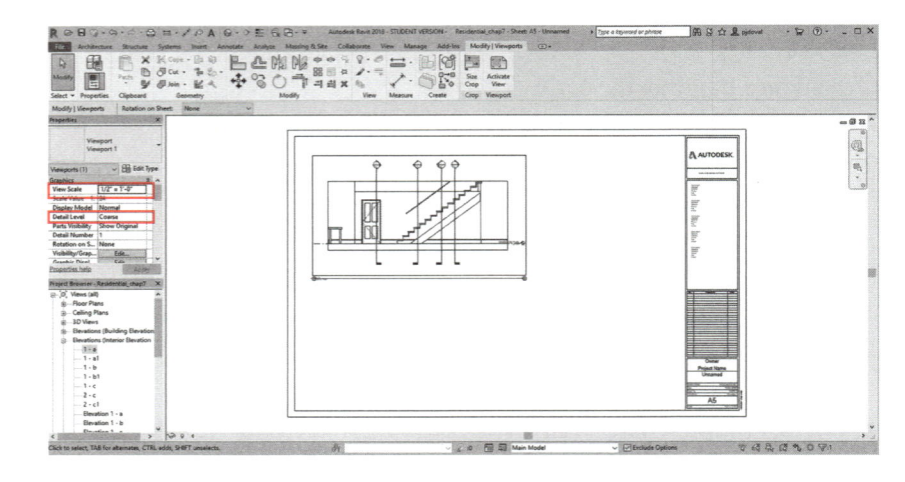

Figure 11.23
Step 3.

STEP 4

You can continue to drag detail drawings from the Project Browser and alter their scale as needed. Once all required drawings are present on the sheet, you can move them around by clicking and dragging them, utilizing the dashed centerlines that appear to keep them aligned.

STEP 5

After placing the images in their final locations, you may find that the numbers for the generated labels are now out of order. Adjust this by clicking on the label to highlight it and changing the Detail Number in Properties. You can also alter the detail name through Properties.

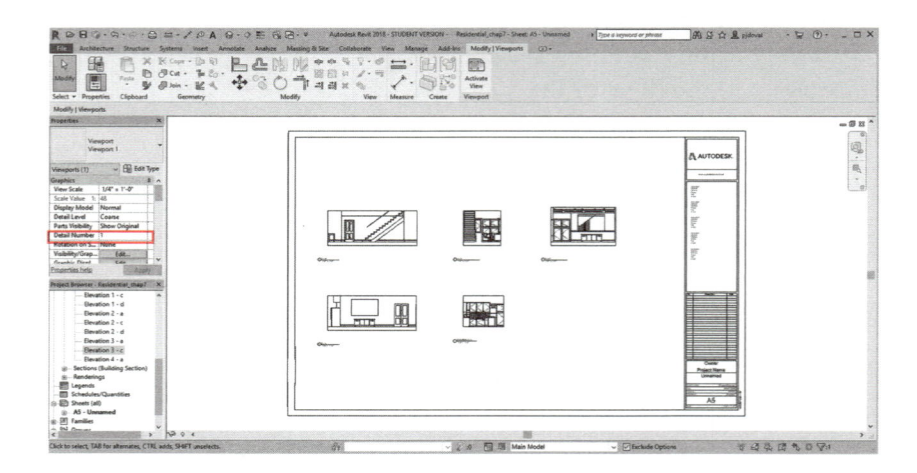

Figure 11.24
Steps 4 and 5.

WHY IS THIS IMPORTANT?

Clear, accurate communication is of the utmost importance when working on a CD set. Plans are passed among experts in architecture, interior design, engineering, and construction and serve as the guide to completing the project and showcasing the scope of the client's needs. It is important to remember that while there would be regular on-site check-ins between experts, drawing mistakes, discrepancies, and omissions can lead to unforeseen time- and cost-consumption. It is better for everyone involved with the project to hold these errors to a minimum.

Figure 11.25
A team of architects, designers, engineers, and contractors reviewing documents on a work site.

CHAPTER REVIEW

1. Why is it important for drawings to be organized in a consistent manner from sheet to sheet? Why is it important that the numbering system is also done in a consistent, yet repetitive, manner?
2. What is the role of the group designation when numbering sheets?
3. What is the roll of the symbol bubble for elevation, section, and detail markers? Why is it important for these bubbles to be accurately labeled?

CHAPTER TERMINOLOGY

construction document set
drawing designation

reference symbol
title block

SAMPLE CD SET STUDIO

The pages that follow show a sample construction document set. This set is a hybrid of the projects and examples explored in this text. The shell of the building can be found in Appendix K for the commercial project, yet the interior has been designed as a residence. It is important to remember to save your work. As seen through multiple examples in this text, existing details can be re-used or edited to meet the needs of a new project. It is suggested that you save any work that you do in order to streamline your design time in the future. This can be seen in this sample CD set, as several examples are copies or edits of work completed in earlier chapters of this text that have been repurposed for this new space.

Drawings have been set up on 24 × 36 sheets and then reduced in size to fit within this text. What this means is that the drawings are properly scaled when reproduced at 24" × 36", but will not read at the correct scale if you were to measure the image in your book.

Please note that there are no schedules shown within this sample set. Several types of drawings, such as furniture plans, finish plans, and lighting plans will typically include a schedule that lists every item that has been specified in that particular category. When grouped with the CD set, it not only allows for cross-referencing among what items have been requested and delivered, but it also instructs the installers on where to place each item.

The chart that follows explains the page designations, the section content, and recommended drawing scales for a CD set. Remember, this process can change depending on the practices within an office or the classroom, and it is always wise to double-check what is expected of you.

Table 11.3 Recommended Page Content and Drawing Scales

Group Number	Content	Commercial Scale	Residential Scale
1	Cover	N/A	N/A
2	Demo/Existing Conditions	1/8" = 1'-0"	1/4" = 1'-0"
3	Dimension plan	1/8" = 1'-0"	1/4" = 1'-0"
4	Building sections & Partition types	1/4" or 1/2" = 1'-0"	3/4" = 1'-0"
5	Building elevations	1/4" or 3/8" = 1'-0"	1/4" = 1'-0"
6	Door & window types	1/2" to 1" = 1'-0"	3/8" to 1 1/2" = 1'-0"
7	Enlarged plans & detail drawings	1/4" = 1'-0" MIN (plans) 1/2" to 1" = 1'-0" (details)	1/2" = 1'-0" MIN (plans) 3/8" to 1 1/2" = 1'-0" (details)
8	Furniture plan & FF&E schedules	1/8" = 1'-0"	1/4" = 1'-0"
9	Finish plan & Finish schedule	1/8" = 1'-0"	1/4" = 1'-0"
10	Ceiling plan, lighting schedule, and ceiling details	1/8" = 1'-0" (plans) 1/2" to 1" = 1'-0" (details)	1/4" = 1'-0" (plans) 3/8" to 1 1/2" = 1'-0" (details)

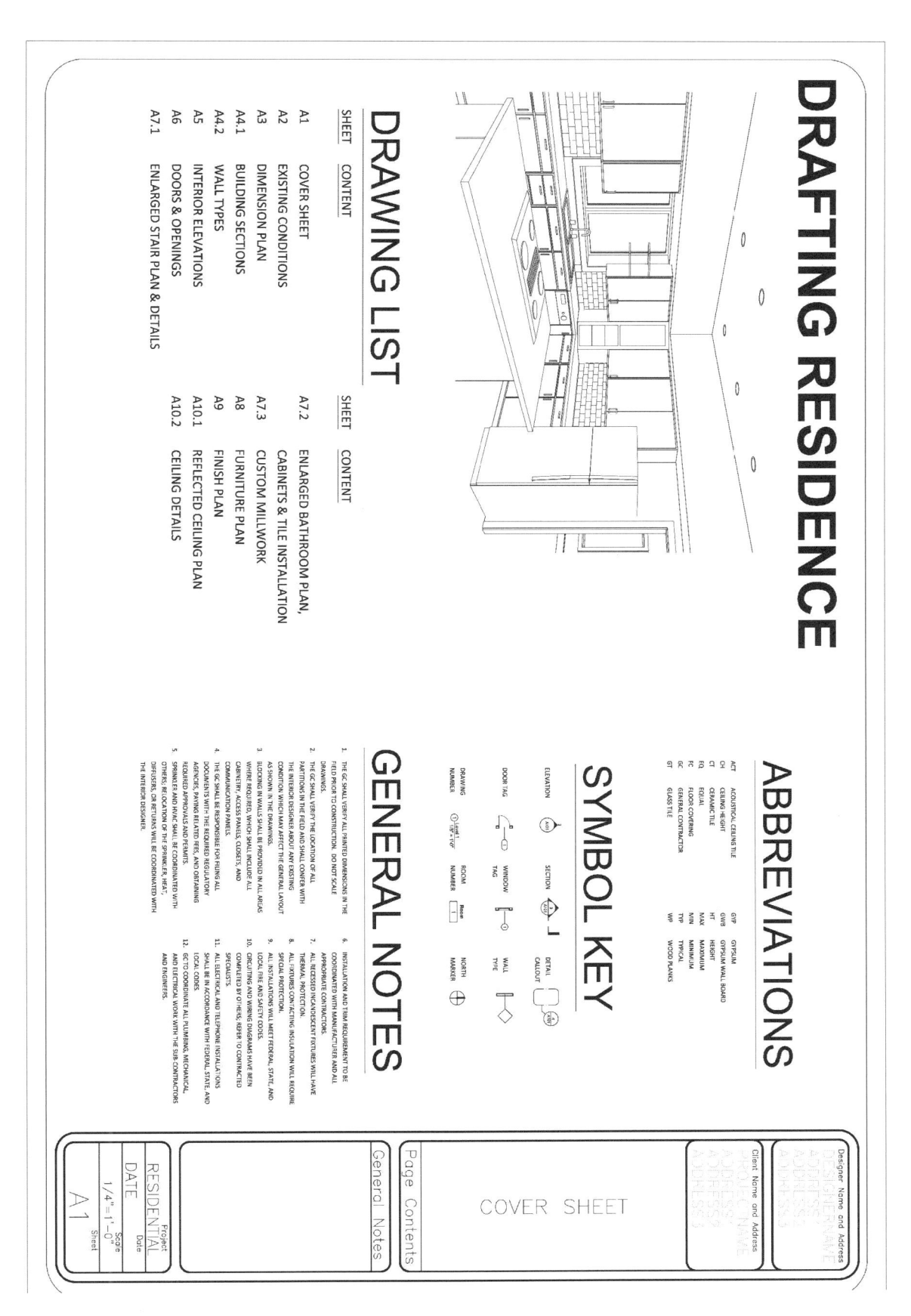

Figure 11.26
Page A1: cover sheet.

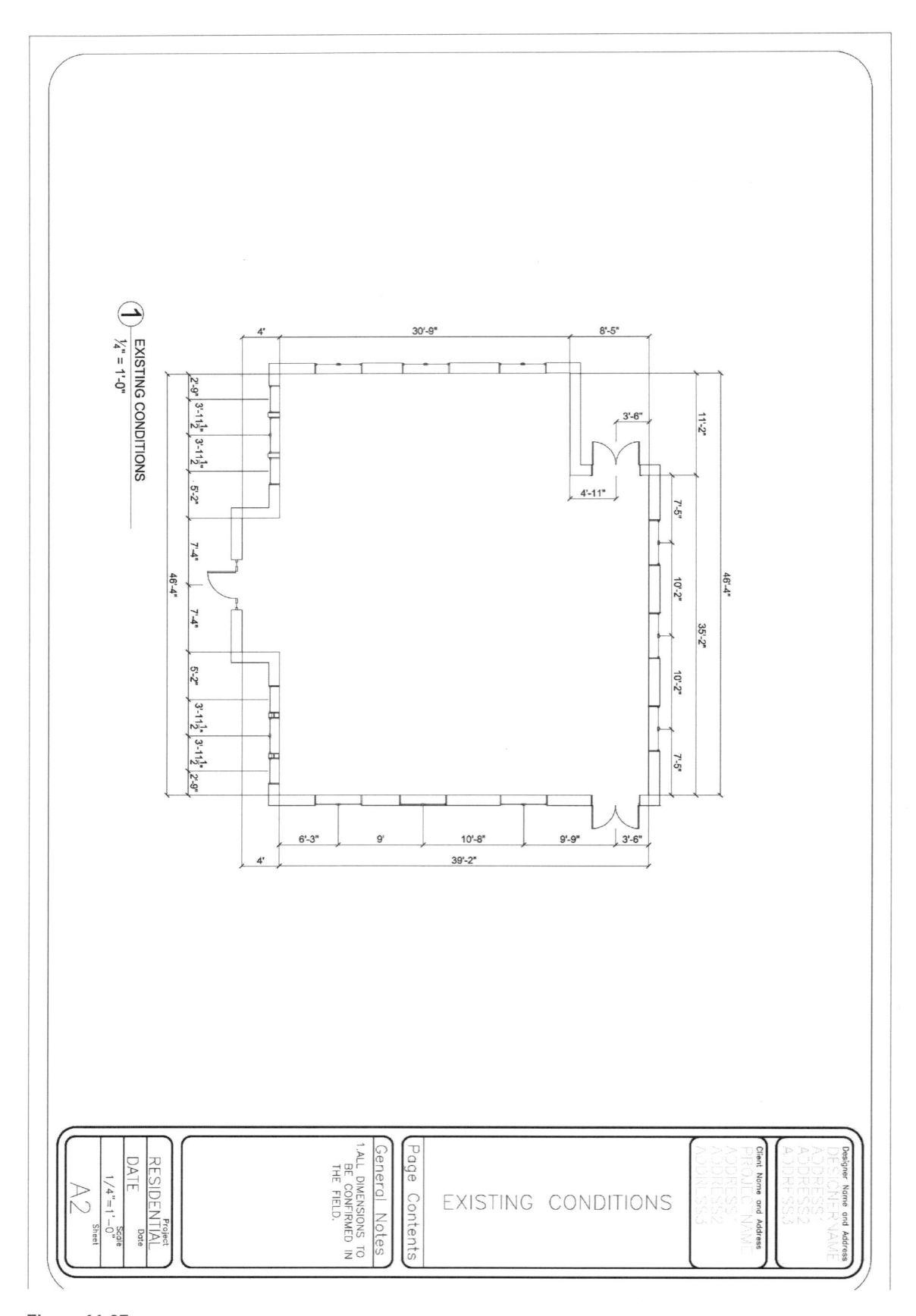

Figure 11.27
Page A2: existing conditions.

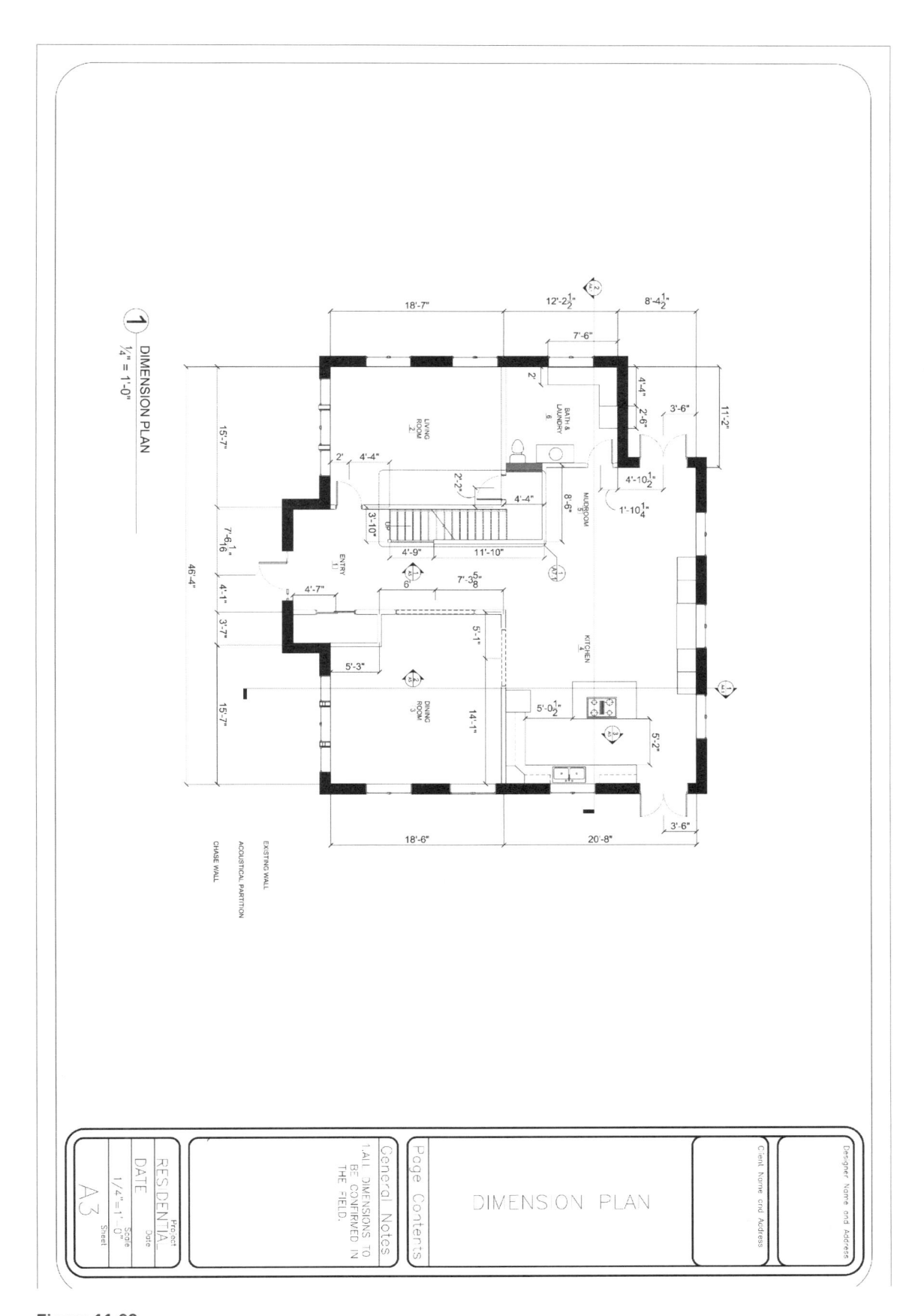

Figure 11.28
Page A3: dimension plan.

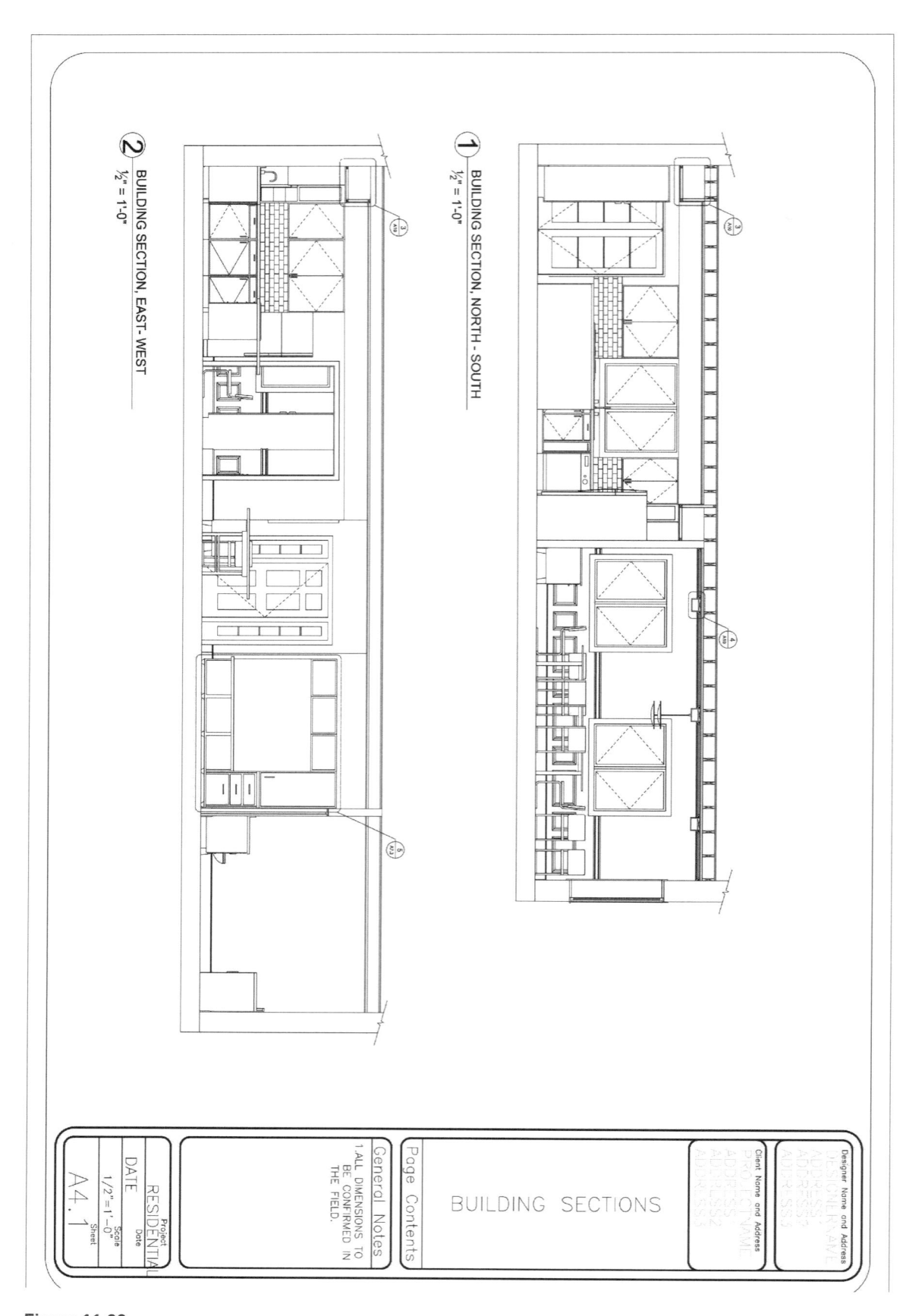

Figure 11.29
Page A4.1: building sections.

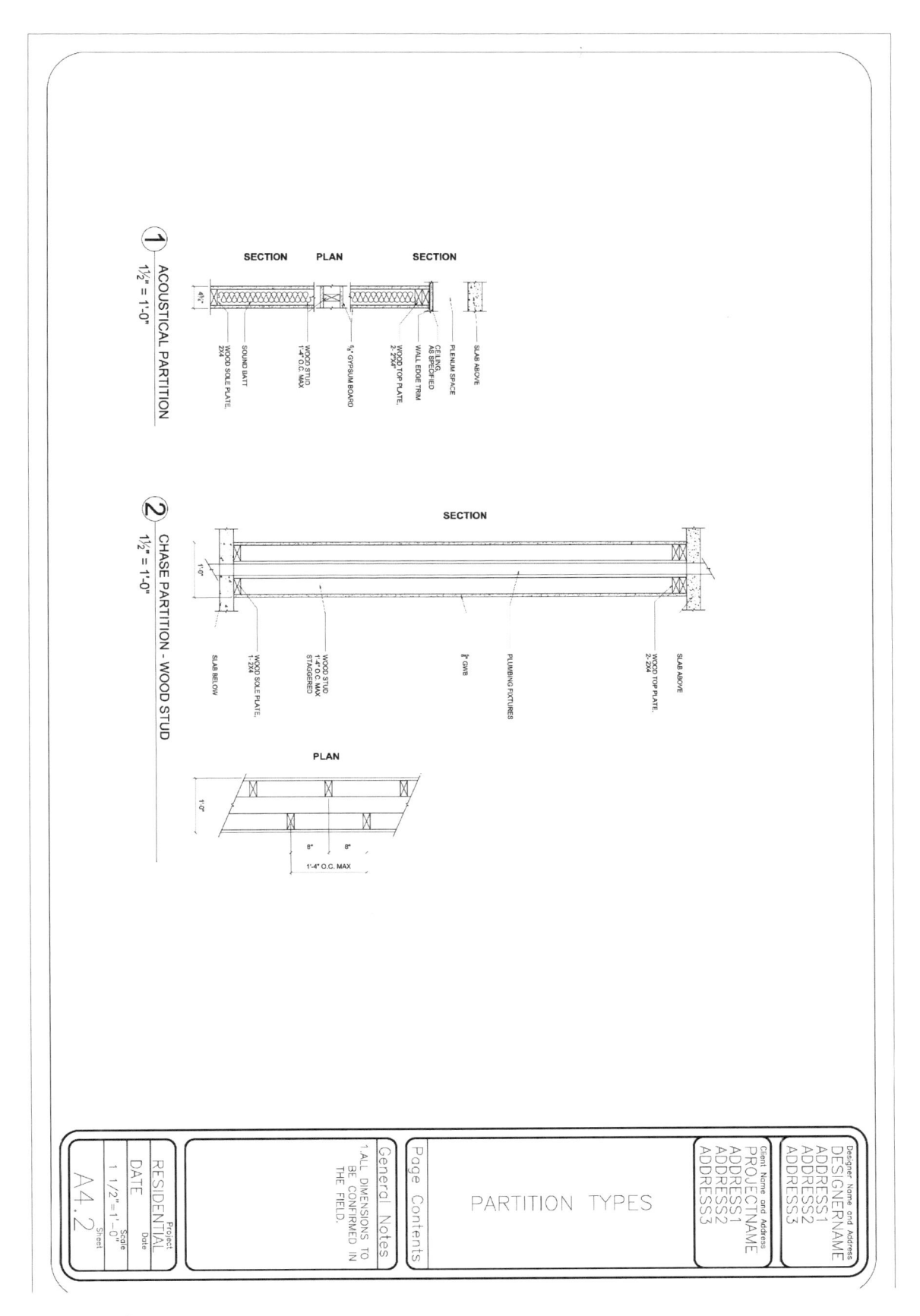

Figure 11.30
Page A4.2: wall types.

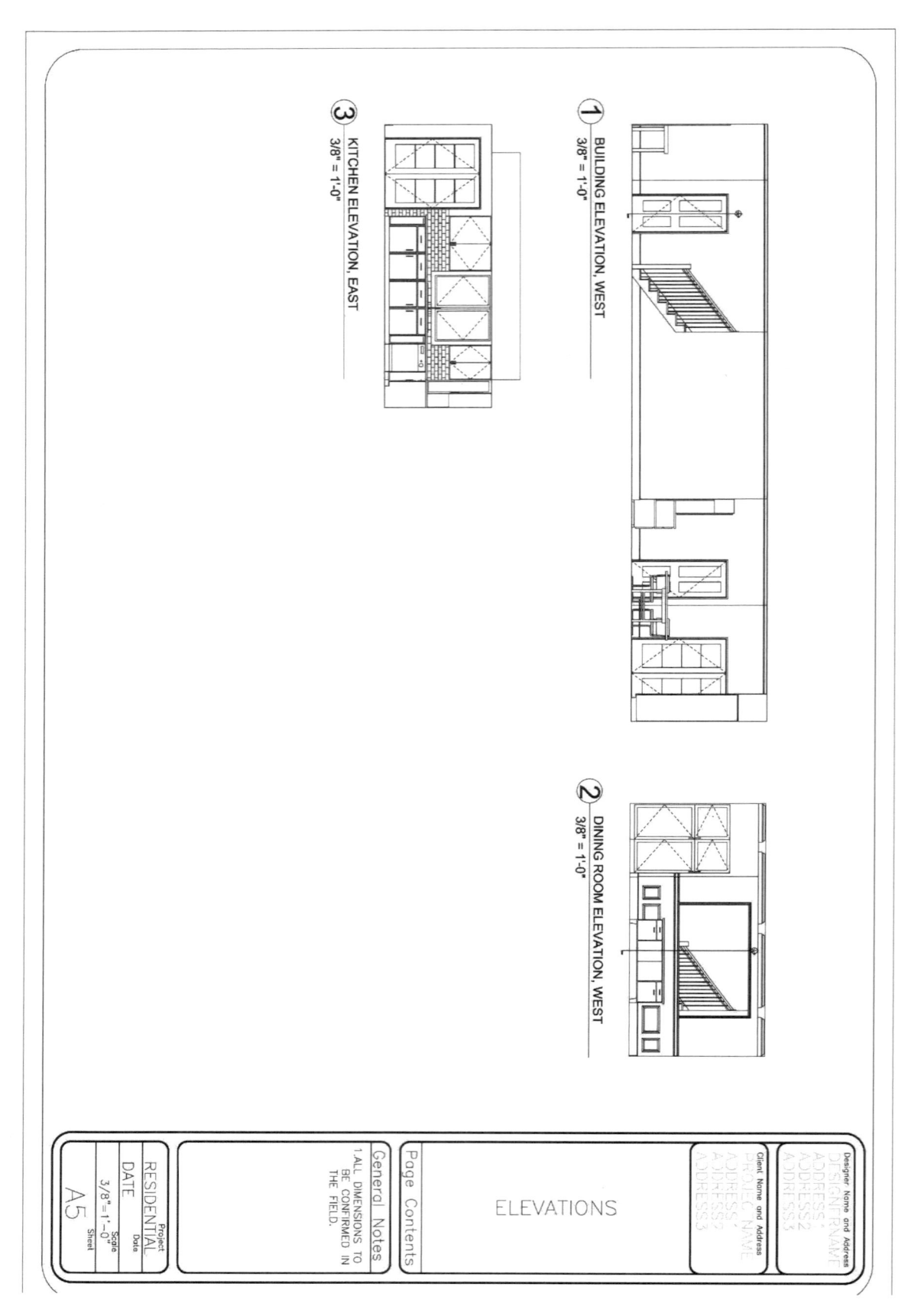

Figure 11.31
Page A5: building elevations.

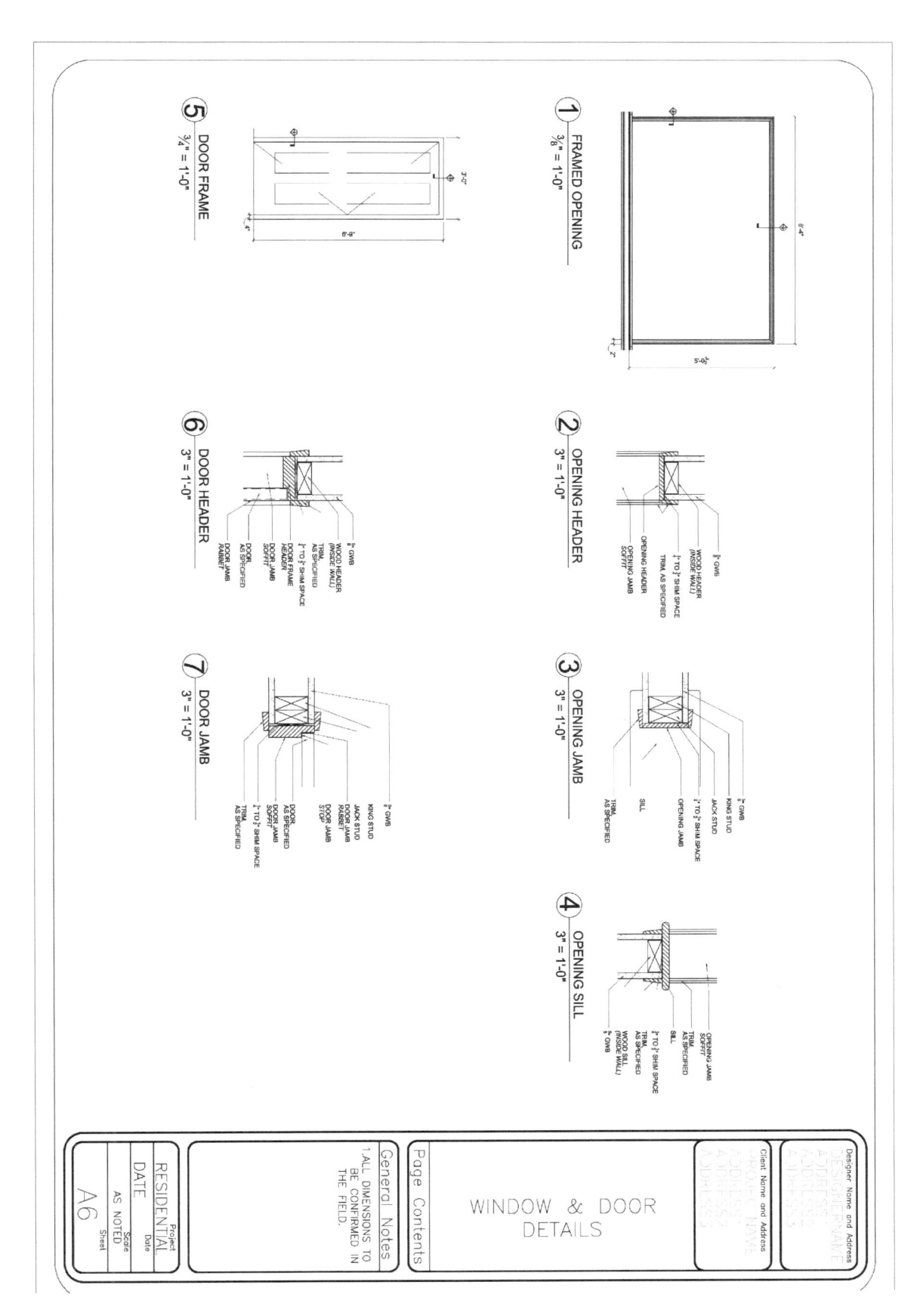

Figure 11.32
Page A6: doors and windows.

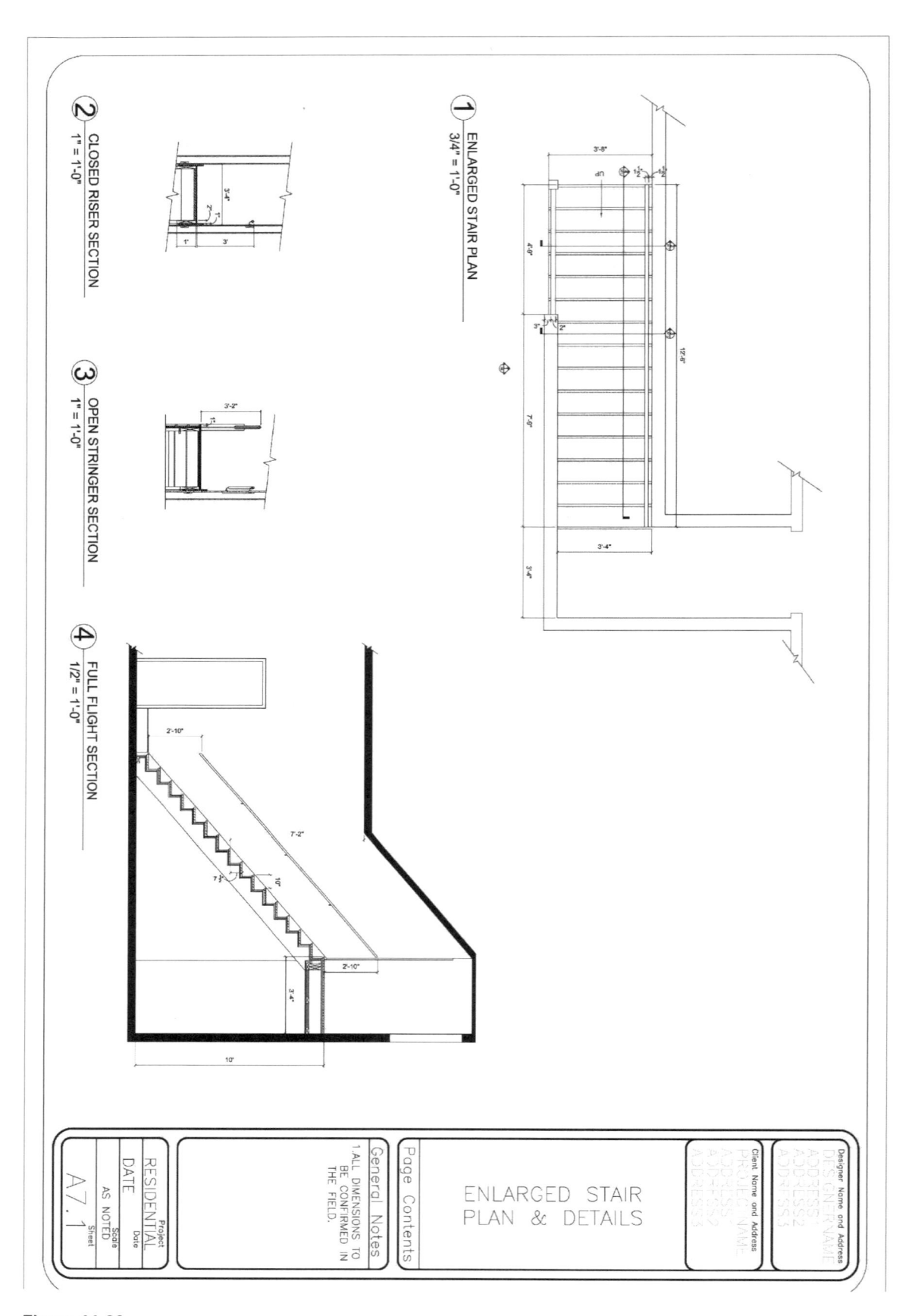

Figure 11.33
Page A7.1: enlarged plans and details.

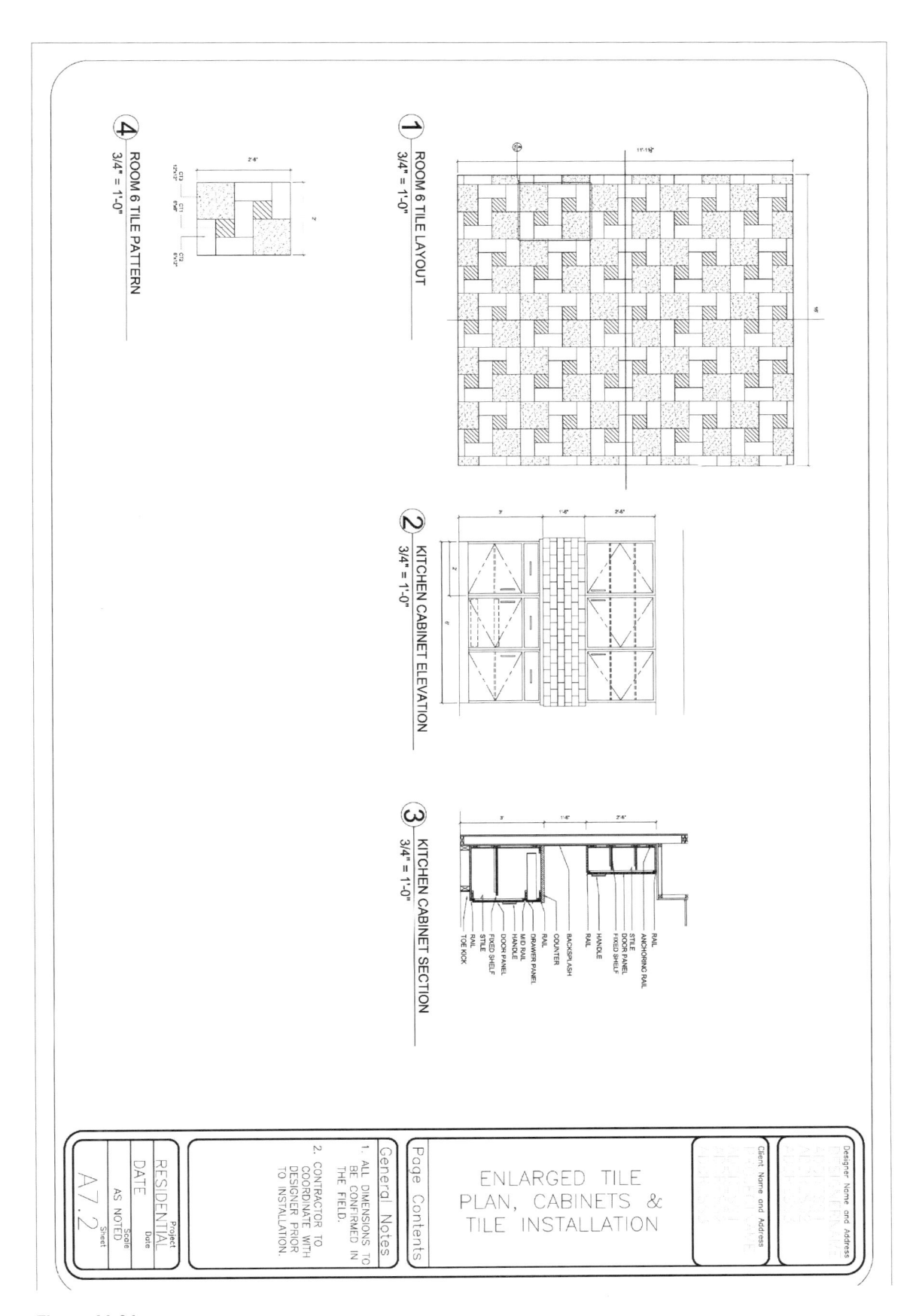

Figure 11.34
Page A7.2: enlarged plans and details.

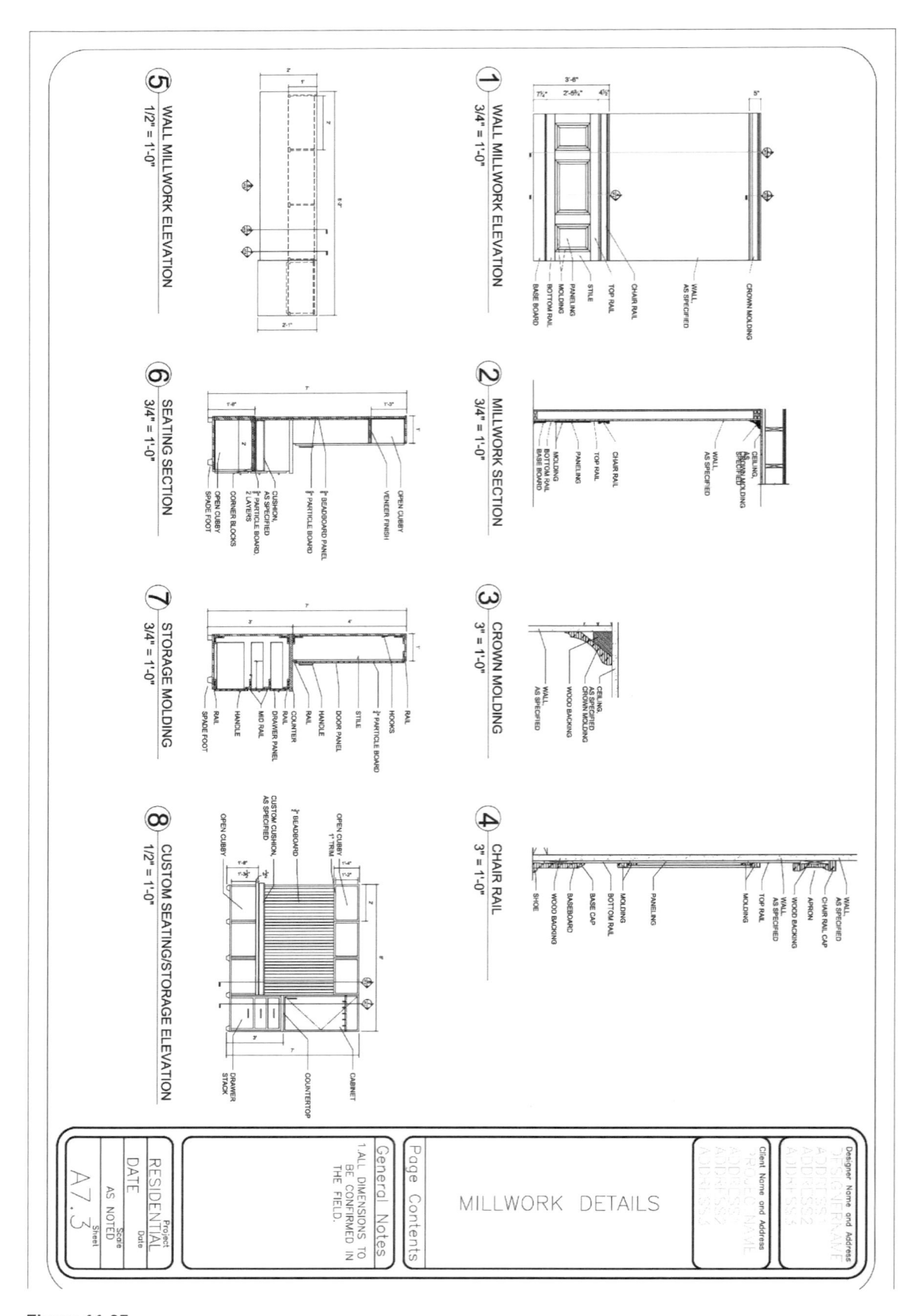

Figure 11.35
Page A7.3: enlarged plans and details.

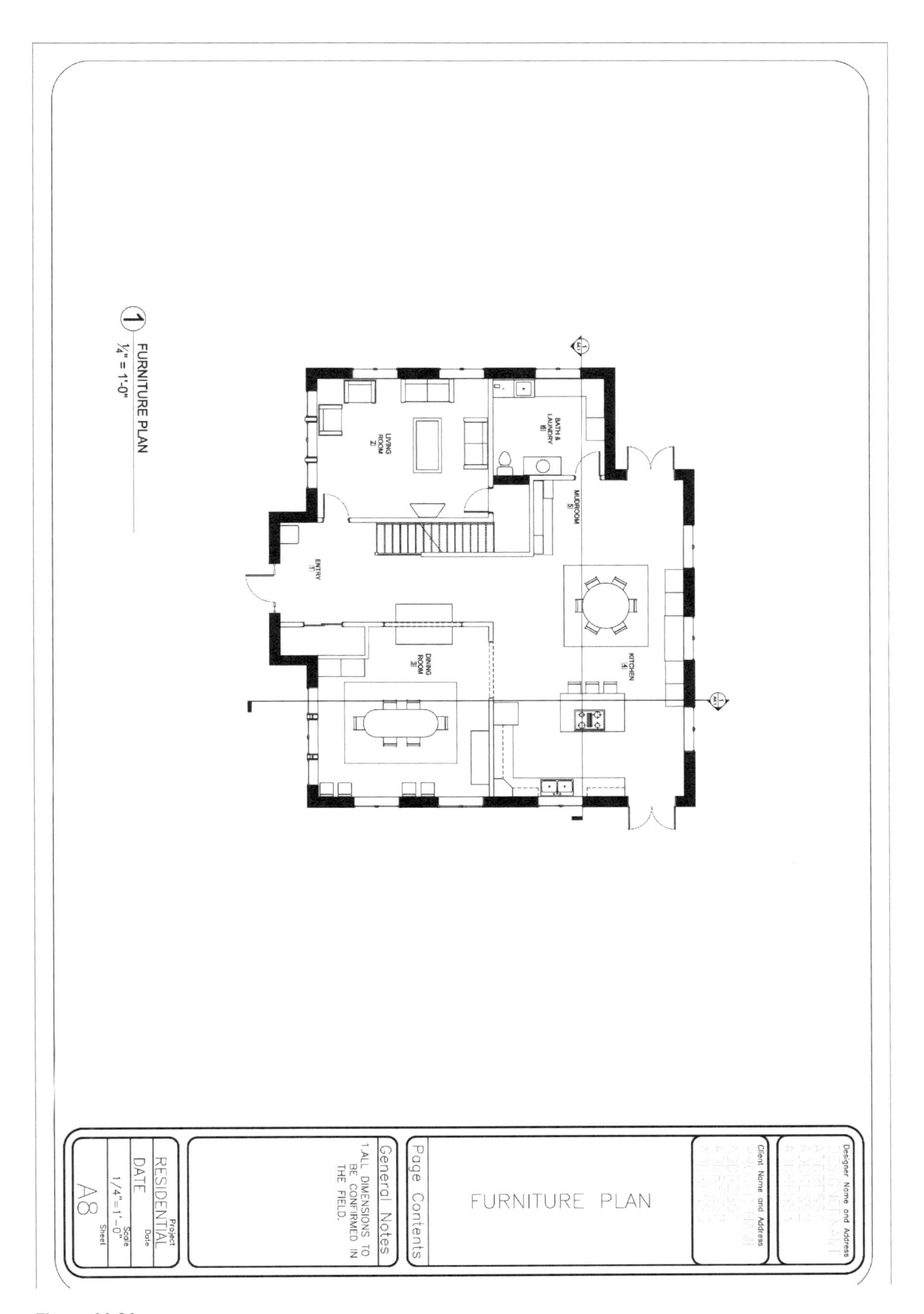

Figure 11.36
Page A8: furniture plan.

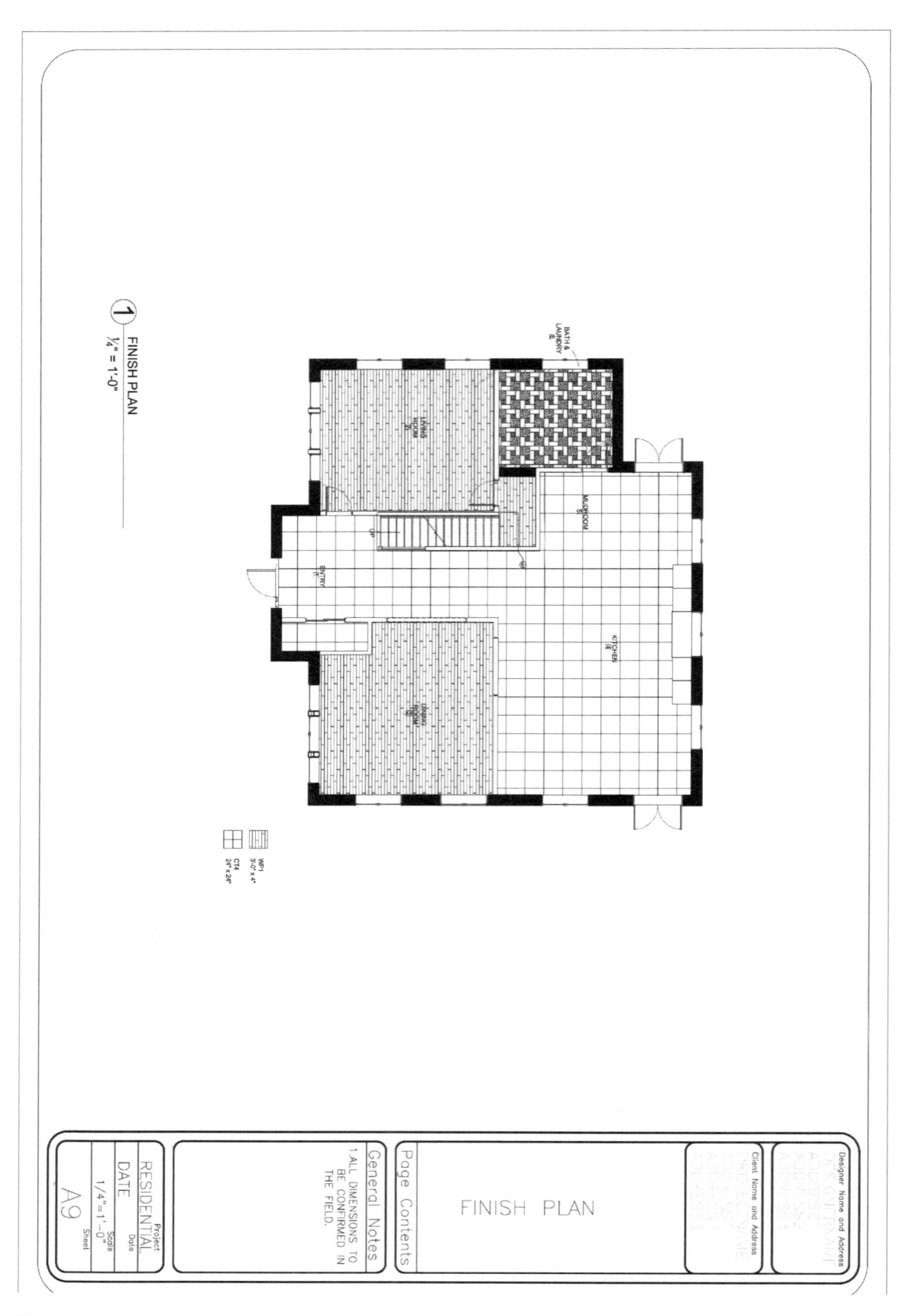

Figure 11.37
Page A9: finish plan.

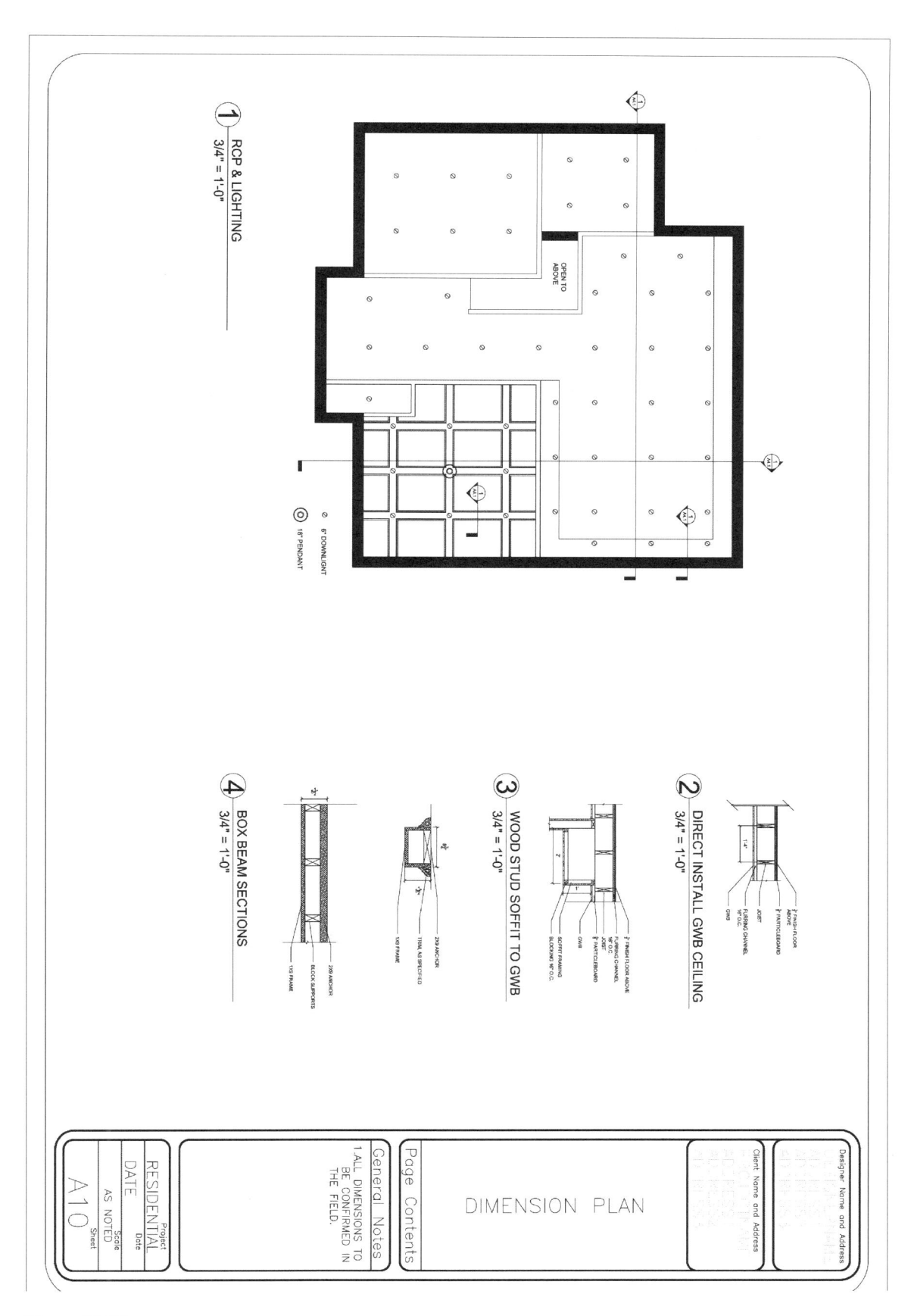

Figure 11.38
Page A10: ceiling plan and details.

CHAPTER REFERENCES

Ballast, David Kent. *Interior Construction & Detailing for Designers and Architects*. Belmont, CA: Professional Publications, Inc., 2013.

Ching, Francis D. *Building Construction Illustrated*. New York: John Wiley & Sons, 2014.

DeChiara, Joseph, Julius Panero, and Martin Zelnik. *Time-Saver Standards for Interior Design and Space Planning*. New York: McGraw-Hill, 2001.

International Code Council. *International Building Code, 2015*. Chicago: International Code Council Publications, 2014.

International Code Council. *International Residential Code, 2015*. Chicago: International Code Council Publications, 2014.

Jefferis, Alan. *Residential Design, Drafting, and Detailing*, 2nd ed. Boston: Cengage Learning, 2013.

Kilmer, W. Otie and Rosemary Kilmer. *Construction Drawings and Details for Interiors*. New York: John Wiley & Sons, 2016.

Kruse, Kelsey and Maryrose McGowan. *Interior Graphic Standards*. New York: John Wiley & Sons, 2003.

United States Department of Justice. *2010 ADA Standards for Accessible Design*. Washington, D.C.: Dept. of Justice, 2010.

Chapter 11: Completing the CD Set
Construction Detailing for Interior Design   11.22

Appendices

APPENDIX A: IBC CODES

APPENDIX B: ADA STANDARDS

APPENDIX C: SYMBOLS, ANNOTATIONS, and MATERIALS

APPENDIX D: CONSTRUCTION MATERIAL GUIDE

APPENDIX E: WALL TYPES

APPENDIX F: DOOR STYLES

APPENDIX G: CEILING STYLES

APPENDIX H: MILLWORK and CABINET STYLES

APPENDIX I: STAIRS, NOSINGS, AND RAILS

APPENDIX J: SAMPLE TILE PATTERNS

APPENDIX K: PROJECT PLAN, SHELL A

APPENDIX L: PROJECT PLAN, SHELL B

Appendix A: IBC Codes

The following table is a compiled list of all the codes utilized in this text. For a complete list of codes, refer to the International Building Codes 2015 or the International Residential Codes 2015 from the International Codes Council.

Table ATA IBC Codes Used in this Text

IBC Code	Topic	Description
803.12	Interior finish stability	Interior finishes, including wall trims, must be fasted to the floor, wall, or ceiling according to manufacturer instructions to ensure that it remains in place during a fire.
		When furring strips are required, the strips may not exceed 1 3/4".
803.13.1	Applying finish materials to rated building elements—Direct attachment	Ceilings that are to be fire-rated must be applied directly to the furring strips above.
803.13.2	Applying finish materials to rated building elements—Suspended ceiling	Suspended ceilings that are to be fire-rated must have a Class A rating.
803.13.4	Material thickness	Materials less than 1/4" can be applied directly to the ceiling without furring strip support, but it cannot be suspended from the ceiling element that supports it.
		Exceptions include noncombustibles or Class A materials.
806.8	Interior floor-wall base	Any floor-wall base that measures less than 6" high must be a Class I or Class II material.
808.1	Suspended acoustical ceilings	Suspended ACT must be used and installed according to manufacturer's directions.
1003.2	Ceiling heights for means of egress	The ceiling in a means of egress must be at least 7'-6" high.
1003.3.1	Ceilings and ceiling mounted objects and headroom	Objects are allowed to extend past the minimum ceiling height if the ceiling over any type of passageway is at least 6'-8".
1003.3.4	Trim projections and accessibility	Any trim that extends into an accessible route cannot reduce the minimum clear width requirements.
1005.3.1	Capacity based on occupant load—Stairs	Calculate the stair capacity by multiplying the occupant load by 0.3" per person, using the occupant load for each floor that would be serviced.
1009.3	Accessible means of egress—Stairs	A flight must have a minimum clear width of 48" between handrails and an area of refuge in order to be considered an accessible means of egress.
1010.1.1	Door size	Doors that are a part of the egress must be a minimum of 32" wide, but may be required to be wider depending on the occupant load of the building.
1010.1.1.1	Projections into clear width	When looking at an 80" door, nothing can project into clear width below 34". Between the measurements of 34"–80", only door closers and stops 4" wide or less may project into the clear width.

Table ATA IBC Codes Used in this Text

IBC Code	Topic	Description
1011.2	Stairway width and capacity	Stairways must be at least 44" wide, unless fewer than 50 people will use the stairs as an accessible means of egress, in which case the minimum width becomes 36".
1011.3	Stairway headroom	A minimum headroom clearance of 80 inches is needed. This must be measured from the edge of the nosing vertically to the ceiling or landing above and must be maintained for the whole width of the flight.
1011.5.2	Riser height and tread depth	Commercial riser heights must be between 4"–7" and the minimum depth a tread can be is 11".
1011.5.5	Nosing and riser profile	Nosings must curve or bevel between 1/16"–9/16" and connect to a solid riser with an angle of 30 degrees or less.
1011.5.5.1	Nosing projection	Nosings can project up to 1 1/4" past the riser below.
1011.5.5.3	Solid risers	Commercial risers must be solid. Stairways that are not a means of egress may have openings between treads, but they must be small enough that a 4" sphere cannot pass through.
1011.6	Landings	Landings must be as deep as the stairway is wide. Commercial straight run stairs may have landings up to 48". Doors that open into landings can project up to 7" into that landing.
1011.7	Stairway construction	Stairs must be built with the same materials permitted for the shell construction of the building. Wood handrails are permitted in all project types.
1011.8	Vertical rise	The vertical rise of a run of stairs cannot exceed 12'-0" without a landing being used.
1011.11	Handrails	Commercial projects require handrails on both sides of a staircase.
1014.2	Handrail height	Handrails must be between 34"–38" above the nosing of each tread.
1014.3.1	Handrail graspability—Type I	Circular cross section handrails must have a diameter between 1 1/4"–2" Non-circular rails must have a perimeter between 4"–6 1/4" and a cross-section between 1"–2 1/4".
1014.3.2	Handrail graspability—Type II	Non-circular rails with a perimeter greater than 6 1/4" must have finger recesses on both sides of the rail. The recess must measure 3/4" from the tallest portion of the rail's profile. This rail must measure between 1 1/4"–2 3/4" wide.
1014.4	Handrail continuity	Commercial handrails must provide continuous support from the bottom to the top of the run without being interrupted by newel posts. Residential handrails may be interrupted by a newel post at a landing.
1014.6	Handrail extensions	Commercial handrails must extend at least 12" past the top riser and 12" plus the depth of one tread past the bottom riser. These rails must then connect to the wall, guard, or newel post. Residential handrails may run from the top riser to the bottom riser with no needed extension.
1014.7	Handrail clearance	A clear space of at least 1 1/2" must be present between the rail and the wall.
1014.8	Handrail projections	Accessible routes require a clear width between handrails of at least 36". Rails may project up to 4 1/2" on each side of the stair.
1015.2	Guardrail placement	Guardrails are required along mezzanines, stairs, ramps and landings that are more than 30" above the floor below.

Table ATA IBC Codes Used in this Text

IBC Code	Topic	Description
1015.3	Guardrail height	Guardrails must be at least 42" high when measured from the floor of a landing or a nosing of a tread.
		Single residential units require guards of at least 34". If the guardrail also acts a handrail, the height must be between 34"–38".
1015.4	Guardrail openings	Commercial guards must be designed so that a 4" sphere cannot pass through any openings.
		Residential guards cannot allow a 4 3/8" sphere to pass through.
1020.1	Corridor construction	Commercial corridors must feature fire-resistance rated materials and must comply with Section 708.
1107.3	Accessible spaces	Spaces that are open to the public or units for people with mobility impairments must have kitchens and bathrooms that are for accessible use.
1107.7.2	Multistory units	Residential units that are constructed to be accessible must have a kitchen and bathroom on the same level as the entrance.
1109.4	Kitchens	Buildings that are accessible must have accessible kitchens.
1109.9	Storage	At least 5% of fixed storage (stationary cabinets and drawers) in accessible buildings must be accessible.
1109.11	Seating at counters	At least 5% of fixed counters in public spaces must be accessible.
2308.5.3.1	Sole plates	Sole plates must be at least as wide as the stud and must be at least 2" thick.
2308.5.3.2	Top plates	Sole plates must be at least as wide as the stud and must be at least 2" thick.
2308.5.3.4	Non-bearing partitions	In partitions that carry no weight, studs must be spaced 24" OC or less.
2308.5.5.3	Nonbearing wood header	Nonbearing interior partitions can be framed with a single header, which must be at least 1 1/2" wide.
R311.7.1	Residential stairway width	Stairs must have at least 36" of clear width. Rails may project up to 4 1/2" into the clear width.
		When handrails are installed on both sides, the clear width can measure at least 31 1/2".
		When a handrail is installed on one side, the clear width can measure 27".
R311.7.3	Residential vertical rise	The vertical rise of a run of stairs cannot exceed 12'-3" without a landing being used.
R311.7.5	Residential treads and risers	For residential projects, the maximum riser height can measure 7 3/4", the minimum tread depth can be 10", and a nosing must be between 3/4" and 1 1/4".
R311.7.5.3	Residential nosings	Nosings may curve up to 9/16" and may project between 3/4"–1 1/4" past the riser.
		Residential treads that are deeper than 11" do not require a nosing projection.
R311.7.6	Residential stair landings	Residential straight run stairs must have landings of at least 36".
R311.7.8	Residential handrails	Residential projects require a handrail on only one side of a staircase, but handrails are permitted to be on both sides.

Appendix B: ADA Standards

The following table is a compiled list of all the standards utilized in this text. For a complete list of codes, refer to the AADAG from the United States Department of Justice.

Table ATB ADA Standards Used in this Text

ADA Code	Topic	Description
201.1	Scope	All new construction projects and existing projects undergoing alteration must comply with ADA code.
		Exceptions may apply based on the scope of the project and the project type.
306.2	Toe clearance	A space measuring at least 9" deep and 30" wide must remain clear between the floor and a constructed element above.
307.2	Protrusion limits	Objects mounted 27"–80" AFF can protrude no more than 4" from the wall surface.
		Handrails may protrude up to 4 1/2".
307.4	Vertical clearance	Vertical clearance must be at least 80" high. Any spaces that are less than 80" must have a guardrail that is at least 27" AFF.
		Exception made for door frames, which can lower the vertical clearance to 78" AFF.
307.5	Required clear width	Any protruding objects cannot reduce the required clear space.
403.5.1	Clear width—walking surface	Accessible routes must be at least 36" wide. Corridors should be a minimum of 60" wide.
404.2.3	Clear width—doors	Door openings must be at least 32". When looking at an 80" door, nothing can project into clear width below 34". Between the measurements of 34"–80", only door closers and stops 4" wide or less may project into the clear width.
504.2	Treads and risers	Treads must be at least 11" deep. Risers must measure between 4"–7" high. Both treads and risers must be uniform in their chosen measurement for the length of the stair run.
504.3	Open risers	Open risers are not allowed in commercial spaces.
504.4	Tread surface	It is recommended that a visual or textural contrast is provided along the nosing of the stair to aid individuals with visual disabilities.
504.5	Nosings	Nosings may project up to 1 1/2" over the tread below.
		Nosing curvature may have a maximum 1/2" radius. Projecting nosings must be curved or beveled.
		Risers may slope up to 30 degrees from vertical.
505.4	Handrail height	Rails must measure between 34"–38" above the nosings of each stair.
505.5	Handrail clearance	A clear space of at least 1 1/2" must be present between the rail and the wall.

Table ATB	ADA Standards Used in this Text	
ADA Code	**Topic**	**Description**
505.7.1	Handrail cross section—Type I	Circular cross section handrails must have a diameter between 1 1/4"–2"
505.7.2	Handrail cross section—Type II	Non-circular rails must have a perimeter between 4"–6 1/4" and a cross-section up to 2 1/4".
505.10.2	Handrail extension—top of stairs	Handrails must extend at least 12" past the top riser and return to the wall, guard, or a newel post.
505.10.3	Handrail extension—bottom of stairs	Handrails must extend at least 12" plus the depth of one tread past the bottom riser and must connect to the wall, guard, or newel post.
804.2.1	Pass through kitchen	Kitchens must have at least 3'-4" of open space between counter fronts and appliances on opposite sides, and feature two entrances.
804.2.2	U-shaped kitchen	When kitchens are enclosed on three sides by walls, cabinets, counters, or appliances, the entrance must be at least 5'-0" of clear space.
804.4.3	Residential kitchen counters	If a residential unit is accessible, there must be clear space for a forward approach to at least 2'-6" of counter that is 34" AFF with knee clearance.
902.3	Work surface height	The top of a work surface must be between 28"–34" AFF.
903.3	Bench size	Benches in public facilities must be at least 42" long and between 20"–24" deep.
903.5	Bench height	Benches in public facilities must have a seating surface between 17"–19" AFF.
904.4	Service counter depth	Accessible service counters must measure the same depth as non-accessible service counters.
904.4.1	Service counter, parallel approach	Accessible service counters are required to be at least 36" long and measure 36" AFF MAX with clear ground space for a side approach to the work surface.
904.4.2	Service counter, forward approach	Accessible service counters are required to be at least 30" long and measure 36" AFF MAX with under counter space meeting code 305 and clear ground space for a forward approach to the work surface.

Appendix C: Symbols, Annotations & Materials

The following diagram is a compilation of just a few drawing symbols that are common in the industry.

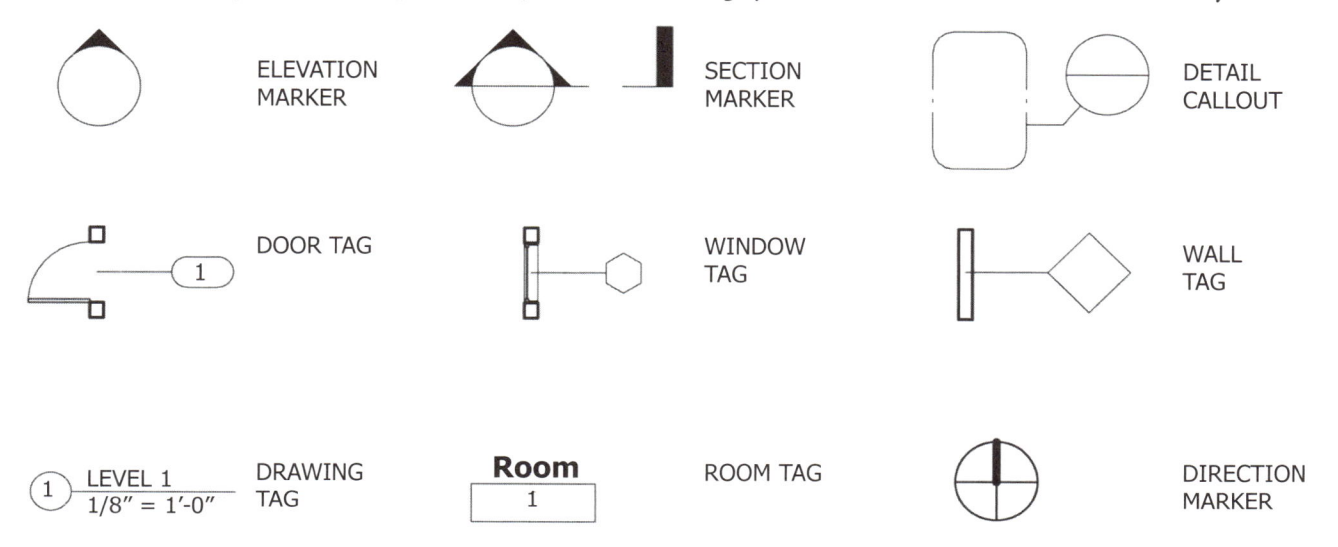

ELEVATION MARKER   SECTION MARKER   DETAIL CALLOUT

DOOR TAG   WINDOW TAG   WALL TAG

LEVEL 1 1/8" = 1'-0" DRAWING TAG   Room 1 ROOM TAG   DIRECTION MARKER

Figure AppC1
Sample of typical drawing symbols.

The following table is a compiled list of just a few of the abbreviations that are common in the industry.

Table ATC Common Abbreviations					
A					
Above Finished Floor	AFF	Acoustical Tile	ACT	Attachment	ATCH
Above Raised Floor	ARF	Adjacent	ADJ	Average	AVG
Above Suspended Ceiling	ASC	Approved	APPD		
Acoustical	ACOUS	Asymmetrical	ASTM		
B					
Back to Back	B/B	Bedroom	BDRM	Blocking	BLKG
Balcony	BALC	Below	BLW	Both faces	BF
Base line	BL	Below Ceiling	BLW CLG		
Baseboard	BB	Below finish floor	BLW FF		
Basement	BSMT	Between	BETW		
C					
Cabinet	CAB	Center to Center	C TO C	Common	COM
Casework	CSWK	Ceramic Tile	CT	Concrete	CONC
Casing	CSG	Change order	CO	Concrete Masonry unit	CMU
Ceiling	CLG	Circle	CIR	Conference	CONF
Ceiling Height	CLG HT	Clear room	CLRM	Coordinate	COORD
Center line	CL	Column	COL		
D					
Detail	DET	Diameter	DIAM	Down	DN
Diagonal	DIAG	Dimension	DIM	Drawing	DWG
E					
Electrical	ELEC	Equal	EQ	Existing	EXST
Elevator	ELEV	Equally spaced	EQL SP		
Entrance	ENTR	Equipment	EQUIP		

(*continued*)

Table ATC Common Abbreviations

F
Face of finish	FOF	Floor finish	FL FIN	From floor below	FFB
Face of studs	FOS	Flooring	FLG	Front	FRT
Face to face	F/F	Fluorescent	FLUOR	Furniture	FURN
Fiberglass	FBG	From floor above	FFA	Furring	FURR

G
General Contractor	GC	Grab bar	GB	Guardrail	GDR
Glass	GL	Grade	GR	Gypsum	GYP
Glass block	GLB	Grout	GT	Gypsum wallboard	GWB

H
Handrail	HNDRL	Height	GT	Hollow metal frame	HMF
Hardware	HDW	Hollow metal door	HMD	Horizontal	HORIZ

I & K
Inside face	IF	Insulation	INSUL	Knockout	KO

L
Linear foot	LF	Load bearing	LDBRG	Lumber	LBR

M
Manufacturing	MFG	Material	MATL	Metal	MET
Masonry	MAS	Maximum	MAX	Mezzanine	MEZZ
Master bedroom	MBR	Mechanical	MECH	Mounted	MTD

N
National Electric Code	NEC	Nominal	NOM	Not to scale	NTS
National Fire Protection Association	NFPA	North	N	Number	NO
Near face	NF	Not applicable	NA		
Near side	NS	Not in contract	NIC		

O
Office	OFF	Opening	OPNG	Overhead	OVHD
On center	OC	Out to tout	O/O		

P
Paint	PNT	Partition	PTN	Perpendicular	PERP
Parallel	PAR	Perimeter	PERIM	Plumbing	PLMB
Particleboard	PBD	Permanent	PERM	Plywood	PLY

R
Recessed	REC	Required	REQD	Riser	R
Rectangular	RECT	Resilient	RESIL	Room	RM
Register	REG	Return	RET	Rough opening	RO
Removable	REM	Right Hand	RH		

S
Schedule	SCHED	Specification	SPEC	Steel	STL
Single	SGL	Square	SQ	Surface	SURF
Sliding door	SLD	Square foot	SQFT	Suspended ceiling	SUSP CLG
Sound transmission class	STC	Square yard	SQ YD	Symmetrical	SYMM
South	S	Stainless steel	SST		

T
Telephone	TEL	Thickness	THK	Top of slab	TSL
Tempered glass	TMPD GL	To floor above	TFA	Tread	T
Temporary	TEMP	To floor below	TFB	Typical	TYP
Terrazzo	TER	Tolerance	TOL		

U
Underwriters Laboratories, Inc.	UL	Unfinished	UNFIN	Unless otherwise noted	UON

V
Veneer	VNR	Vertical	VERT		

W
Wainscot	WSCT	Water resistant	WR	With	W/
Wall to wall	W/W	Waterproof	WP	Without	W/O
Water closet	WC	Width	WD	Wood	WD

The following diagram is a compilation of typical material symbols utilized in the industry; however, it is not necessary for you to utilize these patterns to represent the materials as listed below. You may customize patterns or assign a pattern to a specific material at will, but when using a material pattern in a detail set, annotate the material in the drawings and wherever necessary for clarity.

SECTION VIEW

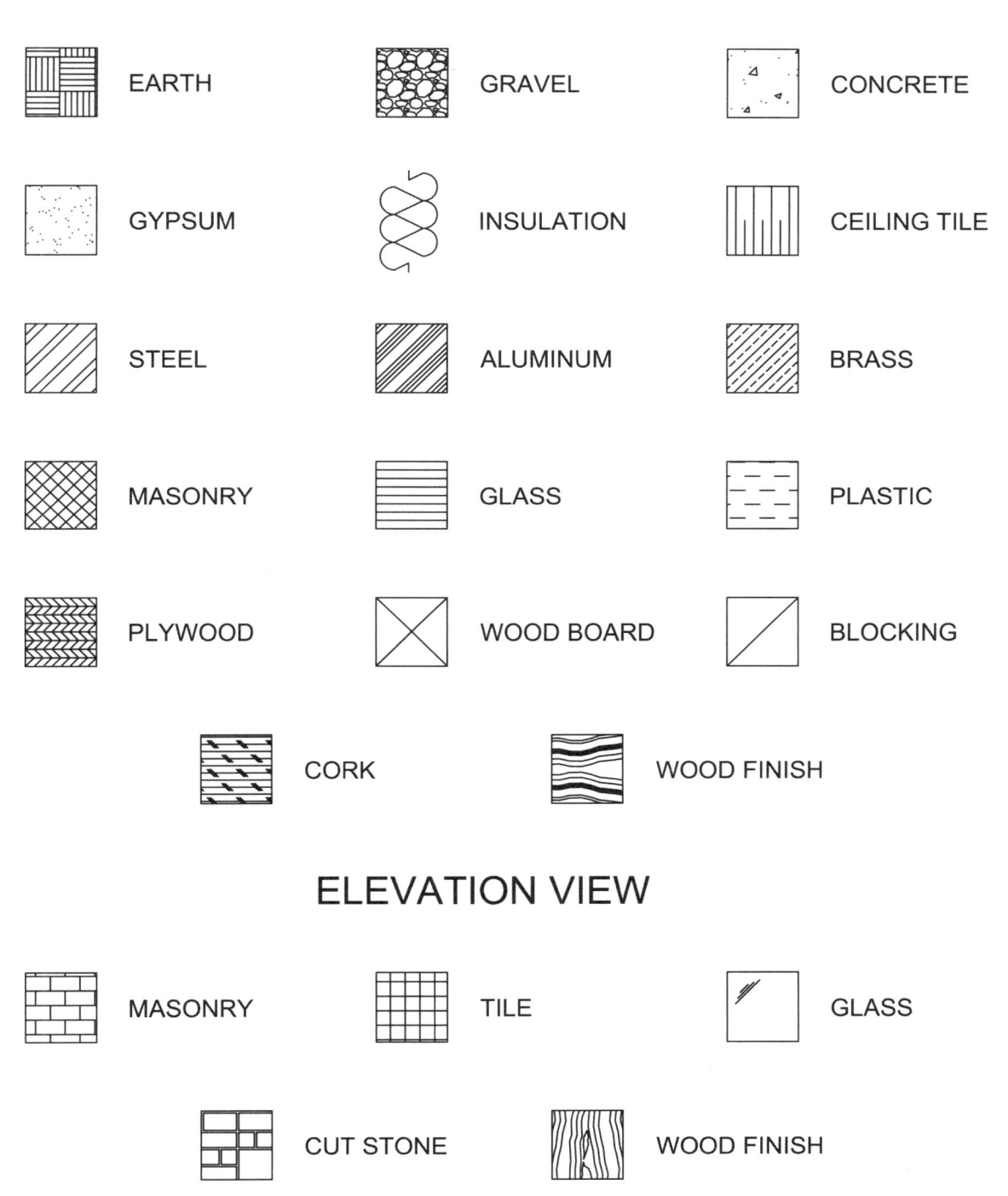

EARTH	GRAVEL	CONCRETE
GYPSUM	INSULATION	CEILING TILE
STEEL	ALUMINUM	BRASS
MASONRY	GLASS	PLASTIC
PLYWOOD	WOOD BOARD	BLOCKING
	CORK	WOOD FINISH

ELEVATION VIEW

MASONRY	TILE	GLASS
	CUT STONE	WOOD FINISH

Figure AppC2
Sample of typical material patterns.

APPENDIX C: SYMBOLS, ANNOTATIONS & MATERIALS | 303

Appendix D: Construction Material Guide

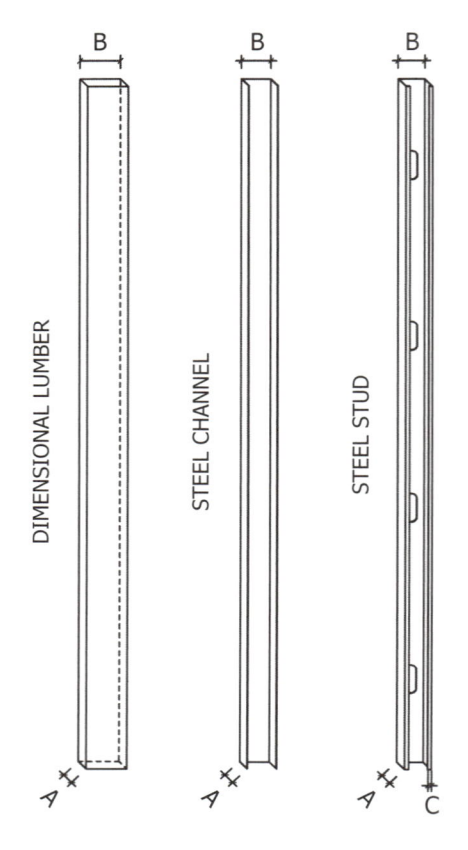

Figure AppD1
Dimensional lumber, steel channel, and steel stud sizes.

Table ATD.1 Sizes of Common Construction Materials

Wood

Dimensional lumber

Nominal	A	B	Nominal	A	B
1 × 2	3/4"	1 1/2"	2 × 2	1 1/2"	1 1/2"
1 × 3	3/4"	2 1/2"	2 × 3	1 1/2"	2 1/2"
1 × 4	3/4"	3 1/2"	2 × 4	1 1/2"	3 1/2"
1 × 6	3/4"	5 1/2"	2 × 6	1 1/2"	5 1/2"
1 × 8	3/4"	7 1/4"	2 × 8	1 1/2"	7 1/4"
1 × 10	3/4"	9 1/4"	2 × 10	1 1/2"	9 1/4"
1 × 12	3/4"	11 1/4"	2 × 12	1 1/2"	11 1/4"

Steel

Steel channel sizes

A	B
1", 1 1/4"	1 5/8"
1", 1 1/4"	2 1/2"
1", 1 1 1/4"	3 5/8"
1", 1 1/4"	4"
1", 1 1/4"	6"

Steel stud width

Letter	Sizes
A	1 3/8", 1 5/8", 2", 2 1/2", 3"
B	2 1/2", 3 1/2", 3 5/8", 4", 5 1/2", 6", 8", 10", 12", 14"
C	3/8", 1/2", 5/8"

Suspension system tiles		Gypsum wallboard sizes			Board sizes		
Style	**Dimensions**	**Style**	**Thickness**	**Sheet size**	**Style**	**Thickness**	**Sheet size**
Panel	12" × 12"	Standard	3/8"	4' × 8'	Plywood	1/4"	4' × 8', 12'
	24" × 24"		1/2"	4' × 8'		1/2"	4' × 8', 12'
	24" × 48"		5/8"	4' × 8', 9', 10', 12', 14'		3/4"	4' × 8', 12'
Plank	5" × 84"	Greenboard	1/2"	4' × 8'	Particleboard	3/8"	4' × 8'
	4" × 48"		5/8"	4' × 8', 9', 10', 12', 14'		1/2"	4' × 8'
		Type X	1/2"	4' × 8'		5/8"	4' × 8'
			5/8"	4' × 8', 9', 10', 12', 14'		3/4"	4' × 8'
						1"	4' × 8'
					Medium Density Fiberboard (MDF)	1/2"	4' × 8'
						3/4"	4' × 8'

Appendix E: Wall Types

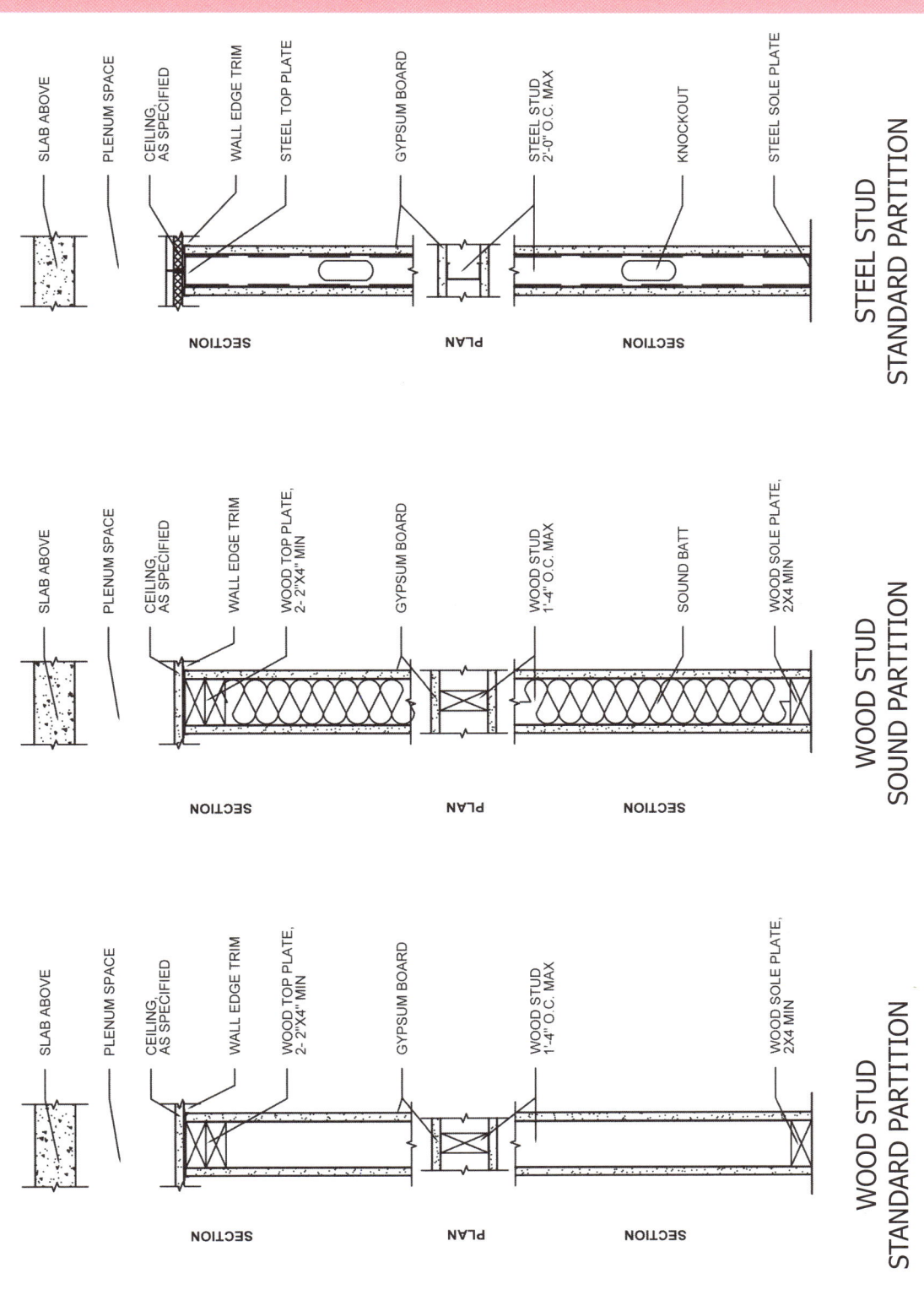

Figure AppE1
Wall types.

APPENDIX E: WALL TYPES | 305

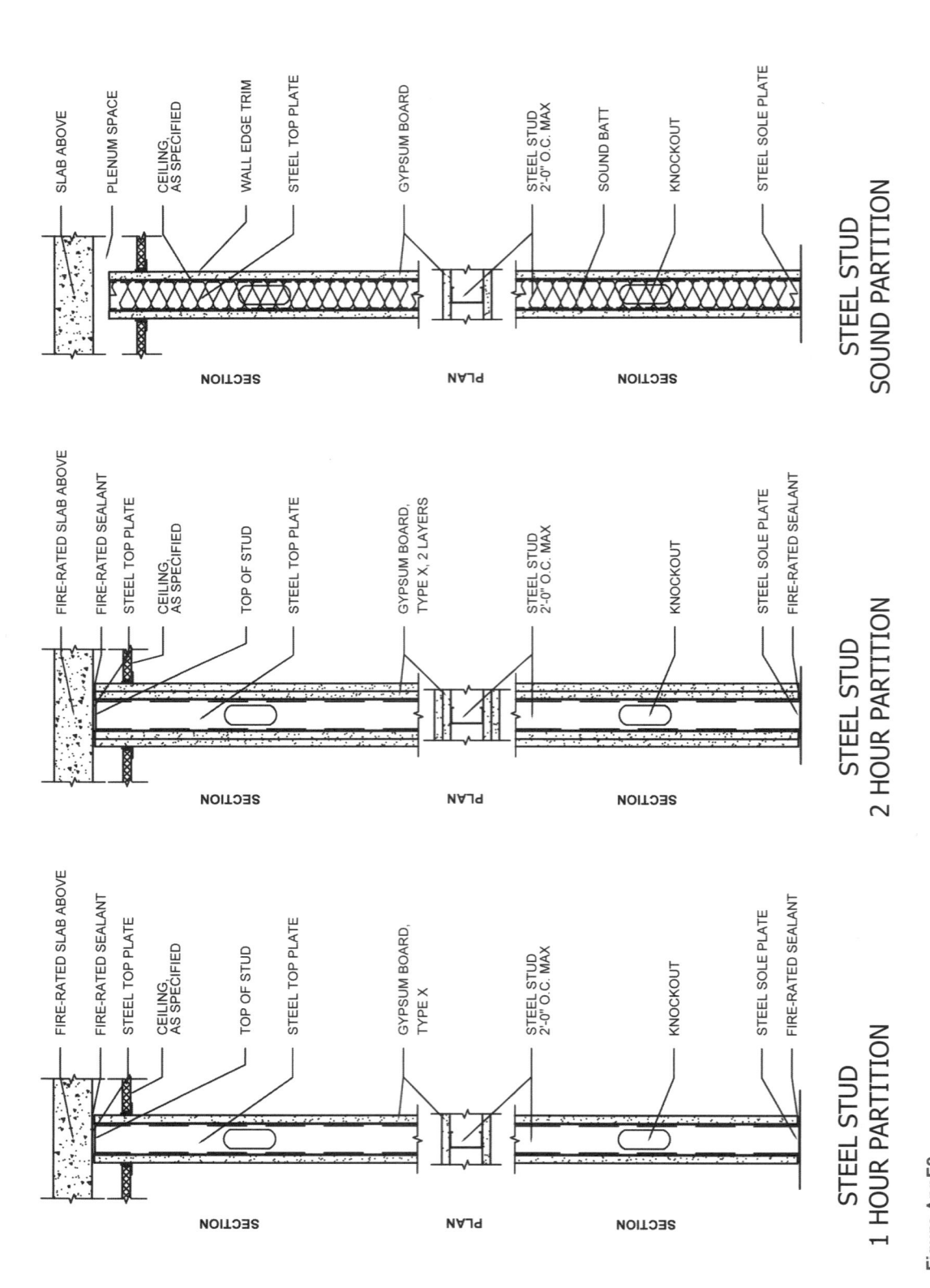

Figure AppE2
Wall types.

306 | APPENDIX E: WALL TYPES

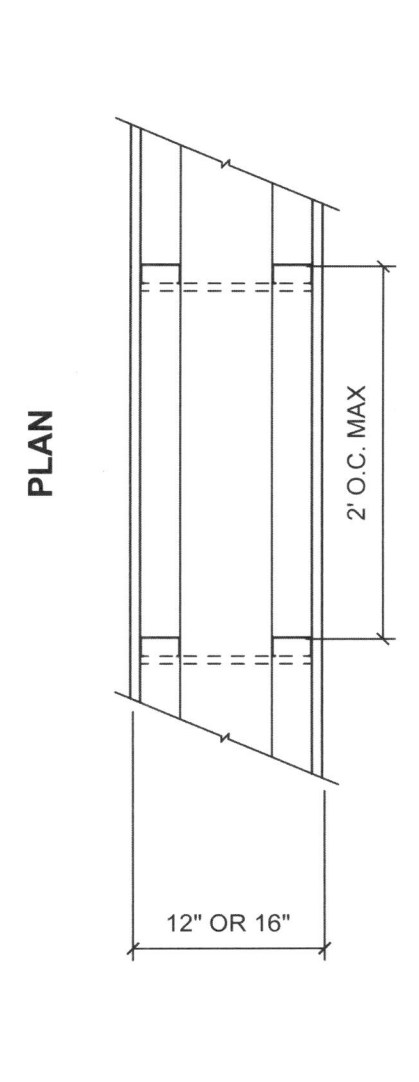

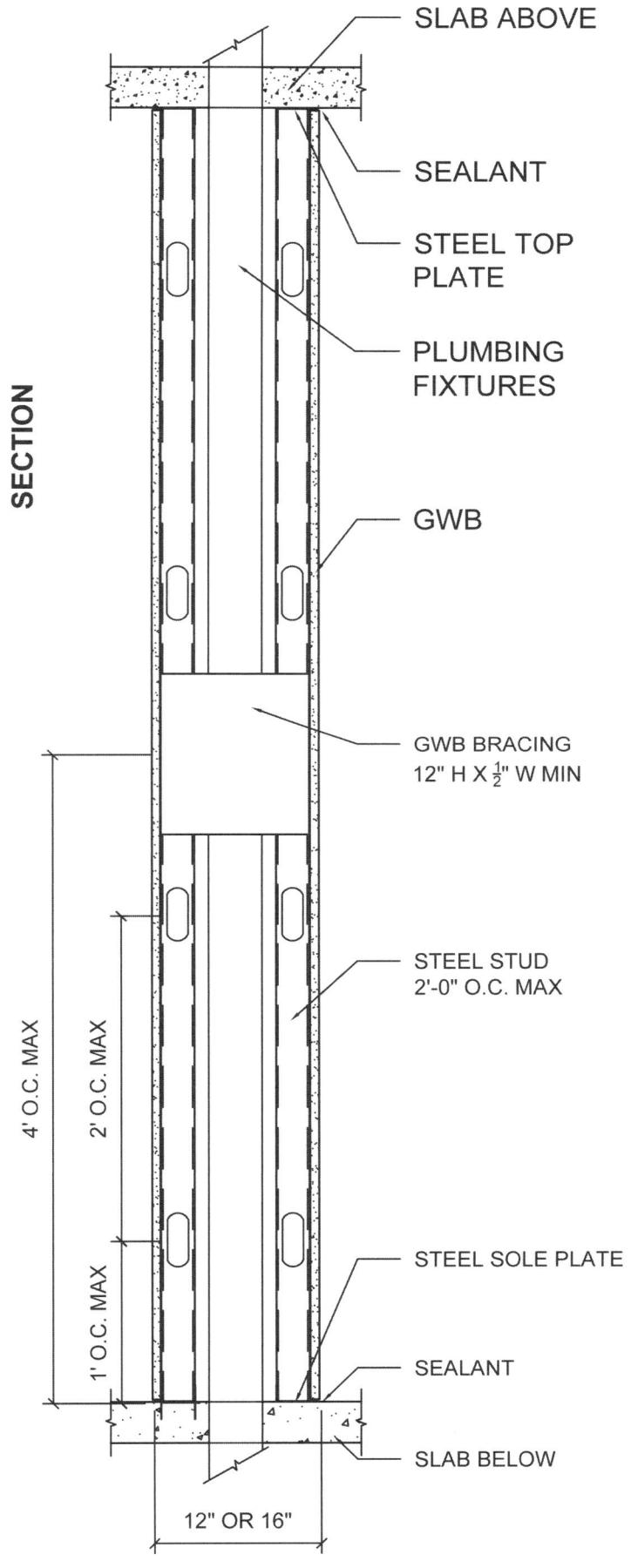

PLAN

2' O.C. MAX

12" OR 16"

STEEL STUD
CHASE PARTITION

SECTION

- SLAB ABOVE
- SEALANT
- STEEL TOP PLATE
- PLUMBING FIXTURES
- GWB
- GWB BRACING 12" H X $\frac{1}{2}$" W MIN
- STEEL STUD 2'-0" O.C. MAX
- STEEL SOLE PLATE
- SEALANT
- SLAB BELOW

4' O.C. MAX
2' O.C. MAX
1' O.C. MAX

12" OR 16"

Figure AppE3
Steel stud chase partition.

APPENDIX E: WALL TYPES | 307

Figure AppE4
Wood stud chase partition.

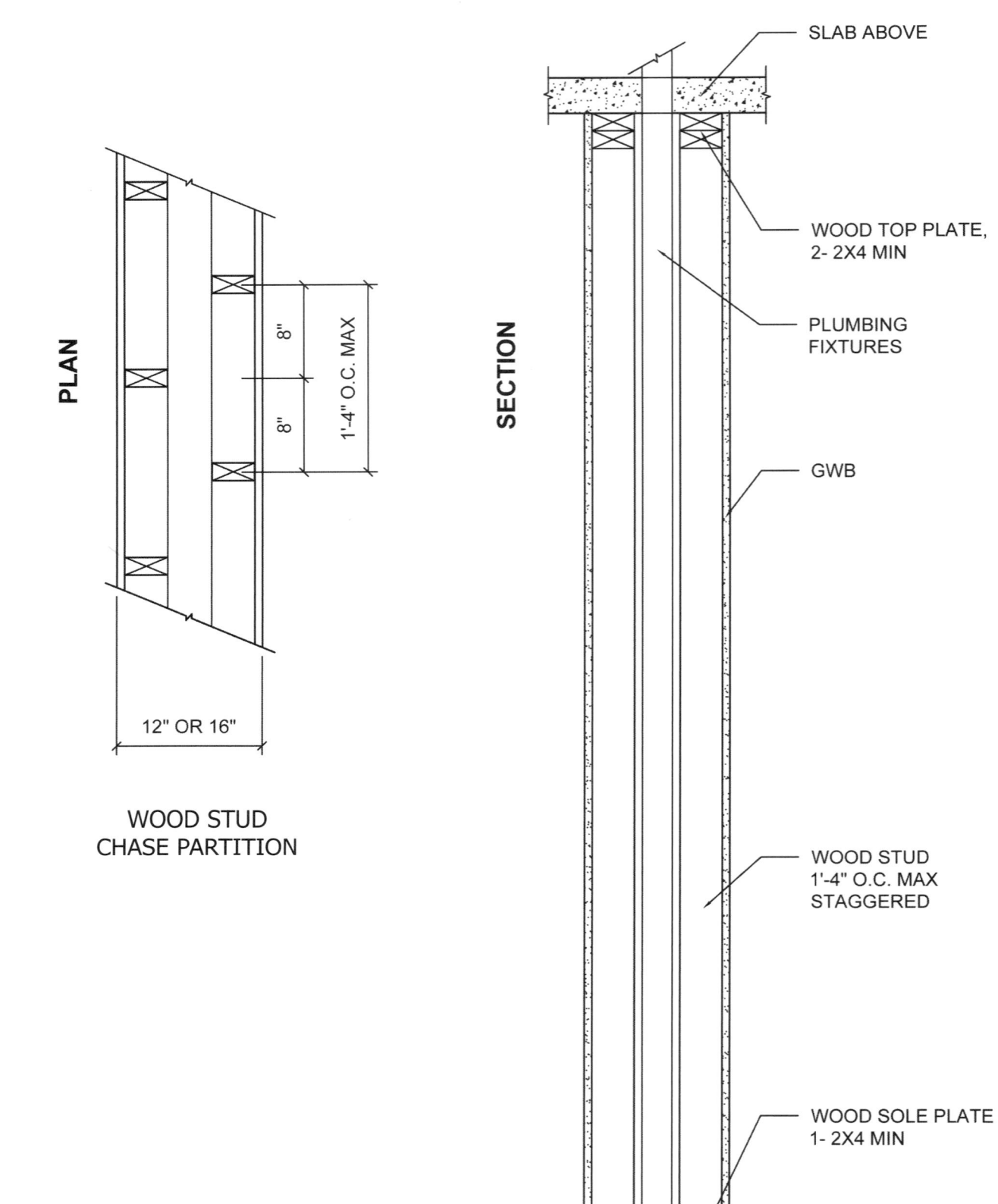

308 | APPENDIX E: WALL TYPES

Appendix F: Door Styles

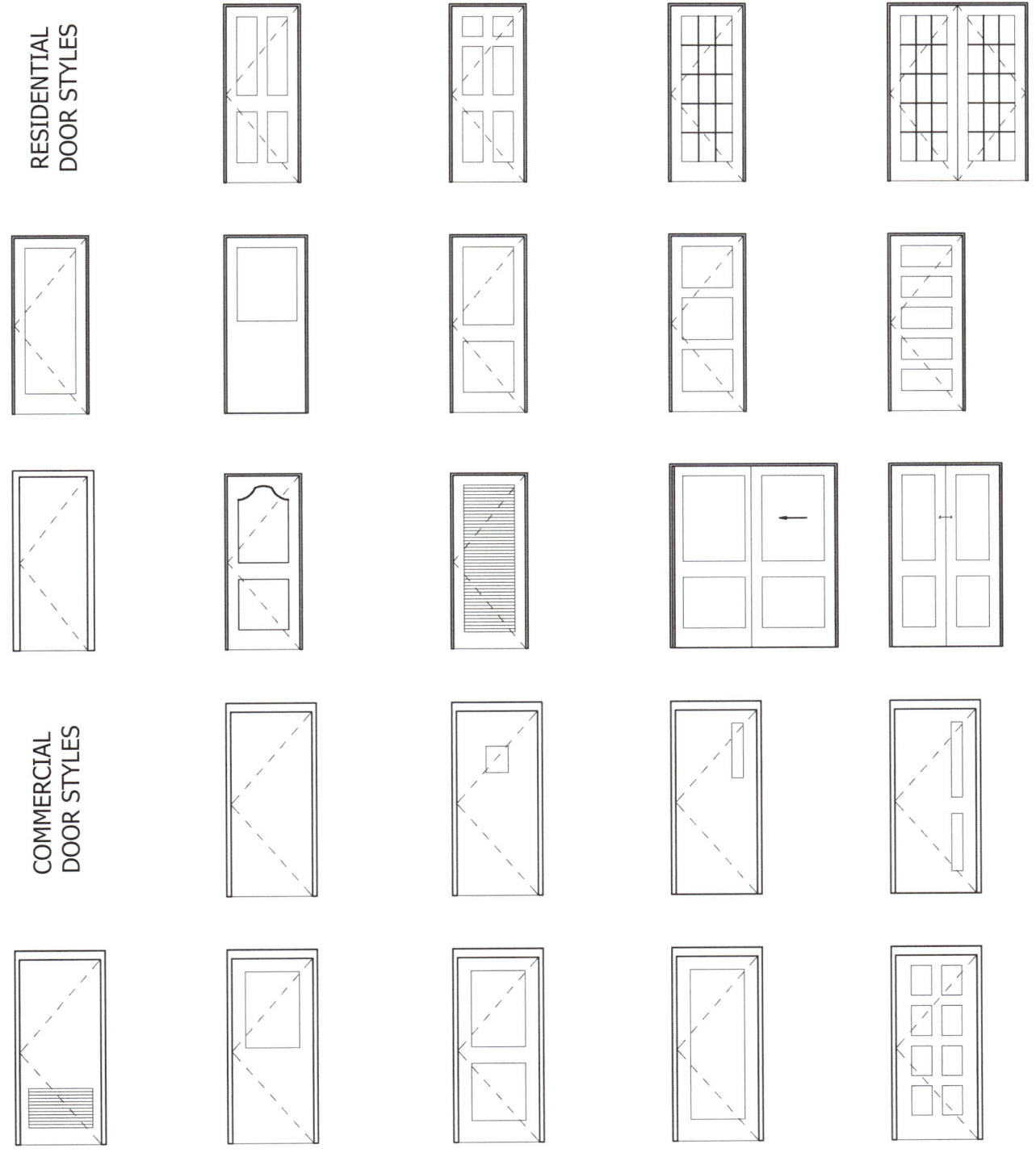

Figure AppF1
A sample of selected residential & commercial door styles.

APPENDIX F: DOOR STYLES

Appendix G: Ceiling Types

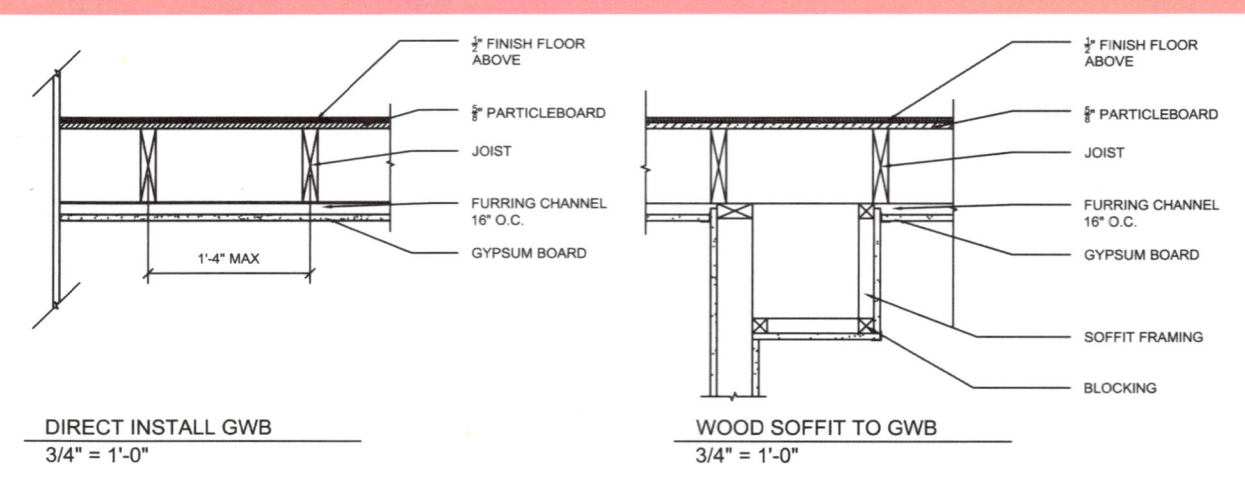

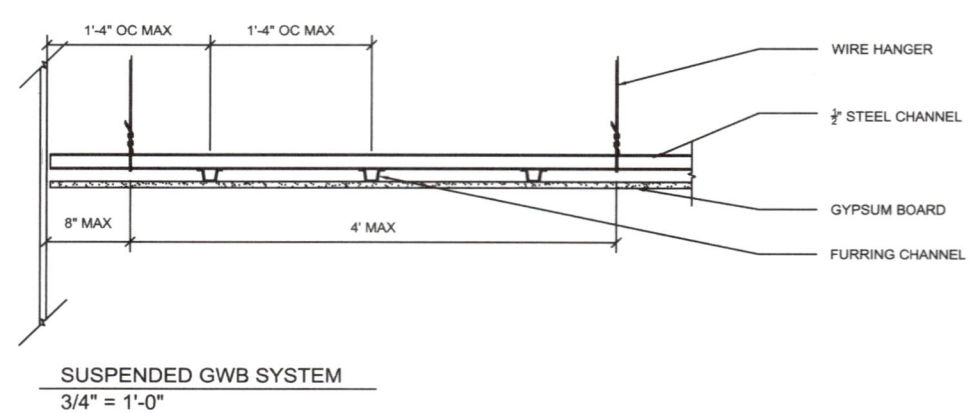

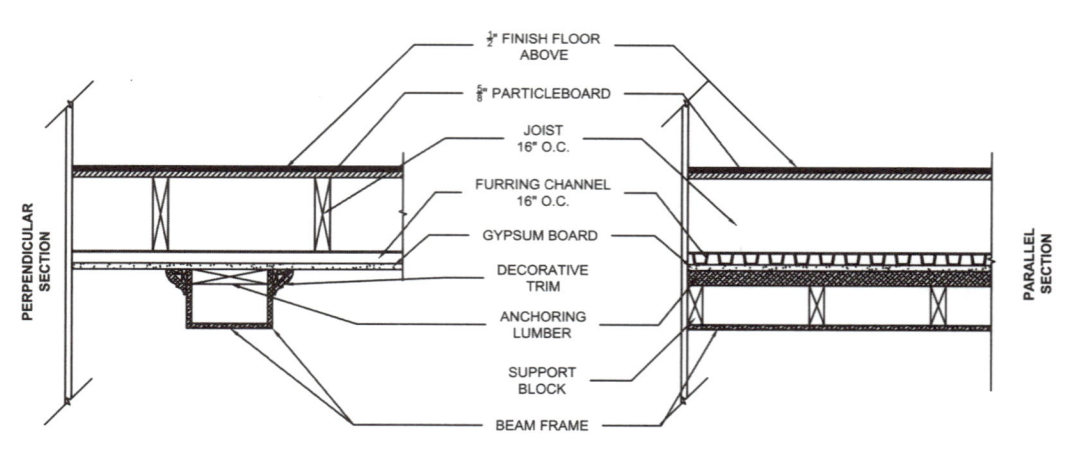

Figure AppG1
Ceiling details.

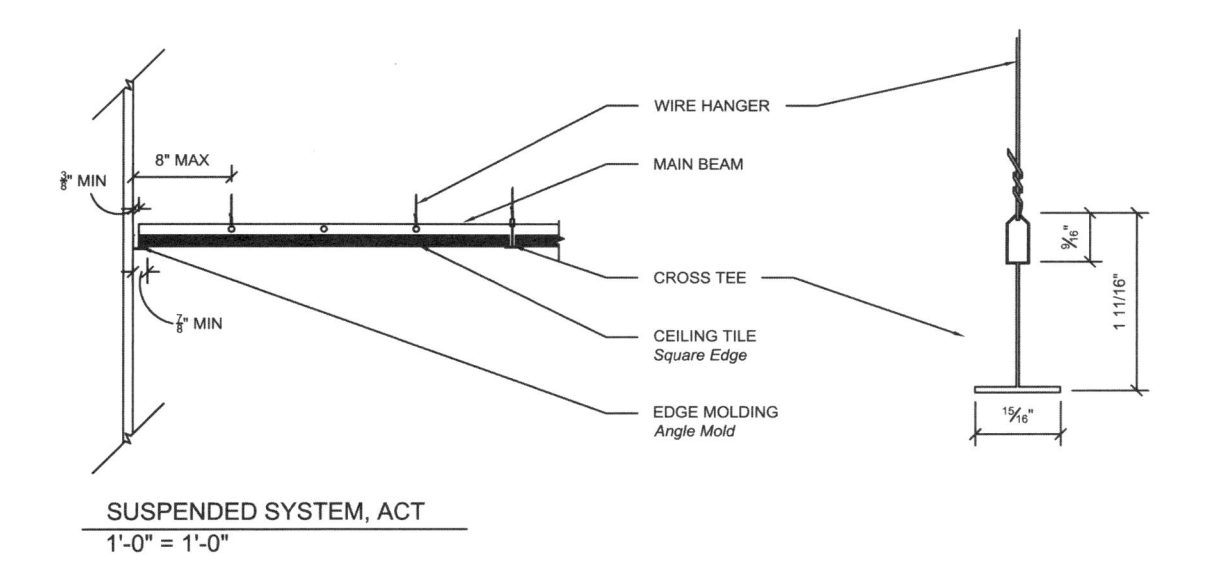

Figure AppG2
Ceiling details.

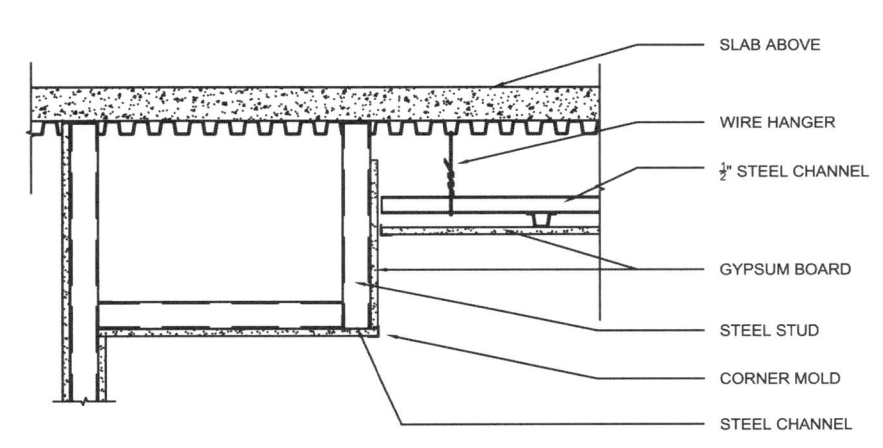

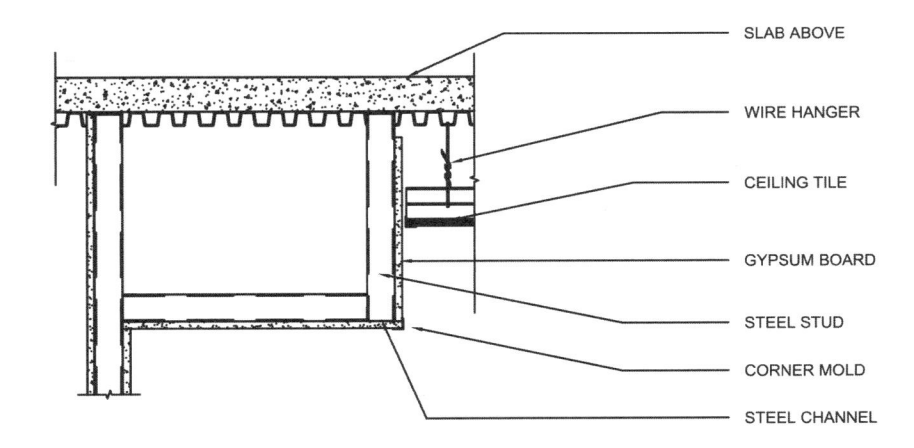

APPENDIX G: CEILING TYPES | 311

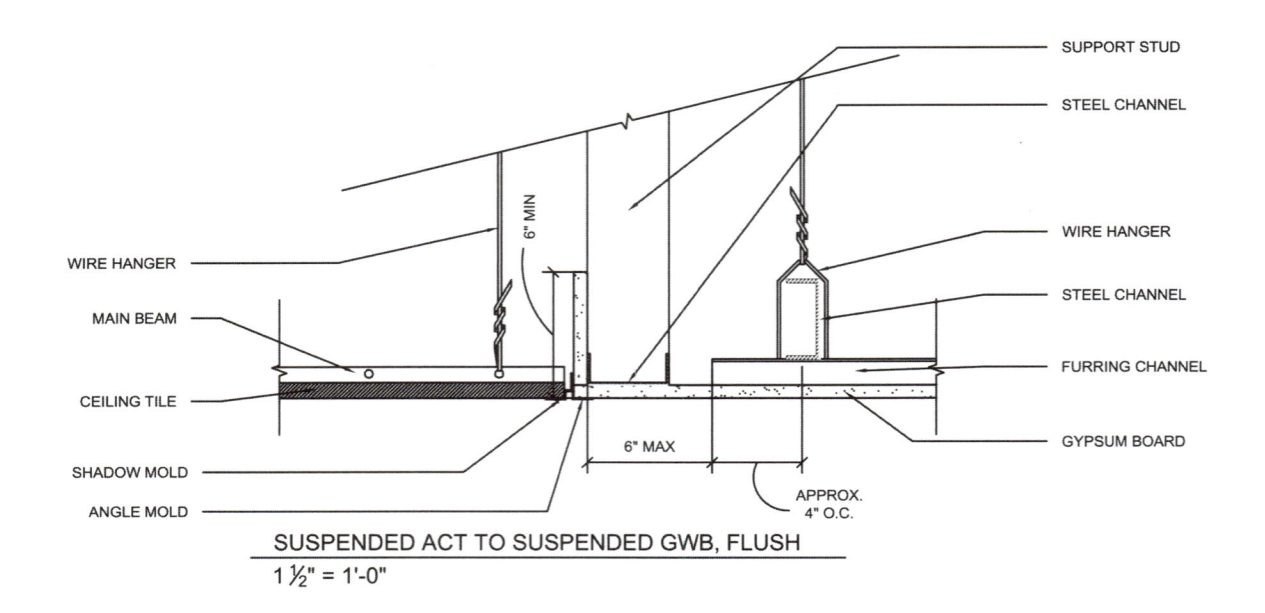

Figure AppG3
Ceiling details.

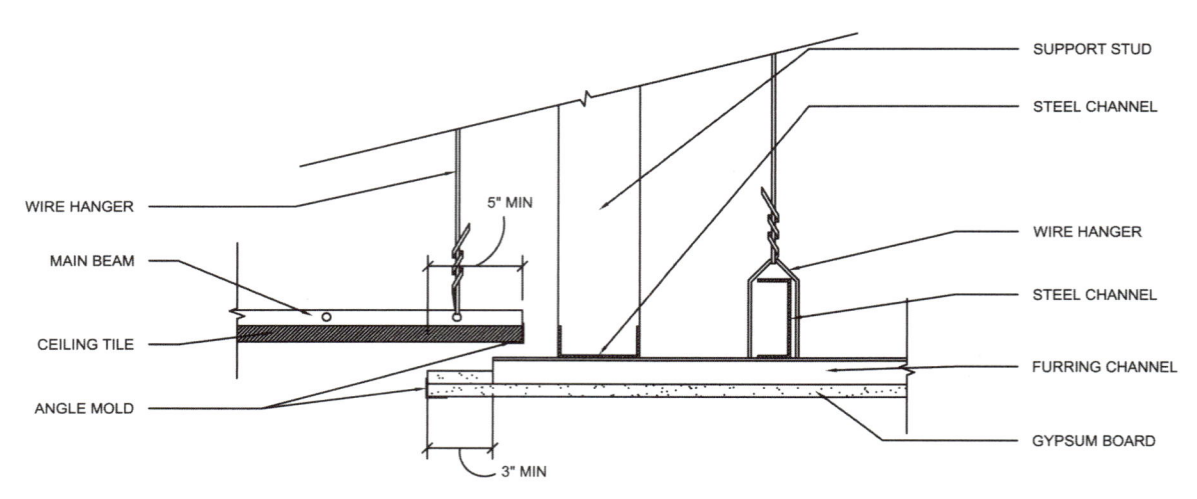

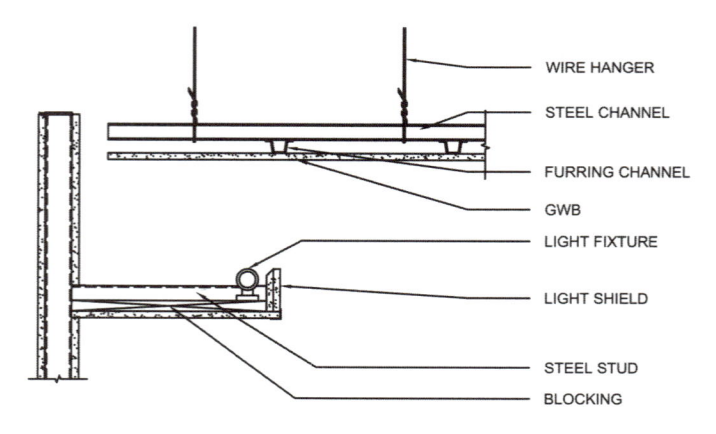

312 | APPENDIX G: CEILING TYPES

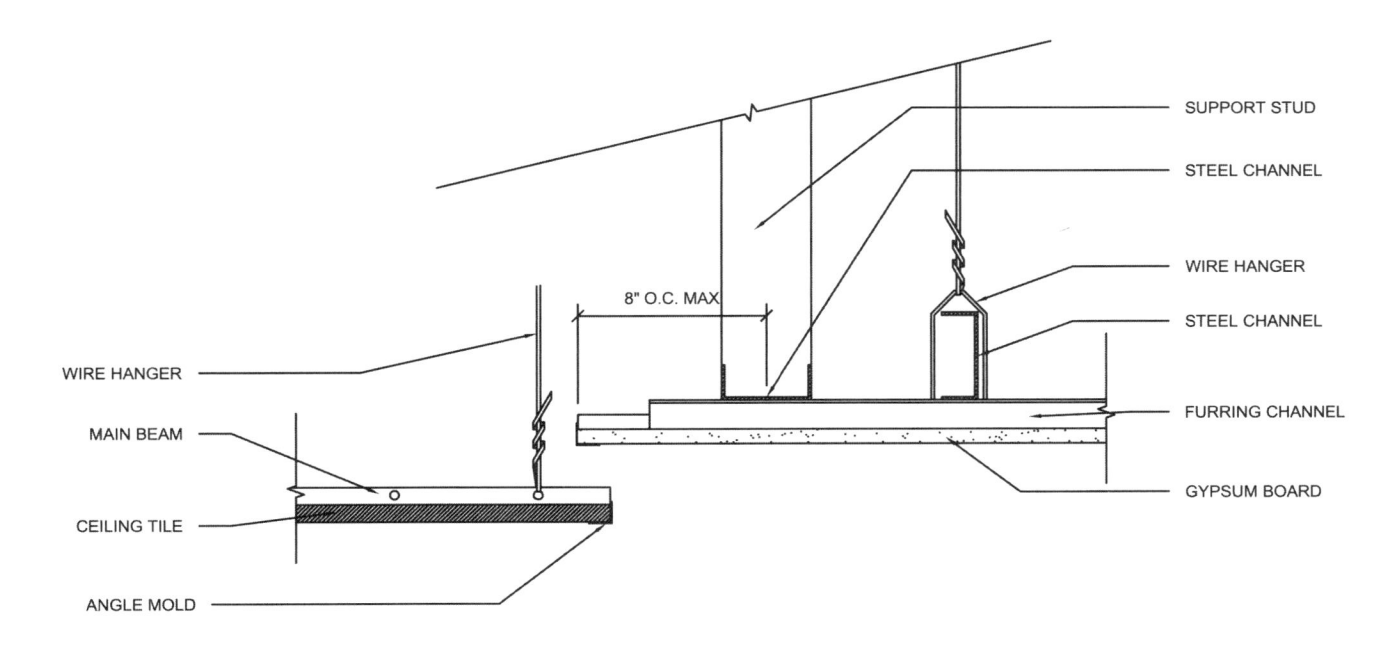

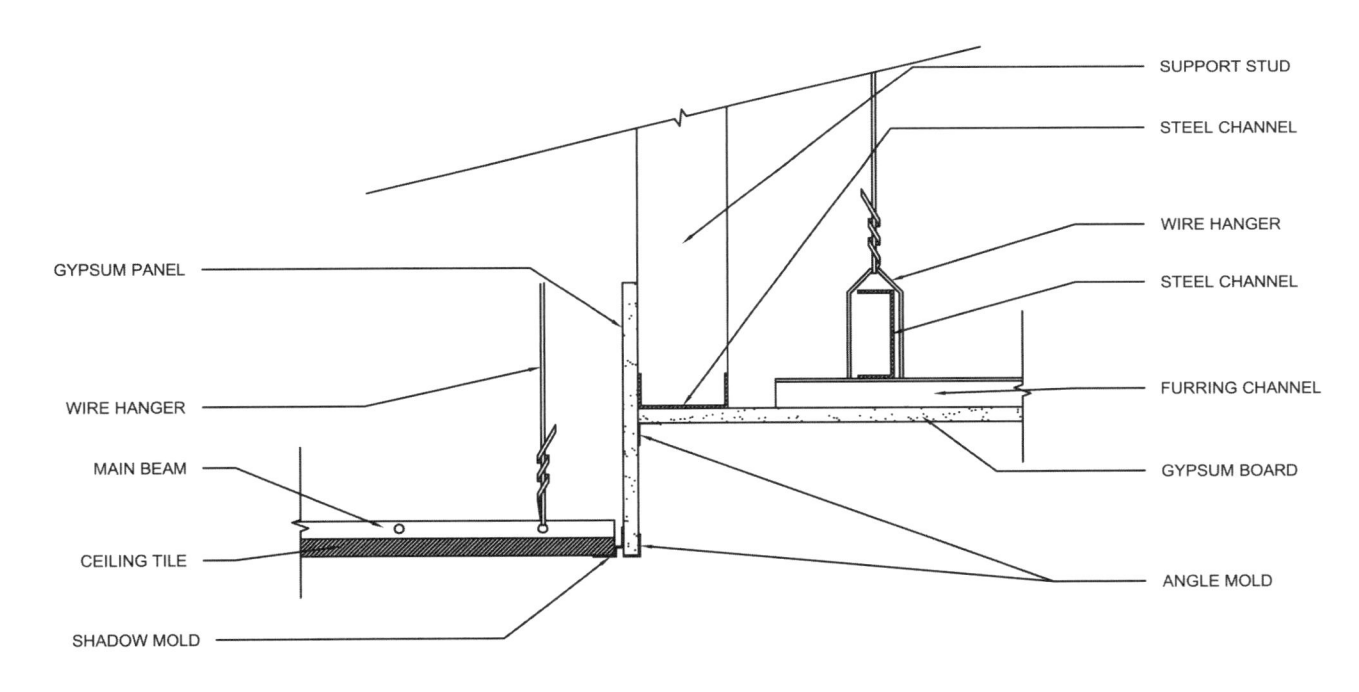

Figure AppG4
Ceiling details.

APPENDIX G: CEILING TYPES

Appendix H: Millwork and Cabinet Styles

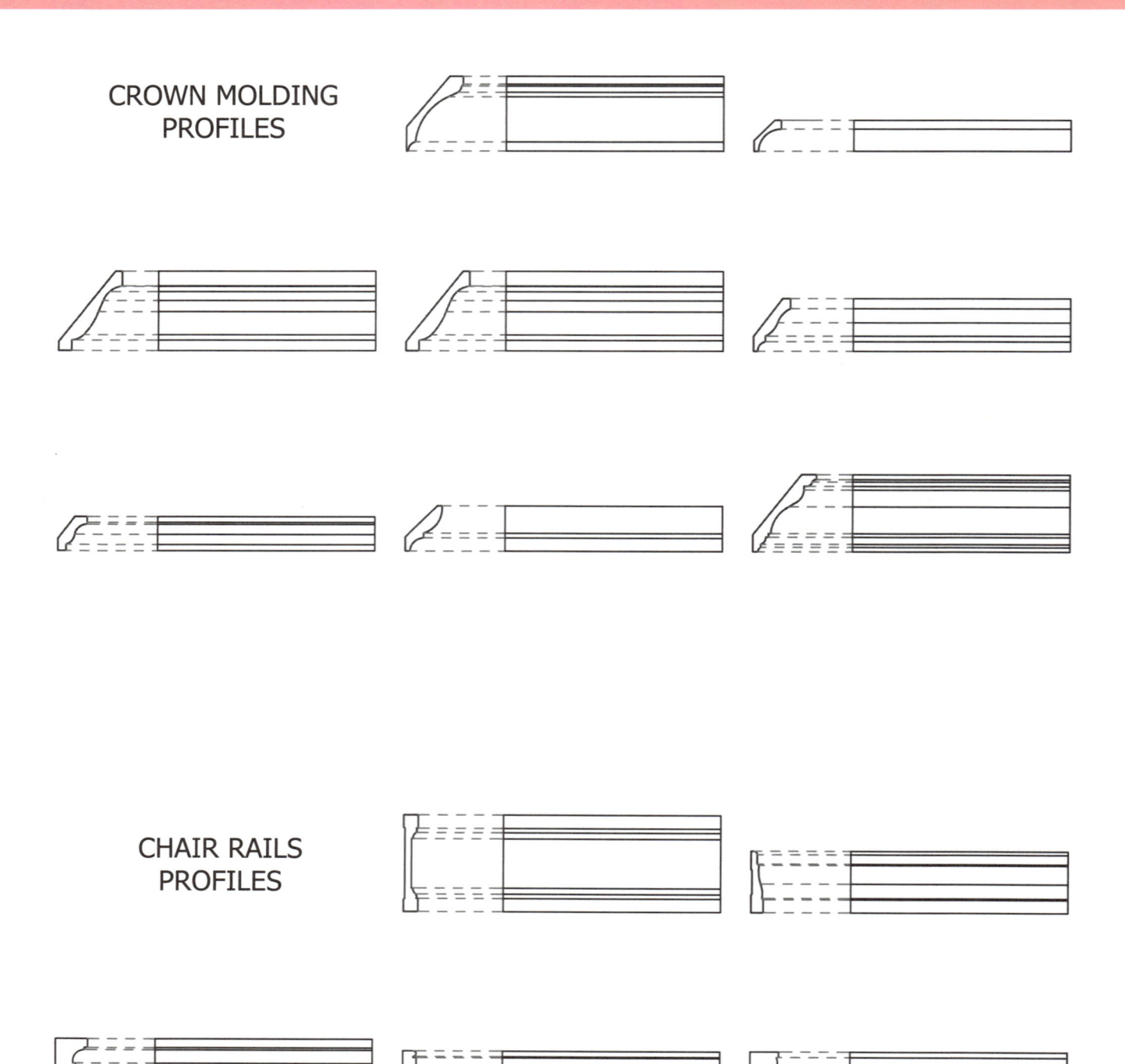

CROWN MOLDING
PROFILES

CHAIR RAILS
PROFILES

Figure AppH1
A sample of selected millwork profiles.

BASEBOARD PROFILES

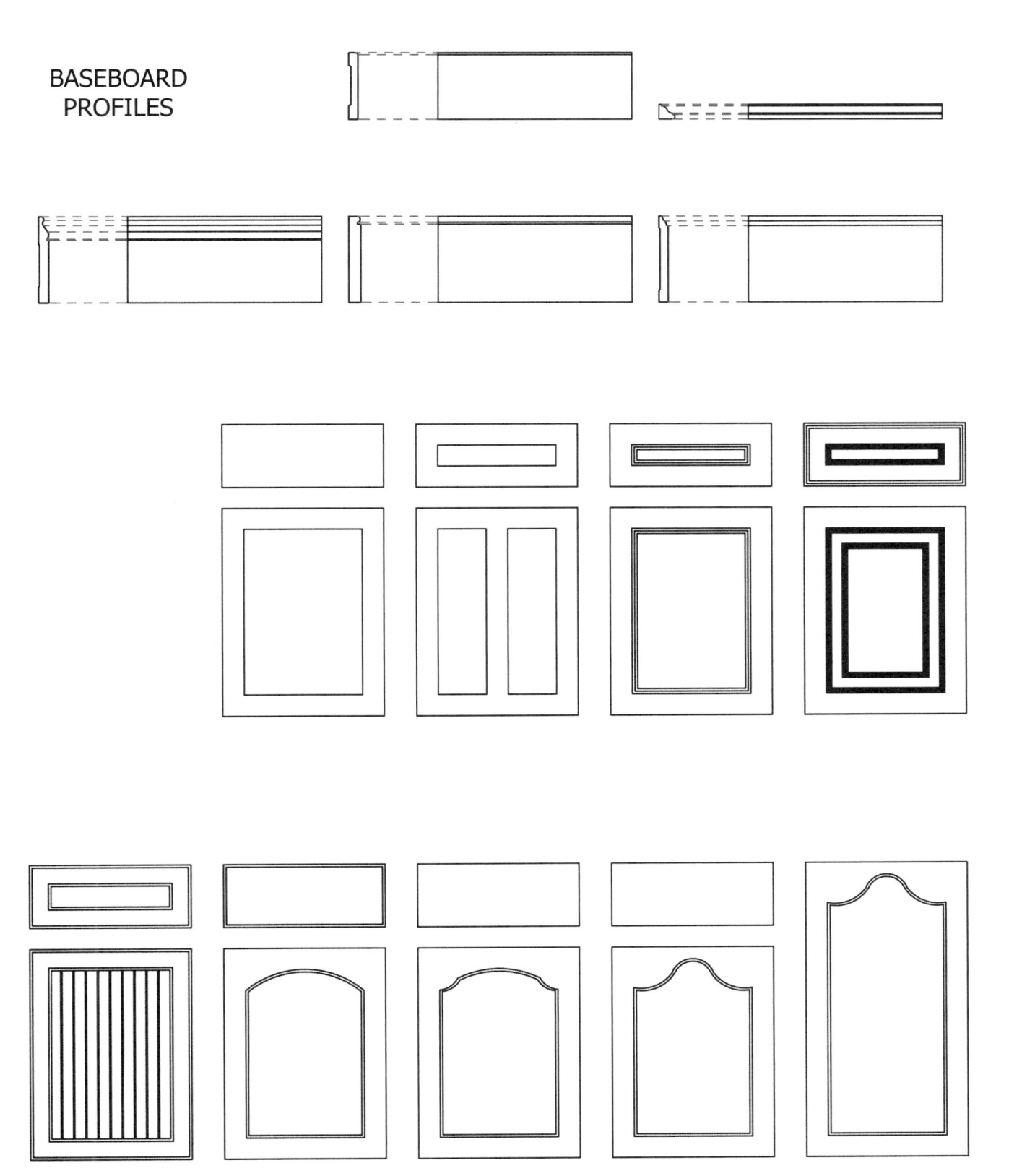

Figure AppH2
A sample of selected millwork profiles.

APPENDIX H: MILLWORK AND CABINET STYLES

Appendix I: Stairs, Nosings, and Rails

Stair dimensions

Direct run dimensions

U- and L-run dimensions

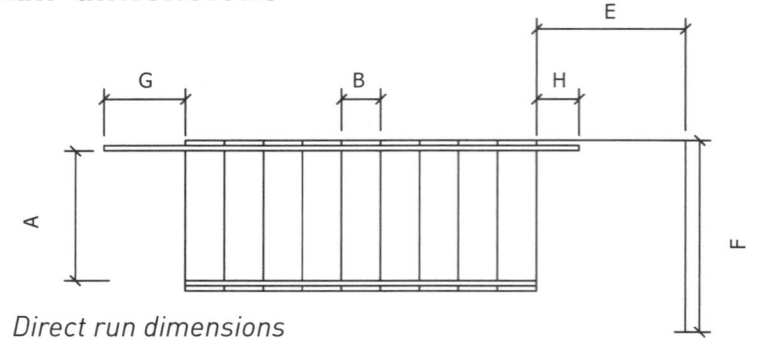

Figure AppI1
Stair layouts and components.

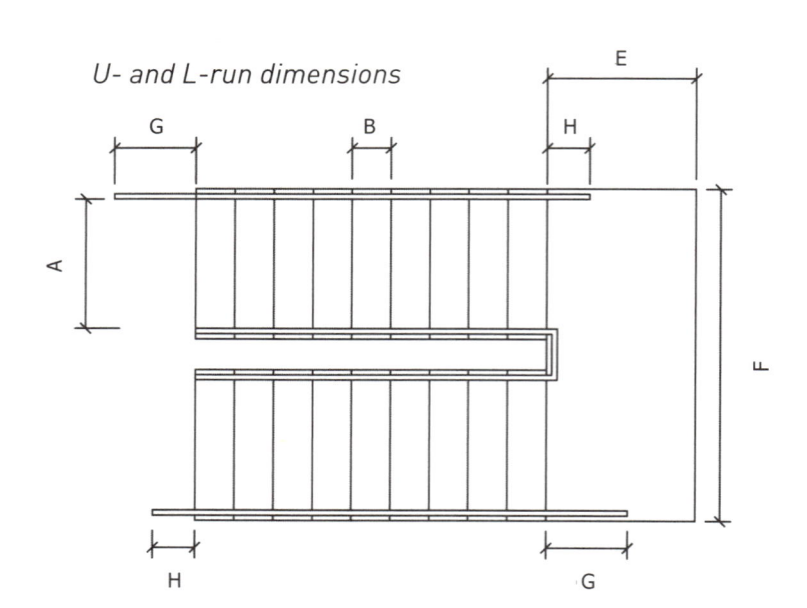

Stair component dimensions

Table AII
Stair Dimensions by Code

Letter	Subject	Commercial	Commercial Egress	Residential
A	Stair clear space width	36" for fewer than 50 people 44" for more than 50 people	48"	
B	Tread depth	11" Min	11" Min	9" Min
C	Riser height	7" Max	7" Max	
D	Nosing depth	1 ½" Max	1 ½" Max	1 ½" Max
E	Landing width			
F	Landing depth			
G	Rail extension (bottom)	Tread depth + 12"	Tread depth + 12"	Not required
H	Rail extension (top)	12"	12"	Not required
I	Handrail height	34"-38" Both sides required	34"-38" Both sides required	34-38" One side required
J	Guardrail height	42" Min	42" Min	34-38" Min When necessary

316 | APPENDIX I: STAIRS, NOSINGS, AND RAILS

Acceptable nose profiles

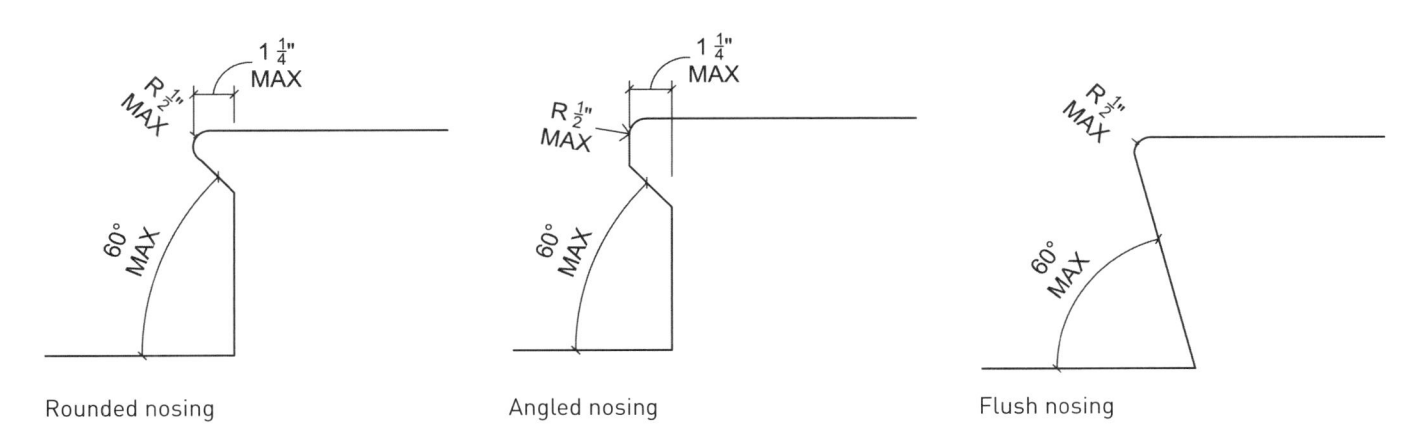

Rounded nosing

Angled nosing

Flush nosing

Figure AppI2
Nosing profiles, per code.

Acceptable rail profiles

Rail profiles that are accepted by both the IBC and the ADA must meet the following criteria:

Circular cross-section

1. The cross-section must measure between 1 1/4" and 2".
2. The graspable portion must maintain a spacing of at least 1 1/2" between the rail and the wall or platform.

Non-circular

1. Extensions of at least 1 1/2" are allowed below the circular cross-section for additional grippable area.

Other profiles that are accepted by both the IBC and ADA must meet additional criteria:

1. Edges must be curved and feature radius of at least 1/8".
2. When outside perimeter must measure between 4" and 6 1/2".
3. The cross-sectional interior dimension must be 2 1/2" or less.

Figure AppI3
Rail profiles, per code.

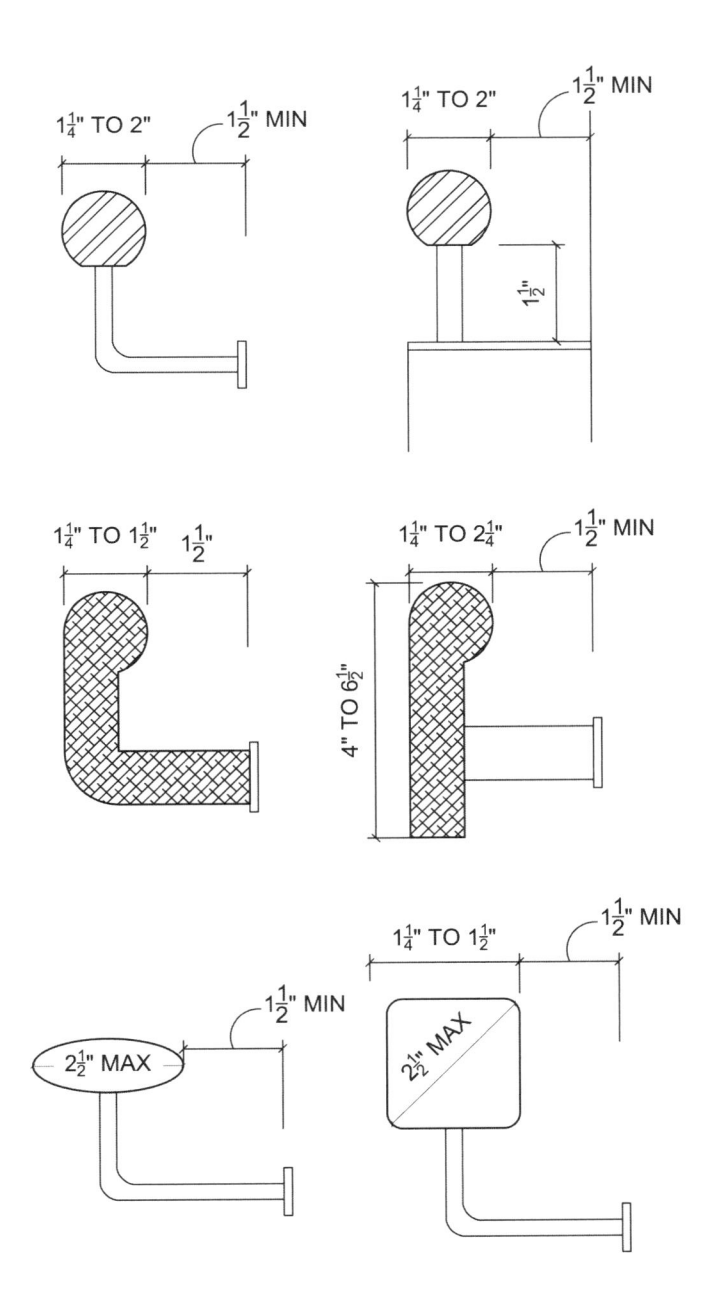

APPENDIX I: STAIRS, NOSINGS, AND RAILS

Appendix J: Sample Tile Patterns

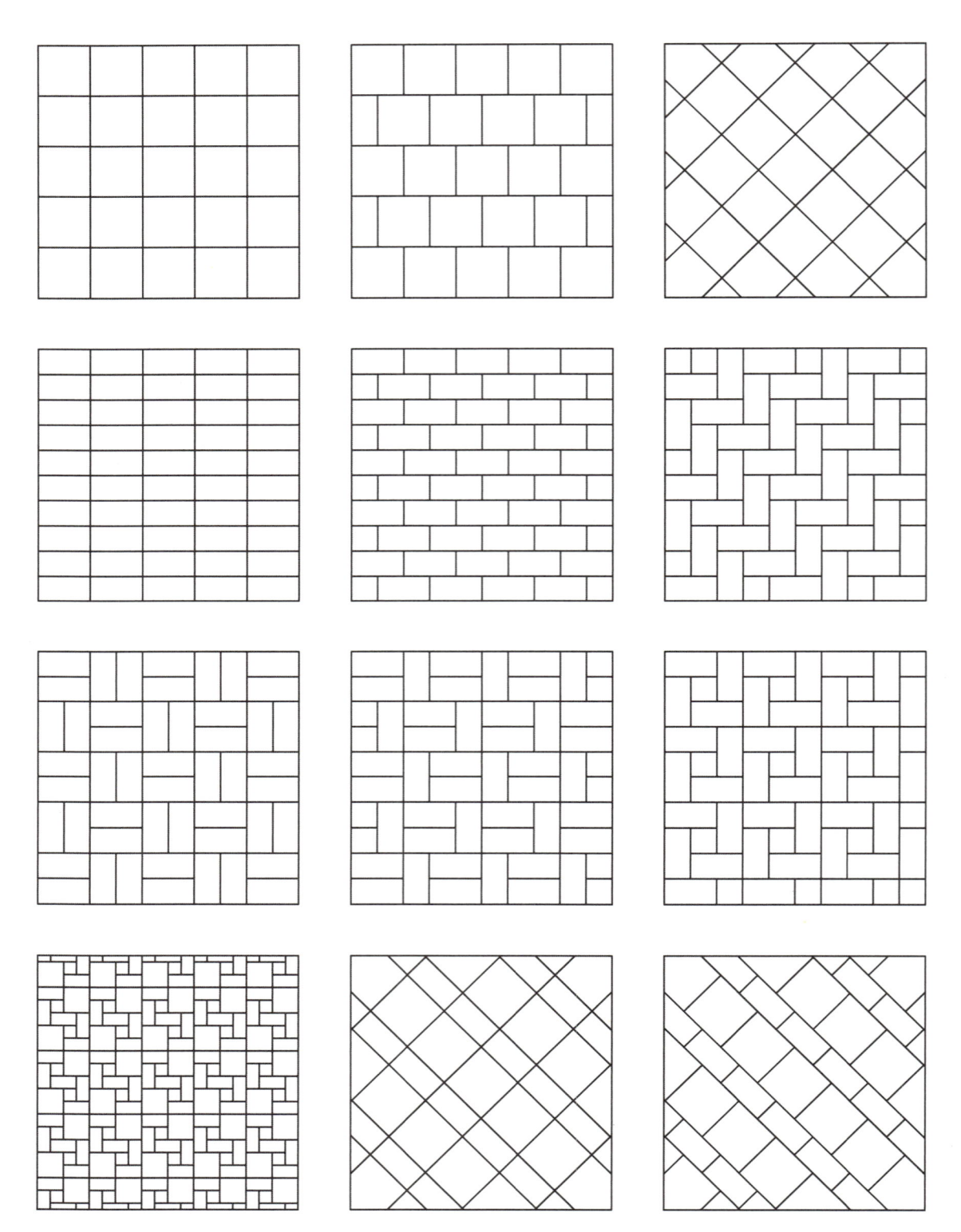

Figure AppJ1 A sample of selected tile patterns.

Appendix K: Project Plan Shell A STUDIO

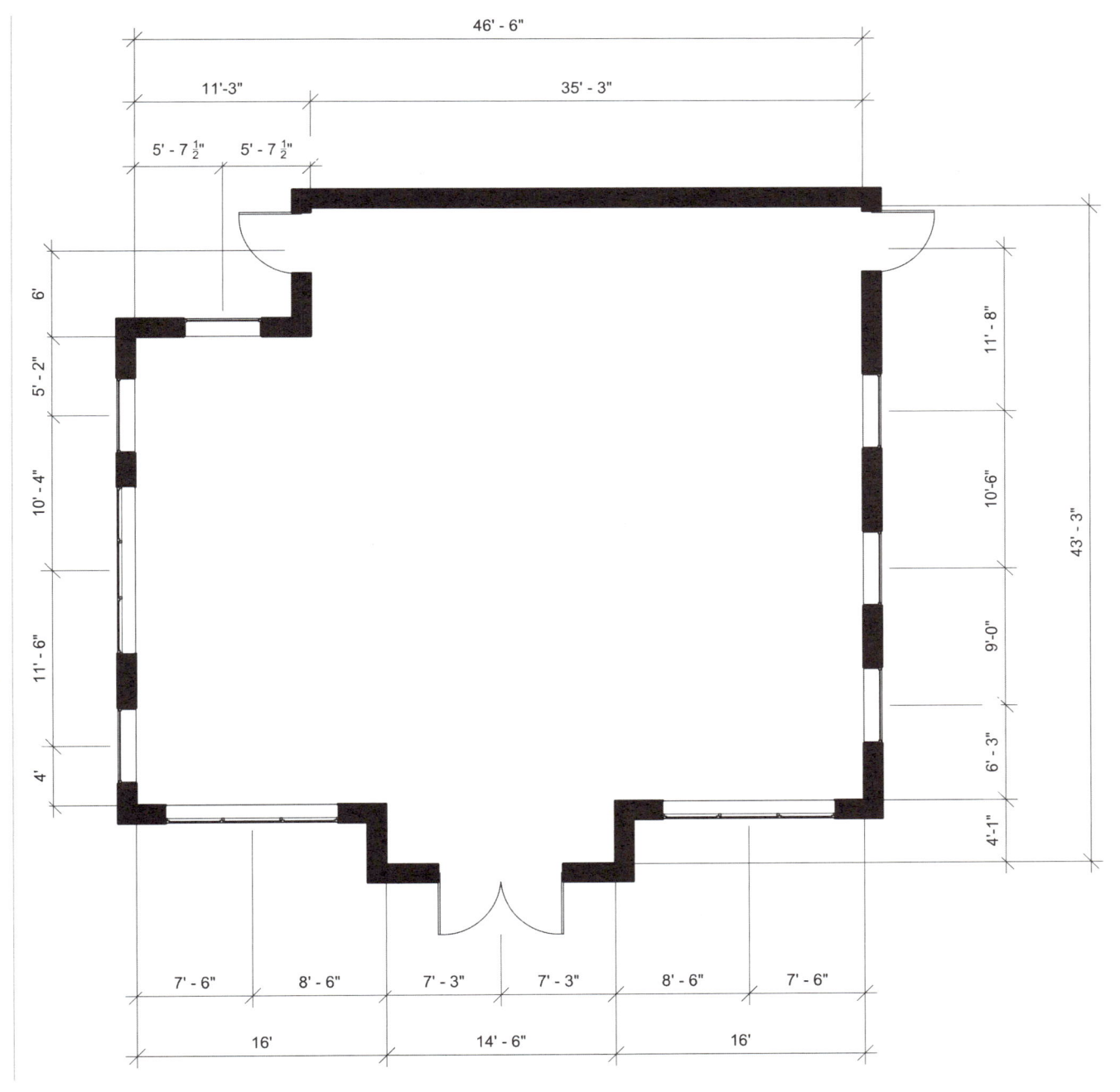

Figure AppK1
Suggested project plan shell A, level 1.

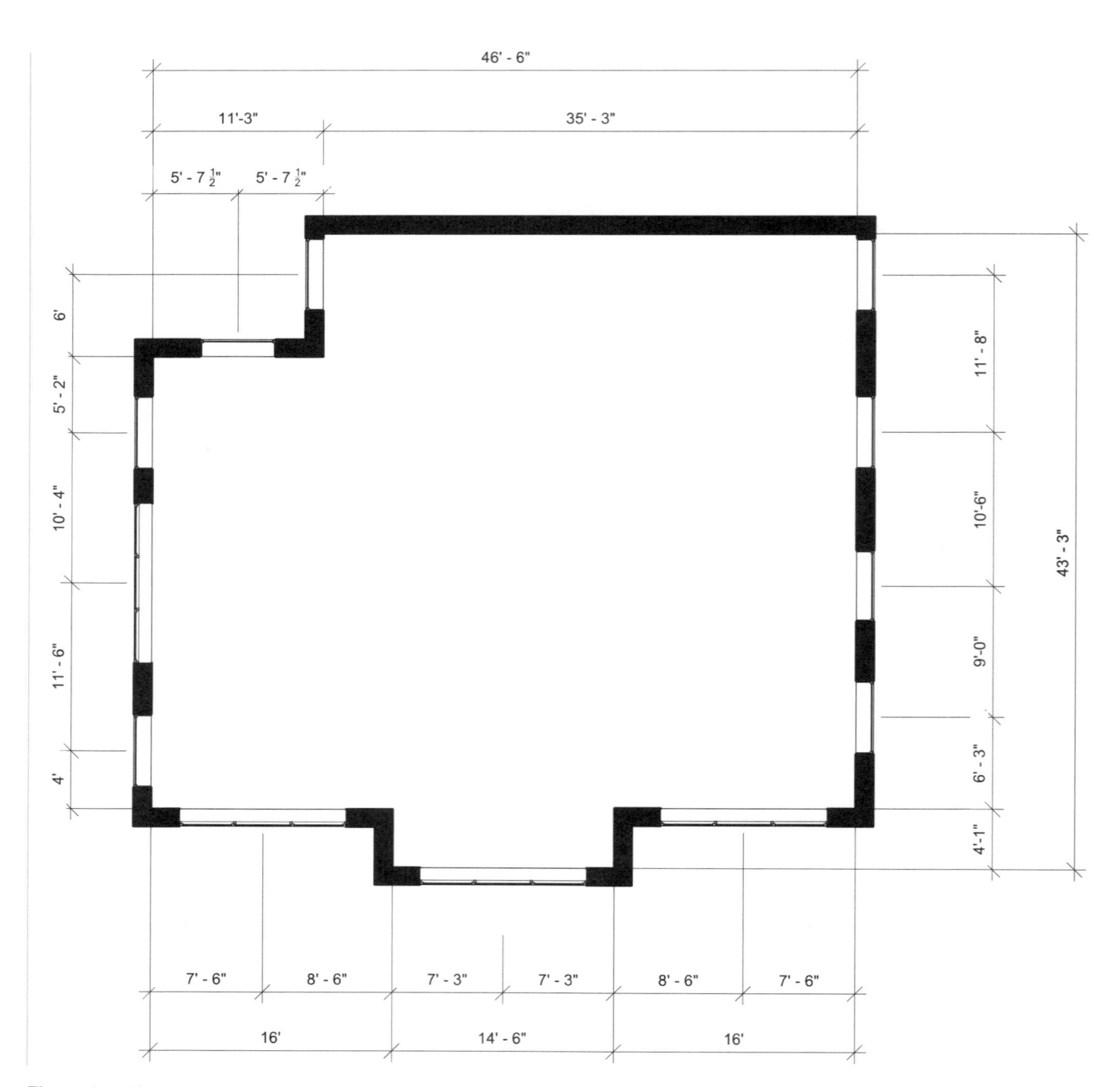

Figure AppK2
Suggested project plan shell A, level 2.

APPENDIX K: PROJECT PLAN SHELL A

Appendix L: Project Plan Shell B STUDIO

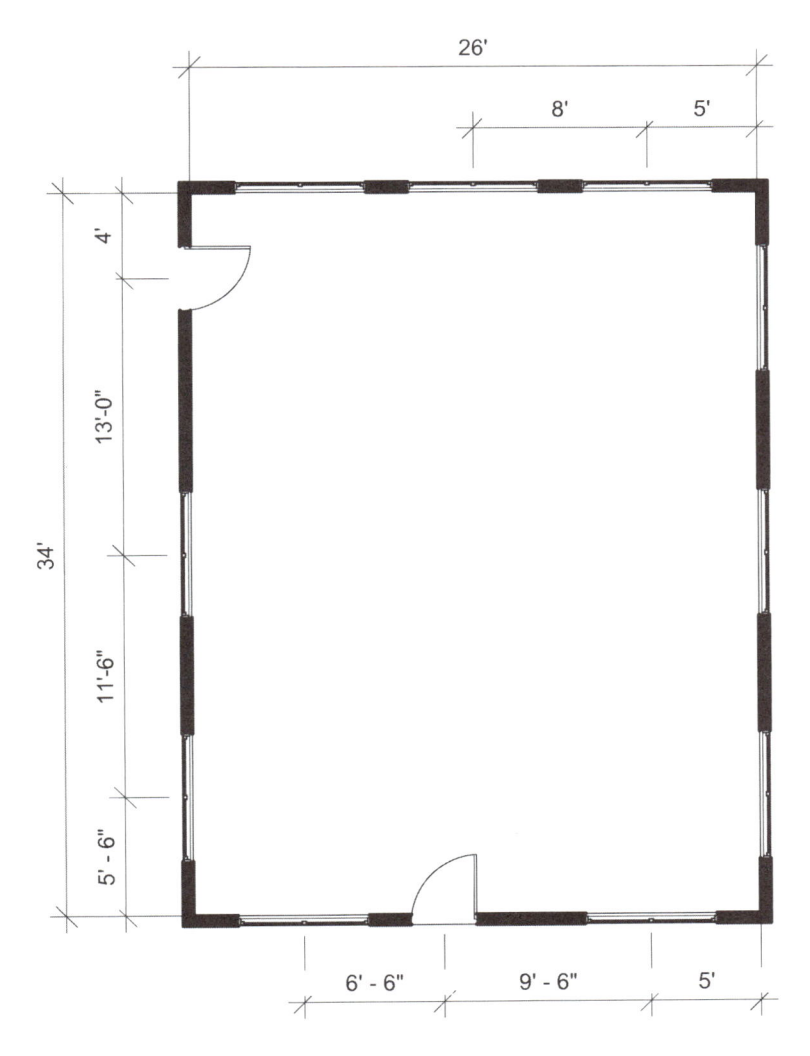

Figure AppL1
Suggested project plan shell B, level 1.

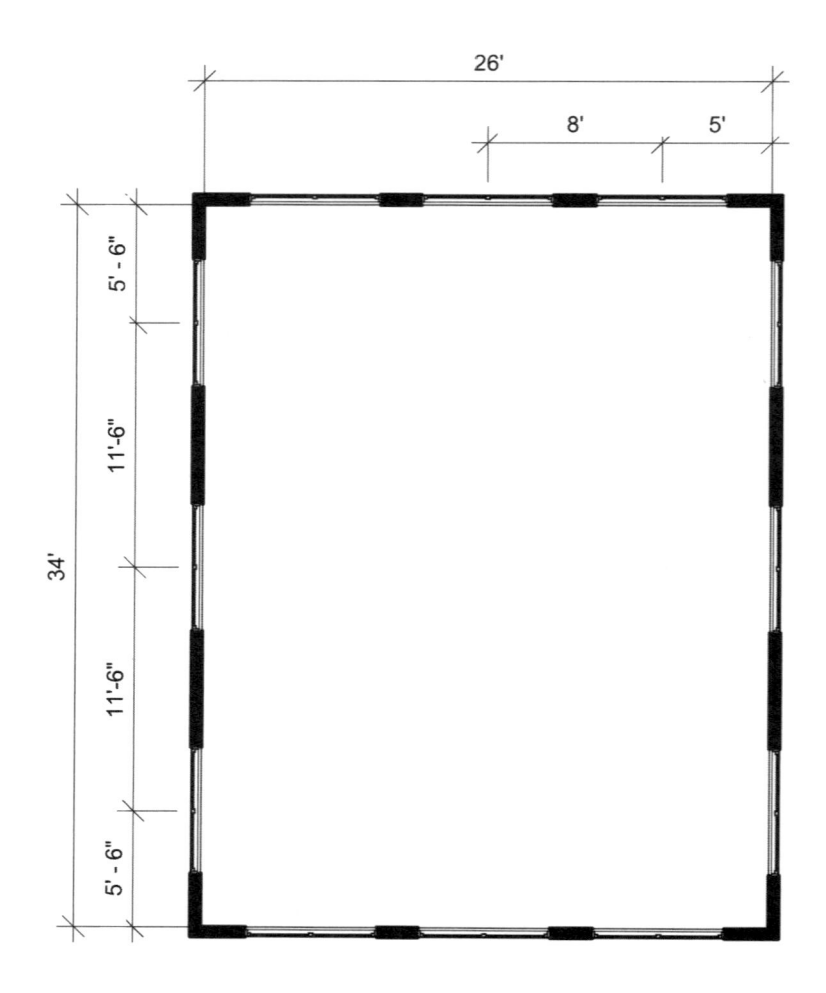

Figure AppL2
Suggested project plan shell B, level 2.

Glossary

acoustical ceiling tile: Modular panels that aid in the absorption of sound. They are the most popular and widely used type of ceiling panel, available in square edge, tegular edge, and concealed-T tiles. See Appendix D for types and common sizes.

acoustical partition: Interior partition that features layers of sound batt to diminish noise transfer from one room to another.

aligned dimension: Dimension stringer that is used to measure between two parallel objects.

Americans with Disabilities Act Accessibility Guidelines: The minimum standards set forth by the Department of Justice to ensure that public buildings are designed with spaces that are inclusive to individuals with disabilities, through barrier-free design, equal accommodations for all, and adapted accommodations.

Americans with Disabilities Act: The 1990 law that bans discrimination against individuals with disabilities. Title III of the law requires public buildings to be accessible to all, resulting in design standards that ensure the inclusion of all within the built environment.

anchoring rails: Horizontal planks running the width of a cabinet, located along the top and bottom of the back panel as a connection point for three parts of the cabinet, adding strength to the construction and creating a plane for wall fasteners.

angle molding: An *L*-shaped trim used along the perimeter of a suspended ceiling.

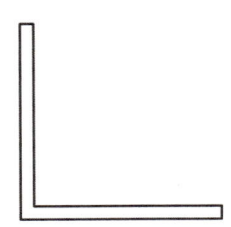

angle supports: *L*-shaped supports that mount the tread and riser to the steel channel.

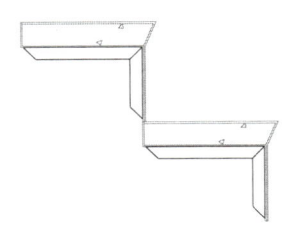

annotation: A notation calling out important information in a drawing. This can be used to create better understanding of the drawing, stress the importance of the element, or indicate information that is not readily apparent. In a construction drawing, this is typically shown with a leader line pointing to the element or through a designer's note to the contractor.

architectural lettering: Uppercase text used to write dimensions, annotations, and notes when drafting.

architectural scale: A three-sided measuring instrument that provides consistent units of measurement for multiple fractional scales.

axonometric: A 3D image of the object or space, with the vertical and horizontal dimensions drawn to scale. This type of drawing will appear skewed along the diagonal.

backbend: The framing members on either side of the throat, which aids in connecting the frame to the wall.

backsplash: A nonporous barrier used along the wall, typically behind counters and sinks as a way to keep the partition from wetness or damage. The barrier is typically composed of a series of tiles but can also be made from stone, metal, or another waterproof product.

balusters: Vertical members that support the handrail or guardrail and aid in both decoration and safety. Balusters must be spaced so that a 4" sphere cannot pass between them.

barrier free: An object or environment designed so that it accessible for all end users.

baseboard: Molding that is used to hide the joint created along the bottom of a wall and the floor. Typically 4" to 7" in height.

base cabinet: A floor-mounted storage unit that may contain shelves or drawers. Base cabinets are typically 32" to 36" high and are topped by a counter.

beadboard: Paneling that is constructed as a thin sheet with carved grooves so that it appears as though multiple planks have been laid side by side.

bearing wall: A wall that supports the weight of the roof and upper levels. Removal of these walls requires alternative support measures. Exterior walls and certain interior walls are load-bearing.

box beam: A decorative, hollow beam that can be added to a ceiling to establish visual interest. The hollow channel that is created lightens the weight on the finished ceiling above and can conceal wires and pipes.

butt joint: The most economical joint, the two boards are laid next to each other (glue) or with one overlapping the other (nail). This joint can be used in furniture and cabinetry or to create a continuous length.

cabinet: A type of storage unit constructed from a system of panels, rails, and stiles, that can be floor- or wall-mounted and utilizes a series of doors, drawers, and shelves, based on the needs of the end user.

cabinet blocking: Framing lumber or aluminum framing that is installed horizontally between studs in partitions where cabinets are set to be installed. The blocking must measure at least 2 × 6 and be aligned with the mounting rail height for the cabinet.

carriage: Elements that are the supports for the treads and risers. When constructed out of wood, the carriages are cut so that the treads and risers can be affixed directly to the carriage, allowing for it to carry the weight of the flight and the users. The number and size of the carriages depends on the width of the flight and the dimensions of the rise and run.

casing: The exposed trim around a window or door, typically made of wood, metal, aluminum, or plastic.

ceiling: A compound construction element that utilizes a support system to attach the finish materials to the structure above and may conceal wires and fixtures.

center line: Dashed lines that mark the center of symmetrical objects.

chair rail: Molding that is mounted along a wall as a means to protect the wall's finish from damage, typically 24" to 36" above the finished floor, but it may be higher.

channel support: Steel tube that supports the front end of a landing for steel stairs.

chase walls: A wall constructed with enough width to conceal plumbing, typically 12" for fixtures on one side and 16" for fixtures on both sides.

clear space: The distance between two objects in which nothing infringes into or interrupts the path of travel.

clip angle: L-shaped metal element that anchor bolts the steel channel to the floor.

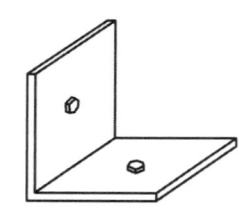

closed stringer: Stairway in which the treads and risers are not visible from the sides because the stringers are covered.

commercial stair: Any staircase in a multi-family home or commercial business. These stairs must be of steel construction.

concealed grid: Suspended acoustical ceiling system where the panels hide the grid from view.

concealed T tile: Grooved ceiling tiles that slide on to the grid tee, allowing for the finished face of the tile to project past the grid and hide the tee above, creating a flush finish between tiles.

construction document set: A collection of interrelated drawings that will act as the instructions for the general contractor to build the project as specified.

cornerblock: A triangular-shaped support that fits into the 90 degree angle created by the sides of a cabinet and helps to hold them together.

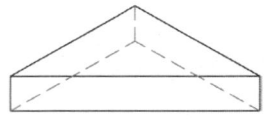

cornice: A ledge that is mounted flush to the top wall just below the ceiling, typically sitting above the crown molding or being directly incorporated into the profile of the crown. This piece typically features a shaped pattern or detail that runs the length of the surface.

counter edge: The curved, finished perimeter of the countertop that protects the end user from being hurt when bumping into the surface.

countertop: Horizontal surface installed on top of base cabinets or along a wall composed of a variety of stone, wood, or composite materials.

cove: Alcoves created in the ceiling or wall planes that eliminate or disguise the typical 90 degree angle formed between the planes. These nooks may simply be used as a decorative element but may also act as housing for hidden lighting within a project.

cove lighting: Indirect lighting that is aimed upward and reflected back down to the room below from an alcove within the ceiling or partition.

cripple stud: A stud that has been shortened for use in supporting openings. These studs appear between the top plate and header, and between the bottom plate and a sill.

cross tee: A lightweight steel runner that acts as the secondary member of a suspended ceiling system, connecting the main beams to one another.

crown molding: An element that disguises the seam where the wall and ceiling meet or can be used at the top of cabinetry or columns. This piece typically features a shaped pattern or detail that runs the length of the surface.

dado joint: A joint that creates a right angle between two pieces of wood, where one piece slides into a notch cut into the other. This notch, referred to as the dado, runs perpendicular to the wood's grain. Typically used within the body of a cabinet or bookcase.

decorative panel: Thin boards or veneered plywood that are carved or embossed with a repetitive pattern.

detail callout: dashed bubble used to refer the reader to an enlarged drawing or more in depth specifics for an element. The numbers and/or letters in the circle refer to the drawing number (top) and the page number (bottom) where the drawing can be found in the construction set.

detail drawing: A plan, elevation, or section shown at a large scale in order to clarify the dimensions, annotations, and finishes for clear communication from the designer to the contractor.

dimension: A measurement indicating the length, width, or thickness of an element. In a construction drawing, this is typically shown with a stringer or leader line, but it may also take the form of an annotation.

direct installation system: System in which the grid or support for the finished ceiling is mounted directly to the structure above. The finished ceiling can be composed of ceiling tiles or gypsum board.

direct run: This type of stair allows for the user to travel from one floor to the next without any landings or returns. Direct runs can only be used when the total rise is less than 12'-0".

double rabbet: A door frame featuring two rabbets separated by a stop, where either side could contain the door.

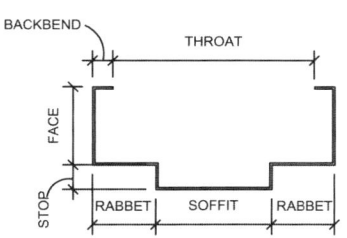

double top plate: The use of two layers of nominal wood boards along the top of a stud wall to join the studs for a wall and support ceiling joists in wood-stud construction.

dovetail joint: A joint created by fitting multiple corresponding pins and tails together. These pins feature a broad base and a taper towards the board, creating triangular shapes that intersect with matching tails. Similar to the finger joint, the dovetail is typically used in furniture and cabinetry as it can give corners a distinct look, but as the work is more involved, it is usually reserved for higher end pieces.

dowel joint: A joint created by drilling cylindrical holes into each piece of wood and then inserting a matching cylindrical pin into the holes. The fit should be tight in order to maintain the strength of the joint, and it can be glued or left without a fastener. Typically used in furniture or cabinetry.

drawer stack: A storage unit in which multiple drawers are stacked one above the other.

drawing designation: An alphanumeric code assigned to each drawing detail within the construction document set, which then organizes them into categories by contractor or field of expertise, drawing type, and page and drawing number.

dropped ceiling: Portion of a ceiling plane that is installed at a lower height than its surrounding planes.

edge molding: Trim used along the perimeter of a suspended ceiling. The two most common edge moldings are the angle molding and the shadow molding.

egress stair: An enclosed, fire-protected stairway that is part of the means of egress for a building.

elevation: A flat view of the face or side of an object. When drawn to scale, this drawing demonstrates height and foreground vs. background.

elevation marker: An icon used to refer the reader to the elevation view from that location on the plan. The numbers and/or letters in the circle refer to the drawing number (top) and the page number (bottom) where the drawing can be found in the construction set. The arrowhead points in the direction of the view.

elevation symbol: An icon used to refer the reader to the elevation view from that location on the plan. The numbers and/or letters in the circle refer to the drawing number (top) and the page number (bottom) where the drawing can be found in the construction set. The arrowhead points in the direction of the view.

exposed grid: Suspended acoustical ceiling system where users below can see the grid that supports the panels.

face frame cabinet: Cabinet that incorporates an assembly of rails and stiles on the front face of its structure to add strength and disguise the construction.

face: The portion of the frame that is visible on either side of the opening and acts as the trim. This can remain plain or be decorative.

Filled Region: Revit tool that creates material designation patterns in an assigned space.

filler bar: A piece of wood supplied by a manufacturer to match the specified casework's finish. These bars can be left plain, but typically they will have a design or pattern carved into them to create a decorative, finished appearance.

finger joint: A joint created by fitting multiple corresponding 90 degree rectangular wedges together. While it may be used in for continuous lengths, this joint is typically used in furniture and cabinetry, as it can give corners a distinct look. Also referred to as a box joint.

flush finish: The meeting point of different materials when they abut at the same height.

frame and panel wainscot: Style of wainscot that is made up of multiple pieces of wood to create a square or rectangle shape with an exposed or framed inner element.

frameless cabinet: Cabinet constructed with thicker sides and without the rail and stile assembly on the front of its structure, allowing for greater access to the interior.

frame: The assembly around a rough opening for a door or window that includes the jamb and header.

French dovetail joint: A joint created by sliding a single dovetail pin into a corresponding tail. Typically used for cabinetry. Also referred to as a sliding dovetail.

frieze: A horizontal band that appears below the cornice, which may be created from wood paneling or plaster. This piece can create a space for your eye to rest or may feature decorative artwork.

full stringer: The finished element that acts as a termination point for the treads and risers and runs along the side of the staircase.

furring channel: A strip of metal that is fastened to the joist above to create a mounting frame for GWB ceilings.

girder: A beam that accepts the weight from above and acts as the main support in the ceiling system.

greenboard: A treated type of gypsum board that has added water-resistant properties, allowing for its installation in spaces that are typically exposed to water, such as a bathroom. Greenboard should not be used alone and should be used under a layer of tiles, as it is not waterproof and can be damaged it if is overexposed to water.

guardrail: A protective rail or barrier that is used on landings or alongside a stair railing and is constructed 42" above the nose or finished floor.

guideline: Lightly drawn continuous lines used as an aid when hand drafting. Guides should never be inked and should be erased whenever possible.

gypsum wallboard: A stacked element comprised of a gypsum core between layers of paper facing used as a surface material for walls and ceilings. Depending on the treatment or material makeup, gypsum board can take on various properties, such as water- or fire-resistance. See Appendix D for types and common sizes.

handrail extension: The portions of the handrail that continue past the top and bottom risers in an effort to provide prolonged support for the end user.

handrail: Support aid along the stairs, secured 34" to 38" above the nosing on one or both sides of the staircase.

hatch: CAD tool that creates material designation patterns in an assigned space.

head: A horizontal framework member that extends between studs to support the structure above in order to form an opening. The top-most element of a door or window.

header: A horizontal framework member that is installed on top of a header plate and extends between studs to support the structure above in order to form an opening. The header is created by rotating a stud so that its widest dimension is parallel with the wall frame. Used in load-bearing, wood-frame walls.

header beam: A horizontal framework member that is installed directly below the top plate and extends between studs to support the structure above in order to form an opening. The header beam is created by rotating studs so that their widest dimension is parallel with the wall frame. Used in load-bearing light gauge steel walls.

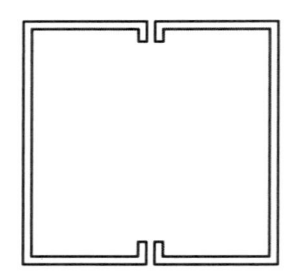

header plate: A horizontal framework member that extends between king studs in a rough opening to support the structure above. May be used in conjunction with a header for a load-bearing wall.

hidden line: A dashed line that depicts elements in a detail drawing that appear either below or behind a surface or overhead objects.

hollow triangle: The gap created between crown molding and the ceiling and wall planes when it is installed. Wood blocking is trimmed to fit inside this triangle for an accurate fit and support.

housed stringer: A type of stringer that is notched so that treads and risers rest inside of the notch and are not visible outside of the staircase. Also called a *closed stringer.*

hutch: An elevated storage component made of some combination of shelves, doors, and drawers.

I-beam: a structural component that appears to have an I-shape in cross-section, with flanges extending equidistant from the central support.

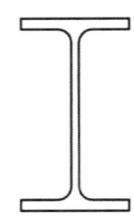

International Building Codes: Created, maintained, and released by the ICC every three years, these model codes are dictate the minimum standards required for egress, circulation, and fire safety.

International Code Council: The organization that writes the codes and standards for construction so that buildings are erected in a manner that protects and promotes the safety and health of the end users.

International Residential Code: Model codes issued by the International Code Council that dictate the minimum standards required for egress, circulation, and fire safety when applied to one- and two-family homes.

jack stud: A stud that has been shortened for use along the sides of openings. These studs are anchored to the king stud and help transfer weight from the header to the sole plate.

jamb: The vertical members of a frame for a window or door.

joinery: An element of woodworking that focuses on creating tight connection points that abut or interlock two pieces of wood through cuts, fasteners, or bonding agents.

joist: Parallel pieces of lumber measuring 2" × 6" minimum that support ceiling and floor systems.

king stud: A full-height stud that anchors from the bottom plate to the top plate and is attached to the header for support.

knockout: A hole cut in a steel stud, usually in an oval or square shape, that allows for wires to be run between studs.

landing: A level area that can be found at the top or bottom of a flight of stairs and, in some cases, between runs of stairs.

leader line: Arrow that extends from an annotation to the object it describes.

ledger board: A level piece of wood that is temporarily mounted to a wall to act as a support shelf for the upper cabinets to sit on during the installation process.

linetype: The characteristic pattern given to a line that has been drawn. The various styles indicate whether the line represents constructed components, hidden elements, or other objects within the drawing.

lineweight: The heaviness of the line that has been drawn. This can be used in conjunction with linetype to differentiate between objects, drawing elements, and drawing types.

***L*-shaped stair:** The *L*-shaped stair features two runs separated by a landing. The first run is a straight run to the landing, while the second run attaches to the landing perpendicular to the first.

main beam: A lightweight steel runner that acts as the chief supporting member of a suspended ceiling system and is anchored to the structure above.

marker bubble: Circle that houses the communicative information for elevations, sections, and details that directs the user as to how to locate related detail drawings. Also referred to as a *callout bubble*.

material designation: A visual depiction of a material that is used to clarify between element layers or to create patterns.

mid rail: A horizontal framing support used between rails when a cabinet has multiple openings, as seen between a drawer and a door.

mid stile: A vertical framing support used between stiles when a cabinet has multiple openings, as seen between doors and drawer stacks or when the opening spans too far a distance between end stiles.

millwork: Ready-made carpentry components that are traditionally made of wood to be installed directly to the walls, ceilings, and floors. These elements include trim, cornices, chair rails, and wainscoting.

mitered edge joint: A 90 degree joint created by uniting two pieces of wood at 45 degree angles. This joint creates the opposite effect of the scarf joint.

model space: The open panel in CAD where unscaled details can be drawn.

model space: The open panel in Revit where unscaled details can be drawn.

mortise and tenon joint: Joint created between two pieces of wood where a notched, rectangular, male connector (tenon) from one piece is inserted in to a matching female connector (mortise) on the other. The fit should be tight in order to maintain the strength of the joint, and it can be glued or left without a fastener. Typically used in furniture or cabinetry.

mounting blocks: 2" × 4" pieces of wood that are anchored to the floor for base cabinets to be placed over.

mounting rails: Pieces of wood that are installed along the front and back of a base cabinet assembly to create a surface to attach the countertop to while also adding constructive strength to the cabinet.

nail plate: Plated steel panels that are installed along the back of a mounting surface if there is a danger of piercing through the surface and damaging electrical or plumbing lines.

nested double joint: A horizontal framework member that extends between king studs in a rough opening to support the structure above. This component is made of three steel channels, one to accept the cripple studs above and two interlocking channels below to support the weight. Used in conjunction with a header beam for load-bearing light gauge steel walls.

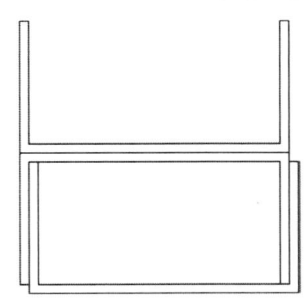

nested header plate: An opening header created by stacking three steel channels in which the lower two channels face each other, with their flanges overlapping, creating a hollow, rectangular shape. The third, and topmost, channel rests above the nested components, facing upward to support the cripple studs above.

newel post: The larger balusters at the top and bottom of a rail.

nonbearing wall: A wall that acts as a space divider and does not bear the weight of the roof or upper levels. Also referred to as a *partition*.

nonegress stair: Any staircase in commercial and multi-family building that is not an enclosed, fire-protected travel path to an exit. These stairs may follow commercial stair codes but are not required to follow the stricter egress stair codes.

nosing: The portion of a tread that projects over the riser below.

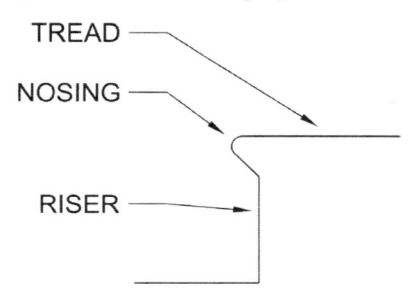

object line: A solid, continuous line that can be used to depict walls, doors, windows, furniture, or lighting within a detail drawing.

open stringer: Stairway in which the treads and risers are visible from the sides because they hang over or are flush with the stringers.

paneling: A millwork wall cover composed of thin boards that are installed directly to the finished wall.

paper space: The layout panels in CAD where details can be scaled and organized in preparation for plotting.

parallel ruler: Horizontal attachment on the drafting board that is capable of sliding up and down to aid in accuracy in 90 degree angles and parallel lines. May be referred to as a *paraline* or replaced by a T-square or drafting machine.

particleboard: An engineered wood panel created by heating and pressing resins and fibers to create a strong, smooth surface suitable for accepting veneer. There are different densities and strengths of particle board available.

partition: A wall that acts as a space divider and does not bear the weight of the roof or upper levels. Also referred to as a *nonbearing wall*.

pattern: A decorative design or alignment of elements.

phantom line: Dashed lines used to aid in the explanation of how to view the space or how elements operate.

plan: A drawing of the building, room, or object as seen from above.

plate rail: Molding placed alone or below the frieze; this decorative length is used for display. The height of the plate rail depends on the height of the room and the other decorative woodwork elements present.

plenum: The space between the finished ceiling and the slab above where the HVAC and electrical systems can be housed.

plywood: An engineered wood panel created by pressurizing thin layers of wood with bonding agents. Strength is gained

profile: The outline or shape of the trim as seen in section, which may be selected for its appearance, historical significance, or simplicity of installation.

rabbet: A groove or cut that creates a joint or space where another piece can fit into it.

rail: A horizontal framing support around an opening. There are typically two: the top rail that runs under the counter and the bottom rail that runs above the toe kick.

rated partition: A wall constructed with fire-rated materials spanning from slab-to-slab.

reception counter: An elevated counter of varying height that appears along the edge of a desk that acts as a joint work surface between an end user and a guest. Also referred to as a reception hutch.

recessed ceiling: Portion of a ceiling plane that is installed at a greater height than its surrounding planes.

reference symbol: A marker representing the existence of an elevation, section, or detail callout on a drawing. The content held within each symbol is used to direct the viewer to a specific sheet and drawing to see the necessary view and construction information. Symbol types have their own unique appearance and purpose.

repeat: Identical duplications of a pattern across a surface.

residential stair: Any staircase in a single-family home. These stairs may be of wood or steel construction.

return: A portion of a desk or work surface that runs perpendicular to the main desk to create added work space, connect the front of a desk to a credenza, and add support.

return: The second portion of a staircase that extends from the first landing to the second landing, allowing the user to reverse direction and end up directly above where they started.

riser: A vertical member at the front of a stair that acts as a support for the tread (see nosing).

rise: The vertical distance between two points used to measure height, such as the distance between the finished floor and a landing.

rough opening: An opening created in the wall to allow for doors or windows to be placed. This opening measures 2" wider and taller than the door or window to be placed in to the wall.

run: The portion of stairs going from one slab to the next or from the slab to a landing.

scale: The ratio between the size of the physical space being designed and the size the space appears as in the drawing.

scarf joint: A 180 degree continuation of two pieces, each of which has a 45 degree angle cut that overlaps. These joints can be glued together or the boards can simply abut and be fastened into place. Typically used for continuous lengths, such as a baseboard, with a minimal seam.

scribing: The process of trimming away a portion of an object so that it fits snuggly against the wall while maintaining evenness.

section: A view of the interior of an object, showing material thicknesses, as seen by "cutting" through the item, typically vertically.

section cut symbol: An icon used to refer the reader to the section drawing based on the object or space that the view "cuts" through. The numbers and/or letters in the circle refer to the drawing number (top) and the page number (bottom) where the drawing can be found in the construction set. The arrowhead and the tail both point in the direction of the view.

shadow molding: A *W*-shaped trim used along the perimeter of a suspended ceiling, which creates a stepped, shadowed appearance.

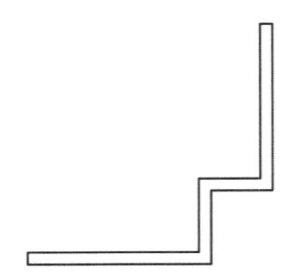

Sheet: The layout panels in Revit where details can be scaled and organized in preparation for plotting.

shim: A wood or metal strip used to aid in leveling plates and frames between structural components and finishing elements.

shim space: The 1/4"– 1/2" gap created between a structural component and a finishing element for the placement of shims to aid in the leveling process.

sill: A horizontal member at the bottom of an elevated opening, such as a window.

single rabbet: A door frame featuring one rabbet that contains a door.

soffit (ceiling): A portion of the ceiling, typically along the wall, that is built at a lower height to establish hierarchy, create a flushed finish, or indicate separate spaces within a single room. The hollow channel that is created lightens the weight on the finished ceiling above and can conceal wires and pipes.

soffit (door): The perpendicular edge to the stop on a door frame. This element can extend from the face to the stop (single rabbet) or can be sandwiched between rabbets (double rabbet).

sole plate: A horizontal member along the bottom of a stud wall. This element joins the studs for the wall and acts as a support for floor joists. Also called the *sill plate*.

spiral stair: A circular or oval staircase with regular, wedge-shaped treads rotating around a central axis.

spline joint: Joint created by inserting a piece of wood or metal between two other pieces of wood that have been notched.

square edge tile: Ceiling tiles featuring a rectangular profile that rest on the grid tee, creating a flush finish between the tiles and the grid.

stair: A means of vertical circulation that allows for the end user to travel from one level to another through a calculated set of steps comprised of treads and risers on a supportive framework.

steel channel: A *C*-shaped metal runner.

steel channel: Elements that are the supports for the treads and risers, acting in the same manner as the carriage and stringers. Treads and risers are affixed directly to the channel, allowing for it to carry the weight of the flight and the users. When constructed out of steel, the channels are hung from the floor above or sit on a bearing plate. The depth of the steel channel must be at least 10".

stile: A vertical framing support. In cabinetry, there are typically two, one on either side of the opening, running from rail to rail.

stop: An element of the door frame that extends into the path of the doorway to provide a closing point between the elements.

straight run: Laid out similarly to the direct run, the straight run features landings between runs, allowing this staircase to be used when the total rise is more than 12'-0".

stringer (dimensions): The device used to notate the dimension on a construction drawing. The stringer is made up of the dimension text, dimension line, the extension line, and an architectural tick.

stringer (stairs): A supportive element that runs along the ends of the treads and risers. The element can be both supportive and decorative.

stud: A vertical framing member that has been mill cut to a specific size. See Appendix G for common sizes.

suspended gypsum system: A framework composed of parallel steel channels supporting perpendicular furrings that are hung from the structure above to hold the gypsum board ceiling and all ceiling-mounted components.

suspended tile system: A grid composed of parallel and perpendicular rails that are hung from the structure above to hold the ceiling tiles and all ceiling-mounted components.

T-bar: The bottom portion of the main beam or cross tee that forms a T-shape on which the ceiling tiles rest or hang.

tegular tile: Notched ceiling tiles that hang on the grid tee, allowing for the finished face of the tile to project past the grid, creating a layered effect.

throat: The open portion of a frame, which fits onto a wall. The size of the throat is dependent on the thickness of the wall.

title block: A strip of information on the drawing sheet that holds project information. This information includes but is not limited to the designer and client's name, building location, the page contents, drawing scale, and the page number.

toe kick: A 3" to 4" notch cut from the bottom of the front of a base cabinet, making room for the users' toes while using the surface and protecting the lower portion of the cabinet from damage.

tongue and groove joint: A joint created by sliding a single rectangular wedge into a corresponding channel. Combination of the finger joint and the French dovetail.

top plate: A horizontal member along the top of a stud wall. This element joins the studs for the wall and acts as a support for ceiling joists.

total rise: The height of a staircase from the floor at the base of first riser to the landing.

total run: The length of a run of stairs from the nose of the first tread to the nose of the landing.

tread: The horizontal portion of a stair on which one places their foot (see nosing).

Type X: A treated type of gypsum board that has added fire-resistant properties, allowing for flame spread to be slowed. Each layer of Type X that is used can provide an hour's worth of resistance when rating a wall assembly (one layer is applicable for a one-hour rating, two layers for two hours, etc.).

***U*-shaped stair:** The *U-shaped* stair features two runs separated by a landing. The first run is a straight run to the landing, while the second run becomes a return, running parallel to the first run.

veneer: A thin layer of wood used as a finish layer for a wooden framework.

vertical rise: The travel distance between landings, which cannot exceed 12'-0".

viewport: The active window on a sheet in CAD or Revit in which an individual detail appears.

wainscot: A type of paneling that is installed between the baseboard and the chair rail but may also be a floor-to-ceiling installation. Wainscot can take the form of a decorative panel or a frame and panel design.

wall cabinet: A storage unit mounted directly to the wall, typically 4'-8" above the finished floor in kitchens and bathrooms but can vary based on the unit's size and function.

wedge: A piece of wood that acts as a shim to ensure a tight fit between the housed stringer and the treads and risers.

winding stair: A winding stair takes the shape of an *L*- or *U*-stair, but wedged shaped treads replace the central landing.

wire hanger: Wire used to secure ceiling systems and components to the structure above (see Figure 6.53).

work triangle: Design concept in which the major appliances (refrigerator, sink, and stove) are close enough for an easy transition from one to the next during the cooking process but spaced out enough that one can still move easily and utilize counter space.

Credits

All illustrations and photographs by PJ do Val unless otherwise indicated.

Chapter 1
1.21 Maxx-Studio/Shutterstock.com
1.22 gargantiopa/iStock.com
1.23 sisoje/iStock.com

Chapter 2
2.1 naito29/shutterstock.com
2.9 Kwanbenz/Shutterstock.com

Chapter 5
5.1 Valentyn Semenov (photovs)/iStock.com
5.5 Christian Delbert/Shutterstock.com
5.6 Vilax/Shutterstock.com
5.27 irisconcept/iStock.com
5.28 Leung Chopan/Shutterstock.com
5.29 Evgeny Sergeev/iStock.com
5.30 Max Krasnov/Shutterstock.com

Chapter 6
6.1 Bigpra/iStock.com
6.3 David Papazian/Shutterstock.com
6.4 Andrey Ezhov/Shutterstock.com
6.12 Artazum/Shutterstock.com
6.14 Iris concept/iStock.com
6.16 Hikesterson/iStock.com
6.44 irisconcept/iStock.com
6.45 Feverpitched/iStock.com
6.46 Richard19981977/iStock.com
6.47 etse1112/iStock.com

Chapter 7
7.1 Ian Dyball/iStock.com
7.2 Scovad/iStock.com
7.3 SafakOguz/iStock.com
7.6 Brett Taylor/iStock.com
7.7 PlusOne/Shutterstock.com
7.8 urfinguss/iStock.com
7.28 alabn/Shutterstock.com
7.29 photographee.eu/Shutterstock.com
7.30 Scovad/iStock.com
7.31 Malkovstock/iStock.com

Chapter 8
8.1 GeorgeVieiraSilva/iStock.com
8.2 SeanPavonePhoto/iStock.com
8.8 photovs/iStock.com
8.14 lisafx/iStock.com
8.16 fatcamera/iStock.com
8.26 in4mal/iStock.com
8.27 archiviz/iStock.com
8.28 hikesterson/iStock.com
8.29 Kaziyeva-Dem'yanenko Svitlana/Shutterstock.com
8.33 B Calkins/Shutterstock.com

Chapter 9
9.1 poligonchik/iStock.com
9.3 antos777/iStock.com
9.5 pio3/Shutterstock.com
9.10 Photo_HamsterMan/iStock.com
9.11 dmitriymoroz/iStock.com
9.13 ismagilov/iStock.com
9.15 Stephen Coburn/Shutterstock.com
9.16 psisa/iStock.com
9.49 rilueda/iStock.com
9.50 KatarzynaBialasiewicz/iStock.com
9.51 egorr/iStock.com
9.52 alabn/iStock.com
9.53 mrtkarabatur/iStock.com

Chapter 10
10.1 CapturePB/Shutterstock.com
10.2 Studio Din/Shtterstock.com
10.3 fallbrook/istock.com
10.4 ImageFlow/Shutterstock.com
10.5 Eviled/Shutterstock.com
10.6 Africa Studio/Shutterstock.com
10.29 Artazum/Shutterstock.com
10.30 LightFieldStudios/iStock.com
10.31 bilanol/Shutterstock.com
10.32 irisconcept/iStock.com

Chapter 11
11.1 Kwanchai_Khammuean/iStock.com
11.2 Rawpixel/iStock.com
11.25 beer5020/iStock.com

Index

abbreviations, 301–302
abstract wall shelving, 261
acoustical ceiling tiles (ACT), 96
acoustical partitions, 56
ADA Accessibility Guidelines (ADAAG), 2
aluminum door, frame and header, 86–87
aluminum window frame, 82–83
Americans with Disabilities Act (ADA) Standards, 2, 299–300
    for cabinetry, 171
    for ceilings, 125
    for custom, 264
    for millwork, 146
    for rails, 225
    for stair, 225
    for walls and openings, 91
anchoring rails, 152
angle supports, 176
annotations, 8, 14, 301–302
    AutoCAD, 27
    hand drafting, 18
    Revit, 41
architectural lettering, 8
architectural scale, 16–17
architectural tick, 7
AutoCAD
    annotations, 27
    detail callout, 32–33
    dimension, 24–26
    important, 33
    linetype, 23
    lineweights, 24
    material designation, 27–29
    scale, 22
    section cut markers, 29–31
axonometric drawings, 4
    axons, 4, 11

backsplash, 149, 151, 230
balusters, 177
baseboards, 129, 130
base cabinet, 148
    elevation, 156–157
    section, 158–161
base cabinet axon, 148, 150
base/wall combination
    elevation, 166
    section, 167

bathroom floor tile pattern, 236–237
bathroom full tile floor plan, 237–239
beadboard, 131
bearing walls, 56
box beams, 99, 118
building elevations, 286
building sections, 284
butt joint, 132

cabinet blocking, 152
cabinetry, 148, 314–315
    ADA Standards for, 171
    base cabinet, elevation, 156–157
    base cabinet, section, 158–161
    base/wall combination, elevation, 166
    base/wall combination, section, 167
    dimensions, standard heights and accessible heights, 154
    IBC Codes for, 171
    important, 168–169
    wall cabinet, elevation, 162–163
    wall cabinet, section, 164–165
CAD, 275–276
    cabinetry, 162
    ceilings, 105
    construction set, 276
    custom details, 243
    millwork, 139
    stairs, 184, 188, 196, 204, 210, 214, 218
    walls and openings, 62
callout marker, 272
case piece elevation, 240–243
casings, 61
ceiling(s), 94, 310–313
    ADA Standards for, 125
    box beams, 118
    direct installed GWB, 114–115
    IBC Codes for, 126
    important, 122–123
    parallel section, 120–121
    perpendicular section, 118–119
    plans, 11
    soffit detail, 116–117
    suspended ACT and GWB systems, 104–107
    suspended ACT systems, 100–101
    suspended GWB cove and recessed ACT system, 108–113
    suspended GWB systems, 102–103

ceiling tile styles, 96
center line, 6
chair rail, 129, 130
channel support, 176
chase walls, 56
clear space, 177
clip angle, 176
closed stringer, 176
commercial stair, 177, 179–180
concealed grid, 96
concealed T tiles, 96
construction document (CD) set, 266
    adding communicative symbols, 271–272
    building elevations, 286
    building sections, 284
    CAD, 275–276
    ceiling plan and details, 293
    cover sheet, 281
    dimension plan, 283
    doors and windows, 287
    enlarged plans and details, 288, 289
    enlarged plans and details, 290
    existing conditions, 282
    finish plan, 291
    furniture plan, 291
    hand drafting, 273–274
    important, 279
    laying out the pages, 268–270
    page content and drawing scales, 280
    page numbering systems, 266–267
    Revit, 277–278
    wall types, 285
construction line, 6
construction material guide, 304
construction plans, close up of, 11
contractors installing, 153
cornerblocks, 148
cornice, 128
counter edge, 151
countertop, 149
cove(s), 99
cove lighting, 99
cover sheet, 281
cripple studs, 59
cross tees, 96
crown molding, 128, 129, 130
cubby and bench section, 248–251
custom
    ADA Standards for, 264
    bathroom floor tile pattern, 236–237
    bathroom full tile floor plan, 237–239
    case piece elevation, 240–243
    combined reception desk dimensions, 231, 232
    cubby and bench section, 248–251
    drawer stack section, 244–247
    kitchen backsplash, 233–235
    reception desk, 252–260
    tile applications, 230
    type of, 230
custom built-in laundry center, 231
custom desk seating, 261

dado joint, 134
decorative panels, 131
detail callout, 9, 20, 271
    AutoCAD, 32–33
    Revit, 50–53
detail drawing, 2
    types of, 2–4
detailing
    characteristics and elements, 4–9
    detail drawing, types of, 2–4
    importance of, 2, 12–13
    place dimensions, 10–11
    starting details, 11
dimension(s), 7, 18
    AutoCAD, 24–26
    hand drafting, 18
    placing of, 10–11
    plan, 10, 283
    reception desk, 232
    Revit, 39–41
    stair, 316
    on walls and openings, 66–67
dimension line, 7
dimension text, 7
direct installation GWB system, 97, 114–115, 122
direct run, 181
    front elevation, 194–197
    plan, 186–189
    section, 198–201, 206
    side elevation, 190–193
door styles, 309
double rabbet, 61
double top late, 58
dovetail joint, 134
dowel joint, 133
drafted exterior elevations, 3D projection of, 11
drafting styles, 7
drawer stack section, 244–247
drawing designations, 267
dropped ceiling, 108

egress stairs, 180
elevation(s), 3, 11
    drafting stud wall, 66–79
    markers, 271
    reception desk, 254–255
elevation symbols, 8, 19, 28–29
    Revit, 44–47
exploded plan, 133
exposed grid, 96
extension line, 7
exterior elevation, 12

face, 61, 149
face framed cabinet, 149
filler bar, 153
finger joint, 134
floor plans, 11
frame, 61, 109
 aluminum door, 86–87
 and panel wainscot, 131
 wooden door, 84–85
frameless cabinet, 149
French dovetail joint, 135
frieze, 129
full stringer, 176
furniture plan, 291
furring channels, 97

girder, 94
greenboard, 56
grid system styles, 96
guardrail, 177
guideline, 6
gypsum wallboard (GWB) systems, 58, 89, 97

hand drafting, 273–274
 architectural scale, 16–17
 detail callout, 20
 dimensions and annotations, 18
 elevation symbol, 19
 important, 20
 linetype, 17
 lineweight, 18
 material designations, 19
 section cut markers, 19
handrail, 177
handrail extensions, 177
hand sketched plan drafts, 12
hatch pattern, 27
header, 59, 61, 83
 aluminum door, 86–87
 wooden door, 83, 84–85
header beam, 59
header plate, 59
hidden line, 6
hollow triangle, 128
horizontal dimensions, 3
housed stringer, 176
hutch, 252

I-beam, 94
illustration, 8
interior partition, 152
International Building Codes (IBC), 2, 179, 296–298
 for cabinetry, 171
 for ceiling, 102, 105, 126
 for millwork, 131, 146
 for rails, 226–227

 for stair, 177, 180, 185, 186, 188, 192, 196, 208, 218, 226–227
 for walls and openings, 66, 72, 85, 92
International Code Council (ICC), 2
International Residential Code (IRC), 2, 179

jack stud, 59
jamb, 61
 aluminum door, 86–87
 wooden door, 83, 85
joinery, 132–135
joists, 94, 96

king studs, 58
kitchen backsplash, 233–235
kitchen paneling, 144
knockouts, 58

landing, 174
laying out, 268–270
leader line, 8, 18, 27
ledger board, 153
linetype, 6, 17
 AutoCAD, 23
 Revit, 37
lineweights, 6, 7, 18
 AutoCAD, 24
 Revit, 38
L-shaped stair, 181

main beam, 95
material, 303
material designations, 8, 19
 AutoCAD, 27–29
 Revit, 42–43
mid rails, 149
mid stiles, 149
millwork, 128, 314–315
 ADA Standards for, 146
 IBC Codes for, 146
 important, 143–144
 joinery, 132–135
 profile, 132
 wall-mounted millwork, elevation, 136–139
 wall-mounted millwork, section, 139–142
 wall-mounted millwork, types of, 128–131
minimalistic kitchen design, 169
mitered edge joint, 133
mitered joint, 133
model space, 22, 36
mortise and tenon joints, 134
mounting blocks, 153
mounting rails, 148

nail plates, 152
nested header plate, 59
newel post, 177

nonbearing, 56
nose profiles, 317
nosing, 175

object line, 6
open stringer, 176

page numbering systems, 266–267
paneling, 131
panel wainscot, 143
paper space, 22
parallel ruler, 17, 18
parallel section, 120–121
particleboard, 232
partition, 56, 57
pattern, 238
perpendicular section, 118–119
phantom line, 6
plans, 2
    ceiling, 11
    dimension, 10
plate rail, 129
plenum space, 95, 95
plywood, 232
profile, 132
project plan, 319–322

rabbet, 61
rails, 149, 177, 317
    ADA Standards for, 226
    IBC Codes for, 226–227
rated partitions, 56
reception counters, 252, 256–257
reception desk, 252–253
    desk hutch section, 258–259
    dimensions, 232
    elevation, 254–255
    full section, 260
    important, 260–262
    reception counter section, 256–257
    reception desk elevation, 254–255
recessed ACT system, 108–113
recessed ceiling, 108
recessed GWB channels, 123
reference symbols, 271
repeat, 238
residential bathroom, 238
residential stairs, 177, 178
return, 182, 252
Revit, 72
    annotations, 41
    cabinetry, 162
    ceilings, 105
    construction document set, 277–278
    detail callouts, 50–53
    dimension, 39–41

elevation symbols, 44–47
important, 53
linetype, 37
lineweight, 38
material designations, 42–43
millwork, 139
scale, 36–37
section cut markers, 48–50
stairs, 184, 185, 196, 214, 218
walls and openings, 72
riser, 175
rough opening, 59
rules of thumb (RoT)
    ceilings, 102, 110
    custom details, 238
    stairs, 180, 185, 199, 204, 216
run, 174

sample tile patterns, 318
scale, 4, 16
    AutoCAD, 22
    Revit, 36–37
scarf joint, 133
scribing, 152
section, 3, 11
section cut markers, 271, 272
    AutoCAD, 29–31
    Revit, 48–50
section cut symbol, 9, 19, 29
shared box beam ceiling, 99
sheet scale, 36–37
shims, 81, 152
shim space, 81
sill, 60
    wooden door, 83
single rabbet, 61
soffit, 61, 98, 116–117, 129
sole late, 58
spiral stair, 182
spline joint, 133
square edge tiles, 96
stair
    ADA Standards for, 225
    commercial, 179–180
    dimensions, 316
    direct run, front elevation, 194–197
    direct run, plan, 186–189
    direct run, section, 198–201, 206
    direct run, side elevation, 190–193
    IBC Codes for, 226–227
    important, 222–223
    layouts, 180–182
    number and height/risers, calculating, 184
    number of treads, calculating, 184
    parts of, 174–177
    residential, 178

run, section, 202–205
    steel U-run, 207–211
    tread depth, calculating, 184
    U-shaped stair, 182
steel channels, 58, 59, 176
steel-frame construction, 59
steel frame partitions, 89
steel girders, 94
steel staircases, 176
steel-stud partition, 58, 64–65, 68–75
stiles, 149
stop, 61
straight run, 181
stringer, 7, 18, 175
stud, 58
suspended ACT systems, 95, 100–101, 104–107
suspended ceiling cove, 99
suspended GWB concealing, 99
suspended GWB cove, 108–113
suspended GWB systems, 102–103, 104–107, 123
suspended gypsum systems, 97
suspended tile system, 95
suspended wood slat ceilings, 122
suspension systems, 95
symbols, 301

T-bar, 96
tegular tiles, 96
title block, 268
toe kick, 149
tongue and groove joint, 135
top plate, 58
total rise, 174
total run, 174
tread, 175
type X gypsum, 56

U-run, 207
    elevation, 221
    plan, 208–211
    section, 212–221
U-shaped stair, 182

vertical dimensions, 3
vertical rise, 174
viewport, 22

wainscot, 130, 131
wall cabinet, 151
    elevation, 162–163
    section, 164–165
wall-mounted millwork
    elevation, 136–139
    section, 139–142
    types of, 128–131
walls and openings, 56–61
    aluminum window frame, header and sill, 82–83
    commercial—aluminum door frame and header, 86–87
    dimensions, drafting based on, 66–67
    important, 88
    steel-stud partition, 64–65, 68–75
    wooden door frame and header, 84–85
    wooden frame opening, 80–81
    wood-stud partition, 62–63, 75–79
wall types, 285, 305–118
winding, 182
wire hangers, 95
wooden door, frame and header, 84–85
wooden frame opening, 80–81
wood joists, 94
wood plank suspension system, 123
wood-stud partition, 62–63, 75–79
work triangle, 154